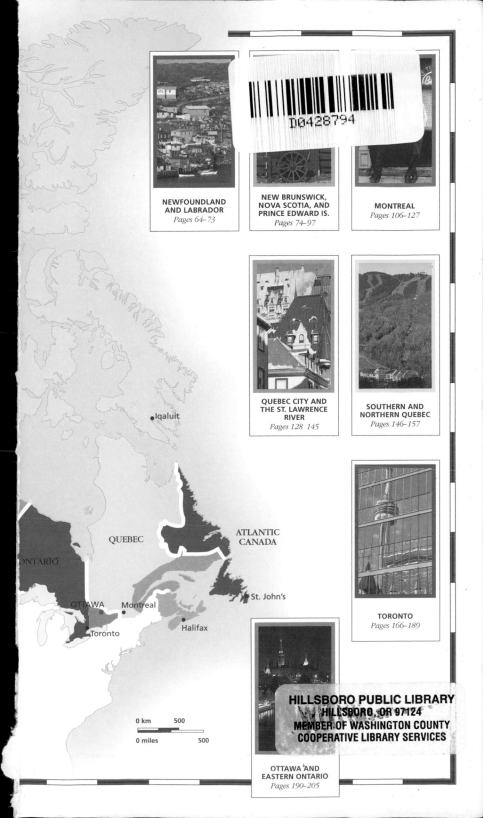

NEWFOUNDLAND
AND LABRADOR
Pages 64–73

NEW BRUNSWICK,
NOVA SCOTIA, AND
PRINCE EDWARD IS.
Pages 74–97

MONTREAL
Pages 106–127

QUEBEC CITY AND
THE ST. LAWRENCE
RIVER
Pages 128–145

SOUTHERN AND
NORTHERN QUEBEC
Pages 146–157

Iqaluit

QUEBEC

ATLANTIC
CANADA

ONTARIO

OTTAWA   Montreal

St. John's

Toronto

Halifax

TORONTO
Pages 166–189

0 km   500

0 miles   500

OTTAWA AND
EASTERN ONTARIO
Pages 190–205

EYEWITNESS TRAVEL

CANADA

EYEWITNESS TRAVEL
CANADA

DK

LONDON, NEW YORK,
MELBOURNE, MUNICH AND DELHI
www.dk.com

PRODUCED BY Duncan Baird Publishers, London, England
MANAGING EDITOR Rebecca Miles
MANAGING ART EDITOR Vanessa Marsh
EDITORS Georgina Harris, Michelle de Larrabeiti, Zoë Ross
DESIGNERS Dawn Davies-Cook, Ian Midson
DESIGN ASSISTANCE Rosie Laing, Kelvin Mullins
VISUALIZER Gary Cross
PICTURE RESEARCH Victoria Peel
DTP DESIGNER Sarah Williams

Dorling Kindersley Limited
PROJECT EDITOR Paul Hines ART EDITOR Jane Ewart
US EDITOR Mary Sutherland EDITOR Hugh Thompson

CONTRIBUTORS
Bruce Bishop, Eric & Katharine Fletcher, Paul Franklin, Sam Ion, Ffion
Llywd-Jones, Helena Katz, Philip Lee, Cam Norton,
Lorry Patton, Sandra Phinney, Geoffrey Roy, Michael Snook, Donald
Telfer, Paul Waters

PHOTOGRAPHERS
Alan Keohane, Peter Wilson, Francesca Yorke

ILLUSTRATORS
Joanna Cameron, Gary Cross, Chris Forsey, Paul Guest, Claire Littlejohn,
Robbie Polley, Kevin Robinson, John Woodcock

Reproduced by Colourscan (Singapore)
Printed and bound by South China Printing Co. Ltd., China

First American Edition, 2000
12 13 14 15 10 9 8 7 6 5 4 3 2 1

Published in the United States by DK Publishing,
375 Hudson Street, New York, New York 10014

Reprinted with revisions 2002, 2004, 2006, 2008, 2010, 2012

Copyright 2000, 2012 © Dorling Kindersley Limited, London
A Penguin Company

A CATALOG RECORD FOR THIS BOOK IS AVAILABLE FROM
THE LIBRARY OF CONGRESS

ISSN 1542-1554
ISBN 978-0-75668-415-0

*Front cover main image: Moraine Lake and Valley of the Ten Peaks
(Wenkchemna Peaks) at sunrise, Banff National Park, Alberta, Canada*

MIX
Paper from
responsible sources
FSC
www.fsc.org   FSC™ C018179

**The information in this
DK Eyewitness Travel Guide is checked regularly.**
Every effort has been made to ensure that this book is as up-to-date
as possible at the time of going to press. Some details, however, such
as telephone numbers, opening hours, prices, gallery hanging
arrangements, and travel information are liable to change. The
publishers cannot accept responsibility for any consequences arising
from the use of this book, nor for any material on third party
websites, and cannot guarantee that any website address in this book
will be a suitable source of travel information. We value the views
and suggestions of our readers very highly. Please write to: Publisher,
DK Eyewitness Travel Guides, Dorling Kindersley, 80 Strand, London,
WC2R 0RL, Great Britain or email travelguides@dk.com.

◁ The dazzling fall foliage of Quebec's maple forests

CONTENTS

The historic reconstruction of
Fortress Louisbourg, Nova Scotia

Moraine Lake in Banff National Park in the Rockies

Château Frontenac in Quebec City

ONTARIO

CENTRAL CANADA

BRITISH COLUMBIA AND THE ROCKIES

NORTHERN CANADA

TRAVELERS' NEEDS

SURVIVAL GUIDE

The Basilica of Sainte-Anne-du-Beaupré in Quebec

INTRODUCING
CANADA

DISCOVERING CANADA

Canada – the world's second largest country after Russia – is a vast land comprising ten provinces and three territories. This young nation, founded in 1867, stretches from the Atlantic to the Pacific to the Arctic Ocean. From rural coastal villages to flat prairies

Cape Sprear, Newfoundland

to teeming metropolises, this vast Commonwealth country offers endless fascinating experiences. This guide divides Canada into 13 regions that will most appeal to travelers. Here you will find a brief overview of each unique region to help you get the most out of your visit.

A deep fjord in Gros Morne National Park, Newfoundland

NEWFOUNDLAND AND LABRADOR

- Striking geography
- Gros Morne National Park
- Viking and Irish heritage
- Seafaring lifestyle

Canadians love their newest province (established in 1949) not only for its rugged landscape of rocky shores, fjords, and sweeping island vistas, but for its people who have inherited the humorous, indomitable spirit of their Irish forbears. St. John's (see pp66–7), the capital city, is a good place to begin your Newfoundland journey, which will probably also lead you to beautiful Gros Morne National Park (see p70) on the western coast, or Terra Nova National Park (see p69) on the eastern side of the island. Labrador, nearby on the Canadian mainland, has a sizable aboriginal population, as well as the town of Happy Valley-Goose Bay (see p73), with its World War II historical background.

NEW BRUNSWICK, NOVA SCOTIA, AND PRINCE EDWARD ISLAND

- Charming seaside villages and towns
- Fortress Louisbourg
- Unique blend of English, Scottish and French Acadian roots
- Great seafood

These three provinces are renowned for their magnificent coastlines. The Bay of Fundy, between Nova Scotia and New Brunswick, has the highest tides in the world, which can be seen at Fundy National Park (see p76). Whale watching in Nova Scotia is a big attraction, but if historical sites beckon, ensure a visit to the amazing reconstruction of Fortress Louisbourg (see pp96–7) on Cape Breton Island. Children's story book heroine Anne of Green Gables has a whole town devoted to her on Prince Edward Island (see pp80–83). Throughout the three provinces, charming Acadian fishing villages

complete with brightly painted lobster boats abound, particularly on the Acadian Peninsula (see p78) and Wolfville (see p85). The area is renowned for fresh seafood.

MONTREAL

- Cosmopolitan flair
- Fine museums
- Delightful ambience of Vieux-Montréal
- Shopping in the Underground City

Canadians are quietly proud of their second largest city which was home to both the 1967 World Exposition and the 1976 Olympic Games (see pp124–5) – and is simply an exciting and fun city to visit at any time of the year. Vieux-Montréal (see pp110–11), the old city built along the shore of the St. Lawrence River, is a charming 18th-century enclave of horse-drawn carriages, boutique hotels, and cafés. The Basilique Notre-Dame-de-Montréal (see p112) is a

The 18th-century charm of Vieux-Montréal

must-see site as is the **Musée des Beaux Arts** *(see p118)*. Shopping is centered on rue Sainte-Catherine, and the nationally famous **Underground City** *(see p119)* is a labyrinthine network with hundreds of shops and restaurants.

Soaring façade of Sainte-Anne-de-Beaupré Basilica in Quebec City

QUEBEC CITY AND THE ST. LAWRENCE RIVER

- **UN World Heritage Site**
- **Historic and political seat of French Canada**
- **Gourmands' paradise**
- **Rare marine wildlife**

Quebec City, with its narrow cobblestone streets which give it a European flavor, is truly representative of French Canada. It was named a UN World Heritage Site in 1985. The small capital of the province of Quebec embraces visitors with a wealth of sights, from the fascinating **La Citadelle** fort *(see pp136–7)*, to the renowned religious shrine of **Sainte-Anne-de-Beaupré** *(see p138)*, and the wondrous cuisine in the restaurants surrounding the imposing hotel, **Château Frontenac** *(see p134)*. Farther afield, you can experience French maritime charm on the **Iles-de-la-Madeleine** *(see p143)* or on the **Gaspé Peninsula** *(see p144–5)*, where there is bountiful seafood and rare marine wildlife.

SOUTHERN AND NORTHERN QUEBEC

- **Farmland in the south**
- **Skiing in the Laurentian Mountains**
- **Canadian Museum of Civilization**
- **Laid-back Gatineau**

Just south of Montreal, rich farming communities straddle the US border around the Appalachian Mountains, particularly at **Sherbrooke** and **Lac Memphrémagog** *(see p148)*. North of the city the magnificent **Laurentian Mountains** *(see p151)*, such as Mont Tremblant, display beautiful colors in the fall and in winter delight skiers and other winter-sports enthusiasts. Across the river from Canada's capital city of Ottawa is the **Gatineau Region** *(see p154)* and the dynamic **Canadian Museum of Civilization** *(see p155)*. For those seeking adventure in the far north of this vast province, **Nunavik** *(see p157)* – not to be confused with the territory of Nunavut – is for the hardiest traveler.

TORONTO

- **Dynamically multicultural**
- **Soaring CN Tower**
- **Renaissance in the arts**
- **Superb shopping and entertainment**

Canada's largest city, with a population of nearly five million people, is a wonder of ethnic diversity, with

Mont Tremblant and Village, a four-season resort in Quebec

disparate cultural and linguistic communities. Under the gaze of the **CN Tower** *(see p172)* – formerly the tallest free-standing structure in the world – is a city that pulses with exciting nightlife, fine and varied dining, and a truly global shopping experience. Stroll around fashionable **Yorkville** *(see p183)* with its cafés and upscale shops, or the colorful and lively **Chinatown** *(see p180)* on Spadina Avenue, with its boisterous streetlife. Toronto is increasingly renowned for its unique architecture, with the one-of-a-kind **Art Gallery of Ontario** *(see pp178–9)* and a bold, futuristic addition to the **Royal Ontario Museum** *(see pp184–5)*. Both museums hold extensive collections. The city has a rich tradition of entertainment, with a wide range of theater, festivals, music, and dance offerings.

The modern Toronto skyline on the north side of Lake Ontario

OTTAWA AND EASTERN ONTARIO

- **National capital region**
- **Camping at Algonquin Provincial Park**
- **Picturesque Kawartha Lakes**
- **National Gallery of Canada**

Ottawa, the nation's delightful capital city, has enough culture and history (and fun things to do) to make for an interesting visit. Your first stop could be the **Parliament Buildings** *(see p192)*, and then a pleasant walk to the **National Gallery of Canada** *(see pp198–9)* for the country's best array of the fine arts. The **Canadian War Museum** *(see p195)* is far from somber, and you can find the best Canadian live music, theater, and dance at the **National Arts Centre** *(see p197)*. The vast **Algonquin Provincial Park** *(see pp204–5)* is rich in wildlife and typifies the great outdoors, as do the **Kawartha Lakes** *(see p202)*.

The copper-roofed Victorian Parliament Buildings in Ottawa

THE GREAT LAKES

- **Point Pelee National Park**
- **Stratford's world-class live classical theater**
- **Thundering Niagara Falls**

The Great Lakes are the life-blood of millions of Canadians and Americans. The cities, towns, and villages that have been built on their shores are verdant, vibrant, and definitely

The breathtaking spectacle at Niagara Falls

visitor-friendly. No visit to this region would be complete without experiencing the majestic **Niagara Falls** *(see pp212–17)*, and the picture-perfect town of Niagara-on-the-Lake. **Point Pelee National Park** *(see p210)* juts out into Lake Erie, offering rural charm and the country's southernmost point. The city of **Stratford** *(see p211)* is renowned in North America for its excellent annual festival of Shake-speare's (and others') works, and **Sainte-Marie-among-the-Hurons** *(see pp220–21)* is a fascinating glimpse of a Jesuit settlement among the Huron natives of the 17th century.

CENTRAL CANADA

- **First Nations culture**
- **Dinosaur Provincial Park**
- **West Edmonton Mall**
- **Polar bear territory**

Roughly the size of Mexico, Central Canada includes the provinces of Manitoba, Saskatchewan, and Alberta. Whether you want to go dinosaur hunting in **Dinosaur Provincial Park** *(see p249)*, or encounter the Royal Canadian Mounted Police at Regina's **RCMP Centennial Museum** *(see p245)*, these sweeping prairies offer a myriad of experiences. You can also learn about First Nations history in **Saskatoon** *(see p246)* or visit polar bears in **Churchill**, Manitoba *(see p253)*. The oil-rich

sands of Alberta fuel not only the economy here, but also keep the gargantuan shopping mecca of **West Edmonton Mall** *(see p250)* busy year-round.

VANCOUVER AND VANCOUVER ISLAND

- **Breathtaking mountain and coastal scenery**
- **Colorful Granville Island in Vancouver**
- **Victoria – a timeless gem**
- **Whale watching in the Pacific Rim National Park**

Sometimes easily confused, British Columbia's capital – the lovely city of **Victoria** *(see pp280–85)* – is situated on Vancouver Island, whereas the striking metropolis of **Vancouver** *(see pp266–77)* is located on the mainland. Among many sights to see in Vancouver are the **Capilano Suspension Bridge** *(see p279)*,

Polar bear and cub near subarctic Churchill, Manitoba

artsy **Granville Island** *(see p274)*, the impressive downtown "wilderness" of **Stanley Park** *(see p275)* and the stunning **UBC Museum of Anthropology** *(see pp276–7)*. Vancouver Island is proud of its impeccably landscaped **Butchart Gardens** *(see p286)* in Brentwood Bay, and the phenomenal nature displays in the **Pacific Rim National Park Reserve** *(see pp288–9)*. Watch out for whales!

Back to nature at Vancouver's Capilano Suspension Bridge

THE ROCKY MOUNTAINS

- **Sublime Banff National Park**
- **Calgary Stampede**
- **Jasper's treasures**
- **Canada Olympic Park**

The "Rockies," as they are affectionately termed, contain no fewer than six national parks, four of which are UNESCO World Heritage sites. **Banff National Park** *(see pp300–303)* was Canada's first, and nearby **Jasper** *(see pp308–11)* is idyllic in both summer and winter. The youthful city of **Calgary** *(see p294)*, a former host of the Winter Olympics and home to the annual ten-day Calgary Stampede festival of all things western, is a lively urban area, so some may prefer quieter cities such as **Cranbrook** *(see p298)*, **Prince George** *(see p312)*, or **Fort Nelson** *(see p313)*. The Rocky Mountains are nearby, silent and impressive sentinels for year-round vacationing.

SOUTHERN AND NORTHERN BRITISH COLUMBIA

- **Bountiful Okanagan Valley**
- **Haida Gwaii and the Haida people**
- **Whistler – host of the 2010 Winter Olympics**
- **Thriving, cultural Nelson**

A climatically diverse province, British Columbia was able to host the 2010 Winter Olympics in **Whistler** *(see p316)*, grow bountiful fruits and vegetables in the **Okanagan Valley** *(see p317)*, and produce some excellent wines at the same time! **Haida Gwaii** *(see p321)* in the north have yet another ecosystem, and are the proud home of the native Haida people, known for their artistry. The town of **Nelson** *(see p318)* in the south also has a thriving cultural scene, and its pretty location on the shores of Kootenay Lake is an envied one.

NORTHERN CANADA

- **Gold Rush history in Dawson City**
- **Inuit art and culture**
- **The Northern Lights**
- **Nunavut, Canada's newest territory**

Multitudes of tourists have yet to discover the barren beauty of Canada's northern regions. Witnessing the

The spectacular Northern Lights, seen in Northern Canada

magical **Northern Lights** *(see p337)* is a definite highlight, as is appreciating the uniqueness of **Inuit art and culture** *(see pp326–7)* by native artisans and musicians. **Dawson City** *(see p336)* in the Yukon is embedded in the Canadian psyche thanks to its rollicking history of the Klondike Gold Rush. The locally produced diamonds are now available worldwide. The Northwest Territories' capital city of **Yellowknife** *(see pp338–9)* is also worth a visit. The territory of Nunavut (formed in 1999), and its capital Iqaluit on **Baffin Island** *(see pp340–41)*, may be remote but offer a once-in-a-lifetime experience.

Epic mountain scenery in the Rockies' Banff National Park

Putting Western and Northern Canada on the Map

Canada lies at the northern end of the American continent and covers 9,970,610 sq km (3,849,652 sq miles). More than 70 percent of this area is uninhabited because of vast tracts of frozen wilderness in the north. In contrast, British Columbia boasts Canada's only temperate rainforest.

Melville Island

Banks Island

Victoria Island

Cambridge Bay

Inuvik

NORTHWEST TERRITORIES

Great Bear Lake

Dawson City

YUKON

CANADA

Yellowknife

Whitehorse

Watson Lake

Hay River

Great Slave Lake

Fort Smith

Thelon

97

Fort Nelson

37

ALBERTA

35

Lake Athabasca

BRITISH COLUMBIA

Fort St. John

Fort McMurray

SASKATCHEWAN

PACIFIC

OCEAN

Haida Gwaii

Prince Rupert

Prince George

97

43

Athabasca

Saskatchewan

Prince Albert

Flin Flon

Edmonton

Red Deer

Banff

Saskatoon

16

Yorkton

Calgary

1

Regina

Vancouver Island

Vancouver

Victoria

Minot

Seattle

90

Portland

15

94

5

UNITED STATES OF AMERICA

80

KEY

- ✈ International airport
- ▬ Highway
- ▬ Major road
- ─ Principal rail routes
- ▪–▪ International border
- --- Provincial border

MILEAGE CHART

10 = Distance in kilometers
10 = Distance in miles

BANFF								
128 80	CALGARY							
3039 1889	2911 1809	DAWSON CITY						
253 157	146 91	1976 1228	RED DEER					
888 552	764 475	2526 1570	610 379	REGINA				
748 465	630 391	2297 1427	476 296	260 161	SASKATOON			
928 577	1057 657	1917 1191	934 580	2424 1506	1677 1042	VANCOUVER		
2513 1562	2385 1482	440 274	2188 1360	2871 1784	2614 1624	2697 1676	WHITEHORSE	
1464 910	1336 830	2942 1828	1186 737	888 552	829 515	3312 2058	3524 2190	WINNIPEG

VANCOUVER AND ENVIRONS

North Vancouver
Coquitlam
Vancouver
Burnaby
Richmond
Surrey

0 km   5
0 miles   5

Vancouver

There are no fast highways that cross Vancouver's center. The Trans-Canada Highway (Hwy 1) passes through the suburb of Burnaby, across Burrard Inlet, to its western end on Vancouver Island.

CANADA

GREENLAND
U.S.A
CANADA
U.S.A
MEXICO

Devon Island
Somerset Island
Prince of Wales Island
Baffin Island
NUNAVUT
Back
Baker Lake
Southampton Island
Hudson Bay
Churchill
Ungava Bay
QUEBEC
MANITOBA
Nelson
Thompson
Belcher Islands
James Bay
Lake Winnipeg
ONTARIO
Seven
Albany
Winnipeg
Thunder Bay
Lake Superior
North Bay
OTTAWA
Fredericton
Sydney
Minneapolis
St. Paul
Lake Michigan
Lake Huron
Montreal
Saint John
Halifax
Toronto
Lake Ontario
Windsor
London
Niagara Falls
Lake Erie
Chicago
New York

0 km   400
0 miles

Putting Eastern Canada on the Map

Most of Canada's 30 million people live close to the US border, in a band that stretches from the east coast across to British Columbia in the west. Over 60 percent of all Canadians are concentrated in the southeast corner of the country, in the provinces of Ontario and Quebec. This is the heartland of Canadian industry, including electronics, hydro-electricity, lumber, and paper. The maritime provinces of Nova Scotia, New Brunswick, and Prince Edward Island are Canada's smallest, but the beauty of their landscapes attracts thousands of tourists each year. Newfoundland and Labrador are also known for their rugged charm.

TORONTO

Toronto
Greater Toronto is Canada's largest city, with a population of 4.6 million. Traffic congestion can be bad, particularly during rush hours, when parking is also expensive.

MILEAGE CHART

CHARLOTTETOWN

10 = Distance in kilometers
10 = Distance in miles

356 / **221**	*FREDERICTON*								
239 / **148**	**473** / **294**	*HALIFAX*							
1149 / **714**	**834** / **518**	**1003** / **623**	*MONTREAL*						
1860 / **1156**	**1510** / **938**	**1925** / **1196**	**676** / **420**	*NIAGARA FALLS*					
1339 / **832**	**1016** / **631**	**1456** / **905**	**200** / **124**	**536** / **333**	*OTTAWA*				
954 / **593**	**598** / **371**	**1071** / **665**	**257** / **160**	**946** / **588**	**724** / **450**	*QUEBEC CITY*			
1412 / **877**	**1267** / **787**	**1512** / **939**	**859** / **534**	**1569** / **975**	**1074** / **667**	**637** / **396**	*SEPT-ILES*		
2794 / **1736**	**2471** / **1535**	**2910** / **1808**	**1654** / **1028**	**1521** / **945**	**1503** / **934**	**1963** / **1220**	**2613** / **1624**	*THUNDER BAY*	
1689 / **1049**	**1366** / **849**	**1806** / **1122**	**549** / **341**	**137** / **85**	**399** / **248**	**809** / **503**	**1449** / **900**	**1384** / **860**	*TORONTO*

KEY

- ✈ International airport
- ▬ Highway
- ▬ Major road
- — Principal rail routes
- ▬ International border
- - - Provincial border

0 km   500

0 miles   500

Montreal

Montreal is a well-established transportation hub. The city is surrounded by a network of highways. The Trans-Canada Highway, a hectic six-lane highway, crosses the city as number 40 , or the Autoroute Métropolitain.

MONTREAL AND ENVIRONS

0 km   5

0 miles   5

A PORTRAIT OF CANADA

Blessed with ancient forests, rugged mountains, and large cosmopolitan cities, Canada is unimaginably vast, stretching west from the Atlantic to the Pacific and north to the Arctic Ocean. Around 20,000 years ago Canada was inhabited by aboriginal peoples, but by the 19th century it had been settled by Europeans. Today, the country is noted as a liberal, multicultural society.

Inuit wooden mask

In part, Canada's heritage of tolerance is a result of its conflict-ridden past. Two centuries of compromise was necessary to fully establish the country. Following fighting between the British and French armies in the 1750s, the British won control of the country in 1759. The self-governing colonies of British North America spent three years hammering out the agreement that brought them together as the Dominion of Canada in 1867. Newfoundland did not become part of the nation until 1949. Powerful regional differences, particularly between French- and English-speaking Canada, meant that the country has had difficulties evolving a national identity. When Pierre Berton, one of Canada's most prolific writers, was prompted to define a Canadian he evaded the question, replying: "Someone who knows how to make love in a canoe."

The second largest country in the world, Canada has a surface area of 9,970,610 sq km (3,849,652 sq miles). Over 40 percent of the land is north of the treeline at 60° latitude; this extraordinarily hostile and sparsely inhabited wilderness is bitterly cold in winter, averaging -30°C (-22°F), and plagued by millions of insects in summer. Not surprisingly, most

The snow-laden rooftops of Quebec City overlooking the St. Lawrence River at dusk

◁ Bull elk grazing in Jasper National Park in the Rocky Mountains

Canadians live in the more temperate regions farther to the south. Of the country's 30 million inhabitants, more than 80 percent live within 200 kilometers (124 miles) of the US border.

FLORA AND FAUNA

In the far north, the permafrost of the treeless tundra (or taiga) supports the growth of only the toughest flora, such as lichen, mosses, and a range of unusually hardy varieties of flowers and grasses. In spring and fall however, the tundra flora bursts into an impressive display of color. Animal life is abundant in this region, and includes the polar bear, arctic fox, wolf, seal, musk ox, and caribou.

Spring flower from the Bruce Peninsula

Farther south, the boreal or coniferous forest covers a wide band from Newfoundland in the east to the Yukon in the west. A variety of trees here, including spruce, balsam fir, and jack pine, provides a home for those animals most typically thought of as Canadian – primarily moose, beaver, lynx, and black bear. The beaver is Canada's national symbol. It was the European fashion for beaver hats that created and sustained the Canadian fur trade and opened up the interior to European settlers, paving the way for the growth of the modern nation.

In the east, deciduous forests containing the emblematic maple are populated by deer, raccoons, and mink. Across central Canada, the grasslands, known as the Prairies, house elk, gophers, and increasing numbers of buffalo.

British Columbia's temperate rain forests are rich in wildlife such as black tail deer, brown bear, and cougar. Rare orchids and ferns grow here, among towering cedars, firs, and spruce trees.

THE FIRST NATIONS

Although thought of as a new country, Canada's prehistory dates back about 20,000 years to the end of the first Ice Age. At that time there was a land bridge joining Siberia to Alaska; Siberian hunter-nomads crossed this bridge to become the first human inhabitants of North America, and over

The bald eagle, a common sight around the Charlotte Island archipelago in British Columbia

the succeeding centuries their descendants gradually moved south. Archaeological digs in the Old Crow River Basin in the Yukon have unearthed a collection of tools believed to date to this initial period of migration. These Siberian nomads were the ancestors of the continent's native peoples.

Inuit children at Bathurst Inlet, Nunavut

By the 16th century, Spanish, French, and Portuguese traders were the first Europeans to have close dealings with the aboriginal peoples of the Americas, whom they named "Indians" in the mistaken belief that they had reached India. The "Indian" appellation stuck, and the "Red" was added by British settlers in the 17th century when they met the Beothuks of Newfoundland, who daubed themselves in red ochre to repel insects. The native peoples of the far north were also given a name they did not want – "Eskimo," literally "eaters of raw meat." Given the history, it is hardly surprising that modern-day leaders of Canada's aboriginal peoples have rejected these names in favor of others: aboriginal, native Canadians, and First Nations are all acceptable, though the people of the north prefer Inuit (meaning "the people"). Included among Canada's native peoples are the Métis, mixed race descendants of aboriginal peoples and French-speaking European traders.

SOCIETY

The official languages of Canada are French and English, and the interplay between Canada's two largest linguistic and cultural groups is evident in the capital city of Ottawa, where every federal speech and bill has to be delivered in both languages. All packaging must also be bilingual. Canada's population is about 24 percent French Canadian, predominantly the descendants of French settlers who came to the colony of New France in the 17th and 18th centuries *(see p45)*. Their English-speaking compatriots are largely descended from 18th- and 19th-century British immigrants.

Canada's reputation as a multicultural society began to be established in the 1800s, when successive waves of immigration, along with various settlement plans, brought people from all over the world to Canada. Today, perhaps the best way to experience this modern country's vibrant cultural mix is to visit its three largest cities – Toronto, Montreal, and Vancouver.

View from Centre Island's parks and gardens on Lake Ontario toward Toronto's CN Tower

Changing of the Guard outside Ottawa's Parliament Building

GOVERNMENT AND POLITICS

Canada is a parliamentary democracy with a federal political system. Each province or territory has its own democratically elected provincial legislature headed by a Premier, and also sends elected representatives to the federal parliament in Ottawa. The House of Commons is the main federal legislature. The Prime Minister is the head of the political structure, as well as an elected member of the House of Commons where he must be able to command a majority. Bills passed in the Commons are forwarded to an upper chamber, the Senate, for ratification. At present, the Prime Minister appoints senators, although there is increasing pressure to make the upper chamber elective too. The nominal head of state is the British monarch, currently Queen Elizabeth II, and her Canadian representative is the Governor-General.

In recent decades, the dominant trend in Canadian politics has been regionalism. The provinces have sought to take back power from the center, which makes it difficult for

The ceremonial unveiling of the new Nunavut flag in 1999

any one political party to win majority support in all parts of the country at once. The most conspicuous aspect of this process has been the conflict over Quebec, where there is a strong separatist movement. Twice since 1980, the Quebecois have been asked to vote in referenda seeking their support to leave Canada and, although the electorate voted "No" both times, it was a close result. The issue of Quebec's relationship with the rest of Canada is still unresolved, and further political disputes seem inevitable.

Since the 1980s aboriginal politics has come to the fore with campaigns for constitutional, land, and mineral rights. The Assembly of First Nations has been at the forefront of the establishment of the Inuit homeland, Nunavut. Current issues include battles for self-government and land claims, as well as hunting and fishing rights.

Canada has played its part in the major events of the 20th century, including both world wars, and today holds a prominent position in international politics. The country is a member of NATO and one of the Group of Eight (G8) countries, which, with the US, UK, Italy, Japan, France, Germany, and Russia, decide on world trade agreements.

ART AND CULTURE

The vast and beautiful landscape of the country is a defining feature of Canadian culture. Outdoor pursuits such as hiking, skiing, and canoeing are high on the list of popular activities. Canadians are also great sports fans, and ice hockey, baseball, basketball, and Canadian football attract huge crowds of spectators, and foster deeply felt allegiances. In addition to their passion for sports, Canadians are also enthusiastic about the arts. This is the country that has produced internationally renowned classical pianist, Glenn Gould, and whose major cities possess well-respected orchestras. Canada has also produced more than its share of popular music stars, from ground breaking singer-songwriters such as Joni Mitchell and Neil Young to more middle-of-the-road artists such as Celine Dion, Bryan Adams, and Shania Twain. Canada's cosmopolitan culture also means that visitors are likely to find a wide choice of music in bars, cafés, and at the country's numerous festivals. All kinds of drama from Shakespeare to new writing can be seen at the renowned Stratford Shakespearean Festival, which is held in Ontario.

International rock star Alanis Morissette

Toronto Maple Leaf legend Mats Sundin

Many Canadian artists have looked to the wilderness as a source of inspiration. The first artist to attempt to express a sense of national identity was Tom Thomson, with his distinctive landscapes of Northern Ontario. He influenced the country's most celebrated group of painters, the Group of Seven *(see pp164–5)*, who evolved a national style of painting capable of representing Canada's wilderness, a theme developed by their contemporaries and successors, notably Emily Carr.

Canada's world-class museums and galleries represent the country's pride in its art collections: the outstanding Art Gallery of Ontario in Toronto

(see pp178–9) has an extensive display of Group of Seven paintings, as well as cutting-edge contemporary art. Major contemporary Canadian artists on the international circuit include Janet Cardiff and Rodney Graham.

Among Canadian writers, there are distinguished practitioners in both English and French, and an impressive list of contemporary novelists includes such prize-winning authors as Margaret Atwood, Carol Shields, Michael Ondaatje, Jacques Poulin, Yann Martel, and Germaine Guèvremont.

The Canadian film industry is thriving, with established directors such as David Cronenberg and Atom Egoyan continuing to create daring films. *Barney's Version*, a critically acclaimed adaptation of Mordecai Richler's 1997 novel, was set and shot in and around Montreal.

Author Margaret Atwood, lauded worldwide

Behind Canada's flourishing cultural life, lies a pride in its history and cosmopolitan heritage, and an affection for the land's daunting beauty.

Landscape and Geology

Canada is the second largest country in the world, covering an area almost as big as Europe. It was created from the world's oldest landmasses. The billion-year-old bowl-shaped Canadian Shield covers much of the country, dipping around Hudson Bay and rising to mountain ranges at its edges. The country is bordered by oceans on three sides, with a coastline 243,800 km (151,400 miles) long and an interior containing some two million lakes. Canada is well known for the diversity of its landscapes: from the frozen, barren north that descends to the mountainous west with its forest and wheat plains, through the wooded, hilly east, and the fertile lowlands of the southeast.

The Great Lakes *region covers 3% of Canada's landmass, and comprises a fertile lowland bowl, vital to its agricultural economy.*

The Interior Plains, *including the prairies, are the principal wheat-growing areas of the country, and range southeast 2,600 km (1,600 miles) from the Cordilleras to the US border. The plains are divided into three huge steppes.*

THE ROCKIES AND THE WESTERN CORDILLERA

This region is part of one of the world's longest mountain chains. In Canada, the Cordillera comprises the Pacific Coastal Mountains and forested basins. Graduated peaks and ridges reveal Ice Age erosion, as does the Columbia Icefield *(see p310)*. The Rockies developed from continental plate movement, which began about 120 million years ago *(see pp258–9)*.

GEOGRAPHICAL REGIONS

Characterized by its variety, Canadian landscape falls into six main areas. The north of the country offers a landscape of tundra, with the far north ice-covered for much of the year. In the west and south, the warmer, fertile lands of the Cordillera and interior plains support the rural population. To the east, the Great Lakes area is an agricultural center. The vast Canadian Shield cradles the plains and rises to form the northern Innuitian region and the Appalachians in the south.

Innuitian Region and Arctic Lowlands

The Rockies & Western Cordillera

Canadian Shield

Interior Plains

Appalachians

Great Lakes

The Appalachians' *rolling landscape is two-thirds woodland and covers both arable lowland areas and the highest peaks in Quebec. These are found on the Gaspé Peninsula, the outer mountain ring of the Canadian Shield highland. Most of the Appalachian mountain chain lies in the US. They are nature's barrier between the eastern seaboard and the continental interior lowlands.*

The Canadian Shield, *formed of the 1,100-million-year-old bedrock of the North American continent, is the core of the country. It spreads out from Hudson Bay for 5 million sq km (1.9 million sq miles). The center is scrub and rock, and rises to steep mountains around the rim.*

The Innuitian *region stretches northward from the Arctic Lowlands' modest height of 100–700 m (330–2,000 ft) above sea level to the peaks of the Innuitian mountain range, at their highest on Ellesmere Island at 2,926 m (9,600 ft). Vigorous glaciation for millenia has developed deep fjords, sharp peaks, and frost patterns on the earth. This region is rich in oil, coal, and gas.*

Canada's Wildlife

By the time it emerged from the last Ice Age 10,000 years ago, Canada had developed a geography and climate that remains one of the most diverse on Earth. In the north, the Arctic weather produces a harsh, barren desert, in darkness for several months and frozen most of the year. By contrast, the country's most southerly province, Ontario, shares a latitude with northern California and offers fertile forests laced with rivers and lakes. In southern Canada, many varieties of wildlife flourish in the coniferous forest that covers the ancient rocks of the Canadian Shield. In the central plain are wheat-filled open prairies. From here, foothills lead to the Rocky Mountains, which gradually roll westward to coastal mountains and the balmy landscape of temperate rainforest along the Pacific coast.

The muskox *is a gregarious herd animal and a remnant of the last Ice Age. Its thick topcoat of guard hair and undercoat of finer, fleecier hair keeps it warm even at –45°C (–50°F).*

THE BOREAL FOREST

The boreal forest extends from eastern Canada, across most of Quebec and Ontario, and into the northern parts of the prairie provinces. It consists of a mix of spruce, pine, birch, and aspen, and occurs mostly on the giant rock outcrop of the Canadian Shield *(see pp22–3).* Dotted with thousands of lakes, it is a rich habitat for some of Canada's best-known wildlife.

THE PRAIRIES

Once referred to as a "sea of grass," the Canadian prairie is now predominantly agricultural in nature, specializing in growing wheat and other grains, and ranching prime beef cattle. While little original prairie wilderness remains, this is still a land of great open spaces that supports a surprising, often rare, wildlife population.

The timber wolf, *or gray wolf, was hunted almost to extinction by 1950. It has now returned to the more isolated parts of its range in the boreal forest.*

The pronghorn *antelope is the last of its species to survive in North America. The fastest American mammal, it can reach speeds of over 75 km (47 miles) per hour.*

The loon *has a haunting call that rings out over northern lakes and is symbolic of the Canadian wilderness.*

The bison *now exists in only two remaining wild herds in Alberta and the Northwest Territories.*

CANADA'S SPORTS FISH

From the northern pike and lake trout in the north to the walleye and smallmouth bass in the south, Canada is blessed with a large number of sports fish species. Some fish that are much sought after as sport in Europe (the common carp, for example) are regarded as "trash," or undesirable, in Canada, and exist in large numbers in lakes and rivers across the Canadian Prairies. The arctic char, plentiful in the far north, is also prized for its taste.

Fishing *is one of Canada's most popular sports and is superbly supported by 37 national parks, each containing plentiful rivers and lakes.*

Salmon migrating *upriver provide an annual challenge for the keen sport fisherman. Canada has half the freshwater in the world, but deep sea angling can also prove rewarding.*

THE ROCKY MOUNTAINS

The Rocky Mountains begin in the foothills of western Alberta and rise into British Columbia. Along with the Columbia Mountains and the coastal mountains, they form a unique environment that ranges from heavily forested lower slopes, through alpine meadows, to snow-covered rocky peaks. This habitat is home to some of the most majestic wildlife in Canada.

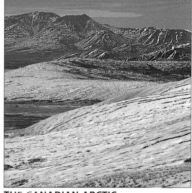

THE CANADIAN ARCTIC

North of the 60th parallel of latitude, the forest yields to arctic tundra and rock. The tundra is mostly bare, and frozen year-round a few inches below the surface, the icy ground being known as permafrost. During the brief summer the top layer thaws, and the Arctic bursts into bloom. Even though the Arctic is a freezing desert with little moisture, wildlife flourishes.

The recurring horns *of a mature male big-horn sheep, found in more remote spots of the Rockies, weigh as much as all its bones put together.*

The great white polar bear *spends most of its life alone, out on the polar ice pack, hunting for seals.*

Canada's grizzly bear *stands up to 2.75 m (8.8 ft) high and weighs up to 350 kg (800 lbs). It feeds on roots, berries, and meat.*

The caribou *is a North American cousin of the reindeer. Caribou in the arctic migrate with the season in herds of 10,000, heading north on to the tundra in spring, south into the forest during winter.*

Multicultural Canada

Canada prides itself on its multiculturalism. The country has evolved a unique way of adjusting to the cultural needs of its increasingly diverse population. In contrast to the US's "melting pot," Canada has opted for what is often called the "Canadian mosaic," a model based on accepting diversity rather than assimilation. The origins of this tolerant and fruitful approach are embedded deep in Canadian history. Fearful of attack by the US in 1793, the British safeguarded the religious and civic institutions of their French-Canadian subjects in the hope that they would not ally with the Americans. This policy set the pattern of compromise that is now a hallmark of Canada. Citizens of British and French ancestry still make up the bulk of the population of 30 million, but there are around 60 significant minorities.

Young Inuit people in traditional dress huddled against the snow

NATIVE CANADIANS

Today there are around one million Native Canadians, though national census figures usually break this group down into three sub-sections – aboriginals (750,000), métis (Indian and French mixed race 200,000), and Inuit (50,000). Of the million, about 60 percent are known as Status Indians, meaning they are officially settled on reserve land. However, over 40 percent of Status Indians now live away from reserve land, and only 900 of Canada's 2,370 reserves are still inhabited. These lands are home to 608 First Nations groups, or bands, which exercise varying degrees of self-government through their own elected councils. Since the 1970s, progressive councils have played a key role in the reinvigoration of

traditional native culture. Most non-Status Native Canadians are now integrated into the rest of Canada's population.

Rarely is the membership of a reserve descended from just one tribe. The largest band is the Six Nations of the Grand River, in Ontario, where the 19,000 inhabitants come from 13 groups including the Mohawk, Delaware, and Seneca peoples.

In the far north, where white settlers have always been rare, the Inuit have a small majority. A result of their self-determination was the creation of Nunavut, a semi-autonomous Inuit homeland comprising 349,650 sq km (135,000 sq miles) of the eastern Arctic, created officially in April 1999. Nunavut means "our land" in the Inuit language, and traditional skills of hunting and igloo-building have been reintroduced to this region.

BRITISH AND IRISH CANADIANS

Canadians of British and Irish descent constitute a large percentage of the country's population. The first English settlers arrived in the wake of the fleets that fished the waters off Newfoundland in the 16th century. Thereafter, there was a steady trickle of English, Scottish, Welsh, and Irish immigrants and several mass migrations, prompted either by adverse politics at home or fresh opportunities in Canada. Thousands of Scots arrived following the defeat of Bonnie Prince Charlie at Culloden in 1746, and the Irish poured across the Atlantic during and after the potato famine (1845–49). When the Prairie provinces opened up in the 1880s and at the end of both World Wars another large-scale migration took place.

These British and Irish settlers did much to shape Canada, establishing its social and cultural norms and founding its legal and political institutions. Canada's official Head of State is still the British monarch.

British poster of the 1920s promoting emigration to Canada

FRENCH CANADIANS

Canada's French-speakers make up about 20 percent of the total population, and are the country's second-largest ethnic group. They are mainly based in Quebec and New Brunswick, but other pockets thrive in other provinces. The French first reached the Canadian mainland in 1535 when Jacques Cartier sailed up the St. Lawrence River in search of a sea-route to Asia. Fur-traders, priests, and farmers followed in Cartier's footsteps and by the end of the 17th century, New France, as the colony was known, was well established. After the British captured New France in the Seven Years' War of 1756–63 *(see pp46–7)*, most French colonists stayed on as British subjects. The French-speakers maintained their own religious and civic institutions and a feeling of independence that has grown over time. Since the 1960s, the constitutional link between Quebec and the rest of the country has been the subject of political debate, with a strong minority of Quebecois pressing for full independence *(see p55)*.

Street scene in Chinatown, Toronto

GERMAN CANADIANS

Although there have been German-speakers in Canada since the 1660s, the first major migration came between 1850–1900, with other mass arrivals following both World Wars. On the whole, the English-speaking majority has absorbed the Germans, but distinctive pockets of German-speakers hold strong today in Lunenburg, Nova Scotia *(see p88)*, and Kitchener-Waterloo in Ontario *(see p218)*. The rural communities surrounding Kitchener-Waterloo are strongholds of the Amish, a German-speaking religious sect, whose members shun the trappings of modern life and travel around on horse-drawn buggies wearing traditional homemade clothes.

German food and drink, especially its beer-making techniques, have added to Canadian cuisine. Ethnic restaurants in German areas still run on traditional lines.

ITALIAN CANADIANS

The widespread Italian presence in Canada can prove hard to see, as, for the most part, all 600,000 immigrants have merged almost seamlessly with the English speakers. There are, however, exceptions; in Toronto, a large and flourishing "Little Italy" neighborhood delights both visitors and the city's epicurean residents. The first major influx of Italian Canadians came in the wake of the civil wars that disrupted Italy in the second half of the 19th century; another wave arrived in the 1940s and 1950s after World War II. Immigration continues into the 21st century, with two percent of Canadians today speaking Italian as their first language.

German beer stein

CHINESE CANADIANS

During the 1850s, Chinese laborers arrived in Canada to work in the gold fields of British Columbia. Thereafter, they played a key role in the construction of the railroads, settling new towns and cities as their work progressed eastward. During this period the Chinese suffered much brutal racism, including laws that enforced statutory discrimination.

A flood of Chinese immigration took place just before the return of Hong Kong to China by the British in 1997. Most settlers chose Toronto, Montreal, and Vancouver, but British Columbia has also gained in popularity. With the Chinese focus on keeping large families together, most new arrivals aim for an established community. About half of all Canada's immigrants today come from Asia. Over two percent of the Canadian population claimed Chinese as their first language in the late 1990s.

UKRAINIAN CANADIANS

Although Ukrainians are a small fraction of the Canadian population, numbering less than three percent, they have had a strong cultural influence, especially in the Prairie Provinces where the cupolas of their churches rise above many midwestern villages. The first major wave of Ukrainian migrants arrived in the 1890s as refugees from Tsarist persecution. The Soviet regime and the aftermath of World War II caused a second influx in the 20th century.

Woman in native Ukrainian dress in Battleford, Saskatchewan

French Canada

"Free Quebec" demonstrator

Many Canadians are quick to point out that Canada's origins are more French than British, that the first European Canadians were explorers from France, and therefore called *canadiens*. French Canadians have had a centuries-long history of conquest and battle to preserve their language and culture, strongest in Quebec and parts of Atlantic Canada. This has left large parts of the country with a French cultural base that lives on in language, religion, and the arts. More recently, the French-Canadian struggle for recognition in the 20th century has left unresolved the issue of Quebec's independence.

The heart of French Canada is Quebec, a province many times the size of France. Here, 85 percent of people count French as their mother tongue. French is not just the language of food, folklore, and love; it is also the language of business, government, and law.

LANGUAGE

French is the joint official language of Canada, but it has mutated in much the same way that North American English has. *Canadiens*, especially those in the bigger cities, have adopted some anglicisms; modern English words relating to industries and trades introduced by English-speakers are favorites. Conversely, some words that have passed out of fashion in France survive here; Canada is one of the few places where a cart remains a *charette*, for example, instead of a *tombereau*, and the *fin-de-semaine* is the time to get away for some relaxation, rather than the now-universal *le weekend*. Young Quebecois in particular are also far more free in using the informal *tu*, than more formal *vous*, than their parents would perhaps consider polite.

Wide varieties exist in the quality and style of French spoken. The Paris-influenced intonation of Montreal's college-educated *haute bourgeoisie*, for example, is quite distinct from the rhythmic gutturals of the Acadian fishermen of the Maritimes. Residents of Quebec's Saguenay-Lac-Saint-Jean region speak a hard, clear French that must sound very like that of their Norman forbears.

Over the years Quebecois have evolved a dialect called *joual*, which is informal, slangy, and peppered with anglicisms. It is also very colorful and viewed with a mix of pride and disdain. The accent may be hard for foreigners to follow.

FOOD

Canadiens have always considered themselves the epicures of Canada, and with some justice, enjoying the delights of the table more passionately than their English-speaking counterparts. Traditional food is rich and hearty. Meat pies are a specialty: *cipaille* comprizes layers of game meat under a flaky crust, and the more common *tourtière* has a filling made of ground beef spiced with cloves. Salmon pie, stews made with pigs' feet, and meatballs in a rich gravy are also typical. Desserts are rich; the Acadian *tarte au sucre* (sugar pie) is popular, as well as *pudding au chomeur* (literally "unemployed pudding"), an upside-down cake with a sweet, caramelized base of sugar baked into a rich batter.

Musician Felix Leclerc was a guardian of Quebec's folk music

MUSIC

Chansoniers are the troubadours of French Canada. Rooted in the traditional music of the first settlers, their haunting songs and simple melodies, such as the ballads of Felix Leclerc, might be melancholy or upbeat, but they are almost always romantic. These folk songs, accompanied by guitar, usually reflect optimism and a deep love for the land. Quebec *chansonier* Gilles Vigneault's *Mon Pays* has become a nationalist anthem for those seeking independence. Of course, French music is not confined to the traditional; there are several successful rock, pop, and independent bands. Acadia's singers are often *chansonières*, including Edith Butler and Angèle Arseneault vividly evoking the sadness and joy of life by the sea.

Sugar pie, a traditional Acadian family dessert, served at celebrations

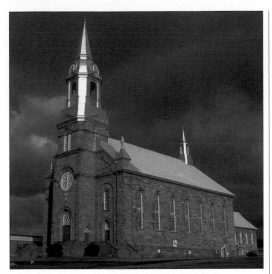

Traditional Catholic church in Cheticamp, Cape Breton Island

FAITH

The first French settlers were Roman Catholic, many very devout and zealous. The founders of Montreal, Paul Chomédy Sieur de Maisonneuve and Jeanne Mance, had hoped to create a new society based on Christian principles. Much of that devotion has evaporated in the modern age, especially in Quebec, which has one of the lowest church-attendance records in the country. Past fidelity has, however, left permanent monuments. Tiny French villages in Quebec and New Brunswick often have huge, stone churches with glittering tin roofs, gilding, and ornate interiors. Some parish churches in Montreal, like the magnificent Basilique Notre-Dame-de-Montréal (see pp112–13), would pass for cathedrals in US cities.

NATIONALISM

There has been a nationalist strain to most *canadien* aspirations since the founding of Modern Canada. Quebecois entered the 1867 Canadian Confederation (see p48) only because French leaders persuaded them that the deal would preserve their faith and language. The 1960s and 1970s took the campaign into a new phase, with the aim being the independence of Quebec, as the politics of mere survival rose to the politics of assertiveness (with French President Charles de Gaulle adding his rallying cry *"Vive le Québec – libre!"* in 1966). Acadians in New Brunswick gained real political power to preserve their unique heritage, Franco-Ontarians fought for control over their own schools, and Manitobans used the courts to force their provincial government to translate all Manitoba statutes into French.

This resurgence of national pride was felt most strongly in Quebec, where the charismatic and popular politician René Lévesque and his Parti-Québécois won the provincial election in 1976 and made outright separatism respectable. The party now regularly wins local elections and has so far held two referenda on independence. Both times Quebecois said no by the narrowest of margins, but the threat still dominates Canada's political life.

SYMBOLS

The Quebec flag has a white cross on a blue background with a white Bourbon lily in each quarter. Acadians have created their own flag by adding a gold star to the French tricolor, which symbolizes *Stella Maris* (Star of the Sea), named after the Virgin Mary. The patron saint of French Canada is St. Jean-Baptiste (St. John the Baptist); parades and parties mark his feast day on June 24. The celebrations take on a strongly nationalist style in Quebec, where the big day is called the *Fête National*. The provincial bird of Quebec is the snowy owl, and the flower remains the white lily, both of which flourish in the province.

Quebec flag with Bourbon lilies

Demonstrators during referendum vote for independence of Quebec

Native Canadians

Native mask
from
Vancouver

Most archaeologists believe that the first inhabitants of North America crossed from Siberia to Alaska around 25,000 years ago. These hunter-nomads came in search of mammoth and bison, the ice-age animals that constituted their basic diet. The first wave of migrants was reinforced by a steady trickle of Siberian peoples over the next 15,000 years, and slowly the tribes worked their way east and south until they reached the Atlantic and South America.

Over the centuries, the descendants of these hunter-nomads evolved a wide range of cultures, which were shaped by their particular environment. In the icy north or across the barren wastes of Newfoundland, life was austere; but the fertile soils of Ontario and the fish-rich shores of British Columbia nourished sophisticated societies based on fishing and farming.

Europeans began to arrive *in numbers during the 17th century. In Newfoundland, the first part of Canada settled by whites, interracial relations were initially cordial but soured when new settlers encroached on ancient hunting grounds. In a pattern repeated across the continent, the native peoples, many dying from European diseases, were driven to inhospitable lands.*

THE IROQUOIS

Spread along the St. Lawrence River and the shores of the Great Lakes, were the Iroquois-speaking tribes, among whom were the Mohawks, the Huron, and the Seneca. These tribes hunted and fished, but they also cultivated beans, pumpkins, squash, and corn, growing everything in abundance for a year-round food supply. This enabled them to live in large villages, often with several hundred inhabitants. Their traditional dwelling was the longhouse, built of cedar poles bent to

An Iroquois-built longhouse

form a protective arch and covered with bark. These settlements were all surrounded by high palisades made of sharpened wooden stakes, a necessary precaution as warfare between the tribes was endemic.

Cornplanter, a 17th-century chief of the Seneca tribe

THE PLAINS PEOPLES

War was also commonplace on the plains of southern Manitoba and Saskatchewan, where the majority Blackfoot tribe was totally reliant on the buffalo: they ate the meat, used the hide for clothes and tents, and filed the bones into tools. The first Blackfoot hunted the buffalo by means of cleverly conceived traps, herding the animals and stampeding them off steep cliffs (see p296). Originally, the horse was unknown to the

Indians on horseback hunting buffalo with arrows

native peoples of the Americas – their largest beast of burden was the dog – but the Spanish conquistadores brought the horse with them when they colonized South America in the 1500s. Thereafter, horses were slowly traded north until they reached the Canadian plains. The arrival of the horse transformed Blackfoot life: it made the buffalo easy to hunt and, with a consistent food supply now assured, the tribe developed a militaristic culture, focusing particularly on the valor of their young men – the "braves."

A Blackfoot camp, showing traditional homes

PEOPLES OF THE PACIFIC COAST

The native peoples of the Pacific Coast were divided into a large number of small tribes such as the Tlingit and the Salish. The ocean was an abundant source of food; with this necessity

taken care of, they developed an elaborate ceremonial life featuring large and lively feasts, the potlachs, in which clans tried

Totem pole in Stanley Park

to outdo each other with the magnificence of their gifts. The peoples of this region were also superb woodcarvers, their most celebrated works of art being totem poles. Each pole featured a myth from the tribe's religion; magical birds and beasts mix with semi-human figures to tell a story in carved panels rising up the pole.

Sqylax tribal celebration in British Columbia

TERMINOLOGY

For Canadians, the words "Eskimo" and "Red Indian" or just "Indian" are unacceptable. They are seen as terms of abuse, as they hark back to times when whites dominated the country and crushed its original population. The word "Eskimo" has been replaced by "Inuit," but modern substitutes for "Indian" are not as clear-cut. Some people choose "aboriginal" or "native," others prefer "indigenous," or speak of Canada's "First Nations." All are acceptable, but it is preferable to determine a specific tribe or band name, such as "Cree" or "Iroquois."

THE INUIT AND THE PEOPLES OF THE NORTHERN FORESTS

Stretching in a band from Alaska to Greenland, the far north was home to the Inuit, nomadic hunters who lived in skin tents in the summer and igloos in the winter. Arctic conditions and limited food supply meant that they foraged in small family groups and gathered together only in special circumstances – during the annual caribou migration, for instance. To the south of the Inuit, and also wide-spread across modern-day Canada, were the tribes of the northern forest, including the Naskapi, the Chipewyan, and the Wood Cree. These tribes were also nomadic hunters, dependent on fish and seal, or deer and moose. Successful hunters earned prestige, and the tribal priest (shaman) was expected to keep the spirit world bene-volent, but there was little other social organization.

An Inuit hunter by his igloo home

Inuit in Caribou parka, checking his harpoon

Paul Okalik, Nunavut's first Premier, at his inauguration

NATIVE CANADIAN ISSUES

Since the 1960s, Canada's native peoples have recovered some of their self-confidence. A key development was the creation of the Assembly of First Nations (AFN), an intertribal organization that has become an influential player on the national scene. In the 1980s, the AFN successfully argued for a greater degree of self-government on the reservations and tackled the federal government on land rights, sponsoring a series of court cases that highlighted the ways the native population had been stripped of its territories. The AFN was also involved in the establishment of Nunavut (see p55), the homeland for the Inuit created in 1999 from part of the former Northwest Territories. By comparison with their white compatriots, Canada's native population remains, nonetheless, poor and disadvantaged. The rectification of historic wrongs will take decades, even assuming that the political will remains strong enough to improve matters.

Art in Canada

Inuit and other First Nations groups have produced art in Canada since prehistoric times: the Inuit carved wood or antler sculptures, and other native groups were responsible for works from rock paintings to richly decorated pottery. Early European immigrants, both French and English, generally eschewed native traditions and followed European forms. Throughout the 19th and early 20th centuries, artists traveled, to Paris, London, and New York to study European art. It was in the 1900s that painters sought to develop a distinctly national style. However, one consistent subject of Canadian painting is the country itself: a preoccupation with its lush forests, stately landscapes, and expanse of freezing northern wilderness. Today, Canadian art reflects a wide range of art movements, with native art in particular fetching high prices among collectors.

On the Saint Lawrence (1897) oil painting by Maurice Cullen

PAINTERS IN THE NEW WORLD

In the 1600s French settlers in Canada either imported religious paintings or commissioned stock subjects to adorn their new churches. Only Samuel de Champlain, the "Father of New France" *(see p45)*, stands out for his sketches of the Huron tribe. After the English conquest in the 1760s, art moved from religion to matters of politics, the land, and the people. Army officers, such as Thomas Davies (1737–1812), painted fine detailed works, conveying their love of the landscape. Artists such as Robert Field (1769–1819), trained in Neo-Classicism, which was prevalent in Europe at the

time, and became very popular, as did Quebec painters Antoine Plamondon (1804–95) and Théophile Hamel (1817–70). Cornelius Krieghoff (1815–72) settled in Quebec and was famous for his snow scenes of both settlers and natives. His contemporary, Paul Kane (1810–71), recorded the lives of the First Nations on an epic journey across Canada. He then completed over 100 sketches and paintings, of which *Mah Min*, or *The Feather*, (c.1856) is one of the most impressive *(see p40)*. During the 19th century, painters focused on the Canadian landscape. Homer Watson (1855–1936)

Lawren S. Harris, painter (1885–1970)

and Ozias Leduc (1864–1955) were the first artists to learn their craft in Canada. Watson said, "I did not know enough to have Paris or Rome in mind. ... I felt Toronto had all I needed." His canvases portray Ontarian domestic scenes.

After Confederation in 1867, the Royal Canadian Academy of Arts and the National Gallery of Canada were founded in 1883. Artists could now train at home, but many still left to study in Paris. Curtis Williamson (1867–1944) and Edmund Morris (1871–1913) returned from France determined to revitalize their tired national art. They formed the Canadian Art Club in 1907, where new schools such as Impressionism were shown. James Wilson Morrice (1865– 1924), Maurice Cullen (1866– 1934), and Marc Aurèle de Foy Suzor-Coté (1869–1937) were key figures in this move toward modernity.

MODERN PAINTERS

Before World War I, Toronto artists criticized the influence of Europe and objected to the lack of a national identity in art. By the 1920s, the most influential set of Canadian artists, the Group of Seven *(see pp164–5)*, had defined Canadian painting in their boldly colored landscapes, such as A.Y. Jackson's *Terre Sauvage* (1913). Though he died before the formation of the Group, Tom Thomson is seen as a major influence. Three painters who came to prominence in the 1930s were influenced by the Group but had very different muses. Each artist was distinguished by a passion for their own province: David Milne (1882–1953), was known for his still lifes; LeMoine Fitzgerald (1890–1956) for his domestic and backyard scenes; and Emily Carr (1871–1945) *(see p282)* for her striking depiction of

Skidegate, Graham Island, BC, (1928) a later work by Emily Carr

the west coast Salish people and their totem poles. Carr was the first woman artist to achieve high regard. A writer as well as painter, her poem *Renfrew* (1929), describes her intense relationship with nature, which was reflected in her paintings: "… in the distance receding plane after plane… cold greens, gnarled stump of gray and brown."

The strong influence of the Group of Seven provoked a reaction among successive generations of painters. John Lyman (1886–1967) rejected the group's rugged nationalism. Inspired by Matisse, he moved away from using land as the dominant subject of painting. Lyman set up the Contemporary Arts Society in Montreal and promoted new art between 1939–48; even Surrealism reached the city.

Since World War II there has been an explosion of new forms based on abstraction. In Montreal, Paul-Emile Borduas (1905–60) and two colleagues formed the Automatists, whose inspirations were Surrealism and Abstract Impressionism. By the 1950s Canadian painters achieved international acclaim. Post-war trends were also taken up in Toronto, where The Painters Eleven produced abstract paintings. Today, artists work across the range of contemporary art movements, incorporating influences from around the world and from Canada's cultural mosaic. Experimental work by painters such as Jack Bush, Greg Carnoe, and Joyce Wieland

continues strongly in the wake of ideas from the 1960s. Canada now boasts a plethora of public and private galleries, and exceptional collections of 20th-century art.

ABORIGINAL ART

The art of the Inuit *(see pp326–7)* and the Northwest First Nations is highly valued in Canada. Pre-historic Inuit finds reveal beautiful objects, from sculpted figurines to carved harpoon heads, which were largely created for religious use. With the arrival of the Europeans the Inuit quickly adapted their artistic skills to make objects for sale such as sculptures made from ivory, bone, and stone. Today, Inuit artists such as Aqghadluk, Qaqaq Ashoona, and Tommy Ashevak are noted for their contribution to contemporary Canadian art, especially their sculpture and wallhangings. The sculpture

Robert Murray's Sculpture

The late Haida sculptor Bill Reid

of the Northwest coast First Nations people is known worldwide, particularly the cedar-wood carvings of Haida artist Bill Reid (1920–98), the totem poles of Richard Krentz, and the Kwa Gulth Big House at Fort Rupert by Chief Tony Hunt.

Painters such as Norval Morisseau, Carl Ray, and Daphne Odjig cover a range of styles, from realism to abstract. Native art celebrates the culture of its people, from their legendary survival skills, tales, and myths, to their land and the fight for its preservation.

SCULPTURE

European sculpture arrived in Canada with the French who created sacred figures to adorn their churches. Sculptors such as Louis Quévillon (1749–1823) carved decorative altarpieces as well as fine marble statues in Montreal. European traditions continued to dominate through the 19th century, and it was not until the 20th century that Canada's new cities began to require civic monuments. The façade of the Quebec Parliament was designed by Louis-Philippe Hébert (1850–1917).

Native subjects were incorporated into much 20th-century sculpture, as were European styles including Art Nouveau and Art Deco. Since the 1960s, sculptors such as Armand Vaillancourt (b.1929) and Robert Murray (b.1936) have sought to develop a Canadian style. Modern materials and the influence of conceptual art inform the work of such current artists as Michael Snow. Their work can be seen not just in museums but also in commercial and civic buildings.

Literature and Music in Canada

As the Canadian poet the Reverend Edward Hartley Dewart wrote in 1864, "A national literature is an essential element in the formation of a national character." Much Canadian literature and music is concerned with defining a national consciousness but also reflects the cultural diversity of the country. Both English and French speakers have absorbed a variety of influences from the US, Britain, and France, as well as from the other nations whose immigrants make up the population. The Europeans' relationship with First Nations peoples has also affected the style and content of much Canadian fiction and poetry, as have the often harsh realities of living in a land of vast wilderness.

Stars of the popular 1934 film *Anne of Green Gables*

NEW BEGINNINGS

Much of the earliest writing in Canada (between the mid-1500s and 1700s) was by explorers, fur traders, soldiers, and missionaries. French lawyer Marc Lescarbot's *Histoire de La Nouvelle France* (1609) is an early example of pioneer commentary and is a lively record of his adventures in Nova Scotia. After the English conquest of 1760, New France was subdued, but by the 19th century, French poets began producing patriotic poems such as *Le Vieux Soldat Canadien* (1855) by Octave Cremazie (1827–79), sparking a renaissance of poetry that continues today.

English writing was concerned with man's struggle with nature and life in the new world. *Roughing it in the Bush* (1852) by Susanna Moodie is a tale of struggles in isolated northern Ontario. British Columbia was the last region to be settled, and a captivating memoir is *A Pioneer Gentlewoman in British Columbia: the recollections of Susan Allison* (1876). Allison came from England to teach in the town of Hope and was the first European woman to make the dangerous journey across the Hope Mountains on horseback. Much 19th-century Canadian fiction romanticizes the past, such as William Kirby's (1817–1906) *Golden Dog* (1877), with its idealized view of 18th-century Quebec. Epic novels of the time focused on native lives and cultures, notably *Wacousta* (1832) by John Richardson (1796–1852). Archibald Stansfield Belaney (1888–1938) took on a new identity as an Ojibway native named Grey Owl (*see p250*), producing some of Canada's best-loved literature. *Pilgrims of the Wild* (1935) tells of his journey to find sanctuary for the over-hunted beaver. *The Adventures of Sajo and her Beaver People* and *Tales of an Empty Cabin* (1935–6) are laments for the wild and lost traditions.

Classics of the early 1900s deal with domesticity. These include *Anne of Green Gables* (1908) by L.M. Montgomery (1874–1942). Humorous writing was led by Stephen Leacock (*see p218*), and Thomas Chandler Haliburton (1796–1865), a judge who created Sam Slick, narrator of *The Clockmaker* (1836). Painter Emily Carr's *A House of all Sorts* (1944) describes her days as a landlady.

POETRY

Early English language poets Standish O'Grady (1793–1841) and Alexander McLachan (1818–96) wrote verse that reflected a colonial point of view. The genre looked critically at an iniquitous motherland (England), while praising the opportunities available in the New World. Creators of a "new" Canadian poetry in the 1870s and 80s used detailed descriptions of landscape to highlight man's efforts to conquer nature. Two notable authors were Charles Mair (1838–1927) and Isabella Valancy Crawford (1850–1887). By the 20th century the idea of the wilderness stayed at the center of Canadian poetry but was written

Internationally renowned poet and songwriter Leonard Cohen

in a sparer style that mirrored the starkness of the Group of Seven's landscape paintings *(see pp164–5)*. Robert Service's (1874–1958) popular ballads deal with history, and he is noted for his gold rush poems such as *The Spell of the Yukon* (1907) and the later *Rhymes of a Roughneck* (1950). John McCrae (1872–1918) wrote one of the most famous World War I poems *In Flanders Fields* (1915).

Modern English and French poetry now has a worldwide audience, with writers such as Anne Wilkinson, Irving Layton, Earle Birney, E.J. Pratt, Leonard Cohen, and Patrick Anderson, whose *Poem on Canada* (1946) looks at the impact of nature on European mentalities. The simple power of French writer Anne Hébert's poems, such as *Le Tombeau des Rois* (The Kings' Tombs) (1953) focuses on the universal themes of childhood, memory, and death. A postwar boom in poetry and fiction was fostered by the Canada Council for the Arts.

Canadian poet Robert Service in 1942

NATIVE CANADIAN WRITING

Despite a powerful oral tradition – where stories are both owned and passed down through families and clans – autobiography, children's books, plays, short stories, poetry, essays, and novels have been produced by Canadian native writers since the 19th century. One of the most popular autobiographies of this period was written by Ojibway native George Copway (1818–69). Titled *The Life, History, and Travels of Kah-ge-ga-ga-bowh* (1847), it had six editions in a year. The first book to be published by a native woman is thought to be *Cogewea, The Half-Blood* (1927), by Okanagan author

Mourning Dove (1888–1936). Another Okanagan novelist, Jeannette Armstrong (b.1948), published *Slash* in 1985. The struggles of a Métis woman in modern Canada are described in the best-selling autobiography of Maria Campbell in *Halfbreed* (1973).

Legend and political campaigning for native rights inform much aboriginal fiction, such as Pauline Johnson's *The White Wampum* (1895) and Beatrice Culleton's *In Search of April Raintree* (1983). The first Inuit work in English was *Harpoon of the Hunter* (1970), a story of coming of age in the northern Arctic by Markoosie (b.1942). One of Canada's top contemporary playwrights is Cree author Thompson Highway (b.1951), whose plays deal with the harsh reality of life on the reservations.

MODERN FICTION

Since the 1940s, many Canadian writers have achieved international fame: Margaret Atwood (b.1939) is well known for her poetry, novels, and criticism, while Carol Shields (1935–2003) won the prestigious Booker Prize for *The Stone Diaries* in 1996. Mordecai Richler (1931–2001) and Robertson Davies (1913–95) are noted for their wry take on contemporary Canadian society. Many authors have reached a wider public through film adaptations of their books. Gabrielle Roy's *Bonheur d'Occasion* (1945) became 1983's *The Tin Flute*; a novel by W.P. Kinsella, *Shoeless Joe* (1982), became *Field of Dreams* in 1989; and the 1996 adaptation

Michael Ondaatje, the acclaimed author of *The English Patient*

of Michael Ondaatje's *The English Patient* (1992) won nine Oscars. There is a strong tradition of short-story writing, one master being Alice Munro (b.1931). Popular history is highly regarded; noted author Pierre Berton (1920–2004) wrote 40 books on the nation's history.

MUSIC IN CANADA

Some of the biggest names in the music industry are Canadian. A strong tradition of folk and soft rock has produced such artists as Leonard Cohen, Kate and Anna McGarrigle, Joni Mitchell, and Neil Young. Other singer/songwriters who have continued the tradition of reflective, melodic hits include Alanis Morissette and k.d. lang; and the Cowboy Junkies and Shania Twain have their own takes on country music. Stars such as Celine Dion and Bryan Adams have made a huge impact in Europe and the US. In the classical sphere, orchestras such as the Montréal Orchestre Symphonique are world famous, as was the pianist Glenn Gould. Jazz is represented by the pianist Oscar Peterson (1925–2007), and every year Montreal hosts a famous festival.

Legendary composer and folk singer Joni Mitchell

Sports in Canada

Canadians are avid sports fans, and most of the country's cities and towns offer visitors a chance to see year-round sports entertainment. Although the official national game is lacrosse – a First Nations game in which the ball is caught and tossed in a leather cradle on a stick – Canadians' greatest enthusiasm is for ice hockey. Baseball, basketball, and Canadian football (similar to the US game) are also big crowd-pullers. Major cities regularly attract international stars to world-class racing, golf, and tennis tournaments. Even small towns provide the chance to watch minor professionals, amateurs, and student athletes. For visitors who prefer participating in sports, Canada offers a broad choice of activities from skiing to golf, fishing, and hiking.

National ice hockey heroes in action during a league game

ICE HOCKEY

The popularity of ice hockey in Canada knows no bounds. Every town has a rink, and every school, college, and university a team. The North American **National Hockey League** (NHL) was founded in 1917, and its principal prize, the Stanley Cup, was instituted in 1892 by Canadian Govenor General, Lord Stanley. Today, the league has 30 teams, 6 of which belong to Canadian cities; the Montreal Canadiens, Calgary Flames, Edmonton Oilers, Toronto Maple Leafs, Ottawa Senators, and the Vancouver Canucks. Although most of the players in both the US and Canada are Canadian, there has been an influx of other nationalities such as Russian, American, and Swedish atheletes playing for the top teams. Renowned for its toughness, the game usually involves a skirmish or two among the players, which often means that this 60-minute game can last up to 3 hours. The season runs from October to April when the play-offs for the Stanley Cup begin.

Hockey stars such as Wayne Gretzky are national icons. He retired in 1999 after 20 years in the game, having captured 61 NHL scoring records.

Tickets to the major games can be hard to come by, and should be booked in advance. It is a good idea to contact the club's ticket lines, or book through **Ticketmaster**. Minor league and college games are easier to get into, and the University of Toronto and York, Concordia in Montreal, and the University of Alberta in Edmonton all have good teams. Tickets can be bought from the local arena, or direct from the administration center, and are usually a great bargain.

BASEBALL

Although baseball is seen as an American sport, the game also has a large following in Canada. There is one Canadian team that plays in the major leagues: the well-known **Toronto Blue Jays**, who won the World Series in 1992 and 1993. Baseball is played in the summer, and the season lasts from April to September (with play-offs through October). It can provide a great family day out, with beer, popcorn, an enthusiastic audience, and plenty of between-inning entertainment, to keep the less baseball-obsessed amused.

The Blue Jays take on their rivals in the Rogers Centre, an architectural marvel with a retractable roof (see p173). Good tickets are easy to come by – just book a day or two in advance. Seats further back are almost always available on the day of the game. Seeing one of the minor league baseball teams can also be fun.

Jose Canseco during his days with the Toronto Blue Jays

FOOTBALL

The Canadian version of football (not soccer) is noted for being a more exciting version of American football. Although the best Canadian players tend to move to the US for higher salaries, the game still attracts substantial home audiences. The Canadian Football League has two divisions of four teams who each play over the July to November season.

The games tend to attract a lively family crowd and are fun, especially around the Grey Cup final. Played on the last Sunday of November, the game is preceded by a week of festivities and a big parade in the host city. Football is also played at most universities, where a Saturday afternoon game makes for an entertaining excursion. The annual college championship game is called the Vanier Cup and is played at Toronto's Skydome and other arenas. Tickets are relatively easy to come by and are reasonably priced.

BASKETBALL

What once was an American passion has now spread around the world to become one of the fastest growing international sports. The game was invented in the United States by a Canadian, Dr. James Naismith, and now enjoys huge popularity in his homeland. The **Toronto Raptors** play in the National Basketball Association, the top professional league in the world, against the likes of the Chicago Bulls, Boston Celtics, Los Angeles Lakers, and New York Knicks. The season lasts from October until late spring, and it is well worth a visit to Toronto's Air Canada Centre to watch one of their fast-paced games. Most of Canada's universities have teams, and although crowds tend to be smaller than those drawn by the professionals,

the competition is fierce and the atmosphere truly exhilarating, especially during the annual national championship tournament played in Halifax each year in March.

Toronto Raptors versus the L.A. Clippers basketball match

GOLF

Canada hosts two major tournaments each year (both in September), which draw large crowds of spectators, as well as the world's greatest players. The biggest is the Canadian Open, usually played at Toronto's Glen Abbey on a course designed by Jack Nicklaus. The annual Greater Vancouver Open is a regular stop on the Professional Golfers' Association tour, although the field is not as strong as that of the Open.

Golf is an immensely popular participation sport, with over 1,700 beautiful courses across the country, from the Banff Springs course in the west to the many rolling fairways of Prince Edward Island in the east.

WINTER SPORTS

Famous for the plentiful snow and sunshine of its cold winters, Canada is one of the top places both to watch and participate in winter sports. Canadian resorts are less crowded than their European counterparts, and are set among some of the most dramatic scenery in the world.

DIRECTORY

National Hockey League
11th Floor, 50 Bay Street, Toronto. **Tel** *(416) 981 2777.*
www.nhl.com

Ticketmaster
(for hockey games)
Tel *(416) 870 8000.*
www.ticketmaster.ca

Baseball
Toronto Blue Jays
Tel *Tickets: (416) 341 1234.*
www.bluejays.com

Football
Canadian Football League
110 Eglinton Avenue W., Toronto. **Tel** *(416) 322 9650.*
www.cfl.ca

Basketball
Toronto Raptors
Tel *Tickets: (416) 815 5600.*
www.raptors.com

Golf
Royal Canadian Golf Association
Tel *(905) 849 9700.*
www.rcga.org

Visitors can enjoy a range of options in resorts across the country, from Whistler in the Rockies to Mont Ste-Anne in Quebec. As well as downhill skiing, it is also possible to try snowboarding, snowmobiling, dogsledding, or even heli-skiing on pristine snow *(see p403).*

Snowboarder descending a slope at speed in powder snow

CANADA THROUGH THE YEAR

Native powwow in Calgary

Seasonal changes in Canada vary greatly across the country, but in general it is safe to say that the winters are long and cold and run from November to March, while spring and fall tend to be mild. British Columbia is the most temperate zone, with an average temperature of 5°C (40°F) in January. July and August are reliably warm and sunny in most places, even the far north, and most outdoor festivals are held in the summer months. There are plenty of events in winter, both indoors and out, some of which celebrate Canadians' ability to get the best out of the icy weather, especially activities such as dogsledding, snowmobiling, and ice-skating. A range of cultural events reflect the country's history, as well as its diverse peoples and culture.

SPRING

March and April bring the country some of its most unpredictable weather, moving from snow to sunshine in a day. In the north this is a time for welcoming the end of winter, while farther south spring is the start of an array of fun festivals.

Dogsledding at Yellowknife's Caribou Carnival in spring

MARCH

The Caribou Carnival
(late March) Yellowknife. A celebration of the arrival of spring, featuring dogsledding, snowmobiling, and delicious local foods.

APRIL

Toonik Tyme *(mid-April)* Iqaluit. This week-long festival includes igloo building, traditional games, and community feasts.

Beaches Easter Parade
(April) Toronto. This annual parade has become a popular spring institution. It follows a route along Queen St. E., between Victoria Park and Woodbine Avenue.
Shaw Festival
(April–October) Niagara-on-the-Lake. Theater festival with classic plays by George Bernard Shaw and his contemporaries *(see p208)*.

SUMMER

Warm weather across most of the country means that there is an explosion of festivals, carnivals, and cultural events, from May through August.

MAY

Canadian Tulipfest *(mid-May)* Ottawa. Colorful display of millions of tulips is the centerpiece for a variety of events.
Banff Festival of the Arts
(May–September) Banff. Two months of opera, music, drama, and dance.

Stratford Shakespearean Festival *(May–November)* Stratford. World-famous theater festival featuring a range of plays from Elizabethan to contemporary works *(see p211)*.
Shorebirds and Friends' Festival *(late May)* Wadena, Saskatchewan. Features guided bird-watching and tours of wildlife habitats.
Vancouver International Children's Festival *(last weekend in May)* Vancouver. Theater, circus, and music for children aged three and up.

JUNE

Pride Week *(early June)* Toronto. A celebration of the gay community, featuring a fun, flamboyant parade.
Grand Prix du Canada *(June)* Montreal. Annual, weekend-long Formula One event.
Midnight Madness *(mid-June)* Inuvik. Celebration of the summer solstice, with parties under the midnight sun.

Vividly colored tulips at Ottawa spring festival, Canadian Tulipfest

Steer wrestling competition in the *Half Million Dollar Rodeo* at Calgary's Stampede

Mosaic – Festival of Cultures *(first weekend in June)* Regina. Cultural events from around the world.

Jazz Fest International *(late June–July)* Victoria. Jazz and blues musicians play in venues all over town.

Red River Exhibition *(late June–July)* Winnipeg. A huge fair with many entertainments.

Festival International de Jazz de Montréal *(late June–July)* Montreal. Famous jazz festival with a number of free outdoor concerts.

Nova Scotia International Tattoo *(late June–July)* Halifax. There are 2,000 participants in one of the world's largest indoor shows.

JULY

Folk on the Rocks *(second weekend)* Yellowknife. Inuit drummers, dancers, and throat singers perform here.

Klondike Days *(July)* Edmonton. Commemorates the city's frontier days.

Calgary Stampede *(mid-July)* Calgary. Ten-day celebration of all things western, including a rodeo *(see p294).*

Molson Indy *(mid-July)* Toronto. Indy car race held at Exhibition Place.

Quebec City Summer Festival *(second week)* Quebec City. Ten days of music and dance.

Just for Laughs Festival *(July)* Montreal. Twelve-day comedy festival with more than 600 comedians from around the world.

Canadian Open Tennis Championships *(July–Aug)* Montreal, Toronto. Major international tennis tournament.

Caribana *(July–August)* Toronto. One of the largest and livliest Caribbean celebrations in North America. The main event is the parade.

Antigonish Highland Games *(mid-July)* Antigonish. Oldest traditional highland games in North America, with pipe bands and dancing.

Ford race car at the Molson Indy meeting held in Toronto

AUGUST

Royal St. John's Regatta *(August 4)* St. John's. Noted as North America's oldest sporting event, features rowing races and a carnival.

Wikwemikong Powwow *(first weekend)* Manitoulin Island. Ojibway native festival with a dancing and drum competition *(see p224).*

Folklorama *(early August)* Winnipeg. Multicultural festival of food, performance, and the arts.

Victoria Park Arts and Crafts Fair *(early August)* Moncton. Atlantic Canada's largest outdoor sale of arts, antiques, and crafts.

Festival Acadien de Caraquet *(early August)* Caraquet. Celebration of Acadian culture and history.

Halifax International Busker Festival *(second week)* Halifax. The best street entertainers from around the world.

Discovery Days Festival *(mid-August)* Dawson City. Commemorates Gold Rush days, with costumed parades and canoe races.

Fringe Festival *(mid-August)* Edmonton. Theater and live music with international performers in the historic Old Strathcona neighborhood.

Canadian National Exhibition *(August–September)* Toronto. Annual fair featuring spectacular air show, concerts, and a casino.

Folkfest *(mid-August)* Saskatoon. Saskatchewan's multicultural heritage celebrated in a variety of events.

Showjumping in the Masters equestrian event held in Calgary

FALL

Cool, but often sunny weather provides the best setting for the dramatic reds and golds of the fall foliage, which are mostly seen in the deciduous forests of the eastern provinces. In Ontario and Quebec, fall signals the end of the humid summer months and heralds crisp days that are perfect for outdoor pursuits.

SEPTEMBER

The Masters *(first week)* Calgary. Equestrian event with top international riders.
First People's Festival *(September)* Victoria. Three days of exhibitions, dancing, and a traditional native gathering known as the potlatch.
Toronto International Film Festival *(September)* Toronto. Movie stars and top directors attend this prestigious festival.

Niagara Grape and Wine Festival *(mid-September)* Niagara Falls. Vineyard tours, wine tastings, and concerts welcome the area's grape harvest.
Flambée des Couleurs *(mid-September–October)* Eastern Townships. Celebrations of glorious fall leaf colors.

OCTOBER

Okanagan Wine Festival *(early October)* Okanagan Valley. Tours and tastings throughout the valley *(see p317).*
Oktoberfest *(mid-October)* Kitchener-Waterloo. Largest Bavarian festival outside Germany *(see p218).*

Traditional Bavarian costumes and music at the Oktoberfest

VANCOUVER

°C/°F			
14/57	**13**/55	**14**/57	
23/73			
5/41		**7**/45	**6**/43
0			**0**/32
6 hrs	9 hrs	4 hrs	2 hrs
90 mm	39 mm	172 mm	214 mm
month **Apr**	**Jul**	**Oct**	**Jan**

TORONTO

°C/°F			
27/81			
12/54	**17**/63	**15**/59	
3/37		**7**/45	
0			**-1**/30
			-8/18
6 hrs	10 hrs	9 hrs	2 hrs
66 mm	74 mm	41 mm	66 mm
month **Apr**	**Jul**	**Oct**	**Jan**

Average daily maximum temperature

Average daily minimum temperature

Average daily hours of sunshine

Average monthly rainfall

Climate

This vast country has a variable climate, despite being famous for having long, cold winters. Most Canadians live in the warmer south of the country, close to the US border. Southern Ontario and BC's south and central coast are the warmest areas, while central and northern Canada have the coldest winters.

OTTAWA

°C/°F			
27/81			
10/50	**14**/57	**13**/55	
0/32		**3**/37	
0			**-6**/21
			-16/3
6 hrs	9 hrs	4 hrs	3 hrs
69 mm	82 mm	67 mm	62 mm
month **Apr**	**Jul**	**Oct**	**Jan**

MONTREAL

°C/°F			
26/79			
11/52	**17**/63	**13**/55	
2/36		**6**/43	
0			**-5**/23
			-13/9
5 hrs	8 hrs	4 hrs	3 hrs
83 mm	98 mm	84 mm	87 mm
month **Apr**	**Jul**	**Oct**	**Jan**

HALIFAX

°C/°F			
23/73			
9/48	**14**/57	**14**/57	
1/34		**7**/45	
0			**0**/32
			-7/19
5 hrs	8 hrs	5 hrs	3 hrs
113 mm	94 mm	120 mm	140 mm
month **Apr**	**Jul**	**Oct**	**Jan**

Celtic Colours *(mid-October)*
Cape Breton Island.
International Celtic music
festival held across the island.

WINTER

Apart from coastal British
Columbia, Canadian winters
are long and cold with lots
of snow. Events focus on
winter sports, with some of
the best skiing in the world
available at such resorts as
Whistler in British Columbia.
The Christmas holidays are a
time of fun activities to cheer
everyone up in the midst of
long, dark days.

NOVEMBER

**Royal Agricultural Winter
Fair** *(early–mid-November)*
Toronto. The world's largest
indoor agricultural fair features
the Royal Horse Show and
the Winter Garden Show.
Canadian Finals Rodeo
(mid-November) Edmonton.
Canada's cowboy champions
are decided at this event.
Winter Festival of Lights *(early
November–mid-January)*
Niagara Falls. Spectacular light
displays and concerts.

DECEMBER

**Canadian Open Sled Dog
Race** *(December)* Fort St
John and Fort Nelson. Snow
sports and family fun-days as
well as dogsled races.

PUBLIC HOLIDAYS

New Years Day (January 1
Good Friday (variable)
Easter Sunday (variable)
Easter Monday (variable)
Vacation for government
offices and schools only.
Victoria Day. (Monday
before May 25)
Canada Day (July 1)
Labour Day (first Monday
in September)
Thanksgiving (second
Monday in October)
Remembrance Day
(November 11)
Christmas Day (December 25)
Boxing Day (December 26)

**An illuminated display of
Christmas decorations**

Christmas Carol Ships Parade
(mid-December) Vancouver.
Boats are beautifully decorated
with Christmas lights, and
cruise Vancouver's waters.

JANUARY

Ice Magic *(mid-January)*
Lake Louise. International ice
sculpture competition
**Techni-Cal Challenge –
Dog Sled Race** *(mid-January)*
Minden. Over 80 teams com-
pete in international races.
Rossland Winter Carnival
(last weekend) Rossland.
Snowboarding contests, a
torchlit parade, and lots of
music and dancing.
Quebec Winter Carnival
(January–February) Quebec.
A famous canoe race across
the St. Lawrence River is just

one attraction at these huge
winter celebrations.
Jasper in January *(last two
weeks)* Jasper. Winter festivities include skiing parties,
races, and food fairs.
**Banff/Lake Louise Winter
Festival** *(last week)* Banff,
Lake Louise. Variety of fun
events, including skating
parties and barn dances.

FEBRUARY

**Yukon Quest International
Sled Dog Race** *(February)*
Whitehorse. Famous 1,600 km
(1,000 mile) race from Fairbanks, Alaska to Whitehorse.
Nova Scotia Icewine Festival
(February) throughout Nova
Scotia. Celebrating the
region's internationally
renowned icewines.
Yukon Sourdough Rendevous
(February) Whitehorse. A
"mad trapper" competition
and an array of children's
events in this winter festival.
Frostbite Music Festival
(third weekend) Whitehorse.
Features a wide range of
music from jazz to rock.
Calgary Winter Festival
(second week) Calgary.
Fun family activities, music,
and feasting.
Festival du Voyageur
(mid-February) Winnipeg.
Celebration of fur trade history
with an enormous street party.
Winterlude *(every weekend)*
Ottawa. A wide array of
activities including ice-
skating on the Rideau Canal.

Two eagle ice sculptures at Ottawa's February festival, Winterlude

THE HISTORY OF CANADA

*C*anada is known for its wild and beautiful terrain, yet with the help of the aboriginal peoples, European settlers adapted to their new land and built up a prosperous nation. Despite continuing divisions between its English- and French-speaking peoples, Canada has welcomed immigrants from around the globe and is respected as one of the most tolerant countries in the world today.

Long before the first Europeans crossed the Atlantic in AD 986, the landscape we now know as Canada was inhabited by various civilizations. Tribes of hunters came on foot, walking across a land bridge that once joined Asia with North America as part of the ancient land mass of Laurasia.

Detail of totem pole made by Haida peoples from the west

winters and brief summers. To the south, the Iroquois settled in forest villages where they lived in longhouses and grew corn as their staple crop.

On the western plains, other tribes depended on the bison for their livelihood, while communities living along the Pacific Coast relied on fishing and trading. Their towering totem poles indicated a rich culture and spiritual belief system.

These first inhabitants, now referred to as the First Nations, endured centuries of hardship and adaptation, eventually developing the skills, technology, and culture required to survive the rigors of life in Canada.

EARLY SURVIVAL

Across most of the country, from the Yukon to the Atlantic, there were two main groups of hunter-gatherers, the Algonquins and the Athapaskans. They lived in small nomadic bands, which developed birch bark canoes and snowshoes to travel across this vast land. Food and clothing were procured through fishing and animal trapping, traditions that gave Canada the lucrative fish and fur trades.

To the north of these two groups were the Innu people, who mastered life in the Arctic, being able to survive in a region of dark, ice-bound

The common bond between all the First Nations, despite their disparate lifestyles, was that they saw themselves as part of nature and not as its masters. They believed the animals they hunted had kindred spirits, and misfortune befell those who offended such spirits by gratuitous killing.

The generosity of the natives toward Europeans may have hastened their own downfall. As Canadian historian Desmond Morton points out: "Without the full... assistance of natives showing the Europeans their methods of survival, their territory, and their resources, the early explorers and settlers would have perished in even greater numbers and possibly abandoned their quest, much as the Vikings had done 500 years before."

TIMELINE

30,000 BC	20,000 BC	10,000 BC	AD1	500	1000	1500

9,000 BC Native peoples are living at least as far south as the Eramosa River near what is now Guelph, Ontario

Viking ship c.980 AD

AD 986 Bjarni Herjolfsson, a Viking sailing from Iceland to Greenland, is the first European to see the coastline of Labrador

1497 John Cabot's first voyage to North America

30,000–10,000 BC Nomadic hunters arrive in North America across a land bridge from Asia

992 Leif "the Lucky" Ericsson visits Labrador and L'Anse aux Meadows, Newfoundland

1003 Thorfinn Karlsefni starts a colony in Labrador (Vinland) to trade with the natives, but it is abandoned two years later because of fighting with the hostile aboriginals

◁ *Mah-Min or The Feather,* painting of an Assiniboine chief by Paul Kane c.1856

THE FIRST EUROPEANS

The Norse sagas of Northern Europe tell how Vikings from Iceland first reached the coast of Labrador in AD 986 and made a series of unsuccessful attempts to establish a colony here. Leif "the Lucky" Ericsson sailed from Greenland in 988, naming the country he found in the west Vinland after the wild grapes found growing in abundance there. Around 1000 AD Thorfinn Karlsefni tried to establish a Vinland colony. Thorfinn's group wintered in Vinland but sailed home to Greenland in the spring, convinced that a colony was impossible as there were too few colonists and the *skraelings* (aboriginals) were hostile. Remarkably, remains of this early Viking settlement were discovered in Newfoundland in 1963 *(see p71)*.

Italian navigator and explorer John Cabot

THE ENGLISH INVASION

In 1497, the Italian navigator John Cabot (1450–98), on the commission of King Henry VII of England, set sail aboard the *Matthew*, bound for America. On June 24, he found a sheltered place on Newfoundland. Here he went ashore with a small party to claim the land for England. He then went on to chart the eastern coastline before sailing home, where he was greeted as a hero.

In May 1498, Cabot sailed again with five ships and 300 men hoping to find the Northwest Passage to China. Harsh weather drove Cabot to relinquish his efforts and head south to Nova Scotia. Cabot then found himself sailing through a sea littered with icebergs. The fleet perished off the coast of Greenland, and English interest in the new land faded.

THE FRENCH ARRIVAL

Originally from the port of St. Malo, explorer Jacques Cartier (1491–1557) made his first voyage to Canada in 1534. He reached Labrador, Newfoundland, and the Gulf of the St. Lawrence before landing on Anticosti Island where he

Map of the voyage of Jacques Cartier and his followers by Pierre Descaliers c.1534–41

TIMELINE

1541 At the mouth of the Cap Rouge River, Cartier founds Charlesbourg-Royal, the first French settlement in America – it is abandoned in 1543

1567 Samuel de Champlain "Father of New France" born

1605 Samuel de Champlain and the Sieur de Roberval found Port Royal, now Annapolis Royal, Nova Scotia

1525	1550	1575	1600

1535 Cartier sails up the St. Lawrence River to Stadacona (Quebec City) and Hochelaga (Montreal)

Jacques Cartier

1608 Champlain founds Quebec City, creating the first permanent European settlement in Canada

1610 Henry Hudson explores Hudson Bay

realized he was at the mouth of a great river. A year later, he returned and sailed up the St. Lawrence River to the site of what is now Quebec City, and then on to a native encampment at Hochelega, which he named Montreal. In 1543, Cartier's hopes for a successful colony died when, after a bitter and barren winter, he and his dispirited group returned to France. Seventy more years would pass before French colonists returned to Canada to stay.

Champlain, "Father of New France," fighting the Iroquois

THE FATHER OF NEW FRANCE

Samuel de Champlain (1567–1635) was a man of many parts – navigator, soldier, visionary – and first made the journey from France to Canada in 1603. While the ship that carried him across the Atlantic lay at Tadoussac, Champlain ascended the St. Lawrence River by canoe to the Lachine Rapids.

Champlain's 1605 attempt to found a colony at Port Royal failed, but in 1608 the seeds of a first tiny French colony at Quebec City were planted, with the construction of three two-story houses, a courtyard, and a watchtower, surrounded by a wooden wall.

The economic engine propelling Champlain was the fur trade. In its name he made alliances with the Algonquins and Hurons; fought their dreaded enemies, the Iroquois; traveled to Huron country, now central Ontario; and saw the Great Lakes. Champlain and the other Frenchmen who followed him not only established lasting settlements in the St. Lawrence Valley but also explored half a continent. They built a "New France" that, at its zenith, stretched south from Hudson Bay to New Orleans in Louisiana, and from Newfoundland almost as far west as the Rockies. In 1612 Champlain became French Canada's first head of government.

Champlain's efforts also helped to create the religious climate that enabled orders such as the Jesuits to establish missions. But his work also laid the seeds of conflict with the English that would last well into the next century and beyond.

Hudson's last voyage

THE HUDSON'S BAY COMPANY

In 1610, English voyager Henry Hudson landed at the bay that still bears his name. The bay's access to many key waterways and trading routes ensured the fortunes of the fur trade. Founded in 1670, the Hudson's Bay Company won control of the lands that drained into the bay, gaining a fur-trading monopoly over the area. The company was challenged only by Scottish merchants who established the North West Company in Montreal in 1783. By 1821, these two companies amalgamated, and the Hudson's Bay Company remains Canada's largest fur trader to this day.

1648–9 The Iroquois disperse the Huron nation and Jesuit father Jean de Brébeuf is martyred during Iroquois raids on Huronia

Engraving of Iroquois

1702 French and British rivalries result in outbreak of Queen Anne's War

| 1625 | 1650 | 1675 | 1700 |

1629 British adventurer David Kirke captures Quebec, but it is returned to France in 1632

Raccoon pelt

1670 The Hudson's Bay Company is founded by royal charter and under-written by a group of English merchants

1676 population of New France swelled to 8,500 by settlers

Anglo-French Hostilities

Throughout the 18th century, hostilities between the French and English in Europe continued to spill over into the New World. By 1713, Britain ruled Nova Scotia, Newfoundland, and the Hudson Bay region and, after the Seven Years War in 1763, all of French Canada.

Anglo-French tensions were exacerbated by religion: the English were largely Protestant and almost all of the French Catholic. This resulted in the colony of Quebec being divided in 1791 into the mainly English-speaking Upper Canada (now Ontario), and majority French-speaking Lower Canada (now Quebec).

Taking advantage of the British conflict with Napoleon in Europe, the Americans invaded Canada in 1812. They were defeated by 1814, but the threat of another invasion colored Canadian history during much of the 19th century.

The Acadian Exodus
French-speaking Acadians were ruthlessly expelled from their homes by the British in the 1750s (see pp62–3).

The Plains Of Abraham, in Quebec, were the site of victory for the British over the French.

General Isaac Brock
Brock's heroic exploits during the War of 1812, such as the capture of an American post at Detroit, buoyed the spirits of the Canadian people.

United Empire Loyalists
The surrender of British General Cornwallis effectively ended the American Revolution (1775–83). A large number of United Empire Loyalists, refugees from the newly formed United States who remained loyal to the British crown, fled to Canada. They swelled the British population by 50,000.

THE SEVEN YEARS WAR

The famous Battle of the Plains of Abraham in 1759 was the last between British and French forces to take place in Canada. The British launched a surprise assault from the cliffs of the St. Lawrence River at a site now known as Wolfe's Cove. Louis Joseph de Montcalm, the French commander, was defeated by General Wolfe and his army. Both generals were killed, and Quebec fell to the British. The war finally ended in 1763 with the Treaty of Paris, which ceded all French-Canadian territory to the British.

Louisbourg
The French fortress of Louisbourg on Cape Breton Island was built between 1720 and 1740, and was the head-quarters for the French fleet until it was destroyed by the British in 1758. Today, the restored fortress is a popular tourist attraction (see pp96–7).

General Wolfe
The distinguished British soldier, shown here fatally wounded at the Plains of Abraham, preceded his 1759 victory in Quebec with the taking of the French fortress, Louisbourg, in 1758.

General Wolfe's forces sailed up the St. Lawrence river overnight, allowing them to surprise the enemy at Quebec.

French Rights
In 1774 the British government passed the Quebec Act, granting French-Canadians religious and linguistic freedom and giving official recognition to French Civil Law.

Wolfe's infantry scrambled up a steep, wooded cliff. They had to defeat an enemy post before the waiting boats of soldiers could join the battle.

TIMELINE

1743 The La Vérendrye brothers discover the Rocky Mountains

1755 Expulsion of the Acadians from Nova Scotia

1758 Louisbourg, the French fortress on Cape Breton Island, falls to the British

Sir Alexander Mackenzie

1793 Scottish explorer and fur trader Alexander Mackenzie crosses the Rockies and reaches the Pacific Ocean by land

| 1720 | 1740 | 1760 | 1780 | 1800 |

1713 British gain control of Nova Scotia, Newfoundland, and Hudson Bay

1759 Wolfe defeats de Montcalm in the Battle of the Plains of Abraham

Medal for the British capture of Quebec 1759

1760 Montreal falls to the British

1774 The Quebec Act grants French colonists rights to their own language and religion

1812 The US at war with Britain until the Treaty of Ghent in 1814

A BRITISH DOMINION

Twenty-five years after the War of 1812 ended in stalemate, violence of a different sort flared in Canada. The English wanted supremacy in voting power and to limit the influence of the Catholic Church. By 1834 the French occupied one quarter of public positions, although they made up three-quarters of the population. Rebellions in Upper and Lower Canada during 1837–38 were prompted by both French and British reformers, who wanted accountable government with a broader electorate. The response of the British Government was to join together the two colonies into a united Province of Canada in 1840. The newly created assembly won increased independence when, in 1849, the majority Reform Party passed an Act compensating the 1837 rebels. Although the Governor-General, Lord Elgin, disapproved, he chose not to use his veto. The Province of Canada now had "responsible government," (the right to pass laws without the sanction of the British colonial representative.)

The rest of British North America, however, remained a series of self-governing colonies that, despite their economic successes, were anxious about American ambitions. Such fears were reinforced by a series of Fenian Raids on Canadian territory between 1866–70. (The Fenians were New York Irish immigrants hoping to take advantage of French Canada's anti-British feeling to help them to secure independence for Ireland.) The issue of confederation was raised and discussed at conferences held from 1864 onward. Only by uniting in the face of this common menace, said the politicians, could the British colonies hope to fend off these incursions.

The new country was born on July 1, 1867. Under the terms of the British North America Act the new provinces of Quebec (Canada East) and Ontario (Canada West) were created, and along with Nova Scotia and New Brunswick became the Dominion of Canada. The new government was based on the British parliamentary system, with a governor-general (the Crown's representative), a House of Commons, and a Senate. Parliament received power to legislate over matters of national interest; defense, criminal law, and trade, while the provinces ruled over local issues such as education.

Representatives meet in London to discuss terms of union

THE METIS REBELLION

Following confederation, the government purchased from the Hudson's Bay Company the area known as Rupert's Land, which extended south and west inland for thousands of kilometers from Hudson's Bay.

Northwest rebel Louis Riel

TIMELINE

1818 Canada's border with the United States is defined as the 49th Parallel from Lake of the Woods to the Rocky Mountains	**1839** Lord Durham issues a report recommending the establishment of responsible government and the union of Upper and Lower Canada to speed the assimilation of French-speaking Canadians		**1849** The boundary of the 49th Parallel is extended to the Pacific Ocean	
1820	**1830**		**1840**	**1850**
1821 Merger of Hudson's Bay and North West Companies	**1837** A general feeling that the government is not democratic leads to violent but unsuccessful rebellions in Upper and Lower Canada		**1841** An Act of Union unites Upper and Lower Canada as the Province of Canada	

The Métis people (descendants of mostly French fur-traders and natives) who lived here were alarmed by the expected influx of English-speaking settlers. In 1869, local leader Louis Riel took up their cause and led the first of two uprisings. The Red River Rebellion was an attempt to defend what the Métis saw as their ancestral rights to this land. A compromise was reached in 1870 and the new province of, Manitoba was created.

Driving home the last spike of the Canadian Pacific Railroad, 1885

However, many Métis moved westward to what was to become the province of Saskatchewan in 1905.

Riel was elected to the House of Commons in 1874 but, in 1875, he emigrated to the US. The government's intention to settle the west led the Métis of Saskatchewan to call Riel home in 1884 to lead the North-West Rebellion. It was short-lived. Defeated at Batoche in May, Riel was ultimately charged with treason and hanged in Regina on November 16, 1885.

BIRTH OF A NATION

The defeat of the Métis and the building of a transcontinental railroad were crucial factors in the settlement of the west. British Columbia, a Crown colony since 1858, chose to join the Dominion in 1871 on the promise of a rail link with the rest of the country. The first train to run from Montreal to Vancouver in 1886 paved the way for hundreds of thousands of settlers in the West in the late 1800s. Prince Edward Island, Canada's smallest province, joined the Dominion in 1873.

In 1898, the northern territory of Yukon was established to ensure Canadian jurisdiction over that area during the Klondike gold rush (see pp50–51). In 1905, the provinces of Saskatchewan and Alberta were created out of Rupert's Land, with the residual area becoming the Northwest Territories. Each province gained its own premier and elected assembly. By 1911 new immigrants had doubled the populations of the new provinces.

For the time being, Newfoundland preferred to remain a British colony, but in 1949 it was brought into Canada as the country's tenth province.

THE METIS PEOPLE

The Métis people of central Canada were descended from native and largely French stock. Proud of their unique culture, this seminomadic group considered themselves separate from the rest of the Dominion. With their own social structure and lifestyle dependent almost entirely on buffalo hunting, they resisted integration. They responded to the unification of the country with two failed rebellions. The Métis won no land rights and were condemned to a life of poverty or enforced integration.

Métis hunt buffalo on the Prairie

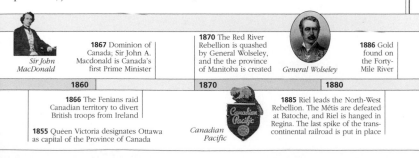

Sir John MacDonald

1867 Dominion of Canada; Sir John A. Macdonald is Canada's first Prime Minister

1870 The Red River Rebellion is quashed by General Wolseley, and the the province of Manitoba is created

General Wolseley

1886 Gold found on the Forty-Mile River

1860	1870	1880

1866 The Fenians raid Canadian territory to divert British troops from Ireland

1855 Queen Victoria designates Ottawa as capital of the Province of Canada

Canadian Pacific

1885 Riel leads the North-West Rebellion. The Métis are defeated at Batoche, and Riel is hanged in Regina. The last spike of the transcontinental railroad is put in place

The Klondike Gold Rush

There had been rumors of gold in the Yukon since the 1830s, but the harsh land, together with the Chilkoot Indians' guarding of their territory, kept most prospectors away. Then, on August 16, 1896 the most frenzied and fabled gold rush in Canadian history started when George Washington Carmack and two Indian friends, Snookum Jim and Tagish Charlie, found a large gold nugget in the river they later named Bonanza Creek. For the next two years at least 100,000 prospectors set out for the new gold fields.

Only about 40,000 prospectors actually made it. Most took boats as far as Skagway or Dyea, on the Alaskan Panhandle, then struggled across the Coast Mountains by the White or Chilkoot passes to reach the headwaters of the Yukon River. From here boats took them 500 km (310 miles) to the gold fields. In all, the gold rush generated Can $50 million, although few miners managed to hold onto their fortunes.

Klondike Entrepreneur
Alex McDonald, a Nova Scotian with a canny business sense, bought up the claims of discouraged miners and hired others to work them for him. Known as "King of the Klondike," he made millions.

The stern wheeler was a steamboat driven by a single paddle at the back.

Skagway, Alaska
The jumping-off point for the Klondike was the tent city of Skagway. There were saloons and swindlers on every corner, and gunfire in the streets was commonplace. The most famous con man was Jefferson Randolph "Soapy" Smith, who died in a shoot-out in 1898.

The Yukon River rises in British Columbia's Coast Mountains, winding for 3,000 km (1,900 miles) to Alaska.

The Mounties Take Control
The safety of the Klondike Gold Rush was secured by Canada's red-coated Mounties. Thanks to them, the rush was remarkably peaceful. A small force of 19 Mounties led by Inspector Charles Constantine were sent to the Yukon in 1895, but by 1898 there were 285, operating out of Fort Herchmer at Dawson.

Klondike Fever
The outside world learnt of the riches in July 1897, when miners docked in Seattle and San Francisco hauling gold. In no time, Klondike fever was an epidemic.

Steamboats and other craft brought thousands of prospectors up the long Yukon River to Dawson, where the boats jostled for space at the dock.

Dawson City
As the gold rush developed in the summer of 1897, the small tent camp at the junction of the Klondike and Yukon rivers grew to a population of 5,000. A year on it had reached 40,000, making Dawson City one of the largest cities in Canada.

Capturing the Mood
Even literature had a place in the Klondike. The gold rush inspired novels such as Call of the Wild *(1903) by Jack London (shown here) and the 1907 verses* Songs of a Sourdough *by poet Robert Service.*

CROSSING THE YUKON RIVER

The ferocious Yukon River rapids in Miles Canyon smashed so many boats to splinters that the Mounties decreed that every boat had to be guided by a competent pilot. Experienced sailors could earn up to Can$100 a trip taking boats through the canyon. Past the canyon, only one more stretch of rapids remained before the Yukon's waters grew calmer all the way to Dawson City.

TIMELINE

1896 George Carmack and two friends, Tagish Charlie and Snookum Jim, strike it rich on Bonanza Creek. Liberal Wilfred Laurier elected as the country's first French-Canadian prime minister

Klondike News 1898

1898 The Yukon is given territorial status, partly to assert British authority in the eyes of the Americans from neighboring Alaska

1896	1897	1898	1899

1897 Steamers from Alaska carry word of the strike to San Francisco and Seattle, setting off a frenzied gold rush

1899 Gold is discovered in Nome, Alaska, and Dawson begins to shrink as people leave to follow the new dream of riches farther west

NEW OPTIMISM AND ARRIVALS

The impact of the Klondike gold rush was felt all over Canada. It led to an expansion of cities such as Vancouver and Edmonton, and the establishment of the Yukon territory. A period of optimism was ush-ered in by the new Liberal government, elected in 1896 under the first French-Canadian premier, Wilfred Laurier, who firmly believed that "the 20th century will belong to Canada."

1914 poster promoting immigration to Canada

The new central Canadian provinces provided a home for European immigrants eager to farm large tracts of prairie land. By 1913, this wave of immigration had peaked at 400,000. Finally Canada began to profit from a prosperous world economy and establish itself as an industrial and agricultural power.

SUPPORTING THE ALLIES

The first overseas test of Canada's mili-tary forces came in 1899, when the Boer War broke out in South Africa; the sec-ond in 1914, when Europe entered World War I. Initially, Laurier was cautious in his approach to the South

African crisis, but pressure from the English-speaking population led to the dispatch of 1,000 soldiers to Cape Town in 1899. Before the Boer War ended in 1902, some 6,000 men had made the journey to serve with the British on the South African battlefields. They returned with a stronger sense of national identity than many of their compatriots at home had expected. But, while the experience of war infused some with a new sense of national unity, it also laid bare divisions. There were fights between French- and English-speak-ing university students, as well as disputes among Ontario conservatives and French-speaking Quebec politicians.

Before matters could come to a head, another crisis loomed. Joining the Allies in Flanders, the Canadians found renewed glory during World War I. Canadian pilot, Billy Bishop, was the Allies' greatest air ace, and another Canadian, Roy Brown, was the pilot credited with downing the Red Baron. Canadian troops were the heroes of two major battles, Ypres (1915) and Vimy Ridge (1917). When peace was declared on November 11, 1918, there were 175,000 Cana-dian wounded, and 60,000 had died for their country.

INDEPENDENT STATUS

Canada had played so significant a role during World War I that it gained recognition as an inde-pendent country, winning rep-resentation in the League of Nations. This independence was confirmed in 1931 with the pass-

Canadians advance at Paardeberg in the Boer War, 1900

TIMELINE

1899 The first Canadians are sent to fight in the Boer War	**1911** Robert Borden and the Conservatives win federal election, defeating Liberal party leader Wilfred Laurier on the issue of the Naval Bill	**1917** Munitions ship explodes in Halifax harbor wiping out 5 sq km (2 sq miles) of the town, killing 2,000, and injuring 9,000	**1918** Canadians break through the German trenches at Amiens beginning "Canada's Hundred Days"

1900	1905	1910	1915	1920

1903 Canada loses the Alaska boundary dispute when a British tribunal sides with the US	**1914** Britain declares war on Germany, automati-cally drawing Canada into the conflict in Europe. The War Measures Act orders German and Austro-Hungarian Canadians to carry identity cards *Dr. Frederick Banting*		**1922** Canadians Charles Best, Frederick Banting, and John MacLeod win the Nobel Prize for the discovery of insulin

ing of the Statute of Westminster, which gave Canada political independence from Britain and created a commonwealth of sovereign nations under a single crown.

However, national optimism was curtailed by the Great Depression that originated with the Wall Street Crash in 1929.

Soup kitchen during the Great Depression

Drought laid waste the farms of Alberta, Saskatchewan, and Manitoba. One in four workers was unemployed, and the sight of men riding boxcars in a fruitless search for work became common.

WORLD WAR II

The need to supply the Allied armies during World War II boosted Canada out of the Depression. Canada's navy played a crucial role in winning the Battle of the Atlantic (1940–43), and thousands of Allied airmen were trained in Canada. Canadian regiments soon gained a reputation for bravery – for example, many died in the 1942 raid on Dieppe. Thousands battled in Italy, while others stormed ashore at Normandy. In the bitter fighting that followed, the Second and Third Canadian Divisions took more casualties holding the beachheads than any unit under British command. It was also the Canadians who liberated much of Holland.

The Canadian prime minister of the day was the Liberal Mackenzie King (1935–48). He ordered a plebiscite to have conscripts sent overseas to meet an infantry shortage in the last months of the war, monitored the building of the Alaska Highway (see pp262–3), and directed a massive war effort.

AN INTERNATIONAL VOICE

When peace finally came in September 1945, Canada had the third-largest navy in the world, the fourth-largest air force, and a standing army of 730,000 men. Although the price Canada had paid during World War II was high – 43,000 people died in action and the national debt quadrupled – the nation found itself in a strong position. A larger population was better able to cope with its losses and much of the debt had been spent on doubling the gross national product, creating durable industries that would power the postwar economy.

German prisoners captured by Canadian Infantry on D-Day, June 6, 1944

1926 The Balfour Report defines British dominions as autonomous and equal in status	Air Canada logo	1937 Trans-Canada Air Lines, now Air Canada, begins regular flights	1942 Around 22,000 Japanese Canadians are stripped of non-portable possessions and interned	1944 Canadian troops push farther inland than any other allied units on D-Day
1925	**1930**	**1935**	**1940**	**1945**
1929 The Great Depression begins	1931 The Statute of Westminster grants Canada full legislative authority	1941 Hong Kong falls to the Japanese, and Canadians are taken as POWs		1945 World War II ends. Canada joins the UN. Canada's first nuclear reactor goes on line in Chalk River, Ontario

Large Canadian grain carrier approaches the St. Lawrence Seaway in 1959 – its inaugural year

Nobel Peace Prize in 1957 for helping resolve the Suez Crisis. Canada is also a respected member of the British Commonwealth, la Francophonie, the Group of Eight industrialized nations, the OAS (Organization of American States), and NATO (North Atlantic Treaty Organization).

THE FRENCH–ENGLISH DIVIDE

Given all these accomplishments, it seems ironic that the last quarter of a century has also seen Canadians deal with fundamental questions of national identity and unity. The driving force of this debate continues to be the historic English–French rivalry. The best-known players of these late 20th-century events are Prime Minister Pierre Trudeau (1968–84) and Quebec Premier René Lévesque (1976–85).

Since World War II, Canada's economy has continued to expand. This growth, combined with government social programs such as old-age security, unemployment insurance, and medicare, means Canadians have one of the world's highest standards of living and a quality of life which draws immigrants from around the world. Since 1945, those immigrants have been made up largely of southern Europeans, Asians, South Americans, and Caribbean islanders, all of whom have enriched the country's multicultural status.

Internationally, the nation's reputation and influence have grown. Canada has participated in the United Nations since its inception in 1945 and is the only nation to have taken part in almost all of the UN's major peacekeeping operations. Perhaps it is only fitting that it was a future Canadian prime minister, Lester Pearson, who fostered the peacekeeping process when he won the

When Jean Lesage was elected as Quebec Premier in 1960, he instituted the "Quiet Revolution" – a series of reforms that increased provincial power. However, this was not enough to prevent the rise of revolutionary nationalists. In October 1970, British Trade Commissioner James Cross and Quebec Labor Minister Pierre Laporte were kidnapped by the French-Canadian terrorist organization, the

Quebec Premier René Levesque and Canadian Prime Minister Pierre Trudeau during the 1980 referendum

TIMELINE

1950 The Canadian Army Special Force joins UN soldiers in the Korean War

1949 New-foundland joins the Confederation. Canada joins NATO

1957 Lester Pearson wins the Nobel Peace Prize for helping resolve the Suez Crisis

Lester Pearson

1965 Canada's new flag is inaugurated after a bitter political debate

1976 The Olympic games are held in Montreal under tight security. René Lévesque and the separatist *Parti Québecois* win a provincial election

Marc Garneau

1980 Quebec votes against separation in the 1980 Quebec Referendum

1984 Aboard the US shuttle *Challenger*, Marc Garneau becomes the first Canadian in space

1950	1955	1960	1965	1970	1975	1980

1990 demonstration for Quebec independence in Montreal

Front du Libération de Québec (FLQ). Cross was rescued by police but Laporte was later found murdered. Trudeau invoked the War Measures Act, sent troops into Montreal, and banned the FLQ. His actions eventually led to nearly 500 arrests.

Trudeau devoted his political life to federalism, fighting separatism, and giving Canada its own constitution. In contrast, Quebec Premier René Lévesque campaigned for a 1980 referendum in Quebec on whether that province should become independent. A majority voted against, but the results were far from decisive, and separatism continued to dominate the country's political agenda. However, in 1982, the Constitution Act fulfilled Trudeau's dream, entrenching federal civil rights and liberties such as female equality.

A MOVE TOWARD CONSERVATISM

In 1984 the leader of the Progressive Conservatives, Brian Mulroney, won the general election with the largest majority in Canadian history. Dismissive of Trudeau's policies, Mulroney's emphasis was on closer links with Europe and, in particular, the US. In the years that followed,

two major efforts were made to reform the constitutional system. The 1987 Meech Lake Accord aimed to recognize Quebec's claims to special status on the basis of its French culture, but Mulroney failed to implement the amendment since it did not obtain the consent of all provinces. The Charlottetown Accord of 1992, which raised the issue of aboriginal self-government, was triggered by Quebec sovereignty issues. The Accord was rejected in a national referendum held in 1992.

Today, many of these reforms are finally in place and hopefully aiding Canadian unity. Quebec's French heritage has official recognition, and the Inuit rule their own territory of Nunavut.

INDEPENDENCE FOR NUNAVUT

On April 1, 1999, Canada gained its newest territory, the Inuit homeland of Nunavut. The campaign for an Inuit state began in the 1960s when the Inuit desire for a political identity of their own was added to aboriginal land claims. Nunavut's first Premier was 34-year-old Paul Okalik, leader of the first-ever Inuit majority government over an 85 percent Inuit population. English is being replaced as the official language by the native Inuktitut, and traditional Inuit fishing and hunting skills are being reintroduced. By 2012, the federal government will invest over Can$1 billion in public services for Nunavut.

Signing ceremony in Iqaluit, April 1, 1999

ATLANTIC CANADA

Introducing Atlantic Canada

Atlantic Canada is renowned for rocky
coastlines, picturesque fishing villages,
sun-warmed beaches, cozy country
inns, and friendly people. Each province
has a distinctive flavor. In northeastern
New Brunswick, French-speaking Acadian
culture flourishes, while the south coast offers
the pristine, tide-carved beauty of the Bay of
Fundy. Nova Scotia, famous for the stunning
natural scenery of the Cabot Trail, is also home to
historic towns like seafaring Lunenburg and Annapolis
Royal, the only town in Canada designated a National
Historic Site. Prince Edward Island is known for its
emerald-green farmland, sandy beaches, and rich lobster
catches. In Newfoundland, the mountains of Gros Morne
National Park rise 800 m (2,625 ft) above sparkling blue
fjords. Labrador offers an imposing and stunning coastal
landscape, often with a backdrop of glittering icebergs.

LABRADOR SEA

● NAIN

LABRADOR

Smallwood
Reservoir
(500)

● CHURCHILL
FALLS

● LABRADOR CITY

Contemporary Acadian homesteads flourish after 400 years
of a unique culture in northeastern New Brunswick

CAMPBELLT●

NEW BRUNSW

The fresh maritime scenery of Two Islands beach, known as "The Brothers" for its
twin offshore islands, in Parrsboro, Nova Scotia

◁ Lobster traps

GETTING AROUND

Air Canada and West Jet offer regular flights throughout the region. The Confederation Bridge connects Borden, Prince Edward Island, to Cape Tormentine in New Brunswick. A ferry travels between Wood Island, Prince Edward Island, and Pictou, Nova Scotia, and another links Digby, Nova Scotia, and Saint John, New Brunswick. Newfoundland must be accessed by air or by ferry from Sydney, Nova Scotia, to either Port aux Basques or Argentia. A high-speed ferry travels between Yarmouth, Nova Scotia, and Bar Harbor and Portland, both in Maine. Bus services cross the provinces, but many areas are remote, so check availability.

LOCATOR MAP

KEY

▨	Highway
▬	Major road
▭	Minor road
═	River

SEE ALSO

- *Where to Stay* pp346–9
- *Where to Eat* pp370–73

Lake Melville

HAPPY VALLEY - GOOSE BAY

ST. ANTHONY

PORT AU CHOIX

GANDER

BONAVISTA

GRAND FALLS

ST. JOHN'S

NEWFOUNDLAND

CORNER BROOK

STEPHENVILLE

ST. PIERRE & MIQUELON ISLANDS (Fr.)

GULF OF ST. LAWRENCE

PORT AUX BASQUES

CAPE BRETON ISLAND

SYDNEY

BATHURST

PRINCE EDWARD ISLAND

BOUCTOUCHE

AMHERST

NOVA SCOTIA

TRURO

ATLANTIC OCEAN

FREDERICTON

WOLFVILLE **HALIFAX**

ANNAPOLIS ROYAL

DIGBY

LUNENBURG

0 km	250
0 miles	250

SHELBURNE

YARMOUTH

Perched on the Atlantic Coast, Quidi Vidi village, one of the oldest in Newfoundland

Maritime Wildlife of Atlantic Canada

The provinces of Atlantic Canada – Nova Scotia, New Brunswick, and Prince Edward Island – along with Newfoundland and Labrador, the Quebec north shore of the St. Lawrence River, and the Gaspé Peninsula, constitute a rich and diverse maritime habitat for wildlife. The climate is dominated by the ocean, being influenced by the moderating Gulf Stream that flows north from the Caribbean and by the southward flow of icy waters, often bearing icebergs, from the Canadian Arctic. The terrain of the eastern Canadian coastline varies from rocky headlands to soft, sandy beaches. Both sea and land mammals inhabit this coast, as do hundreds of species of seabird.

The piping plover *is a small, endangered shore bird that lives and breeds along the Atlantic coast of Canada.*

SHORELINE HABITAT

The maritime shoreline encompasses rocky cliffs, sandy beaches, and salt-flat marshes. Moving a little inland, the landscape shifts to bog, forest, and meadow. It is an inviting habitat for many smaller mammals such as raccoons and beavers, and also provides a home for a diversity of bird life. Where the shoreline meets the water, fertile intertidal zones are a habitat for mollusks, algae, and invertebrae.

The river otter *lives in "families," frequenting rivers, lakes, and ocean bays, in its search for fish.*

The common puffin *is a shoreline bird, which lives on cliff edges and is characterized by a brightly colored bill and its curious, friendly nature.*

The raccoon, *with its ringed tail and black-masked face, preys upon fish, crayfish, birds and their eggs.*

The beaver, *symbol of Canada, lives in marshy woodland near streams and rivers. It gnaws down trees, using them to build dams and its lodge.*

OCEAN HABITAT

The sea around Atlantic Canada is influenced by the cold Labrador Current flowing from the north, the Gulf Stream from the south, and the large outflow of fresh water at the mouth of the St. Lawrence River. The region is home to myriad ocean creatures, and the highest tides in the world at the nutrient-rich Bay of Fundy. Off Newfoundland lie the Grand Banks, once one of the Earth's richest fishing grounds. Over-fishing has endangered fish stocks, and quotas are now limited.

The adult blue whale *is the world's largest mammal, reaching up to 30 m (100 ft) long. Today, whale-watching is a growing eco-tourism enterprise, particularly in Digby, where this and other species congregate.*

Lobster, *a favorite seafood of the area, is caught in traps set near the shore. Rigid conservation rules have been put in force to protect its numbers.*

The Atlantic salmon, *unlike its Pacific cousins, returns to its home stream to spawn several times during its lifetime. Atlantic salmon are renowned sport fish (see p25).*

Bottle-nosed dolphins, *characterized by their long beaks and "smiles," live off the east coast, in both New Brunswick and Nova Scotia.*

SEABIRDS OF THE ATLANTIC COAST

The maritime coast of eastern Canada is a perfect environment for seabirds. Rocky cliffs and headlands provide ideal rookeries. The rich coastal waters and intertidal zones ensure a generous larder for many species, including the cormorant and storm petrel. Some Atlantic Coast seabirds are at risk due to environmental changes, but puffins and razorbills, in particular, continue to thrive.

The double-crested cormorant *or "sea crow," as it is sometimes known, is a diving fishing bird, capable of capturing food as deep as 10 m (30 ft) under water.*

Leach's storm-petrel *is part of the Tubenose family of birds, whose acute sense of smell helps them navigate while out at sea.*

The Acadians

Few stories surrounding the settlement of the New World evoke as many feelings of tragedy and triumph as the tale of the Acadians. Colonizing Nova Scotia's fertile Annapolis Valley in the 1600s, 500 French settlers adopted the name Acadie, hoping to establish an ideal pastoral land. They prospered and, by 1750, numbered 14,000, becoming the dominant culture. The threat of this enclave proved too much for a town run by the British, and in 1755 the Acadians were expelled overseas, many to the US. When England and France made peace in 1763, the Acadians slowly returned. Today their French-speaking culture still thrives in some areas.

Acadian women *play a part in summer festivals, displaying local woolcraft and linen textiles.*

Ile Sainte-Croix *was the earliest Acadian settlement, established by the French in New Brunswick in 1604. The neat, spacious layout of the village is typical.*

ACADIAN FARMING

As hardworking farmers, Acadians cleared the land of the Annapolis Valley, built villages, and developed an extensive system of dikes to reclaim the rich farmland from tidal waters. Summer crops were carefully harvested for the winter; potatoes and vegetables were put in cellars, and hay stored to feed cattle and goats. By the 19th century, Acadian farmers had expanded their crop range to include tobacco and flax.

An important crop, hay was raked into *"chafauds,"* spiked haystacks that dried in the fields for use as winter animal feed.

The Expulsion of the Acadians *took place in August 1755. British troops brutally rounded up the Acadians for enforced deportation. Over 6,000 Acadians were put on boats, some bound for the US, where they became the Cajuns of today. Some returned in later years, and today their descendants live in villages throughout Atlantic Canada.*

The Acadian people *maintained a traditional farming and fishing lifestyle for centuries, re-created today at the Village Historique Acadien* (see p79).

The Church of Saint Anne *in Sainte-Anne-du-Ruisseau represents Acadian style in its fresh simplicity and elegance. Catholicism was very important to the Acadians, who turned to their priests for succour during the 1755 diaspora.*

Acadian musicians *have reflected their culture since the 17th century. Playing lively violin and guitar folk music, they are known for their upbeat tunes and ballads of unrequited love and social dispossession.*

Acadian life revolved around the farmsteads in each community. Men tilled the fields and fished while women helped with the annual harvest.

HENRY WADSWORTH LONGFELLOW

One of the most popular poets of the 19th century, both in the US and Europe, the American Henry Longfellow (1807–82) is best known for his long, bittersweet narrative poems. Based on the trials and injustices of the Acadian civilization, *Evangeline*, published in 1847, traces the paths of a young Acadian couple. The poem, now regarded as a classic, stirringly records Evangeline's tragic loss in this land intended as an idyll when their love was destroyed through the upheavals and expulsion of the 18th century: "Loud from its rocky caverns, the deep-faced neighbouring ocean [sings], List to the mournful tradition sung by the pines of the Forest, … List to a Tale of Love in Acadie, home of the happy."

NEWFOUNDLAND AND LABRADOR

With towering peaks, vast landscapes, and 17,000 km (10,500 miles) of rugged coastline, Newfoundland and Labrador displays wild, open spaces and grand spectacles of nature. In this captivating land, massive icebergs drift lazily along the coast, whales swim in sparkling bays, and moose graze placidly in flat open marshes.

Newfoundland's west coast offers some of the most dramatic landscapes east of the Rockies. The granite mountains of Gros Morne National Park shelter deep fjords, while the eastern part of the island has a more rounded terrain, featuring the bays and inlets of Terra Nova National Park. Part of the area's appeal is retracing the history of past cultures that have settled here, including Maritime Archaic Indians at Port au Choix, Vikings at L'Anse-Aux-Meadows, and Basque whalers at Red Bay in the Labrador Straits.

SIGHTS AT A GLANCE

Historic Towns and Cities
Gander ⑨
Happy Valley-
 Goose Bay ⑯
Labrador City ⑱

Nain ⑮
St. John's ①
Trinity ⑥

National Parks
Gros Morne National Park ⑪
Terra Nova National Park ⑦

**Historic Sites and Areas
of Natural Beauty**
Avalon Peninsula ②
Battle Harbour ⑭

Bonavista Peninsula ⑤
Burin Peninsula ③
Churchill Falls ⑰
Labrador Straits ⑬
Northern Peninsula ⑫
Notre Dame Bay ⑧
Saint-Pierre and Miquelon
 Islands ④
The Southwest Coast ⑩

KEY

✈ International airport
▭ Major road
— Major rail routes
▪— International border

0 km   200
0 miles   200

◁ **The weathered seaside fishing villages of Newfoundland have relied on the fishing trade for centuries**

St. John's ●

Italian explorer Giovanni Caboto (John Cabot) *(see p44)* aroused great interest in Newfoundland (after his 1497 voyage on behalf of Henry VII of England) when he described "a sea so full of fish that a basket thrown overboard is hauled back brimming with cod." Cabot started a rush to the New World that made St. John's a center of the fishing industry, and North America's oldest set-

Pendant in local museum

tlement. Today, St. John's still bustles with the commerce of the sea: fishing, oil exploration, and the ships of a hundred nations waiting to be serviced. The people of St. John's are known for their friendliness, a delightful counterpoint to the harsh, rugged beauty that surrounds this historic town.

Downtown St. John's, seen from the approach by sea

Exploring St. John's

The capital of Newfoundland is easily explored on foot. Most of the sights are within a short distance of each other moving east along Water Street. Approaching by sea offers the best view of the harbor, in particular the steep cliff-lined passage on the east side where pastel-colored old houses cling to the rocks.

⊞ Murray Premises

cnr Water St. & Beck's Cove.
◯ *8am–10:30pm daily.* ♿
At the west end of Water Street stands Murray Premises. Built in 1846, these rambling brick and timberframe buildings are the last remaining examples of the large mercantile and fish-processing premises that were common on the St. John's waterfront. Murray Premises once bustled with the work of shipping cod to world markets. It narrowly escaped destruction in a huge fire that engulfed the city in 1892, and the buildings mark the western boundary of the fire's devastation. Now a Provincial Historic Site, the restored buildings are home

to a boutique, hotel, offices, and a fine seafood restaurant, hung with photographs that re-call the busy town of the 1900s.

🏛 The Rooms

9 Bonaventure Ave. *Tel (709) 757 8000.*
◯ *10am–5pm Mon–Sat (to 9pm Wed, Thu; Museum & Art Gallery also open noon–5pm Sun).* ◐ *Jan 1, Mon mid-Oct–May; Dec 25.* **www.**therooms.ca
A major landmark, The Rooms is a modern facility housing three provincial institutions: the Provincial Archives; the Museum of Newfoundland, which charts the province's history over the past 9,000 years; and the Art Gallery of Newfoundland and Labrador, which showcases the work of local, national, and international artists.

⊞ The Waterfront

Water St. *Tel (709) 576 8106.* ♿
Tracing the edge of St. John's waterfront, Water Street is the oldest public thoroughfare in North America, dating to the late 1500s when trading first started in the town. Once a brawling wharfside lane of gin mills and brothels, Water Street

and Duckworth Street now offer an array of gift shops, art galleries, and some of New-foundland's top restaurants. Harbour Drive, along the waterfront, is a great place to stroll, while George Street is the hub of the city's nightlife.

⊞ East End

King's Bridge Rd. 🛈 *(709) 576 8106.*
The East End is one of St. John's most architecturally rich neighborhoods, with narrow, cobblestone streets and elegant homes. Commissariat House, now a provincial museum, was built in 1836 and was once the home of 19th-century British officials. Nearby Government House, built during the 1820s, is the official residence of the province's Lieutenant Governor.

⊞ The Battery

Battery Rd. 🛈 *(709) 576 8106.*
The colorful houses clinging to sheer cliffs at the entrance to the Harbour are known as the Battery. With the look and feel of a 19th-century fishing village, this is one of St. John's most photographed sites. The community is named for the military fortifications built here over centuries to defend the harbor. Local residents used the battery's guns in 1763 to fight off Dutch pirate ships.

🛡 Signal Hill Historic Site of Canada

Signal Hill Rd. *Tel (709) 772 5367.*
◯ *Visitor Centre: Jun–Sep: 8:30am–8pm; Sep–Oct: 8:30am–4:30pm; Oct–May: 8:30am–4:30pm Mon–Fri.* ◐ *Jan 1 Dec 25, 26.* 🎞 ♿
This lofty rise of land presents spectacular views of the open Atlantic, the harbor entrance, and the historic splendor of the city of St. John's.

View of Signal Hill from St. John's picturesque fishing harbor

The Cabot Tower as it rises above Signal Hill over the harbor

🏛 Cabot Tower

Signal Hill Rd. **Tel** (709) 772 5367.
⏰ Jun–Sep: 8:30am–9pm; Sep–May: 9am–5pm. ♿

The building of Cabot Tower at the top of Signal Hill began in 1897 to celebrate the 400th anniversary of Cabot's arrival. On summer weekends, soldiers in period dress perform 19th-century marching drills, with firing muskets and cannon. It was here that another Italian, Guglielmo Marconi, received the first transatlantic wireless signal in 1901.

🏛 Quidi Vidi Village

Quidi Vidi Village Rd. **Tel** (709) 729 2977. ⏰ daily.

On the other side of Signal Hill, the weathered buildings of ancient Quidi Vidi Village nestle around a small harbor. Visitors can browse through the eclectic collection of antiques for sale at Mallard Cottage, dating back to the 1750s. Above the village, the Quidi Vidi Battery was a fortified gun emplacement built in 1762 to defend the entrance of Quidi Vidi Harbour. Today, the site is a reconstruction of the small barracks that soldiers lived in. Guides in period military dress are on hand to relate tales of their lives and hardships.

🌿 Pippy Park

Nagles Place. **Tel** (709) 737 3655.
⏰ daily. ♿
Visitors are sometimes startled to see moose roaming free in St. John's, but it happens often in this 1,400-ha (3,460 acre) nature park, 4 km (2 miles) from the town center. The park is also home to the ponds and gardens of the local Botanical Gardens. The only Fluvarium in North America is based

here too, featuring nine underwater windows that look onto the natural activity of a rushing freshwater trout stream.

🏛 Cape Spear Lighthouse Historic Site of Canada

Tel (709) 772 5367. ⏰ mid-May–mid-Oct: 10am–6pm daily; grounds open all year. 🎫 ♿
Ten km (6 miles) southeast of town, Cape Spear marks the most easterly point in North America. Set atop seaside cliffs, the majestic Cape Spear Lighthouse has long been a symbol of Newfoundland's independence. Two lighthouses sit here. The original, built in 1836 and the oldest in Newfoundland, stands beside a graceful, modern, automated lighthouse, added in 1955.

ST. JOHN'S CITY CENTER

Cabot Tower ⑥
East End ③
Murray Premises ①
Signal Hill ⑤
The Battery ④
The Waterfront ②

Key to Symbols see back flap

Whale- and bird-watching boats tour the Avalon Peninsula frequently

Avalon Peninsula ❷

🚌 St. John's. 🚢 Argentia.
ℹ️ Dept. of Tourism, Confederation Building, St. John's (709) 576 8106.

The picturesque community of Ferryland on the Avalon Peninsula is the site of a large-scale archeological excavation of Colony Avalon, a settlement founded by English explorer Lord Baltimore and 11 settlers in 1621. This was Baltimore's first New World venture, intended to be a self-sufficient colony engaged in fishing, agriculture, and trade, with firm principles of religious tolerance.

By the end of the following year there were 32 settlers. The population continued to grow, and for many years it was the only successful colony in the area. Although excavations to date have unearthed only five percent of the colony, it has proved to be one of the richest sources of artifacts from any early European settlement in North America. Over half a million pieces have been recovered, such as pottery, clay pipes, household implements, and structural parts of many buildings, including defensive works, a smithy, and a waterfront commercial complex. An interpretive center tells the story of the colony and a guided tour includes the chance to watch archeologists working on site and in the laboratory.

GATHERALLS BOAT TOURS PARKING
Boat-tour sign in Witless Bay

At the southern end of the peninsula, **Cape St. Mary's Ecological Reserve** is the only nesting seabird colony in the province that can be approached on foot. A short trail leads along spectacular seacliffs to a site where over 8,000 golden-headed gannets nest on a rock just a few yards over the cliff.

On the southwest side of the peninsula, overlooking the entrance to the historic French town of Placentia, visitors can stroll through **Castle Hill National Historic Site**. These French fortifications dating back to 1632 protected the town, and the site of the remains offers fine coastal views.

🐦 Cape St. Mary's Ecological Reserve
off Route 100. **Tel** (709) 277 1666. ☐ year round. **Interpretive Centre** ☐ May–Oct: daily. 🏬 ♿

🏰 Castle Hill National Historic Site of Canada
Jerseyside, Placentia Bay. **Tel** (709) 227 2401. ☐ late Jun–Aug: 8:30am–8pm; Sep–mid-Jun: 8:30am–4:30pm. 🏬 ♿ 📷

Burin Peninsula ❸

🚌 St. John's. 🚢 Argentia.
ℹ️ Columbia Drive, Marystown Jun–Nov: (709) 279 1211; Dec–May: (709) 279 1887.

The Burin Peninsula presents some of the most dramatic and impressive scenery in Newfoundland. Short, craggy peaks rise above a patchwork green carpet of heather, dotted by scores of glittering lakes. In the fishing town of Grand Bank, **The Provincial Seaman's Museum** is a memorial to Newfoundland seamen who perished at sea. The nearby town of Fortune offers a ferry to the French-ruled islands of Saint-Pierre and Miquelon.

🏛 The Provincial Seaman's Museum
Marine Drive. **Tel** (709) 832 1484. ☐ May–Oct: daily. ♿ limited. 📷

Saint-Pierre and Miquelon Islands ❹

🏘 6,400. 🛬 ✈️ 🚢 ℹ️ 4274 Place de General DeGaulle (508) 41 20 00. www.st-pierre-et-miquelon.com

These two small islands are not Canadian but French, and have been under Gallic rule since 1783. Saint-Pierre, the only town on the island of the same name, is a charming French seaside village, complete with gendarmes, bicycles, and fine French bakeries where people line up every morning for fresh baguettes. The **Saint-Pierre Museum** details the history of the islands, including their lively role as a bootlegger's haven during Prohibition in the 1930s when over three million cases of liquor passed

The Newfoundland Ferry collects visitors for Saint-Pierre and Miquelon

Cape Bonavista Lighthouse, built on the spot believed to be John Cabot's first landing place in the New World

through this tiny port annually. Many of the harborfront warehouses originally built for this trade are still standing.

A daily ferry leaves Saint-Pierre for the smaller village of Miquelon. Miquelon Island is made up of two smaller islands, Langlade and Grand Miquelon, joined by a narrow, 12-km (7-mile) long strand. The road across this sandy isthmus crosses grassy dunes where wild horses graze and surf pounds sandy beaches.

🏛 **Saint-Pierre Museum**
Rue du 11 Novembre. **Tel** (508) 410 135. ◯ Jun–Oct: Tue–Sun. 🎫 ♿

Bonavista Peninsula ❺

📷 St. John's. 🚢 Argentia. ℹ️ Discovery Trail Tourism Association (709) 466 3845. **www**.thediscoverytrail.org

Bonavista Peninsula juts out into the Atlantic ocean, a rugged coastal landscape of seacliffs, harbor inlets, and enchanting small villages such as Birchy Cove and Trouty.

The town of Bonavista is believed to be where Italian explorer John Cabot (see p44) first stepped ashore in the New World. His monument stands on a high, rocky promontory, near the Cape Bonavista Lighthouse, built in 1843.

Along the Bonavista waterfront, the huge 19th-century buildings of Ryan Premises,

once a busy fish merchants' processing facility, are now restored as a National Historic Site. Ryan Premises include three large buildings where fish were dried, stored, and packed for shipping, and displays on the history of the fisheries in North America. The waterfront salt house offers local music.

Trinity ❻

🏞 300. ℹ️ Trinity Interpretation Centre, West St (709) 464 2042/0592.

The charming village of Trinity, with its colorful 19th-century buildings overlooking the blue waters of Trinity Bay, is easily one of the most beautiful Newfoundland communities. Best explored on foot, Trinity has a range of craft shops and restaurants. The **Trinity Museum** contains over 2,000 artifacts, illustrating the town's past.

Also here is Hiscock House, a turn-of-the-century home, restored to the style of 1910, where merchant Emma Hiscock ran the village store, forge, and post office while raising her six children.

🏛 **Trinity Museum**
Church Rd. **Tel** (709) 464 3599. ◯ mid-Jun–mid-Oct: 10am–5:30pm daily. 🎫 📷

Terra Nova National Park ❼

Trans-Canada Hwy. 📷 from St. John's. ◯ May–mid-Oct: daily. 🎫 ♿ 🚗 limited. ℹ️ Glovertown (709) 533 2801. **www**.pc.gc.ca

The gently rolling forested hills and deep fjords of northeastern Newfoundland are the setting for Terra Nova National Park. The park's Marine Interpretation Centre offers excellent displays on the local marine flora and fauna, including a fascinating underwater video monitor that broadcasts the busy life of the bay's seafloor. Whale-watching tours are also available.

A lookout over Terra Nova National Park

Notre Dame Bay ❽

🚗 Gander. 🚢 Port-aux-Basques.
ℹ️ Notre Dame Junction, Rte 1.
www.kittiwakecoast.ca

On the east side of Notre
Dame Bay, traditional Newfoundland outports maintain a
way of life that echoes their
history. The **Twillingate
Museum**, located in an
elegant Edwardian rectory in
Twillingate, has several rooms
furnished with period antiques.
Also on display are aboriginal
artifacts collected from nearby
sites, and marine memorabilia
recounting the region's
fascinating shipping history.
   Boat tours take passengers
out into the bay for a close-
up look at the huge icebergs
that float by in spring and
summer, and to see the many
whales that roam about offshore. Nearby Wild Cove and
Durrell are romantic villages.

The elegant Edwardian rectory that
houses the Twillingate Museum

Gander ❾

🏔️ 10,000. ✈️ ⌧ ℹ️ 109 Trans-
Canada Hwy (709) 256 7110.

Best known for its illustrious
aviation history, Gander is a
small town and a useful tourist
center for fuel and food. In
Grand Falls-Windsor, 100 km
(57 miles) west
of Gander,

A mamateek dwelling reveals a past way of life in Grand Falls Indian village

the Mary March Regional
Museum, named after the last
survivor of the now extinct
Beothuk people, traces 5,000
years of human habitation in
the Exploits Valley. Throughout
Newfoundland, the Beothuks
were decimated by disease
and genocide between 1750
and 1829. Behind the museum,
visitors can take a guided tour
through the historic village.

The Southwest Coast ❿

🚗 Ferry dock terminal. 🚢 Port-aux-
Basques. ℹ️ Port-aux-Basques (709)
695 3688.

In southern Newfoundland
a 45-km (28-mile) coastal
drive along Route 470 from
Channel Port-aux-Basques to
Rose Blanche leads through a
landscape of ancient, jagged,
green mountains and along a
rocky, surf-carved shoreline.
Near Rose Blanche, a 500-m
(545-yd) boardwalk trail
winds through bright wild-
flower-strewn heath to the
impressive Barachois Falls.
There is a charming picnic
spot at the foot of the 55 m
(180 ft) falls. The area is

noted for its many shipwrecks,
and so the Rose Blanche
Lighthouse, built in 1873,
stands in defiant splendor
atop the harbor headland.

Gros Morne National Park ⓫

Tel (709) 458 2417. 🚗 Corner
Brook. 🚢 St. Barbe. ◐ daily. 🈲
♿ 🛒 **www**.pc.gc.ca

A United Nations World
Heritage Site, Gros Morne
is Newfoundland's scenic
masterpiece. Here the Long
Range Mountains rise 700 m
(2,000 ft) above blue fjords
that cut into the coastal range.
Some of the world's oldest
mountains, these are pre-
Cambrian and several million
years older than the Rockies.
   The best way to see the park
is on a boat tour along Western
Brook Pond, a narrow fjord
cradled between soaring cliffs
where waterfalls vaporize as
they tumble from great heights.
Wildlife, including
moose, caribou,
and eagles, is
frequently
seen and
heard.

The Long Range Mountains in Gros Morne National Park, seen from a walkway in the park

For hotels and restaurants in this region see p346 and p370

Northern Peninsula Tour ⑫

Road sign on Hwy 430

A land of legends and mystery, the Northern Peninsula of Newfoundland offers adventurous travelers the chance to experience over 40 centuries of human history, from early aboriginal people through colonization to today's modern fishing life. The road north travels along a harsh and rocky coast. Along the way, important historic sites, such as L'Anse-aux-Meadows, tell the story of the earlier cultures who chose this wild land as their home.

TIPS FOR DRIVERS

Tour length: 430 km (267 miles) along Hwy 430.
Starting point: Deer Lake, at junction of Hwy 1.
Stopping off points: Gros Morne's Wiltondale Visitors' Centre and Tablelands; Port au Choix National Historic Site; Grenfell Museum in St. Anthony.

Port au Choix ⑤
This historic site is dedicated to exhibitions of Maritime Archaic Indians and Dorset Eskimos who lived here in 2000 BC and AD 500.

Hawke's Bay ④
A whaling station early in the 20th century, Hawke's Bay boasts excellent salmon fishing waters.

The Arches ③
This lovely spot is named for three limestone arches that are probably 400 million years old.

Gros Morne National Park ②
This fine place has a reputation as one of the most beautiful parks in the whole of Canada.

L'Anse-aux-Meadows National Historic Site ⑥
This historic settlement takes visitors back to AD 1000, with eight reconstructions of the wood and sod buildings built and used by Viking settlers when they landed here.

Deer Lake ①
A good fuel and refreshment center for those starting on the tour, Deer Lake and its surrounding area is remarkable for its jagged landscape, salmon river (the Humber), forests, lakes, and farms.

KEY

▬ Tour route

= Other roads

0 km   25

0 miles   25

Fishermen's huts in the village of Red Bay on the coast of Labrador

Labrador Straits ⓭

📧 Blanc Sablon. ℹ️ Forteau (709) 931 2013. **www**.labradorcoastal drive.com

Hauntingly beautiful coastal landscapes explain why the Labrador Straits is a popular place to visit in this province. A summer ferry service crosses the straits from Newfoundland to Blanc Sablon, Quebec, just a few kilometers from the Labrador border. From there, an 85-km (53-mile) road leads along the coast through a wild countryside of high, barren hills, thinly carpeted by heath and wind-twisted spruce.

The Labrador Straits was an important steamship route in the mid-19th century. To aid navigation in the often treacherous waters, the Point Amour Lighthouse was built in 1854 near L'Anse-Amour. Now a Provincial Historic Site, this 30-m (109-ft) tower is the second-tallest lighthouse in Canada. Visitors can ascend the tower for stunning views of the Labrador coast.

Along the road to the lighthouse is a monument that marks the site of the Maritime Archaic Burial Mound National Historic Site, North America's oldest burial mound, where a Maritime Archaic Indian child was laid to rest 7,500 years ago.

At the end of Rte. 510 lies **Red Bay National Historic Site**. Here visitors can take a short boat ride to an island where 16th-century Basque whalers operated the first factory in the New World. A tour around the island leads past the foundations of the shanties, shipworks, and cooper shops

where as many as 1,500 men worked each season, rendering whale oil for lamps in Europe.

🏛 Red Bay National Historic Site
Route 510. **Tel** (709) 920 2142. ☐ Jun–early Oct: daily. 🏛 ♿

Battle Harbour ⓮

✉️ 🛥 ℹ️ Mary's Harbour, Newfoundland (709) 921 6216. **www**.battleharbour.com

Once considered the unofficial capital of Labrador (from the 1870s to the 1930s), Battle Harbour, a small settlement on an island just off the southern coast of Labrador, was a thriving fishing community during the late 18th and 19th centuries. In 1966, the dwindling population was relocated to St. Mary's on the mainland, but all of the

town's buildings, many of which date back 200 years, were left standing, and in the 1990s the town was restored. Today, visitors can tour the island and get a taste of the way life was in coastal Labrador a century ago.

Nain ⓯

🚶 1,150. ✈️ 🛥 ℹ️ Town Council, Nain (709) 922 2842.

Traveling north, Nain is the final community of more than a few hundred people. The town can be reached by a coastal boat service that carries passengers and freight, but no cars. A large part of Nain's small population is Inuit and the town is home to many of Labrador's most prominent Inuit artists. The Torngasuk Cultural Center has a gift shop with CDs and books by local artists for sale. The staff here can also put visitors in touch with local soapstone sculptors.

Nearby Hopedale was the site of one of the many Moravian Missions built in Labrador. Today the main feature in Hopedale is the **Hopedale Mission National Historic Site**. Visitors can tour the Mission, constructed in 1782, which

Inuit children in Nain

is the oldest woodframe building in Atlantic Canada. Both the Mission and other structures were

Battle Harbour Island with icebergs on the horizon

A snowy street in Nain during the long winter

built in Germany, shipped across the Atlantic, and reassembled here.

🏛 Hopedale Mission National Historic Site

Agvituk Historical Society, Hopedale. **Tel** (709) 933 3881. ⬜ daily. 📷

The Moravian Church in Happy Valley-Goose Bay

Happy Valley-Goose Bay ⓖ

🏚 8,000 ✈ 🚢 ℹ Labrador, Lake Melville Tourism Association (709) 896 3489. 📷 book ahead.

The largest town in the wilderness of Central Labrador, Happy Valley-Goose Bay was a strategically important stopover for transatlantic flights during World War II. German, Italian, and British pilots now train at the NATO base here.

Today, the town is home to the Labrador Heritage Museum, where exhibitions depict its fascinating history. It pays particular attention to the life of trappers, with displays that include animal furs, trapper's tools, and a traditional tilt (wilderness shelter).

Churchill Falls ⓗ

ℹ Churchill Falls Development Corporation (709) 925 3335. 📷 obligatory, book ahead.

The town of Churchill Falls is ideally placed for visitors to stock up on supplies, fill up with gas, and check tyres as there are no service stations between Happy Valley-Goose Bay and Labrador City. Churchill Falls is famous as the site of one of the largest hydro-electric power stations in the world. Built in the early 1970s, the plant is an extraordinary feat of engineering, diverting the Churchill River (it is Labrador's largest) and its incredible volume of water to power the underground turbines that produce 5,225 megawatts of power – enough to supply the needs of a small country. Guided tours are available of this impressive complex.

Labrador City ⓘ

🏚 7,700. ✈ 🚢 ℹ Labrador West Tourism Development Corporation (709) 944 7631.

In the midst of ancient tundra, Labrador City is a mining town that shows the modern, industrial face of Canada. The town is home to the largest open-pit iron mine in the world and the community has largely grown up around it since the late 1950s. The historic building that once held the town's first bank is now the Height of Land Heritage Centre, a museum of photographs, artifacts, and displays dedicated to preserving the history of the development of Labrador.

The vast open wilderness surrounding Labrador City, with its myriad pristine lakes and rivers, is renowned as a sportsman's paradise that attracts hunters and anglers from around the world. Every March, this region sponsors the Labrador 150 Dogsled Race, which has become one of the world's top dogsledding competitions. The western Labrador wilderness is also home to the 700,000 caribou of the George River herd. The herd moves freely through the area for most of the year, grazing the tundra in small bands. Professional outfitters take groups of visitors out to track the herd through the region. Many tourists make the trip to admire the animals.

THE LABRADOR COASTAL FERRY

The Labrador Coastal Ferry is the primary mode of transportation for many communities along the Coast. Departing from St. Anthony in northern Newfoundland, the ferry round-trip takes 12 days, visiting up to 48 communities, delivering goods, passengers, and supplies in each port. Half the passenger space is for tourists, half for locals. Along the way, the ferry calls at the historic port of Battle Harbour and travels into fjords. Icebergs are a common sight.

NEW BRUNSWICK, NOVA SCOTIA, AND PRINCE EDWARD ISLAND

The beauty and lure of the sea is always close at hand here. Stunning coastal scenery, picturesque centuries-old villages, world-class historic sites, and a wealth of family attractions have turned these three Maritime Provinces into one of Canada's top vacation destinations. New Brunswick's ruggedly beautiful Bay of Fundy is matched by the gently rolling landscape of Acadian villages tucked into quiet coves and long sandy beaches. With its sparkling bays and ancient weathered fishing towns, Nova Scotia embodies the romance of the sea. Elegant country inns and historic sites bring the past to life. Canada's smallest province, Prince Edward Island, is known for its vibrant green farmlands, red bluffs, deep blue waters, and golf courses, and is enjoyed by cyclists, anglers, and hikers.

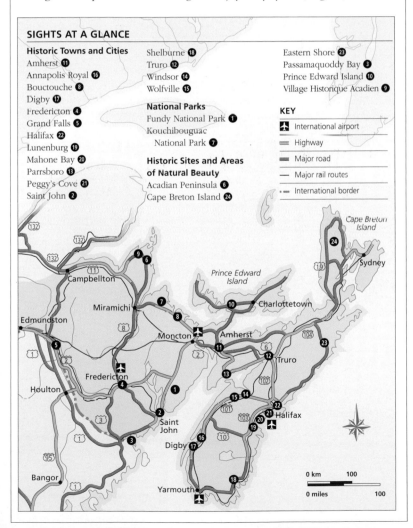

SIGHTS AT A GLANCE

Historic Towns and Cities
Amherst ⑪
Annapolis Royal ⑯
Bouctouche ⑧
Digby ⑰
Fredericton ④
Grand Falls ⑤
Halifax ㉒
Lunenburg ⑲
Mahone Bay ⑳
Parrsboro ⑬
Peggy's Cove ㉑
Saint John ②

Shelburne ⑱
Truro ⑫
Windsor ⑭
Wolfville ⑮

National Parks
Fundy National Park ①
Kouchibouguac
  National Park ⑦

Historic Sites and Areas of Natural Beauty
Acadian Peninsula ⑥
Cape Breton Island ㉔

Eastern Shore ㉓
Passamaquoddy Bay ③
Prince Edward Island ⑩
Village Historique Acadien ⑨

KEY

✈ International airport

━ Highway

━ Major road

— Major rail routes

∎–∎ International border

Humpback whales at play in the Bay of Fundy

Fundy National Park ❶

Tel (506) 887 6000. 🚗 Moncton. 🚌 Sussex. 🚢 Saint John. ⏰ daily. 🏛 May–Oct. ♿ ▣
www.pc.gc.ca

Along New Brunswick's southern shore, the tremendous tides of the Bay of Fundy are a powerful feature of everyday life. Twice a day, over 100 billion tons of water swirl into and out of the bay, creating a tidal shift of up to 15 m (48 ft) and carving out a stunning wild and rocky shoreline.

One of the best places to experience these world-famous tidal wonders is at Fundy National Park, which is filled with wildlife and hiking trails. Here at low tide, visitors can walk out for over a kilometer. The Bay is a favorite with naturalists, who study the fascinating creatures that live half their lives under water and the other half above.

Moose in Fundy National Park

Saint John ❷

🏘 70,000. ✈ 🚗 🚢 ℹ City Hall, King St. (506) 658 2990. **www**.tourismsaintjohn.com

New Brunswick's second city, Saint John, still retains the charm of a small town. In 1785, 14,000 loyalists escaping the turmoil of the American Revolution built Saint John in under a year.

More recently, restoration has made Saint John's historic center a delightful place to explore. The Old City Market is a working public market, with colorful produce stacked high, fresh seafood vendors, cafés, and an excellent traditional fish restaurant.

In nearby Market Square, an airy atrium links buildings that were once the city's center of commerce. Here visitors will find upscale restaurants and stores. Market Square is also the home of the lively **New Brunswick Museum**. Three floors offer clever and entertaining exhibits on New Brunswick's geological, cultural, and natural history. Children particularly enjoy the Hall of Whales and the three-level Tidal Tube in which water rises and falls, re-creating the height of the tides roaring away just outside.

Nearby, the Loyalist House Museum is located in an impressive Georgian house built by Loyalist David Merritt in around 1810. Inside, the house has been renovated to reflect the lifestyle of a wealthy family of that time, with authentic period furnishings.

🏛 New Brunswick Museum
Market Square. **Tel** (506) 643 2300. ⏰ daily ⏰ Nov–mid-May: Mon. 🏛 ♿

Passamaquoddy Bay ❸

🚗 St. Stephen. 🚢 Black's Harbour & Letete. ℹ St. Andrew's Tourism Bureau (506) 529 3556.

There is a genteel historic charm to the villages surrounding the island-filled waters of Passamaquoddy Bay, and none is more charming or intriguing than the lovely resort town of St. Andrews-by-the-Sea. The beautifully maintained Fairmont Algonquin Resort, with its elegant grounds and 18-hole golf course, recalls early 20th-century days when St. Andrews was renowned as an exclusive getaway of the rich and powerful.

In town, Water Street is lined with intriguing boutiques, craft shops, and fine restaurants housed in century-old buildings. At the town dock, tour companies offer numerous sailing, whale-watching, and kayaking adventures. Nearby, the elegant Georgian home built for Loyalist Harris Hatch in 1824 is now the location of the **Ross Memorial Museum** which contains an extensive collection of antiques and art assembled early in the 20th century.

Two ferries leave from the St. George area nearby for Campobello and Grand Manan Islands, 20 km (12 miles) and 30 km (18 miles) south respectively of St. Andrews.

View of Saint John from the Saint John River

The charming Victorian vista of Fredericton seen from across the Saint John River

The Roosevelt Campobello International Park is a 11-sq-km (4-sq-mile) preserve on Campobello Island built around the elegant summer home of US President Franklin D. Roosevelt. The 34-room Roosevelt Cottage has been restored, and includes historic and personal artifacts belonging to Roosevelt and his family.

Renowned for its rugged coastal beauty, Grand Manan Island has high rocky cliffs, picturesque fishing villages, and brightly painted boats resting against weathered piers. It is popular with bird-watchers as it attracts large flocks of seabirds annually.

🏛 The Ross Memorial Museum
188 Montague St. **Tel** (506) 529 5124. ◯ late May–early Oct: Mon–Sat.

Fredericton ❹

🏚 48,000. ⊠ 🚉 ℹ Carlton Tourism Division (506) 460 2041. **www**.tourismfredericton.ca

Straddling the Saint John River, Fredericton is New Brunswick's provincial capital. Its Victorian homes and waterfront church make it one of the prettiest small cities in Atlantic Canada. Several historic buildings reflect the town's early role as a British military post. The **Beaverbrook Art Gallery** contains an impressive collection of 19th- and 20th-century paintings, including Salvador Dali's masterpiece *Santiago el Grande* (1957).

King's Landing Historical Settlement, 37 km (22 miles) west of Fredericton is a living history museum that re-creates daily life in a rural New Brunswick village of the 19th-century. Over a hundred costumed workers bring villagers' homes, church, and school to life.

🏛 Beaverbrook Art Gallery
703 Queen St. **Tel** (506) 458 8545. ◯ daily. 📷 🚻 📷 **www**.beaverbrookartgallery.org

🏚 King's Landing Historical Settlement
Rte 2, W of Fredericton. **Tel** (506) 363 4999. ◯ Jun–early Oct: 10am–5pm daily. 📷 🚻 partial.

Grand Falls ❺

🏚 5,900. 🚉 ℹ Malabeam Reception Centre. 📷

From Fredericton to Edmundston, the Saint John River flows through a pastoral valley of rolling hills, woods, and farmland. The town of

Grand Falls consists of one well-appointed main street, which is a useful refreshment stop. The town was named Grand Falls for the mighty cataract the Saint John's River creates as it tumbles through Grand Falls Gorge. Framed by parkland, the surge of water drops more than 25 m (40 ft). Over time it has carved a gorge 1.5 km (1 mile) long, with steep sides as high as 70 m (200 ft) in places.

Upriver and north through the valley, the town of Edmundston offers the **New Brunswick Botanical Garden**. Paths lead through eight themed gardens and two arboretums that provide dazzling input for the senses. Bright colors, delicate scents, and even soft classical music delight visitors.

🌿 New Brunswick Botanical Garden
Saint-Jacques, Edmundston. **Tel** (506) 737 4444. ◯ May–Oct: 9am–dusk daily. 📷 **www**.umce.ca/jardin

The deep waterfall valley of Grand Falls Gorge

Endless sandy beaches stretch to the horizon at Kouchibouguac National Park

The Acadian Peninsula ⑥

🚉 Bathurst. 🚌 Bathurst.
⛴ Dalhousie. 🛈 Jun–Sep: Water
St., Campbellton (506) 789 2367;
Oct–May: Campbellton Chamber of
Commerce (506) 759 7856.

The quiet coastal villages, beaches, and gentle surf of the Acadian peninsula have made it a favorite vacation destination. Established here since the 1600s, the Acadians have long enjoyed a reputation for prosperous farming, pretty villages and a strong folk music tradition *(see pp62–3)*.

In Shippagan, the small fishing town at the tip of the mainland, the **Marine Centre and Aquarium** holds tanks with over 3,000 specimens of Atlantic sealife and displays on local fishing industries.

Nearby, the Lamèque and Miscou islands are connected by causeways to the mainland. On Miscou Island, a 1-km (0.5-mile) boardwalk leads through a peat bog with signs about this unique ecosystem. The 35-m (85-ft) high Miscou Lighthouse is the oldest operating wooden lighthouse in Canada.

Home to many Acadian artists, Caraquet is the busy cultural center of the peninsula. On the waterfront, adventure centers offer guided kayak trips on the Baie des Chaleurs. For those wanting an introduction to the story of the Acadians, the **Acadian Wax Museum** features a self-guided audio tour past 23 tableaus from Acadian history. The scenes begin with the founding of the

"Order of the Good Times" at Annapolis Royal in 1604 and focus on the expulsion of 1755.

🐟 Marine Centre and Aquarium
100 Aquarium Street, Shippagan.
Tel (506) 336 3013. ⬜ mid-May–mid-Oct: 10am–6pm daily. 🎫 ♿

🏛 Acadian Wax Museum
Rte 11, Caraquet. **Tel** (506) 284 2591. ⬜ Jun–Sep: daily. 🎫 ♿

Kouchibouguac National Park ⑦

Tel (506) 876 2443. 🚉 Newcastle.
🚌 Newcastle. ⛴ Miramichi.
⬜ daily. **www**.pc.gc.ca

The name of this park comes from the native Mi'kmaq word for "River of Long Tides." The park's 238 sq km (92 sq miles) encompass a salt-spray world of wind-sculpted dunes, salt marshes packed with wild life, and 25 km (16 miles) of fine sand beaches, as well as excellent terrain for cyclists. A popular activity is the Voyager

Marine Adventure, a three-hour canoe paddle to offshore sandbanks where hundreds of gray seals relax in the sun.

Bouctouche ⑧

🏘 2,400. 🚌 🛈 Jun–Sep: 14 Acadia St. (506) 743 8811; Oct–May: Bouctouche Chamber of Commerce (506) 759 7856. **www**.bouctouche.org

A seaside town with a strong Acadian heritage, Bouctouche is home to **Le Pays de la Sagouine**. This theme village is named for La Sagouine, the wise washerwoman created by Acadian authoress Antonine Maillet (b. 1929). Theatrical shows here act out her tales.

Nearby, the Irving Eco-Centre studies and protects the beautiful 12-km (8-mile) network of dunes, saltmarshes, and beach that extend along the entrance to Bouctouche Harbour.

🎭 Le Pays de la Sagouine
57 Acadia St. **Tel** 1 800 561 9188.
⬜ mid-Jun–Sep: 10am–6pm daily.

The raised boardwalk at the Irving Eco-Centre, La Dune de Bouctouche

Village Historique Acadien ❾

After the tragic deportation of 1755–63 *(see p62–3)*, Acadians slowly returned to the Maritimes, clearing new farmlands and rebuilding their way of life. The Village Historique Acadien portrays a rural Acadian community between 1770 and 1939. The village's 45 restored historic buildings, including several working farms, cover 364 ha (900 acres). Throughout the village, period-costumed bilingual guides re-create the daily activities of the 19th century. Visitors can ride in a horse-drawn wagon, watch the work of the blacksmith, print shop, or gristmill, and also tour working farms and homes where women are busy spinning, weaving, and cooking.

VISITORS' CHECKLIST

Route 11, 10 km (6 miles) W of Caraquet. *Tel (506) 726 2600.* from Bathurst. Jun–Oct: 10am–6pm daily. late Oct– May.

School and Chapel
Through centuries of turmoil, Catholicism was a vital mainstay of the Acadian people. Priests were also schoolteachers; education was highly prized by the community.

Men in horse-drawn cart
Traditional methods are used on the farms; tilled by local people arriving each day, the harvest is moved in carts to barns for winter.

Cooper's Shop Tinsmith
Lobster Pound

The Chapel was built by pioneer Acadians and dates from 1831.

Doucet Farm was first built in 1840 and has been fully restored to its original appearance.

Mazerolle Farm sells fresh bread and rolls, which are baked daily in a large oven in the farmhouse.

Poirier
Tavern

Savoie House
Education Centre

Robin
shed

Godin
House

The Visitors' Reception Centre offers an audiovisual presentation, and typical Acadian food in its restaurant.

Forge
In many ways the center of the community, the blacksmith was a feature of every Acadian village, repairing farm equipment and shoeing horses for the people of the area.

0 m   100

0 yards   100

Prince Edward Island ⑩

Beautiful and pastoral, Prince Edward Island is famous for its lush landscapes. Wherever you look, the island's rich colors, emerald green farmlands, red-clay roads, and sapphire sea, seem to combine and recombine in endless patterns to please the eye. The island is also a popular destination for golfers who come to tee off on some of Canada's best courses, as well as a haven for sun worshipers who revel in the sandy beaches that ring the island. Prince Edward Island seems made for exploring at a leisurely pace. Meandering coastal roads present an ever-changing panorama of sea, sand, and sky. Small historic towns are home to elegant country inns and art galleries. In the evenings, the island's famous lobster suppers await, caught fresh daily from the Atlantic Ocean.

Green Gables House
Set amid leafy green paths, this 19th-century home was the setting for the popular Anne of Green Gables *tales.*

Malpeque Bay
Cabot Beach Provincial Park covers part of the bay. Ten million of the world-famous Malpeque oysters are caught here each year.

North Cape

Mill River

Portage

EGMONT BAY

Malpeque

Cavendish

Kensington

Hunter River

Victoria

Cedar Dunes Provincial Park features a restored 1875 lighthouse, sandy beaches, and a large coastal campground.

KEY

▬	Major road
═	Minor road
▭	Rivers
—	National Park boundaries
⛴	Ferry
✕	Airport
☀	Viewpoint

STAR SIGHTS

★ PEI National Park

★ Charlottetown

Main street, Summerside
This quiet city with its attractive tree-lined streets is known for its Lobster Carnival *each July.*

Confederation Bridge, opened in 1997 at a total cost of Can$900m, runs for 13 km (8 miles) to the mainland.

0 km   100
0 miles   100

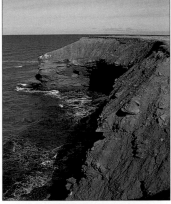

★ Prince Edward Island National Park

Characterized by 40 km (25 miles) of coastline leading onto red cliffs, pink and white sand beaches, and mild seas, this park offers unbeatable sport and vacationing facilities and has an educational Visitors' Centre for those interested in its marine wildlife.

East Point Lighthouse
The island's easternmost point is home to a 19th-century lighthouse with a restored radio room. Now unmanned and fully automatic, it is open to visitors.

★ Charlottetown

Elegant 19th-century row houses characterize the streets of this sleepy town, the smallest of Canada's provincial capitals; in 1867 the Confederation of Canada was decided here.

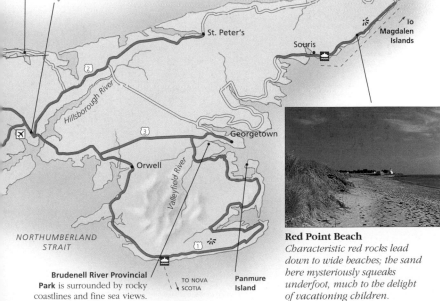

St. Peter's

Io Magdalen Islands

Souris

Hillsborough River

Georgetown

Valleyfield River

Orwell

NORTHUMBERLAND STRAIT

Brudenell River Provincial Park is surrounded by rocky coastlines and fine sea views.

TO NOVA SCOTIA

Panmure Island

Red Point Beach
Characteristic red rocks lead down to wide beaches; the sand here mysteriously squeaks underfoot, much to the delight of vacationing children.

Exploring Prince Edward Island

The smallest province in Canada, Prince Edward Island's concentration of activity means every corner of the island is accessible. Charlottetown, known as the birthplace of Canada, is centrally located, and its tree-lined streets make a gentle start to exploring the outlying country. Red clay roads guide the visitor through farms and fishing villages to tiny provincial parks scattered throughout the island. Traveling the north coast takes in the splendid rolling green scenery of PEI National Park, with its famous beaches, while southward, warm swimming spots abound.

the park's western end, the Homestead Trail leads for 8 km (5 miles) through rustic green woodlands and meadows.

The park's quieter eastern side features a long stretch of pristine beach and dunes, and a scenic coastal road. The Reeds and Rushes Trail is a lovely short boardwalk track leading to a freshwater marsh pond where local species of geese and duck nest and feed.

Fishing huts overlooking French River near Cavendish

🌺 Prince Edward Island National Park

Charlottetown. 🚢 Wood Islands.
ⓘ (902) 672 6350. ◌ daily. 🎫 ♿
www.pc.gc.ca

Cavendish

This is such a busy little town that it can be hard to see the gentle, pastoral home of the *Anne of Green Gables* novels. The best place to get in touch with its charm is at the site of **Lucy Maud Montgomery's Cavendish Home**, where the author lived for many years, a simple and authentic site. The town is also the location of **Green Gables**, the novels' fictional 19th-century home.

🏛 Lucy Maud Montgomery's Cavendish Home

Route 6. *Tel* (902) 963 2231. ◌ mid-May–mid-Oct: 10am–5pm daily. 🎫 ♿

🏛 Green Gables

Route 6. *Tel* (902) 963 7874.
◌ daily by appointment. ♿

Cavendish
Routes 6 & 13. ⓘ (902) 963 7830.

Prince Edward Island National Park

Green Gables is part of Prince Edward Island National Park, whose western entrance is in Cavendish. This is the park's busier side. The soft sand and gentle surf of Cavendish Beach make it one of the most popular beaches in the province. The park's coastal road leads to North Rustico Beach, which is a favorite with sightseers. At

The South Coast

Enchanting vistas are found along the roads of the south shore, between Confederation Bridge and Charlottetown. Visitors will also find Victoria-by-the-Sea, a small village that is home to some of the island's most interesting craftshops.

En route to Charlottetown, visitors can make a short detour to **Fort Amherst-Port-la-Joye National Historic Site**. It was here, in 1720, that the French built the island's first permanent settlement. The British captured it in 1758, and built Fort Amherst to protect the entrance to Charlottetown Harbour. While the fort is long gone, the earthworks can still be seen in the park-like surroundings.

🏛 Fort Amherst-Port-la-Joye National Historic Site of Canada

Rocky Point. *Tel* (902) 566 7626.
◌ mid-Jun–Aug: daily. 🎫 ♿

The red bluffs of Cavendish Beach, one of the most favored spots in Prince Edward Island National Park

For hotels and restaurants in this region see pp347–9 and pp371–3. For transport information see p421

View of 19th-century church at Orwell Corner Historic Village

Panmure Island

The natural beauty of the island's eastern area is easy to experience on Panmure Island, south of Georgetown. Level roads make it popular with cyclists. In summer, the octagonal wooden **Panmure Island Lighthouse** is open, and the view from the top takes in a long vista of the island's beaches, saltmarshes, and woodlands The lighthouse still guides ships into port as it did when it was first built in 1853.

Panmure Island Lighthouse
Panmure Island. **Tel** (902) 838 3568.
Jul–Aug: 9am–7pm daily.

Orwell Corner Historic Village

Just outside of the small hamlet of Orwell, Orwell Corner Historic Village re-creates the day-to-day life of a small 19th-century crossroads community. Orwell Corner was thriving until well into the 20th century, when changes in transportation and commerce lessened the importance of the settlement. This charming villlage was restored and opened in 1973. Among the buildings are a blacksmith's, church, schoolhouse, and Clarke's store, the social center of the village. Upstairs is the workshop of Clarke's seamstresses, who made dresses for local ladies.

Just 1 km (0.5 mile) away is the **Sir Andrew Macphail Homestead**. This Victorian house and its surroundings were the much-loved home of Macphail, a local doctor, journalist, teacher, and soldier who counted among his friends prime ministers and acclaimed writers such as

Kipling. The house features many exhibits dealing with Macphail's life. Outside, trails wind through deep woodlands.

Orwell Corner Historic Village
Orwell. **Tel** (902) 651 8513.
May–Oct: daily.

Sir Andrew Macphail Homestead
off Rte 1, Orwell. **Tel** (902) 651 2789.
Jun–Sep: 10am–5pm daily.

Charlottetown

The birthplace of Canada is a charming small city. Along Peake's Quay, sailboats lie snug against marina piers, and the waterside buildings are home to intriguing shops and restaurants. The elegant **Confederation Centre of the Arts** hosts an array of live entertainment including the popular musical *Anne of Green Gables*. **Province House National Historic Site** is where the 1864 Charlottetown

Conference was held, which led to the formation of Canada as a nation. Several rooms have been meticulously restored to their 19th-century character. **Ardgowan National Historic Site** was once the home of William Pope, one of the Fathers of Confederation.

Confederation Centre of the Arts
145 Richmond St. **Tel** (902) 628 1864. daily.

Province House National Historic Site of Canada
165 Richmond St. **Tel** (902) 566 7626. daily; call ahead for hours.

Ardgowan National Historic Site
Mount Edward Rd. **Tel** (902) 566 7050. daily.

Charlottetown
Water St. (902) 368 4444.
www.city.charlottetown.pe.ca

Historic homes in Great George Street, Charlottetown

LUCY MAUD MONTGOMERY

The island's most famous author, Lucy Maud Montgomery, was born in Cavendish in 1874. Nearby Green Gables House became the setting of her internationally best-selling novel, *Anne of Green Gables* (1908), set in the late 19th century. The manuscript was accepted only on the sixth attempt. To date, millions of copies of *Anne* have been published, in 16 languages. In 1911, Lucy married and moved to Ontario, where she raised two sons. She continued to write, producing 17 more books, ten of which feature Anne, with all but one set on Prince Edward Island. She died in 1942 and was buried overlooking the farms and fields of her beloved native Cavendish, the Avonlea of which she wrote so often.

Author Lucy Maud Montgomery

Amherst ⓫

🏙 9,500. 🚗 ℹ Rte 104, exit 1
(902) 667 8429.

A busy commercial and
agricultural town, Amherst
overlooks the world's largest
marsh, the Tantramar. Along
its edge, hayfields grow on
land reclaimed by Acadian-
built dikes in the 1600s. **The
Cumberland County Museum**
is located in the family home
of Senator R.B. Dickey, one of
the Fathers of Confederation.
It focuses on the area's
industrial development, as well
as local and natural history.
  Nearby are **Fort Beauséjour**
and its museum, and the
archaeological digs at the
Acadian village of Beaubassin.

🏛 **Cumberland County
Museum**
150 Church St. **Tel** (902) 667 2561.
⬤ Tue–Sat. 🎫 👤

🏚 **Fort Beauséjour**
Trans-Canada Hwy 2, Exit 513A.
⬤ Jun–mid-Oct: daily. 🎫 👤 📷

Truro ⓬

🏙 11,700. 🚉 🚗 ℹ Victoria
Square (902) 893 2922.

Located at the hub of Nova
Scotia's main transportation
routes, Truro is the site of a
unique geographical phenomenon, the tidal bore. As the
great Fundy tides return
landward, sweeping into the
Minas Basin, they generate a
wave, or "bore," that is driven
for several kilometers up the
rivers that empty into the
back of the basin. An
information display next

Façade of Haliburton House in Windsor, home of the famous humorist

to the Salmon River explains
each process and posts the
tidal times. On the nearby
Shubenacadie River, visitors
can ride the bore in rafts. The
waves generated can reach
2 m (7 ft) in height, creating
a churn of whitewater that
the rafts race through as they
follow it for miles upstream.

Parrsboro ⓭

🏙 1,500. ℹ Main St. (902)
254 3266.

Located on the north shore of
the Minas Basin, Parrsboro is
famous as the home of the
world's highest
tides, which reach
over 15 m (50 ft)
in height.
Rockhounds
are drawn to
the Minas Basin
whose beaches are
scattered with semi-
precious gems and fossils.
The displays at **Fundy Geological Museum** in Parrsboro
feature superb examples of
local amethysts. There are also
dinosaur footprints and bones.

Prosauropod dinosaur skull
from Fundy Museum

🏛 **The Fundy Geological
Museum**
6 Two Islands Rd. **Tel** (902) 254
3814. ⬤ Jun–mid-Oct: daily; late
Oct–May: Tue–Sun. 🎫 👤

Windsor ⓮

🏙 3,800. 🚗 ℹ Hwy 101, exit 6
(902) 798 2275.

A quiet town whose elegant
Victorian homes overlook the
Avon River, Windsor was the
home of Judge Thomas
Chandler Haliburton, lawyer,
historian, and the author of
the Canadian "Sam Slick" stories, which achieved enormous
popularity in the mid-1800s.
Haliburton was one of the first
widely recognized humorists
in North America. His clever,
fast-talking character Sam Slick
was a Yankee clock peddler
who coined idiomatic terms
such as "the early
bird gets the
worm," and
"raining cats
and dogs."
His elegant
home is now the
**Haliburton House
Provincial
Museum**. Surrounded by
gardens that Haliburton tended
and loved, the house is
furnished in Victorian period
antiques and contains many
of his personal possessions,
including his writing desk.

🏛 **Haliburton House
Provincial Museum**
414 Clifton Ave. **Tel** (902) 798 2915.
⬤ Jun–mid-Oct: daily. 🎫 👤 limited.

Two Island Beach in Parrsboro, famous for the two large rock outcrops known as the "Brothers Parrsboro"

For hotels and restaurants in this region see pp347–9 and pp371–3

Wolfville ⑮

🏠 3,700. ℹ️ Willow Park (902) 542 7000.

The home of the acclaimed Acadia University, Wolfville and the surrounding countryside radiate a truly gracious charm. Here the green and fertile Annapolis Valley meets the shore of the Minas Basin, and keen visitors can follow country roads past lush farmlands, sun-warmed orchards and gentle tidal flats.

Much of the valley's rich farmland was created by dikes built by the Acadians in the 1600s. After the Great Expulsion of 1755, the British offered the land to struggling New England villagers on the condition that the entire village would relocate. These hardworking settlers, known as Planters, proved so successful that the towns of the Annapolis Valley flourished.

Wolfville is a pretty town of tree-lined streets and inviting shops and restaurants. Nearby, the town's Visitor Information Center marks the start of a 5-km (3-mile) trail along the Acadian dikes to the graceful church at the **Grand Pré National Historic Site**. When the British marched into the Acadian village of Grand Pré in August 1755, it marked the beginning of the Great Uprooting, *Le Grand Dérangement*, which eventually forced thousands of Acadians from Nova Scotia *(see pp62–3)*. In 1921 a stone church modeled after French country churches was built on the site of the old village of Grand Pré as a memorial to this tragedy. The French Cross marks the spot where the Acadians boarded the ships. Visitors can also stroll around the garden grounds, where a statue of Evangeline, the heroine of Longfellow's epic poem about the Acadians, stands waiting for her lover, Gabriel. The site's information center features exhibits on the Acadians and their history. After the Great Uprooting, many families hid locally, while some returned in later years.

Longfellow's Evangeline

🏛 Grand Pré National Historic Site

Hwy 101, exit 10. **Tel** (902) 542 3631. ⬜ May–Oct: daily. 🅿️ ♿

Annapolis Royal ⑯

🏠 550. 🚌 ℹ️ Prince Albert Rd. (902) 532 2562.

Toward the eastern end of the Annapolis Valley is the historic town of Annapolis Royal, the first capital of the colony of Nova Scotia. The British-built **Fort Anne National Historic Site** witnessed many battles between the English and the French for control of the area.

The nearby fur-trading post of Port Royal *(see p45)*, the first European settlement in the New World north of Florida, was built in 1605 by Samuel de Champlain. **The Port Royal National Historic Site** is an exact replica of the original colony, based on French farms of the period, from plans drawn by Champlain.

Kejimkujik Park entrance sign

An hour's drive inland from Annapolis Royal lies **Kejimkujik National Park**, which covers 381 square km (148 sq miles) of inland wilderness laced with lakes and rivers. The park has many paddling routes and 15 hiking trails, ranging from short walks to a 60-km (37-mile) perimeter wilderness and wildlife trail.

🏛 Fort Anne National Historic Site

St. George St. **Tel** (902) 532 2397. ⬜ daily (Oct 16–May 14: by appt; call (902) 532 2321). 🅿️ ♿

🏛 Port Royal National Historic Site

15 km W. of Annapolis Royal. **Tel** (902) 532 2898. ⬜ May–Oct: 9am– 5:30pm (to 6pm Jul & Aug). 🅿️ ♿

🗻 Kejimkujik National Park

Hwy 8. **Tel** (902) 682 2772. ⬜ daily. 🅿️ mid-May–Oct. ♿

Digby ⑰

🏠 2,100. ✈️ 🚌 🚢 ℹ️ Shore Rd (902) 245 5714.

This fishing town is synonymous with the plump scallops that are the prime quarry of its fishing fleet. The area around Digby also offers splendid scenery and is the starting place for a scenic trip along Digby Neck to the rocky coastal landscape of beautiful Long and Brier Islands.

The waters off Long and Brier Islands brim with finback, minke, and humpback whales, and whale-watching tours are one of the region's favorite pastimes. Some visitors may even glimpse the rare right whale, as about 200 of the 350 left in the world spend their summers in the Bay of Fundy.

Children having fun in a canoeing lake at Kejimkujik National Park

Riverfront houses at Bridgewater near Lunenburg, Nova Scotia ▷

The Dory Shop Museum in Shelburne, center of local boat-building

Shelburne ⑱

🏠 *2,000.* 🚌 **ℹ** *Dock St. (902) 875 4547.*

A quiet historic town nestled on the shore of a deep harbor, Shelburne was founded hastily by 3,000 United Empire Loyalists fleeing persecution after the American Revolution in 1775. More loyalists followed over the next few years, and Shelburne's population swelled to 16,000, making it at the time the third-largest town in British North America. Over time, many of those settlers relocated to Halifax or returned to England, leaving behind the fine 18th-century homes they had built.

A walk along Water Street leads past some of the town's most attractive historic homes to the **Dory Shop Museum**. This two-storey structure has been a commercial dory (flat-bottomed) boat building shop since its founding in 1880. During the days of the Grand Banks schooner fleet, Shelburne dories were famous for their strength and seaworthiness. The museum's first floor features displays on the

industry and the salt-cod fishery. Upstairs, skilled shipwrights demonstrate the techniques of dory building that have changed little in a century.

The 1995 film *The Scarlet Letter* was shot in Shelburne, with the whole main street becoming a movie set. The town is also home to the only active cooperage in Canada.

🏛 Dory Shop Museum
Dock St. **Tel** *(902) 875 3219.*
⭘ *Jun–Sep: daily.* 🈺 **&** *limited.*

Lunenburg ⑲

🏠 *2,600.* 🚌 **ℹ** *May–Sep: (902) 634 8100; Oct–Apr: (902) 634 3170.*
www.*explorelunenburg.ca*

No town captures the seafaring romance of Nova Scotia as much as Lunenburg. In the mid-1700s the British, eager for another loyal settlement, laid out a town plan for Lunenburg. They then offered the land to Protestant settlers from Germany. Although these were mainly farmers, they soon turned to shipbuilding and fishing. In 1996 the town was declared a UNESCO World

Heritage Site, one of the best-preserved planned settlements in the New World. Lunenburg is also the home port of *Bluenose II*, a replica of Canada's most famous schooner.

The **Fisheries Museum of the Atlantic** fills several buildings along the waterfront. Its docks are home to the *Theresa E. Conner*, the last of the Grand Banks Schooners, and the side-trawler, *Cape Sable*.

🏛 Fisheries Museum of the Atlantic
Bluenose Dr. **Tel** *(902) 634 4794.*
⭘ *mid-May–mid-Oct: daily; late Oct–May: Mon–Fri.* 🈺 **&** *limited.*

One of Mahone Bay's three waterfront churches

Mahone Bay ⑳

🏠 *990.* 🚌 **ℹ** *South Shore Tourism Association (902) 634 8844.*
www.*mahonebay.com*

The small seaside town of Mahone Bay has been called the "prettiest town in Canada." Tucked into the shores of the bay that shares its name, the waterfront is lined with historic homes

View of the Lunenberg Fisheries Museum of the Atlantic along the town's romantic waterfront

dating to the 1700s, and at the back of the harbor three stately churches cast their reflection into the still waters.

The town has attracted some of Canada's finest artists and craftspeople, whose colorful shops line the main street. The small **Settlers Museum** offers exhibits and artifacts relating to the town's settlement by foreign Protestants in 1754, and its prominence as a boat-building center. There is also a collection of 18th- and 19th-century ceramics and antiques.

🏛 **Settlers Museum**
578 Main St. *Tel* (902) 624 6263.
◯ Jun–Sep: Tue–Sun.

Peggy's Cove ㉑

🏚 60. 🍴 Sou'wester Restaurant (902) 823 2561.

Peggy's Cove Lighthouse stands atop wave-worn granite rocks and is one of the most photographed sights in Canada, a symbol of Nova Scotia's enduring bond with the sea. The village, with its colorful houses clinging to the rocks, and small harbor lined with weathered piers and fish sheds, has certainly earned its reputation as one of the province's most picturesque fishing villages. This is a delightful place to stroll through, but visitors may want to avoid midday in summer, when the number of tour buses can be a distraction. Early morning and late afternoon are the most peaceful times. Just outside the village is a memorial to the victims of the 1998 Swissair crash.

The village was also the home of well-known marine artist and sculptor, William E. deGarthe (1907–83). Just above the harbor, the deGarthe Gallery has a permanent exhibition of 65 of his best-known paintings and sculptures.

Right outside the gallery, the Memorial is a 30-m (90-ft) sculpture created by deGarthe as his monument to Nova Scotian Fishermen. Carved into an outcropping of native granite rock, the sculpture depicts 32 fishermen, and

The best-known symbol of Atlantic Canada, Peggy's Cove Lighthouse

their wives and children. The large angel in the sculpture is the original Peggy, sole survivor of a terrible 19th-century shipwreck, for whom the village was named.

Halifax ㉒

See pp90–91.

The Eastern Shore ㉓

🚉 Halifax. 🚌 Antigonish. 🚢 Pictou. 🛈 Canso (902) 366 2170.

A tour along the Eastern Shore is a trip through old-world Nova Scotia, through towns and villages where life has changed little since the turn of the 20th century. The tiny house and farm that comprise the Fisherman's Life Museum in Jeddore, Oyster Ponds (60 km/37 miles east of Halifax) was the home of an inshore fisherman, his wife,

and 13 daughters around 1900. Today, the homestead is a living-history museum where guides in period costume (many of them wives of local fishermen) reenact the simple daily life of an inshore fishing family, still the heart of Nova Scotia culture. Visitors who arrive at midday may be invited to share lunch cooked over a woodburning stove. There are also daily demonstrations that include rug-hooking, quilting, and knitting, and visitors can tour the fishing stage where salted fish were stored.

Sherbrooke Village is the largest living-history museum in Nova Scotia. Between 1860 and 1890, this was a gold and lumber boomtown. As the gold ran out, Sherbrooke once again became a sleepy rural village. In the early 1970s, 25 of Sherbrooke's most historic buildings were restored. Within the village, scores of costumed guides bring 19th-century Nova Scotia to life. A ride on a horse-drawn wagon offers an overview of the town; the drivers share bits of local history as the horses trot along the village roads. At the Apothecary, visitors can watch the careful mixing of patent medicines, and those interested in the Ambrotype Studio can dress in period costumes, sitting very still while the vintage camera records their image on glass. Just outside town a massive waterwheel turns, powering the Lumber Mill.

🏛 **Sherbrooke Village**
off Hwy 7. *Tel* (902) 522 2400.
◯ Jun–Oct: daily. ⌨

The Apothecary at the living history museum Sherbooke Village

Halifax ㉒

With its bustling waterfront, pretty parks, and unique blend of modern and historic architecture, Halifax is a fascinating city. Its cultured flavor belies its 250-year history as a brawling military town. Founded in 1749 by General George Cornwallis, Halifax was planned as Britain's military center north of Boston.

Town memorial to merchant seamen

The city has a long history of adventure, being the town where legalized pirates, or privateers, brought captured ships to be shared with the crown. On December 6, 1917, the city was devastated by the explosion of a French ship in the harbor. Today, Halifax is best known as one of Canada's foremost centers of higher learning and has many colleges and five universities.

Exploring Halifax

This is an easy town to explore on foot, as many of the better museums, historic sites, shops, and restaurants are located within the fairly contained historic core.

Downtown, leading west from Brunswick Street, is hilly and green, ideal for a leisurely walk to appreciate the old-style architecture. Citadel Hill offers excellent views of the city, the harbor, and Dartmouth.

🏠 Historic Properties

1869 Upper Water St. **Tel** (902) 429 0530. ⬜ daily. &
The Historic Properties are a wharfside collection of very old stone and timber-frame structures, which were originally built in the 19th century to hold the booty captured by privateers. Today, they house an intriguing collection of specialty and gift shops, pubs, and fine restaurants. This is one of the city's favorite gathering spots on warm summer nights, with crowds of strollers enjoying the lights of the harbor and music drifting from nearby pubs.

🏛 Maritime Museum of the Atlantic

1675 Lower Water St. **Tel** (902) 424 7490. ⬜ May–Oct: daily; Nov–Apr: Tue–Sun. 🎫 & 📷 on request.
This harborfront museum offers extensive displays on Nova Scotia's seafaring history, including small craft, a restored chandlery, and, at the dock outside, the elegantly refitted 1913 research vessel *Acadia*. The museum's most popular exhibit is the *Titanic* display, which offers artifacts recovered from the ship. There are fragments of the ship's grand staircase, as well as a mural-sized photo showing the staircase in its original state. After the 1912 catastrophe, many of the bodies that were recovered were brought to Halifax, and 150 are buried at Fairview Cemetery.

🏠 Harbourfront

ℹ (902) 490 5946.
The Harbourfront Walkway, features interesting gift shops, cafés, and restaurants in historic settings along the boardwalk. This delightful promenade leads to the Dartmouth Ferry, North America's oldest town ferry. A trip round the harbor is an inexpensive way to enjoy a panorama of Halifax.

🏠 Government House

1200 Barrington St.
The current home of Nova Scotia's lieutenant-general, this beautiful building is not open to the public but well worth exterior inspection for its historic and architectural interest. Its Georgian façade lends an urban grandeur. Completed in 1807, Government House cost over £30,000 (Can$72,000), a huge amount for a humble fishing village.

The bandstand of Halifax Public Gardens, framed in flowers

🏠 Pier 21

1055 Marginal Road **Tel** (902) 425 7770. ⬜ May–Oct: daily; Nov–Apr: Wed–Sat. 🎫 & www.pier21.ca
Canada's entry point for more than a million immigrants and refugees, Pier 21 is now a National Historic Site. It offers powerful and emotional displays and fascinating images.

🍂 Halifax Public Gardens

Spring Garden Rd. **Tel** (902) 490 4894. ⬜ mid-Apr–Nov: daily. & limited.
Created in 1836, the Public Gardens are a beautiful 7-ha (17-acre) oasis of Victorian greenery and color in a bustling city. A peaceful place to

The waterfront of Halifax, seen from the town ferry

stroll, the gardens' paths wind past duck ponds, fountains, and a seemingly endless array of vivid flower beds. In the center of the gardens, an ornate bandstand is the site of Sunday concerts. On weekends, craftspeople gather outside the park's cast-iron fence to display their varied and colorful wares.

✠ Halifax Citadel National Historic Site

Citadel Hill. *Tel (902) 426 5080.*
◯ *May–Oct: daily. Grounds: all year.*
🌿 *summer.* ♿ ✦
Overlooking the city, this huge star-shaped fortress has a commanding view of the world's second-largest natural harbor. Built between 1828 and 1856, the citadel and its outlying fortifications provided a formidable defense. Visitors can stroll the parade grounds where the kilted regiment of the 78th Highlanders perform with twice-daily musket drills.

Halifax's famous town clock, built in 1803 as a gift from British royalty

✠ Old Town Clock

Citadel Hill.
At the base of Citadel Hill stands the city's most recognized landmark, the Old Town Clock. The clock was a gift in 1803 from Edward, the British Duke of Kent and then military commander, who had a passion for punctuality. He designed the clock with four faces so that both soldiers

VISITORS' CHECKLIST

🏔 *394,000.* ✈ *35 km (22 miles)
N of the city.* 🚌 🚆 *6040 Almon
St.* 🛈 *1595 Barrington St. (902)
490 5946.* 📷 *Nova Scotia
International Tattoo (Jul); Atlantic
Jazz Festival (Jul); International
Busker's Festival (Aug).*
www.*destinationhalifax.com*

and citizens would arrive at their appointed destinations on time.

✠ Province House

1726 Hollis St. *Tel (902) 424 4661.*
📷 *Jul–Aug: 9am–5pm Wed–Fri;
Sep–Jun: 9am–4pm Mon–Fri.* ♿
Built between 1811 and 1819, Province House is the oldest seat of government in Canada. In 1864 the Fathers of Confederation held two days of meetings here on the formation of Canada *(see p48)*. Visitors can tour the rooms where these plans were laid.

HALIFAX CITY CENTER

Key to Symbols *see back flap*

0 meters 250
0 yards 250

Cape Breton Island ㉔

Magnificent natural beauty is the attraction on Cape Breton. Every year thousands of people travel the famous Cabot Trail through the craggy splendor of Cape Breton Highlands National Park *(see p94–5)*. But Cape Breton's beauty is not limited to these two renowned sights; it can be found along inviting country roads and in the less explored corners of this green, fertile island. Particularly stunning are the Mabou Highlands, which cradle the gentle waters of Lake Ainslee, Bras d'Or Lake where eagles soar over scenic shores, and romantic coastal villages such as windswept Gabarus. The reconstructed 18th-century French garrison and village, Fortress Louisbourg, is also highly popular.

Glenora Whisky

St. Pierre Church at Cheticamp
Built in 1883, the silver spire of this church is typical of Catholic style. The church is in the center of the town of Cheticamp, which offers whale-watching opportunities and is the focus of the 3,000-strong local Acadian community.

Glenora Distillery
Located on the scenic Ceilidh Trail, Glenora was Canada's first single-malt distillery and is renowned for its Glen Breton Rare, a 10-year-old whisky. Visitors can also enjoy a pub, an inn, and a gift shop.

Lake Ainslee
This tranquil lake, encircled by scenic roads, attracts many bird species, such as ospreys and loons, which feed on its shores.

Margaree Harbour

Mabou

Port Hastings

Isle Madame

St. F

KEY

▬	Major road
═	Minor road
▬	Scenic route
—	River
ℹ	Visitor information
❊	Viewpoint
✈	Airport
—	National Park boundary
⛴	Ferry

0 km 15

0 miles 15

VISITORS' CHECKLIST

ℹ️ Causeway, Port Hastings (902) 425 5781. ✈ Sydney. 🚢 from Halifax. ⛴ from Port aux Basques & Argentia, Newfoundland. **www**.cbisland.com

Cabot Trail Highway
This sublime 300-km (186-mile) drive around the island's northwest and its national park attracts more visitors each year.

CAPE BRETON HIGHLANDS NATIONAL PARK

Bay St. Lawrence

Ingonish Beach

Sydney Mines coastal town dates back to the 1700s, with mining shafts that reach 5 km (3 miles) out to sea.

Bird Islands

St. Ann's

Sydney
The third-largest town in Nova Scotia, Sydney is a comparatively small town with a long history as a mining center. The main draw today is its heritage housing.

The Alexander Graham Bell Museum sits on the shores of Bras d'Or Lake, Bell's summer home for 30 years. Plans, copies, and prototypes of many of his most famous inventions can be seen here.

Glace Bay

Baddeck

St. Andrew's Channel

Iona

Big Pond

as d'Or Lake

Gabarus

Pioneer cottages
These 19th-century settlers' cottages in Iona's Highland Village are fully restored.

Fortress Louisbourg
The reconstructed fort and village is ideal for a walk and tour through the 1744 past of French Canada. Attractive hiking trails surround the site (see pp96–7).

Exploring Cape Breton Island

Cape Breton fresh lobster

The largest island in Nova Scotia, Cape Breton has a wild beauty and grandeur that makes for some of the most impressive scenery in Canada. From the rolling highlands, sprinkled with sparkling streams, to fine sandy beaches, the island's 300-km (200-mile) Cabot Trail provides one of the most memorable tours in Canada. Other inviting country roads lead to the stunning Mabou Hills, surrounding Lake Ainslee, and to romantic little towns including Baddeck and the Acadian settlement of Cheticamp near the green Margaree Valley.

Lobster fishing boats in the Main à Dieu harbor on Cape Breton Island

Cape Breton Highlands National Park

In 1936 the Canadian Government set aside the 950 sq km (366 sq miles) of magnificent highlands in the northern tip of Cape Breton Island to form Cape Breton Highlands National Park. The park contains some of Canada's most famous scenery, with its mountains, green wilderness, and windswept coastal beauty. The best-known feature of the park is the spectacular 106-km (66-mile) section of the Cabot Trail highway, which traces much of the park's boundary in a loop from Cheticamp to Ingonish.

The Cabot Trail is the primary route through the park, and most attractions are found along it. Entering the park, the trail ascends along the flanks of the coastal mountains. The 24 look-out points on this stretch present far-reaching views of the highlands rising from the sea. Continuing inland, the trail travels across the highland plateau. Just past French Lake, the short Bog Walk is a

boardwalk trail through marshes, with educational panels that describe this unique bog-bound ecosystem, which is home to rare orchids. Visitors may even catch a glimpse of the park's many moose grazing here in a wetland marsh.

Crossing the French and Mackenzie Mountains, the trail descends dramatically to the charming old community of Pleasant Bay. It then re-enters the highlands, crossing

Picturesque Ingonish Beach on Cape Breton Island

North Mountain, which, at 457-m (1,500-ft), is the highest point in the park. The trail descends into the Aspy River Valley, where a gravel road leads to the base of the 30-m (100-ft) high Beulach Ban Falls.

At Cape North, another side road leads to the scenic whale-watching destination of Bay St. Lawrence just outside the park. Farther on, the Scenic Loop breaks away from the Cabot Trail and follows the coast, offering awesome views as it descends to White Point. This road rejoins the Cabot Trail to the east, where it reaches the resort town of Ingonish. The Highland Links Golf Course here is ranked among the top golf courses in Canada.

✦ Cape Breton Highlands National Park
ℹ️ Cheticamp. *Tel (902) 224 2306.*
⭕ daily. ▨ ♿ limited.
www.pc.gc.ca

Baddeck

Across the lake from the estate of Alexander Graham Bell, who loved the little town, Baddeck lies in rich farmland and is very much the island's premier resort destination. Set on the northwest side of Bras d'Or Lake, Baddeck is still the small, friendly town that charmed visitors in the 19th century. All amenities are within walking distance. The town's main street follows the waterfront and is lined with shops, cafés, and restaurants. Boat cruises around the lake are available from several places on Water Street by the shore.

The town's top attraction is the **Alexander Graham Bell National Historic Site**. The museum here contains the world's largest collection of photographs, artifacts, and documents about the life of this famous humanitarian and inventor. There are early telephones and several of his later inventions, including a copy of his HD-4 Hydrofoil.

Baddeck
ℹ️ Port Hastings (902) 625 4201.

�🏛 Alexander Graham Bell National Historic Site
559 Chebucto St (Hwy 205).
Tel (902) 295 2069. ⭕ May–Oct: daily; Nov–Apr: by appt. ▨ ♿

A fly-fisher tries his hand in the salmon- and trout-filled waters of the Margaree River

Margaree River Valley

Small and emerald green, the Margaree River Valley is a favorite with hikers, antique-hunters, and sightseers. The river has attracted salmon and trout anglers in large numbers since the mid-19th century.

In the little town of North East Margaree, the tiny but elegant **Margaree Salmon Museum** will fascinate even non-anglers with its beautiful historic rods and reels.

Paved and gravel roads follow the Margaree River upstream to the scenic spot of Big Intervale, where the headwaters come tumbling out of the highlands. For a taste of Gaelic culture, follow the Ceilidh Trail all the way to the **Glenora Distillery**, Canada's first single-malt distillery.

🎣 Margaree Valley
ℹ️ *Margaree Fork (902) 248 2803.*

🏛 Margaree Salmon Museum
60 E. Big Interval Rd. **Tel** *(902) 248 2848.* ⭕ *mid-Jun–mid-Oct: 9am–5pm daily.* 📷 ♿ *limited.*

🏛 Glenora Distillery
Route 19/Ceilidh Trail. **Tel** *(902) 258 2662.* ⭕ *daily.* 📷

Cheticamp

This vibrant town is the largest Acadian community in Nova Scotia. Its beautiful Saint Pierre Church is visible from miles out at sea. The Acadians of Cape Breton are skilled craftspeople, and the town's seven cooperatives produce pottery and hooked rugs. Cheticamp's best-known rug hooker was Elizabeth Le-Fort, whose large and intricate works depicting prominent moments in history have hung in the Vatican and in the White House. Several of her finest rugs are on display at the **Dr. Elizabeth LeFort Museum** at Les Trois Pignons.

Cheticamp is also a popular whale-watching destination; tours are available for seeing many varieties of whale.

🏛 Dr. Elizabeth LeFort Museum
15584 Main St. **Tel** *(902) 224 2642.* ⭕ *May–Oct: daily.* 📷

Sydney

The only city on Cape Breton Island, Sydney is the third-largest town in Nova Scotia. Boasting the biggest steel plant in North America, the town is the region's industrial center. Despite this, Sydney has a small, attractive historic district around the Esplanade, with several restored buildings, such as Cossit House and Jost House, both dating from the 1870s. Downtown, boutiques, stores, and restaurants can be found along the town's main drag, Charlotte Street.

🏨 Sydney
ℹ️ *Sydney (902) 539 9876.*

ALEXANDER GRAHAM BELL

Alexander Graham Bell was born in 1847 in Scotland. Bell's mother was deaf, and, as a child, he became fascinated by speech and communication. In 1870, Bell and his family moved to Ontario *(see p218)*. His work involved transmitting the voice electronically, and he began experimenting with variations of the technology used by the telegraph. In 1876 he transmitted the world's first telephone message, "Watson, come here, I want you." With the patenting of his invention,

Alexander Graham Bell

Bell secured his role as one of the men who changed the world. In 1877, Bell married Mabel Hubbard, one of his deaf students. In 1885, the couple visited Cape Breton, where Bell later built his beautiful estate, Beinn Bhreagh, by Bras d'Or Lake. There he lived and worked each summer until he died in 1922. In Baddeck, the Alexander Graham Bell Museum focuses on his life and varied work.

Fortress Louisbourg

Built between 1713 and 1744, the magnificent Fortress Louisbourg was France's bastion of military strength in the New World. Today, it is the largest military reconstruction in North America. Visitors stepping through the fortress gate enter the year 1744, when war had just been declared between France and England. Inside, scores of historically costumed guides bring the excitement of an 18th-century French trading town to life. The streets and buildings are peopled with merchants, soldiers, fishmongers, and washerwomen, all going about the daily business of the 1700s. From the lowliest fisherman's cottage to the elegant home of the Chief Military Engineer, attention to detail throughout is superb. The costumed interpreters offer information about the fortress, its history, and the lives of people they portray.

Costumed interpreter

Overview of the Fortress
The seat of government and the central command of French military power in the New World, the Fortress was home to a town of thousands.

0 meters   50

0 yards   50

The Quay and Frederic Gate
The Quay was the center of commercial activity in the town. It is still central to the fort, as many activities now take place at the Gate's imposing yellow arch.

STAR FEATURES

★ King's Bastion

★ Engineer's Residence

★ **The Engineer's Residence**
Responsible for all public construction projects at the fortress, the engineer was one of the most important and powerful men in the community.

VISITORS' CHECKLIST

Rte. 22 SW of Louisbourg. *Tel* (902) 733 2280. ☐ May, Jun, Sep & Oct: 9:30am–5pm daily; Jul & Aug: 9am–6pm. ⊠ ☐ ☐ ☐
⊓ ☐ www.louisbourg.ca/fort

★ King's Bastion
The largest building in the Citadel, the King's Bastion Barracks was home to the 500 French soldiers who lived, ate, and slept here.

The Icehouse was used to store fresh food for the Governor's table.

Officers' rooms

King's Bakery
Visitors can buy warm bread from this working bakery that produced the soldiers' daily rations.

The Forge
Traditional skills are in evidence here, with costumed workers demonstrating exactly the carefully learned craft of the 18th century.

The Guardhouse held the vital human line of defense; guards were stationed here while on duty.

The Dauphin Gate
Soldiers in historic uniforms at the gate challenge visitors, just as they would have in 1744. The gate's artistic details are based on archeological relics from the original gate recovered in the 1960s.

QUEBEC

Introducing Quebec

Quebec is the largest of Canada's provinces and the biggest French-speaking territory in the world, with many of its seven million citizens holding firm to the language and culture inherited from their French ancestors. Landscapes range from pastoral valleys and villages along the American border, to vast expanses of tundra on the shores of Hudson Bay. At Quebec's heart is the St. Lawrence River. Its north shore begins with the scenic Charlevoix region edging a wilderness of lakes, forest, and tundra that stretches to the Hudson Strait, past one of the world's largest power projects at James Bay. To the south lies the mountainous Gaspé Peninsula. There are two major cities; multiethnic Montreal, and Quebec City, the provincial capital and North America's only walled city.

Huds Stra

Hudson Bay

James Bay

RADISSO

The picturesque lakeside resort of St- Jovite in the Laurentian Mountains set amid a backdrop of magnificent fall colors

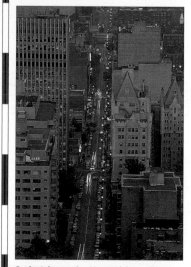

Quebec's largest city, Montreal, has a vibrant downtown area that comes to life after dark

VAL D'OR

0 km   100

0 miles   100

KEY

▬ Highway

▬ Major road

═ River

SEE ALSO

• *Where to Stay* pp349–53

• *Where to Eat* pp373–8

SOUTHERN AND
NORTHERN QUEBEC

QUEBEC CITY AND THE
ST. LAWRENCE RIVER

MONTREAL

Infantrymen parade in La Citadelle
(see pp136–7) overlooked
by Château Frontenac

Ungava
Bay

QUEBEC

SEPT-ILES

ILE D'ANTICOSTI

GASPÉ

138

BAIE-
COMEAU

GASPÉ
PENINSULA

CHIBOUGAMAU

132

167

TADOUSSAC

155

CHICOUTIMI

175

40

QUEBEC CITY

SHERBROOKE

MONTRÉAL 20

HULL

GETTING AROUND

Airports serve every major city. Bus services
tour the whole province and include Voyageur
Lines, Orléans Express, and smaller regional
services. Greyhound buses, based in the US,
travel to Montreal. Limocar bus travel covers
the Laurentian Mountains and Autobus Viens
serves the Eastern Townships. Rail services are
limited to the southern part of Quebec. The
region also has a comprehensive network of
high standard highways for exploring by car.

Maple Forests

The red maple leaf of Canada

Long the pride of Quebec and Ontario, there is more to Canada's ancient maple forests than their annual display of beauty. Every fall, turning leaves splash crimson and orange across the south, but it is in springtime that the trees give up their most famous product: maple syrup. Extracting techniques which were developed by native peoples were passed to Europeans in the 17th century. Traditional methods changed little until the 1940s, when part of the process was mechanized. Many age-old methods remain, however, including the final hand-stirring of the syrup.

Maple trees, either red maple *(Acer rubrum)* or sugar maple *(Acer saccharum)*, grow to heights of well over 30 m (100 ft), with thick trunks a meter (3 ft) in diameter. While their main product is the syrup, the hard wood is used for furniture and, of course, the leaf itself is the national symbol of Canada, officially established on the flag in 1965.

Collecting sap from trees *by tapping maple trunks is the first step. Cuts are made low in the wood in spring as sap rises.*

Transporting the sap *in large barrels on a horse-drawn sleigh through the snowy forests is traditional. In the 1970s this was largely replaced by a network of plastic tubing that take the sap directly from tree trunks to the sugar shacks.*

Sugar shacks *are built in the forest in the center of the sugar bush, the cluster of maple trees that are producing sap. Men and women alike work long hours at slowly evaporating the sap, reducing it to syrup. Quebecois have their own rite of spring: when the first syrup is ready, it is poured onto the crisp snow outside the shacks to make a tasty frozen taffy.*

MAPLE SYRUP PRODUCTS

Although 80 percent of Canada's annual maple harvest eventually becomes maple syrup, there is more to the industry than simply a sweet sauce. Boiled for longer, the syrup hardens into a pale golden sugar that can be used to sweeten coffee or eaten like candy. Maple butter, which is whipped with sugar, is also popular. Savory products benefit too; ham and bacon can be cured in syrup, which is delicious. The sweet-toothed people of Quebec use the syrup to make sugar pie, a tart with a sweet, fudge filling.

Maple products are used in a variety of foods, both sweet and savory

Maple syrup

Syrup is graded according to quality; clear golden fluid, produced at the start of the season, is the most prized, and is generally bottled. Later, darker syrup is used in cooking, and the final, even darker, batch makes a base for synthetic flavors or syrups. Over Can$100 million is spent annually on maple products.

THE STORY OF MAPLE SYRUP

The first maple-sugar farmers were native Canadians. Long before European settlers arrived in the 16th century, tribes all over Northeast America sweetened savory dishes with syrup. An Iroquois legend tells the story of a chief in ancient times who, hurling an ax at a tree, found it stuck in the trunk at the end of the next day, dripping sweet fluid. That night the chief's wife boiled the day's hunt in the sap, and the syrup was born. Folk tales apart, it is certain that native people discovered the sap and techniques for refining it, few of which have changed, and passed their knowledge to Europeans freely.

Boiling maple sap *involves 40 liters (88 pts) of sap to create one liter (2.2 pts) of syrup. The gold color and maple flavor develop as distillation takes place. The paler first syrup of the season is the most valuable.*

Transforming sap into maple syrup *takes place very slowly. The sap bubbles over a wood fire (maple wood is prefered) until about 98 percent of its water content evaporates. Modern processes use mechanized evaporators to boil the sap and draw off the steam, but even hi-tech methods still require a final hand-stirred simmering.*

The St. Lawrence Seaway

Extending from the Gulf of St. Lawrence on the Atlantic coast to Duluth at the western end of Lake Superior in Minnesota, the St. Lawrence Seaway and Great Lakes System flows across North America for over 3,700 km (2,300 miles). The St. Lawrence Seaway itself stretches 553 km (344 miles) from Montreal to Lake Erie and covers 245,750 square km (95,000 sq miles) of navigable water. Open from March to December, it is the world's longest deep-draft inland waterway. Ships carry a huge quantity of domestic traffic, but over 60 per cent of the total freight travels to and from overseas ports, mainly from Europe, the Middle East, and Africa. Traffic varies: cargoes of grain travel in superships alongside pleasure boats.

LOCATOR MAP

▨ *The St. Lawrence Seaway*

THE HISTORY OF THE SEAWAY

The Seaway has ancient beginnings: in 1680, French monk Dollier de Casson started a campaign to build a mile-long canal linking Lac St. Louis and Montreal, which was finally opened in 1824 as the Lachine Canal. In 1833, the first Welland Canal (from Lake Ontario to Lake Erie) opened. The fourth Welland Canal was the first modern part of the Seaway to be built in 1932. 1951 brought US and Canadian cooperation to bear on a new seaway, which began in Canada in 1954. On April 25, 1959, the Seaway opened, linking the Great Lakes to the world.

Pleasure boats
cruise the Seaway near the Thousand Islands by Kingston, Ontario. Each summer, small craft take advantage of the excellent sailing and waterskiing available in this section of the Seaway.

The *D'Iberville*, **first ship to cross the Seaway**

Ottawa

O N T A R I O

Kingston

Toronto

Lake Ontario

↗ LAKE HURON

U N I T E D

S T A T E S

Lake Erie

| 0 km | 100 |
| 0 miles | 100 |

KEY

⚓ Lock

Montreal *is the historic beginning of the Seaway. It was here that the first link was built to the lakes during the 18th century, opening up pathways to the center of North America. The Seaway is open nine months each year, despite much freezing weather.*

Cargo ships *carry iron ore, grain, coal, and other bulk commodities through the waterway: more than 2 billion tons of cargo have been shipped since 1959. Canada's heavy industry could not continue without the Seaway.*

GULF OF ST. LAWRENCE

Quebec City

QUEBEC

St. Lambert Lock *bypasses the Lachine Rapids west of Montreal. The Seaway is a watery stair-case to America's heartland. The process involves raising and lowering the ships the height of a 60-story building.*

Montreal

CONSTRUCTION OF THE SEAWAY

In 1895, the US and Canadian governments appointed a Deep Waterways Commission to study the feasibility of what was to become today's St. Lawrence Seaway; it reported in favor of the project two years later. After 50 years of intercountry wrangling, the jointly financed project was begun on August 10, 1954 – in the words of Canadian Prime Minister Louis St. Laurent "a bond rather than a barrier between Americans and Canadians." The massive undertaking was beset with problems not previously encountered, especially the discovery of ancient rock formations so hard that new machinery had to be created to dig through them. All work, including relocating villages and dredging the existing canals, had to be carried out with minimum disruption to the daily boat, rail, and car traffic of major cities. Nonetheless, the four-year construction was completed almost to the day.

Welland Canal

Lake St. Francis

Lake St. Louis

St. Lawrence River

Lake Erie

Lake Ontario

The Seaway in profile with locks and rising water levels

MONTREAL

Montreal is the second largest city in Canada. The pious 17th-century French founders of this vibrant island metropolis might be a little surprised to have produced a place that revels so much in its reputation for joie de vivre, but at least their edifices remain: the spires of some of Canada's finest churches still rise above the skyline.

Montreal's location at the convergence of the St. Lawrence and Ottawa rivers made it Canada's first great trading center. It was founded in 1642 by a group of French Catholics as a Christian community and port. Much of its economic power has now moved west to Toronto, and what makes Montreal interesting today is a cultural, rather than a geographical, confluence. About 70 percent of its 3 million residents are of French descent, another 15 percent have British origins, and the rest represent nearly every major ethnic group. Many speak three or more languages. The communities form a kind of mosaic, with the anglophones in the west, the francophones in the east, and other ethnic communities in pockets all over the island. There is nothing rigid about these divisions: Anglophones eat and drink in the restaurants and bistros of the historic French district, and francophones visit the traditionally English area. The most interesting neighborhoods sprawl along the southern slopes of Mont-Royal – the 234-m (767-ft) hill from which the city derives its name. Vieux-Montréal's network of narrow, cobblestone streets huddles near the waterfront, while the main shopping area is farther north along Rue Sainte-Catherine. It extends below the city's surface in the maze of tunnels that connect the Underground City, the complex of homes, stores, and leisure venues that spreads out beneath the bustling city. Other modern attractions include the Olympic Park stadium and the Musée d'Art Contemporain, built in the 1990s to complement Montreal's fine historic museums.

Visitors admiring the skyline of Montreal

◁ Waiters posing outside a typically French traditonal bistro in downtown Montreal

Exploring Montreal

Montreal occupies a 50-kilometer (30-mile) long island at the confluence of the St. Lawrence and the Ottawa River. The city core, where many sights are found, is fairly compact and lies to the south and east of Montreal's main landmark, Mont-Royal. Vieux Montréal, the old city, is nestled on the shore of the St. Lawrence, while the modern downtown lies between it and Mont-Royal. Streets follow a fairly consistent grid pattern making the city easy to navigate.

The skyscrapers of downtown Montreal at dusk

KEY

- Street-by-Street map: *see pp110–11*
- ✈ International airport
- 🚉 Railroad station
- 🚌 Bus terminus
- ⛴ Ferry boarding point
- ℹ Visitor information
- 🅿 Parking
- Ⓜ Métro station
- ▬ Highway
- ▬ Major road
- ▬ Pedestrian walkway

SIGHTS AT A GLANCE

Historic Buildings and Areas
Château Ramezay ❸
Chinatown ❼
Lachine ㉗
McGill University ⑬
Place des Arts ❾
Plateau Mont-Royal ❽
Rue Sherbrooke ⑲
Sir George Etienne-Carter National Historic Site ❹
Square Dorchester and Place du Canada ⑯
Underground City ⑮
Vieux Port ❶

Parks and Gardens
Jardin Botanique de Montréal ㉓
Olympic Park pp124–5 ㉒
Parc Mont-Royal ㉑

Islands
Ile Notre-Dame ㉕
Ile Sainte-Hélène ㉔

Churches and Cathedrals
Basilique Notre-Dame-de-Montréal pp112–13 ❷
Cathédrale Marie-Reine-du-Monde ⑰
Christ Church Cathedral ⑪
Oratoire St-Joseph ⑳

Museums and Galleries
Centre Canadien d'Architecture ⑱
Centre d'Histoire de Montréal ❻
Centre des sciences de Montréal ❺
Maison Saint-Gabriel ㉖
McCord Museum of Canadian History ⑫
Musée d'Art Contemporain pp116–17 ❿
Musée des Beaux-Arts pp118–19 ⑭

Mont Royal

Parc Jeanne-Mance

PARC MONT-ROYAL

Parc Rutherford

Lac aux Castors

Guy Concor

GETTING AROUND

A tunnel and 15 bridges link Montreal island to the mainland, and the Ville-Marie Expressway carries road traffic right into its heart. The most convenient way to get around within the city is on the métro and bus system, which service most sites of interest.

LOCATOR MAP

MONTREAL

SEE ALSO

• *Where to Stay* pp349–51

• *Where to Eat* pp373–5

0 meters 500

0 yards 500

GREATER MONTREAL

Longueuil

Côte St-Luc

Lac St-Louis

Brossard

0 km 3

0 miles 3

Street-by-Street: Vieux-Montréal

Montreal's founders, led by Paul Chomédy de Maisonneuve, built the Catholic village of Ville Marie, that was to become Montréal, on the Saint Lawrence river in 1642. Missionary efforts failed to flourish, but the settlement blossomed into a prosperous fur-trading town with fine homes and a stone stockade. As Montreal expanded in the mid-20th century, the old city, Vieux-Montréal, fell into decline. In 1980, however, the district underwent a renaissance. The remaining 18th-century buildings were transformed into the restaurants, bistros, and boutiques that are so fashionable today, especially those of rue Notre-Dame and rue St-Paul.

View from the river
This clutch of historic streets leading down to the great St. Lawrence River is a district of romance and charm in the midst of this modern city.

★ Basilique Notre-Dame
One of the most splendid churches in North America, the city's 1829 Catholic showpiece has a richly decorated and colorful interior ❷

Pointe-à-Callière Archeological Museum
An underground tour here leads visitors past excavated ruins and early water systems dating from the 17th century.

STAR SIGHTS

★ Basilique Notre-Dame

★ Château Ramezay

Hôtel de Ville
The city hall was created in French Second Empire style in 1872–78, and restored to its glory in 1922. The marble hall features a statue of the first mayor.

LOCATOR MAP
See Montreal Map pp108–109

RUE BONSECOURS

RUE NOTRE-DAME

RUE SAINT-CLAUDE

PLACE JACQUES CARTIER

SAINT VINCENT

RUE SAINT PAUL

RUE DE LA COMMUNE

PROMENADE DES ARTISTES

Chapelle Notre Dame-de-Bonsecours
Long the spiritual home of Quebec's sailors, this church has fine views of the river from its tower.

Marché Bonsecours
The neo-Renaissance façade of this elegant building conceals its lively history, from its early 19th-century days as Canada's Parliament to a thriving time as a vegetable market.

★ **Château Ramezay**
Once the home of Montreal's governing city council, this 18th-century building pays tribute to the settling of Quebec with its fine museum of early tools and artifacts ③

| 0 meters | 100 |
| 0 yards | 100 |

KEY

– – – Suggested route

Vieux-Port ❶

333 Rue de la Commune.
Tel *(514) 496 7678.* 🚇 *Central Station.* 🚌 *55, 515.* 🚍 *Terminus Voyager.* 🚇 *Square Victoria.*
www.oldportofmontreal.com

In its glory days of the 19th century, the Vieux-Port of Montreal was one of the most important inland harbors in North America, but it declined in the early 20th century. By the late 1980s, the Canadian government had begun to transform it into one of the most popular parks in Montreal. Its 12.5 km (8 miles) of waterside walkways and open grassy fields blend almost seamlessly into the

Cyclists enjoying the waterfront promenade, Vieux-Port

lovely streets of Vieux-Montréal, giving the old city a wide window onto the river.

The port has a bustling, recreational atmosphere. On summer afternoons, visitors and Montrealers alike stroll, cycle, or in-line skate along the Promenade du Vieux Port.

Château Ramezay ❸

280 Rue Notre Dame E. **Tel** *(514) 861 3708.* 🚇 *VIA Rail.* 🚌 *14, 55, 515.* 🚍 *Terminus Voyager.* 🚇 *Champ-de-Mars.* ⏰ *Jun–Sep: 10am–6pm daily; Oct–May: 10am–4:30pm Tue–Sun.* ⏰ *Jan 1, Dec 25.* 📷 ♿
📱 **www.**chateauramezay.qc.ca

When Montreal's 11th governor, Claude de Ramezay, arrived in the city in 1702, he was homesick for Normandy and decided to build a residence that was reminiscent of the châteaux back home, with stone walls, dormer windows, and copper roof. The squat round towers, added in the 19th century, reinforce the effect. Many

Basilique Notre-Dame-de-Montréal ❷

In the center of Place d'Armes sits the Basilica, Montreal's grandest Catholic church. Originally built in the 17th century, a new building was commissioned in 1829. American architect James O'Donnell excelled himself with a vast vaulted cavern that combined elements of Neo-Classical and Neo-Gothic design, and provides 3,000 seats in the nave and two tiers of balconies. Splendidly redecorated in the 1870s, the intricate woodcarving is the work of Canadian craftsman Victor Bourgeau.

The main altar is surrounded by delicate pine and walnut woodcarving.

The nave is illuminated by a rose window under an azure ceiling.

★ Reredos
The focus of the nave is backed by azure, beneath a golden starry sky.

STAR SIGHTS

★ Reredos

★ Pulpit

★ Pulpit
This ornate construction was sculpted by Philippe Hébert. The prophets Ezekiel and Jeremiah stand at its base.

of de Ramezay's governor successors lived here and the building also housed the West India Company. This is one of the most impressive remnants of the French regime open to the public in Montreal.

The château has been restored to its original style. Of particular interest is the Nantes Salon, with its 18th-century carved paneling by the French architect Germain Boffrand.

Uniforms, documents, and furniture on the main floor reflect the life of New France's ruling classes, while the cellars depict the doings of humbler colonists. The scarlet automobile, made for the city's first motorist, is an interesting sight.

Sir George-Etienne Cartier National Historic Site ❹

458 Rue Notre Dame E. **Tel** (514) 283 2282. 🚇 Central Station. 🚌 🚇 Terminus Voyager. 🚇 Champ-de-Mars. ⬚ Apr–May, Sep–Dec: 10am–noon & 1–5pm Wed–Sun; Jun–Aug: 10am–6pm daily. ● Jan–Mar. ♿ 🎫 📷

George-Etienne Cartier (1814–73) was a Father of Confederation (*see p48*) and one of the most important French-Canadian politicians of his day. This national historic site comprises two adjoining graystone

Ormolu clock at the Etienne-Cartier

houses owned by the Cartiers on the eastern edge of the old town. One is dedicated to Cartier's career as a lawyer, politician, and railroad-builder. In this house, you can sit at a round table and listen in either French or English to a very good summary of the political founding of modern Canada.

The second house focuses on the Cartiers' domestic life and the functioning of a Victorian upper middle-class family. Visitors can wander through formal rooms full of rich furniture and listen to snatches of taped conversation from "servants" talking about their lives.

The twin towers rise 69 m (226 ft) above the basilica and are visible across the old city.

The Vieux Séminaire dates from 1685 and still belongs to the Sulpician Fathers, the priests who also run the basilica. It is the oldest building in Montreal.

VISITORS' CHECKLIST

110 Rue Notre Dame W, Place d'Armes. **Tel** (514) 842 2925. 🚇 Place d'Armes. ⬚ 8am–5pm daily. ♿ 📷 🎫 daily. www.basiliquenddm.org

Pipe Organ
The renowned maker Casavant built the organ above the north door in 1891. Recitals are still held frequently.

Stained-glass windows
The basilica's beautiful windows were imported from Limoges in 1930. Each tells a story of Montreal's past; this shows New World pioneer Maisonneuve climbing Mont Royal in 1643.

Children playing outside the Centre des sciences de Montréal

Centre des sciences de Montréal ❺

King Edward Pier. **Tel** (514) 496 4724. 🚇 Central Station. 🚌 Terminus Voyager. 🚇 Champs-de-Mars.
🕐 9:30am–9pm Mon–Sat, 9:30am–6pm Sun.

Dominating the Vieux-Port's King Edward Pier, this huge, airy building is home to a number of permanent and temporary exhibitions that focus on technology, engineering, and science, as well as other subjects. Among its permanent displays, the Centre features an interactive look at the workings of the human brain and the chance for you to save humanity in the game "Mission Gala." The exhibits were produced in collaboration with Quebec's Ministry of Education and are designed to appeal to children.

Attached to the Centre des sciences de Montréal is the IMAX Telux theater that shows educational documentaries in 3-D on its immense screen.

Centre d'Histoire de Montréal ❻

335 Place d'Youville.
Tel (514) 872 3207. 🚌 61.
🚇 Square Victoria. 🕐 Tue–Sun.
⬤ mid-Dec–mid-Jan. 📷

The exhibits in this museum trace the history of Montreal from the first Indian settlements to the modern age, with the focus on everyday life. The museum is housed in a handsome, red-brick fire station

with a gracefully gabled roof built in 1903. There are two floors of permanent exhibits. On the first floor, "Montreal, 5 Times" traces five passages in Montreal's history, beginning in 1535 with the meeting of First Nations peoples and European explorers and ending with the cultural boom of the 1960s. The second floor houses "Montreal of 1000 Faces," focusing on trade and immigration through the city's history. News reel footage from the 1930s, 1940s and 1950s is fun and informative, while a third floor observation deck offers a scenic view of the Old Port and Old Montreal.

Centre d'Histoire de Montréal

Chinatown ❼

🚇 Champ-de-Mars; Place des Arts.

The name has become a little anachronistic, as many of the restaurants and shops in this 18-block district just northeast of the Old City are now owned by Vietnamese and

Thai immigrants. Most arrived in Montreal in the wake of 20th-century upheavals in Southeast Asia. The Chinese, however, were here first. They began arriving in large numbers after 1880, along with many European immigrants. The Chinese community stuck together in this corner of the city in an attempt to avoid discrimination from some of the town's residents. As they grew more prosperous, many of the descendants of the first immigrants moved to the wealthier areas of Montreal, leaving Chinatown to the elderly and to the newly arrived. Many thousands of them now return during the weekends, making the narrow streets busy and full of people shopping for silk, souvenirs, vegetables, records, and barbecued meat.

Restaurants specialize in a range of delicious cuisines, serving Szechuan, Cantonese, Thai, Vietnamese, and Korean food, fragrantly filling the air with the smell of hot barbecued pork and aromatic noodles.

For those seeking respite from the bustle of the streets and their vibrant market stalls, there is a lovely little garden dedicated to the charismatic Chinese leader Sun Yat-sen on Clarke Street. Other features of the area include two large, Chinese-style arches, which span de la Gauchetière Street, and, strangely enough, a pair of authentic pagodas on the roof of the modern Holiday Inn hotel.

A brightly colored market stall in vibrant Chinatown

Locals picnicking in the leisurely atmosphere of the Parc Lafontaine in Plateau Mont-Royal

Plateau Mont-Royal ❽

Tel Tourisme Montreal: (514) 844 5400. 🚇 *Sherbrooke; Mont-Royal.*

No neighborhood captures the essence of Montreal more fully than the Plateau. Its main thoroughfares are lined with bistros, bookstores, boutiques, and sidewalk cafés. Nightclubs veer from the eccentric to the classic, and eateries from snack bars and sandwich shops to some of the best dining locations in the city. Jazz bars, too, are popular in this area and range from the decorous to the distinctly shady.

The area's residents are a mix of students, working-class French-speakers, trendy young professionals, and ethnic families with roots in Europe and Latin America. They congregate either in Parc Lafontaine, a neighborly expanse of green with an outdoor theater, or in "Balconville," a distinctly Montrealer institution linked to the duplexes and triplexes that many residents live in. To save interior space, these stacks of single-floor flats are studded with balconies linked to the street by fanciful, wrought-iron stairways. Although treacherous in winter, in summer they are decked with flowers and barbecue grills, and become centers for parties, family gatherings, and picnics.

The large working-class families for whom these homes were built in the early part of the century lived very modestly, but they managed to amass enough money to build impressively large and beautiful parish churches, notably the Eglise Saint-Jean-Baptiste. The Catholic bourgeoisie lived just a little farther south, in gracious Second-Empire homes on Rue Saint-Denis or Carré Saint-Louis, one of the prettiest squares in the city.

Place des Arts ❾

260 Blvd. de Maisonneuve W. *Tel (514) 842 2112.* 🚇 *Place des Arts.* www.pdarts.com

This complex of halls and theaters is Montreal's prime center for the performing arts. Both the Opéra de Montréal (Montreal Opera) and the Orchéstre Symphonique de Montréal (Montreal Symphony Orchestra) make their home in the Salle Wilfrid Pelletier, the largest of the center's five halls. The buildings of Place des Arts share a modern, spacious central plaza with the outstanding Musée d'Art Contemporain *(see pp116–17).*

Place des Arts, Montreal's top entertainment venue

Musée d'Art Contemporain ⑩

Opened in 1964, the Museum of Contemporary Art is the only institution in Canada dedicated exclusively to modern art. Located in downtown Montreal, more than 60 percent of the approximately 7,500 paintings, drawings, photographs, videos, and installations in the permanent collection are by Quebec artists. Works date from 1939, but the emphasis is on the contemporary. There are also works by innovative international talents, such as the controversial Bill Viola, Louise Bourgeois, and Andrès Serrano. The exhibits are in wide, well-lit galleries whose elegance helped to earn the Musée a Grand Prix from Montreal Council. The exhibition space is built around a rotunda, which runs up through the core of the building.

Les Dentelles de Montmirail
Natalie Roy's 1995 landscape (detail shown) is part of a large collection of modern Quebec art.

First floor

★ **Niagara Sandstone Circle** *(1981)*
English sculptor Richard Long's work is literally ground breaking. Using materials from the natural environment, which itself is the theme of the work, his careful geometric placing acts as a spur to meditation.

Street Level

KEY

▢	Permanent exhibition space
▢	Temporary exhibition space
▢	Pierre Granche sculpture
▢	Movie theater
▢	Video gallery
▢	Multimedia gallery
▢	Theater/Seminar hall
▢	Art workshops
▢	Nonexhibition space

Entrance Hall
The museum uses this airy modern space, hung in places with pieces from its collection, for special events and receptions. A pleasant first-floor restaurant overlooks the hall.

STAR EXHIBITORS

★ Pierre Granche

★ Richard Long

MUSEUM GUIDE

Only a small proportion of the exhibits in the museum are on permanent display. They occupy the upper floor space along with rotating and visiting items. There is also a sculpture garden, accessible from the main museum building, that has rotating exhibits and is a good spot to rest during a tour of the galleries.

★ **Comme si le temps … de la rue** *(1991–2)*
Pierre Granche's permanent outdoor installation is based on Egyptian mythological figures whose shapes symbolize Montreal. Created to contrast with its urban milieu, the work exudes humor and poetry.

Main Entrance

Museum façade
Built in the 1990s, the MAC building shows 320 artworks, taken from their much larger rotating collection.

Christ Church Cathedral ⓫

1444 Union Ave. *Tel* (514) 843 6577. ⊟ Central Station. ⊞ 15. ⊟ McGill. ◯ 8am–5:30pm daily. ⅃

Architect Frank Wills completed Christ Church in 1859 as the seat of the Anglican bishop of Montreal. This graceful Gothic limestone building, with a triple portal and a tall slender spire, has exterior walls decorated with gargoyles. The church was too heavy for the land, and the stone spire was replaced in 1940 with a treated aluminum steeple. Many local workers find respite at noon concerts in the cathedral's cool, dim interior with its pointed arched nave and magnificent stained-glass windows, some from the William Morris studio in London

Inuit slippers at the McCord Museum

Christ Church Cathedral, based on a 14th-century English design

McCord Museum of Canadian History ⓬

690 Rue Sherbrooke W. *Tel* (514) 398 7100. ⊟ Central Station. ⊞ 24. ⊟ McGill. ◯ 10am–6pm Tue–Fri; 10am–5pm Sat & Sun. ● Mon. ⅃ **www**.mccord-museum.qc.ca

Lawyer David Ross McCord (1844–1930) was an avid collector of virtually everything that had to do with life in Canada, including books, photographs, jewelry, furniture, clothing, documents, papers, paintings, toys, and porcelain. In 1919, he gave his considerable acquisitions to McGill University with a view to establishing a museum of Canadian social history. That collection, now more than 120,000 artifacts, is housed in a stately limestone building that was once a social center for McGill students. The museum has a good section of early history, as well as exceptional folk art. A particularly fine collection of Indian and Inuit items features clothing, weapons, jewelry, furs, and pottery. A separate room is devoted to the social history of Montreal. The museum's most celebrated possession is a vast collection of photographs that chronicle every detail of daily life in 19th-century Montreal.

McGill University ⓭

845 Rue Sherbrooke W. *Tel* (514) 398 4455. ⊟ Central Station. ⊞ 24. ⊟ McGill. ◯ 9am–6pm Mon–Fri. ⌧ book in advance. ⅃ **www**.mcgill.ca

When it was founded in 1821, Canada's oldest university was set on land left for the purpose by fur trader and land speculator James McGill (1744–1813). The university's main entrance is guarded by the Classical Roddick Gates. Behind them an avenue leads to the domed Neoclassical Arts Building, which is the oldest structure on campus.

The rest of the 70 or so buildings range from the ornately Victorian to the starkly concrete. One of the loveliest is the **Redpath Museum of Natural History**, which holds one of the city's most eclectic and eccentric collections. A huge number of fossils, including a dinosaur skeleton, sit alongside African art, Roman coins, and a shrunken head.

⌂ **Redpath Museum of Natural History**
859 Rue Sherbrooke W. *Tel* (514) 398 4086. ◯ 9am–5pm Mon–Fri; 1pm–5pm Sun. ● Sat. ⅃

Musée des Beaux Arts ⑭

The oldest and largest art collection in Quebec is
housed in two dramatically different buildings that face
each other across Rue Sherbrooke. The Michal
and Renata Hornstein Pavilion, fronted with four white
marble pillars, faces the huge concrete arch and tilting
glass front of the Jean-Noël Desmarais Pavilion. The
former focuses on Canadiana, with Inuit art, furniture,
and church silver from early settlers, and paintings from
the 18th century to the 1960s. The galleries in the
Desmarais Pavilion (illustrated here) focus on European
art from the Middle Ages to the 20th century, especially
the Renaissance. Linking the two pavilions is the gallery
of ancient cultures, with rich collections of artifacts,
including Roman vases and Chinese incense boxes.

**Façade of Jean-Noël
Desmarais Pavilion**
*Opened in 1991, the larger
pavilion contains a collection that has grown from
1,860 to about 26,000 pieces.*

★ **Portrait of a Young
Woman** *(c.1665)*
*This famous work origi-
nated in Rembrandt's
native Holland. Painted
in characteristically
realist style, the sitter's
pensive concentration
is thrown into sharper
relief by the deep
black background.*

MICHAL AND RENATA
HORNSTEIN PAVILION

Connected to the Desmarais Pavilion by
an underground tunnel that contains an
exhibition on ancient cultures, this gallery is
dedicated to pre-1960 America and includes
Meso-American, Inuit, and Amerindian art,
as well as early European-style furniture,
domestic silver, and decorative art. Later
galleries follow the history of Canadian
painting, from church sacred art to early
native studies by wandering
artist Paul
Kane and the
impressionism
of James Wilson
Morrice. The Group
of Seven and Paul-
Emile Borduas are among
those representing the
20th century.

Level 3

**18th-century
silver teapot**

**Access to
the Michal
and Renata
Hornstein
Pavilion**

Level S2

STAR EXHIBITS

★ Man of the House of
  Leiva by El Greco

★ Portrait of a Young
  Woman by Rembrandt

Level 4

★ **Man of the House
of Leiva** *(1590)*
*El Greco's haunting
portrayals of the
Spanish aris-
tocracy are a
Renaissance
highlight.*

GALLERY GUIDE
*The exceptional painting
collections are contained on
levels 3 and 4 of the Desmarais
Pavilion. Level 2 offers a
fine café. The museum
shop and main entrance
are on level 1. Lower
level S2 has contem-
porary art galleries
and tunnel access
to the Michal and
Renata Hornstein
Pavilion.*

KEY

☐ Contemporary art

☐ Art of ancient cultures

☐ 19th-century European art

☐ African art

☐ Old Masters

☐ Temporary exhibitions

☐ Nonexhibition space

**A street-level entrance to the
labyrinthine Underground City**

Underground
City 15

Central Station. Terminus
Voyager. Peel, McGill, Bonaventure.

When Montreal opened its
first métro (or subway)
lines in 1966, it inadvertently
created a whole new layer of
urban life – the Underground
City. It is theoretically possible
to lead a rich life in Montreal
without once stepping outside.
The first métro stations had
underground links to just the
two main train stations, a few
hotels, and the shopping mall
under the Place Ville-Marie
office tower. This has turned

into a vast network of over
30 km (19 miles) of well-lit,
boutique-lined passages that
includes more than 1,600
shops, 200 restaurants, hotels,
film theaters, and concert halls.

Square Dorchester
and Place du
Canada 16

1001 Rue Square Dorchester.
Tel (514) 873 2015. Central
Station. Terminus Voyager.
Peel, Bonaventure, Lucien-L'Allier.

These two open squares create
a green oasis in downtown
Montreal. On the north side
of Boulevard René-Lévesque,
statues including Canada's
first French-Canadian prime
minister, Sir Wilfrid Laurier,
share Square Dorchester with
a war memorial. On Place
du Canada a statue of the
country's first prime minister,
Sir John A. Macdonald,
looks out over the stately
Boulevard René-Lévesque.
   The buildings surrounding
the park are eclectic. The mix
includes a Gothic church, a
shiny, black bank tower and
the Sun Life Building (1933),
a huge stone fortress that
housed the British Crown
Jewels during World War II.

Varied architecture, from historic to post-modern, in Square Dorchester

Montreal skyline at night ▷

Marie-Reine-du-Monde façade with statues of Montreal's patron saints

Cathédrale Marie-Reine-du-Monde ⑰

1085 Rue Cathédrale. *Tel (514)*
866 1661. 🚇 *Central Station.*
🚌 *Terminus Voyager.* 🚇 *Bonaventure.*
🕐 *7am–6:15pm Mon–Fri,*
7:30am–6:15pm Sat, Sun. ♿

When Montreal's first Catholic
cathedral burned down in
1852, Bishop Ignace Bourget
decided to demonstrate the
importance of the Catholic
Church in Canada by building
a new one in a district
dominated at the time by
the English Protestant
commercial elite.
To show his flock's
loyalty to the Pope,
he modeled his
new church on
St. Peter's Basilica
in Rome.
   The cathedral,
which was com-
pleted in 1894,
has dimensions
that are a quarter
of those of St.
Peter's. The statues
on the roof repre-
sent the patron saints of all
the parishes that constituted
the Montreal diocese in 1890.
The magnificent altar canopy,
a replica of the one Bernini
made for St. Peter's, was
cast in copper and gold
leaf. Another reminder of
Bourget's loyalty to Rome
can be found on the pillar in
the northeast corner of the
church. Here lies a marble
plaque listing the names of
all the Montrealers who
served in the Papal armies
during the Italian war of
independence in the 1850s.

The altar canopy in the
cathedral

Centre Canadien d'Architecture ⑱

1920 Rue Baille. *Tel (514) 939 7000.*
🚇 *Central.* 🚌 *Terminus Voyager.*
🚇 *Guy Concordia.* 🕐 *11am–6pm*
Wed–Sun, 11am–9pm Thu. ● *Mon*
& Tue. 📷 ♿ ✔ *book ahead.*

Visitors enter through an
unobtrusive glass door
in an almost windowless
façade of gray limestone that
fronts this large U-shaped
building. Well-lit exhibition
rooms house a series of
regular exhibits in rotation.
The three primary exhibits
focus on architec-
ture, design and
landscape
architecture.
The two arms of
the modern
building embrace
the ornate, grand
Shaughnessy
Mansion, which
faces Boulevard
René-Lévesque
Ouest. Now part
of the Centre, the
house was built
in 1874 for the president of
the Canadian Pacific Railway,
Sir Thomas Shaughnessy,
and has an art-nouveau
conservatory with an
intricately decorated ceiling.
   The Centre is also a major
scholarly institution. Its
extensive collection of
architectural plans,
drawings, models, and
photographs is the most
important of its kind
anywhere. The library alone
has in excess of 215,000
volumes on the world's most
significant buildings.

Rue Sherbrooke ⑲

🚇 *Central Station.* 🚌 *Terminus*
Voyager. 🚇 *Sherbrooke.*

In the latter half of the 19th
century, Montreal was one
of the most important cities in
the British Empire. Its traders
and industrialists controlled
about 70 percent of Canada's
wealth, and many built themselves fine homes on the
slopes of Mont Royal in an
area that became known as
the Golden, or Square, Mile.
Rue Sherbrooke between Guy
and University were their Main
Street, and its shops, hotels,
and churches were the most
elegant in the country.
   Some of that elegance
survived the modernizing
bulldozers of the 1960s. Holt
Renfrew, Montreal's upscale
department store, and the
stately Ritz-Carlton Hotel still
stand. So do two exquisite
churches, the Presbyterian
St. Andrew and St. Paul, and
the Erskine American United
at the corner of avenue du
Musée, which boasts stained-
glass windows by Tiffany.
Boutiques, bookstores, and
galleries fill many of the rows
of graystone townhouses.
Millionaires not quite wealthy
enough to make it into the
Square Mile built graceful row
homes on rues de la Mont-
agne, Crescent, and Bishop
nearby. Many of these now
house trendy shops and bistros.
   Farther west is the Grande
Seminaire, where Montreal's
Roman Catholic archdiocese
still trains its priests.

Historic home on Rue Sherbrooke,
the "Golden Square Mile"

For hotels and restaurants in this region see pp349–51 and pp373–5. For transport information see p418

Montreal's largest shrine, Oratoire Saint-Joseph, showing the steps climbed annually by pilgrims

Oratoire Saint-Joseph ⑳

3800 Chemin Queen Mary. *Tel (514) 733 8211.* ⬜ Central Station. ⬜ Terminus Voyager. ⬜ Côte des Neiges. ⬜ daily. ♿

Every year, two million pilgrims climb the 300 steps to the entrance of this enormous church on their knees. Their devotion would no doubt please Brother André (1845–1937), the truly remarkable man responsible for building this shrine to the husband of the Virgin Mary. It began when he built a hillside chapel to St. Joseph in his spare time. Montreal's sick and disabled joined him at his prayers, and soon there were reports of miraculous cures. Brother André began to draw pilgrims, and the present oratory was built to receive them. He is buried here and was beatified in 1982.

The church's octagonal copper dome is one of the biggest in the world – 44.5 m (146 ft) high and 38 m (125 ft) wide. The interior is starkly modern; the elongated wooden statues of the apostles in the transepts are the work of Henri Charlier, who was also responsible for the main altar and the huge crucifix. The striking stained-glass windows were made by Marius Plamondon. The main building houses a museum depicting André's life. Beside the crypt church, a votive chapel is ablaze with hundreds of flickering candles that have been lit by hopeful pilgrims.

Parc Mont-Royal ㉑

Tel (514) 843 8240. ⬜ Central Station. ⬜ 11. ⬜ Mont-Royal. ⬜ 6am–midnight daily. ♿

The steep green bump that rises above the city center is only 234 m (767 ft) high, but Montrealers call it simply "the mountain" or "la montagne." Jacques Cartier gave the peak its name when he visited in 1535 and it, in turn, gave its name to the city. The hill became a park in 1876 when the city bought the land and hired Frederick Law Olmsted, the man responsible for designing New York's Central Park, to landscape it. Olmsted tried to keep it natural, building a few lookouts linked by footpaths. Succeeding generations have added a manmade pond (Beaver Lake), a 30-m high (98-ft) cross made of steel girders, and the Voie Camilien Houde, a thoroughfare that cuts through the park from east to west.

The mountain's 101 ha (250 acres) of meadows and hardwood forests still offer Montrealers a precious escape from urban life, as well as spectacular views of the city. The wide terrace in front of the Chalet du Mont-Royal pavilion looks out over the skyscrapers of the down-town core. The northern boundary of the park abuts two huge cemeteries, the Catholic Notre-Dame-Des-Neiges and the old and stately Protestant Mount Royal Cemetery, where many of Canada's finest rest.

A typical view of Montreal from the top of lofty Parc Mont-Royal

Olympic Park ㉒

Penguin at the Biodome

Designed for the 1976 Olympic Games, Montreal's Olympic Park showpieces a number of stunning modern buildings. Paris architect Roger Taillibert created the Stadium, now known to many Montrealers as "The Big Owe," a reference not only to its round shape but the Can$1.61 billion it cost to build. The stadium, seating 56,000, is used today for concerts by international stars, as well as for big exhibitions, and as a modern attraction in a historic city. Arching up the side of the stadium is the Montreal Tower, with its fine views. Nearby, the Biodome environmental museum replicates four world climates.

Aerial view of Olympic Park
An exceptional tourist attraction, the park can be toured fully during the day. Another popular way to visit is for a concert or sporting event.

The Biodome was first used as a velodrome for the 1976 Olympics – hence the unusual cycling hat design of its roof.

★ Biodome
Here are stunning re-creations of climate zones: a steamy rainforest, the freezing Polar World, the fertile forests of the Laurentian Mountains, and the fish-filled St. Lawrence ecosystem.

Sports Centre
Should any visitor become inspired by the international-standard sport on offer at the stadium, this fully equipped center offers unbeatable facilities, including a 15-m (50-ft) deep scuba diving pool.

★ Montreal Tower

At 175 m (575 ft) this is the world's tallest inclined tower, arching over the stadium in a graceful sweep. A cable car takes visitors up the side of the tower to its large viewing deck in less than two minutes.

VISITORS' CHECKLIST

3200 Viau St. *Tel* (514) 252 4737. 🚇 Viau and Pie-IX. 🕐 Jun–Sep: 9am–8pm daily; Oct–May: 9am–5pm daily. www.rio.gouv.qc.ca

The stadium roof was originally intended to be retractable. However, due to structural problems, it was replaced in 1998 by a detached, permanently closed roof.

★ Olympic Stadium

The first event to take place in this cavernous space was the spectacular opening ceremonies of the 1976 Summer Olympic Games.

Viewing Deck

This glass platform provides some stunning views of the city. Signs point out sights of interest that can be as far as 80 km (50 miles) away.

A cable car shoots up the side of the tower at speed; tickets can be combined with a guided tour of the Stadium or Biodome.

| 0 meters | 50 |
| 0 yards | 50 |

STAR SIGHTS

★ Olympic Stadium

★ Montreal Tower

★ Biodome

PLAN OF THE OLYMPIC PARK AREA

1 Sports Field
2 Pierre-Charbboneau Centre
3 Maurice-Richard Centre
4 Biodome
5 Olympic Stadium
6 Sports Centre
7 Botanical Gardens

The Jardin Botanique is an oasis of calm away from the rush of the city

Jardin Botanique de Montréal ㉓

4101 Rue Sherbrooke E. *Tel (514)
872 1400.* 🚇 *Pie-IX.* ◯ *May–Oct:
9am–6pm daily; Nov–Apr: 9am–5pm
Tue–Sun.* 🖫 🛈 ♿

Montreal's botanical garden is
among the largest in the
world, a fine accomplishment
for this northern city
with a brutal climate.
Its 75-ha (182-acre)
enclose 30 outdoor
gardens, 10 green-
houses, a "courtyard
of the senses" in
which blind
interpreters help
visitors discover the
touch and smell of
exotic flowers, and
a bug-shaped
Insectarium full of
creepy-crawlies, both
preserved and living. Its most
peaceful havens are the 2.5-ha
(6-acre) Montreal–Shanghai
Dream Lake Garden, a delightful replica of a 14th-century
Ming garden, and the exquisite
Japanese Garden.

**Bonsai tree at the
Jardin Botanique**

Ile-Sainte-Hélène ㉔

20 Chemin Tour de Lille. *Tel (514)
872 6120.* 🚇 *Jean Drapeau.*
⛴ *Vieux-Port.* ◯ *6am–midnight
daily.* ♿

This small forested island in
the middle of the St. Lawrence
River has played a major role
in Montreal's emergence as a
modern city. Originally named
after Samuel de Champlain's
wife *(see p45),* Ile-Sainte-Hélène

was the site of Expo '67,
the world fair that brought
millions of visitors to the city
in the summer of 1967.

Several reminders of those
days remain – most notably
La Ronde, the fair's amusement park, and the dome that
served as the United States
Pavilion. This is now the
Biosphere, an interpretive
center that examines the
Great Lakes and
St. Lawrence River
system. Between the
dome and the roller
coasters is the Fort
de l'Ile-Sainte-
Hélène, built in 1825
to protect Montreal
from a potential
American attack.
Its red stone walls
enclose a grassy
parade square that is
used today by
members of the Olde 78th
Fraser Highlanders and the
Compagnie Franche de la
Marine, re-creations of two
18th-century regimental

military formations that fought
each other over the future of
New France until 1759. The
fort also houses the **Musée
David M. Stewart**, a small and
excellent museum of social
and military history with
educational activities for
schools and younger visitors.

🏛 **Musée David M. Stewart**
20 Chemin Tour de Lille. *Tel (514)
861 6701.* ◯ *10am–5pm Wed–Mon.*
● *Jan 1, Dec 25.* 🖫

Ile-Notre-Dame ㉕

110 Rue Notre-Dame. *Tel (514) 872
6120.* 🚇 *Central Station.*
🚌 *Terminus Voyager.* 🚌 *Place
d'Armes.* ◯ *6am–midnight daily.* ♿

This 116-ha (286-acre) wedge
of land encircled by the
St. Lawrence Seaway did not
exist until 1967, when it was
created with rock excavated
for the Montreal métro
system. It shared Expo '67
with Ile-Sainte-Hélène, and
today the two islands
constitute the Parc Jean-
Drapeau. Ile-Notre-Dame's
most popular attraction by far
is the monumental Casino de
Montréal, a province-owned
gambling hall housed in the
old French and Quebec
pavilions. Every day,
thousands line up at its
tables and slot machines.
The casino never closes.
There are more refined
entertainments – a rowing
basin, excavated for the
1976 Olympics, superb floral
gardens, and a carefully
filtered body of water, which
is the site of the city's only

Built for Expo '67, the Biosphere has displays on Canadian river systems

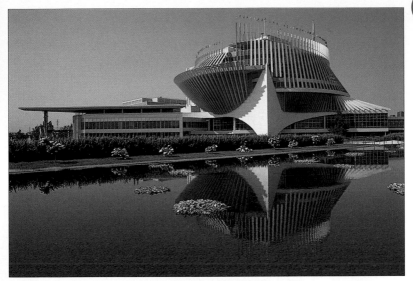

The province-owned Casino on Ile-Notre-Dame is open to the hopeful 24 hours a day

swimming beach. Ile-Notre-Dame's Circuit Gilles Villeneuve, named for the Canadian champion, plays host to NASCAR races.

Maison Saint-Gabriel ㉖

2146 Place de Dublin. **Tel** (514) 935 8136. 🚇 Charlevoix. 🚌 57. ⭘ late Jun–Sep: Mon–Sat; Sep–Jun: Tue–Sun. 🎟️ 🔦 🛈 obligatory.

This isolated little fragment of New France at first appears lost among the apartment buildings of working-class Pointe-Saint-Charles. It was a farm when the formidable Marguerite Bourgeoys, Montreal's first schoolteacher and now a canonized saint, bought it in 1668 as a residence for the religious order she had founded in 1655.

The house, rebuilt in 1698 after a fire, is a fine example of 17th-century architecture, with thick stone walls and a steeply pitched roof built on an intricate frame of original heavy wooden timbers.

Marguerite Bourgeoys and her tireless sisters worked the farm and ran a school on the property for native and colonial children. They also housed and trained the *filles du roy* (the "king's daughters"),

orphaned young girls sent abroad to be the women of his new colony. The house's chapel, kitchen, dormitory, and drawing rooms are full of artifacts dating from the 17th century. These include a writing desk the saint used herself and a magnificent vestment and cope, embroidered in silk, silver, and gold by a wealthy hermit who lived in a hut on the property.

Lachine ㉗

Blvd. St. Joseph. **Tel** (514) 873 2015. 🚇 Lionel Groulx. 🚌 191.

Lachine comprises a suburb of southwest Montreal and includes a small island of the same name west of the Lachine Rapids, where the St. Lawrence River widens to form Lac-Saint-Louis. Lachine is now part of Montreal, but has a long history of its own. The old town along Blvd. Saint-Joseph is charming. Many of its fine old homes have become restaurants and bistros with outdoor terraces that overlook Parc René-Lévesque and the lake. One of the oldest houses, built by merchants in 1670, is now the **Musée de Lachine**, a historical museum and art gallery. The **Fur Trade at Lachine National Historic Site**

is a building dedicated to the fur trade, which for years was Montreal's main support.

The Lachine Canal, built in the 19th century to bypass the rapids, links the town directly to the Vieux-Port. The canal itself is now blocked to shipping, but the land along its banks has been turned into parkland with a bicycle trail.

🏛️ **Musée de Lachine**
1 Chemin du Musée. **Tel** (514) 634 3478. ⭘ Apr–Nov: 11:30am–4:30pm Wed–Sun. 🛈 reserve.

🏛️ **Fur Trade at Lachine National Historic Site**
1255 Blvd. St. Joseph. **Tel** (514) 637 7433. ⭘ Apr–mid-Oct: daily; rest of year: by reservation only. 🎟️ 🔦 🛈

A view of the historical Musée de Lachine from the reclaimed canal

QUEBEC CITY AND THE ST. LAWRENCE RIVER

The heart and soul of French Canada, Quebec City sits overlooking the St. Lawrence River on the cliffs of Cap Diamant. As provincial capital, the city is the seat of regional government, and nowadays is the heart of French-Canadian nationalism. Parisian in atmosphere, with every tiny street worth visiting, Quebec City is almost entirely French-speaking. The European ambiance, architecture, and the city's crucial historical importance all contributed to it being named as a United Nations World Heritage Site in 1985. One of the world's great waterways, the St. Lawrence River is home to rare marine wildlife. Right and minke whales swim as far upstream as Tadoussac and feed at the mouth of the Saguenay River. The Laurentian Mountains rise up above the St. Lawrence on the north shore, a year-round natural playground. Nearer Quebec City, the rich scenery of the Charlevoix region is among the most beautiful in the country, contrasting with the soaring cliffs and wilderness of the Gaspé Peninsula. Offshore, Ile d'Anticosti is a stunning nature preserve.

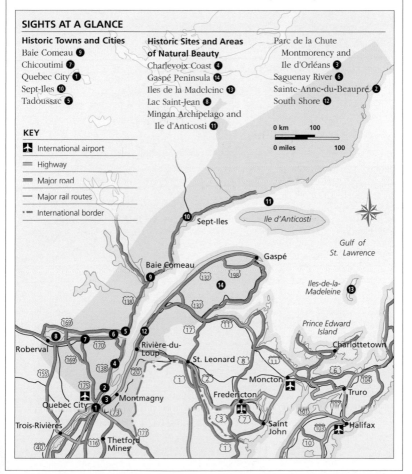

SIGHTS AT A GLANCE

Historic Towns and Cities
Baie Comeau ⑨
Chicoutimi ⑦
Quebec City ①
Sept-Iles ⑩
Tadoussac ⑤

Historic Sites and Areas of Natural Beauty
Charlevoix Coast ④
Gaspé Peninsula ⑭
Iles de la Madeleine ⑬
Lac Saint-Jean ⑧
Mingan Archipelago and Ile d'Anticosti ⑪

Parc de la Chute Montmorency and Ile d'Orléans ③
Saguenay River ⑥
Sainte-Anne-de-Beaupré ②
South Shore ⑫

KEY

✈ International airport

═ Highway

▬ Major road

— Major rail routes

•– International border

0 km   100
0 miles   100

Sept-Iles
Ile d'Anticosti
Gulf of St. Lawrence
Gaspé
Baie Comeau
Iles-de-la-Madeleine
Prince Edward Island
Roberval
Rivière-du-Loup
Charlottetown
St. Leonard
Montmagny
Moncton
Fredericton
Truro
Quebec City
Trois-Rivières
Saint John
Halifax
Thetford Mines

◁ The historic architecture of Quebec City's Lower Town

Street-by-Street: Quebec City ●

One of the oldest communities on the
American continent, Quebec City was discovered as an Iroquois village by the French
explorer Jacques Cartier and founded as a city
in 1608 by explorer Samuel de Champlain *(see
p45)*. The British gained dominance over the
city and the rest of the province at the Plains
of Abraham battle just outside the city walls in
1759. Today the town is renowned as the heart
of French Canada. The oldest part of the city is
Basse-Ville, or Lower Town, which was renovated in the 1970s. With its winding staircases
and cafés, it is a charming destination.

**★ Basilique
Notre-Dame-
de-Québec**
*This 1647 cathe-
dral provides a
rich setting for
relics from early
French rule in
Quebec, and
Old Master
paintings.*

Musée du Fort
*Military history is
brought to life here in
sound-and-light shows
reenacting six Quebec
sieges and battles, and
numerous war relics.*

**Holy Trinity Anglican
Cathedral**
*An elegant 1804 stone Neo-
Classical façade conceals
an English oak interior.*

Château Frontenac
*Quebec City's best-known
landmark has risen over the
city since 1893, and has
618 luxurious guest rooms.*

| 0 meters | | 100 |
| 0 yards | | 100 |

KEY

– – – Suggested route

Musée de la Civilisation

Human history through the ages is explored in this airy modern building linked to historic houses in the rest of the town, including Maison Chevalier.

VISITORS' CHECKLIST

167,500. ✈ 16 km (10 miles) west of the city. 🚊 450 Rue de Gare-du-Palais. 🚌 320 Rue Abraham-Martin. ⛴ 10 Rue des Traversiers. ℹ 835 Avenue Wilfrid-Laurier (418) 641 6290. 🎊 Winter Carnival (Jan–Feb); Summer Festival (Jul). **www**.quebecregion.com

★ Place Royale

A virtual microcosm of Canadian history, Place Royale has experienced a renaissance, and the surrounding streets, with their 18th- and 19th-century architecture, have been sandblasted back to their original glory.

The funicular travels from Terrasse Dufferin to Lower Town, providing excellent aerial views of the historic city center.

STAR SIGHTS

★ Place Royale

★ Basilique Notre-Dame

Maison Chevalier

Linked with the Musée de la Civilisation, this home built for an 18th-century merchant showcases the decorative arts. Quebec furniture and the famous Quebec silverware feature in every room, as well as exhibits showing how well-to-do families lived in the 18th and 19th centuries.

Quebec City

Containing the only walled city north of the Rio Grande, Quebec City has narrow cobblestone streets and 18th-century buildings that lend a European air to this small provincial capital, just 55 square km (21 square miles). Most of the sights are packed into one accessible corner, above and below the Cap Diamant cliffs, with the Citadel rising up protectively at the top of the cliff. As Quebec's capital, the city is home to the provincial parliament, the Assemblée Nationale, which conducts its debates almost entirely in French in splendid chambers behind the ornate early 19th-century façade of the grandiose Hôtel du Parlement.

Château Frontenac dominates the skyline of Quebec City

Exploring Quebec City

Most of the main sights are easily reached on foot. The city can conveniently be divided into three parts. Basse-Ville, or Lower Town, is the oldest part, and rambles along the St. Lawrence River at the foot of Cap Diamant. Above lies the walled city, Haute-Ville, or Upper Town. This area is full of shops and restaurants, similar to the Basse-Ville, but both Catholic and Protestant cathedrals are here, as is the imposing Château Frontenac. Beyond the walls stretches Grande Allée, with the Hôtel du Parlement where the provincial parliament of Quebec sits.

🏛 Terrasse Dufferin

Sweeping along the top of Cap Diamant from Château Frontenac to the edge of the Citadel, this boardwalk is well equiped with benches and kiosks, and offers unmatched views of the St. Lawrence River, the Laurentian Mountains, and Ile d'Orleans. During the freezing Quebec winter, the municipal authorities install an ice slide for toboggans on the terrace, known as Les Glissades de la Terrasse.

🍁 Parc des Champs-de-Bataille

835 Ave. Wilfrid Laurier. *Tel (418) 648 4071.* ⬜ *daily.* 🚻

Once a battlefield where the future of Canada was decided, the National Battlefields Park is now a delightful grassy recreation ground, with grand monuments and a dedicated fountain the only clues to the area's bloody and dramatic history. On September 13, 1759, British regulars under General James Wolfe defeated the French army on this clifftop field, the Plains of Abraham, just outside the walls of Quebec *(see pp46–7)*, establishing permanent British rule in Canada. In 1908, the 100-ha (250-acre) battlefield was turned into one of the largest urban parks in North America.

Joan of Arc at Parc-des-Champs de Bataille

🏛 Assemblée Nationale

Ave. Honoré-Mercier & Grande Allée E. *Tel (418) 643 7239.* 🚻 🎫 *daily.*

The Assemblée Nationale, Quebec's provincial parliament, meets just outside the walls of the Old City in this graceful Second-Empire building, completed in 1886 as a showcase of provincial history. Niches along the imposing façade and up the sides of the tall central tower display 22 bronze figures, each representing a person who played a vital role in Quebec's development. The first inhabitants of the territory are honored in a bronze rendition of a First Nations family by the main door. Inside, the blue chamber is the hub of Quebec's political activity.

🏛 Fortifications de Québec

Tel (418) 648 7016. ⬜ *Apr–Oct: daily.* 📷 🚻

After a century of peace, the fortifications that had secured Quebec since their completion by the British in 1760 were transformed in the 1850s from a grim military necessity into this popular attraction. On the city's northern and eastern edges, low ramparts studded with cannons defend the clifftop, with the walls on the western side reaching 2.5 m (10 ft). Two elegant gates, the Saint-Jean and the Saint-Louis, pierce the western stretch. Visitors can walk along the top of the walls for 4 km (3 miles).

Quebec's 18th-century fortifications in the Parc d'Artillerie

Abundant produce stalls draw crowds at the market in Vieux Port

🏛 Vieux Port

ℹ 100 Quai Saint Andre. **Tel** (418) 648 3300. 👤

This delightful area has its focus around the old harbor northeast of the walled city. In contrast to the crammed heritage of much of the Lower Town, Vieux Port is an airy riverside walking site, full of new and restored modern attractions. Boat cruises downriver to the Chute Montmorency waterfalls (see p139) are available. Waterfront walks pass chic boutiques, apartment blocks, the city's concert stadium, and shops in trendy warehouse settings.

🏛 Musée de la Civilisation

85 Rue Dalhousie. **Tel** (418) 643 2158. ◯ late Jun–early Sep: daily; late Sep–early Jun: Tue–Sun. 🗓 👤 www.mcq.org

Top contemporary Canadian architect Moshe Safdie designed this modern limestone and glass building in Basse-Ville to house Quebec's museum of history and culture. Although highly up-to-date in feel, the construction has won several prizes for blending in well with its historic surroundings. Three heritage buildings are part of the museum's structure including Maison d'Estebe, an 18th-century merchant's house. The museum also uses another nearby 18th-century house, Maison Chevalier, for displaying Quebec architecture and furniture in period setting.

Museum exhibits include "Encounters with the First Nations," and the remains of a 250-year-old French flat-bottomed boat. Many exhibits are hands on, and, during workshops for families, participants are encouraged to try on costumes from different eras.

Antique and modern architecture of the Musée de la Civilisation

QUEBEC CITY

KEY

■ Street-by-Street map: see pp130–31

0 meters 250
0 yards 250

Key to Symbols see back flap

▦ Place Royale

Rue Saint Pierre. **Tel** *(418) 646 3167.*
Of all the squares in Canada,
Place Royale has undoubtedly
the most history. Samuel de
Champlain, the founder of
Quebec, planted his garden
on this site, and the French
colonial governor Frontenac
turned it into a market in 1673.
A bust of Louis XIV was in-
stalled in 1686, and the square
was named Place Royale.

Today it remains much as it
did in the 18th century, exud-
ing an air of elegance and delicate grandeur. A cobblestone
court in the center of Basse-
Ville, Place Royale is surrounded by steep-roofed
early 18th-century buildings
with pastel-colored shutters
that were once the homes of
wealthy traders. The square
declined in the 19th century
but is now fully restored and
a favorite for street performers.

Rue du Petit Champlain bustling with shoppers

⛫ Rue du Petit Champlain

below Dufferin Terrace in Old City.
Tel *(418) 692 2613.* ♿ *partial.*
www.quartierpetitchamplain.com
The aptly named Escalier
Casse-Cou, or Breakneck Stairs,
descends from Haute-Ville past
several levels of gift shops to
end on this narrow little
walkway in the oldest part of
the town. French artisans built
homes here as early as the
1680s, and Irish dockworkers
moved to the area in the 19th
century. Much of the historic
architecture remained, but the
area fell into decline early in
the 20th century. The workers'
homes have been transformed
into 50 art and speciality
shops and restaurants, and the
short pedestrian walkway has
become one of the liveliest
spots in old Quebec City. While
often crowded, some interesting boutiques can be found.

A familiar landmark of the city, the 600-room Château Frontenac hotel

▦ Place d'Armes

French colonial soldiers once
used this attractive, grassy
square just north of Château
Frontenac as a parade ground,
but its uses today are more
congenial. Open horse-drawn
carriages wait here to offer
visitors a journey that reveals
the square in all its charm. In
the center, the
Monument de
la Foi commem-
orates the 300th
anniversary of
the 1615 arrival of
Catholic Recollet
missionaries. On
the southwest
corner next to
the fine Anglican
cathedral, lies the
grand early 19th-
century Palais de
Justice. The Musée
du Fort opposite contains a
large scale model of Quebec
City in the 19th century.

▦ Château Frontenac

1 Rue des Carrières. **Tel** *(418) 692
3861.* ♿ *(see p352)*
The steep, green copper-
roofed landmark that dominates the skyline of Old Quebec
is a luxury hotel, built by the
Canadian Pacific Railway on
the heights overlooking the
St. Lawrence River. In the
19th century, US architect
Bruce Price designed the hotel
as a French-style château on
a huge scale, with dozens of
turrets, towers, and a high
copper roof studded with
rows of dormer windows.
Building continued for almost
a century after the first section
of the hotel was opened in
1893, with a final part completed in 1983. Made from

brick and stone, the hotel now
has over 600 rooms. The public
salons are sumptuous and elegant; Salon Verchère and the
Champlain are the most visited.

⛪ Basilique Notre-Dame-de-Québec

Place de l'Hôtel de Ville. **Tel** *(418) 694
0665.* ⦿ *8:30am–4pm daily.* ♿
This magnificent cathedral
is the principal seat of the
Roman Catholic archbishop of
Quebec, whose diocese once
stretched from here to Mexico.
Fire destroyed the first two
churches on the site before
1640, and the first cathedral
built here was torn down by
the British in 1759. A fourth
version burned down in 1922.
The present cathedral replaced
it in the style of the 1647
original. Some modern materials, including concrete, steel,
and plaster, have been used to
re-create the light feel; glow-
ing stained-glass windows,
richly gilded decoration, and
the graceful baldachin over the
main altar add to the effect.

Imposing façade of the Basilique-Notre-Dame-de-Québec

🚽 Rue du Trésor
off Place d'Armes.
This tiny alley just across rue
de Buade from Holy Trinity
cathedral is something of a
Quebecois institution. Closed
to cars, the little street is packed in summer with visitors
eager to have their portraits
drawn, painted, or caricatured
by the dozens of street artists
who gather here. Browsing
for sketches and watercolors
of Quebec scenes can be fun.

🔒 Holy Trinity Anglican Cathedral
31 Rue des Jardins. *Tel (418) 692
2193.* ⬚ *daily.* ♿
After worshiping for nearly a
century in the city's Catholic
churches, in 1804 the Anglicans
of Quebec finally had their
own cathedral built at state
expense. Their new mother
church was the first
Anglican cathedral
outside Britain and
is modeled on
London's huge Neo-
Classical St. Martin's
in the Fields. To this
day, gifts from
England remain,
including the prayer
book and Bible don-
ated by the British
King George III. Cut from
the King's Windsor Forest in
England, the pews are of oak,
and the eight-bell peal is the
oldest in Canada. In the summer artists and artisans fill the
verdant church grounds.

🔒 Monastère des Ursulines
Rue Donnacona. *Tel (418) 694 0694.*
⬚ *daily.* ♿
In 1639, Mère Marie de
l'Incarnation brought the Ursuline order of nuns to Quebec
and oversaw the construction
in 1641 of the nunnery, which
later burned down. Today, visitors can see the Saint-Augustin
and Saint-Famille wings, which
date from a period of rebuilding between 1686 and 1721.
Surrounded by fruit orchards,
the charming complex has
gradually evolved over the
past four centuries. One of the
buildings is North America's
oldest girls' school.
Nearly a hundred nuns still
live and work here, so access
is limited. The beautifully
decorated chapel and French

The Hôtel de Ville seen from the small park in its grounds

Reliquary from the Ursuline Convent

antiques, including Louis XIII
furniture, scientific instruments,
paintings, and embroideries,
are displayed in the
Musée des Ursulines
within the monastery.
The museum also
tells the story of the
nuns' educational
and missionary
achievements. Mère
Marie completed the
first Huron, Algon-
quin and Iroquois
dictionaries. Copies
are on display, along with embroidery and liturgical clothes
from the 17th to 19th centuries.

🚽 Hôtel de Ville
Côte de la Fabrique. *Tel (418) 691
4606.* ⬚ *Interpretive Centre: late
Jun–Sep: daily; Oct–Jun: Tue–Sun.* ♿
This imposing building stands
at the western end of the rue
de Buade, a popular gathering
place for Quebec artists offering their wares. Built in 1833,
and still the town hall to the
city, it is the grounds that are

the focus for the city's people.
The small park here holds
theater performances in the
summertime and is a meeting
place for festival-goers.

🚽 Séminaire de Québec
2 Côte de la Fabrique. *Tel (418) 692
2843.* ⬚ *summer.* ✔ *obligatory.*
📷 ♿
In 1663, the first bishop of
Quebec, Francois Laval, built
a seminary next to his cathedral to train Catholic priests
for his huge diocese. Over the
centuries it has been added to
and now forms a graceful
complex of 17th , 18th , and
19th-century buildings centered on a peaceful courtyard.
Within the seminary, visitors
can admire the excellent 18th-
century paneling that covers
the walls of the chapel. The
Musée de l'Amérique Française
is part of the complex and
has a wonderfully eclectic collection, including a converted
chapel decorated with fascinating wooden *trompe l'oeils.*

The 19th-century interior of the chapel at the Séminaire de Québec

La Citadelle

Both the French and British armies contributed to the building of this magnificent fort. The French started construction in 1750, with work completed in 1831 by the British. The purpose of the fort was to defend Quebec against an American attack that never came.

Regimental stained glass beaver badge

Today the fortifications are a pleasant walkway that provides a tour around the star-shaped fortress. The Citadelle is home to the famous French Canadian regiment the Royal 22^e (Van Doos). Because the Citadelle is still a working military barracks, visitors can see the regiment perform their daily tasks as well as their parade drill.

The Fortifications
From the mid-19th century, the Citadelle served as the eastern flank of Quebec City's defenses.

Old Military Prison

Cap Diamant is the highest point of the Cape Diamond cliffs, from which the Lower Town descends.

Governor-General's residence
This splendid mansion with its double central staircase and marble hall has been the official home of Canada's governors-general since the 19th century.

Trenches around the Citadelle have always been key defensive structures.

Cape Diamond Redoubt
The oldest building in the Citadelle, the Redoubt dates back to 1693 when it was built under the leadership of the French Count Frontenac as a first citadel for Quebec. Now home to relics of war, the Redoubt offers fine views of the St. Lawrence River.

The Vimy Cross was erected in memory of the Canadians who fell at the WWI battle of Vimy Ridge in 1917.

Chapel
A key part of the fortress, this private chapel used to be a British powder magazine and is now used for ceremonial purposes.

★ **Changing of the Guard, Parade Square**
Every day from June to Labour Day, the Changing of the Guard takes place. The ceremonial dress of the 22^e, scarlet tunic and blue trousers, is of British design.

The Barracks
As a fully operational military site, the barracks is home to Canada's most dashing regiment, the 22^e, who fought with bravery in both world wars.

Plains of Abraham

The Prince of Wales Bastion contains a now disused powder magazine. Built in 1750, it once stored 2,388 barrels of gunpowder.

Ticket booth

0 meters	25
0 yards	25

Entrance to the Citadelle

STAR SIGHTS

- ★ Changing of the Guard
- ★ Dalhousie Gate

★ **Dalhousie Gate**
One of the original structures remaining from the 19th century, Dalhousie Gate is surrounded by portholes and gun fittings. These helped the four-pointed fortress to cover its north, south, and west flanks with defensive fire.

Sainte-Anne-de-Beaupré ❷

One of Canada's most sacred places, the shrine to the mother of the Virgin Mary was originally built in the 17th century. In 1650 a group of sailors who landed here after surviving a shipwreck vowed to build a chapel in honor of Saint Anne, the patron saint of those in shipwrecks. Over 1.5 million visitors now visit every year, including an annual pilgrimage on Saint Anne's Feastday on July 26. This medieval-style basilica was built in the 1920s, and was the fifth church to be built on this site. In the entrance stand two columns of crutches, testimony to the faith of generations of Roman Catholics. The dome-vaulted ceiling is decorated with gold mosaics portraying the life of Saint Anne. She is represented in a large gilt statue in the transept, cradling the Virgin Mary.

Statue of Saint Anne
The focus of the upper floor, the richly decorated statue sits in front of the relic of Saint Anne, presented to the shrine by Pope John XXIII in 1960.

Stained-glass windows show the progress of pilgrims through the shrine, with the rose window as centerpiece.

PLAN OF THE SHRINE

1 Basilica   4 Museum
2 Monastery   5 Blessing Office
3 Church store

THE BASILICA

In 1876, Saint Anne was proclaimed patron saint of Quebec, and in 1887 the existing church was granted basilica status. The Redemptorist order became the guardians of the shrine in 1878.

Entrance to Basilica's upper floor

Bright mosaic floor tiles echo ceiling patterns

★ The Basilica
There has been a church on this site since 1658. In 1922, the previous basilica burned down. Today's version was built in 1923 and consecrated in 1976.

STAR SIGHTS

★ The Basilica

★ Pietà

★ **Pietà**
A faithful copy of Michel-angelo's original in St. Peter's, Rome, this shows Christ at his death.

Montmorency Falls at Ile d'Orléans, Quebec's most dramatic waterfall

Basilica interior
Lit by sun streaming through the stained-glass windows, the cream and gold interior is decorated in every corner.

Parc de la Chute Montmorency and Ile d'Orléans ❸

ℹ Montmorency Falls (418) 663 3330. 🕐 Jan–mid-Apr: 10am–4pm Sat & Sun; mid-Apr–mid-Jun, Sep & Oct: 9am–6pm daily; mid-Jun–Aug: 8:30am–7:30pm daily. ● Nov & Dec. 🚻 mid-Apr–Oct. ℹ Ile d'Orléans Tourist Centre, 490 Cote du Pont, St. Pierre (418) 828 9411.

Located 7 km (4.5 miles) east of Quebec City, Montmorency Falls is Quebec's most celebrated waterfall. Higher than Niagara Falls, the cascade is created as the Montmorency River empties out into the St. Lawrence River – a total of 30 m (100 ft) higher than the 56-m (175-ft) plunge of Niagara Falls from the Niagara River to Lake Ontario. The park surrounding the Falls offers a suspension bridge, an aerial tram, and a series of trails that climb the surrounding cliffs.

A bridge nearby crosses the river to the Ile d'Orléans, which is covered with flowers, strawberry fields, and farmland. The villages give a fascinating look at rural life in Quebec.

Charlevoix Coast ❹

ℹ 495 Blvd. de Comporte, La Malbaie (418) 665 4454. **www**.tourisme-charlevoix.com

The Charlevoix Coast runs 200 km (130 miles) along the north shore of the St. Lawrence River, from Sainte-Anne-de-Beaupré in the west to the mouth of the Saguenay. A UNESCO World Biosphere Reserve because of its fine examples of boreal forest, the area is a slim band of flowery rural beauty on the southern edge of tundra that stretches northward. Gentle valleys protect old towns reaching to the river, with coastal villages sheltering beneath tall cliffs. Lying in a fertile valley is the exceptionally pretty Baie-Saint-Paul, its streets lined with historic houses and inns.

Just 35 km (21 miles) north of Baie-Saint-Paul lies the **Parc des Grands Jardins**, a vast expanse of lakes and black-spruce taiga forest with a herd of caribou. Small mountains offer walking and hiking. Farther downstream is the tiny and tranquil island Ile-aux-Coudres. The lush, green farmland here is sprinkled with historic farms and a windmill.

🏛 **Parc des Grands Jardins**
Rte. 381. **Tel** (418) 439 1227. 🕐 May–Oct: daily; Nov–Apr: Sat & Sun. 🚻

Moulin de L'Ile-aux-Coudres, in the Charlevoix region

The town of Tadoussac at the confluence of the St. Lawrence and Saguenay rivers

Tadoussac ❺

🏠 850. 🚗 🚢 🚹 *197 Rue des Pionniers (418) 235 4744.*

Lined with boutiques, the old streets of this little town make a gentle start to exploring the local stretch of the St. Lawrence River. In 1600, French traders picked the village as the site of the first fur-trading post in Canada, noticing that for generations native Indians had held meetings here to trade and parley. In the 19th century, even while the fur trade was still a force, steamships began to transport well-heeled tourists to the village for a taste of its wilderness beauty.

Justifying two centuries of tourism, the scenery here is magnificent. Backed by rocky cliffs and towering sand dunes, Tadoussac's waterfront faces over the estuary at the confluence of the St. Lawrence and Saguenay rivers. In the town, the re-creation of the original 17th-century fur-trading post and the oldest wooden church in Canada, the Petite Chapelle built in 1747, are popular.

However, the main attraction in Tadoussac lies offshore. Whale-watching tours offer trips into the estuary to see many species at close quarters. The thriving natural conditions in the estuary support a permanent colony of white beluga whales, which are joined in summer by minke, fin, and blue whales.

Saguenay River ❻

🚆 *Jonquière.* 🚗 *Chicoutimi.* 🚹 *412 Blvd. Saguenay Est 100, Chicoutimi (418) 543 9778.* **www.**tourisme saguenaylacsaintjean.net

The Saguenay River flows through the world's southernmost natural fjord. This was formed from a retreating glacier splitting a deep crack in the Earth's crust during the last Ice Age, 10,000 years ago. Inky waters, 300 m (985 ft) deep in places, run for 155 km (95 miles) beneath cliffs that average 450 m (1,500 ft) in height. Due to the exceptional depth, ocean liners can travel up to Chicoutimi on the river.

Running from Lac St. Jean to the St. Lawrence estuary, the Saguenay is best known for its lush borderlands and the wildlife that thrives in its lower reaches. Much of the pretty Bas Saguenay, the southern half of the river, is a federal marine park. A colony of a thousand whales lives here.

Beautiful views of the length of the fjord are available on the western shore at Cap Trinité, a cliff that rises 320 m (1,050 ft) over the channel, with a well-known 10-m (33-ft) statue of the Virgin Mary surveying the scenery from the lowest ledge.

Chicoutimi ❼

Saguenay. 🏠 *64,600.* 🚆 *Jonquière.* 🚗 *Chicoutimi.* 🚹 *412 Blvd. Saguenay Est 100 (418) 543 9778.*

Snug in the crook of mountains on the western shore of the Saguenay, Chicoutimi is one of northern Quebec's most expansive towns, despite its modest population. The cultural and economic center of the Saguenay region, Chicoutimi's waterfront district has now been restored. A stroll along the riverside offers good views of the surrounding mountains and the confluence of the Chicoutimi, Du-Moulin, and Saguenay rivers.

Once a center for the paper trade, Chicoutimi still features a large pulp mill, the **Pulperie de Chicoutimi**. Although no longer operational, the plant can be toured, and an adjacent museum shows visitors the intricacies of this long-standing Quebecois industry, which once supplied most of North America's paper needs.

🏛 **Pulperie de Chicoutimi**
300 Dubuc. **Tel** *(418) 698 3100.*
◯ *late Jun–Sep: 9am–6pm daily.* ♿

Waterside view of a section of the deep Saguenay fjord

A Tour of Lac-Saint-Jean **8**

In the midst of the rocky, spruce-covered wilderness that characterizes central Quebec, Lac-Saint-Jean is an oasis of tranquillity. Dairy farms, charming villages such as Chambord, and warm sandy beaches border the lake itself, which covers 1,000 sq km (386 sq miles). The lake and its rolling green landscape fill a crater-sized basin left by advancing glaciers at the end of the last Ice Age. Tiny rivers flow to the lake and tumble dramatically down the basin's steep walls into the blue waters, to be reborn as the source of the Saguenay River.

TIPS FOR DRIVERS

Starting point: Chambord.
Length: 230 km (144 miles).
Getting around: This is a long, though relaxed drive, and the road is well maintained. Inns and restaurants offer rest on the way in most towns and villages, including Mashteuiatsh. Small side roads make peaceful diversions.

Parc National de la Pointe-Taillon ⑥
Stretching into a peninsula, this park is excellent for cycling and hiking, but is best known for its fine, long beaches.

Chambord ①
Sailing and swimming are top activities here, especially for children and families.

KEY

▬ Tour route
═ Other roads
⁑ Viewpoint

Dolbeau ⑤
Most visitors to Dolbeau arrive in July for the ten-day Western Festival, which features rodeos and cowboys in Stetsons.

Mashteuiatsh, Pointe-Bleu ④
This Montagnais Indian village is open to visitors who can see at first hand age-old methods of carving, hunting, weaving, and cooking.

Roberval ③
This little village has a charming waterfront, from which spectators can see the finish of the swimming contest to cross the lake, which has taken place each July since 1946.

Village Historique de Val-Jalbert ②
This outdoor museum is dominated by the 70-m (200-ft) Ouiatchouan waterfall, which once acted as power for a pulp mill here in the 1920s.

Daniel Johnson Hydroelectric Dam, north of Baie-Comeau

Baie-Comeau ❾

🏃 26,700. ✈ 🚉 ⛴ ⓘ 337 La Salle (418) 294 2876.

This small town owes its entire existence to the US newspaper, the *Chicago Tribune*, which in 1936 built a mill near the mouth of the Manicougan River to supply its newspaper presses with paper. Declared a historic district in 1985, Baie-Comeau's oldest area is the Quartier Amélie, with rows of fine homes and an impressive hotel dating from the 1930s.

Paper production remains a vital industry in this area, but Baie-Comeau is most important today as a gateway to the enormous Manic-Outardes hydroelectric power complex, situated along Hwy 389, from 22 km (14 miles) to 200 km (130 miles) north of town. The most spectacular example is Manic-5, 190 km (115 miles) from Baie-Comeau. Its gracefully arched Daniel Johnson Dam holds back a vast reservoir that fills a crater geophysicists believe might have been created by a meteorite several millennia ago.

Sept-Iles ❿

🏃 29,000. 🚉 🚉 ⛴ ⓘ 1401 Boulevard l'Aure (418) 962 1238.

Until the 1950s, Sept-Iles led a quiet existence as a historic, sleepy fishing village. However, after World War II, the little settlement, set on the shores of a large, circular bay, drew the attention of large companies to use as a base for expanding the iron mining industry in northern Quebec. Now the largest town along the north shore of the Gulf of St. Lawrence, Sept-Iles has turned into Canada's second largest port as part of the St. Lawrence Seaway. A boardwalk along the waterfront offers visitors the chance to see the large ships in action, and to observe close-up the workings of a busy modern dock.

Although boasting the best of modern marine technology, the town also offers a reminder of its long-standing history. Vieux Poste near the center of the town is a fine reconstruction of a native trading post, where the original inhabitants of the area met to barter furs with French merchants. A small museum with aboriginal art and artifacts sells native crafts.

Despite its industrial importance, Sept-Iles is an area of considerable natural beauty.

Sept-Iles from the air, showing the bustling dock in action

Miles of sandy beaches rim the nearby coastline, and the salmon-rich Moisie River flows into the Gulf of St. Lawrence just 20 km (12 miles) east of the town. The seven rocky islands that gave the city its name make up the Sept-Iles Archipelago Park.

Ideal for campers and hikers with its beaches and nature trails, one of the seven islands, Ile Grand-Basque, is a popular local camping spot. Another small island, Ile du Corossol, has been turned into a bird sanctuary that teems with gulls, terns, and puffins, and can be toured with a guide. Cruises are available for guided trips between islands.

Mingan Archipelago and Ile d'Anticosti ⓫

🚉 Sept-Iles. ⛴ Sept-Iles. ⓘ 1401 Boulevard l'Aure (418) 962 1238.

Barely visited until recently, this unspoiled and unsettled area is fast gaining in popularity for its harsh landscape, rich wildlife, and untouched ecosystems. In 1984, the Mingan Archipelago islands became Canada's first insular national park. Puffins, terns, and several gull species find refuge in the Mingan Archipelago Wildlife Park, which comprises all 40 of the Mingan Islands that scatter along the north shore of the Gulf of St. Lawrence. Gray, harbor, and harp seals all cluster along the tiny coves and bays, and fin whales are occasional visitors. As well as the abundant wildlife, the islands are famous for their bizarre monoliths. Eroded over many centuries by the sea, these limestone carvings have surreal shapes. The best-known rocks look strikingly like flowerpots, with grasses sprouting from their peaks. Visitors can book a trip to admire this unique manifestation of nature by boat.

Until 1974, the Ile d'Anticosti, east of the archipelago, was private property – all 8,000 sq km (3,090 sq miles) of it. The past owner, French chocolate tycoon Henri Menier, bought

"Flowerpot" limestone monoliths at Mingan Archipelago National Park

the island in 1895 and stocked it with a herd of white-tailed deer for his friends to hunt. Now numbering 120,000, the deer herd is firmly ensconced but can still be hunted. Wildlife abounds; over 150 species of bird live in the relatively unspoiled forest and on the beaches. The village of Port Menier has 300 residents and acts as the local ferry terminus and lodging center.

Seal at Ile d'Anticosti

South Shore ⑫

🚉 Rivière-du-Loup. ✈ Rivière-du-Loup. ⛴ Rivière-du-Loup. 🏠 Rivière-du-Loup (418) 867 3015, 1 888 825 1981. **www**.riviereduloup.ca

Communities here can trace their roots back to the old 18th-century settlers of New France. Dotted along the flat, fertile farmland of the south shore of the St. Lawrence River west of Gaspé and inland toward Montreal, the villages cover the area between the region's largest towns of Montmagny and Rimouski. Rivière-du-Loup, a seemingly unremarkable town in this stretch, provides for many people a taste of true Quebec. Featuring an ancient stone church that rears above the skyline, the old town rambles along hilly streets, and its old 18th-century cottages have an appealing French atmosphere. From the peak of the old town, views across the river valley are lovely. Other villages in this area feature unusual attractions. Farther along the main Route 132, Trois-Pistoles boasts a history that goes back to 1580, when Basque whalers arrived. The offshore Ile aux Basques was a whaling station in the 16th century, and today can be visited to tour the nature preserve in its place. Toward the region's commercial center, Rimouski, lies Parc Bic, a small preserve of 33 square km (13 square miles) dedicated to the two forest zones, deciduous and boreal, it encloses, and its varied coastal wildlife.

Iles-de-la-Madeleine ⑬

🏠 128 Chemin Principal, Cap-aux-Meules (418) 986 2245. **www**.tourismeilesdelamadeleine.com

The few fishing families who make their homes on this remote archipelago in the middle of the huge gulf of St. Lawrence have taken to painting their cottages in an assortment of mauves, yellows, and reds. The river gives striking views of the little communities on their low-lying, windswept islands, but the islands themselves have more to offer the visitor who makes the boat trip to see them. As well as the charming ancient villages, they are home to what are reputed to be some of the most relaxing beaches in Canada, celebrated for their fine sand and sheltered position.

Painted fisherman's cottage on L'Ile-du-Havre-Aubert, Iles-de-la-Madeleine

Gaspé Peninsula Tour ⑭

Popularly known as La Gaspésie, the Gaspé Peninsula stretches out north of New Brunswick to offer Quebec's wildest and most appealing scenery. As the peninsula spreads east, clumps of trees become dense pine forests, and the landscape becomes rough and rocky; cliffs along the northern coast reach 500 m (1,500 ft). The Chic-Choc mountains reach heights of 1,300 m (4,000 ft) and provide some of the province's best hiking. Shielded by the mountains, the southern coast harbors 18th-century fishing villages, inland fruit farms, exotic gardens, and wilderness national parks.

Parc National de la Gaspésie ③
Over 800 sq km (300 sq miles) of rough terrain mark a change from boreal to subalpine forest.

Cap Chat ②
Named for a nearby cat-shaped rock, Cap Chat boasts the tallest windmill in the world at 110 m (330 ft).

Grand Métis ①
This small town is home to one of Canada's most beautiful gardens, an exotic haven of over 1,000 rare species.

QUEBEC CITY

Sainte-Flavie

Matane

RESERVE FAUNIQUE DE MATANE

Amqui

Causapscal

Roumbierville

0 km   20

0 miles   20

Carleton ⑧
Founded in 1766 by Acadians fleeing the Great Expulsion in Nova Scotia *(see pp62–3)*, Carleton today is a pleasant, relaxed resort town. Quality hotels and restaurants line the airy streets, and many visitors enjoy the mild coastal climate.

Vallée de la Matapédia ⑨
Starting at the confluence of two excellent salmon-fishing rivers, the picturesque Matapédia Valley is crisscrossed by covered bridges. Concealing long-established fruit farms, the valley's elm and maple trees show stunning fall colors.

Sainte-Anne-des-Montes ④
The entrance to Gaspé's park and the wildlife reserves of the Chic-Chocs, this 19th-century village has fine restaurants, and good salmon fishing nearby.

TIPS FOR DRIVERS

The main road on this tour is Hwy 132, which follows the coastline from Grand Métis along the peninsula in a round trip. While too long to complete in a day, the journey can be broken in many of the local villages. Trips into the interior on the secondary road 299 are ideal for seeing the rocky wilderness.

Mont-Louis
⑤
Grande-Vallée
132

Murdochville
198
6

RESERVE FAUNIQUE DES CHIC-CHOCS
Gaspé

299

7

Grand Rivière

Maria
New Richmond
Mont Saint-Pierre ⑤
The gateway for visits to the Chic-Choc mountains, this village is also a beach center for hang gliding.

132
New-Carlisle

Parc National du Canada Forillon ⑥
The park contains the tail end of the Appalachian Mountains, now cliffs worn into rugged formations by the sea.

Rocher Percé ⑦
Situated out to sea south of the small town of Percé, this famous pierced landmark is the result of tidal erosion. In the 1930s, Percé became a popular spot for Canadian artists and still contains many galleries.

KEY

▅	Tour route
＝	Other roads
▲	Camp grounds
ℹ	Visitor information
☀	Viewpoint

SOUTHERN AND NORTHERN QUEBEC

The vast area of land that stretches across Quebec from the Ontario boundary to historic Quebec City is rewarding in its diversity. In the south, the rich hilly farmland of the Appalachians and scarlet forests of maple trees attract many visitors each year, while the stark beauty of Nunavik's icy northern coniferous forests bursts into a profusion of wildflowers in spring, alongside the largest hydroelectric projects in the world. The center of the region is Quebec's natural playground, the Laurentian Mountains, a pristine lake-filled landscape offering fine skiing on ancient mountains. Populated by native people until Europeans arrived in the 16th century, the area was fought over by the French and British until the British gained power in 1759. Today French-speakers dominate.

SIGHTS AT A GLANCE

National Parks
Parc National de
la Mauricie **⑤**

Historic Towns and Cities
Gatineau **⑫**
Joliette **⑦**
Oka **⑨**
Rouyn-Noranda **⑮**

Sainte-Croix **③**
Sherbrooke **②**
Terrebonne **⑧**
Trois Rivières **⑥**
Val d'Or **⑭**

**Historic Sites and Areas
of Natural Beauty**
James Bay **⑯**
Lac Memphrémagog **①**
Laurentian Mountains **⑪**
Nunavik *(not shown on map)* **⑰**

Reserve Faunique
La Vérendrye **⑬**
Richelieu Valley **④**
Sucrerie de la Montagne **⑩**

KEY

✈ International airport

═ Highway

▬ Major road

— Major rail routes

•─• International border

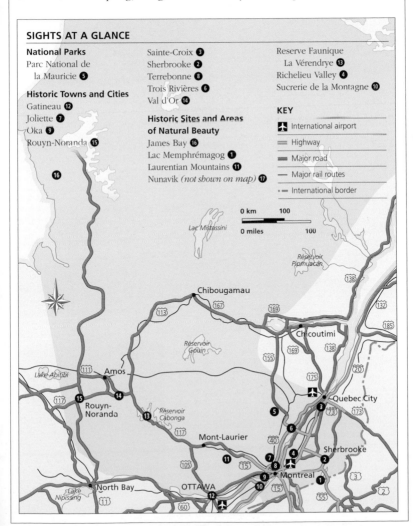

0 km 100

0 miles 100

⚹ Colorful houses in St. Jovite, with the Laurentian Mountains rising behind

Church by Lac Memphrémagog

Lac Memphrémagog ❶

🚉 Magog. 🚢 Magog.
ℹ️ 55 Cabana St., Magog 1
(800) 267 2744. **www**.tourisme-
memphremagog.com

This area belongs to the Eastern Townships, or the "Garden of Quebec" that stretches from the Richelieu River valley to the Maine, New Hampshire and Vermont borders in the US. Set among rolling hills, farmland, woods, and lakes in a landscape similar to the Appalachians, the Townships are among Canada's top maple syrup producers *(see pp102–3)*.

Lac Memphrémagog itself is long, narrow, and surrounded by mountains. It even boasts its own monster, a creature named Memphré, first spotted in 1798. The lake's southern quarter dips into the state of Vermont, so it is no surprise that the British Loyalists fleeing the American Revolution were this region's first settlers. Their influence can be seen in the late 19th-century redbrick and wood-frame homes of lakeside villages such as enchanting Georgeville and Vale Perkins, and in the resort city of Magog at the northern end of the lake.

Benedictine monks from France bought one of the lake's most beautiful sites in 1912 and established the Abbaye Saint-Benoît-du-Lac. Today the monks produce cider and a celebrated blue cheese called l'Ermite. They are also renowned for Gregorian chant, and visitors can hear them sing mass in the abbey church.

Sherbrooke ❷

🏘️ 140,000. ✈️ 🚌 🚆 ℹ️ 2964 King St. W. 1 (800) 561 8331, (819) 821 1919. **www**.sdes.ca

The self-styled "Queen of the Eastern Townships," Sherbrooke is indeed this region's industrial, commercial, and cultural center. The city lies in a steep-sided valley, with the historic quarter delightfully situated among the rolling farmlands of the Saint-François and Magog Rivers. The first settlers were British Loyalists from the New England states. Although their heritage survives in the fine old homes and gardens of Sherbrooke's North Ward and in street names, today the city is overwhelmingly French speaking. From the town center runs the Riverside Trail, a lovely waterfront park with 20 km (12 miles) of cycling and walking trails along the banks of the Magog River.

Sainte-Croix ❸

🏘️ 2,600. ℹ️ 6375 rue Garneau (418) 926 2620.

A charming, wooden manor house with bold sweeping front steps, pillars, and carved curlicues is the grandest old house in this pretty riverside town. It is the centerpiece of **Domaine Joly-De-Lotbinière**, a stunning estate built in 1851 by the local squire (seigneur). The house is surrounded by banks of geraniums and terraces of walnut trees stretching down to the river. Rare plant finds include 20 red oaks estimated to be more than 250 years old. The gardens are best known, however, for cultivating blue potatoes.

🏛️ **Domaine Joly-De-Lotbinière**
Rte. de Pointe-Platon.
Tel (418) 926 2462. ◻ mid-May–mid-Oct: 10am–5pm daily. 🅿️ 🔵 partial.

Richelieu Valley ❹

ℹ️ 1080 Chemin des Patriotes Nord, Mont Saint-Hilaire (450) 536 0395, 1 888 736 0395. **www**.vallee-du-richelieu.ca

This fertile valley follows the 130-km (80-mile) Richelieu River north from Chambly to Saint-Denis. **Fort Chambly**, also known as Fort St. Louis, in the industrial town of Chambly along the valley on the Montreal Plain, is the best preserved of a series of ancient buildings that the French erected to defend this vital waterway from Dutch and British attack. Built from solid stone in 1709 to replace the original wooden fortifications set up in 1655, the fort is well preserved. A museum in Saint-Denis commemorates Quebecois patriots who fought in the failed 1837 rebellion against British rule.

A sign to Fort Chambly in the Richelieu Valley

Today the river flows past attractive villages surrounded by orchards and vineyards; Mont Saint-Hilaire affords fine views of Montreal, and is famed for its apple plantations. Its 19th-century church was declared a historic site in 1965 and features paintings by Canadian Ozias Leduc *(see p32)*.

🏛️ **Fort Chambly**
2 Richelieu St., Chambly. **Tel** 1 (888) 773 8888 or (450) 658 1585.
◻ Apr–Oct: 10am–5pm Wed–Sun (mid-May–Aug: daily); Mar & Nov: weekdays for groups by appt. 🅿️

Mont Saint-Hilaire, Richelieu Valley

Canoeists on Lac Wapizagonke in Parc National de la Mauricie

Parc National de la Mauricie ❺

off Hwy 55 N. Shawinigan.
Tel (019) 530 3232. 🚉 Shawinigan.
⬜ daily. 🅿️ 🚻 partial. 💶 for a
fee. **www**.pc.gc.ca

Campers, hikers, canoeists, and cross-country skiers love this 536-sq km (207-sq mile) stretch of forest, lakes, and pink Precambrian granite. The park includes part of the Laurentian Mountains *(see p151)*, which are part of the Canadian Shield, and were formed between 950 and 1,400 million years ago. La Mauricie's rugged beauty is also accessible to motorists, who can take the winding 63-km (40-mile) road between Saint-Mathieu and Saint-Jean-de-Piles.

Another great drive starts at Saint-Jean-de-Piles and has good views of the narrow Lac Wapizagonke Valley. With trout and pike in the lake, the area is an angler's delight. Moose and bear roam wild in the park.

Trois-Rivières ❻

🏠 52,000. ✈️ 🚉 🚌 ⛴️ 🚻 ℹ️ *1457
Rue Notre Dame (819) 375 1122,
1 800 313 1123.*

Quebec is one of the major paper producers in North America, and Trois-Rivières, a pulp and paper town, is a main center of that industry in the province. This fact often hides the rich historical interest that Trois-Rivières has to offer. The first colonists arrived here in 1634 from France and, although not many of the colonial dwellings remain, the city's charming old section has a number of 18th- and 19th-century houses and shops, many of which have been converted into cafés and bars.

Ursuline nuns have been working in the city since 1697, and the core of the old city is the **Monastère des Ursulines**, a rambling complex with a central dome, a chapel, and a little garden that is now a public park. Rue des Ursulines features several little old houses with varying architectural styles.

The church of the Monastère des Ursulines in Trois-Rivières

Also here is an 18th-century manor house, the 1730 Manoir Boucher-de-Niverville, which contains the local chamber of commerce and rotates displays on the rich history of the area around the Eastern Townships.

🏛️ **Monastère des Ursulines**
734 Ursulines. *Tel* (819) 375 7922.
⬜ Mar & Apr: Wed–Sun; May–Nov: Tue–Sun; Nov–Feb: call ahead. 🅿️

Joliette ❼

🏠 31,100. 🚌 ℹ️ *500 rue Dollard (450) 759 5013.*

Two Catholic priests are responsible for turning the industrial town of Joliette on the Assomption River into a cultural center. In the 1920s, Father Wilfrid Corbeil founded the Musée d'Art de Joliette, whose permanent collection ranges from medieval religious art to modern works. In 1974, Father Fernand Lindsay started the Festival International de Lanaudière, a series of summer concerts by some of the world's best-known musicians.

The nearby town of Rawdon, 18 km (11 miles) west, has a deserved reputation as a place of great natural beauty. Trails wind away from the small town alongside the Ouareau River, leading to the picturesque, rushing Dorwin Falls.

Terrebonne ❽

🏚 *36,680.* 🚌 🚆 🚍 ℹ️ *3645 Queen Street (1 800 363 2788).*

Just northwest of the outer fringe of Montreal's suburbs, this historic little town on the Mille-Iles River was founded in 1673, but a fire in 1922 engulfed many of its original buildings. However, some graceful 19th-century homes remain, on rue Saint-François-Xavier and rue Sainte-Marie, many of them converted into restaurants and bistros. The town's real gem is the **Ile-des-Moulins**, a pre-industrial complex of living history in the middle of the Mille-Iles River, with water-powered mills for grinding grain, carding wool, and sawing lumber. One of the biggest buildings on the site is the three-floor factory that was the first large-scale bakery in Canada. It was built by the Northwest Company in 1803 to make the saltless ship's biscuits that sustained the *voyageurs* who paddled west every year to collect furs for the company.

Terrebonne is also the center of Quebec's horse-riding culture. Popular with locals, rodeo and ranching events take place regularly.

🏭 **Ile-des-Moulins**
Autoroute 25, exit 22 E. **Tel** *(450) 471 0619.* ⬜ *Jun–Sep: 1–9 pm daily.*
♿ www.ile-des-moulins.qc.ca

The Oka ferry as it travels across the Lake of Two Mountains

Oka ❾

🏚 *3,840.* 🚌 🚆 ℹ️ *183 rue des Anges (450) 479 8337.*

The prettiest way to approach this village north of Montreal is on the small ferry that chugs across the Lake of Two Mountains from Hudson. Framed by mountains and orchards, from the water the small Neo-Romanesque 1878 church is visible through the trees. Oka's **Abbaye Cistercienne** was founded by a group of monks who moved to Canada from France in 1881. The decor of the abbey church is somewhat stark, in the Cistercian tradition, but the Neo-Romanesque architecture is gracefully simple and the gardens peaceful. The abbey closed in 2009, but the abbey shop still operates, selling the soft Oka cheese that the monks have developed. Nearby, the Parc d'Oka covers about 20 sq km (7 sq miles) of ponds and forests. It features the best beach and campground in the Montreal area, attracting sports lovers and visitors year-round.

Quebecois Maple Syrup

🏛 **Abbaye Cistercienne**
1600 Chemin d'Oka. **Tel** *(450) 479 6170.* ⬜ *8am–8pm Mon–Sat.* ⬛ *lunchtimes.* **www.** abbayeoka.com

Sucrerie de la Montagne ❿

10 km South of Rigaud. 🚌 **Tel** *(450) 451 0831.* ⬜ *year round but call ahead.* ♿ 🚗 *obligatory.* 🖼 **www.**sucreriedelamontagne.com

This typically Canadian treat is set in a 50-ha (120-acre) maple forest on top of Rigaud Mountain near Rang Saint-Georges, Rigaud. It is entirely devoted to the many delights of Quebec's most famous commodity, the maple tree and its produce *(see pp102–3).* The site features a reconstructed 19th-century sugar shack, where collected maple sap is distilled and boiled in large kettles to produce the internationally renowned syrup. Over 20 rustic buildings house a fine bakery, a general store, and comfortable cabins for overnight guests. The heart of the complex is a huge 500-seat restaurant that serves traditional banquets of ham, pea soup, baked beans, pork rinds (called *oreilles du Christ*, or Christ's ears), and pickles, and dozens of maple-based products, including syrup, sugar, candies, taffy, muffins, and bread. Folk music accompanies the nightly feast. The tour includes a thorough explanation of the maple syrup-making process, which is generally thought to have originated with the native people. They later imparted their secrets to European settlers, whose traditional methods are still in use today.

Rue-St-Louis Church in Terrebonne

Laurentian Mountains Tour ⓫

Cycle sign

This whole region, from the lively resort of Saint-Sauveur-des-Monts in the south to north of Sainte Jovite, is nature's own amusement park, full of beautiful lakes, rivers, hiking and cycling trails, and ski runs visited all through the year. The mountains are part of the ancient Laurentian Shield and are a billion years old. Dotted with pretty, old French-style towns, this is a superb area to relax in or indulge in some vigorous sports in the many national parks.

TIPS FOR DRIVERS

Although the 175-km round tour of the Laurentian Mountains can be made from Montreal in a day on Hwy 15, the region is best seen and enjoyed by taking advantage of the slower, but more scenic, Hwy 117. There may be traffic congestion at the peak times of July through August and from December to March.

Sainte Jovite ④
Full of historic architecture, this village lies in a wooded valley.

La Conception ⑤
Plenty of tiny hotels and street cafés add to the charm of this old village.

Mont Tremblant ⑥
The tallest of the Laurentian range with a vertical rise of about 645 m (2,454 ft), this is a popular international four-season resort.

Saint Faustin ③
Saint-Faustin has an important role as the starting-off point for trips around the area. Local woods contain an interpretive center with flora and fauna trails.

Sainte-Agathe-des-Monts ②
The largest town in the Laurentians provides busy café society all year round. Lac des Sables in town offers beaches and lake cruises.

Val Morin ①
This enchanting village is a charming introduction to the area, with traditional French homes and churches.

KEY

▬ Tour route

═ Other roads

0 km   3

0 miles   3

The impressive beauty of Quebec's thundering Montmorency Falls ▷

Gatineau ⑫

Meditation center

Gatineau (known as Hull until 1992), is based just across the river from Ottawa in the province of Quebec, and, as a result, many federal bureaucracies have their headquarters here. For years, Gatineau has been a more relaxed and fun-loving counterpart to the capital, an attitude that reveals itself even in its officialdom – City Hall, for instance, boasts a meditation center.

From Hull's establishment in 1800, the city's liquor laws were far more lenient than Ottawa's, and so this was where Ottawa politicians came to party (the city still has a lower drinking age). Gatineau contains one of Canada's best museums, the Canadian Museum of Civilization, which provides a fascinating tour of Canada's history over the past 1,000 years.

VISITORS' CHECKLIST

🏙 228,000. ✈ Ottawa International 12 km (8 miles) south of the city. 🚌 200 Tremblay Rd, Ottawa. ℹ La Maison du Tourisme, 103 Rue Laurier (819) 778 2222, 1 800 265 7822. 🎪 Fall Rhapsody (Sep/ Oct). www.outaouais-tourism.ca

🌿 Gatineau Park

Hwy 5. **Tel** (819) 827 2020, 1 800 465 1867. ◯ daily.
This 360 sq km (140 sq miles) oasis of lakes and rolling hills between the Gatineau and Ottawa Rivers is a weekend playground for city residents. The park contains fragments of Gothic buildings, collected by the former Prime Minister, William Lyon MacKenzie-King.

Casino du Lac Leamy

1 Casino Blvd. **Tel** (819) 772 2100, 1 800 665 2274. ◯ 9am–4am daily. ♿
Four million visitors a year are lured to this glittering Casino, which is equipped with 1,300 slot machines and 45 gaming

Gaming room in the casino

tables. Owned by the Quebec Government, the Casino opened in 1996 and is set in a park full of flowers and fountains.

🏛 Alexandra Bridge

Built in 1900, this handsome steel-framed bridge spans the Ottawa River and links Ontario to Quebec. From footpaths, drivers' lanes, and cycle routes, the bridge offers fine views of the river, the Canadian Museum of Civilization, and the Parliament Buildings in Ottawa.

🏛 Maison du Citoyen

25 Laurier St. **Tel** (819) 595 7100. ◯ 8:30am–4:30pm Mon–Fri. ⬤ public holidays. ♿
The heart of this modern complex is a vast atrium, the Agora, meant to serve as an all-weather gathering place for Gatineau's citizens, as well as an airy meditation center for the city's workers. Opening from it are City Hall, a library, a theater, and an art gallery.

🏛 Promenade du Portage

Linked with the city bridges, this main route downtown is a good shopping center with large stores and lively cafés. After dark the area and nearby Place Aubry become the focus of the city's excellent nightlife.

GATINEAU CITY CENTER

Alexandra Bridge ①
Canadian Museum of Civilization ②
Maison du Citoyen ③
Promenade du Portage ④

Casino du Lac Leamy

BOULEVARD SACRÉ-COEUR
RUE ST-REDEMPTEUR
RUE ST-HYACINTHE
RUE ST-HENRI
RUE ARTHUR-GUERTIN
RUE EDGAR-CHENIER
RUE CHAMPLAIN
RUE LAURIER
Parc Dupuis
RUE LAVAL
RUE KENT
RUE DE VERDUN
Parc Jacques-Cartier
RUE ST-ÉTIENNE
RUE ST-ÉTIENNE

BOULEVARD ST-LAURENT

Gatineau Park
RUE CHARLEVOIX
Alexandra Bridge ①
Parc Fontaine
RUE PAPINEAU
OTTAWA
RUE ST-REDEMPTEUR
RUE EDDY
RUE FRONTENAC
RUE LAVAL
RUE KENT
RUE CHAMPLAIN
BOULEVARD MAISONNEUVE
② Canadian Museum of Civilization
RUE DE L'HÔTEL-DE-VILLE
RUE ST-JACQUES
RUE WRIGHT
④
RUE LAURIER
③ Maison du Citoyen
RUE WELLINGTON
PROMENADE DU PORTAGE
RUE LAURIER
RUE EDDY

0 meters 300
0 yards 300

Ottawa International Airport 12 km (8 miles)

Key to Symbols see back flap

Canadian Museum of Civilization

This museum was built in the 1980s to be the storehouse of Canada's human history. The architect, Douglas Cardinal, wanted the undulating façades of both buildings to reflect the Canadian landscape. The more curved hall is the Canadian Shield Wing, home to the museum's offices. The Glacier Wing displays the exhibits. Its entry is stunning; the dramatic interior of the Grand Hall contains a forest of totem poles. Canada Hall traces the progress of the Canadian people from the Vikings through early settlers to the present day. The Children's Museum is delightfully diverting. The fourth level holds an archive, which is open to the public.

VISITORS' CHECKLIST

100 Laurier St. **Tel** (819) 776 7000, 1 800 555 5621.
◻ May–mid-Oct: 9am–6pm daily; mid-Oct–May: 9am–6pm Tue–Sun. 🎫 ♿ 🍴 ☐ 📷
🚉 🚌 **www.**civilization.ca

The museum façade echoes the rolling Canadian landscape

Canada Hall is a mazelike journey that traces the country's history from Norse settlers and colonial times to Victorian villages.

Level Three

David M. Stewart Salon

Level Two

Main Entrance

The Children's Museum
This extremely popular space contains a "world tour" of interactive exhibits, a busy international market, and this brightly decorated Pakistani trolleybus.

Level One

Library

★ The Grand Hall
Lit by windows three stories high, totem poles from the West Coast line the Grand Hall; each pole tells a native myth in wood carving.

KEY TO FLOOR PLAN

◻	Canada Hall
◻	Children's Museum
◼	Canadian Postal Museum
◻	First Peoples Hall
◻	Pacific Coast Aboriginal Exhibits
◻	W.E. Taylor Salon
◻	Grand Hall
◻	IMAX/OMNIMAX' movie theater
◻	Special exhibitions
◼	Nonexhibition space

STAR SIGHT

★ The Grand Hall

The wildlife preserve of La Vérendrye, seen from the air

Reserve Faunique La Vérendrye ⑬

Tel (819) 736 7431. 🚗 Maniwaki.
◯ summer. ♿ partial.

This wildlife preserve is situated approximately 471 km (292 miles) to the northwest of Montreal on Hwy 117. It is celebrated for long, meandering waterways and streams and, with thousands of kilometers of canoe trails, is a legend among canoeists. Its rivers are usually gentle, and the 13,000 sq km (5,000 sq miles) of wilderness are home to large numbers of moose, bear, deer, and beaver. The land is practically untouched, but there are several campgrounds here for those who seek a truly peaceful break. In season, anglers can try for walleye, pike, lake trout, and bass. Hwy 117 traverses the park, providing access to many of its lakes and rivers, and is the starting point of hiking trails.

A moose at La Vérendrye

Val d'Or ⑭

🏙 35,000. 🚗 🛈 1070 3rd Ave. E. (819) 824 9646.

Val d'Or is principally a mining town and is the major center in the northwestern part of Quebec. The town sights here are not architectural but vivid living history attractions of mines and historic villages

from the area's heritage of lumber trade and mining. Miners have been digging gold, silver, and copper out of the ground around Val d'Or since the 1920s. A climb to the top of the 18-m (60-ft) Tour Rotary on the edge of town shows many still-active mineheads.

La Cité de l'Or is a popular attraction, built around the abandoned Lamaque Goldmine, formerly one of the richest sources of gold in the area. In its heyday of the early 20th century, the mine had its very own small town site with a hospital, a boarding house for all single workers, and neat streets lined with little log cabins for married men and their families. The mine managers had more elaborate homes nearby, and there was a sumptuous guesthouse for visiting executives. Much of the Village Minier de Bourlamaque remains intact and was declared a historic site in 1979. Visitors can tour the village, the old analysis office and laboratories, and the minehead. For an extra fee, fascinating tours in coveralls and helmets are available down the 90 m (300 ft) mine shaft.

🏛 La Cité de l'Or
90 Ave. Perrault. *Tel* (819) 825 7616.
◯ Jun–Sep: 9am–6pm daily. 📷 ♿ partial.

Rouyn-Noranda ⑮

🏙 26,450. ✈ 🛈 191 Ave. du Lac (819) 797 3195, 1 888 797 3195.

As with all developed areas in the north of Quebec, towns here are based on heavy industry. Rouyn and Noranda sprang up virtually overnight in the 1920s when prospectors found copper in the region. They merged into one city in 1986 but are quite different places. Noranda on the north shore of Lake Osisko is a carefully planned company town with its own churches and schools, built to house the employees of the now-defunct Noranda copper mine. The lawns and tree-lined streets have an almost English air. Nowadays its residents are likely to be employed in surrounding mines. The Horne Smelter, one of the biggest in the world, is based just outside the center of town and can be visited by arrangement.

Rouyn, on the south shore of the lake, is less structured and more commercial. It is also where Noranda residents used to go for recreation, and it is useful as a refreshment and fuel center for those traveling to the northern wilderness. The **Maison Dumulon**, a reconstruction of Rouyn's first post office and general store, celebrates its pioneer spirit with displays on the first settlers.

🏛 Maison Dumulon
191 Ave. du Lac. *Tel* (819) 797 7125.
◯ Jun–Sep: daily; Oct–Jun: Wed–Sun. ⬤ Jan 1, Dec 25. 📷 ♿

Copper being smelted into huge nuggets for export, Noranda

Herds of caribou migrate south in summer across the Hudson Bay area into Nunavik

James Bay 🄰

🛈 *Tourisme Quebec (877) 266 5687.*

The thinly populated municipality of James Bay is roughly the size of Germany, which makes it much larger than most other municipalities in the region – about 350,000 square km (135,000 square miles). Its landscape, lakes, scrubby trees, and early pre-Cambrian rock is hardly urban, changing from forest to taiga to tundra and becoming gradually more inaccessible in the frozen northern parts. However, what the region lacks in infrastructure it makes up for amply in power capacity. Its six major rivers, which all flow into the Bay, can produce enough electricity to light up the whole of North America. So far, the Quebec government has spent over Can$20 billion in building a third of the number of dams for what is already one of the biggest hydroelectric projects in the world. Five power plants produce nearly 16,000 megawatts of electricity to power much of Quebec and parts of the northeastern US. Le Grand 2 (known as LG 2) is the biggest dam and underground generating station in the world.

The main town in the area is the small settlement of Radisson. A functional but useful tourist center, Radisson also offers good views of the surrounding country. Not all of the Bay's 215 dams and dikes can be seen, but the massive dams and series of reservoirs, especially LG 2, which is just east of town, are visible from above.

One of the vast power stations at James Bay

Nunavik 🄱

🛈 *Association touristique du Nunavik (819) 964 2002, 1 888 594 3424.* **www**.nunavik-tourism.com

In the far north of Quebec, the municipality of Nunavik covers an area slightly larger than continental Spain. Its inhabitants number about 7,000, nearly all of them Inuit, who live in 14 communities along the shores of Hudson Bay, the Hudson Strait, and Ungava Bay. Nunavik is Quebec's last frontier, a wild and beautiful land that is virtually inaccessible except by airplane. Caribou herds, polar bears, and musk oxen roam the taiga coniferous forest and frozen Arctic tundra that covers this region. Seals and beluga whales can be found swimming in its icy waters.

Kuujjuaq, near Ungava Bay, is Nunavik's largest district, with a population of just over 1,400. This is a good jumping-off point for expeditions to the valley of Kangiqsujuaq near Wakeham Bay and the rugged mountains around Salluit.

Visitors come to Nunavik and Kuujjuaq to appreciate the many varieties of wildlife which roam freely in their natural setting. Summer is the best time for a trip; temperatures rise, but the ground remains frozen all year round. The region has no railroads (and hardly any roads) and should be explored only in the company of a seasoned and reliable guide. Many Inuit groups and communities offer guide services and the opportunity to experience life on the land with Inuit families. Visitors should be prepared for a very warm welcome and the chance to sample traditional Inuit foods and hospitality.

A man fishing from a small boat in Combermere, Eastern Ontario ▷

ONTARIO

Introducing Ontario

The sheer size of Ontario is daunting. It is Canada's second-largest province, covering over one million square miles and stretching all the way from the Great Lakes on the US border to the frozen shores of Hudson Bay. Northern Ontario is relatively inaccessible, but this wild and stunningly beautiful region of turbulent rivers, deep forests, and Arctic tundra can be reached by air, and by the occasional scenic road and railroad. Much of the north is also sparsely populated, in striking contrast to the fertile lands farther south, and bordering Lake Ontario, which have attracted many thousands of immigrants. Both Toronto, Canada's biggest city, and Niagara Falls, the country's leading tourist destination, are here.

The world's second-tallest free-standing structure, Toronto's CN Tower, at night

WOODLAND CARIBOU NATIONAL PARK

PICKLE LAKE

RED LAKE
105
Lac Seul
599
Lake Nipigon
DRYDEN
17
NIPIGON
THUNDER BAY
11
Lake Superi

0 km   150

0 miles   150

A tour boat approaches the spectacular Horseshoe Falls at Niagara

GETTING AROUND

Among several highways skirting the northern shore of Lake Ontario, the main ones are Hwy 401, from Toronto to Montreal in the east and Windsor in the west, and the Queen Elizabeth Way (QEW), from Toronto south to Niagara Falls. Niagara Falls, Toronto, and Ottawa are linked by bus and rail. Hwy 400 runs north from Toronto to Parry Sound, where it becomes Hwy 69 up to the Trans-Canada Highway. Buses also cover northerly routes.

**The Neo-Gothic splendor of Ottawa's Parliament
Buildings seen from the top of Nepean Point**

Hudson Bay

AKIMISKI
ISLAND

ONTARIO

11 HEARST
COCHRANE

17 101

WAWA

11

SUDBURY   NORTH BAY

SAULT
STE. MARIE   17   69   11   ALGONQUIN
PROVINCIAL
PARK   OTTAWA
401

TOBERMORY   MIDLAND   7
KINGSTON

Lake
Huron   TORONTO   Lake
Ontario

21   NIAGARA ON
THE LAKE
KITCHENER
STRATFORD   HAMILTON
LONDON   NIAGARA FALLS
402
401   Lake
Erie

KEY

▬ Highway

▬ Major road

▭ Minor road

═ River

SEE ALSO

The Hudson's Bay Company

The Hudson's Bay Co. crest

The Hudson's Bay Company was incorporated by King Charles II of England on May 2, 1670. His decision was prompted by the successful voyage of the British ship *Nonsuch*, which returned from the recently discovered Hudson's Bay crammed with precious beaver furs. The king granted the new company wide powers, including a monopoly of trading rights to a huge block of territory bordering the Bay, then known as Rupert's Land. The Company was ordered to develop links with the native Americans of Rupert's Land, and trade took off swiftly. Here fashion played a part: the ladies and gentlemen of 18th-century Europe were gripped by a passion for the beaver hat, and the demand for beaver pelts became almost insatiable.

European fur couriers *rapidly built up a roaring trade with native fur trappers, which came to follow a seasonal pattern.*

Fort Yukon 1846-1869

Fort Good Hope 1821

Fort Simpson 1821

Fort St. James 1821

Edmonton 1795

Cumberland House 1774

Fort Victoria 1843

LANDS AND TRADING POSTS

From 1670 onward, trading goods were dispatched from England to the Company's main trading sites around Hudson Bay, modest stockaded settlements with safe stores for the merchandise. Larger outposts gradually became self-sufficient, catering to newer, smaller posts as the Company moved ever westward. By 1750, HBC camps were established at the mouths of all the major rivers flowing into Hudson Bay. James Bay's Fort Albany had a jail, a hospital, a smithy, a cooperage, a canoe-building jetty, and sheep and cattle barns, while gallant efforts were made to grow crops. Main trading posts serviced a network of smaller seasonal outposts. They continued their expansion west until the transfer of land rights to the new country of Canada in 1870.

KEY

🛖 Trading post

- - Trading route

〰 1670 boundary of Rupert's Land

The Seven Oaks Massacre *of June 1816 in Manitoba occurred when HBC workers clashed with the rival North West Company, and 20 men were killed. The two companies agreed in 1821 to join territories and increased in power.*

English traders *assembled a variety of goods to trade with local tribes in return for the winter's supply of pelts. Transported by ship in spring, the merchandise ranged from trinkets to more substantial items including blankets, knives, and guns.*

THE CHANGING FORTUNES OF HBC

HBC reigned supreme in Canada until the 1840s, but civil disobedience led the British to relinquish claims to Washington State and Oregon in 1846, establishing the US border. No longer able to enforce its monopoly, HBC sold its land to Canada in 1870, retaining only areas around the trading posts. They were in key locations, which boosted HBC's expansion into real estate and retail in the 20th century. Today HBC is one of Canada's top companies, but it is majority-owned by a US firm.

The Bay in Vancouver, one of HBC's modern department stores

0 km   500

0 miles   500

The beaver's coat *is at its thickest and most valuable in winter, when the natives ventured out into the ice and snow to trap the animal. In spring Indian trappers delivered bundles of soft pelts to the Company's trading posts, in exchange for goods.*

Company sailboats *first carried materials to trade with native peoples. As the Company grew, it transported building materials, food, and seeds to set up what became sizeable settlements. Ships returned with up to 16,000 beaver pelts.*

The Group of Seven

Tom Thomson,
(1877–1917)

Formed in 1920, the Group of Seven revolutionized Canadian art. Mostly commercial artists working in an Ontario art firm, this small band of painters was inspired by a colleague, Tom Thomson. An avid outdoorsman, Thomson started making trips in 1912 into the wilderness of northern Ontario to produce dozens of brightly colored, impressionistic sketches. His friends realized that he was taking Canadian art in a new direction – these landscapes of their country were largely free of the rigid European focus that had characterized painting until then and a nationalist movement had begun. After World War I and the death of Thomson in 1917, these same friends started the Group and held their first exhibition in Toronto in 1920. Many of the paintings shown depicted Nova Scotian, Ontarian and Quebec wildernesses; a new art was born that forged a sense of national pride between the people and their land in this young country.

The Red Maple *is A.Y. Jackson's vibrant landmark of 1914, embodying the Group aim of creating a national consciousness.*

Edge of the Forest (1919) *by Frank Johnston is just one of the Group's works that illustrates their statement: "Art must grow and flower in the land before the country will be a real home for its people." Using the impressive surroundings of their homeland, the Group painters developed a spontaneous technique.*

Above Lake Superior *was painted by Lawren Harris in 1922. Known for his simple, heroic images, Harris captures the harsh, exhilarating climate of the Great Lakes region in winter, known as "the mystic north." Harris believed that spiritual fulfillment could best be obtained by studying landscape. The Group also held the ethos that truly meaningful expression was accomplished only when the the subject of the work was one the viewer shared with the artist, in this case local landscape.*

Falls, Montreal River
(1920) was painted by
J. E. H. MacDonald, who
chose Algoma as his work
base. Each of the Group
had a preferred individual
region in which they
found most inspiration,
mostly in Ontario.
Sketching trips regularly
took place in summer, with
painters showing each
other favorite areas.

THE GROUP OF SEVEN

Based in a converted railway boxcar, the members hiked and boated to favorite places in Algonquin Park, Georgian Bay, Algoma, and Lake Superior to produce new art for their country. Following the 1920 exhibition, entitled The Group of Seven, their striking paintings immediately became popular and the Group went on to exhibit together almost every year. Native inspiration was vital to the Group's subject and technique. The apparently raw and coarse methods were a rejection of the heavy, realist oils produced in Europe at the time. Luminous colors and visible brushstrokes led one critic to remark that the Group had "thrown [their] paint pots in the face of the public." The Group held their final show in 1931 and disbanded the following year to make way for a wider group of painters from across Canada, the Canadian Group of Painters. Founders of a distinctive Canadian art movement based on a love of their country's natural beauty, the Group of Seven painters remain particularly celebrated in Canada and are still given prominence in top galleries across Ontario and the rest of the country today.

The photograph below, taken at Toronto's Arts & Letters Club in 1920, shows, from left to right: Varley, Jackson, Harris, Barker Fairley (a friend and writer), Johnston, Lismer and MacDonald. Carmichael was not present.

AUTUMN, ALGOMA *(1920)*

This richly decorated canvas shows the extraordinary evening colors of the fall in Ontario. Algoma was J.E.H. MacDonald's chosen region, a Canadian Eden in northern Ontario that acted as his inspiration and where he regularly made sketching trips. MacDonald records uniquely Canadian subjects in this painting; the blazing foliage and looming pines serve to record and thus establish a Canadian identity. Influenced by the stark landscapes produced in Scandinavia from around 1900, MacDonald focuses on the chill drama in this scene to add a grandeur to his beloved landscape.

The Group of Seven in 1920

TORONTO

Toronto has shed its prim, colonial image to become one of North America's most dynamic cities, a cosmopolitan mix of eight million inhabitants drawn from more than one hundred ethnic groups. Reveling in its position as the financial and commercial center of Canada, Toronto also boasts fine art museums, suave café-bars, and luxury stores.

Located on the north shore of Lake Ontario, Toronto was originally a native Indian settlement dating from the 17th century, and, after 1720, a French fur-trading post. Fought over by the US and Britain in the War of 1812 *(see p45)*, Toronto has since been a peaceful city, growing dramatically after World War II, with the arrival of over 500,000 immigrants, especially Italians and, most recently, Asians.

The first place to start a visit is the CN Tower, formerly the world's tallest tower and the city's most famous tourist attraction. From the top, it is easy to pick out the sights of the city, and from the bottom, a short stroll leads to the Rogers Centre or the banking district. To the north of downtown is the boisterous street-life of Chinatown and the superb paintings of the Art Gallery of Ontario. Beyond sits the University of Toronto, on whose perimeters lies the fine Royal Ontario Museum and two delightful specialty collections, the Gardiner Museum of Ceramic Art and the Bata Shoe Museum. A quick subway ride takes the visitor north to Casa Loma, an eccentric Edwardian mansion, and Spadina House, the elegant Victorian villa nearby. Many more attractions are scattered around the periphery, including Toronto Zoo and the Ontario Science Centre. The McMichael Canadian Art Collection, in nearby Kleinburg, contains an outstanding collection of paintings by the Group of Seven, among many others, in a pastoral setting.

Toronto's café society doing what it does best in the downtown area

◁ The spire of the CN Tower rearing above the city reflected in an office building

Exploring Toronto

Toronto is a large, sprawling city that covers over 640 sq km (398 sq miles) on the north side of Lake Ontario. The center offers a pleasant mix of office blocks, leafy residential streets, and shopping areas, while outer areas, such as North York and Scarborough, are more residential and spread out. The downtown core, encompassing the business district and Chinatown, is bordered by College and Front on the north and south, and Jarvis and Spadina on the east and west.

SIGHTS AT A GLANCE

**Historic Areas
and Buildings**
Casa Loma **23**
Chinatown **13**
First Post Office **9**
Fort York **24**
Little Italy **25**
Mirvish Theatres **7**
Ontario Parliament
   Buildings **16**
Royal York Hotel **3**
Spadina House **22**
Toronto City Hall **12**
University of Toronto **15**

Parks and Gardens
The Beaches and
   Scarborough Bluffs **28**
Ontario Place **26**
Queen's Park **17**
Toronto Island **27**
Toronto Zoo **29**

Modern Architecture
CN Tower p172 **1**
Rogers Centre **2**

**Museums, Galleries,
and Concert Halls**
*Art Gallery of Ontario
   pp178–9* **11**
The Bata Shoe Museum **20**
Black Creek
   Pioneer Village **31**
Four Seasons Centre for
   the Performing Arts **5**
George R. Gardiner Museum
   of Ceramic Art **18**
Hockey Hall of Fame **4**
McMichael Canadian Art
   Collection **32**
Ontario Science Centre **30**
Roy Thomson Hall **8**
*Royal Ontario Museum
   pp184–5* **19**
Toronto Dominion Gallery
   of Inuit Art **6**

Shopping Areas
Kensington Market **14**
Queen Street West **10**
Yorkville **21**

GETTING AROUND

Toronto's public transportation is excellent. The subway lines follow the main arteries: Bloor/Danforth (east–west) and Yonge/University (north–south). Buses and streetcars serve the areas around each sub-way station. The GO Transit train service links Toronto to the suburbs.

TORONTO AND ENVIRONS

North York

Vaughan

Scarborough

Rexdale

Mississauga

Lake Ontario

0 km   5

0 miles   5

Toronto's CN Tower dominates the city skyline

LOCATOR MAP

KEY

⬛	Downtown: see pp176–7
⬛	Harbourfront: see pp170–71
✈	International airport
⛴	Ferry boarding point
🚆	Railroad station
Ⓜ	Subway station
ℹ	Visitor information
🅿	Parking
━━	Highway
━━	Major roads
──	Pedestrian walkway

SEE ALSO

• *Where to Stay* pp354–5

• *Where to Eat* pp378–81

For additional map symbols *see back flap*

Street-by-Street: Harbourfront

Toronto's harbourfront has had a varied history.
Lake Ontario once lapped against Front Street,
but the Victorians reclaimed 3 km (1.5 miles) of
land to accommodate their railroad yards and
warehouses. Ontario's exports and imports were
funneled through this industrial strip until the 1960s,
when trade declined. In the 1980s the harbourfront
had a new lease on life, when planners orchestrated
the redevelopment of what has now become
10 sq km (4 sq miles) of reclaimed land. It now
boasts grassy parks, walkways, smart apartments,
many of the city's best hotels, and a cluster of tourist
sights in and around the Harbourfront Centre.

★ **View from the CN Tower**
Once the world's tallest building, the CN Tower offers views of up to 160 km (100 miles) over Ontario, and a glass floor for those with iron nerves ❶

FRONT ST. W.

LAKE SHORE

Metro Toronto Convention Centre
Split into north and south arenas, the center is used for large-scale business shows as well as trade and consumer exhibitions for the public.

★ **Rogers Centre**
Using enough electricity to light the province of Prince Edward Island, a performance at the vast Rogers Centre stadium is an unforgettable experience ❷

Charter boats
Sailing out into Lake Ontario and around the three Toronto Islands provides fine views of the city. Small sailboats, motorboats, and tours are available.

0 m	150
0 yards	150

KEY

– – – Suggested route

For hotels and restaurants in this region see pp354–5 and pp378–81. For transport information see pp418–19

LOCATOR MAP
See pp168–9

Toronto Harbourfront
*The harbourfront is a pleasing and relaxing addition to the city.
Modern attractions consolidate Toronto's standing as the third-
largest theater and dance center in the world.*

Molson Amphitheatre
*Classical and modern
performances run through
the summer evenings in this
open-air concert venue.
Part of the Harbourfront
Centre arts complex, nearby
attractions include theater,
dance, and film screenings.*

The Gardiner Expressway
divides the city center from the
waterfront and leads west to
Niagara Falls *(see pp212–15).*

The Power Plant
Contemporary
Art Gallery hosts
changing exhi-
bitions of major
international
artists.

Queen's Quay
*The focus of activity on the
harborfront, Queen's Quay
is a lively area for visitors.
Lined with cafés and restaurants, the walkway offers lakeside views as well as street
performers and gift shops.*

STAR SIGHTS

★ Rogers Centre

★ CN Tower

CN Tower ❶

At 553 m (1,815 ft) high, the CN Tower was once the tallest free-standing structure in the world. In the 1970s, the Canadian Broadcasting Company (CBC) decided to build a new transmission mast in partnership with Canadian National (CN), the railroad conglomerate. The CN Tower was not originally designed as the world's tallest spire, but it so overwhelmed the city's visitors that it soon became one of Canada's prime tourist attractions. The tower houses the largest revolving restaurant in the world, which rotates fully every 72 minutes.

VISITORS' CHECKLIST

301 Front St. W. **Tel** 416 868 6937. ☐ 10am–10pm daily. ● Dec 25. www.cntower.ca

The Sky Pod is reached by its own elevator and is the highest accessible point on the tower at 447 m (1,465 ft).

The 360 Restaurant
Award-winning cuisine is available as the restaurant revolves, allowing diners a spectacular view while they dine.

The interior lookout level offers visitors the chance to observe the city in comfort, away from the wind; signs identify main Toronto landmarks.

The exterior lookout level is protected by steel grilles and illustrates how exposed the tower is, especially in windy weather.

The CN Tower from the Lake
The tower offers fantastic views in every direction. On a clear day it is possible to see as far south as Niagara Falls (see pp212–15).

Glass Floor
The ground is 342 m (1,122 ft) beneath this thick layer of reinforced glass, and even the courageous may feel a little daunted.

The outside elevators are glass-fronted and take visitors shooting up the outside of the Tower to the upper levels. Speeds take your breath away and make your ears pop; the elevators can reach the top in under a minute.

The inside staircase is the longest in the world, with 1,776 steps. Climbing the steps as part of a charity event is a popular fund-raising activity in Toronto.

View of the City from the Lookout Level
At 346 m (1,136 ft) above the city, the Look-out Level provides panoramas of Toronto from interior and exterior galleries.

Rogers Centre ❷

1 Blue Jay Way. *Tel 416 341 3034.*
🚊 Union. ◯ *daily.* 📷 ♿ ✓
www.rogerscentre.com

Opened in 1989, the Rogers
Centre was the first sports
stadium in the world to have a
fully rectractable roof. In good
weather, the stadium is open
to the elements, but in poor
conditions the roof moves into
position, protecting players and
crowd alike. This remarkable
feat of engineering is based on
simple principles; four gigantic
roof panels are mounted on
rails and take just twenty
minutes to cover the playing
area. The design is certainly
innovative and eminently practical, but the end result looks
sort of like a giant hazelnut.
However, the building's looks
are partially redeemed by a
matching pair of giant-sized
cartoon-sculptures on the
outside wall showing spectators
at an imaginary game, the
creation of a popular contemporary artist, Michael Snow.

The Rogers Centre is home
to two major sports teams, the
Toronto Argonauts from the
Canadian Football League,
and the Toronto Blue Jays of
Major League Baseball. The
Rogers Centre is also used for
special events and concerts.
Guided tours allow a close
look at the mechanics of the
roof and include a 20-minute
film outlining the story of its
ground-breaking construction.

Lavish interior lobby of the Royal York

Royal York ❸

100 Front St. W. *Tel 416 368 2511.*
🚊 *Union.* ♿

Dating from 1929, the Royal
York has long been Toronto's
preeminent hotel, its plush
luxury easily outshining its
rivals. It was built
opposite the city's main
train station for the
convenience of visiting
dignitaries, but for
thousands of
immigrants, the hotel
was the first thing
they saw of their new
city, giving it a
landmark resonance
beyond its immediate
commercial purpose.
The Royal York was
designed by the Montreal
architects Ross and
Macdonald in contemporary
Beaux Arts style with a

**Doorman of the
Royal York**

tumbling, irregular façade
that resembles a large
French château. Inside, the
public areas are lavish and
ornate, with slender galleries
providing extra grace and
charm. The Royal York has
been revamped over the years
and remains a favorite with
high-powered visitors,
which have included
visiting royalty.

Union Station, across
the street from the
Royal York, was also
designed by Ross and
Macdonald. The earlier
building of the two, it
shares a similar Beaux
Arts style. The long
and imposing stone
exterior is punctuated
by stone columns, and
on the inside, the cavernous
main hall has a grand
coffered ceiling supported by
22 sturdy marble pillars.

The retractable roof of the Rogers Centre rears above the playing field, site of many football and baseball games

For hotels and restaurants in this region see pp354–5 and pp378–81. For transport information see pp418–19

Modern exterior of the Four Seasons Centre for the Performing Arts

Hockey Hall of Fame ❹

Brookfield Place, 30 Yonge St.
Tel *416 360 7765.* 🚇 *Union Station.*
◯ *Jun–Sep: 9:30am–6pm Mon–Sat,*
10am–6pm Sun; Oct–May: 10am–
5pm Mon–Fri, 9:30am–6pm Sat,
10:30am–5pm Sun. ◑ *Jan 1,*
Dec 25. 🎦 ♿ **www**.hhof.com

The Hockey Hall of Fame is
a lavish tribute to Canada's
national sport, ice hockey *(see
p36)*. Hockey, both ice and
grass, originated in Canada;
from its simple winter
beginnings on frozen lakes and
ponds, the game now ignites
Canadian passions like no
other. The Hall of
Fame's ultra-modern
exhibition area is
inventive and
resourceful, with
different sections
devoted to particular
aspects of the game.
There are displays on
everything from the
jerseys of the great
players, including
Wayne Gretzky and
Mario Lemieux, to a replica of
the Montréal Canadiens' locker
room in the old Forum.

The Stanley Cup at the
Hockey Hall of Fame

Another section traces the
development of the goalie's
mask from its beginnings to the
elaborately painted versions of
today. Interactive displays
abound, and visitors can stop
pucks fired by virtual players.
A small theater shows films of
hockey's most celebrated
games. A separate area displays
a collection of trophies, including the Stanley Cup, hockey's
premier award, donated by
Lord Stanley in 1893.

Four Seasons Centre for the Performing Arts ❺

145 Queen St. W. **Tel** *416 363
8231.* 🚇 *Osgoode.* ♿
www.fourseasonscentre.ca

The Four Seasons Centre for
the Performing Arts is Canada's
first purpose-built opera and
ballet house. Completed in
2006, it is home to both the
Canadian Opera Company and
the National Ballet of Canada.
With the world's longest
freespan glass staircase and a
horseshoe-shaped, European
style auditorium featuring
phenomenal advancements in
modern engineering
and accoustical
design, it stages a
full range of operatic
repertoires, from
chamber pieces by
Mozart and Handel, to
some of the monumental
19th- and 20th-century
works, such as
Wagner's *Ring
Cycle*, which
require an orchestra
of over 100 musicians.

The world-class Canadian
Opera Company, under
the directorship of
Alexander Neef, is
the largest producer
of opera in Canada.
The National
Ballet of
Canada, with
Karen Kain as
Artistic Director,
is the country's
premiere dance
company, with
more than
60 dancers.

Toronto Dominion Gallery of Inuit Art ❻

79 Wellington St. West. **Tel** *416 982
8473.* 🚇 *Union Station.* ◯ *8am–
6pm daily (10am–4pm Sat, Sun).* ♿

The Toronto Dominion Centre
consists of five jet-black skyscrapers, a modern tribute to
the Toronto Dominion Bank.
The southern tower displays a
strong collection of Inuit Art
on two levels of its foyer. The
exhibits were assembled as a
centennial project in the 1960s.
They bought over 100 pieces
in a variety of materials, including caribou antler and walrus
ivory, but the kernel of the
collection is the stone carving.
Soapstone sculptures on display
show mythological beasts and
spirits as well as scenes from
everyday life. Some of the
finest were carved by Johnny
Inukpuk (b.1911), whose
Mother Feeding Child (1962)
and *Tattooed Woman* (1958)
have a raw, elemental force.

Mirvish Theatres ❼

260 and 300 King St. W. **Tel** *416
872 1212.* 🚇 *St. Andrew.* 🚋 *King
504/503.* ♿

In the 1960s, the Royal
Alexandra Theatre was about
to be flattened by bulldozers
when the flamboyant "Honest
Ed" Mirvish, the king of the
bargain store, came to the
rescue. Mirvish saved a fine
Edwardian theater, whose
luxurious interior of red velvet,
green marble, and flowing
scrollwork once made it the

The Royal Alexandra, one of the Mirvish Theatres

Toronto's fashionable café society on Queen Street West

most fashionable place in Toronto. Nowadays, the Royal Alex stages well-known plays and big-hit Broadway musicals. Evening performances are extremely popular, and booking ahead is required. Early arrivals can enjoy the original Edwardian features in the bar before the show. Next door is the Princess of Wales Theatre, which is used for Broadway-style musicals.

Roy Thomson Hall ❽

60 Simcoe St. *Tel* 416 872 4255.
St. Andrew. for performances.
http://roythomson.com

This Arthur Erickson-designed concert hall is home to the Toronto Symphony Orchestra, but jazz, pop, rock, and world music artists have also graced its stage. The Roy Thomson Hall is also used as a screening venue for the Toronto International Film Festival.

First Post Office ❾

260 Adelaide St. E. *Tel* 416 865 1833.
King, Queen. 501, 504.
Jarvis 141. 9am–4pm Mon–Fri, 10am–4pm Sat & Sun. by appt.

In 1829, the British House of Commons founded their colonial postal service and five

years later established a post office in a far-flung outpost of the newly created town of Toronto. Remarkably, Toronto's First Post Office has survived, weathering many attempts by the city to have it demolished. The only remaining example in the world of a post office dating from the British North American postal era still in operation, the First Post Office functions fully. Visitors make the trip to write a letter with a quill pen and seal it themselves with hot wax. Today's mail, however, is processed by the national service, Canada Post. After a devastating fire in 1978, the building was refurbished to its former carved and decorated appearance using historical city archive records.

Young visitors on Queen Street West

Queen Street West ❿

Osgoode. Queen 501.

Through the day and into the small hours of the morning, Queen Street West buzzes. Students and trendsetters reinvigorated this old warehouse area in the 1980s, but nowadays the street is more varied, with chic designer stores, downbeat bars, and stylish cafés mixed in with more mainstream offerings from the big chain stores. The chief merrymaking is concentrated between University and Bathurst, a good place for budget restaurants and bars.

Worker at Toronto's First Post Office stamping mail by hand

Street-by-Street: Downtown

Throughout the 19th century, Yonge Street was the commercial focus of Toronto, lined with scores of shops and suppliers. It also separated the city ethnically. In 1964, with the building of the new City Hall and Nathan Phillips Square just across from Old City Hall, Toronto's center of gravity shifted to Queen Street. South of Queen Street lay the banking district, where old Victorian buildings were replaced from the 1960s onward by gleaming concrete-and-glass tower blocks. The re-invigorated Harbourfront, with its yachts and cafés, provides light relief from the busy atmosphere. Yonge Street is now best known for the Eaton Centre emporium, one of the world's biggest malls.

Textile Museum of Canada
This international collection features over 12,000 examples of fabrics, embroidery, and clothing through the ages.

Campbell House Museum
This 19th-century home is a period piece from the days of the Victorian bourgeoisie.

KEY

– – – Suggested route

MCCAUL STREET

ST. PATRICK STREET

SIMCOE STREET

UNIVERSITY AVENUE

★ **Art Gallery of Ontario**
With exhibits ranging from the 14th to the 21st centuries, the AGO is also home to a number of works by Edgar Degas. ⑪

STAR SIGHTS

★ Art Gallery of Ontario

★ Toronto City Hall

Toronto Eaton Centre
If Toronto has a specific core, it is outside the Eaton Centre shopping mall at the Yonge and Dundas intersection. Its size has made it a tourist attraction in its own right.

LOCATOR MAP
See Toronto Map pp168–9

Yonge Street
is the main north–south thoroughfare of the city.

Church of the Holy Trinity
This charming Anglican church was built in the 19th century and features an elegant interior.

Nathan Phillips Square
is a lively gathering place for concerts, festivals, and civic celebrations.

0 meters 100
0 yards 100

★ Toronto City Hall
Open since 1965, this controversial development has slowly become popular with locals, who use the plaza as a skating rink in winter 12

Old City Hall
In sharp contrast to its ultra-modern replacement across the street, the elegant 19th-century Old City Hall now operates as a provincial courthouse.

Art Gallery of Ontario ⑪

Founded in 1900, the Art Gallery of Ontario holds one of Canada's most extensive collections of fine art and modern sculpture. This modern structure houses European works by Rembrandt, Gainsborough, van Gogh, and Picasso; a superb collection of Canadian art, including the Group of Seven work *(see pp164–5);* Inuit art; and the world's largest public collection of works by British sculptor Henry Moore. In 2008 the gallery reopened after a major expansion, designed by architect Frank Gehry, to accommodate an unprecedented gift of 2,000 works from a private collection.

Hina and Fatu (1892), Paul Gauguin

★ **African Art Collection**
This late-18th-/early-19th-century reliquary figure from Gabon is just one of many exhibits in the African Art Collection that aims to show the relationships between art and culture in Africa.

★ **Henry Moore Sculpture**
The museum houses the world's largest public collection of works by Henry Moore, including Draped Reclining Figure *(1952–3).*

Massacre of the Innocents *(c.1609–11)*
Peter Paul Rubens's early 17th-century masterpiece, discovered in 2001, is a highlight of the European Art collections.

KEY

- ☐ Contemporary art
- ☐ European art
- ☐ Temporary exhibitions
- ☐ Canadian art
- ☐ African art
- ☐ Prints, drawings, and photographs
- ☐ Nonexhibition space

Dundas Street

STAR EXHIBITS

- ★ The West Wind
- ★ Henry Moore Sculpture
- ★ African Art Collection

Fourth floor

Third floor

Second floor

Fifth floor

VISITORS' CHECKLIST

317 Dundas St. W. *Tel* 416 979 6648. 🚇 St. Patrick. 🚌 505. ◯ 10am–5:30pm Tue–Sun (to 8:30pm Wed). 🎟 ♿ 🚫 📷 🍴 🖥 🏪 www.ago.net

Revamped Façade

The modern extension of the Art Gallery of Ontario was designed by Toronto-born architect Frank Gehry. It is his first building in Canada.

★ **The West Wind** (*1917*)
Tom Thomson's painting inspired a distinctive Canadian style exemplified by the "Group of Seven."

First floor/ street level

Main entrance

Concourse

GALLERY GUIDE

The second floor houses several excellent collections of Canadian painting, with works by the "Group of Seven" (see pp164–5), and Inuit art. It also houses a significant collection of African art and the Henry Moore Centre, which is home to Moore's sculptures, bronzes, and plaster casts. European art is found mainly on the first floor.

Scene in the Northwest (*c.1845*)
This painting by Canadian artist Paul Kane shows British surveyor Captain John Henry Lefroy. It is part of the collection of Canadian art from the middle of the 19th century.

Built in the 1960s, the ultra-modern design of Toronto City Hall is internationally renowned

Toronto City Hall ⑫

100 Queen St. W. & Bay St. *Tel* 416 392 8016. 🚇 Queen, Osgoode. 🚋 Queen 501. ⏱ 8:30am–4:30pm Mon–Fri. ♿

Completed in 1964, Toronto's City Hall was designed by the award-winning Finnish architect Viljo Revell. At the official opening, the Prime Minister Lester Pearson announced, "It is an edifice as modern as tomorrow," but for many cityfolk tomorrow had come too soon and there were howls of protests from several quarters. Even now, after nearly 40 years, the building appears uncompromisingly modern. It is the epitome of 1960s urban planning, with two curved concrete and glass towers framing a central circular building where the Toronto councils meet. Nearby, the Old City Hall is a grand 19th-century neo-Romanesque edifice whose towers and columns are carved with intricate curling patterns.

Chinatown ⑬

🚋 Dundas 505, College 506, Spadina 510.

The Chinese community in Toronto numbers around 283,000, nearly ten percent of the city's total population. There have been several waves of Chinese migration to Canada, the first to British Columbia in the late 1850s during the Gold Rush. The first Chinese to arrive in Toronto came at the end of the 19th century as workers on the Canadian Pacific Railway, settling in towns along the rail route. The Chinese found work in the Toronto laundries, factories, and on the railways. The last immigration wave saw prosperous Hong Kong Chinese come to live in Toronto in the 1990s. Chinese Canadians inhabit every part of the city but are concentrated in four Chinatowns, the largest and liveliest of which is focused on Spadina Avenue, between Queen and College streets, and along Dundas Street, west of the Art Gallery of Ontario. These few city blocks are immediately different from their surroundings. The sights, sounds, and smells of the neighborhood are reminiscent not of Toronto but of Hong Kong. Stores and stalls spill over the sidewalks, offering a bewildering variety of Chinese delicacies, and at night bright neon signs advertise dozens of delicious restaurants.

Vivid restaurant signs in Chinatown

Kensington Market ⑭

Baldwin St. & Augusta Ave. 🚋 Dundas 505, College 506, Spadina 510.

Kensington Market is one of Toronto's most distinctive and ethnically diverse residential areas. It was founded at the turn of the 20th century by East European immigrants, who crowded into the patchwork of modest houses near the junction of Spadina Avenue and Dundas Street, and then spilled out into the narrow streets to sell their wares. The bazaar they established in their small 1930s houses has been the main feature of the area ever since.

Today, Jewish, Polish, and Russian stall owners and shopkeepers rub shoulders with Portuguese, Jamaican, East Indian, Chinese, and Vietnamese traders in a vibrant street scene that always excites the senses. The focal point of this open-air market is Kensington Avenue, whose lower half, just off Dundas Street, is crammed with thrift shops selling all manner of trendy retro bargains, from original punk gear to flares. Kensington Avenue's upper half is packed with fresh food stores filled with produce from every corner of the globe, ranging from iced fish to stacks of cheeses and exotic fruits.

A Torontonian samples exotic nuts in the bazaar of Kensington Market

Façade of the Ontario Parliament Building, home of the provincial legislature since 1893

University of Toronto ⑮

2/ King's College Circle. **Tel** 416 978 2011. 🚇 St. George, Queen's Park. 🚋 College 506. ♿

The University of Toronto grew out of a Royal Charter granted in 1827 by King George IV to Toronto's King's College. Seen by the church as challenging its control of education, the new institution weathered accusations of godlessness and proceeded to swallow its rivals, becoming in the process one of Canada's most prestigious universities.

This unusual history explains the rambling layout of the present campus, a leafy area sprinkled with colleges. The best-looking university buildings are near the west end of Wellesley Street. Here, on Hart House Circle, lie the delightful quadrangles and ivy-clad walls of Hart House (1919), built in imitation of some of the colleges of Oxford and Cambridge universities in Britain, and the Soldiers' Tower, a neo-Gothic memorial to those students who died in both world wars. Nearby, King's College Circle contains University College, an imposing neo-Romanesque edifice dating from 1859, Knox College with its rough gray sandstone masonry, and the fine rotunda of the university's

Convocation Hall. A visit to the campus can be peacefully rounded off by a short stroll along Philosophers' Walk, where the manicured lawns lead to Bloor Street West.

Reminiscent of old British universities, the University of Toronto

Ontario Parliament Building ⑯

Queen's Park. **Tel** 416 325 7500. 🚇 Queen's Park. 🚋 College 506. ⏰ 8:30am–5pm Mon–Fri, 9am–4:30pm Sat & Sun. ♿ 🎥 10am–4pm.

There is nothing modest about the Ontario Parliament Building, a vast pink sandstone edifice opened in 1893 that dominates the end of University Avenue. Ontario's

elected representatives had a point to make. The province was a small but exceedingly loyal part of the British Empire and clamored to make its mark and had the money to do so. Consequently, the Members of Provincial Parliament (MPPs) commissioned this immensely expensive structure in the Romanesque Revival style. Finished in 1892, its main façade is a panoply of towers, arches, and rose windows decorated with relief carvings and set beneath a series of high-pitched roofs.

The interior is of matching grandeur. Gilded classical columns frame the main staircase and enormous stained-glass windows illuminate long and richly timbered galleries. The chamber is a lavish affair, with a wealth of fine wooden carving that carries epithets urging good behavior, such as "Boldly and Rightly," and "By Courage, not by Craft."

In 1909, a fire razed the west wing, which was rebuilt in Italian marble. The stone was very expensive, so the MPPs were annoyed to find that a large amount of the marble was blemished by dinosaur fossils, which can still be seen today in the west hallway. Visitors can sometimes watch the parliament in session.

The Parliament Buildings, viewed from inner-city Queen's Park

Queen's Park ⑰

College St. & University Ave.
Tel *416 325 7500.* 📍 *College 506.*
📍 *Queen's Park.* ♿

Despite being ringed by a road that links two of downtown's busiest streets, Queen's Park is a peaceful and pleasant grassy space, perfect for catching your breath when visiting the closely packed sights in the surrounding area. The park is fringed to the west by the 19th-century buildings of the University, while the Royal Ontario Museum and the George R. Gardiner Museum of Ceramic Art lie to the north. Since the Legislative Buildings lie right in the middle of the park, its tranquility is occasionally broken by political protesters and special interest groups loudly proclaiming their displeasure with the provincial government.

Gardiner Museum of Ceramic Art ⑱

111 Queen's Park. **Tel** *416 586 8080.*
📍 *Museum.* 🕐 *10am–6pm Mon & Thu; 10am–9pm Fri, 10am–5pm Sat & Sun.* ● *Jan 1, Dec 25.* 📷 ♿
www.gardinermuseum.on.ca

Opened in 1984, the Gardiner Museum of Ceramic Art is the only showcase of its kind in North America dedicated solely to pottery and porcelain. Skillfully displayed, the collection traces the history of ceramics, with a detailed focus on its principal developmental stages. These start with Pre-Columbian pottery, and the museum has fascinating displays of ancient pieces from Peru and Mexico that incorporate several grimacing fertility gods.

The Greeting Harlequin Meissen ceramic figure

Examples of brightly colored *maiolica* (glazed, porous pottery), includes painted pots made first in Mallorca, then Italy, from the 13th to the 16th centuries. Cheerfully decorated everyday wares are complemented by later Renaissance pieces relating classical myths and history. English delftware (tin-glazed earthenware) is also well represented in the collection. The Renaissance pieces gathered from Italy, Germany, and England are superb – particularly the collection of *commedia dell'arte* figures.

These are derived from the Italian theatrical tradition of comic improvisation with a set of stock characters, notably the joker Harlequin. Intricately decorated in rainbow colors, these figurines were placed on dinner tables by the aristocracy to delight, impress, or even to woo their special guests.

Porcelain here is stunning, with many examples of exquisite Meissen from 1700 to 1780. Packed in its own specially made leather carrying case to accompany a fine lady owner on her travels, a special feature is the embellished tea and chocolate service dating from the early 18th century. Each tiny cup has individual, intricate sailing scenes surrounded in gold. The porcelain collection also contains over 100 carved or molded scent bottles from all over Europe.

Royal Ontario Museum ⑲

See pp184–5.

The Bata Shoe Museum ⑳

327 Bloor St. W. **Tel** *416 979 7799.*
📍 *St. George.* 🕐 *10am–5pm Mon–Wed, Fri & Sat, 10am–8pm Thu, noon–5pm Sun.* ● *Jan 1, Good Friday, Jul 1, Dec 25.* 📷 ♿
www.batashoemuseum.ca

The Bata Shoe Museum was opened in 1995 to display the extraordinary range of footwear collected by Sonja Bata, a member of the eponymous shoe manufacturing family, a worldwide concern that sells footwear in 60 countries. To be sure her collection was seen to best effect, Sonja had the prestigious contemporary Canadian architect Raymond Moriyama design the building – an angular modern affair complete with unlikely nooks

The modern exterior of the Bata Shoe Museum

and crannies created to look like a chic shoebox.

The collection is spread over several small floors and features three special exhibitions developing a particular theme, as well as regularly rotated items selected from the museum's substantial permanent collection. More than a temple to fashion, the museum treats shoes as important ethnological pieces, illustrating not only changes in technology, but also shifting values and attitudes. Entire ways of life can be gleaned from the design of these beautiful objects, from climate and profession to gender and religion.

One fixed feature in the museum is the exhibition entitled "All About Shoes," which provides the visitor with an overview of the functions and evolution of footwear. It begins with a plaster cast of the earliest-known footprint, discovered four million years after it was made in Tanzania, and has an interesting section on medieval pointed shoes. A second permanent feature is the section on celebrity footwear. This rotating display could include Marilyn Monroe's red stiletto heels, a pair of Elton John's platforms, or Michael Johnson's gold lamé sprinting shoes. A fashion section, called Fashion Afoot, includes *haute couture* shoes by Roger Vivier and Christian Louboutin. There is also a display of unusual and improbable footwear including unique French

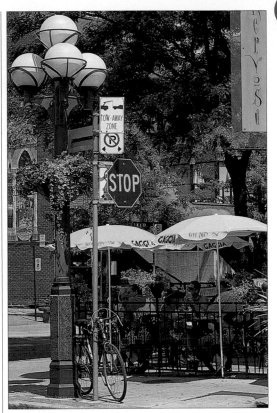

A lazy Sunday afternoon at Café Nervosa in trendy Yorkville

chestnut-crushing boots and a pair of US army boots made for use in the Vietnam War, whose sole is shaped to imitate the footprint of an enemy Vietcong irregular.

Yorkville ㉑

🚇 Bay.

In the 1960s, tiny Yorkville, in the center of the city, was the favorite haunt of Toronto's hippies. With regular appearances by counter-cultural figures such as Joni Mitchell, it was similar to New York's Greenwich Village. The hippies have now moved on, and Yorkville's modest brick and timber terrace houses have either been colonized by upscale shops and fashionable restaurants, or converted into bijou townhouses. Designer boutiques, specialty bookstores, private

art galleries, fine jewelers, and quality shoe stores all jam into the neighborhood, attracting shoppers in droves. The area is a lovely place to sit at an outdoor café, nursing a cappuccino and watching the crowds. Yorkville and Cumberland Avenues are the center of all this big spending, as are the elegant and discreet shopping complexes that lead off them, especially the deluxe Hazelton Lanes, at the corner of Yorkville Avenue, which houses trendy upscale brands. The dropout philosophy has been thoroughly replaced by very chic stores – some of the most exclusive retail outlets in the country are found here. Although the recession in the 1990s affected trade somewhat, the area is still prosperous and thriving. Café society really takes off at night, but Yorkville can be an expensive place to have fun.

Traditional Indian *Paduka* footwear, the Bata Shoe Museum

Royal Ontario Museum ⑲

Founded in 1912, the Royal Ontario Museum (ROM)
holds a vast and extraordinarily wide-ranging collection
drawn from the fields of fine and applied art, the natural
sciences, and archaeology. Special highlights include the
dinosaur gallery, and an Asian Arts gallery featuring
Chinese sculpture and architecture and Japanese art
and culture. The ROM has undergone a major
transformation over the years, and many galleries have
been restored. The Michael Lee-Chin Crystal addition
is a bold chrystalline formation designed by architect
Daniel Libeskind, which contains a main museum
entrance and cutting-edge galleries.

KEY

- ☐ Samuel Hall Currelly Gallery
- ☐ Asian and Middle Eastern Arts
- ☐ Natural History
- ☐ Textiles, costume and glass
- ☐ Canada Galleries
- ☐ World Cultures
- ☐ Michael Lee-Chin Crystal spaces
- ☐ Non-exhibition space

GALLERY GUIDE

*The museum has an exceptional
array of themed galleries, spanning
both World Cultures and Natural
History. With six million objects in
the ROM's collections, there is something new to discover around every
corner. The Canada Galleries are
located on the first floor.*

The futuristic-looking Royal Ontario Museum

The Green Room
*This elegant English parlour
dates from the 1750s. One
of several room settings
featured in the European
galleries, it boasts the
original green paneled
walls popular among the
gentry of the time.*

Learning Centre
& Library

Canada Gallery: First Peoples
*This spacious gallery celebrates Canadian
culture, with a dynamic approach to the
country's aboriginal traditions. Many
of the unique and vibrant aboriginal
artifacts are displayed for the first time.*

STAR EXHIBITS

★ Dinosaur Gallery

★ Galleries of Africa:
  Egypt

Level 1
(below)

Theater

Garfield Weston
Exhibition Hall

Fifth floor
Restaurant
Lounge

Fourth
floor

Institute for
Contemporary
Culture

Curatorial
Centre

Third
floor

Second floor

Museum Store

First floor
(street level)

Main entrance

★ Galleries of Africa: Egypt
*With a large collection of
mummies, burial masks,
and domestic artifacts, the
Egyptian collection contains
the remains of a buried court
musician, in a painted
golden coffin so intricate that
scholars dare not open it.*

Stuffed Albatross
*This huge bird has a
wingspan of 3 m
(9 ft). It is a main
feature of the bird
gallery, which offers
interactive exhibits.*

Bat Cave
*Painstakingly reconstructed
from a 4-km (2-mile) long
Jamaican bat cave, some
3,000 wax and vinyl bats
fly to greet the visitor in
this eerie darkened cavern.*

★ Dinosaur Gallery
*The most popular gallery in the
ROM is now on the second floor of
the Michael Lee-Chin Crystal, with
dinosaur skeletons set in simulations
of the Jurassic Age and animation
techniques as used in the 1990s
blockbuster* Jurassic Park.

Spadina Museum, Historic House & Gardens ㉒

285 Spadina Rd. *Tel* 416 392 6910. 77+, 127. Dupont. Jan–Apr: noon–5pm, Sat & Sun; May–Aug: noon–5pm, Tue–Sun; Sep–Dec: noon–4pm, Tue–Fri; noon–5pm, Sat & Sun. Mon; Dec 25, 26, Jan 1. obligatory.

James Austin, first president of the Toronto Dominion Bank, had this elegant Victorian family home built on the bluff overlooking Spadina Avenue in 1866. The last of the Austins, Anna, moved out in 1982. She left the building, its contents and gardens to the Historical Board of Toronto. This authentic family home illustrates the decorative tastes of four gen-

erations of well-to-do Canadians. The general ambience appeals, but there are several enjoyable features, notably the Art Nouveau frieze in the Billiard Room and a trap door in the Palmroom that allowed gardeners to tend to the plants unseen by the family.

The front door of Spadina House with garlanded Victorian columns

Fort York ㉔

100 Garrison Rd. *Tel* 416 392 6907. 511, 509. daily. Good Fri, Dec 18–Jan 2 approx.

The British built Fort York in 1793 to reinforce their control of Lake Ontario and, from this, Toronto grew. The weaknesses of the fort were exposed when the Americans overran it after a long battle in the War of 1812 (*see p47*). After the war, the British strengthened the fort, and its garrison gave a boost to the local economy. The military compound has been painstakingly restored, and its barracks, old powder magazine, and officers' quarters make for a pleasant visit. It is the largest collection of War of 1812 buildings in Canada.

Casa Loma ㉓

This unusual Gothic revival house was designed by E.J. Lennox, the man responsible for Toronto's Old City Hall. With its combination of architectural elements, the house is a remarkable tribute to Sir Henry Pellatt (1859–1939), one of the most influential industrialists of early 20th century Canada. He made a fortune in hydroelectric power during the early 1900s, harnessing the strength of Niagara Falls for electricity. In 1906, Pellatt decided to build himself a castle. Three years and Can$3.5 million later, construction was halted due to the outbreak of World War I.

The Study hid secret doors in its wooden panels, one leading to Sir Henry's wine cellar.

★ **The Great Hall**
Oak beams support a ceiling 18-m (60-ft) high, in a hall featuring a 12-m (40-ft) tall bay window.

The Terrace looks over delightful formal gardens and a fountain against a backdrop of hills and rhododendron forest.

The Bathroom was designed for Sir Henry's personal use. It contains a free-standing shower with six heads and features lavish decoration.

Fresh vegetables on sale in Little Italy

Little Italy

College St. W. 512. 207
Queen's Quay W. 416 203 2500.

There are half a million
people of Italian descent
resident in Toronto. The first
major wave of Italian migrants
arrived between 1885 and
1924. Italians have been in
Toronto since 1830, and their
sense of community, together

with the instability of
Italy after World War II,
led to another large
influx in the 1940s
and 1950s. Italians live
and work in every
corner of the city, but
there is a focus for
the community in the
lively "Corso Italia,"
or Little Italy, whose
assorted stores, cafés,
and restaurants run along
St. Clair Avenue West.

Though the architecture is at
best unremarkable, many
houses are brightly painted in
the traditional colors of red,
green, and white. More European touches appear in the
proliferation of espresso bars,
and cinemas showing Italian
films. The typically Mediterranean food offered by the
many sidewalk cafés is terrific.

Ontario Place

955 Lakeshore Blvd. W. *Tel* 416 314
9900. Union Station. 509, 511.
mid-May–Sep: 10am–midnight.
www.ontarioplace.com

This excellent theme park will
appeal to families with young
children. Built over Lake
Ontario on three artificial
islets, the clean and fairly
tame fun is largely waterbased
with paddle boats, log flumes,
water slides, and splash
ponds. The atmosphere
changes at night when large
pop concerts are staged at the
Molson Amphitheatre. The
globular Cinesphere houses
the first ever permanent IMAX
theater. This large format
cinema technology was
developed in Toronto by the
IMAX Corporation in 1967.

**Façade of house and
formal gardens**
*Five acres (2 ha) of garden
add to the charm of the
estate with perennial
borders, roses, lawns,
and woodland.*

VISITORS' CHECKLIST

1 Austin Terrace. *Tel* 416 923 11
71. Dupont. 9:30am–5pm
daily. Jan 1, Dec 25.
www.casaloma.org

★ Conservatory
*White walls offset the
Victorian stained-glass
dome. The marble flower-
beds conceal steam pipes
for the rare plants.*

STAR SIGHTS

★ The Great Hall

★ Conservatory

Visitors on the bicycling paths on the Toronto Islands

The Toronto Islands ㉗

🚢 Queen's Quay. 🛈 207 Queen's Quay W. 416 397 2628.
www.toronto.ca/parks/island

In Lake Ontario, just offshore from the city, the three low-lying Toronto Islands, connected by footbridges, shelter Toronto's harbor and provide easy-going recreation in a car-free environment. Here, amid the cool lake breezes, visitors can escape the extremes of the summer heat, which can reach up to 35°C (95°F). In good weather there are views of the top of the CN Tower *(see p172)*.

It takes about half an hour to walk from one end of the islands to the other. In the east is Ward's Island, a sleepy residential area with parkland and wilderness; Centre Island, home to the Centreville Amusement Park for children, is in the middle, and to the west lies the isle of Hanlan's Point with the Islands' best beach.

The Beaches and Scarborough Bluffs ㉘

Beaches 🚋 Queen 501. **Bluffers Park** 🚇 Victoria Park, then 🚌 Kingston Rd 12+. 🛈 207 Queen's Quay W. 416 203 2500.

The Beaches is one of Toronto's most beguiling neighborhoods, its narrow leafy streets running up from the lakeshore and lined by attractive brick houses with verandas. The area lies to the east of downtown, between Woodbine Avenue and Victoria Park Avenue. Queen Street East, the main thoroughfare, is liberally sprinkled with excellent cafés and designer clothes shops. The Beaches was a restrained and quiet neighborhood, but its long, sandy beach and boardwalk have made it extremely fashionable – real estate prices have risen dramatically. Rollerblading and cycling are popular here – a 3-km (2-mile) path travels through the area and is very busy in summer, as is the large public swimming pool. The waters of Lake Ontario are not ideal for swimming, but those planning to do so can call 416 392 7161 for updated water-quality reports. Windsurfing boards can be rented easily.

At its eastern end, the Beaches borders Scarborough, the large suburb whose principal attraction is also along the rocky lakeshore. Here, the striking Scarborough Bluffs, outcrops of rock made from ancient sands and clay, track along Lake Ontario for 16 km (10 miles). A series of parks provides access: Scarborough Bluffs and the Cathedral Bluffs parks offer great views of jagged cliffs, and Bluffers Park is ideal for picnics and beach trips. Layers of sediment from five different geological periods can be seen in the rocks around the park.

Toronto Zoo ㉙

361A Old Finch Ave., Scarborough.
Tel 416 392 5900. 🚇 Kennedy, then 🚌 86A (in summer). ⏰ May–Sep: 9am–7pm daily; Sep–Apr: 9am–6pm daily. ⏰ Dec 25. 🎫 ♿ 📷
www.torontozoo.com

Toronto has one of the world's best zoos. It occupies a large slice of the Rouge River Valley, and is easily accessible by public transportation and car.

The animals are grouped according to their natural habitats, both outside, amid the mixed forest and flatlands of the river valley, and inside within a series of large, climate-controlled pavilions.

Visitors can tour the zoo by choosing one of the carefully marked trails, or hop aboard the Zoomobile, a 30-minute ride with commentary that gives an excellent overview. It takes about four hours to see a good selection of animals, including such Canadian species as moose, caribou, and grizzly bear. Splash Island provides a spot for young visitors to cool off in the water, amid walrus and beaver sculptures.

A mother and baby orangutan at Toronto Zoo

A tinsmith takes a break outside his store in Black Creek Pioneer Village

Ontario Science Centre ⓰

770 Don Mills Rd. *Tel* 416 696 3177. Eglinton or Pape, then Eglinton 100 or Don Mills 25. 10am–5pm daily. Dec 25 www.osc.on.ca

One of Toronto's most popular sights, the Ontario Science Centre attracts children in droves. They come for the center's interactive displays and hands-on exhibits exploring and investigating all manner of phenomena, from the Solar System to the human brain. Attractions include a spelunking cave, a science arcade, and an IMAX theater. Visitors can land on the moon, travel to the end of the universe, or have hair-raising fun on a Van de Graaff generator.

Black Creek Pioneer Village ⓱

Cnr Steeles Ave. W. & Jane St. *Tel* 416 736 1733. Finch, then 60. May & Jun: 9:30am–4:30pm Mon–Fri, 10am–5pm Sat & Sun; Jul–Sep: 10am–5pm daily; Sep–Dec: 9:30–4pm Mon–Fri, 10am–4:30pm Sat & Sun. Jan–May; Dec 25.

Over the years, some 40 19th-century buildings have been moved to historic Black Creek Pioneer Village in the northwest of the city

from other parts of Ontario. Inevitably, the end result is not entirely realistic – no Ontario village ever looked quite like this – but this living history showpiece is still great fun. Staff in period costume demonstrate traditional skills such as candlemaking, baking, and printing. Among the more interesting buildings are the elegant Doctor's House from 1860, and the Lasky Emporium general store, which is open and trading, selling baking products to visitors. The Tinsmith Shop is manned by skilled craftsmen, and there is a Masonic Lodge meeting room too.

Four buildings are credited to Daniel Stong, a 19th-century pioneer; his pig house, smoke house, and two contrasting homes – the first and earlier dwelling is a crude log shack, the second a civilized house with a brick fireplace, outside of which is a herb garden.

McMichael Canadian Art Collection ⓲

10365 Islington Ave., Kleinburg. *Tel* (905) 893 1121. Islington, then 37, then 13 (limited service). 10am–4pm Mon–Sun. Dec 25. www.mcmichael.com

On the edge of Kleinburg, about 30 minutes' drive north of downtown Toronto, Robert and Signe McMichael built themselves a fine log-and-stone dwelling overlooking the forests of the Humber River Valley. The McMichaels were also avid collectors of Canadian art, and in 1965 they donated their house and paintings to the government. The art collection has been greatly increased and, with over 6,000 pieces, is now one of the most extensive in the province.

Most of the McMichael is devoted to the work of the Group of Seven (see pp164–5), with a whole string of rooms displaying an eclectic selection of their works. The keynote paintings are characteristically raw and forceful landscapes illustrating the wonders of the Canadian wilderness. Each of the group has been allocated a separate area, and both Tom

Bill Vazan's "Shibagau Shard" at the McMichael

Thomson (a famous precursor of the group) and Lawren Harris are well represented. There are also sections devoted to contemporary Inuit and Native American art, including the sculpture *Bases Stolen from the Cleveland Indians and a Captured Yankee* (1989) by the artist Gerald McMaster (b.1953).

The log and stone façade of the McMichael Art Collection building

OTTAWA AND EASTERN ONTARIO

Eastern Ontario is justly famous for its history and natural beauty. The myriad lakes and waterways that dominate the landscape here once served as trade highways through the wilderness for native people and explorers. Today they form a beautiful natural playground, with spectacular opportunities for outdoor activities such as boating, fishing, hiking, and skiing. The St. Lawrence is one of the world's great waterways and has its source near the small, historic city of Kingston. North of Lake Ontario lies the Canadian Shield, with the ancient lakes, rocks, and forest that epitomize Canada. A favorite with many Canadian vacationers, Algonquin Provincial Park is one of the country's most famous wilderness areas. Also popular is the picturesque Kawartha Lakes region. Rising majestically over the Ottawa River, Canada's capital is a storehouse of national history and stately architecture that attracts over 7.7 million visitors each year.

SIGHTS AT A GLANCE

Historic Towns and Cities
Barry's Bay ⑬
Combermere ⑪
Eganville ⑫
The Haliburton Highlands ⑩
Kingston ⑤
North Bay ⑮

Ottawa ①
Prescott ③
Upper Canada Village ②

National and Provincial Parks
Algonquin Provincial Park ⑭
Serpent Mounds Park ⑧

Islands and Waterways
Kawartha Lakes ⑨
Prince Edward County ⑦
Rideau Canal ⑥
The Thousand Islands ④

KEY
✈ International airport
═ Highway
▬ Major road
— Major rail routes
·— International border

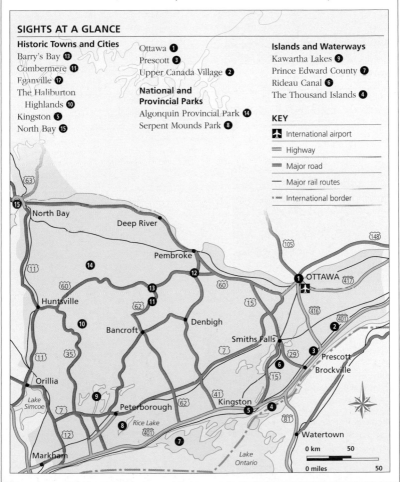

◁ Pleasure boats on the Rideau Canal at night overlooked by Ottawa's imposing Parliament Buildings

Street-by-Street: Ottawa ❶

Ottawa was a compromise choice for Canada's capital, picked in part because of the rivalry between the English and French and the cities that grew into today's urban giants, Toronto and Montreal. This compromise has from its foundation in 1826, grown into a city with an identity all its own. Named capital of the Dominion of Canada in 1857, Ottawa has a fine setting on the banks of the Ottawa and Rideau rivers. Far more than just the political capital, the city has grown into a mix of English and French residents and historic and modern buildings with plenty of attractions to keep its six million annual visitors busy.

A member of the RCMP leading his horse by the Parliament buildings

Centennial Flame was first lit in 1967 to commemorate a century o Confederation. It burns continually

★ **Parliament Buildings**
The Changing of the Guard takes place outside daily from June to August. The spectacular cere-mony adds to the grandeur of this seat of government.

WELLINGTON STREET

Rideau Canal
Built in the early 19th century, the Canal is now a playground for visitors, its banks lined with grassy cycling and walking paths.

National War Memorial
Annually, on November 11, a memorial service takes place here to honor Canada's war veterans.

Fairmont Chateau Laurier
is a luxury hotel, and arguably Canada's most famous. It has offered sumptuous accommo-dation to Canada's great and good since it was built in 1912.

Major's Hill Park
This peaceful, open-air space in the heart of the busy capital is marked by a statue of an Anishinabe scout, in honor of the First Nations' role in the development of Canada.

VISITORS' CHECKLIST

785,000. ✈ 18 km (12 miles) south of the city. 🚌 265 Catherine St. 🚆 200 Tremblay Rd. 🛈 Canada's Capital Information Centre, 90 Wellington St. (613) 239 5000. 🎿 Winterlude (Feb), Canadian Tulip Festival (May). **www**.canadascapital.gc.ca

Nepean Point
is a spot from which the whole of central Ottawa can be seen.

0 meters 100
0 yards 100

KEY

– – – Suggested route

Royal Canadian Mint
This Can$20 Olympic skiing coin was created by the Mint as a souvenir for the 1988 Winter Olympic Games in Calgary. The mint produces only special edition and investment pieces.

★ National Gallery
Featuring more than 25,000 artworks, this is the country's premier collection of the fine arts, housed in this outstanding granite and glass building.

STAR SIGHTS

★ National Gallery

★ Parliament Buildings

Exploring Ottawa

The core of the capital is relatively contained, and many of the top sights can be easily accessed on foot. Traveling south through the city, the Rideau Canal is Ottawa's recreation ground year round, from boating and strolling during summer to skating across its icy surface in the freezing Canadian winter. The National Arts Centre is a focus for theater, opera, and ballet; history and art buffs can spend days visiting museums and galleries, both large and small. Ottawa is a city of festivals too; notably Winterlude, a three-weekend February celebration, while in spring the Canadian Tulip Festival transforms the city into a sea of flowers. Canada Day celebrations, on July 1, also attract thousands of visitors.

Antique doll's dress, Bytown

Away from downtown, it may seem that the suburban National Capital Region is overflowing with museums for every enthusiast. Attractions include the Central Experimental Farm and the Canada Aviation Museum.

Cash register from a 19th-century shop at the Bytown Museum

Ottawa's majestic Gothic Parliament Buildings

🏛 Parliament Buildings

Parliament Hill. **Tel** *(613) 992 4793.*
⬜ *daily.* ◑ *Jul 1.*
Dominating the skyline, the country's government buildings overlook downtown Ottawa in a stately manner. Undaunted by the tall buildings that have crept up around them in the 150 years since they became Ottawa's center of power, the East and West Blocks glow green above the city because of their copper roofing. The neo-gothic sandstone buildings were completed in 1860. Located on a 50-m (165-ft) hill, the Parliament offers a view of the Ottawa River. The Parliament

Buildings are distinctly reminiscent of London's Westminster, both in their Victorian Neo-Gothic style and in their position. Partly destroyed in a fire in 1916, all the buildings are now restored to their former grandeur.

The Parliament Buildings can be toured year round, including when the Government, Commons, and Senate are in session. Hand-carved sandstone and limestone characterize the interior of the government chambers. In the summertime, Mounties patrol the neat, grassy grounds outside the Parliament, where visitors mingle and spot politicians. On July 1, which is Canada Day, Parliament Hill is the site of a large outdoor concert and celebration. Thousands flock to the area to listen to music and watch the fireworks.

🏛 Bytown Museum

Ottawa Locks. **Tel** *(613) 234 4570.*
⬜ *May–Oct: daily.* 🎫
Bytown, the capital's original name, changed to Ottawa in 1855. Located east of Parliament Hill and beside the Rideau Canal, in Ottawa's oldest stone building (1827), the Bytown Museum is a well-appointed place to learn

Key to Symbols *see back flap*

KEY

▇ Street-by-Street map: *see pp192–3*

more about local history. Colonel John By, the officer in charge of building the Rideau Canal, set up his headquarters here in 1826. While work was underway, the building, also known as the Bytown, was used to store military equipment and cash. The ground floor houses an exhibit on the construction of the Rideau Canal. Also very enjoyable

The elegant Zoé's Lounge bar at the Château Laurier Hotel

is the focus on domestic life of the early 19th century, with a wide variety of homey artifacts on display.

| 0 meters | 500 |
| 0 yards | 500 |

🏨 Fairmont Château Laurier Hotel

1 Rideau St. **Tel** (613) 241 1414. **Fax** (613) 562 7031. ♿
This wonderful stone replica of a French château is a fine example of the establishments built by railroad companies in the early 1900s. It has attracted both the great and the good since it opened as a hotel in 1912. Centrally located at the foot of Parliament Hill, its interior features large rooms with high ceilings, decorated with Louis XV-style reproductions. The hotel attracts an upscale clientele, including celebrities and government mandarins. Zoé's Lounge, a restaurant

Demob sign at the War Museum

with soaring columns, chandeliers and palms, lit by an atrium, is a wonderful place for lunch, as is the larger restaurant, Wilfrid's.

🏛 Canadian War Museum

1 Vimy Pl. **Tel** (819) 776 8600, 1 800 555 5621. ⬜ May, Jun, Sep–mid-Oct: 9am–6pm daily (to 8pm Thu; from 9:30am Sat, Sun); Jul, Aug: 9am–6pm daily (to 8pm Thu, Fri; from 9:30am Sat, Sun); mid-Oct–Apr: 9am–5pm Tue–Sun (to 8pm Thu; from 9:30am Sat, Sun). 🐾 free Jul 1. ♿ www.warmuseum.ca
Canadians may have a reputation as a peaceful people but they have seen their share of the world's battlefields. This museum, housed in a stunning modern building close to Parliament Hill, looks at the country's military history and at how this history has shaped the nation and its people. Exhibits range from the earliest wars fought on Canadian soil between the French and the British, to the American invasion of 1812, the Boer War of 1899, and Canada's role in the two world wars. The LeBreton Gallery houses an extensive collection of military technology including vehicles, artillery, and other artifacts. There is also a collection of war art representing both world wars. The museum's Regeneration Hall, with its view of the Peace Tower on Parliament Hill, represents hope for a better future.

🏛 Royal Canadian Mint

320 Sussex Dr. *Tel (613) 993 8990.*
🔵 *daily.* 📷 ♿ 🎫 *obligatory.*
Founded in 1908 as a branch
of the British Royal Mint, this
no longer produces regular
Canadian cash currency.
Instead, it strikes many special-
edition coins and Maple Leaf
bullion investment coins. The
mint also processes about 70
percent of the country's gold
in its refinery, which is among
the largest in North America.

The building was refurbished
fully in the 1980s and now
offers guided tours. These are
available daily, but coinage
fanatics must make reservations
in advance to see the process
that turns sheets of metal into
bags of shiny gold coins.

The façade of Ottawa's imposing Cathédrale Notre Dame

🏛 Cathédrale Notre-Dame

Cnr Sussex Dr. & St. Patrick St.
Tel (613) 241 7496. 🔵 *daily.* ♿
Built between 1841 and 1865,
Notre Dame, with its twin
spires, is Ottawa's best-known
Catholic church. It is situated
in the Byward Market area and
features a spectacular Gothic-
style ceiling. The windows,
carvings, and the huge pipe
organ are also well worth
seeing. Philippe Parizeau
(1852–1938) carved the woodwork in mahogany. In niches
around the sanctuary, there
are wooden etchings of
prophets and apostles, crafted
by Louis-Philippe Hebert
(1850–1917), now painted to
look like stone. Joseph Eugene
Guiges, the first bishop of
Ottawa, oversaw the completion of Notre Dame, and his
statue is outside the basilica.

Byward Market is known as a lively area of Ottawa

🏛 ByWard Market

Byward St. *Tel (613) 562 3325.*
🔵 *daily.* 🔴 *Jan 1, Dec 25 & 26.* ♿
limited. **www**.byward-market.com
This neighborhood bustles all
year round; outdoors in the
summer, inside in winter. The
area is located just east of
Parliament Hill, across the
Rideau Canal, and offers a
colorful collection of craft
shops, cafés, boutiques, bistros,
nightclubs, and farmers' market
stalls. Special attractions
include the food market in the
Byward Market Building on
George Street, and the cobble-
stoned Sussex Courtyards. The
cafés are among Ottawa's
most popular places to lunch.

⚓ Laurier House

335 Laurier Ave. E. *Tel (613) 992
8142.* 🔵 *Apr–late May: 9am–5pm
Mon–Fri; late May–Oct: 9am–5pm
daily.* 📷 ♿
Now a national historic site,
Laurier House, a Victorian
town house built in 1878,
served as the chief residence
of two notable Canadian
prime ministers, Sir Wilfrid

Laurier and William Lyon
Mackenzie King. Beautifully
furnished throughout, it houses
memorabilia, papers, and
personal possessions of both
former national leaders.

Rideau Canal

ℹ *Tel (613) 283 5170.*
Built in the mid-19th century,
the Rideau Canal travels
through lakes and canals from
Ottawa to the city of Kingston
(see p200). The canal flows
through the capital, providing
an attractive pastoral sight,
with its walking and cycling
paths bordering the water.
Once used for shipping, the
canal is now a recreational
area. In summer, visitors stroll
along its banks, while through
Ottawa's freezing winter the
canal turns into the city's skating rink, popular with locals
during the winter festival.

🌾 Central Experimental Farm

Experimental Farm Dr, cnr Prince of
Wales and Carling Ave. *Tel (613)
230 3276.* 🔵 *9am–5pm daily.*
🔴 *Dec 25.* 📷 ♿ 🎫
The CEF is a national project
researching all aspects of
farming and horticulture. It
also offers some of the best
floral displays in the country,
including lilacs, peonies, and
roses. There is an ornamental
flower show and an
arboretum with over 2,000
varieties of trees and shrubs.
The farm's livestock barns
and show cattle herds are
especially popular with
children, and everybody
loves the tours of the 4-sq-km
(1.5-sq-mile) site in wagons
drawn by huge, magnificent
Clydesdale horses.

Children can get close to animals at the Central Experimental Farm

The waterside restaurant at the National Arts Centre, seen from the Rideau Canal

🏛 National Arts Centre

53 Elgin St. **Tel** (613) 947 7000.
⬭ daily. 🖼 🎦 obligatory. ♿
www.nac-cna.ca

Completed in 1969, the National Arts Centre has three stages, an elegant canal-side restaurant, and a summer terrace. The building, designed by noted Canadian architect Fred Neubold, comprises three interlocking hexagons opening onto good views of the Ottawa River and the Rideau Canal. Many exponents of Canadian and international dance, theater, and musical forms, including the National Arts Centre Orchestra, perform here regularly. The center's Opera auditorium seats 2,300; Theatre Hall, with its innovative apron stage, seats 897; the Studio, a marvelous venue for experimental productions, comfortably seats 300. The center is extremely popular and reserving well in advance is recommended.

🏛 Currency Museum

245 Sparks St. **Tel** (613) 782 8914.
⬭ May–Sep: 10:30am–5pm Mon–Sat, 1–5pm Sun; Oct–Apr: 10:30am–5pm Tue–Sat, 1–5pm Sun.
www.currencymuseum.ca

Based in the Bank of Canada building, the National Currency Museum features displays that trace the history of money through the ages. This is a fascinating place to learn about the unusual variety of things used as Canadian currency over the years, including whales' teeth, glass beads, grain, paper, and metal. The emphasis of the exhibition is on Canadian currency in all its forms. Visitors can also see the workings of the National Bank.

🏛 Canada Science and Technology Museum

1867 St. Laurent Blvd.
Tel (613) 991 3044. ⬭ 9am–5pm daily (early Sep–Apr: closed Mon) 🖼
www.sciencetech.technomuses.ca

Discover a whole new world at this interactive museum, whose exhibits include a wide range of fascinating displays exploring Canada's space history, transportation through the ages, and modern and industrial technology. A vintage steam locomotive can be boarded (for a 10-minute ride, Jul–Sep only) and the more modern-minded may enter a mini-control room and pull levers to launch a make-believe rocket. Children and adults can also join a mission to save a colony on Mars.

🏛 Canada Aviation and Space Museum

Aviation & Rockcliffe Parkways.
Tel (613) 993 2010. ⬭ May–early Sep: daily; early Sep–Apr: Wed–Sun.
🖼 www.aviation.technomuses.ca

This huge building near Rockcliffe Airport houses over 130 aircraft, which have flown both in war and peace. A replica of the famous 1909 *Silver Dart*, the first aircraft to fly in Canada, is here, as is the nose cone from the *Avro Arrow*, the supersonic superfighter that created a political crisis in Canada when the government halted its development in the 1950s. The *Spitfire*, valiant friend of the Allies in World War II, features alongside historic bush planes such as the *Beaver* and early passenger carrier jets. Displays detail the exploits of Canadian war heroes, plus era aircraft, while the interactives along the Walkway of Time trace the history of world aviation.

Model of a rocket at the National Museum of Science and Technology

National Gallery of Canada

Opened in 1988, the National Gallery of Canada
provides a spectacular home for the country's impressive collections of art. Located near the heart of the
capital, architect Moshe Safdie's memorable pink
granite and glass edifice is architecture as art in its
own right. The National Gallery is one of
the three larget museums in the counry, and is
Canada's top art gallery, with excellent collections of both national and international
exhibits. The museum is a short stroll from
the Rideau Canal and Major's Hill Park.

No.29 *(1950)*
*A vivid example of Jackson Pollock's
idiosyncratic drip technique, this was
part of an enormous canvas carefully
cut into sections, hence its title, No. 29.*

Library

Level 2

★ **Rideau Street Chapel**
*Set in a peaceful inner court-
yard, this 1888 chapel was
saved from bulldozers nearby
and moved here for safety.*

GALLERY GUIDE
*On its first level the gallery houses the
world's largest collection of Canadian art.
It also features international displays and
major traveling exhibitions. The second level
contains the European and American Galleries
and the gallery of prints, drawings, and photographs. Visitors can relax in the two courtyards
or in the fine café.*

STAR EXHIBITS

- ★ Rideau Street
  Chapel

- ★ The Jack Pine by
  Tom Thomson

KEY

- ☐ Special exhibition space
- ☐ Canadian gallery
- ☐ Contemporary art
- ☐ European and American galleries
- ☐ Prints, drawings, and photographs
- ☐ Inuit art
- ☐ Non-exhibition space

Inuit sculpture
*This is represented in ancient
and modern forms;* Aurora
Borealis decapitating a young
man *dates from 1965.*

National Gallery façade
In addition to displays of painting, prints, architecture, and photography, the gallery holds regular events for the performing arts, including movies, lectures, and concerts.

VISITORS' CHECKLIST

380 Sussex Dr.
Tel (613) 990 1985. 3.
May–Sep: 10am–5pm
Fri–Wed, 10am–8pm Thu;
Oct–Apr: 10am–5pm Wed,
Fri–Sun, 10am–8pm Thu.
Jan 1, Good Friday, Dec 25.
for special exhibitions.
11am & 2pm.
www.gallery.ca

★ **The Jack Pine** *(1916)*
In many ways the father of Canada's nationalist art movement of the early 20th century, the Group of Seven, Tom Thomson first attracted notice with his vivid, sketchy, impressionist paintings of Ontario landscape, here shown with a brightly colored oil of a provincial tree framed in wilderness.

Level 1

Virgin and Child with an Angel *(c.1535–1539)*
Francesco Salviati (1510–1563) was taught by painter Andrea del Sarto in Florence. The placement of the divine group in a grotto, with a landscape in the distance, recalls Sarto's work.

Ground Level

Auditorium

Water Court
This delightful airy space is a sharp contemporary contrast to the treasures of yesteryear that abound in the rest of the gallery. Water Court is used as a contemplative gallery for sculpture.

Lecture room

Main entrance

Upper Canada Village ❷

🖼 *Morrisburg.* 🚌 ℹ *Morrisburg*
1 800 437 2233. **www**.upper
canadavillage.com

This recreated 19th-century
town is made up of 40
authentic pre-Confederation
(1867) buildings, relocated
from the surrounding area to
save them from flooding during
construction of the St. Lawrence
Seaway in the 1950s. Today, it
is preserved as a tourist
attraction and is a colorful
reminder of the province's
social history. Costumed
villagers work in the blacksmith's forge and the sawmill
while tinsmiths and cabinet-
makers employ the tools and
skills of the 1860s. A bakery,
cheese factory, and general
store are in operation. History
is also reflected in nearby
**Battle of Crysler's Farm Visitor
Centre**, a memorial to those
who died in the War of 1812.

**🛡 Battle of Crysler's Farm
Visitor Centre**
Prescott, Exit 758 off Hwy 401.
***Tel** (613) 543 3704.* ⬜ *mid-May–
mid-Oct: 9:30am–5pm daily.* 🎫 ♿

Prescott ❸

🏘 *4,100.* 🚌 ℹ *360 Dibble St W.
(613) 925 2812.* **www**.prescott.ca

The major attractions in this
19th-century town are its
architecture and access to the
St. Lawrence River. Prescott's
refurbished waterfront area
and its busy marina make for
a pleasant waterside stroll.

**The 1838 lighthouse overlooks the
pleasure boats of Prescott's marina**

The Shakespearean
Festival here attracts
visitors from around
the world, as does the
excellent scuba diving.
There are 22 wrecks
that sank between
the late 19th- and
mid-20th-centuries
within an hour's drive.
  **Fort Wellington
National Historic Site**,
east from the center of
town, attracts many
visitors. Originally built
during the War of 1812
and rebuilt in 1838, four
walls and some
buildings remain.
These include a stone
blockhouse which is
now a military museum,
incorporating refur-
bished officers' quarters.

🏛 Fort Wellington
Prescott. ***Tel** (613) 925 2896.*
⬜ *late May–mid-Oct: daily.* ♿

The Thousand Islands ❹

ℹ *2 King St. East, Gananoque (613)
382 3250.* **www**.gananoque.com

The St. Lawrence River, one
of the world's great waterways,
is a gateway for ocean-going
vessels traveling through the
Great Lakes. Few stretches of
the trip compare in charm or
beauty to the Thousand
Islands, an area that
contains a scattering of
over a thousand tiny
islands, stretching from
just below Kingston
downriver to the water-
side towns and cities of
Gananoque, Brockville,
Ivy Lea, and Rockport.
Cruising opportunities
abound from the
Kingston boarding site.
  River sights include the
curious Boldt's Castle, a
folly built on one of the
islands by millionaire
hotelier Boldt and
abandoned in grief
when his wife died in 1904. It
was Oscar, Boldt's head chef
at the Waldorf Astoria who,
entertaining summer guests at
the castle, concocted Thousand
Island salad dressing. Land-
lubbers will enjoy the scenery

A sailboat travels the Thousand Islands

from the Thousand Islands
Parkway, which runs from the
pretty town of Gananoque to
Mallorytown Landing.

Kingston ❺

🏙 *153,000.* ✈ 🚌 🚌 ⛴
ℹ *209 Ontario St. (613) 548 4415.*
www.tourism.kingstoncanada.com

Once a center for ship building
and the fur trade, Kingston
was briefly (1841–44) the capital of the United Province of
Canada *(see pp49)*. Constructed
by generations of shipbuilders,
the city's handsome
limestone buildings reflect
a dignified lineage. The
host of the 1976 Olympic
Games regatta,
Kingston is still one
of the freshwater
sailing capitals of
North America and
the embarkation point
for many local cruises.
It is also home to more
museums than any
other town in Ontario.
  Universally popular, the
restored British bastion
**Fort Henry National
Historic Site of Canada** is
a living military museum
brought to life by guards in
bright scarlet period uniforms
who are trained in drills,
artillery exercises, and
traditional fife and drum
music of the 1860s. Canada's

**Guard at
Fort Henry**

top Army Training University is also based in the city and The Royal Military College Museum, housed in a 1846 Martello Tower, tells the story of today's cadets and their forebears.

West of the downtown area lies the **Marine Museum of the Great Lakes**. There are displays on the history of the Great Lakes and the ships that sailed on them, including the first ship built for the Lakes here in 1678. The museum also contains a 3,000-ton icebreaker, a fine example of shipbuilding in the last century. Modern-day technology is explored at Kingston Mills, the lock station at the southern end of the Rideau Canal, where boats are lifted 4 m (13 ft).

🛡 Fort Henry
Kingston. **Tel** (613) 542 7388.
☐ mid-May–late Sep: daily. 🎫 ♿
www.forthenry.com

🏛 Marine Museum of the Great Lakes
55 Ontario St. **Tel** (613) 542 2261.
☐ Apr–Oct: 10am–5pm daily; Nov–May: 10am–4pm Mon–Fri. 🎫 ♿
www.marmuseum.ca

Rideau Canal ❻

ℹ 34 Beckwith St. South, Smiths Falls
Tel (613) 284 0505. ☐ May–Oct.

The Rideau Canal, originally a defensive barrier protecting Canada against the Americans and finished in 1832, stretches for 200 km (125 miles). The best way to enjoy this sparkling necklace of scenic waterway is by boat. A great feat of 19th-century engineering,

A view of the Rideau Canal as it travels through Westport village

Historic house along the main street of Picton in peaceful Quinte's Isle

which includes 47 locks and 24 dams, the system allows boaters to float through tranquil woods and farmland, scenic lakes, and to stop in quaint villages, as well as visit the **Rideau Canal Museum** at Smith's Falls. The canal north of Kingston also contains a number of provincial parks which offer canoe trails. Also popular is the 400-km (250-mile) Rideau Trail, a hiking system linking Kingston and Canada's capital city, Ottawa.

🏛 Rideau Canal Museum
34 Beckwith St. S. **Tel** (613) 284 0505. ☐ mid-May–mid-Oct: daily; mid-Oct–mid-May: by appt. 🎫 ♿

Prince Edward County ❼

ℹ 116 Main St., Picton. **Tel** (613) 476 2421. **www**.pec.on.ca

Charming and known for its relaxed pace and old-fashioned hospitality, Prince Edward County is surrounded by Lake Ontario and the Bay of Quinte, and is sometimes referred to as Quinte's Isle. The island is renowned for its two camping and sunbathing beaches in Sandbanks Provincial Park. There, mountains of fine sand reach 25 m (82 ft) and are considered one of the most significant fresh-water dune systems in the world.

United Empire Loyalists (see p46) settled in the County following the American Revolution (1775), founding engaging small towns and a strong farming industry.

Visitors can absorb the local historic architecture by traveling along the country roads and the Loyalist Parkway, either cycling or by car, pausing to appreciate the island's charming views.

Serpent Mounds Park ❽

Rural route 2 in Keene. **Tel** (705) 295 6879. 🚉 Coburg. 🚉 Peterborough. ☐ mid-May–mid-Oct: 9am–8pm daily. 🎫 ♿

Situated on the shore of Rice Lake, Serpent Mounds is a historic native Indian burial ground. A grove of aging oak encloses nine burial mounds of an ancient people who gathered here more than 2,000 years ago. The only one of its kind in Canada, the largest mound has an unusual zigzag appearance, said to represent the shape of a moving snake. The site is still sacred to native people. Rice Lake, which offers shady picnic spots and excellent fishing, provides a pleasant backdrop.

On the tiny Indian River 9 km (5 miles) away, Lang Pioneer Village is a more traditional representation of Canada's past, featuring 20 restored 19th-century buildings, heritage gardens, and farmyard animals. Visitors can watch an ancient restored grist mill in action, and workers in period costumes display ancient skills. Blacksmiths and tinsmiths ply their trade in an authentic smithy and will give lessons.

Lush bullrushes surround a pond in Petroglyphs Provincial Park

Kawartha Lakes ❾

ℹ️ *Peterborough (705) 742 2201.*
🚉 *Peterborough.* 🚌 *Cobourg.*
www.thekawarthas.net

The Kawartha Lakes are part of the 386-km (240-mile) Trent–Severn Waterway that runs from Lake Ontario to Georgian Bay and was originally built in the 19th century. Today the area is a playground for vacationers, with water-based activities including cruises and superb fishing. Renting a houseboat from one of the coastal villages is a popular way of exploring the locality. At the center of the region lies the friendly city of Peterborough, notable for its university, pleasing waterfront parks, and the world's largest hydraulic liftlock. Thirty-four km (21 miles) north lies the Curve Lake Indian Reserve's famous Whetung Gallery, one of the best places locally for native arts and crafts.

Petroglyphs Provincial Park, 55 km (34 miles) to the north of Peterborough, is better known to locals as the "teaching rocks" for the 900-plus aboriginal rock carvings cut into the park's white marble outcrops. Rediscovered in 1954, these wonderfully preserved symbols and figures of animals, boats, spirits, and people were made by spiritual leaders to record their dreams and visions. Today the stones are housed in a huge glass building, built around them in 1984 to protect them from frost. The stones remain respectfully regarded to this day as a sacred site by native peoples.

🌿 **Petroglyphs Provincial Park**
2249 Northey's Bay Rd, Woodview, off Hwy 28. **Tel** *(705) 877 2552.*
◯ *May–Oct: 10am–5pm daily.* ♿

The Haliburton Highlands ❿

ℹ️ *Haliburton (705) 286 1777.*
www.haliburtoncounty.ca

The Haliburton Highlands are one of Ontario's year-round outdoor destinations, renowned for their forests, lakes, and spectacular scenery. In the summer, thousands of visitors enjoy boating, fishing, and swimming in this region. In fall, busloads of tourists travel to appreciate the celebrated seasonal colors; others come for the deer hunting. Winter brings skiers and snowboarders.

The village of Haliburton is found along scenic Highway 35, which winds its way through exceptional scenery from Minden north to the considerable charms of Dorset. The fire tower atop a rock cliff overlooking the village gives spectacular views of the Lake of Bays and the surrounding area. This spot is a fantastic viewing point for the myriad colors of Ontario's fall trees with their lovely bright red and orange shades.

The Madonna at Pioneer Museum

Combermere ⓫

🏛️ *250.* ℹ️ *Ottawa Valley Tourist Association, 9 International Dr., Pembroke (613) 732 4364.*
www.ottawavalley.org

The village of Combermere is a central point for people heading to a number of provincial parks in Eastern Ontario, including Algonquin *(see pp204–5)*, Carson Lake, and Opeongo River. It is a good tourist center for fuel and refreshments. A few kilometers (2 miles) south of Combermere lies the **Madonna House Pioneer Museum**. Founded by Catherine Doherty, this Catholic lay community has grown to have mission outposts around the world. It is managed by volunteers, who live on its cooperative farm, and who dedicate themselves to fundraising. Since 1963, a recycling program has been raising money for the world's poor.

🏛️ **Madonna House Pioneer Museum**
Hwy 517. **Tel** *(613) 756 3713.* ◯ *mid-May–mid-Oct: 10am–5pm Tue–Sat.*

Golfers taking a break between games to enjoy the Haliburton scenery

Farm cottages outside Barry's Bay, home to many Ontarian craftspeople

Eganville ⑫

🏠 1,300. ⓘ Ottawa Valley Tourist Association, 9 International Dr., Pembroke (613) 732 4364.

This highway 60 village with its little restaurants and gas station provides a handy tourist center for visitors to this picturesque region. Local attractions include the **Bonnechere Caves**, 8 km (5 miles) away. The caves were at the bottom of a tropical sea 500 million years ago. Gradually raised over millennia from the ocean bed, they are covered with fossils of primitive life forms. The privately owned site is open for tours in summer.

⋂ Bonnechere Caves
Tel (613) 628 2283. ◯ May–early Sep: daily; late Sep–Oct: Sat & Sun. 🖼

Barry's Bay ⑬

🏠 1,250. ⓘ Ottawa Valley Tourist Association, 9 International Dr., Pembroke (613) 732 4364.

An attractive little town, Barry's Bay has a sizeable Polish population, as does its neighbor Wilno, site of the first Polish settlement in Canada. The area is home to many craftspeople and artisans, who sell their wares in the local villages. Barry's Bay is also popular for stores selling outdoor gear and watersport equipment. Year-round sports facilities can be found at nearby Kamaniskeg Lake and Redcliffe Point, both of which are popular places for renting cottages. Perched high on a hill, nearby Wilno overlooks scenic river valleys and boasts the fine church and grotto of St. Mary's.

Algonquin Provincial Park ⑭

See pp204–205.

North Bay ⑮

🏠 56,000. ✈ 🚌 🚗 ⓘ 1375 Seymour St. (705) 472 8480.

Billing itself as the Gateway to the Near North, North Bay sits at the eastern end of Lake Nippissing, 350 km (217 miles) north of Toronto. The region's most famous natives are undoubtedly the Dionne quintuplets. Born in 1934, the Quints' original modest family homestead has been relocated and now forms the town's popular **Dionne Quints Museum**.

Lake Nippissing nearby is famous for its fishing and wilderness scenery. Boat cruises across the lake follow the old French explorers' route. North Bay is a good starting-point for trips to the area's many vacation camps.

🏛 Dionne Quints Museum
17 Seymour St. **Tel** (705) 472 8480. ◯ mid May–mid-Oct: daily. 🖼 &

THE DIONNE QUINTS

The hamlet of Corbeil experienced a natural miracle on May 28, 1934: the birth of the Dionne quintuplets; Annette, Emilie, Yvonne, Cecile, and Marie, the five identical girls born to Oliva and Elzire Dionne. The Quints' combined weight at birth was only 6.1 kg (13 lbs 5 oz), and the babies' lungs were so tiny that small doses of rum were required daily to help them breathe. Experts put the chances of giving birth to identical quintuplets at 1 in 57 million. The girls became international stars, attracting countless visitors to North Bay during the 1930s. A Quint industry sprang up with curiosity-seekers flocking to watch the young girls at play. The Dionne homestead was moved to North Bay in 1985, and visitors can travel back over 60 years to marvel anew at the birth of the Quints in this small farmhouse.

Algonquin Provincial Park ⑭

"Moose Crossing"

To many Canadians, Algonquin, with its lush maple and pine woods, sparkling lakes, and plentiful wildlife, is as familiar a symbol of Canada as is Niagara Falls. Founded in 1893, this is the oldest and most famous park in Ontario, stretching across 7,630 sq km (2,946 sq miles) of wilderness. Wildlife abounds; visitors have a chance to see beavers, moose, and bears in their natural habitats, and the park echoes with the hauntingly beautiful call of the loon, heard often in northern Ontario. Every August, on Thursday evenings, "wolf howls" are organized, whereby park staff attempt to elicit answers from these native animals by imitating their cries. Opportunities for outdoor activities are plentiful; most visitors like to try one of the 2,000 km (1,243 miles) of canoe routes through the forested interior.

Killarney Lodge
This is one of the park's rental lodges, rustic buildings that are popular during the spring, summer, and fall.

The Algonquin Gallery
exhibits various international art displays, with a focus on nature and wildlife. Painters featured have included Tom Thomson, precursor of the famous Group of Seven *(see pp164–5).*

Moose near Highway 60
Visitors can usually spot a few moose each day, especially near lakes and salty puddles by roadsides, which these huge animals seem to love.

Canoe Lake
Two thousand kilometers (1,243 miles) of canoe trails surround the park. They range from beginner and family routes, some as short as 6 km (4 miles), to 70-km (50- mile) treks for the experienced. Routes are well planned and marked.

Lake Opeongo
With over 2,400 lakes, Algonquin is justly celebrated for its matchless fishing opportunities. Lake Opeongo, one of the largest in the park, is famous for its abundance of lake trout and smallmouth bass.

VISITORS' CHECKLIST

Hwy 60. **Tel** (705) 633 5572. ◯ daily. 🚌 from Toronto in summer. 🏕 for camping. 🍴 some lodges. 🌐 **www**.algonquinpark.on.ca

Park Visitor Centre
Opened in 1993 to celebrate Algonquin's centenary, the Centre contains a museum with displays on the park's wildlife and natural history.

Radiant Lake

Lake Travers

Petawawa River

Lake Lavieille

Opeongo

The **Algonquin Logging Museum** tells the story of this traditional local trade, illustrated by a river dam and log-moving "alligator."

Whitney

0 km — 10
0 miles — 10

KEY

━━ Major road

═══ Minor road

--- Provincial Park boundary

△ Campsite

ℹ Visitor information center

☀ Viewpoint

⛵ Canoe route access

Brewer Lake
This scenic fishing lake is situated on the Highway 60 corridor. A 56-km (35-mile) journey through the park, this beautiful route is popular with daytrippers and those wishing to catch the major sights in limited time.

THE GREAT LAKES

The varied charms of the Canadian Great Lakes region, from the sleepy little farming towns bordering Lake Erie to the island-studded bays of Lake Huron and the wilderness encircling Lake Superior, tend to be obscured by the fame of Niagara Falls. One of the world's most famous sights, the falls occur where the Niagara River tumbles 50 meters (164 ft) between Lakes Erie and Ontario. Native tribes once lived on the fertile land around the area's lakes and rivers, but fur traders used the lakes as a vital waterway. The War of 1812 resulted in British Canada securing trade rights to the northern lakeshores. Between 1820 and 1850 settlers established farms, and mining and forestry flourished in Canada's then richest province. Today, the Trans-Canada Highway follows the northern shores of Lakes Huron and Superior for over 1,000 km (620 miles), traveling through the untamed scenery of Killarney Park, past picturesque old towns such as Sault Ste. Marie, and eventually reaching the bustling port of Thunder Bay.

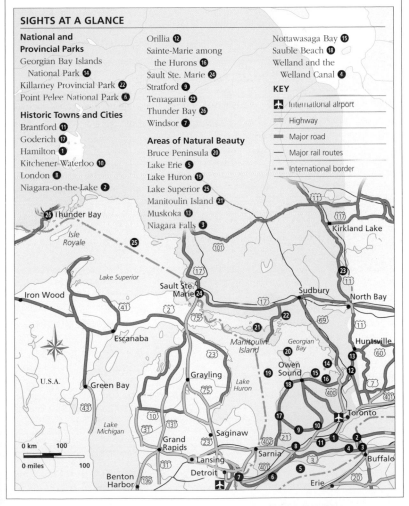

SIGHTS AT A GLANCE

National and Provincial Parks
Georgian Bay Islands National Park ⑭
Killarney Provincial Park ㉒
Point Pelee National Park ⑥

Historic Towns and Cities
Brantford ⑪
Goderich ⑰
Hamilton ①
Kitchener-Waterloo ⑩
London ⑧
Niagara-on-the-Lake ②

Orillia ⑫
Sainte-Marie among the Hurons ⑯
Sault Ste. Marie ㉔
Stratford ⑨
Temagami ㉓
Thunder Bay ㉖
Windsor ⑦

Areas of Natural Beauty
Bruce Peninsula ⑳
Lake Erie ⑤
Lake Huron ⑲
Lake Superior ㉕
Manitoulin Island ㉑
Muskoka ⑬
Niagara Falls ③

Nottawasaga Bay ⑮
Sauble Beach ⑱
Welland and the Welland Canal ④

KEY

✈ International airport
═ Highway
▬ Major road
— Major rail routes
·—· International border

⊲ The warm colors of Killarney Provincial Park reflected in the tranquil waters of Cranberry Lake

The imposing façade of Dundurn Castle in Hamilton

Hamilton ❶

🏙 *500,000.* ✈ 🚂 🚌 🚢
ℹ *34 James St. S. (905) 546 2666.*
www.tourismhamilton.com

The city of Hamilton sits at the extreme western end of Lake Ontario, some 70 km (44 miles) from Toronto. Its specialty is steel, and the city's mills churn out around 60 percent of Canada's total production. Despite the town's industrial bias, it possesses some enjoyable attractions. **Dundurn Castle** is a Regency-style villa dating from the 1830s, whose interior holds a fine collection of period furnishings. It was built for the MacNabs, one of the most influential families in Ontario, who included in their number Sir Allan Napier MacNab, a Premier of Canada from 1854–6.

Another sight is the **Royal Botanical Gardens**, comprising forests, marshes, and small lakes over some 1,093 ha (2,700 acres) on the north side of Hamilton harbor. Among the notable gardens here are a fine Rose Garden; the Laking Garden with its peonies and irises; and the heavily perfumed Lilac Garden. The Rock Garden, built in 1935, contains an ampitheater, conifers, and cherry trees.

Also in town, the Canadian Warplane Heritage Museum has a display of more than 30 operational aircraft dating from World War II to the jet age.

🏛 **Dundurn Castle**
610 York Blvd. **Tel** *(905) 546 2872.*
◯ *mid-May–early Sep: 10am–4pm daily; early Sep–mid-May: noon–4pm Tue–Sun.* 🎟 ♿ *partial.*

🌷 **Royal Botanical Gardens**
680 Plains Rd. West. **Tel** *(905) 527 1158.* ◯ *daily.* 🎟 ♿ *partial.*

Niagara-on-the-Lake ❷

🏙 *15,000.* 🚢 ℹ *26 Queen St. (905) 468 4263.* **www**.niagaraonthelake.com

Niagara-on-the-Lake is a charming little town of elegant clapboard mansions and leafy streets set where the mouth of the Niagara River empties into Lake Ontario. The town was originally known as Newark and under this name it became the capital of Upper Canada (as Ontario was then known) in 1792. It was to be a temporary honor. Just four years later, the British decided to move the capital farther away from the US border, and chose York (now Toronto) instead. It was a wise decision. In 1813, the Americans crossed the Niagara River and destroyed Newark in the War of 1812 *(see pp46–7)*.

Rose in the Royal Botanical Gardens

The British returned after the war to rebuild their homes, and the Georgian town they constructed has survived pretty much intact.

Today, visitors take pleasure in exploring the town's lovely streets, but there is one major attraction, **Fort George**, a carefully restored British

---

stockade built in the 1790s just southeast of town. The earth and timber palisade encircles ten replica buildings including three blockhouses, the barracks, a guard house, and the officers' quarters. There is also a powder magazine store, where all the fittings were wood or brass, and the men donned special shoes without buckles to reduce the chance of an unwanted explosion. Guides in old-style British military uniforms describe life in the fort in the 19th century.

Niagra-on-the-Lake is also home to the annual Shaw Festival, a prestigious theatrical season featuring the plays of George Bernard Shaw and other playwrights, which runs from April to November.

🏛 **Fort George**
Queen's Parade, Niagara Pkwy.
Tel *(905) 468 6614.* ◯ *May–Oct: 10am–5pm daily.* 🎟 ♿

Gardens in front of an early 19th-century inn at Niagara-on-the-Lake

Niagara Falls ❸

See pp212–15.

Welland and The Welland Canal ❹

🏙 *50,000.* ✈ 🚌 ℹ *Seaway Mall, 800 Niagara St. (905) 735 8696.* **www**.wellandcanal.com

An important steel town, Welland is bisected by the famous Welland Canal, which was built to solve the problem of Niagara Falls. The Falls

Aerial view of the small village of Long Point on the shore of Lake Erie

presented an obstacle that made it impossible for boats to pass between lakes Ontario and Erie. Goods had to be unloaded on one side of the Falls and then carted to the other, a time-consuming and expensive process. To solve the problem, local entrepreneurs dug a canal across the 45-km (28-mile) isthmus separating the lakes early in the 19th century, choosing a route to the west of the Niagara River.

The first **Welland Canal** was a crude affair, but subsequent improvements have created today's version, which has eight giant locks adjusting the water level by no less than 99 m (324 feet). A remarkable feat of engineering, the canal is capable of accommodating the largest of ships. You can drive alongside the northerly half of the canal, on Government

Road from Lake Ontario to Thorold, where seven of the eight locks are situated. The viewing platform at Lock No. 3 provides a great vantage point and has an information center detailing the canal's history.

Welland boasts another eye-catching attraction: 28 giant murals decorate some of the city's downtown buildings.

Lake Erie ➎

ℹ️ 660 Garrison Rd., Fort Erie (905) 871 1332, 1 888 270 9151.

Lake Erie is named after the native people who once lived along its shores. The Erie were renowned for their skills as fishermen. Some 400 km (249 miles) long and an average of 60 km (37 miles) wide, Lake Erie is the shallowest of

the Great Lakes and separates Canada from the US. Its northern shore is one of the most peaceful parts of Ontario, with a string of quiet country towns and small ports set in rolling countryside. Three peninsulas reach out from the Canadian shoreline, one of which has been conserved as the Point Pelee National Park, home to a virgin forest and, during spring and summer, thousands of migrating birds.

About 30 km (19 miles) south of Niagara Falls, the small town of Fort Erie lies where the Niagara River meets Lake Erie, facing its sprawling US neighbor, Buffalo. The massive Peace Bridge links the two, and most people cross the border without giving Fort Erie a second look. They miss one of the more impressive of the reconstructed British forts that dot the Canada-US border. Old **Fort Erie** is a replica of the stronghold, destroyed by the Americans in the War of 1812. Entry is across a draw-bridge, and the interior holds barracks, a powder magazine, officers' quarters, and a guard room. The fort's battlefield is the site of one of the War of 1812's bloodiest battles, fought here during the siege of the fort in 1814.

🏛️ **Fort Erie**
350 Lakeshore Rd. **Tel** (905) 871 7211. ⭕ mid-May–Oct: daily.
📷 ♿ partial.

A merchant ship on the Welland Canal near the town of Welland

Point Pelee National Park ❻

Tel *(519) 322 2365.* 🚇 *Windsor.*
🚌 *Windsor.* ⬜ *daily.* 🅿️ ♿ ✉️
www.pc.gc.ca

A long, fingerlike isthmus,
Point Pelee National Park
sticks out into Lake Erie for
20 km (12 miles) and forms
the southernmost tip of
Canada's mainland. The park
has a wide variety of habitats
including marshlands, open
fields, and ancient deciduous
forest. These woods are a
rarity, as they are one of the
few places in North America's
Carolinian Life Zone where
many of the trees have never
been logged. The profusion
of species creates a junglelike
atmosphere, with red cedar,
black walnut, white sassafras,
hickory, sycamore, and sumac,
all struggling to reach the light.
This varied vegetation attracts
thousands of birds, which visit
on their spring and fall migrations. Over 370 species
have been sighted
here, and they can be
observed from look-
out points and forest
trails. Every fall, hosts
of orange-and-black
monarch butterflies
can also be seen
here. A marshland
boardwalk trail
winds through Point Pelee and
has good observation spots
along the way. Bikes and
canoes can be rented at the
start of the boardwalk, and
there is a concession stand
here. Farther into the park, the
visitor center features displays
of local flora and fauna.

Water cascades at the main entrance of Windsor's fashionable Casino

Windsor ❼

🏙️ *216,000.* ✈️ ✕ 🚌 🚉 ℹ️ *333
Riverside Drive W. (519) 255 6530,
1 800 265 3633.*

A car manufacturing town,
just like its American neighbor
Detroit, Windsor and its
factories produce hundreds
of US-badged vehicles every
day. Windsor has clean,
tree-lined streets and
a riverside walkway,
but its most noted
attraction is a trendy
river-side Casino that
draws thousands of
visitors. The city
has many lively
bars and cafés, the
best of which are
along the first three blocks of
the main street, Ouellette. Also
of interest, the nearby **Art Gallery of Windsor**, is noted for
its excellent visiting exhibitions.
It is possible to relive the
days when the town was a
bootleggers' paradise by taking
a guided tour of the Hiram

**Contemporary painting
at Windsor Art Gallery**

Walker Distillery: during
Prohibition millions of bottles
of alcohol were smuggled from
Windsor into the US across
the Detroit River.
From Windsor, it is an easy
20-km (12-mile) drive south
along the Detroit River to the
British-built Fort Malden at
Amherstburg. Not much is left
of the fort, but there is a neatly
restored barracks dating from
1819, and the old laundry now
holds an interpretation center.
This relates the fort's role in
the War of 1812 *(see pp46–7)*,
where the English plotted to
invade the US.

🏛️ **Art Gallery of Windsor**
401 Riverside Dr. W. **Tel** *(519) 9770
013.* ⬜ *Wed–Sun.* 🅿️ *donation.* ♿

London ❽

🏙️ *356,000.* ✈️ ✕ 🚌 🚉 ℹ️ *267
Dundas St. (519) 661 5000, 1 800
265 2602.* **www.**londontourism.ca

Likeable London sits in the
middle of one of the most
fertile parts of Ontario and is
the area's most important town.
It is home to the respected
University of Western Ontario,
which has a striking modern
art gallery and a campus with
dozens of Victorian mansions.
In addition, the few blocks
that make up the town center
are notably refined and well
tended. The finest buildings
in the center are the two 19th-
century cathedrals, St. Paul's,
a red-brick Gothic Revival
edifice built for the Anglicans
in 1846, and the more ornate,
St. Peter's Catholic Cathedral

Kayakers alongside the boardwalk at Point Pelee National Park

erected a few years later. In the northwest of the city, the London Museum of Archeology focuses on the 1,100-year history of the settlement of the area. The Lawson Iroquoian Village here is a reconstruction of a 500-year-old village, once occupied by the Neutral Indians, with elm longhouses and cedarwood palisades.

Reconstruction of a 500-year-old house at Lawson Indian Village

Stratford ⑨

🏃 30,000. 🚉 🚌 47 Downie St. 1 800 561 7926. www.welcometo stratford.com

In 1830, an innkeeper called William Sargint opened the "Shakespeare Inn" beside one of the rough agricultural tracks that then crisscrossed southern

---

THE UNDERGROUND RAILROAD

Neither underground nor a railroad, the name "Underground Railroad" (UGRR) was founded by abolitionists in the 1820s. The UGRR helped slaves from the southern United States to escape to both Canada and the free northern states. It was a secretive organization, especially in the South where the penalties for helping a slave to escape were severe. Slaves were moved north from safe house to safe house right up to the end of the American Civil War in 1865. Reverend Josiah Henson was one of those who escaped on the UGRR, and later founded a school for ex-slaves. Harriet Beecher Stowe's 1851 abolitionist novel *Uncle Tom's Cabin* was based on his life story.

Reverend Josiah Henson

Ontario. The farmers who settled nearby called the local river the "Avon" and named the town that grew up here "Stratford," after William Shakespeare's home town.

In 1952, local journalist Tom Patterson (1920–2005) organized a Shakespeare Festival. This first event was a humble affair held in a tent, but since then the festival has grown into one of Canada's most important theatrical seasons, lasting from May to early November (www.stratfordfestival.ca). The leading plays are still Shakespearean, but other playwrights are showcased too, including modern works.

Stratford is an attractive town with plenty of green lawns, riverside parks, and swans. The town is geared toward visitors, offering countless guesthouses and several good restaurants. The visitor center produces a book with information and photographs of all the town's bed-and-breakfasts. They also organize heritage walks through the town, which pass its many historic buildings. One of the town's architectural highlights is the Victorian town hall, with its turrets. Stratford has a plethora of art galleries, as well as craft boutiques and other stores.

Stratford's River Avon and Huron Street bridge, overlooked by the distinctive Victorian courthouse

Niagara Falls ❸

Although the majestic rumble of the falls can be heard from miles away, there is no preparation for the sight itself, a great arc of hissing, frothing water crashing over a 57-m (188-ft) cliff amid dense clouds of drifting spray. There are actually two cataracts to gaze at as the speeding river is divided into twin channels by Goat Island, a tiny spray-soaked parcel of land. On one side of Goat Island is the Canadian Horseshoe Falls, and on the far side, across the border, is the smaller American Falls. Stunning close-up views of the falls are available from the vantage point of the Maid of the Mist boat trips. Even better is the walk down through a series of rocky tunnels that lead behind Horseshoe Falls, where the noise from the crashing waters is deafening.

American Falls
The Niagara River tumbles over the 260-m (850-ft) wide American Falls.

Rainbow Bridge
From the elegant span of the Rainbow Bridge there are panoramic views over the falls. The bridge itself crosses the gorge between Canada and the US. Here, on sunny days, rainbows rise through the spray.

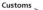

Customs

Bird Kingdom is Canada's only indoor aviary and features over 300 exotic birds.

Clifton Hill
This street boasts a range of attractions. Ripley's Believe it or Not Museum features a dog with human teeth as just one of its offerings.

STAR SIGHTS

★ Horseshoe Falls

★ Maid of the Mist boat trip

VISITORS' CHECKLIST

130 km (84 miles) SW of Toronto.
▣ from Toronto.
▣ from Toronto. ℹ Niagara
Falls Tourism, 5515 Stanley Ave.,
Niagara Falls (905) 356 6061 or
1 (800) 563 2557.
www.discoverniagara.com

★ Horseshoe Falls
*Shaped like a horseshoe,
this is the larger set of falls
at Niagara, being some
670 m (2,200 ft) wide and
57 m (188 ft) high.*

The Minolta Tower, like the Skylon
Tower, offers panoramic views of the
whole area. Three observation decks
look out over the falls.

| 0 meters | 250 |
| 0 yards | 250 |

Journey Behind the Falls
*An elevator from the Horseshoe
Falls leads to the Journey
Behind the Falls, where a
series of rocky tunnels take
visitors behind a wall of water
so thick it blocks out daylight.*

★ Maid of the Mist boat trip
*These intrepid vessels gets very close
to the foot of the falls. Raincoats are
supplied as passengers can expect
to get wet on this thrilling trip.*

Skylon Tower
*The tower has an observation
deck, which gives a bird's-
eye view of the falls. It is also
open at night so visitors can
see the floodlit waters.*

Exploring Niagara Falls

Niagara Falls is a welcoming little town that stretches along the Niagara River for about 3 km (2 miles). Renowned as a honeymoon destination, the town is well equipped to satisfy the needs of the 16 million people who visit the falls each year. It is divided into three main sections: to the south are the falls themselves, and these are flanked by a thin strip of parkland that stretches out along the river bank as far as Clifton Hill, the glitziest street in Ontario, lined with garish amusement park attractions. To the west is the main motel strip, Lundy's Lane. To the north, on Bridge Street, lies the business district and the train and bus stations.

Horseshoe Falls

Named for their shape, the 675-m- (2,200-ft-) wide and 52-m- (170-ft)- high Horseshoe Falls are formed by the turbulent waters of the Niagara River roaring over a semicircular cliff to plunge into the bubbling cauldron below. By these means the Niagara River adjusts to the differential between the water levels of lakes Erie and Ontario, which it connects. The falls remain an awe-inspiring sight, despite the fact that the flow of the river is regulated by hydroelectric companies, which siphon off a substantial part of the river to drive their turbines. One result has been a change in the rate of erosion. By the 1900s, the falls were eroding the cliff beneath them at a rate of 1 m (3 ft) a year. Today, the rate is down to 30 cm (1 ft) a year.

The Maid of the Mist pleasure trip

☷ Maid of The Mist

5920 River Rd. *Tel (905) 358 5781.*
◯ *mid-May–Oct: daily.* 🗺 ⅚
www.maidofthemist.com
The best way to appreciate the full force of the falls is to experience the Maid of the Mist boat trip. Boats depart from the jetty at the bottom of

Clifton Hill and head upriver to the crashing waters under the falls. Raincoats are provided on this invigorating and wet trip.

A wax museum and an array of other attractions at Clifton Hill

Clifton Hill

This short, steep street runs up from the edge of the Niagara River gorge and is lined with a string of fast food restaurants and tourist attractions. The flashing lights and giant advertising billboards point the way to such sights as the Guinness Book of World Records, House of Frankenstein, That's Incredible Museum, Houdini's Museum and Ripley's Believe it or Not! Museum, where visitors can speak to a genie in a crystal bottle and see oddities such as a man with a greater-than-usual number of pupils in his eyes.

White Water Walk

4330 Niagara Pkwy. *Tel (905) 374 1221.* ◯ *daily.* 🗺 ⅚
www.niagaraparks.com
The great force of the Niagara River's torrent is best admired from down at the bottom of the canyon. The Great Gorge

The dramatic arc of thundering waters at Horseshoe Falls

For hotels and restaurants in this region see pp358–9 and pp383–4

Wooden boardwalk along the Niagara River at the Great Gorge Adventure

Adventure provides this close-up view by means of a tunnel and an elevator, which lead from the top of the gorge to a riverside boardwalk. The whirlpools and rapids here are some of the most spectacular, yet treacherous, in the world.

The Old Scow

Just above the falls, stranded on the rocks in the middle of the river, is the Old Scow, a flat-bottomed steel barge that was shipwrecked in August 1918. It was being towed across the Niagara River by a tugboat when the lines snapped. The scow hurtled towards the falls, getting within 767 m (2,460 ft), of the brink, and the two-man crew appeared to be doomed. Luckily the boat grounded itself on this rocky ledge just in time. The crew's ordeal was, however, far from over: they had to wait another 29 hours before being finally winched to safety. The Old Scow has been rusting away on the rocks ever since.

🦋 Niagara Glen Nature Reserve

3050 River Road. *Tel* (905) 358 8633. ◯ daily.

The small Niagara Glen Nature Reserve lies 7 km (4 miles) downriver from the falls. This segment of the gorge has been preserved in pristine condition, with bushes and low trees tumbling down the rocky cliffside. This is how it may have looked before the coming of the Euro-

peans. Seven different hiking trails lead past boulders, caves, and wild flowers. The walks are easy on the way down but a steep climb on the way up.

Whirlpool Aerocar

3850 Niagara Pkwy. *Tel* (905) 354 5711. ◯ daily, weather permitting 📷 www.niagaraparks.com

The Niagara River makes a dramatically sharp turn about 4.5 km (3 miles) downstream from the falls, generating a vicious, raging whirlpool, one of the most lethal stretches of water in the whole of North America. The effect is created when the river pushes against the north-west side of the canyon, only to be forced to turn around in the opposite direction. The most stunning view of the whirlpool rapids is from the

Butterfly at the Botanic Gardens and Conservatory

Aerocar, a specially designed cable car that crosses the gorge, high above the river. A different perspective of the falls can be seen from here.

🦋 Niagara Parks Botanical Gardens and Butterfly Conservatory

2565 Niagara Pkwy. *Tel* (905) 358 0025. ◯ daily. 📷 for conservatory. ♿ www.niagaraparks.com

The Niagara Parks Botanical Gardens are located 9 km (6 miles) downstream from the falls and comprise over 40 ha (99 acres) of beautifully maintained gardens divided into several different zones. One of the prettiest areas in summer is the rose garden, which displays over 2,400 different varieties. The extensive annual garden, which houses many rare species imported from all parts of the globe, puts on a year-round show. The gardens also include an arboretum that has examples of many different types of trees from beech and mulberry to magnolia and yew.

The butterfly conservatory is even more popular. At the beginning of a visit, a video is shown in the theater. The film explains the life cycle of a butterfly, from egg and larvae through to the emergence of the adult. Over 2,000 butterflies are housed in a huge heated dome where they fly free – one of the largest collections in the world. A series of pathways pass through the dome, leading past the lush tropical flora on which the butterflies make their homes.

The Whirlpool Rapids are best seen from the Spanish Aero Car

Tourists get a close-up view of the magnificent frothing waters of Niagara's Horseshoe Falls ▷

Alexander Graham Bell's study at the Bell Homestead in Brantford

Kitchener-Waterloo ⑩

🏛 350,000. 🚉 🚌 ℹ️ 79 St. Joseph St. (519) 585 7517, 1 800 265 6959. www.explorewaterlooregion.com

Originally called Berlin by the German immigrants who settled here in the 1820s, the town was renamed Kitchener (after the British Empire's leading general) during World War I. Today, the town is a supply center for the surrounding farming communities, including religious groups such as the Mennonites *(see box).* Visitors can see the fascinating sight of traditionally dressed Mennonites in their horse-drawn buggies around town. Every year, these descendants of German immigrants organize the nine-day **Oktoberfest**, a celebration of German culture, with everything from sausages with sauerkraut to lederhosen and lager.

Fruit seller in Brantford

Brantford ⑪

🏛 97,000. ✈️ 🚉 🚌 ℹ️ 399 Wayne Gretzky Pkwy (519) 751 9900.

Brantford is an unassuming manufacturing town that takes its name from Joseph Brant (1742–1807), the leader of a confederacy of tribes called the Six Nations. An Iroquois chief himself, Brant settled

here in 1784. He soon decided that the interests of his people lay with the British, and his braves fought alongside the Redcoats during the American War of Independence (1775–83). Sadly, he had chosen the losing side and, after the war, his band was forced to move north to Canada, where the British ceded the natives a piece of land at Brantford. The Iroquois still live in this area, and host the Six Nations Pow Wow, featuring traditional dances and crafts, and held here every August. Brantford is also known for its association with the telephone. In 1876, the first ever long-distance call was made from Brantford to the neighboring village of Paris by Alexander Graham Bell (1847–1922), who had emigrated from Scotland to Ontario in 1870. Bell's old home, conserved as the **Bell Homestead National Historic Site**, is located on the outskirts of town. The site has two buildings: Bell's homestead is furnished in period style and houses displays on his inventions as well as telling the story of the telephone; the other, containing the first Bell company office, was moved here from Brantford in 1969.

Brantford is also the birthplace of native poet and author E. Pauline Johnson.

🏚 **Bell Homestead National Historic Site**
94 Tutela Heights Rd. **Tel** (519) 756 6220. ◯ 9:30am–4:30pm Tue–Sun. ⬤ Jan 1, Dec 25. 🎫 &

Orillia ⑫

🏛 29,000. 🚉 ℹ️ 50 Andrew St. S. (705) 325 1311.

Orillia is a pleasant country town that was the home of the novelist and humorist Stephen Leacock (1869–1944). Leacock's tremendously popular *Sunshine Sketches of a Little Town* poked fun at the vanities of provincial Ontario life in the fictional town of Mariposa. His old lakeshore home has been conserved as the **Stephen Leacock Museum**, containing original furnishings as well as details of his life.

Orillia lies along a narrow strip of water linking Lake Couchiching to Lake Simcoe (once a Huron fishing ground) and is a good base from which to cruise both lakes. On the shore, Orillia's Centennial Park has a marina and a long boardwalk that stretches all the way to Couchiching beach.

🏛 **Stephen Leacock Museum**
50 Museum Drive, Old Brewery Bay. **Tel** (705) 329 1908. ◯ daily. 🎫 &
www.leacockmuseum.com

Bethune Memorial House in the town of Gravenhurst, Muskoka

Muskoka ⑬

🏛 55,000. 🚉 Gravenhurst. 🚌 Huntsville. ℹ️ 1342 Hwy 11 North RR #2, Kilworthy (705) 689 0660, 1 800 267 9700.

Muskoka comprises an area north of Orillia between the towns of Huntsville and Gravenhurst. In summer, city folk stream north to their cottages here. The center of this lake country is Gravenhurst, a resort at the south end of

For hotels and restaurants in this region see pp358–9 and pp383–4

Lake Muskoka. Here, a small museum is devoted to the life and work of Doctor Norman Bethune (1890–1939), who pioneered mobile blood transfusion units during the Spanish Civil War. Bethune Memorial House is the doctor's birthplace, and it has been restored in late 19th-century style.

Windsurfing off Turgean Bay Island in Georgian Bay

Georgian Bay Islands National Park ⑭

Tel (705) 526 9804. 🚉 Midland. ☐ daily. 🍂 summer. ♿ 🅿️ www.pc.gc.ca

The deep-blue waters of Georgian Bay are dotted with thousands of little islands, often no more than a chunk of rock guarded by a windblown pine. The bay is large, beautiful, and flows into Lake Huron. Sixty of its islands have been incorporated into the Georgian Bay Islands National Park. The park's center is Beausoleil

THE MENNONITE RELIGIOUS COMMUNITY

The Mennonite Christian sect was founded in Europe in the early 16th century. The Mennonites were persecuted because they refused to swear any oath of loyalty to the state or take any part in war. In the 17th century, a group split off to form its own, even stricter, sect. These Ammanites (or Amish) emigrated to the US and then to Ontario in 1799. The old-order Amish own property communally and shun modern machinery and clothes, traveling around the highways in distinctive horse-drawn buggies and dressed in traditional clothes.

Amish couple driving a buggy

Island, the hub of the area's wide range of facilities.

Beausoleil is also crossed by scenic hiking trails, but it is important to come properly equipped since it is a remote spot. The only way to reach the island is by water taxi from the hamlet of Honey Harbour. The journey takes about forty minutes. Day trips around the islands are also available from the "Day Tripper's Ferry."

Nottawasaga Bay ⑮

🚉 Barrie. 🚉 Wasaga Beach. ℹ️ 550 River Rd. W., Wasaga Beach 1 888 227 8667. www.wasagabeach.com

Part of scenic Georgian Bay, Nottawasaga Bay is one of the region's most popular vacation destinations. Wasaga Beach has miles of golden, sandy beach and many chalets and cottages. As well as swimming and sunbathing, there is the curious Nancy Island Historic Site, behind Beach Area 2. The site

has a museum which houses the preserved HMS *Nancy:* one of few British boats to survive the War of 1812 *(see pp46–7).*

There are more naval relics in Penetanguishene, just to the east of Nottawasaga Bay, where Discovery Harbour is a superb reconstruction of the British naval base that was established here in 1817. Along the inlet are replicas of the barracks, blacksmiths' workshops, houses, and the original 1840 Officers' Quarters. The harbor holds a pair of replica sailing ships, the *Tecumseh* and the *Bee,* built to 19th-century specifications. In the summer, volunteers organize sailing trips for visitors, who are expected to lend a hand during the voyage.

To the west of Nottawasaga Bay lies Owen Sound. Once a tough Great Lakes port, this is now a quiet place with a Marine-Rail Museum devoted to the town's past. Displays include photographs of Victorian ships and sailors.

Discovery Harbour, Nottawasaga Bay's restored British naval base

Sainte-Marie-among-the-Hurons ⑯

17th-century Iroquoian jug

Sainte-Marie-among-the-Hurons is one of Ontario's most compelling attractions. Located 5 km (3 miles) east of the town of Midland, the site is a reconstruction of the settlement founded here among the Huron natives by Jesuit priests in 1639. The village is divided into two main sections, one for Europeans (complete with a chapel and workshops), the other for Hurons, with a pair of bark-covered longhouses. Marking the boundary between the two is the small church of Saint Joseph, a simple wooden building where the Jesuits set about trying to convert the Hurons. Their efforts met with a variety of reactions, and the complex relationship between the two cultures is explored here in detail.

Exterior of Longhouse
The exterior of the longhouse had bark-covered walls built over a cedar pole frame that was bent to form an arch.

In the hospital the Jesuits used French medicines with limited success. The Huron had no resistance to European diseases such as influenza and measles.

★ Fireside Gathering
Inside the longhouse, fish, skins, and tobacco were hung from the ceiling to dry. An open fire burned through the winter. The smoke caused health problems to the Huron.

Church of Saint Joseph
This is the grave site of two Jesuit priests, Jean de Bré-beuf and Gabriel Lalement, who were captured, bound to the stake, then tortured to death by the Iroquois.

Ojibway Wigwam by the Palisades
This wigwam is built to Ojibway design and lies next to the wooden palisade which encloses the mission. It is believed that the Jesuits built these to make visiting Ojibway feel at home.

STAR FEATURES

★ Fireside Gathering in Longhouse

★ Traditional Crafts

VISITORS' CHECKLIST

Hwy 12 (5 km, 3 miles east of
Midland). **Tel** *(705) 526 7838.*
May–Oct: 10am–5pm daily.
www.hhp.on.ca

★ Traditional Crafts
*The costumed guides here have been trained in the trad-
itional crafts employed by both the Huron and the French,
including 17th-century cooking and blacksmith's work.*

The blacksmith's shop was
important as Sainte-Marie
needed essential items such
as hinges and nails, often
made by using recycled iron.

The carpenter's shop
had an abundant supply
of local wood, and craftsmen from France were
employed by the priests
to build the mission.

Interior of Chapel
*The old chapel has been care-
fully re-created and, with
the light filtering in through
its timbers, it is easy to imagine what it was like for the
priests as they gathered to say
mass each day before dawn.*

Entrance

Bastions helped defend
the mission from attack.
Built of local stone to
ward off arrows and mus-
ket balls, they also served
as observation towers.

0 meters   25
0 yards   25

The Cookhouse Garden
*At Sainte-Marie, care is taken
to grow crops the Huron way,
with corn, beans, and squash
planted in rotation. This system provided a year-round
food supply, which was supple-
mented with meat and fish.*

Goderich ⑰

🏛 *7,600.* ⊠ 🚉 *cnr Hamilton St. & Hwy 21.* **Tel** *(519) 524 6600, 1 800 280 7637.*

Goderich is a charming town overlooking Lake Huron at the mouth of the Maitland River. It was founded in 1825 by the British-owned Canada Company, which had persuaded the Ontario government to part with 1 million ha (2.5 million acres) of fertile land in their province for just twelve cents an acre, a bargain of such proportions that there was talk of corruption. Eager to attract settlers, the company had the Huron Road built from Cambridge, in the east, to Goderich. The town was laid out in a formal manner, with the main streets radiating out from the striking, octagon-shaped center.

Goderich possesses two excellent museums. The first, the **Huron County Museum**, houses a large collection of antique farm implements, as well as a military gallery and a reconstruction of a 19th-century town street, with store fronts and a real locomotive. There is also a huge, steam-driven thresher. The **Huron Historic Gaol National Historic Site**, built between 1839 and 1842, is an authentically preserved Victorian prison. Fascinating tours are available of its dank cells, the original jailers' rooms, and the Governor's 19th-century house. The town is also renowned for its sunsets, particularly as viewed from the shore of Lake Huron.

The golden sands of Sauble Beach on the shore of Lake Huron

♛ Huron Historic Gaol National Historic Site
181 Victoria St. N. **Tel** *(519) 524 2686.* ◯ *May–Sep: 10am–4:30pm Mon–Sat, 1–4:30pm Sun.* 📷

🏛 Huron County Museum
110 North St. **Tel** *(519) 524 2686.* ◯ *May–Sep: 10am–4:30pm Mon–Sat, 1–4:30pm Sun.* 📷 ♿

Sauble Beach ⑱

🚌 *Owen Sound.* 🚉 *RR1, Sauble Beach (519) 422 1262.* **www**.*saublebeach.com*

One of the finest sandy beaches in Ontario, Sauble Beach stretches for 11 km (7 miles) along the shores of Lake Huron. Running behind this beach is a long, narrow band of campsites, cabins, and cottages. The center of the resort is at the pocket-sized village of Sauble Beach, with a population of only five hundred. The quiet back streets of the village also offer friendly guesthouses and B&Bs. The most attractive and tranquil camping is at Sauble Falls Provincial Park, north of the beach.

Lake Huron ⑲

🚉 *Sarnia, Southern shore (519) 336 3232.* 🚉 *Barrie, Georgian Bay (705) 725 7280, 1 800 263 7745.* **www**. *georgianbaytourism.on.ca* 🚉 *Sault Ste. Marie, North shore (705) 945 6941.*

Of all the Great Lakes, it is Lake Huron which has the most varied landscapes along its shoreline. To the south, the lake narrows to funnel past the largely industrial towns of Sarnia and Windsor on its way to Lake Erie while its southeast shore is bounded by a gentle bluff, marking the limit of one of Ontario's most productive agricultural regions. Farther north, the long, thin isthmus of Bruce Peninsula stretches out into Lake Huron, signaling a dramatic change in the character of the lakeshore. This is where the southern flatlands are left behind for the more rugged, glacier-scraped country of the Canadian Shield. This transition can be seen clearly in the area of Georgian Bay. This is an impressive shoreline of lakes, forests, beaches, and villages that attracts large numbers of visitors. The lake's island-sprinkled waters are a popular area for water sports. Outdoor activities here include swimming, hiking, and fishing.

Historic storefront in the charming town of Goderich

For hotels and restaurants in this region see pp358–9 and pp383–4

Bruce Peninsula Tour ⑳

The 100-km (62-mile) Bruce Peninsula divides the main body of Lake Huron from Georgian Bay and also contains some of the area's most scenic terrain. Bruce Peninsula National Park lies along the eastern shore and boasts craggy headlands and limestone cliffs with several hiking paths. Beyond the port of Tobermory, at the peninsula's tip, Fathom Five Marine National Park, comprises 19 uninhabited islands. The park is popular with divers because of its clear waters and amazing rock formations.

TIPS FOR WALKERS

Tour Route: The route follows Route 9 and Hwy 6. It can be reached from Owen Sound in the south, or Tobermory in the north. *Length:* 100 km (62 miles). *Stopping-off points:* Diving trips and tours to Flowerpot Island leave from Tobermory, which also has good accommodation.

Stokes Bay ①
The hamlet of Stokes Bay, with its sandy beaches and good fishing, is typical of the villages here. It is close to the the peninsula's main sights.

Cabot Head ②
The Cabot Head Lighthouse and keeper's house can be reached via the scenic coast road from the village of Dyer's Bay.

Fathom Five Marine Park ⑤
Off the northern tip of the peninsula, the park's boundaries enclose an area around 19 islands. Divers are drawn here by the clear, calm waters and shipwrecks.

Bruce Peninsula National Park ③
The park's rugged cliffs are part of the Niagara Escarpment, a limestone ridge that stretches across southern Ontario and along the peninsula.

Dyer's Bay

Miller Lake

Ferndale

Barrow Bay

Hope Bay

Pike Bay

Wiarton

Tobermory ④
At the northern tip of the peninsula, this small fishing village is a hub for tourist acitivties in the area. Ferries to Flowerpot Island leave from here.

Flowerpot Island ⑤
The only island in Fathom Five Marine Park with basic facilities, it is noted for the rock columns that dot the coastline.

| 0 km | 5 |
| 0 miles | 5 |

KEY

▬ Tour route

═ Other roads

☀ Viewpoint

Manitoulin Island ㉑

🏠 *12,600.* 🚌 🚶 *70 Meredith St, Little Current (705) 368 3021.*

Hugging the northern shores of Lake Huron, Manitoulin Island is, at 2,800 sq km (1,100 square miles), the world's largest freshwater island. A quiet place of small villages, rolling farmland, woodland, and lakes, its edges are fringed by long, deserted beaches. The lake's North Channel separates Manitoulin from the mainland, its waters attracting summer sailors, while hikers come to explore the island's trails.

The Ojibway people first occupied the island more than 10,000 years ago, naming it after the Great Spirit – Manitou, (Manitoulin means Spirit Island). First Nations peoples still constitute over a quarter of the island's population. Every August they celebrate their culture in one of Canada's largest powwows, the Wikwemikong (Bay of the Beaver).

On the north shore, Gore Bay houses five tiny museums that focus on the island's early settlers. Nearby, the island's largest settlement is Little Current, a quiet town with a handful of motels and restaurants. From May to September the Chi Cheemaun car ferry connects Tobermory on the Bruce Peninsula to Manitoulin Island.

Gore Bay on Manitoulin Island

Reflections in George Lake, Killarney Provincial Park

Killarney Provincial Park ㉒

Tel (705) 287 2900. 🚌 *Sudbury.* ○ *daily.* 🅿 *for some facilities.*

Killarney Provincial Park is a beautiful tract of wilderness with crystal-blue lakes, pine and hardwood forests, boggy lowlands, and the spectacular La Cloche Mountains, which are known for their striking white quartzite ridges. This magnificent scenery has inspired many artists, particularly members of the Group of Seven *(see pp164–5),* one of whom, Franklin Carmichael, saw the park as Ontario's most "challenging and gratifying landscape." The park's 100-km (62-mile) La Cloche Silhouette Trail takes between a week and ten days to complete and attracts numbers of serious hikers to its stunning views of the mountains and of Georgian Bay. Canoeists can paddle on the park's many lakes and rivers by following a network of well-marked canoe routes.

Temagami ㉓

🏠 *1,000.* 🚌 🚶 *Chamber of Commerce, Lakeshore Rd. (705) 569 3344.*

The tiny resort of Temagami and its wild surroundings have long attracted fur traders and trappers, painters, and writers, most famously Grey Owl *(see p250),* the remarkable Englishman who posed as a Native Canadian and achieved celebrity status as a naturalist and conservationist in the 1930s. The resort sits on the distinctively shaped Lake Temagami, a deep lake with long fjords and bays as

One of Lake Temagami's numerous canoe routes

For hotels and restaurants in this region see pp358–9 and pp383–4

well as 1,400 islands, which are crisscrossed by numerous scenic canoe routes, hiking and mountain bike trails.

Even more remote is the Lady Evelyn Smoothwater Wilderness Park, farther to the west. The only way in is by canoe or float plane from Temagami, but the reward is some of Ontario's most stunning scenery. Much more accessible is the 30-m (98-ft) high Temagami Fire Tower lookout point, which provides panoramic views of the surrounding pine forests, and the charming Finlayson Provincial Park, a popular place to picnic and camp; both are located on Temagami's outskirts.

Sault Ste. Marie ❷

🏃 75,000. ✕ 🚊 🚌
ℹ 99 Foster Dr. (705) 759 5442.

Where the rapids of St. Mary's River link Lake Superior to Lake Huron sits the attractive town of Sault Ste. Marie, one of Ontario's oldest European communities. The town was founded as a Jesuit mission and fur trading post by the French in 1688. Called the "Sault" (pronounced "Soo") after the French word for "rapids," the trading station prospered after 1798 when the rapids were bypassed by a canal. Since then, the canal has been upgraded time and again, and today transports the largest of container ships to the interior, thereby maintaining a thriving local economy.

Although there are regular boat trips along the canal, visitors are drawn to Sault Ste. Marie's main tourist attraction, the **Algoma Central Railway**, which offers day-long rail tours from the city into the wilderness. The train weaves north through dense forest, past secluded lakes and over yawning ravines to reach the spectacular scenery of Agawa Canyon where there is a two-hour break for lunch.

In town, the Roberta Bondar Pavilion is a huge tentlike structure decorated with murals depicting Sault's history. Named after Canada's first female astronaut, who

Canal locks at Sault Ste. Marie

was on the *Discovery* mission in 1992, the pavilion is also the venue for concerts, exhibitions, and a summer farmers' market.

🚂 Algoma Central Railway
129 Bay St. **Tel** (705) 946 7300.
⭕ Jun–mid-Oct: once daily. 🖼 🕎

Lake Superior ❷

ℹ Ontario Travel Information Centre, Sault Ste. Marie (705) 945 6941.

The least polluted and most westerly of the Great Lakes, Lake Superior is the world's largest body of freshwater, with a surface area of 82,000 sq km (31,700 sq miles). It is known for sudden violent storms, long a source of dread to local sailors. The lake's northern coast is a vast weather-swept stretch of untamed wilderness

dominated by dramatic granite outcrops and seemingly limitless forest. This challenging area is best experienced in Pukaskwa National Park and Lake Superior Provincial Park, both reached via the Trans-Canada Highway (Hwy 17) as it cuts a dramatic route along the lake's north shore.

Thunder Bay ❷

🏃 109,000. ✈ ✕ 🚊 ℹ Terry Fox Information Centre, Hwy 11/17 E. (807) 983 2041, 1 800 667 8386.

On the northern shore of Lake Superior, Thunder Bay is Canada's third-largest freshwater port, its massive grain elevators dominating the city's waterfront. Grain is brought to Thunder Bay from the prairies farther west before being shipped to the rest of the world via the Great Lakes.

The town was originally established as a French trading post in 1679. These early days are celebrated at Old Fort William, a replica of the old fur trading post, with costumed traders, French explorers, and natives. Fort William was amalgamated with the adjacent town of Port Arthur to form Thunder Bay in 1970.

🏰 Old Fort William
Off Broadway Ave. **Tel** (807) 473 2333. ⭕ mid-May–mid-Oct: 9am–5pm daily. 🖼 🕎 www.fwhp.ca

Lake Superior, the world's largest freshwater lake

Hoodoos near Drumheller ▷

CENTRAL CANADA

Introducing Central Canada

Central Canada covers the provinces of Manitoba, Saskatchewan, and eastern Alberta and encompasses the most productive agricultural and energy-rich part of the country. The region is dominated by prairie, (often associated with borderless fields that stretch to the horizon) and covers a vast area of the western interior, which is the size of Mexico. The region is not all prairie, but has a variety of landscapes, from the forested aspen parkland to the west and north of the plains to the tundra of northern Manitoba and the rocky desert of the badlands in the south.

The Broadway Bridge and central Saskatoon overlooking the South Saskatchewan River

Grain elevators and wheat cars punctuate the vast fields of the Canadian prairies

For additional map symbols see back flap

GETTING AROUND

Winnipeg, Edmonton, Regina, and Saskatoon, the four main cities of the region, are well served by public transportation, with regular air, train, and bus connections from British Columbia and other provinces. All four cities also have international airports. From Winnipeg, the Trans-Canada Highway follows the route established in the 19th century by the Canadian Pacific Railway, going 1,333 km (828 miles) west to Calgary. The more scenic Yellowhead Highway starts at the Forks in Winnipeg and runs through Yorkton and Saskatoon, reaching Edmonton at 1,301 km (808 miles), continuing on through Jasper National Park and British Columbia.

KEY

▬	Highway
▬	Major road
—	River
--	Provincial boundaries

Hudson Bay

MANITOBA

● **LYNN LAKE**

● **THOMPSON**

106

● **FLIN FLON**

● **THE PAS**

6

60

10

Lake Winnipeg

3

● **YORKTON**

16

● **DAUPHIN**

6

● **PORTAGE LA PRAIRIE**

1

WINNIPEG

EGINA

The prairies of Manitoba, one of Canada's richest agricultural areas

0 km	150
0 miles	150

SEE ALSO

Dinosaurs and Prehistoric Canada

It is easier to imagine gunslingers and coyotes in the desert-like badlands of the Red Deer River Valley in Alberta than it is to envisage the dinosaurs who once lived in this region. Over 75 million years ago the area was a tropical swamp, similar to the Florida Everglades, and the favored habitat of these huge reptiles, which dominated the Earth for some 160 million years. All the dinosaur specimens found here originate from the Cretaceous period (144–65 million years ago). Dramatic changes in the region's weather patterns, from wet and tropical to dry desert, helped to preserve an incredible number of dinosaur remains in the area. Today, the Dinosaur Provincial Park is a UNESCO World Heritage Site.

LOCATOR MAP

This Triceratops skull *shows the dinosaur's flaring bony frill, which protected its neck from attack. Its two horns were an awesome 1 m (3 ft) long. More types of horned dinosaurs have been found here in Alberta than anywhere else.*

Trained staff carefully dig out a groove around the bone while it is still in the ground. Once removed it will be carefully matched to its adjoining bone.

The Magnolia *is thought to be one of Earth's first flowering plants, or angiosperms, and became widespread during the Cretaceous period.*

Joseph Burr Tyrrell *found the first important dinosaur skeleton sections in the Red Deer River Valley, Alberta, in 1884. A geologist, Tyrrell stumbled across the skull of a 70 million-year-old Albertosaurus while surveying coal deposits. Subsequently, palaeontologists rushed here to search for fossils. Drumheller's Royal Tyrrell Museum of Palaeontology is named after him (see p248).*

An artist's re-creation *of the Cretaceous landscape depicts the types of flora living at the time. Tree ferns dominated the country, and grew in large forests to heights of 18 m (60 ft). Similar species still grow in the tropics.*

Horseshoe Canyon *lies along the Red Deer River, its high, worn hills visibly layered with ancient sediments. Ice Age glaciers eroded the layers of mud and sand that buried the remains of dinosaurs and plants. Erosion continues to form this barren, lunar landscape, exposing more bones, petrified wood, and other fossils.*

This dinosaur nest *on display at the Royal Tyrrell Museum was discovered at Devil's Coulee, Alberta, in 1987, and contains several embryos and eggs of the plant-eating Hadrosaur.*

The Royal Tyrrell *Field Station in the Dinosaur Provincial Park opened in 1987, and offers visitors interpretive displays explaining the history of the area's dinosaurs.*

SIMULATED DINOSAUR DIG

The Royal Tyrrell Museum offers the chance to experience the thrill of excavation on a realistic dinosaur dig, designed for ages 10 and older. Using the real tools and techniques of palaeontology, and with Museum science educators as guides, visitors can uncover casts of dinosaur bones, map the quarry, make a field jacket, and learn how to read fossils. There is also a 90-minute hike through the Badlands where visitors can prospect for fossils and investigate real dinosaur remains.

The leg bone of a duck billed dinosaur is revealed to be complete. Beneath it another piece of bone has been covered with strips of plaster of Paris to protect it during transportation to a laboratory.

The reconstructed skeleton *of an Albertosaurus towers over the Dinosaur Hall at the Royal Tyrrell Museum. The first dinosaur discovered in the area, Albertosaurus was a fierce meat-eating predator. Despite being eight meters (26 ft) long and weighing some two tons (2,032 kg), this dinosaur was capable of reaching speeds of 40 km/h (25 mph).*

Canadian Mounties

The Royal Canadian Mounted Police are a symbol of national pride. Canada's first Prime Minister, Sir John A. Macdonald, founded the North West Mounted Police in 1873 in Ontario after violence in the west of the country (between illicit liquor dealers and local natives) reached a climax with the Cypress Hills Massacre *(see p247)*. Marching west, the Mounties reached the Oldman River, Alberta, 70 km (43 miles) west of the Cypress Hills, where they built Fort Macleod in 1874. The principal aims of the Mounties were to establish good relations with the aboriginal peoples of the Prairies and to maintain order over new settlers in the late 1800s. The Mounties won respect for their diplomacy, policing the Canadian Pacific Railway workers and the Klondike Gold Rush in the Yukon during the 1890s. In recognition of their service they gained the Royal prefix in 1904.

Traditional Mountie

The lush Cypress Hills *were the site of a gruesome massacre which led to the founding of the North West Mounted Police.*

The march west *covered 3,135 km (1,949 miles) from Fort Dufferin, Manitoba to southern Alberta. A force of 275 men, 310 horses, and cattle, was sent to catch the illicit whiskey traders operating in the west. Battling with extreme temperatures, plagues of insects, and lack of supplies, the Mounties arrived at the Oldman River in 1874.*

THE LONG MARCH

Sioux Chief Sitting Bull

Inspector James M. Walsh sealed the Mounties' reputation for bravery when he took only six men on a parley with Sioux Chief Sitting Bull. The Sioux had retreated to the area after their defeat of US General Custer at the Battle of the Little Big Horn in 1876. Although the Sioux were the traditional enemies of the local Blackfoot and Cree Indians, there was no fighting after the arrival of the Mounties. Walsh's force succeeded in enforcing law and order across mid-west Canada, winning respect for their diplomacy. Blackfoot native chief Crowfoot praised their fairness saying, "They have protected us as the feathers of a bird protect it from winter."

James M. Walsh

The adventures of the *pioneering Mounties have long been a source of inspiration to countless authors and filmmakers. Square-jawed and scarlet clad, the Mountie was the perfect hero. Perhaps the best-known "Mountie" film was the 1936 "Rose Marie" starring crooner Nelson Eddy and Jeanette MacDonald.*

The skilled horsemen of the Musical Ride are selected after two years on the force. The officers then begin seven months of intensive training.

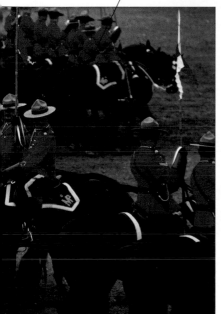

THE MUSICAL RIDE

The Musical Ride is a thrilling spectacle of 32 riders and horses performing a series of traditional cavalry drills set to music. The drills have not changed since their original use in the British army over a century ago. Staying in tight formation, the horses do the trot, the canter, the rally, and the charge. Every summer the Ride is performed in different venues across Canada and the US.

As an enduring symbol of Canada *the image of the Mounties has adorned everything from postage stamps and currency to this 1940s promotional tourist poster for Lake Louise in Banff National Park.*

32 specially bred horses take part in the Musical Ride. A mixture of thoroughbred stallion crossed with black Hanoverian mare, the horses train for two years.

Today's Mounties *are a 28,000-strong police force responsible for the enforcement of federal law across Canada. Their duties range from counting migratory birds to exposing foreign espionage. Jets, helicopters, and cars are all used by modern Mounties.*

CENTRAL CANADA

Central Canada covers a vast region of boreal forest and fertile grasslands, often known as the Prairies, which traverses Manitoba, Saskatchewan, and part of Alberta. Originally, First Nations peoples lived here, and depended on the herds of buffalo that provided them with food, shelter, and tools. By the end of the 19th century the buffalo were hunted almost to extinction. European settlers built towns and farms, some taking native wives and forming a new cultural grouping, the Métis. By the 20th century the area's economy came to rely on gas, oil, and grain. Today the Prairies, punctuated by striking, tall grain elevators, are known for the surprising variety of their landscape and the intriguing history of their towns.

SIGHTS AT A GLANCE

Historic Towns and Cities
Batoche National
 Historic Site **28**
Churchill **32**
Dauphin **8**
Duck Lake **29**
Edmonton **23**
Flin Flon **31**
Fort Qu'appelle **10**
Gimli **5**
Lethbridge **18**
Maple Creek **16**
Medicine Hat **17**
Moose Jaw **12**
North Battleford
 and Battleford **27**
Portage La Prairie **6**

Red Deer **21**
Regina **11**
Saskatoon **13**
Selkirk **3**
Steinbach **2**
The Pas **30**
Vegreville **24**
Winnipeg **1**
Yorkton **9**

Rivers and Lakes
Lake Winnipeg **4**

National and Provincial Parks
Cypress Hills Interprovincial
 Park **15**
Dinosaur Provincial Park **20**
Elk Island National Park **22**

Grasslands National Park **14**
Prince Albert National Park **26**
Riding Mountain
 National Park **7**
Wood Buffalo National Park **25**

Museums
Royal Tyrrell Museum **19**

KEY

✈	International airport
=	Highway
▬	Major road
—	Major rail routes
·—·	International border

0 km 250

0 miles 250

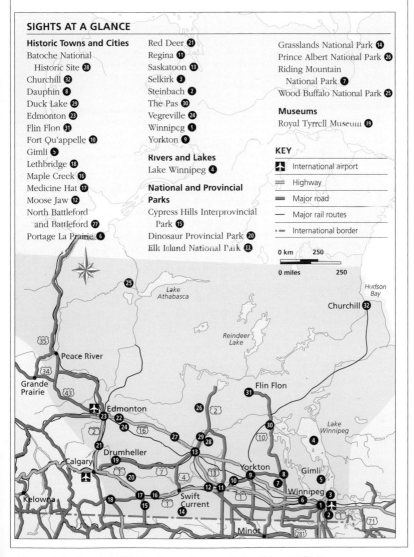

◁ A young Indian dancer in traditional costume performs a centuries-old dance in Alberta

Winnipeg ❶

Winnipeg is a cosmopolitan city located at the geographic heart of Canada. Over half of Manitoba's population live here, mostly in suburbs that reflect the city's broad mix of cultures. Winnipeg's position, at the confluence of the Red and Assiniboine rivers, made it an important trading center for First Nations people going back some 6,000 years. From the 1600s Europeans settled here to trade fur. During the 1880s grain became the principal industry of the west, aided by a railroad network routed through Winnipeg. Today, this attractive city, with its museums, historic buildings, and excellent restaurants, makes for an enjoyable stay.

Exploring Winnipeg

Most of Winnipeg's sights are within easy walking distance of the downtown area. The excellent Manitoba Museum of Man and Nature and the Ukrainian Cultural Centre lie east of the Exchange District.

At the junction of the Red and Assiniboine rivers lies The Forks, a family entertainment center devoted to the city's history. At the junction of Portage and Main streets, lie the city's financial and shopping districts with their banks and malls.

🚉 St. Boniface

Riel Tourism, 219 Provencher Blvd. **Tel** 1(866) 808 8338. ☐ Mon–Sat. 🖕
Canada's second-largest French-speaking community outside of Quebec lives in the historic district of St. Boniface. This quiet suburb faces The Forks across the Red River and was founded by priests in 1818 to care for the Métis (see p49) and the French living here. In 1844 the Grey Nuns built a hospital that now houses the St. Boniface Museum.

Priests built the Basilica of St. Boniface in 1818. Although the building was destroyed by fire in 1968, its elegant white façade is one of the city's best-loved landmarks. Métis leader Louis Riel was buried here after his execution following the rebellion at Batoche in 1881.

🏛 Manitoba Children's Museum

45 Forks Market Rd. **Tel** (204) 924 4000. ☐ daily. 🎫 🖕 www. childrensmuseum.com
Located within The Forks complex, this museum provides a series of enticing hands-on exhibits aimed at children from the ages of 3 to 11. In the All Aboard gallery children can play at being train drivers for a day on a reconstructed 1952 diesel engine while learning the history of Canada's railroad. They can also browse the internet or produce a TV show in a studio.

🚉 The Forks National Historic Site

401–25 Forks Market Rd. **Tel** (204) 957 7618. ☐ grounds: daily; office: Mon–Fri. 🎫 special events. 🖕
The Forks National Historic Site celebrates the history of the city. The river port, warehouses, and stables of this once bustling railroad terminus have now been restored.

The stable buildings, with their lofty ceilings, skylights, and connecting indoor bridges, house a flourishing market offering a range of specialty food, fresh produce, meat, and fish. Crafts, jewelry, and folk art are sold from the converted hayloft.

Set in 23 ha (56 acres) of parkland, The Forks has an open-air amphitheater, and

The brightly colored main entrance to the Manitoba Children's Museum

Cruise boats and canoes can be hired from The Forks harbor

a tower for a spectacular six-story-high view of the Winnipeg skyline. The river-side walkway also offers fine views of the city center and St. Boniface.

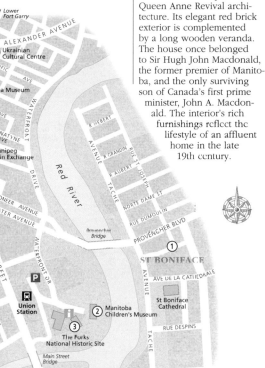

WINNIPEG TOWN CENTER

VISITORS' CHECKLIST

🏠 650,000. ✈ 12 km (8 miles) NW of city. 🚉 cnr Main St. & Broadway. 🚌 Greyhound Canada Station, cnr Portage Ave. & Colony St. 🛈 Destination Winnipeg, 259 Portage Ave. *Tel* (204) 943 1970, 1 800 665 0204. 🎭 Festival Voyageur (Feb); Red River Exhibition (Jun); Winnipeg Intl Children's Festival (Jun); Folklorama (Aug).

🏛 Dalnavert

61 Carlton St. *Tel* (204) 943 2835. ◻ Wed–Sun. 🎟 ♿ 📷
Built in 1895, this beautifully restored Victorian house is an excellent example of Queen Anne Revival architecture. Its elegant red brick exterior is complemented by a long wooden veranda. The house once belonged to Sir Hugh John Macdonald, the former premier of Manitoba, and the only surviving son of Canada's first prime minister, John A. Macdonald. The interior's rich furnishings reflect the lifestyle of an affluent home in the late 19th century.

The Golden Boy statue adorns the dome of the Legislative Building

🏛 Legislative Building

Cnr Broadway & Osborne. *Tel* (204) 945 5813. ◻ Mon–Fri for tours. ♿
The Legislative Building is built of a rare and valuable limestone complete with the delicate remains of fossils threaded through its façade. The building is set in 12 ha (30 acres) of beautifully kept gardens dotted with statues of poets such as Robert Burns of Scotland, and Ukrainian Taras Ahevchenko, which celebrate the province's ethnic diversity.

🏛 Winnipeg Art Gallery

300 Memorial Blvd. *Tel* (204) 786 6641. ◻ Tue–Sun. 🎟
This gallery boasts the largest collection of contemporary Inuit art in the world, with over 10,000 carvings, prints, drawings, and textiles. Especially striking is the large four-panel fabric collage wall-hanging, "Four Seasons of the Tundra" by Inuit artist Ruth Qaulluaryuk. The Gallery also contains Gothic and Renaissance altar paintings and tapestries donated by Irish peer Viscount Gore.

🏛 Exchange District and Market Square

Albert St. *Tel (204) 942 6716.*
www.exchangedistrict.org

When the Canadian Pacific Railway decided to build its transcontinental line through Winnipeg in 1881, the city experienced a boom that led to the setting up of several commodity exchanges. Named after the Winnipeg Grain Exchange, this district was soon populated with a solid array of handsome terracotta and cut stone hotels, banks, warehouses, and theaters. The Exchange District is now a National Historic Site and has been restored to its former glory. It now houses boutiques, craft stores, furniture and antique stores, galleries, artists' studios, and residential lofts.

The center of the district is Old Market Square, a popular site for staging local festivals and outdoor concerts.

🏛 Ukrainian Cultural and Educational Centre

184 Alexander Ave. E. *Tel (204) 942 0218.* ⬭ *10am–4pm Mon–Sat, 2–5pm Sun.* 🚻

Housed in an attractive 1930s building in the Exchange District, this institute was founded to celebrate the history and culture of Canada's second-largest ethnic grouping.

The center's museum, gallery, and research library are known for their collection of wood carvings, vibrant textiles, and collection of elaborately decorated, often hand-painted, *pysanky* (Easter eggs). The Harvest of Dreams exhibit tells the story of how the first Ukrainians arrived in Canada.

Original 19th-century walls enclose the buildings at Lower Fort Garry

🏛 Lower Fort Garry

5981 Hwy 9. *Tel (204) 785 6050, 1 877 534 3678.* ⬭ *May–Sep: 9am–5pm daily.* 🅿 🚻 **www**.pc.gc.ca

Located 32 km (20 miles) north of Winnipeg on the banks of the Red River, Lower Fort Garry is the only original stone fur-trading post left standing in Canada. The Fort was established in 1830 by George Simpson, the governor of the Hudson's Bay Company's northern division, whose large house is now one of the fort's major attractions.

An interactive display is the highlight in the reception center. Inside, several buildings have been restored, including the clerk's quarters and the store with its stacks of furs.

🏛 Royal Canadian Mint

520 Lagimodière Blvd. *Tel (204) 983 6429, 1 866 822 6724.* ⬭ *9am–5pm daily (Sep–mid-May: Tue–Sat).* ⬤ *Jan 1, Dec 25.* 🅿 🚻 ☑ **www**.mint.ca

The Royal Canadian Mint is housed in a striking building of rose-colored glass. The mint produces more than four billion coins annually for Canadian circulation, as well as for 60 other countries including Thailand and India.

🍃 Assiniboine Park

2355 Corydon Ave. *Tel (204) 986 5537.* ⬭ *daily.* 🚻

Stretching for 153 ha (378 acres) along the south side of the Assiniboine River, Assiniboine Park is one of the largest urban parks in central Canada.

One of the park's best-loved attractions is the Leo Mol Sculpture Garden, which has some 50 bronze sculptures by the celebrated local artist. The park's Conservatory offers a tropical palm house which has seasonal displays of a wide range of flowers and shrubs. The park also features an English garden, a miniature railroad, and a fine example of a French formal garden. The old refreshment pavilion is now the Pavilion Gallery, which focuses on local artists. A large outdoor bandshell houses live music.

The Assiniboine Park Zoo contains over 250 different species, specializing in cold-hardy animals from the northern latitudes and mountain ranges such as polar bears, cougars, elk, and bald eagles. The zoo houses a large statue of Winnie the Bear, thought to be modeled on the Winnie the Pooh of the A.A. Milne books.

The park's numerous cycling and walking trails are popular in summer, as is cross-country skiing, skating, and tobogganing in winter.

Sculpture in the Leo Mol garden, Assiniboine park

A pink glass pyramid houses Canada's Royal Mint

For hotels and restaurants in this region see pp359–60 and pp384–5. For transport information see pp420–21

The Manitoba Museum

Outstanding displays of the region's geography and people are imaginatively presented at this excellent museum, which opened in 1970. The visitor proceeds through chronologically organized galleries with displays that range from pre-history to the present day. Each geographical area also has its own gallery: from the Earth History Gallery, which contains fossils up to 500 million years old, to the re-creation of Winnipeg in the 1920s, including a cinema, and a dentist's office. One of the museum's biggest draws is a full-size replica of the Nonsuch, a 17th-century ketch.

VISITORS' CHECKLIST

190 Rupert Ave. **Tel** (204) 956 2830. ▣ 11. ◯ 10am–4pm Tue–Fri, 11am–5pm Sat, Sun (May–Aug: 10am–5pm daily). ▦ ⌖ ▯
▣ www.manitobamuseum.ca

KEY

☐ Orientation Gallery

☐ Earth History Gallery

☐ Arctic/Sub-Arctic Gallery

☐ Boreal Forest Gallery

☐ Grasslands Gallery

☐ Discovery Room

☐ Urban Gallery

☐ Nonsuch Gallery

☐ Hudson's Bay Company Gallery

☐ Parklands/Mixed Woods Gallery

☐ Temporary exhibits

☐ Non-exhibition space

Moose Diorama
A moose and her calf among the conifers of the boreal forest are part of a display that includes a group of Cree people rock painting and gathering food before the harsh winter sets in.

Boreal Mezzanine

Earth History Mezzanine

GALLERY GUIDE

The galleries are arranged on two levels, with steps connecting to mezzanines in the Earth History and Boreal Forest galleries. Part of a three-story addition houses the museum's Hudson's Bay Company collection.

Main entrance

Nonsuch Gallery
This two-masted ketch, built in England in 1968, is a replica of the Nonsuch that arrived in Hudson Bay in 1688 in search of furs.

Buffalo Hunt
A Métis hunter chasing buffalo symbolizes the museum's focus on man's relationship with his environment.

Prairie fields bloom with color across Central Canada during summer ▷

Ploughing with horses at the Mennonite Heritage Village, Steinbach

Steinbach ❷

🏠 13,000. ✈ 🚌 ℹ Hwy 12N. (204) 326 9566.

About an hour's drive south-east of Winnipeg, Steinbach is a closely knit community with impressive businesses in trucking, printing, manufacturing, and especially car dealerships. These are run largely by the Mennonites, members of a Protestant religious sect who are noted for their fair dealing.

Steam Engine at the Mennonite Heritage Village

The Mennonites arrived in Steinbach on ox-drawn carts in 1874, having fled from religious persecution in Russia. Despite not having a rail link, the town thrived, as the Mennonites were good farmers and, later, car dealers (despite preferring not to use cars themselves). The nearby **Mennonite Heritage Village** re-creates a 19th-century Mennonite settlement, with some buildings dating from the 1870s, and a church and school furnished to the period. Its restaurant serves home-made meals such as borscht, a soup made with cabbage, and cream according to a traditional recipe. The store offers locally crafted items, including Victorian candy.

🏛 **Mennonite Heritage Village**
Hwy 12 North. **Tel** (204) 326 9661, 1 866 280 8741. ⏱ May–Sep: daily; Oct–Apr: Tue–Fri. 🔲 🚻 www.
mennoniteheritagevillage.com

Selkirk ❸

🏠 9,600. 🚌 ℹ Red River North Tourism, 18 Main St. (204) 482 2020. **www**.redrivernorthtourism.com

Named after the fifth Earl of Selkirk, Thomas Douglas, whose family had an interest in the Hudson's Bay Company, Selkirk was established in 1882 when settlers arrived along the shores of the Red River. Today, on Main Street, a 7.5-m (25-ft) high statue of a catfish proclaims Selkirk as the "Catfish capital of North America." Sport fishing is a year-round activity, attracting enthusiasts from across North America.

The city's Marine Museum displays six restored historic ships, including the 1897 S.S. *Keenora*, Manitoba's oldest steamship.

Lake Winnipeg ❹

🖼 Winnipeg. 🖼 Winnipeg. ℹ Travel Manitoba (204) 927 7800, 1 800 665 0040. **www**.travelmanitoba.com

Lake Winnipeg is a huge stretch of water some 350 km (217 miles) long that dominates the province of Manitoba, connecting the south of the province to the north at Hudson Bay via the Nelson River. Today, the resorts that line the lake are popular with locals and visitors alike.

Numerous beaches line the southeastern coast of the lake, including Winnipeg Beach, with one of the best windsurfing bays on the lake. A wood carving of an Indian head by native artist Peter "Wolf" Toth stands in the local park. Called *Whispering Giant*, the sculpture honors the Ojibwa, Cree, and Assiniboine First Nations people of Manitoba.

Grand Beach in the **Grand Beach Provincial Park** has long powdery-white sand beaches and huge grass-topped dunes over 12 m (39 ft) high. Stretching back from the beach, the marsh, which is also known as the lagoon, is one of the park's treasures, and supports many species of birds, such as the rare and endangered Piping Plover.

Moving west from the lake, **Oak Hammock Marsh** provides an important habitat for over 300 species of birds and animals. The marsh's tall grass prairie, meadows, and aspen-oak bluffs house birds such as the ruff (a shorebird), the

Historic ships outside the Marine Museum of Manitoba in Selkirk

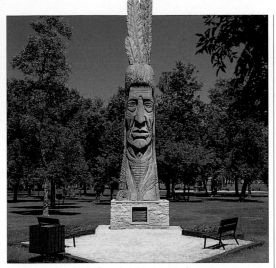

Carved cedar sculpture in the park at Winnipeg Beach

garganey (a duck), and the sharp-tailed sparrow.

Farther north, **Hecla/ Grindstone Provincial Park** occupies a number of islands in the lake. A causeway links the mainland to Hecla Island, which was originally inhabited by the Anishinabe (Ojibwa) people. The first European settlers here were Icelanders who arrived in 1875. Today, the seaside village of Hecla is a pretty open-air museum featuring several restored 19th-century buildings. From Hecla there are many hiking and biking trails that lead to viewpoints for sightings of waterfowl such as great blue herons and the rare western grebe.

🍁 **Grand Beach Provincial Park**
Hwy 12, nr Grand Marais. *Tel* (204) 754 5040. ☐ daily. 📷 ♿ partial.

🍁 **Hecla/Grindstone Provincial Park**
Hwy 8, nr Riverton. *Tel* (204) 378 2261. ☐ daily. ♿

Gimli ❺

🏠 2,100. 🚌 🛈 Centre St. (204) 642 7974.

Located on the western shores of Lake Winnipeg, Gimli is the largest Icelandic community outside Iceland. The settlers arrived, having gained the rights to land, at nearby Willow

Creek in 1875. They soon proclaimed an independent state, which lasted until 1897 when the government insisted that other immigrants be allowed to settle in Gimli. Today, the **New Iceland Heritage Museum** tells the story of the town's unusual history.

Gimli has a distinctly nautical atmosphere, with cobbled sidewalks leading down to a picturesque harbor and a wooden pier. At the Icelandic Festival of Manitoba, held every August, visitors can play at being Vikings, participate in games, listen to folk music, and eat Icelandic specialties.

About 25 km (15 miles) west of Gimli, the Narcisse Wildlife Management Area has been set up to preserve the habitat

Statue of a Viking in the village of Gimli

of thousands of red-sided garter snakes that can be seen here during early spring and early fall, on a specially designated short trail.

🏛 **New Iceland Heritage Museum**
The Waterfront Centre, Unit 108, 94 First Ave. *Tel* (204) 642 4001. ☐ 9am–4pm daily. 📷 ♿

Portage la Prairie ❻

🏠 13,000. 🚌 ✈ 🛈 97 Sask Ave. E. (204) 239 8334.

Portage la Prairie lies at the center of a rich agricultural area growing wheat, barley, and canola. The town is named after the French term for an overland detour, as Portage la Prairie lies between Lake Manitoba and the Assiniboine River, which formed a popular waterway for early travelers. Today, this thriving farming community contains the Fort La Reine Museum and Pioneer Village, on the site of the original fort built by the French explorer, La Vérendrye, in 1738. The museum offers exhibits of tools and photographs detailing 19th-century prairie life. The popular railroad display features a caboose, a watchman's shack, and the cigar-stained business car of Sir William Van Horne, founder of the Canadian Pacific Railroad. Pioneer Village successfully re-creates a 19th-century settlement with authentic stores and a church.

Pioneer Village, part of the Fort La Reine complex at Portage la Prairie

Riding Mountain National Park ❼

Hwys 10 & 19. **Tel** *(204) 846 7275.* ◯ *daily.* 🎦 ♿ *partial.* **www**.pc.gc.ca

One of western Manitoba's most popular attractions, Riding Mountain National Park is a vast 3,000-sq-km (1,158-sq-miles) wilderness. The best hiking trails and some of Manitoba's most beautiful scenery are to be found in the center of the park, where a highland plateau is covered by forests and lakes. To the east, a ridge of evergreen forest including spruce, pine, and fir trees houses moose and elk. A small herd of bison can also be found in the park near Lake Audy. Bison were reintroduced here in the 1930s after they had been hunted out at the end of the 19th century. The most developed area here is around the small settlement of Wasagaming where information on the park's network of trails for cycling, hiking, and horseback riding is available. Canoes are also available to rent for exploring the park's biggest lake, Clear Lake.

Wasagaming is the park's main settlement, and its facilities include hotels, restaurants, and campgrounds.

One of a small herd of bison at Riding Mountain National Park

Dauphin ❽

🧍 *7,900.* ✈ 🚉 🚌
ℹ *100 Main St. S. (204) 622 3140.*

A pleasant tree-lined town, Dauphin was named after the King of France's eldest son by the French explorer La Vérendrye. Located north of Riding Mountain National Park, Dauphin is a distribution-and-supply center for the farms of the fertile Vermilion River valley. The Fort Dauphin Museum in town is a replica of an 18th-century trading post. Exhibits include a

trapper's birchbark canoe and several early pioneer buildings, including a school, church, and blacksmith's store.

Today, the town's distinctive onion-shaped dome of the Church of the Resurrection is a tribute to Dauphin's Ukrainian immigrants who began to arrive in 1891. A traditional Ukrainian meal, including savory stuffed dumplings *(piroggi)*, forms part of a tour of the church.

Yorkton ❾

🧍 *17,000.* ✈ 🚉 ℹ *Jct Hwy 9 & Hwy 16 (306) 783 8707, 1 877 250 6454.* **www**.tourismyorkton.com

Founded as a farming community in 1882, Yorkton is located in central Saskatchewan. The striking architecture of its churches, especially St. Mary's Church, reflects the town's Ukrainian heritage. The church was built in 1914. Its 21-m (68-ft) high dome, icons and paintings are stunning. The Yorkton branch of the **Western Development Museum** (one of four in the province) tells the story of immigrants to the region.

🏛 Western Development Museum
Hwy 16A. **Tel** *(306) 783 8361.* ◯ *9am–6pm Mon–Fri; noon–5pm Sat, Sun, daily in summer.* 🎦 ♿

The magnificent dome at St. Mary's Church, Yorkton

The elegant façade of Motherwell Homestead

Fort Qu'Appelle ❿

🧍 *2,000.* **www**.fortquappelle.com

Named after an 1864 Hudson's Bay Company fur trading post, the picturesque town of Fort Qu'Appelle is located between Regina and Yorkton on Highway 10. The **Fort Qu'Appelle Museum** is built on the site of the old fort and incorporates a small out-building that was part of the original structure. The museum houses native artifacts such as antique beadwork and a collection of pioneer photographs.

The 430-km (267-mile) long Qu'Appelle River stretches across two-thirds of southern Saskatchewan. At Fort Qu'Appelle the river widens into a string of eight lakes bordered by several provincial parks. Scenic drives through the countryside are just one of the attractions of the valley.

About 30 km (19 miles) east of Fort Qu'Appelle is the **Motherwell Homestead National Historic Site**. This gracious stone house with extensive ornamental gardens was built by politician William R. Motherwell. Motherwell introduced many agricultural improvements to the area and was so successful that, after living in poverty for 14 years, he rose to become agriculture minister of Saskatchewan between 1905 and 1918.

🏛 Fort Qu'Appelle Museum
cnr Bay Ave. & Third St. ◯ *Jun–Aug: 1–5pm daily.* 🎦 ♿ *limited.*

🚩 Motherwell Homestead
Off Hwy 22. **Tel** *(306) 333 2116.* ◯ *May–Sep: daily.* 🎦 ♿ *limited.*

Regina ⓫

🏙 199,000. 🚏 ✈ 🚉 🛈 Hwy 1 E
(306) 789 5099, 1 800 661 5099.
www.reginaroc.com

Regina is a friendly, bustling city and the capital of Saskatchewan. The city was named for Queen Victoria by her daughter, Princess Louise, who was married to the Governor General of Canada. Regina was established in 1882 after starting life as a tent settlement called Pile O'Bones. This is a derivation of "oskana" (a Cree word meaning buffalo bones), from the piles of bones left behind after hunting.

Today, Regina is a thriving modern city whose highrise skyline contrasts with the 350,000 trees of the man-made Wascana Centre, a 9-sq-km (3.5-mile) urban park containing a vast man-made lake. The lake's Willow Island is a popular site for picnics and can be reached by ferry. The park is also a

Canadian goose in Wascana Centre Park

haven for some 60 species of waterfowl, including Canada geese. The **Royal Saskatchewan Museum** is housed in the park and focuses on the story of the area's First Nations peoples from earliest times to the present day. There are lectures by tribal elders on the land and its precious resources, as well as murals, sculptures, and paintings by contemporary Saskatchewan native and non-native artists.

One of several murals on downtown buildings in Moose Jaw

The original headquarters for the North West Mounted Police lies west of the city center. Today, the Royal Canadian Mounted Police Barracks trains all Canada's Mounties and is also the site of the **RCMP Heritage Centre**. Here, the story of the Mounties is told from their beginnings following the Cyprus Hills Massacre in 1873 (see p247). Among the highlights are the ceremonies and drills that are regularly performed by special trained groups of Mounties, including the Sergeant Major's Parade, the Musical Ride, and Sunset Retreat Ceremonies.

🏛 **Royal Saskatchewan Museum**
2445 Albert St. **Tel** (306) 787 2815. ⬜ daily. ⬤ Dec. 25. ♿ **www**.royalsaskmuseum.ca

🏛 **RCMP Heritage Centre**
5907 Dewdney Ave. W. **Tel** (306) 522 7333. ⬜ daily. ♿ **www**.rcmpheritagecentre.com

Moose Jaw ⓬

🏙 34,300. ✈ 🚉 🛈 99 Diefenbaker Dr. (306) 693 8097, 1 866 693 8097.

The quiet town of Moose Jaw was established as a railway terminus by the Canadian Pacific Railroad in 1882. A terminus for the American Soo Line from Minneapolis, Minnesota soon followed. Today, a series of murals celebrates the lives of the early railroad pioneers and homesteaders, decorating 29 buildings around downtown's 1st Avenue. Nearby, River Street has a concentration of 1920s hotels and warehouses that reflect Moose Jaw's time as "sin city" during the 1920s – when Prohibition in the United States meant that illegally produced liquor was smuggled from Canada to Chicago, by gangsters such as the infamous Al Capone.

The Moose Jaw branch of the Western Development Museum focuses on transportation, particularly the railroad.

Cadets of the Royal Canadian Mounted Police Academy in Regina are put through their paces

Traditional powwow dancer in Wanuskewin Park, Saskatoon

Saskatoon ⑬

👥 224,000. ✈ ☒ ▯ ▯
🛈 202 Fourth Ave. N. (306) 242
1206, 1 800 567 2444.
www.tourismsaskatoon.com

Founded in 1882 by Ontario Methodist John Lake as a temperance colony, Saskatoon is located in the middle of prairie country. Today, the city is an agricultural and commercial hub, and a busy regional center for cattle ranchers and wheat farmers from surrounding communities. The region's history is told in Saskatoon's branch of the Western Development Museum, which focuses on the town's boom years in the 1900s, re-creating the bustling main street of a typical prairie

town, including its railroad station and a hotel.

The South Saskatchewan River meanders through the city and is bounded by many lush parks, including the outstanding 307-ha (760-acre) **Wanuskewin Heritage Park**. The park is devoted to First Nations history, with archaeo-logical sites that confirm the existence of hunter-gatherer communities some 6,000 years ago. Some of the digs are open to the public, and the excellent park interpretive center has an archaeological lab explaining current research. The park's wooded hills and marshy creeks are still held to be sacred lands by the Northern Plains peoples who act as interpretive guides. Easy-to-follow trails lead the visitor past tipi rings, buffalo trails, and a buffalo jump *(see p296)*.

The riverbank also houses two museums, The Ukrainian Museum of Canada with its brightly colored traditional textiles, and the Mendel Art Gallery, with First Nations and Inuit pottery and glassware.

🌺 **Wanuskewin Heritage Park**
Off Hwy 11. **Tel** *(306) 931 6767.*
◯ *daily.* ● *Good Fri, Dec 25.* 🄸
🄳 *limited.* **www**.wanuskewin.com

Black-tailed prairie dog

Grasslands National Park ⑭

Jct Hwys 4 & 18. 🛈 *Val Marie (306)
298 2257.* 🚍 *Val Marie.* ◯ *daily.*
🄳 *partial.* **www**.pc.gc.ca

Situated in the southwest corner of Saskatchewan, Grasslands National Park was set up in 1988 to preserve one of the last original prairie grasslands in North America. The park is an area of climatic extremes where summer temperatures can be as high as 40 °C (104 °F), and winter ones as low as -40 °C (-48 °F). This environment supports a range of rare wildlife, including short-horned lizards and ferruginous hawks. The rugged landscape along the Frenchman River valley is the only remaining habitat of the black-tailed prairie dog in Canada. Visitors may hike and camp in the park, but facilities are basic.

East of the park is the strik-ing, glacially formed landscape of the **Big Muddy Badlands**. In the early 1900s, caves of eroded sandstone and deep ravines provided hideouts for cattle thieves such as Butch Cassidy and Dutch Henry.

🎯 **Big Muddy Badlands**
Off Hwy 34. **Tel** *(306) 267 3312.*
Tours in summer from Coronach. 🄸

Buttes (isolated flat-topped hills) in the Big Muddy Badlands seen from Grasslands National Park

Cypress Hills Interprovincial Park 🟝

Hwy 41. 🔲 *(403) 893 3833.*
🔲 *daily.* 🔲 *partial.*
www.cypresshills.com

Crossing the border between Saskatchewan and Alberta, the Cypress Hills Interprovincial Park offers fine views of the plains from its 1,400-m (4,593-ft) high peaks. The park's landscape is similar to the foothills of the Rocky Mountains, with its lodgepole pine forests and abundant wild flowers. Walking trails through the park offer the visitor the chance to see moose, elk, and white-tailed deer, as well as the 220 or more species of bird that stop here during migration, such as the rare trumpeter swan and mountain chickadee.

In the eastern section of the park, in Saskatchewan, **Fort Walsh National Historic Site** houses a reconstruction of Fort Walsh, which was built in 1875 by the Mounties to keep out the illicit whiskey traders who were causing trouble among the natives. Nearby, the trading posts involved in the illegal liquor trade, Farwells and Solomons, have been reconstructed. Costumed guides tell the story of the Cypress Hills Massacre.

🔲 **Fort Walsh National Historic Site**
Cypress Hills Interprovincial Park.
Tel *(306) 662 2645.* 🔲 *May–Sep: 9:30am–5:30pm daily.* 🔲

Maple Creek 🟝

🔲 *2,300.* 🔲 🔲 *Hwy 1 West (306) 662 4005.*

Located on the eastern edge of the Cypress Hills and affectionately known as "Old Cow Town," Maple Creek was established as a ranching center in 1882. The town still has a look of the Old West with trucks and Stetson-wearing ranchers filling the downtown streets. Maple Creek's many original 19th-century storefronts include the elegant Commercial Hotel with its marble-floored lobby.

High Level Bridge over the Oldman River, Lethbridge

The oldest museum in the province, the Saskatchewan Old Timers' Museum, boasts a collection of pictures and artifacts telling the story of the NWMP, the natives, and the early settlement of the area.

Medicine Hat 🟝

🔲 *61,000.* 🔲 🔲 🔲 *8 Gehring Rd. SW. (403) 527 6422, 1 800 481 2822.* **www**.tourismmedicinehat.com

The south Saskatchewan River Valley is the picturesque setting for the town of Medicine Hat, the center of Alberta's gas industry. Founded in 1883, Medicine Hat is noted for Seven Persons Coulee, once a substantial native camp and buffalo jump and now one of the most important archaeological sites of the northern plains. Evidence that aboriginal peoples lived here over 6,000 years ago has been garnered from finds including bones, tools, and arrowheads. Tours of the site are available.

Lethbridge 🟝

🔲 *86,700.* 🔲 🔲 🔲 *2805 Scenic Dr. S. (403) 331 0022, 1 866 213 4070.* **www**.lethbridge.ca

Coal, oil, and gas are the basis of Lethbridge's success. Alberta's third-largest city was named after mine-owner William Lethbridge in 1885, but First Nations peoples such as the Blackfoot Indians have inhabited the area since prehistoric times.

Lying on the banks of the Oldman River, Lethbridge is home to the notorious Fort Whoop-up, established in 1869 by whiskey traders John Healy and Alfred Hamilton for the sole purpose of profiting from the sale of illicit, and often deadly, whiskey. Many Indians, drawn by the lure of the drink, were poisoned or even killed by the brew, which was made with substances such as tobacco and red ink. Today, a replica of Fort Whoop-up has a visitor's center that describes the history of the trading post.

CYPRESS HILLS MASSACRE

On June 1, 1873 a group of whiskey traders attacked an Assiniboine camp, killing several women, children, and braves in retaliation for the alleged theft of their horses by natives. Many native people had already died from drinking the traders' liquor, which was doctored with substances such as ink and strychnine.

The massacre led to the formation of the North West Mounted Police. Their first post at Fort Macleod in 1874, and another at Fort Walsh in 1875, marked the end of the whiskey trade and earned the Mounties the natives' trust.

Two Assiniboine Indians from an engraving made in 1844

Royal Tyrrell Museum 🌀

The museum's Albertosaurus logo

The outstanding Royal Tyrrell Museum was opened in 1985 and is the only museum in Canada devoted to 4.5 billion years of the Earth's history. The layout of the exhibits enables visitors to follow the course of evolution through displays of dinosaurs and fossils from different ages. The museum uses interactive computers, videos, and three-dimensional dioramas to re-create distinct prehistoric landscapes, bringing the age of the dinosaurs and the study of palaeontology to life.

VISITORS' CHECKLIST

Hwy 838, 6 km NW of Drumheller. *Tel* (403) 823 7707, 1 888 440 4240. 🚌 Calgary. ⏰ May–Sep: daily; Oct–Apr: Tue–Sun. 🎫 ♿ www.tyrrellmuseum.com

KEY

- ☐ Cretaceous Alberta Gallery
- ☐ Lords of the Land
- ☐ Discoveries
- ☐ Burgess Shale
- ☐ Dinosaur Hall
- ☐ Bearpaw Sea
- ☐ Reptile Hall
- ☐ Mammal Hall
- ☐ Cretaceous Garden
- ☐ Terrestrial Palaeozoic
- ☐ Discovery Room
- ☐ Ice Ages Gallery
- ☐ Non-exhibition space

Dinosaur Hall
In Dinosaur Hall, a T-rex towers over a display of some 35 complete dinosaur skeletons.

The Ice Ages Gallery displays skeletons and fossils of the giant woolly mammoths, mastodons, bison, and sabre-toothed tigers that inhabited North America.

GALLERY GUIDE

The collection is housed on several levels reached by a series of ramps. Each area contains a display on an era of geological time. Introductory exhibits on fossils and dinosaurs are followed by displays on prehistoric mammals and the Ice Ages. The largest and most popular part of the museum is the Dinosaur Hall.

MUSEUM-ORGANIZED TREKS

Visitors on a trek through the Badlands

The Royal Tyrrell Museum has a Field Centre within Dinosaur Provincial Park *(see opposite)*. As well as interesting displays on the park's history, the Field Centre is the starting point for guided tours (by bus or on foot) that allow participants to learn more about the creatures that populated ancient Alberta. There is also a self-guided walking tour.

Black Beauty Skull
This T-rex was found in the Crowsnest Pass area of south-western Alberta. The black discoloration was the result of a chemical reaction as the skeleton fossilized.

Elk Island National Park's largest lake, Astotin Lake, is skirted by a popular hiking trail

Dinosaur Provincial Park ⑳

Rte 544. *Tel* (403) 378 4342. ☐ daily. 🎫 ♿ partial.

Two hours' drive southeast of the town of Drumheller, the UNESCO World Heritage Site of Dinosaur Provincial Park, established in 1955, contains one of the world's richest fossil beds. Located along the Red Deer River Valley, the park includes dinosaur skeletons mostly from the late Cretaceous Period, about 75 million years ago *(see pp230–31)*. More than 300 mostly intact skeletons have been made here and more than 30 institutions worldwide have specimens from this valley on display.

From Drumheller it is possible to drive the 48-km (30-mile) loop **Dinosaur Trail** through the "Valley of the Dinosaurs." The trail passes the Royal Tyrrell Museum, takes in stunning views of strange badlands landscape from highpoints such as Horseshoe Canyon, and leads to intriguing rock hoodoos.

> 💥 **Dinosaur Trail**
> ℹ️ Drumheller (403) 823 1331.

Red Deer ㉑

🏙️ 83,000. 🚉 ℹ️ Sports Hall of Fame, Hwy 2 (403) 346 0180. **www**.tourismreddeer.net

Located midway between Calgary and Edmonton, this bustling city was founded in 1882 by Scottish settlers as a stopover point for travelers. A modern city with good cultural and recreational facilities, Red Deer is the hub of central Alberta's rolling parkland district. The city has some interesting buildings, such as the award-winning St. Mary's Church, and the landmark Water Tower, known as the "Green Onion." The city's beautiful reserve of Waskasoo Park is located along the Red River.

Elk Island National Park ㉒

Hwy 16. *Tel* (780) 992 5790. ☐ daily. 🎫 ♿ partial. **www**.pc.gc.ca

Established in 1906 as Canada's first animal sanctuary, Elk Island became a national park in 1913. It offers a wilderness retreat only half-an-hour's drive from Edmonton. This 194 sq km (75 sq miles) park provides a habitat for large mammals such as elk, the plains bison, the rarer, threatened wood bison, and moose. The park's landscape of transitional aspen parkland (an area of rolling meadows, woodlands, and wetlands) is, according to the World Wildlife Fund for Nature, one of the most threatened habitats in North America.

Aspen trees grow mostly on dry ridges, while balsam, poplar, and white birch grow near wet areas. Plants such as sedges and willows also thrive in the wetlands alongside a host of birds such as the swamp sparrow and yellow warbler.

Elk Island is a popular day trip from Edmonton as well as being a picturesque weekend picnic spot for locals. There are 13 hiking trails of varying difficulties and lengths. During the summer a wide range of activities is available in the park including swimming, canoeing, and camping. Cross-country skiing is the most popular winter activity.

Hoodoos, towers of rock sculpted by erosion, near Drumheller

Ice Palace at West Edmonton Mall

Edmonton ㉓

🚶 1 million. ✈ ⊠ 🚉 🚌 ℹ 990 Jasper Ave. (780) 496 8400, 1 800 463 4667. **www**.edmonton.com/tourism

Edmonton spans the valley of the North Saskatchewan River and sits in the center of Alberta province, of which it is the capital. Established as a series of Hudson's Bay Company trading posts in the 1790s, this city is now the focus of Canada's thriving oil industry.

Edmonton's downtown area is centered on Jasper Avenue and Sir Winston Churchill Square, where modern high-rises sit among shops and restaurants. The gigantic **West Edmonton Mall** contains over 800 stores, an amusement and water park, over 100 restaurants, a bowling center, an ice rink, and 27 movie theaters. In contrast is one of Alberta's oldest buildings, the delightful Alberta Legislature, opened in 1913. Overlooking the river, on the site of the old Fort Edmonton, the building has beautiful landscaped grounds.

Southwest of downtown, Fort Edmonton Park re-creates the original Hudson's Bay Company fort with reconstructions of street areas in 1885 and 1920. Here visitors can experience past times, wandering around original shops and businesses, as well as taking rides on a horse-drawn wagon, steam train, or street car.

West of downtown is the Royal Alberta Museum with natural history displays; to the northwest is the Telus World of Science, which boasts an IMAX theatre, Observatory, and Star Theatre.

🏬 **West Edmonton Mall**
170th St. & 87th Ave. **Tel** (780) 444 5200. ◯ daily. ♿

Vegreville ㉔

🚶 5,300. 🚌 ℹ at giant Pysanka (780) 632 2606.

Along the Yellowhead Hwy, heading eastward from Edmonton, lies the predominantly Ukrainian town of Vegreville. Its community is famous for producing traditionally Ukrainian, highly decorated Easter eggs (or pysanki). Visible from the road is a giant pysanka covered with intricate bronze, gold, and silver designs that tell the story of the region's Ukrainian settlers, and celebrates their religious faith, bountiful harvests, and the protection they received from the RCMP. The egg is 7 m (23 ft) high, and is made of over 3,500 pieces of aluminum.

A giant decorated Easter egg celebrates Vegreville's heritage

Wood Buffalo National Park ㉕

Main access: Fort Smith, NWT. **Tel** (867) 872 7900. ◯ daily. 🏞 **www**.pc.gc.ca

The largest national park in Canada, Wood Buffalo is about the size of Denmark, covering an area of 44,807 sq km (17,474 sq miles). The park was made a UNESCO World Heritage Site in 1983 because of the range of habitat it offers for such rare species of animal as the wood bison or buffalo.

There are three different environments here: fire-scarred forest uplands; a large, poorly drained plateau filled with streams and bogs; and the Peace-Athabasca Delta, full of sedge meadows, marshes, and shallow lakes. Sightings of bald eagles are common, and the park is the only remaining natural nesting site of the rare whooping crane and peregrine falcon in the world.

THE GREY OWL STORY

Long before conservation became popular, the renowned naturalist by the name of Grey Owl, took up the cause. Inspired by his Mohawk wife, Anahareo, he wrote the first of several best-selling books, *Men of the Last Frontier*, in 1931, the same year he became the official naturalist of Riding Mountain National Park. He built a cabin on the peaceful shores of Lake Ajawaan from where he ran a beaver protection program. When Grey Owl died of pneumonia in 1938, there was uproar when a newspaper discovered that he was really an Englishman. Born in Hastings in 1888, Archibald Stansfield Belaney took on the identity of Grey Owl when he returned to Canada after World War I. He wore buckskins and wore his hair in Apache-style braids. A generation later Grey Owl's legacy remains the protection of Canada's wildlife.

Grey Owl feeding a beaver

Prince Albert National Park 26

Established in 1927, Prince Albert National Park covers 3,875 sq km (1,500 sq miles) of wilderness, from the gently rolling terrain of aspen parkland in the south to the spruce and fir trees of the northern boreal forest. These distinct environments house different wildlife populations, with moose, wolf, and caribou in the forests, and elk, bison, and badger in the parkland. The center of the park, and the most accessible areas for visitors, are the hiking and canoeing trails around the Kingsmere and Waskesiu Lakes. The townsite of Waskesiu is the best place from which to begin exploring the park.

VISITORS' CHECKLIST

Off Hwy 2. **Tel** (306) 663 4522.
Nature center.
May–Aug: 8am–8pm daily.
Dec 25 & 26.
www.pc.gc.ca/princealbert
www.waskesiu.org

KEY

— Major road

= Minor road

-- Hiking route

— Rivers

Camping

Picnic area

Visitor information

Grey Owl's cabin by Ajawaan Lake
A 20-km (12-mile) trail leads to Grey Owl's log cabin, "Beaver Lodge."

Beach resort at Waskesiu Lake
The village of Waskesiu offers visitors a wide range of facilities, including stores, hotels, and a sandy lakeside beach.

Kingsmere Lake

Crean Lake

The Hanging Heart Lakes form a waterway that leads to Lake Crean – one of the popular canoe trips in the park.

The Nature Centre explains the park's ecology.

Waskesiu Lake

Waskesiu

PRINCE ALBERT

0 km 3
0 miles 3

View over Waskesiu Lake
Fall foliage across the boreal forest seen around the lake from Kingsmere Road.

Kingfisher trail is a popular 13-km (8-mile) walk by Waskesiu lake.

Gun with carriage at Fort Battleford National Historic Site

North Battleford and Battleford ㉗

🏛 16,500. 🚌 ℹ️ *Visitors' center, jct Hwys 16 & 40 (306) 445 2000, 1 800 243 0934.* **www**.tourism battlefords.com

North Battleford and Battleford, together known as The Battlefords, face each other across the North Saskatchewan River Valley. Named after a ford in the Battle River, the area was the site of age-old conflicts between the Blackfoot and Cree. An important early settlement in the West, it was chosen as the seat of the North-West Territories government from 1876 to 1882. Today, the communities are thriving industrial centers, although the North Battleford branch of the Western Development Museum focuses on rural life.

The **Allen Sapp Gallery** displays works by Allen Sapp, one of Canada's best-loved contemporary artists. His simple, delicately colored paintings and drawings celebrate the traditions of the Northern Plains Cree community.

Between the Saskatchewan and Battle rivers is the **Fort Battleford National Historic Site** containing a well-restored North-West Mounted Police post. The stockade has original buildings, including the lookout point in the commander's residence, officers' quarters, and restored barracks now housing a museum. Costumed guides tell the story of the time when 500 settlers took refuge in the stockade during the North-West Rebellion.

🏛 **Allen Sapp Gallery**
1 Railway Ave. *Tel (306) 445 1760.* ⭕ *Jun–Sep: daily; Oct–May: 11am–5pm Wed–Sun.* ♿

🎖 **Fort Battleford National Historic Site**
Off Hwy 4. *Tel (306) 937 2621.* ⭕ *mid-May–mid-Sep: daily; Oct–Apr: by appointment.* 📷 ♿

Batoche National Historic Site ㉘

Rte 225 off Hwy 312. *Tel (306) 423 6227.* ⭕ *May–Sep: daily.* 📷 ♿

The original village of Batoche was the site of the Métis's last stand against the Canadian Militia, led by Louis Riel and Gabriel Dumont in 1885 *(see p49)*.

From the 17th century, white fur traders in the west had married Indian wives and adopted tribal languages and customs. The resulting mixed raced peoples, the Métis, had originally rebeled in 1869 in the Winnipeg area in defense of their land rights. When history began to repeat itself in 1885, Métis rebels recalled Riel from exile in Montana to declare a provisional government at Batoche. Violence erupted on May 9, 1885 into what was to become known as the North-West Rebellion. Riel surrendered, was tried for treason, and hanged in Regina.

Today, the Batoche National Historic Site of Canada occupies the site of the village and battlefield. The 6-sq-km (2.5-sq-miles) park houses the bullet-ridden St. Antoine de Padou Church and Rectory as well as the cemetery where the Métis leaders are buried. An interpretive center features an audio-visual presentation telling the history of Batoche and the rebellion through the eyes of the Métis.

St. Antoine de Padou Church and Rectory at Batoche National Historic Site

For hotels and restaurants in this region see pp359–60 and pp384–5

POLAR BEARS

Known as the "Lord of the Arctic," the magnificent polar bear can weigh as much as 650 kg (1,433 lb). In the fall the bears begin to congregate along the bay east of Churchill waiting for ice to form in order to hunt seals. Their acute sense of smell can detect a scent up to 32 km (20 miles) away and pick up the presence of seals under 1 m (3 ft) of snow and ice.

Up to 150 bears pass by and through Churchill during the season. The best way to view them is in a tundra buggy, a large buslike vehicle that is warm, safe, and elevated over 2 m (6.5 ft) from the ground.

The majestic polar bear

Duck Lake ❷⁹

🏠 *670.* 🚌 ℹ️ *301 Front St. (306) 467 2057.* **www**.*louisrieltrail.com*

A little to the west of the small farming village of Duck Lake lies a plaque commemorating the first shots fired in the North-West Rebellion. On March 26, 1885, a police interpreter and a Cree emissary scuffled during a parley, and the officer was killed. During the ensuing battle, 12 NWMP officers and six Métis died. The Battle of Duck Lake is depicted in a series of murals at the town's interpretive center.

The Pas ❸⁰

🏠 *15,000.* 🚉 🚌 ℹ️ *324 Ross Ave. (204) 623 7256.*

Once a key fur-trading post dating back some 300 years, The Pas is now a major industrial distribution and transportation center for Manitoba's northwest. Nearby Clearwater Lake Provincial Park is named for the lake itself, which is said to be so clear that it is possible to see the bottom at 11 m (35 ft). The park also offers a walking trail through "the caves," a geological phenomenon where rock masses split away from cliffs to create huge crevices that provide shelter for a number of animals, including black bears, moose, wolves, and foxes.

Flin Flon ❸¹

🏠 *5,600.* ✈️ 🚌 ℹ️ *Hwy 10A (204) 687 4518.*

Steep hilly streets reflect the fact that Flin Flon lies on Precambrian rock (as old as the formation of the Earth's crust itself, roughly 3.8 billion years ago), and the area is famous for its distinctive greenstone. The town bears the name of a fictional character of a popular novel, *The Sunless City* by J.E.P. Murdock. The book was read by a prospector at the time he staked his claim here in 1915. Copper and gold are still mined in Flin Flon, but visitors mostly come to experience the vast wilderness of the nearby Grass River Provincial Park.

The distinctive Grass River, where strings of islands dot the countless lakes of the river system, has been a trade route for centuries, used by both natives and, later, European explorers and fur traders to travel from the northern forests to the prairies. Today, visitors may follow the historic route on guided canoe tours as well as fishing for northern pike, lake trout, turbot, and perch.

Churchill ❸²

🏠 *1,000.* ✈️ 🚉 ℹ️ *211 Kelsey Blvd. (204) 675 2022.*

Located at the mouth of the Churchill River on Hudson Bay, the town retains the look of a basic pioneer town, with no luxury hotels, no paved roads, and few trees. This vast Arctic landscape is snow-free only from June through to the end of August. Churchill has no road access and can be reached by plane or train from Winnipeg, Thompson, and The Pas. Despite its remote situation, Churchill was an important point of entry into Canada for early European explorers and fur traders arriving by boat in the 18th century. The Hudson's Bay Company established an outpost for fur-trading here in 1717.

Today, visitors come to see the polar bears, beluga whales, and the splendid array of tundra flora in this region. In the spring and fall the tundra's covering of moss, lichens, and tiny flowers bursts into an array of reds, violets, and yellows. In the summer beluga whales move upriver to the warmer waters and can be seen from boat trips or on scuba dives.

Polar bear warning sign near Churchill

Lake Louise, Alberta ▷

BRITISH COLUMBIA AND THE ROCKIES

Introducing British Columbia and the Rockies

The dramatic beauty of British Columbia and the Rockies' mountain ranges, forests, and lakes make it a much visited area. There is a wide variety of landscapes available here, from the northern Rockies with their bare peaks, to the south's Okanagan Valley with its orchards and vineyards. The region's temperate climate means that BC has more species of plants and animals than anywhere else in the country.

Millions of visitors come here every year, drawn by a wide range of outdoor activities. To the west, Vancouver Island offers ancient rainforest and the impressive coastal scenery of the Pacific National Park Reserve. Lying between the Pacific Ocean and the Coast Mountains, Vancouver is a stunningly attractive city, with good transportation links to the rest of the region, including Calgary in the east.

Rainforest in Gwaii Haanas National Park Reserve and Haida Heritage Site on Haida Gwaii

Illuminated by over 3,500 lights, Victoria's Parliament Buildings are reflected in the waters of Inner Harbour on Vancouver Island

SEE ALSO

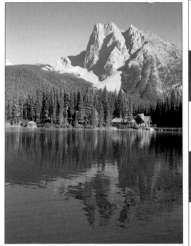

Snow-covered peaks reflected in the waters of
Emerald Lake in the Rockies' Yoho National Park

GETTING AROUND

The Trans-Canada Highway (Hwy 1) is the
major highway that leads to the rest of the
province from Vancouver, passing through the
gold rush route along the Fraser Canyon, then
on to Alberta. From Hope, there are two more
roads leading to the interior: the Coquihalla
Highway (Hwy 5) travels to Kamloops and
beyond, until it connects to Hwy 16, which
cuts through Jasper National Park; and Hwy 3
runs east and west through BC. VIA Rail
runs a scenic route from Vancouver to Jasper.
Bus routes cover most destinations.

0 km   100

0 miles   100

KEY

Trans-Canada Highway (Hwy 1)

Highway or major road

River

-- Provincial boundaries

The Rocky Mountains

Orchid found in the Rockies

The Canadian Rocky Mountains are a younger section of the Western Cordillera, a wide band of mountain ranges that stretch from Mexico to Canada. Formed between 120 and 20 million years ago, they include some of Canada's highest peaks, the 325-sq-km (125-sq-mile) Columbia Icefield, and glacial lakes. In summer wild flowers carpet the alpine meadows; in winter both visitors and locals take advantage of the snow-covered slopes to indulge in winter sports. The flora and fauna of the Canadian Rockies are protected within several National Parks; the most noted being Banff, Jasper, and Yoho *(see pp300–311)*, which houses the renowned Burgess Shale fossil beds.

BRITISH
COLUMBIA   ALBERTA

Vancouver US-Canada Border

LOCATOR MAP

■ *The Canadian Rockies*

Watson Lake

Fort Nelson

The Liard River Hot Springs, are located along the famous Alaska Highway *(see pp262–3)*. They are the result of surface water trickling down through cracks and fissures to the superheated rocks of the Earth's crust, which reach temperatures of 1,000 °C (1,832 °F). Steam is then released and rises to the surface where it condenses as water.

Rocky Mountain Trench

Fort St. John

Dawson Creek

Grande Prairie

Jas

Prince George

Fraser River

Hoodoos are
mushroom-shaped pedestals of rock, sculpted by wind and sand. These are found among the bare peaks of Muncho Lake Provincial Park, at the northern end of the Canadian Rockies.

Kamloops

From the Icefields Parkway *(Hwy 93), a scenic route that runs from Lake Louise in Banff National Park to Jasper, it is possible to view the saw-toothed appearance of the youngest peaks in the range. These were formed during the last episode of uplift, about 20 to 15 million years ago. Older ranges such as the Appalachians (see p23) have rounded tops formed by long-term erosion.*

Maligne Canyon *is a 50-m deep (164-ft), limestone gorge in Jasper National Park. The canyon was formed by the melt-waters of a glacier that once covered the valley. Today, the Maligne River rushes through this narrow channel, which also drains a series of underground caves.*

The Lewis Overthrust *in Waterton Lakes National Park is a geological phenomenon. When rocks were moving east during the formation of the Rockies, a single mass composed of the lowest sedimentary layer of the Rockies – known as the Lewis Thrust – came to rest on top of the prairies.*

0 km   100
0 miles   100

Field • Banff • Calgary

MOUNT ROBSON

COLUMBIA ICEFIELDS

Kelowna

The Burgess Shale fossil beds in Yoho National Park are a UN World Heritage Site and contain fossils dating from the Cambrian to the Permian ages some 570–290 million years ago. There are two main fossil beds; Walcott's Quarry, and Mt. Stephen, known for its wealth of trilobite (Cambrian marine animal) fossils.

THE FORMATION OF THE ROCKY MOUNTAINS

There are three main forces responsible for the formation of the Rocky Mountains. First, large areas of the Earth's crust (known as tectonic plates), constantly moving together and apart, created uplift. Second, the North American plate was subducted by the Pacific plate, which caused a chain of volcanoes to form from the molten rock of the oceanic crust. Third, erosion caused by the Ice Ages, as well as rivers and wind, deposited sedimentary rocks on the North American plate, which was then folded by more plate movement between 50 and 25 million years ago. The Rockies' jagged peaks reflect their recent formation.

Volcanoes   North America Plate

Pacific Plate

1 Some 150 million years ago, the Pacific plate moved east, adding to the molten rock from great depths of the North American Plate. This then rose up to form the Western Cordillera Mountains.

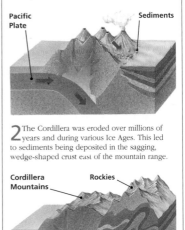

Pacific Plate   Sediments

2 The Cordillera was eroded over millions of years and during various Ice Ages. This led to sediments being deposited in the sagging, wedge-shaped crust east of the mountain range.

Cordillera Mountains   Rockies

3 Around 50 million years ago, the Pacific plate continued to push east, forcing the Cordillera range eastward, compressing sedimentary rocks, folding and uplifting them to form the Rockies.

Forestry and Wildlife of Coastal British Columbia

From its southern border with the United States to the northern tip of Haida Gwaii, the coastal region of British Columbia ranks as the richest ecological region in Canada. The warm waters of the north Pacific Ocean moderate the climate, creating a temperate rainforest teeming with life such as the black tail deer, black bear, and cougar. Dense forest still covers many islands, bays, and inlets along the coast, and is home to a large number of plant and animal species, including some of the tallest trees in Canada. Douglas Fir and Sitka Spruce can grow as high as 91 m (300 ft).

Trumpeter swans *are so-called for their distinctive brassy call. They are found on marshes, lakes, and rivers.*

TEMPERATE RAINFOREST HABITAT

High rainfall and a mild climate have created these lush forests of cedar, spruce, and pine, with their towering Douglas Firs and Sitka Spruces. Housed beneath the dripping forest canopy is a huge variety of ferns, mosses, and wild flowers, including orchids. Today, environmentalists campaign to protect these ancient forests from the threat of logging.

Bald eagles, *with their distinctive white heads, can be seen in large numbers diving for fish in the ocean near Haida Gwaii. The area is noted for having one of the largest bald-eagle populations in BC.*

The white black bear, *also known as the kermode or "spirit bear," is unique to coastal British Columbia. It is related to the black bear, and is an agile salmon catcher.*

Harlequin ducks *are small and shy, and the males have striking markings. A good swimmer, the harlequin enjoys fast-flowing rivers and the strong surf of the Pacific.*

Black tail deer *are found only on the north Pacific coast. They are the smallest member of the mule deer family and are preyed on by cougars in the area.*

SALMON

BC's coastal waters are home to five Pacific salmon species: pink, coho, chinook, sockeye, and chum. Together they support one of the main commercial food fisheries in the world, though numbers are declining in some parts of BC. Pacific salmon spawn in freshwater streams only once in their life, then die. Their offspring migrate downstream and out to sea, where they grow to adults ranging in size from 7 kg (15 lb) to over 45 kg (100 lb). At maturity they swim long distances upstream in order to return to the waters of their birth.

Chinook Salmon *leaping while swimming upstream to spawn.*

Sockeye Salmon *are highly prized in BC's fishing industry for their firm, tasty flesh.*

COASTLINE HABITAT

The warm waters of the north Pacific Ocean provide a habitat for more species of wildlife than any other temperate coastline. This distinctive region is characterized by having thousands of islands and inlets, which provide a home for a range of animals. Mammals such as gray, humpback, and orca whales can be seen here, as can sea otters, seals, and sea lions.

Northern sea lions *live in colonies along the rocky BC coast. Large, lumbering animals, they have short "forearms" that enable them to move on land.*

The glaucous gull *is a large, gray-backed sea gull, which nests along coastal cliffs, and on the numerous small islands here.*

Killer whales *(or orcas) are found off the sheltered eastern coast of Vancouver Island and up BC's mainland coast. They are known as "killer" because they feed on other mammals.*

Sea otters *were hunted, almost to extinction, for their thick fur coats. Today, these playful creatures are numerous off the coast of mainland BC and Vancouver Island.*

The Alaska Highway

The building of the Alaska Highway was an extraordinary achievement. Winding through 2,451 km (1,523 miles) of wilderness, mountains, muskeg (moss-covered bog), and forest, the first road was completed in 1942, only eight months and twelve days after construction began. Linking the United States to Alaska through British Columbia, it was built after the Japanese attacked Pearl Harbor in 1941, as a military supply route and to defend the northwest coast of Alaska.

Today, the original gravel road has been replaced by a two-lane, mostly asphalt highway. The highway's many curves are gradually being straightened, shortening its total length, and the present road now covers 2,394 km (1,488 miles).

LOCATOR MAP

■ Map area

YUKON

FAIRBANKS

Destruction Bay

Haines Junction

Johnson's Crossing

KLUANE NATIONAL PARK

Kluane National Park and Reserve *contains some of the most dramatic scenery to be seen along the highway. The Kluane Mountains are among the highest in Canada, and icefields cover around half of the park's area.*

Whitehorse *is the capital of the Yukon and the center of the province's forestry and mining industries. The town, at mile 910 of the highway, retains a frontier atmosphere, and it is still possible to hear coyotes at night.*

LLEWELLYN GLACIER PROVINCIAL PARK

Historical Mile 836 marks the site of the Canol Project. This oil pipeline was built alongside the highway, to aid the military effort. The pipe ran an incredible 965 km (600 miles) to an oil refinery in Whitehorse.

Teslin Lake *derives its name from the Tlingit language, meaning "long and narrow waters." The highway follows the 130-km long (80-mile) stretch of water, lined by snow-capped peaks. Today, the area attracts anglers eager to catch the plentiful trout, grayling, and pike, and hunters looking for game.*

The Alaska Highway in winter *is often covered in snow and affected by frost heave. Since it was opened to the public in 1949, teams of maintenance workers have ensured that the road is open year round.*

CONSTRUCTION OF THE HIGHWAY

The Alaska Highway was built in under nine months by US army engineers and Canadian construction workers. The recruiting poster for workers warned: "This is no picnic… Men will have to fight swamps, rivers, ice, and cold. Mosquitoes, flies, and gnats will not only be annoying but will cause bodily harm. If you are not prepared to work under these… conditions, DO NOT APPLY."

The workers shared mobile army camps that were moved along the route as construction progressed. If a company got stuck in one of many dismal swamps, they employed such techniques as laying corduroy – where whole trees were laid side by side, then spread with gravel. In some places en route as many as five layers were required.

Bogged-down truck waits for corduroy to be laid

The Peace River Valley section of the highway winds through fertile farmland, between Dawson Creek and Fort St. John. Before the Peace River suspension bridge was built in 1943, travelers crossed the river by ferry.

Watson Lake

MUNCHO LAKE PROVINCIAL PARK

Fort Nelson

BRITISH COLUMBIA

Kechika River

KWADACHA WILDERNESS PROVINCIAL PARK

SPATSIZI PLATEAU WILDERNESS PROVINCIAL PARK

T. EDZIZA OVINCIAL PARK

Fort St. John

Dawson Creek

Peace River

Historic Mile 588 or "Contact Creek" is the point where two teams of builders, from the north and south, met in 1942.

The Sign Post Forest *at Watson Lake has over 65,000 signs. The first was erected in 1942 by a GI missing his hometown of Danville, Illinois.*

| 0 km | 100 |
| 0 miles | 100 |

KEY

▬ Alaska Hwy

═ Other roads

▢ National and Provincial Parks

- - Provincial boundaries

VANCOUVER AND VANCOUVER ISLAND

L ooking out toward the waters of the Georgia Strait, Vancouver occupies one of the most beautiful settings of any world city. The coastal mountains form a majestic backdrop for the glass towers and copper-topped skyscrapers of the city. It was Captain James Cook who claimed the area for the British when he stepped ashore at Nootka Sound, Vancouver Island, in 1778. Until then the area had been inhabited for more than 10,000 years by the First Nations peoples, whose cultural heritage is celebrated in two of Canada's best museums: the UBC Museum of Anthropology in Vancouver and Victoria's Royal BC Museum. Established as a city after a fire destroyed the fledgling town of Granville in 1886, Vancouver offers historic districts, lush gardens, and wilderness parks within its environs. A short ferry ride away, Vancouver Island's world-famous Pacific Rim National Park is a major whale-watching center.

SIGHTS AT A GLANCE

Vancouver
(See pages 266–79) ❶ – ❽

Vancouver Island Gardens and Areas of Natural Beauty
Butchart Gardens ⓴

Cowichan District ㉒
Port Renfrew ㉑
Telegraph Cove ㉙

Historic Towns and Cities
Campbell River ㉘
Chemainus ㉓

Nainamo ㉔
Port Alberni ㉕
Tofino ㉖
Victoria ⓳

National Parks
Pacific Rim National Park Reserve ㉗

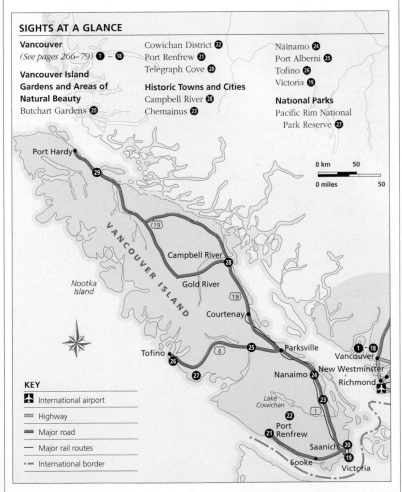

KEY

✈ International airport
═ Highway
▬ Major road
— Major rail routes
•–• International border

◁ Detail from Haida totem pole carved from cedar wood representing a double-headed snake

Exploring Vancouver

The heart of Vancouver is its downtown area, a finger of land bounded by the waters of English Bay. The city center radiates from Robson Square. The 405-ha (1,000-acre) Stanley Park occupies the tip of the peninsula, next to the West End. The historic Chinatown and Gastown districts are close to Main Street, the city's south to north axis.

SIGHTS AT A GLANCE

Historic Streets and Buildings
Chinatown ②
Old Hastings Mill Store ⑫

Parks and Gardens
Capilano Suspension Bridge ⑰
Dr. Sun Yat-Sen Chinese Garden ①
Grouse Mountain ⑯
Lighthouse Park ⑱
Lynn Canyon Park and
    Ecology Centre ⑮
Queen Elizabeth Park
    and Bloedel Conservatory ⑨
Stanley Park ⑬
VanDusen Botanical
    Garden ⑩

Modern Architecture
BC Place Stadium ④

Museums and Galleries
Museum of Vancouver and
    H.R. MacMillan Space Centre ⑦
Science World ③
*University of British Columbia Museum
    of Anthropology pp276–7* ⑪
Vancouver Art Gallery ⑤
Vancouver Maritime Museum ⑥

Shopping Areas
Granville Island ⑧
Lonsdale Quay Market ⑭

GREATER VANCOUVER

West Vancouver
North Vancouver
Burnaby
Vancouver

0 km   5
0 miles   5

KEY

	Waterfront and Gastown: *see pp268–9*
✈	International aiport
🚇	SkyTrain station
🚌	Bus station
⛴	SeaBus station
🚉	Railroad station
ℹ	Visitor information
P	Parking
▬	Highway
▬	Major road
▬	Pedestrian walkway

For additional map symbols *see back flap*

LOCATOR MAP

CALGARY

VANCOUVER

SEE ALSO

• *Where to Stay* pp360–62

• *Where to Eat* pp385–8

| 0 meters | 500 |
| 0 yards | 500 |

GETTING AROUND

Vancouver's transportation system includes the SeaBus, bus, and SkyTrain, one of the longest automated light rapid transit systems in the world. The Canada Line is a tunnel connecting the waterfront to Richmond and the airport. The SeaBus runs between Lonsdale Quay in North Vancouver and Waterfront Station downtown, where it is possible to connect with the bus and SkyTrain system. Many Vancouverites commute by car, and rush hour traffic is to be avoided because access to downtown is limited to a few bridges, including the hectic Lion's Gate Bridge.

Vancouver's stunning harbor with mountains as a backdrop

Street-by-Street: Waterfront and Gastown

One of Vancouver's oldest areas, Gastown faces the waters of Burrard Inlet and lies between Columbia Street in the east and Burrard Street in the west. The district grew up around a saloon, opened in 1867 by "Gassy" Jack Deighton whose statue can be seen on Maple Tree Square. Today, Gastown is a charming mix of cobblestone streets, restored 19th-century buildings, and storefronts. Chic boutiques and galleries line Powell, Carrall, and Cordova streets. Restaurants and cafés fill the mews, courtyards, and passages. Two eateries open onto Blood Alley, named for the city's first slaughterhouses. On the corner of Water and Cambie streets, visitors can hear the musical chimes of the steam clock every 15 minutes, as well as be entertained by street performers.

★ Canada Place
Canada Place is a waterside architectural marvel of white sails and glass that houses a hotel, two convention centers, and a cruise ship terminal.

The SeaBus
Stunning views of the harbor can be seen from the SeaBus, a catamaran that ferries passengers across Burrard Inlet between the central Waterfront Station and Lonsdale Quay in North Vancouver.

The Waterfront Station occupies the imposing 19th-century Canadian Pacific Railroad building.

★ Harbour Centre Tower
The Harbour Centre is a modern high-rise building best known for its tower. Rising 177 m (581 ft) above the city, on a clear day it is possible to see as far as Victoria on Vancouver Island.

STAR SIGHTS

★ Canada Place

★ Harbour Centre Tower

Water Street
Much of the quaint charm of Gastown can be seen here. Water Street boasts gas lamps and cobblestones, as well as shops, cafés, and the famous steam clock.

LOCATOR MAP
See map pp266–7

Steam Clock
The world's first steam clock is still maintained by the man who built it in the 1970s. It toots every 15 minutes on the corner of Water and Cambie streets.

"Gassy" Jack Statue
Gastown is named after "Gassy" Jack Deighton, an English sailor noted both for his endless chatter and for the saloon he opened here for the local saw-mill workers in 1867.

The Inuit Gallery
on Water Street offers a variety of original Inuit art such as jewelry and paintings.

WATERFRONT ROAD EAST

0 meters 100
0 yards 100

WATER STREET

Shopping on Cordova St West
is a delightful experience with its range of small galleries and trendy boutiques.

Triangular Building
Reminiscent of New York's Flatiron Building, this striking structure was built in 1908–9 as a hotel and forms the corner of Alexander and Powell streets. It is now an apartment building.

KEY

– – – Suggested route

Peaceful pavilion in the Dr. Sun Yat-Sen Classical Chinese Garden

Dr. Sun Yat-Sen Classical Chinese Garden ❶

578 Carrall St. **Tel** *(604) 662 3207.* 🚉 & 🚉 *Central Station.* 🚌 *19, 22.* 🚢 *Downtown terminal.* 🕐 *Summer: 10am–6pm; winter: 10am–4:30pm.* 🔴 *Jan 1, Dec 25.* 💰 📷 👤 **www**.vancouverchinesegarden.com

Opened in 1986, the first full-sized Ming Dynasty-style classical Chinese garden built outside of China offers a refuge from Vancouver's bustling city center. The garden owes its tranquillity to ancient Taoist principles, which aimed to create a healthy balance between the contrasting forces of man and nature.

Over 50 skilled craftsmen came from Suzhou, China's Garden City, to construct the garden, using traditional tools and techniques. Pavilions and walkways were all built with materials from China. Many of the plants and trees symbolize different virtues. Willow is a symbol of feminine grace, and the plum and bamboo represent masculine strength. Complimentary Chinese tea rounds out the soothing atmosphere.

Chinatown ❷

Pender St. 🚉 *East Hastings & East Pender Sts router.*

Vancouver's Chinatown is older than the city itself. In 1858 the first wave of Chinese immigrants was drawn to Canada by the promise of gold. The Canadian Pacific Railroad attracted even more Chinese workers in the 1880s with jobs to build the new railroad. Today Chinatown stretches from Carrall to Gore Streets and still provides a warm welcome for more recent Asian immigrants.

Declared an historic area in 1970, Chinatown has restored many of its notable houses with their elaborately decorated roofs and covered balconies. The main drag, Pender Street, is the best place to view the architectural details that decorate the upperstories of the buildings, such as highly painted wooden balconies.

Bilingual sign in Chinatown

Street signs with colorful Chinese characters add to the authentic atmosphere.

Whether buying mouth-watering duck, or watching the spicy dumplings known as won tons being made at top speed, or settling down to taste the myriad dishes available in numerous fine restaurants, the main attraction for the visitor is food. There is also a fascinating range of stores, from bakeries selling a selection of savory and sweet buns to traditional herbalists, and jewelers specializing in jade. In contrast to the bustling markets there are also several relaxing tearooms, as well as the nearby Dr. Sun Yat-Sen Chinese Garden, which also offers tea and cakes and has weekly evening concerts of Chinese music under the soft light of lanterns throughout the summer.

Science World ❸

1455 Quebec St. **Tel** *(604) 443 7443.* 🚉 *Central Station.* 🚉 *Central Station.* 🕐 *10am–5pm Mon–Fri, 10am–6pm Sat & Sun.* 🔴 *Dec 25.* 💰 👤 **www**.scienceworld.ca

Overlooking the waters of False Creek, near the Main Street Railway Station, stands the 47-m- (155-ft-) high steel geodesic dome that now houses Vancouver's science

The striking geodesic dome housing Vancouver's interactive Science World

museum, Science World.
The dome was designed for
Expo '86 and inspired by American inventor R. Buckminster
Fuller. It is now one of the
city's most striking landmarks.
The highly interactive science
museum moved into the
structure in 1989.

In the Eureka Gallery,
visitors can design their own
inventions. The Sara Stern
Search Gallery lets visitors
touch the furs and bones of
animals, while the Illusions
Gallery boggles the mind with
its many optical tricks and
displays. For 2- to 6-year-olds,
the Kidspace Gallery provides
a safe and colorful environment for learning and play.

The museum is renowned
for its OMNIMAX® Theatre,
located at the top of the
dome, where a huge screen
shows films of flights through
such epic landscapes as
Mount Everest and the Grand
Canyon, as well as Kelly
Slater surfing in Tahiti.

BC Place Stadium ❹

777 Pacific Blvd. **Tel** (604) 669
2300. 🚇 Stadium. ◯ varies,
depending on scheduled events.
📷 ✔ May Oct: Tue–Fri. ♿
www.bcplacestadium.com

Standing out from the city's
skyline, the state-of-the-art,
retractable roof of the BC Place
Stadium was unveiled in 2011.
When the arena opened in
1983, it had a white fabric roof
and was the first covered
stadium in Canada and the
largest air-supported dome in
the world. The versatile
stadium is able to convert in a
matter of hours from a football
field seating 60,000 people to
a more intimate concert bowl
seating up to 30,000.

Among the famous guests
who have visited the dome
are Queen Elizabeth II and
Pope John Paul II. Visitors
hoping to catch a glimpse of
a celebrity or two can take
behind-the-scenes tours to the
locker rooms, playing fields,
and media lounges. The
stadium also houses the
**BC Sports Hall of Fame and
Museum**, which chronicles

The large white dome of BC Place Stadium

the history of the region's
sporting heroes.

🏛 **BC Sports Hall of Fame
and Museum**
BC Place Stadium. **Tel** (604) 687
5520. ◯ 10am–5pm daily. 📷 ♿
www.bcsportshalloffame.com

Vancouver Art Gallery ❺

750 Hornby St. **Tel** (604) 662 4719.
🚇 Central Station. 🚇 Central
Station. 🚌 3. ◯ 10am–5pm daily
(to 9pm Tue; admission by donation).
📷 ♿ www.vanartgallery.bc.ca

What was once British
Columbia's imposing pro-
vincial courthouse now
houses the Vancouver Art
Gallery. The building was
designed in 1906 by Francis
Rattenbury, an architect known
for the Gothic style of Victoria's
Parliament building and the
Empress Hotel (see p280).
The interior was modernized
in 1983 by Arthur Erikson,
another noted architect, who

Decorative Victorian features on
the Vancouver Art Gallery façade

designed the UBC Museum of
Anthropology (see pp276–7).

The Vancouver Art Gallery
presents a full range of
national and international
art by groundbreaking
contemporary artists and
major historical figures,
including the most significant
body of work by British
Columbian artist Emily Carr.
The gallery also houses a
permanent collection of
10,000 works of art. Visitors
can take part in talks and
tours, or visit interpretive
sites and learning centers,
as well as the Gallery Café
and the Gallery Store.

Vancouver Maritime Museum ❻

1905 Ogden Ave. **Tel** (604) 257
8300. 🚇 & 🚇 Central Station.
◯ 10am–5pm daily (Sep–mid-May;
Tue–Sun). ● Dec 25. 📷 ♿ www.
vancouvermaritimemuseum.com

Celebrating Vancouver's history
as a port and trading center,
this museum's star feature is
the schooner, St. Roch. Built
as a supply ship for the
Mounties in 1928, in 1940–42
St. Roch was the first ship to
navigate the Northwest
Passage in both directions.

Other displays include Map
the Coast, which tells the story
of British Captain George
Vancouver and the crews of
the Chatham and the
Discovery, who charted the
inlets of the coast of BC in
1792. The Children's Maritime
Discovery Centre has a powerful telescope through which
the busy port can be viewed.

Steel sculpture in front of the Museum of Vancouver's distinctive façade

Museum of Vancouver and H.R. MacMillan Space Centre ❼

1100 Chestnut St., Vanier Park. *Tel* (604) 736 4431; Space Centre (604) 738 7827. 🚉 Central Station. 🚌 Central Station. 🚏 22. ⏲ 10am–5pm Mon–Wed, Fri–Sun; until 8pm Thu. 📷 ♿ **www**.museumof vancouver.ca, **www**.spacecentre.ca

Located in Vanier Park near the Vancouver Maritime Museum *(see p271)*, the Museum of Vancouver is a distinctive addition to the city's skyline. Built in 1967, the museum's curved, white, concrete roof is based on a First Nations hat. Outside, a stunning sculpture, which looks like a giant steel crab, sits in a fountain on the museum's south side.

Displays here include the Orientation Gallery, which re-creates British Columbia's rocky coastline and mountainous interior. Vancouver's history is explored from the culture of the First Nations of the area to the city's pioneering days, celebrated in a series of black-and-white photographs. The museum is also noted for its depiction of everyday life, with exhibits such as an 1880s Canadian Pacific Railroad car, and the 1950s gallery, with a vintage Ford Thunderbird and a working jukebox.

At the same location, the H.R. MacMillan Space Centre is popular with both children and adults, who can explore the universe in the Planetarium and in the GroundStation Canada Theatre.

Granville Island ❽

1661 Duranleau St. *Tel* (604) 666 5784. 🚉 Central Station. 🚌 Central Station. 🚏 50. ⏲ Market: 9am–7pm daily; other stores: 10am–7pm daily. ♿ **www**.granvilleisland.com

Today, this once down trodden industrial district has a glorious array of stores, galleries, and artists' studios in its brightly painted warehouses and tin sheds. The fire of 1886 destroyed almost all of fledgling Vancouver and drove people south across the water to Granville Island and beyond. Many of the early buildings were constructed on land reclaimed in 1915 to cope with the burgeoning lumber and iron industries.

Granville Island Brewing Company sign

There are very few chain stores on the island, and the smaller stores are known for their variety, originality, and quality, displaying a range of local arts and crafts such as rugs, jewelry, and textiles.

The island is also a center for the performing arts and boasts several music, dance, and theater companies.

A daily public market offers a cornucopia of foods that reflect Vancouver's ethnic diversity. Waterside cafés and restaurants occupy the False Creek Shore where there was once a string of sawmills.

Queen Elizabeth Park and Bloedel Conservatory ❾

Cambie St. *Tel* Conservatory: (604) 257 8584. 🚌 15. ⏲ Conservatory: 10am–5pm daily (May–Aug: 9am–8pm). 📷 for Conservatory. ♿

Queen Elizabeth Park is located on Little Mountain, Vancouver's highest hill (152-m/499-ft), and has fine views of the city. Despite being built on the site of two former stone quarries, the park's gardens are continually in bloom, beginning in early spring when multicolor tulips cover the hillsides.

The plastic-domed Bloedel Conservatory is perched on top of the hill, and grows plants from many climactic zones in the world, from rainforest plants and trees to desert cacti. There are also free-flying colorful tropical birds and fishponds filled with Japanese carp.

The plastic dome of the Bloedel Conservatory in Queen Elizabeth Park

A dazzling fall display of reds and oranges, one of many attractions in Stanley Park

VanDusen Botanical Garden ⑩

5251 Oak St. **Tel** *(604) 878 9274.*
🚇 *Central Station.* 🚇 *Central Station.* 🚌 *17.* ⭘ *10am–dusk daily.*
⛔ *Dec 25.* ♿&
www.vandusengarden.org

This 22-ha (55-acre) garden was opened in 1975. In 1960 the land was under threat from its original owners, the Canadian Pacific Railroad, who wanted to build high-rise apartments. It took a campaign by local people and a donation from Mr W.J. VanDusen, a wealthy local business-man, to save the site.

Today, visitors enjoy a spectacular display of over 7,500 families of plants from 6 continents, set among lakes and marble sculptures. The Perennial Garden is filled with roses in summer, while September heralds the blazing reds and oranges of fall. The Visitor Center is leading the Garden's green initiatives: the roof uses solar panels and collects rainwater to be used throughout the gardens.

University of British Columbia Museum of Anthropology ⑪

See pp276–7.

Old Hastings Mill Store ⑫

1575 Alma Rd. **Tel** *(604) 734 1212.*
🚌 *4th Ave. route.* ⭘ *Feb–May, Oct–Nov: 1–4pm Sat & Sun; Jun–Sep: 11am–4pm Tue–Sun.* ⛔ *Dec & Jan.*
Donation. &

The Old Hastings Mill Store was Vancouver's first general store and post office and one of the few wooden buildings to survive the Great Fire of 1886. Built in 1865, it was moved by barge from its original site at Gastown in 1930 to the shores of Jericho Beach and then to its present home on Alma Street, at the corner of Point Grey Road. Starting in the 1940s, local people contributed a variety of historic artifacts, and today the house is an interesting small museum. Behind the pretty clapboard exterior, the museum's exhibits include a range of Victorian artifacts such as a horse-drawn cab, several antique sewing machines, and

Marble statue in Botanical Gardens

The Old Hastings Mill Store, one of Vancouver's oldest buildings

an extensive collection of native artifacts including an impressive range of hand-woven baskets.

Stanley Park ⑬

2099 Beach Ave. **Tel** *(604) 257 8400.*
🚇 *Central Station.* 🚇 *Central Station.* 🚌 *123, 135.* ⛴ *Horseshoe Bay.* ⭘ *daily.* &

This is a magnificent 404-ha (1,000-acre) park of tamed wilderness, just a few blocks from downtown, that was originally home to the Mus-queam and Squamish native Canadians. Named after Lord Stanley, Governor General of Canada, the land was made a park by the local council in 1886. It offers visitors the opportunity to experience a range of typical Vancouver attractions. There are beaches, hiking trails, and fir and cedar woods as well as wonderful views of the harbor, English Bay, and the coastal moun-tains. Bicycles can be rented for the popular ride around the 10-km (6.5-mile) perimeter seawall. The park is also home to the **Vancouver Aquarium Marine Science Centre** where visitors can watch dolphins and beluga whales through the glass of enormous tanks.

➤ **Vancouver Aquarium Marine Science Centre**
Stanley Park. **Tel** *(604) 659 3474.*
⭘ *Jun–Aug: 9:30am–7pm daily; Sep–May: 9:30am–5pm daily.* 🍽
🅿 & **www.**vanaqua.org

University of British Columbia Museum of Anthropology ⑪

Founded in 1947, this outstanding museum houses one of the world's finest collections of Northwest coast native peoples' art. Designed by Canadian architect Arthur Erickson in 1976, the museum is housed in a stunning building overlooking mountains and sea. The tall posts and huge windows of the Great Hall were inspired by the post-and-beam architecture of Haida houses and are a fitting home for a display of full-size totem poles, canoes, and feast dishes. Through the windows of the Great Hall, the visitor can see the magnificent outdoor sculpture complex, which includes two houses designed by contemporary Haida artist Bill Reid.

★ The Great Hall
The imposing glass and concrete structure of the Great Hall is the perfect setting for totem poles, canoes, and sculptures.

OUTDOOR HAIDA HOUSES AND TOTEM POLES

Set overlooking the water, these two Haida houses and collection of totem poles are faithful to the artistic tradition of the Haida and other tribes of the Pacific northwest, such as the Salish, Tsimshan, and Kwakiutl. Animals and mythic creatures representing various clans are carved in cedar on these poles and houses, made between 1959 and 1963 by Vancouver's favorite contemporary Haida artist Bill Reid and Namgis artist Doug Cranmer.

Carved red cedar totem poles

Climbing figures
These climbing figures are thought to have decorated the interior of First Nations family houses. Carved from cedar planks, the spare style is typical of Coast Salish sculpture.

Ceramic jug
This beautifully decorated jug was made in Central Europe in 1674 by members of the Anabaptist religious sect. The foliage motifs are in contrast to the freely sketched animals that run around the base.

STAR EXHIBITS

★ The Great Hall

★ The Raven and the First Men by Bill Reid

★ **The Raven and the First Men** *(1980)*
Carved in laminated yellow cedar by Bill Reid, this modern interpretation of a Haida creation myth depicts the raven, a wise and wily trickster, trying to coax mankind out into the world from a giant clamshell.

VISITORS' CHECKLIST

6393 NW Marine Drive.
Tel (604) 822 5087. 4 UBC,
10 UBC. Apr–Sep: 10am–
5pm daily (to 9pm Tue); Oct–
May: 10am–5pm Wed–Sun (to
9pm Tue). Dec 25 & 26.
www.moa.ubc.ca

GALLERY GUIDE
The museum's collections are arranged on one level. The Ramp gallery leads to the Great Hall, featuring the cultures of Northwest coast First Nations peoples. The Multiversity Galleries contain artifacts from other cultures, and a range of 15th- to 19th-century European ceramics is housed in the Koerner European Ceramics Gallery.

Wooden Frontlet
Decorated with abalone shell, this wooden frontlet was a ceremonial head-dress worn only on important occasions such as births and marriages.

Red cedar carved front doors
This detail comes from the set of stunning carved red cedar doors that guard the entrance to the museum. Created in 1976 by a group of First Nations artists from the 'Ksan cultural center near Hazelton, the doors show the history of the first people of the Skeena River region in British Columbia.

KEY

☐	The Great Hall
☐	Bill Reid Rotunda
☐	Multiversity Galleries
☐	Koerner European Ceramics Gallery
☐	Temporary exhibition space
☐	Michael M. Ames Theatre
☐	Non-exhibition space

Lonsdale Quay Market ⑭

123 Carrie Cates Ct., North Vancouver. **Tel** (604) 985 6261. 🚌 Lonsdale. ⏱ 9am–7pm daily. ♿ www.lonsdalequay.com

The striking concrete-and-glass building housing the Lonsdale Quay Market forms part of the North Shore SeaBus terminal. The market has a floor devoted to food – everything from fresh-baked bread to blueberries – as well as an array of cafés and restaurants that serve a variety of ethnic cuisines. On the second floor, visitors will find specialty shops offering a wide choice of hand-crafted products and gift items from local designers, as well as Kid's Alley, a row of child-oriented shops. The complex includes a hotel and spa, a pub, and a nightclub.

The modern fountain at Lonsdale Quay

Lynn Canyon Park and Ecology Centre ⑮

3663 Park Rd. **Tel** (604) 990 3755. 🚆 Hastings. 🚌 Lonsdale Quay, then bus 228 or 229. ⏱ daily. **Ecology Centre** Jun–Sep: 10am–5pm daily; Oct–May: 10am–5pm Mon–Fri, noon–4pm Sat & Sun. ⏹ Jan 1, Dec 25 & 26. 🎫 donation. 📷 🖥 www.dnv.org/ecology

Located between Mount Seymour and Grouse Mountain, Lynn Canyon Park is a popular hiking destination

Panoramic view of Vancouver's skyline from Grouse Mountain

noted for its lush second-growth temperate rain forest. The original 90-meter (295-ft) trees were logged in the early 20th century and a few of the huge stumps with circumferences of up to 11 meters (36 ft) can still be seen lying on the forest floor. Some of the stumps have springboard notches left by lumberjacks of the time.

Several marked trails, some of them steep and rugged, lead through the canyon, with longer hikes heading into surrounding park land. Many of the trails, however, are gentle strolls through Douglas fir, western hemlock, and western red cedar. If you venture far enough into the forest it is possible to see black bears, cougars, and blacktail deer, but most visitors keep to the main trails where they are more likely to see squirrels, jays, woodpeckers, and banana slugs, which can grow to lengths of 26 cm (10 inches). There are wonderful views from the 50-m (164-ft) high suspension bridge that crosses the canyon. From here, it's a short walk to 30 Foot Pool, a popular summer spot for sunbathing and swimming. A 40-minute walk takes hikers to the beautiful Twin Falls.

The nearby Ecology Centre offers guided walks, shows natural history films, and features interesting displays on the ecology of the area.

Grouse Mountain ⑯

6400 Nancy Greene Way. **Tel** (604) 980 9311. 🚌 Lonsdale Quay. 🚌 236. ⏱ 9am–10pm daily. 🎿 ♿ 🍴 🖥 www.grousemountain.com

From the summit of Grouse Mountain visitors experience the grandeur of BC's dramatic landscape and stunning views of Vancouver. On a clear day it is possible to see as far as Vancouver Island in the west, the Coastal Mountains to the north and toward the Columbia Mountains in the east.

A tough 3-km (2-mile) trail goes to the top of the 1,211-m (3,973-ft) mountain, but most visitors choose to take the Skyride cable car. In the summer there are many activities including mountain bike tours, nature walks, and hang-gliding competitions, not to mention logger sports such as chain-saw sculpture shows. In the winter, the summit has all the amenities of a ski resort, including ski schools, 26 ski runs, equipment rental, snowboarding, and 13 illuminated slopes for night skiing.

At the Refuge for Endangered Wildlife, an enclosed natural habitat that is home to two orphaned grizzly bears and three gray wolves, wildlife rangers give daily talks. The Theatre in the Sky presents a video that takes viewers on an aerial tour of BC; another video tells the tale of the orphaned bears.

The Skyride cable car, Grouse Mountain

Capilano Suspension Bridge ⑰

3735 Capilano Rd., North Vancouver. **Tel** (604) 985 7474. 🚌 Highlands 236. ☐ daily (hours vary according to season). 🔴 Dec 25. 🎫 🎥 May–Oct. 🚻 🛗 www.capbridge.com

The Capilano Suspension Bridge has been a popular tourist attraction since it was built in 1889. Pioneering Scotsman George Grant Mackay, drawn by the wild beauty of the place, had already built a small cabin overlooking the Capilano Canyon. Access to the river below was almost impossible from the cabin, and it is said that Mackay built the bridge so that his son, who loved fishing, could easily reach the Capilano River.

The present bridge, which dates from 1956 and is the fourth to be constructed here, hangs 70 m (230 ft) above the canyon and spans 137 m (450 ft), making it one of the longest such bridges in the world. Nature lovers are drawn by the views and the chance to wander through old-growth woods (old trees that have never been felled) past trout ponds and a 61-m (200-ft) waterfall. The Treetops Adventure attraction includes seven suspension bridges through evergreens, taking you up 30 m (100 ft) above the forest floor.

Atkinson Lighthouse

Lighthouse Park ⑱

Off Beacon Lane, West Vancouver. **Tel** (604) 925 7000 ☐ 6am–10pm daily.

Named after the hexagonal lighthouse built at the mouth of Burrard Inlet in 1910 to guide ships through the foggy channel, Lighthouse Park is an unspoiled area with 75 ha (185 acres) of old growth forest and wild, rocky coast. The trees here have never been logged and some of the majestic Douglas firs are over 500 years old.

There is a variety of hiking trails in the park, some leading to a viewpoint near the 18-m (60-ft) Point Atkinson Lighthouse. On a clear day one can see stunning vistas across the Strait of Georgia all the way to Vancouver Island. A 2-hour hike leads through about 5 km (3 miles) of old-growth forest, taking walkers through the fairly rugged terrain of moss-covered gullies and steep rocky outcrops with breath-taking views of the sea and surrounding area. Wear good walking shoes or boots, stay on the trails and be prepared for inclement weather.

The drive to the park itself is spectacular. Scenic **Marine Drive** winds along the West Vancouver coastline edging past beaches, clinging to rocky shoreline and passing some of Canada's priciest real estate. On the way, there are a couple of towns that are worth a stop. **Ambleside** has a long beach, which is a favorite with families and dogs but packed on sunny summer weekends. From here there are great views of Stanley Park and the Lion's Gate Bridge. A seawall walkway leads to Dundarave Pier, with panoramic views sweeping from Vancouver right around to the Strait of Georgia. **Dundarave** itself is a small village with a pleasing cluster of shops, cafés, and restaurants, as well as a beach that is not so busy as the beach at Ambleside.

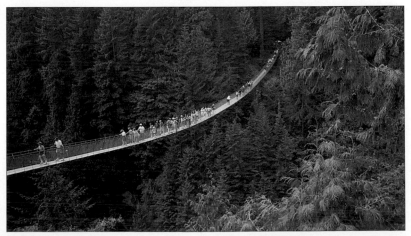

The Capilano Suspension Bridge crossing the dramatic and tree-covered Capilano Canyon

Victoria ⓳

A quiet, attractive city, Victoria's reputation for having an old-fashioned, seaside-town atmosphere is enhanced in the summer by the abundance of flowers in hanging baskets and window boxes that decorate every lampost, balcony, and storefront. Established as a Hudson's Bay Company fur-trading post in 1843 by James Douglas, Victoria had its risqué moments during its gold rush years (1858–63), when thousands of prospectors drank in 60 or more saloons on Market Square. Victoria was established as the provincial capital of British Columbia in 1871 but was soon outgrown by Vancouver, now BC's largest city. Today, Victoria is still the province's political center as well as one of its most popular attractions for visitors.

Fishing boats and pleasure craft moored in Victoria's Inner Harbour

Octagonal main dome in the Parliament Buildings

Exploring Victoria

A stroll along Victoria's Inner Harbour takes in many of the city's main attractions, such as the Royal British Columbia Museum with its dramatic depictions of the geology and native cultures of the region. Dominating the area are two late 19th-century buildings: the Fairmont Empress Hotel and the Parliament Buildings, designed by noted architect, and Victoria's adopted son,

Francis Rattenbury. Between Fort Street and View Street is the four-story shopping mall, the Bay Centre. Bastion Square, with its restaurants and boutiques, lies to the south of Market Square and its restored 1850s buildings.

🏛 Parliament Buildings

501 Belleville St. **Tel** (250) 387 3046. ◯ 9am–5pm Mon–Fri. ◯ Jan 1, Dec 25. 🔄 🗹 Mon–Fri (summer: 6pm Mon–Fri, weekends).
Victoria's many-domed Parliament Buildings are an impressive sight, particularly at night when the façades are illuminated by thousands of lights. Designed by Francis Rattenbury, the buildings were completed in 1897. Rattenbury, a 25-year-old British architect who had arrived in British Columbia only the year before, won a provincial competition to design the new Parliament Buildings. He went on to design several of the province's structures, including the nearby Fairmont Empress Hotel.

The Parliament Buildings illuminate the waters of the Inner Harbour

The history of British Columbia is depicted throughout the Parliament Buildings. A statue of explorer Captain George Vancouver is perched on top of the main dome. Inside, large murals show scenes from the past.

SIGHTS AT A GLANCE

Bastion Square ②
Beacon Hill Park ⑩
Carr House ⑪
Fairmont Empress Hotel ⑤
Helmcken House ⑨
Maritime Museum of
British Columbia ③

Market Square ①
Parliament Buildings ⑥
Royal BC Museum ⑦
See pp284–5
The Bay Centre ④
Thunderbird Park ⑧

**Bastion Square is a popular lunch
spot for locals and visitors**

(Map area)

Victoria Airport
25 km (15 miles)

CENTENNIAL
SQUARE

City Hall

CORMORANT STREET

PANDORA AVENUE

JOHNSON STREET

YATES STREET

VIEW STREET

FORT STREET

BROUGHTON STREET

COURTNEY STREET

BURDETT AVE

airmont
mpress Hotel

DOWNTOWN

Terminal

Royal BC
Museum

Helmcken
House ⑨

rbird
k

South
Park

Beacon Hill
Park ⑩

AMES BAY

BLANSHARD STREET

QUADRA STREET

DOUGLAS STREET

BROAD STREET

The Bay
Centre ④

NEY STREET

OLDT ST

FAIRFIELD ROAD

HUMBOLDT STREET

ACADEMY CLOSE

SOUTHGATE STREET

QUADRA ST

DOUGLAS STREET

Craigdarroch Castle

Art Gallery of Greater Victoria,
Government House

0 meters   250

0 yards   250

Key to Symbols see back flap

🏨 Fairmont Empress Hotel

721 Government St.
Tel (250) 384 8111.
☐ daily. 🚻
Completed in 1908 to
a Francis Rattenbury
design, the Empress
is one of Victoria's
best-loved sights.
Close to the Parliament
Buildings, the Empress
Hotel overlooks the
Inner Harbour and
dominates the skyline
with its ivy-covered
Edwardian splendor.
Visitors are welcome to
sample the luxurious
decor of the hotel's
public bars and lounges,
such as the Empress
Room, and the Palm
Court with its lovely
Tiffany-glass dome.

🏨 Bastion Square

Government St. **Tel** (250) 885 1387.
☐ daily. 🚻
This beautifully restored square
faces Victoria's picturesque
harbor and contains some of
the city's oldest 19th-century
buildings. What were once
luxury hotels and offices,
built during the boom era of
the late 1800s, now house
several eclectic restaurants.
Restoration began in 1963
when it was discovered that
the Hudson's Bay Company's
fur-trading post Fort Victoria,
established in 1843, once
stood on this site. Today, this
pedestrian square includes

the MacDonald Block building, built in 1863 in Italianate
style, with elegant cast-iron
columns and arched windows.
The old courthouse, built in
1889, houses the Maritime
Museum of British Columbia.
In summer, both visitors
and workers lunch in the
courtyard cafés.

🏨 Market Square

560 Johnson St. **Tel** (250) 386
2441. ☐ 10am–5pm daily.
🔵 Jan 1, Dec 25. 🚻 limited.
www.marketsquare.ca
Two blocks north of Bastion
Square on the corner of Johnson Street, Market Square has
some of the finest Victorian
saloon, hotel, and store
façades in Victoria. Most of
the buildings were built in the
1880s and 1890s, during the
boom period of the Klondike
Gold Rush. After decades of
neglect, the area received a
face-lift in 1975. The square
is now a shoppers' paradise,
with a variety of stores selling
everything from books and
jewelry to musical instruments
and other arts and crafts.

One of the giant totem poles on display at Thunderbird Park

✤ Thunderbird Park

Cnr Belleville & Douglas Streets.
This compact park lies at the entrance to the Royal British Columbia Museum *(see pp284–5)* and is home to an imposing collection of plain and painted giant totem poles. During the summer months it is possible to watch native artists in the Thunderbird Park Carving Studio producing these handsome carved totems. The poles show and preserve the legends of many different tribes from the aboriginal peoples of the Northwest Coast.

🏛 Helmcken House

10 Elliot St. Square. *Tel (250) 356 7226.* ◯ *May–Oct: 10am–5pm daily; Nov–Apr: noon–4pm Thu–Mon.* 🖼 ♿ 📷
Located in Elliot Square in the Inner Harbour area, the home of Hudson's Bay Company employee Dr. John Sebastian Helmcken was built in 1852 and is thought to be one of the oldest houses in British Columbia. The young doctor built his house with Douglas fir trees felled in the surrounding forest. This simple but elegantly designed clapboard dwelling contains many of the original furnishings, including the piano, which visitors are permitted to play. Among other exhibits are a collection of antique dolls and the family's personal belongings, such as clothes, shoes, and toiletries.

🏛 Maritime Museum of British Columbia

28 Bastion Square. *Tel (250) 385 4222.* ◯ *10am–5pm daily.* 🖼 **www**.mmbc.bc.ca
At this fascinating three-story museum of coastal history, exhibits tell the stories of the giant canoes of the Coast Salish First Nations Peoples. Other displays include the tall ships of the first European explorers, pirate ships, and whalers. Tumultuous tales of coastal shipwrecks are gruesomely captivating. On the top floor is the former courtroom of the notorious Sir Matthew Baillie Begbie, also known as the "Hanging Judge." The 19th-century courtroom is preserved in all its glory.

🏬 The Bay Centre

1150 Douglas St. *Tel (250) 952 5690.* ◯ *10am–6pm Mon–Wed & Sat, 10am–9pm Thu–Fri, 11am–6pm Sun.* ♿ **www**.thebaycentre.ca
The Bay Centre is a shopping mall within walking distance of the Inner Harbour and was intially built behind the façades of several historic buildings on Government Street. The Driard Hotel, designed in 1892 by John Wright, was saved from demolition by a public campaign, as were the fronts of the 1910 Times Building and the fine, 19th-century Lettice and Sears Building. Behind these elegant façades, there are three floors of stores selling everything from fashion and gifts to handmade chocolates and gourmet food.

🏬 Carr House

207 Government St. *Tel (250) 383 5843.* ◯ *11am–4pm Tue–Sat* 🖼 ♿ 📷 **www**.emilycarr.com
Emily Carr, one of Canada's best-known artists *(see pp32–3)*, was born in 1871 in this charming, yellow clapboard house. It was built in 1864 by prominent architects Wright and Saunders, under instruction from Emily's father, Richard Carr. Located just a few minutes walk from Inner Harbour, both the house and its English-style garden are open to visitors. All the rooms are appropriately furnished in late 19th-century period style, with some original family pieces. Visitors can see the dining room where Emily taught her first art classes to local children. Emily's drawing of her father still sits upon the mantel in the sitting room where, as an eight-year-old, she made her first sketches.

The Carr House where renowned painter Emily Carr was born

🌿 Beacon Hill Park

Douglas St. **Tel** *(250) 361 0600.*
⬜ *daily.* ♿
In the late 19th century this delightful park was used for stabling horses, but in 1888 John Blair, a Scottish landscape gardener, redesigned the park to include two lakes and initiated extensive tree planting. Once a favorite haunt of artist Emily Carr, this peaceful 74.5-ha (184 acre) park is now renowned for its lofty old trees (including the rare Garry oaks, some of which are over 400 years old), picturesque duck ponds, and a 100-year-old cricket pitch.

🏛 Art Gallery of Greater Victoria

1040 Moss St. **Tel** *(250) 384 4101.*
⬜ *10am–5pm Tue–Sat; 10am–9pm Thu, noon–5pm Sun.* 📷
www.aggv.ca
This popular gallery's contemporary facilities are located in the heritage neighborhood of Rockland, a few blocks west of Craigdarroch Castle. Inside, visitors will find a diverse presentation of exhibitions, including contemporary, Canadian, heritage, and national touring exhibitions. On permanent exhibition is the work of British Columbia's premier artist, Emily Carr, featuring her paintings of the British Columbian coastal forests and depictions of the lives of native peoples, as well as excerpts from her writings and archival photographs.

Shinto shrine detail at the Art Gallery

In its quaint courtyard garden, the gallery also houses the only original Japanese Shinto shrine in North America.

⛪ Craigdarroch Castle

1050 Joan Cres. **Tel** *(250) 592 5323.*
⬜ *Jun–Sep: 9am–7pm daily; Oct–May: 10am–4:30pm daily.*
⬛ *Jan 1, Dec 25, 26.* 📷
www.craigdarrochcastle.com
Completed in 1890, Craigdarroch Castle was the pet project of respected local coal millionaire Robert Dunsmuir. Although not a real castle, the design of this manor home was based on that of his ancestral home in Scotland and mixes several architectural styles such as Roman and French Gothic.

When the castle was threatened with demolition in 1959, a group of local citizens formed a society that successfully battled for its preservation. Today, the restored interior of the castle is a museum that offers an insight into the lifestyle of a wealthy Canadian entrepreneur.

The castle is noted for having one of the finest collections of Art Nouveau lead-glass windows in North America, and many of the rooms and hallways retain their patterned wood parquet floors and carved paneling in white oak, cedar, and mahogany. Every room is filled with opulent Victorian furnishings from the late 19th century and decorated in original colors such as deep greens, pinks, and rusts. Several layers of the paint have been painstakingly removed from the drawing room ceiling to reveal the original hand-painted and stenciled decorations beneath, including wonderfully detailed butterflies and lions.

A tower at Craigdarroch Castle in the French Gothic style of a château

⚜ Government House

1401 Rockland Ave. **Tel** *(250) 387 2080.* ⬜ *daily (gardens only).* ♿
www.ltgov.bc.ca
The present Government House building was completed in 1959 after fire destroyed the 1903 building, which was designed by renowned architect Francis Rattenbury.

As the official residence of the Lieutenant Governor of British Columbia, the Queen's representative to the province, the house is not open to the public, but visitors can view 5.6 ha (14 acres) of stunning public gardens with beautiful lawns, ponds, an English country garden, and a Victorian rose garden. From Pearke's Peak, a mount formed from the rocky outcrops that surround the property, there are marvelous views of the grounds.

The 1959 Government House, built with blue and pink granite

The Royal British Columbia Museum

The Royal British Columbia Museum tells the story of this region through its natural and human history. The museum is regarded as one of the best in Canada for the striking way it presents its exhibits. A series of imaginative dioramas re-create the sights, sounds, and even smells of areas such as the seashore, the ocean, and the coast forest, all of which occupy the second floor Natural History Gallery.

The region's history is presented on the third floor, including a reconstruction of an early 20th-century town. Visitors can experience the street life of the time in a cinema showing silent films and a saloon. The collection of native art and culture in the First Peoples Gallery includes a ceremonial Big House.

Third Floor

19th-century Chinatown
As part of an 1875 street scene, this Chinese herbalist's store displays a variety of herbs used in traditional Chinese medicine.

★ First Peoples Gallery
Made of cedar bark and spruce root in around 1897, this hat bears the mountain goat crest of the raven clan.

First Nations' Ceremonial Masks
The mouse, raccoon, and kingfisher are carved on these masks belonging to the Martin family, who wore them to dance on ceremonial occasions.

KEY TO FLOOR PLAN

- ☐ First Peoples Gallery
- ☐ Modern History Gallery
- ☐ Feature exhibits
- ☐ Natural History Gallery
- ☐ National Geographic IMAX theater
- ☐ Non-exhibition space

Exterior of the museum
The museum's main exhibits building was opened in 1968 after years of having to occupy several sites in and around the Legislative Buildings. The museum also houses provincial archives and a cultural precinct.

Modern History Gallery

A variety of streets, stores and public buildings, from the 1700s to 1990s, are re-created in this gallery. Here, the Grand Hotel occupies an authentic wooden sidewalk.

VISITORS' CHECKLIST

675 Belleville St. **Tel** *1 888 447 7977* or *(250) 356 7226.* 🚌 *5, 28, 30.* ⭕ *9am–5pm daily.* ⬤ *Jan 1, Dec 25.* 📷 🚻 🛗 📷 📷 📷
www.royalbcmuseum.bc.ca

★ Natural History Gallery

A full-size prehistoric tusked mammoth guards the entrance to the Natural History Gallery which includes several lifelike dioramas that re-create British Columbia's coastal forests and ocean life since the last Ice Age.

★ Seashore Diorama

This diorama uses sound, film, lighting, and realistic animals such as this northern sea lion.

Second Floor

GALLERY GUIDE

The main exhibits of the museum are housed on the second and third floors. The Natural History Gallery, on the second floor, reconstructs a range of environments from the Coast Seashore to the Old Growth Forest displays. The third floor has the First Peoples and Modern History galleries.

STAR EXHIBITS

★ Seashore Diorama

★ Natural History Gallery

★ First Peoples Gallery

First Floor

Main Entrance

The lily pond in the formal Italian garden at Butchart Gardens

Butchart Gardens ⑳

800 Benvenuto Ave., Brentwood Bay.
Tel (250) 652 4422, 1 866 652 4422.
🚌 Victoria. 🚌 Victoria. ◐ 9am
daily; closing times vary by season. 📷
♿ www.butchartgardens.com

These beautiful gardens
were begun in 1904 by Mrs.
Jennie Butchart, the wife of a
cement manufacturer. When
her husband moved west to
quarry limestone near Victoria,
Mrs. Butchart began to design
a new garden, which would
stretch down to the water at
Tod Inlet. When the limestone
deposits ran out, Mrs Butchart
decided to add to her burgeoning garden by landscaping the
quarry site into a sunken garden which now boasts a lake
overhung by willow and other
trees laden with blossom in
spring. A huge rock left in
the quarry was turned into a
towering rock garden. Today
visitors can climb stone steps
to see stunning views from
the top. As their popularity
grew, so the gardens were
filled with thousands of rare
plants collected from around
the world by Mrs Butchart.
Today, the gardens are
arranged into distinct areas.
There is a formal Italian garden
with a lily pond that features
a fountain bought in Italy by
the Butcharts in 1924. The
rose garden is filled with the
scent of hundreds of different
blooms in summer. During
the summer the gardens are
illuminated and play host to
evening musical performances.

Port Renfrew ㉑

🚶 200. 🏠 2070 Phillips Rd., Sooke
(250) 642 6351.

Port Renfrew is a small,
friendly fishing village and
ex-logging town. A popular
daytrip from Victoria, the
town offers visitors access
to Botanical Beach where a
unique sandstone shelf leaves
rock pools filled with marine
life such as starfish at low tide.
Port Renfrew is famed for its
hiking along old logging roads:
the Sandbar Trail goes through
a Douglas fir plantation to a
large river sandbar where it is
possible to swim at low tide.
A more serious hike is the
47-km (29-mile) Juan de Fuca
Marine Trail from Port Renfrew
to China Beach. This trail offers
a range of hikes, from treks
lasting several days to short
beach walks. The town is one
of two starting points for the
West Coast Trail in Pacific Rim
National Park *(see pp288–9)*.

Cowichan District ㉒

🚌 & 🚌 from Duncan. ℹ️ 381A
Trans-Canada Hwy, Duncan (250)
746 4636, 1 888 303 3337.

Located on the south central
coast of Vancouver Island,
about 60 km (37 miles) north
of Victoria, the Cowichan
District incorporates both the
Chemainus and Cowichan
Valleys. Cowichan means
"warm land" in the language
of the Cowichan peoples, one
of British Columbia's largest
First Nations groups; the area's
mild climate means the waters
of Cowichan Lake are warm
enough to swim in during the

summer months. The largest
freshwater lake on the island,
Lake Cowichan offers excellent
fishing, canoeing, and hiking.
Between the town of
Duncan and the lake lies the
Valley Demonstration Forest,
which has scenic lookouts
and signs explaining forest
management. Duncan is
known as the City of Totems
as it displays several poles in
the downtown area. The
Quw'utsun' Cultural and Conference Centre shows films on
the history of the Cowichan
Tribe. The gift shop sells traditional artifacts including
Cowichan sweaters. You can
also visit a First Nations carver
in his studio at the Maritime
Centre in Cowichan Bay.

Stunning vista over Lake Cowichan
in the Cowichan Valley

Chemainus ㉓

🚶 4,100. 🚌 🚌 ⛴ ℹ️ 9796
Willow St. (250) 246 3944.
www.chemainus.bc.ca

When the local sawmill closed
in the late 1970s, picturesque
Chemainus transformed itself
into a major attraction with the
painting of giant murals around
the town that depict the history
of the region. Local artists
continued the project and today
there are more than 40 murals
on the outside walls of local
buildings, based on real events

First Nations' faces looking down from a Chemainus town mural

Pleasure craft and fishing boats moored in Nanaimo harbor

in the town's past. Larger-than-life images of Cowichan natives, pioneers, and loggers have revitalized the town. Visitors enjoy browsing in the town's various antique stores and relaxing in the many pleasant sidewalk cafés.

Environs

Some 70 km (45 miles) south of Chemainus, Swartz Bay is the departure point on Vancouver Island for ferries to the Southern Gulf Islands and the mainland. Visitors are drawn to the 200 mostly uninhabited islands by their tranquility and natural beauty. It is possible to stroll along empty beaches where sightings of eagles and turkey vultures are common. There are fishing charters for visitors who enjoy catching salmon and cod, and kayaking tours offering stops on isolated shores to view otters, seals, and marine birds.

Salt Spring is the most populated Gulf island, with about 10,500 inhabitants. In the summer, visitors come to wander around the pretty village of Ganges, where a busy marina surrounds the wooden pier. The village offers stores, cafés, galleries, and colorful markets.

Nanaimo ㉔

🏠 78,800. ✈ 🚉 🚌 🚢 ℹ 2290 Bowen Rd. (250) 756 0106, 1 800 663 7337. **www**.tourismnanaimo.com

Originally the site of five Coast Salish native villages, Nanaimo was established as a coal-mining town in the 1850s.

As the second-largest city on Vancouver Island, Nanaimo has plenty of malls and businesses along the Island Highway, but it is the Old City Quarter on the waterfront in the heart of downtown Nanaimo that visitors enjoy most.

The Old City Quarter has many 19th-century buildings, including the Nanaimo Court House, designed by Francis Rattenbury in 1895. The **Vancouver Island Conference Centre** includes a re-creation of an old schoolroom, a First Nations exhibit, and a Sports Hall of Fame. Other exhibits include native artifacts displayed in a village diorama.

🏛 Vancouver Island Conference Centre
101 Gordon St. **Tel** (250) 244 4050. ☐ 10am–5pm daily. 🗎 ♿ 🗎 book in advance.

Port Alberni ㉕

🏠 25,000. 🚉 🚌 🚢 ℹ 2533 Port Alberni Hwy (250) 724 6535.

Port Alberni sits at the head of Alberni Inlet, which stretches 48 km (30 miles) from the interior of Vancouver Island to the Pacific Ocean in the west. The town now depends upon hikers, kayakers, and wildlife watchers, and it is a popular haunt for salmon fishers. Every year the Salmon Derby and Festival offers thousands of Canadian dollars for the biggest fish caught during the last weekend in August. The town's other attractions include a 1929 locomotive offering train rides along the waterfront during the summer from the 1912 Port Alberni Railway Station to the steam operated MacLean Sawmill.

Many visitors come to cruise on the freighter M.V. *Frances Barkley.* The ships deliver mail down the inlet, as well as offering trips to Ucluelet, Bamfield, and other way-points near the Pacific Rim National Park. It also carries kayaks and canoes for those hoping to sail around the Broken Group Islands *(see p288).*

Just east of Port Alberni, it is possible to hike among awe-inspiring old growth Douglas firs and red cedars in the outstanding Cathedral Grove, located in the MacMillan Provincial Park.

A carved eagle soars over Port Alberni Pier

A 1929 steam locomotive offering rides along Port Alberni's waterfront

Tofino ❷❻

🏠 1,700. 🛈 455 Campbell St. (250) 725 3414.

Once a timber town, Tofino is now a busy tourist center for the Pacific Rim National Park Reserve (see below). Its sandy beaches and woodland trails attract visitors all year round; in the summer, surfing, hiking, kayaking, and whale-watching also draw the crowds. The Pacific Rim National Park Reserve begins just past the junction of Tofino/Ucluelet.

In Tofino, the **Eagle Aerie Gallery** displays works by First Nations artist Roy Vickers, while **The Whale**

Centre Maritime Museum showcases artifacts from local shipwrecks and First Nations history. It also organizes whale-watching excursions.

Just north of Tofino, the UNESCO Biosphere Reserve of Clayoquot Sound features a diverse range of ecosystems, including islands, mountains, and temperate rainforests. Boating and paddling day

Sunset at Chesterman Beach, Tofino

trips can be arranged through several tour operators in Tofino, and hiking trails are easily accessible on a few islands.

🏛 **Eagle Aerie Gallery**
350 Campbell St. **Tel** (250) 725 3235. ⬤ 9:30am–5:30pm daily.

🏛 **The Whale Centre Maritime Museum**
411 Campbell St. **Tel** (250) 725 2132. ⬤ 9am–8pm daily.
www.tofinowhalecentre.com

Campbell River ❷❽

🏠 32,000. 🛈 1235 Shoppers Row (250) 830 0411. **www.**
campbellrivertourism.com

Located on the northeast shore of Vancouver Island, Campbell River is renowned as a center for salmon fishing.

Pacific Rim National Park Reserve ❷❼

The Pacific Rim National Park Reserve is composed of three distinct areas: Long Beach, the West Coast Trail, and the Broken Group Islands, all of which occupy a 130-km (80-mile) strip of Vancouver Island's west coast. The park is a world famous area for whale-watching, and the Wickaninnish Interpretive Centre off Hwy 4 has the latest information on their movements. Long Beach offers a range of hiking trails, with parking at all trail heads and beach accesses. The most challenging hike is the 75-km (47-miles) West Coast Trail, between Port Renfrew and Bamfield. The Broken Group Islands are popular with kayakers.

The Broken Group Islands
This is an archipelago of some 100 islets popular with kayakers and scuba divers.

The Schooner Cove Trail is one of nine scenic and easy-to-follow trails along the sands of Long Beach.

Tofino

LONG BEACH

Port Albion

Ucluelet

The Wickaninnish Interpretive Centre has viewing platforms for whale-watching.

Long Beach
The rugged, windswept sands of Long Beach are renowned for their wild beauty, with crashing Pacific rollers, unbeatable surfing opportunities, rock pools filled with marine life, and scattered driftwood.

Dodd Island

Turret Island

Effingham Island

The crashing waters of Elk Falls along the Campbell River

which follow the fish up river. Visitors can rent a fishing boat or try their luck catching fish from the 183-m (600-ft) Discovery Pier in the town.

Just 3 km (1.8 miles) north west of Campbell River, Elk Falls Provincial Park houses large Douglas Fir forests and several waterfalls, including the impressive Elk Falls.

The waters of Discovery Passage are on the migration route for five major species of salmon, including the giant Chinook. There are boat tours,

Telegraph Cove ㉙

Port McNeill. 1594 Beach Drive, Port McNeill (250) 956 3131.

Located on the northern end of Vancouver Island, Telegraph Cove is a small, picturesque boardwalk village, with distinctive high wooden houses built on stilts that look

over the waters of Johnstone Strait. In summer, the Northern resident killer whales, drawn to the area by the migrating salmon, come to cavort on the gravel beds in the shallow waters of Robson Bight, an ecological reserve established in 1982. Visitors may view the antics of the whales from tour boats or from Port McNeill.

Killer whales in the waters of Johnstone Strait, Vancouver Island

WHALE WATCHING

Migrating gray whales

More than 20 species of whale are found in British Columbia's coastal waters. Around 22,000 gray whales migrate annually from their feeding grounds in the Arctic Ocean to breed off the coast of Mexico. The whales tend to stay near to the coast and often move close enough to Vancouver Island's west shore to be sighted from land. From March to August there are daily whale-watching trips from Tofino and Ucluelet.

West Coast Trail
This trail passes stunning scenery, including moss-draped rainforest and deep, rocky gullies.

VISITORS' CHECKLIST

Hwy 4. **Tel** (250) 726 7721. from Port Alberni. daily. Mar–Sep. www.pc.gc.ca

KEY

▬	Major road
═	Minor road
▪▪	West Coast Trail
▬	National Park boundary
▬	Rivers
🔺	Camping
🏕	Picnic areas
ℹ	Tourist information
�◁	Viewpoint

Bamfield

0 km 10
0 miles 10

Port Renfrew

At the Nitinat Narrows hikers on the West Coast Trail must take a short ferry ride across this pretty waterway. The trail is open from May to September.

THE ROCKY MOUNTAINS

The Canadian Rockies occupy a band of the provinces of British Columbia and Alberta nearly 805 km (500 miles) wide, and are part of the range that extends from Mexico through the US into Canada. Between 65 and 100 million years ago, a slow but massive upheaval of the Earth's crust caused the rise of the Rocky Mountains and the dramatic, jagged appearance of their peaks, 50 of which are over 3,048 m (10,000 ft) high. A region of spectacular beauty, the landscape of the Rockies is dominated by snow-topped peaks, luminous glaciers, and iridescent glacial lakes, now protected in a series of national parks. The discovery of natural hot springs at Banff in 1883 prompted the federal government to create Canada's first national park. Since 1984 Banff, Jasper, Yoho, and Kootenay parks have become UNESCO World Heritage sites.

SIGHTS AT A GLANCE

Historic Towns and Cities
Calgary ❶
Cranbrook ❼
Fernie ❺
Fort Macleod ❷
Fort Nelson ⓵⓽
Fort St. John ⓵⓼
Grande Prairie ⓵⓻
Prince George ⓵⓺
Radium Hot Springs ❿

National and Provincial Parks
Banff National Park ⓵⓷
Glacier National Park ❾
Jasper National Park ⓵⓹
Kootenay National Park ⓵⓵
Muncho Lake Provincial Park ⓶⓪
Waterton Lakes National Park ❸
Yoho National Park ⓵⓸

Historical Sites and Places of Natural Beauty
Crowsnest Pass ❹
Fort Steele Heritage Town ❻
Kananaskis Country ⓵⓶
The Purcell Mountains ❽

KEY

✈ International airport
═ Highway
▬ Major road
— Major rail routes
╍ International border

0 km   150
0 miles   150

◁ Skilled horsemanship on display at the Calgary Exhibition and Stampede

Calgary **❶**

Blackfoot shirt in Glenbow Museum

Established in 1875, Calgary is famous for hosting the Winter Olympics of 1988, and for its Stampede. Calgary covers the largest area of any city in Alberta, and lies between the eastern foothills of the Rockies and the Prairies. It is a sophisticated place, with skyscrapers, galleries, and theaters, but it retains the air of a frontier town where pick-up trucks and cowboy boots are not out of place. The city's western atmosphere belies the fact that its modern skyline has grown since the oil boom of the 1960s. Noted for its proximity to Banff National Park, Calgary's center, with its offices and stores, is 128 km (79 miles) east of Banff Townsite *(see p303)*.

Calgary Tower surrounded by the skyscrapers of the city's skyline

Calgary Tower
9th Ave. & Centre St. SW.
***Tel** (403) 266 7171.* ◯ *daily.*
🎦 ♿ www.calgarytower.com
The Calgary Tower is the city's third-tallest structure, with two elevators that hurtle to the top in 62 seconds, and two emergency staircases composed of 802 steps apiece. From street level to the top, Calgary Tower measures 191 m (627 ft). At the top there is a restaurant and an observation deck, both of which offer incredible views across to the Rockies and eastward over the vast plains of the Prairies.

Art Central
100 7th Ave. SW.
***Tel** (403) 543 9600.* ◯ *daily.* ♿
www.artcentral.ca
A former bowling alley and pool hall at the corner of Centre Street and 7th Avenue, in downtown Calgary, this building underwent a complete overhaul in 2004 and reinvented itself as a

visual arts complex. Spread out over three levels, Art Central accommodates 57 individual spaces for studios, galleries, eclectic boutiques, and artist exhibitions and demonstrations. The complex also houses a restaurant and café.

Shopping at a designer boutique in downtown Eau Claire Market

Eau Claire Market
200 Barclay Parade SW. ***Tel** (403) 264 6450.* ◯ *daily.* ♿
Housed in a brightly colored warehouse, this market provides a welcome contrast to the surrounding office blocks downtown. Located on the Bow River, opposite Prince's Island Park, it offers specialty stores selling a fine variety of gourmet foods, contemporary arts, craft markets, cinemas, cafés, and restaurants. Walkways connect to a footbridge that leads to Prince's Island Park. The market will be undergoing a complete renovation during 2012.

Some of the shops and exhibition spaces inside Art Central

MEMORIAL DRIVE

Prince's Island Park ⑨

EAU CLAIRE AVENUE
Eau Claire Market ⑧
1ST AV

Calgary Chinese Cultural Centre
2ND A
3RD AV

5TH STREET SW
4TH STREET SW
3RD STREET SW
2ND STREET SW

4TH   AVENUE   SW

5TH   AVENUE   SW

6TH   AVENUE   S

7TH AVE

Bus Terminal
2 km (1.2 miles)
STEPHEN AVE MALL

9TH AVENUE S

Canada Olympic Park

Heritage Park
Historic Village

10TH AVENUE SW

Key to Symbols *see back flap*

SIGHTS AT A GLANCE

Art Central ⑥
Calgary Chinese Cultural Centre ⑦
Calgary Tower ⑤
Eau Claire Market ⑧
EPCOR Centre for the Performing Arts ④
Fort Calgary ②
Glenbow Museum ③
Prince's Island Park ⑨
St. George's Island ①

♣ Prince's Island Park

The pretty Prince's Island Park lies close to the city center on the banks of the Bow River. This tiny island is connected to the city via several bridges, including a pedestrian bridge at the end of 4th Street SW. During hot summers, visitors and locals picnic under the cool shade of the park's many trees, as well as using its walking and biking trails.

⊞ Calgary Chinese Cultural Centre

197 1st St. SW. *Tel (403) 262 5071.*
☐ daily. ⬚ for museum. ♿
www.culturalcentre.ca
Located in downtown Calgary, the Chinese Cultural Centre was completed in 1992. It is modeled on the 1420 Temple of Heaven in Beijing, which was used exclusively by emperors.

Blue tiles inside the dome of the Calgary Chinese Cultural Centre

The center was built by artisans from China using traditional skills.

The Dr. Henry Fok Cultural Hall is the highlight of the building with its 21-m-high (70-ft) ceiling and an impressive dome adorned with dragons and phoenixes. Each of the dome's four supporting columns is decorated with lavish gold designs, which represent the four seasons.

VISITORS' CHECKLIST

🏠 904,987. ✈ 17 km (10.5 miles) NE of city. 🚌 Greyhound Bus Station, 877 Greyhound Way SW. ℹ Tourism Calgary 200, 238 11th Avenue SE. (403) 263 8510, 1 800 661 1678. 🎪 Calgary Stampede (Jul); Calgary Folk Festival (Jul); Taste of Calgary (Aug). www.tourismcalgary.com

🏛 Glenbow Museum

130 9th Ave. SE. *Tel (403) 268 4100.*
☐ daily. ⬚ ♿ www.glenbow.org
Located in the heart of downtown Calgary, the Glenbow Museum is one of western Canada's largest museums, hosting three major temporary exhibitions annually, in addition to having over 20 permanent galleries. The museum houses an excellent collection of Canadian and contemporary art, as well as a wide range of objects that chronicle the history of the Canadian West through First Nations and pioneer artifacts. An extensive military collection includes medieval armor and Samurai swords. Glenbow's gallery, Nitsitapiisinni, traces the story of the Blackfoot people.

🎭 EPCOR Centre for the Performing Arts

205 8th Ave. SE. *Tel (403) 294 9494.*
☐ daily. ⬚ www.epcorcentre.org
Opened in 1985, this large complex houses four theaters and a concert hall, as well as having five rental boardrooms. Located in the heart of the city on Olympic Plaza, the center has staged events as diverse as k.d. lang concerts and the High Performance Rodeo.

The lobby of the EPCOR Centre for the Performing Arts

Mountie's cabin in the Interpretive Centre at Fort Calgary Historic Park

🚩 Hunt House
and Deane House

806 9th Ave. SE. *Tel* (403) 290
1875. ⭕ Deane House: daily. 🖼
The Hunt House lies across
the Elbow River from the Fort
Calgary Interpretive Centre.
This small log house is one
of the few buildings left from
the original settlement of
Calgary in the early 1880s.

Nearby Deane House was
built for the Superintendent of
Fort Calgary, Captain Richard
Burton Deane, in 1906. Today,
the house is a restaurant where
visitors can enjoy a meal in a
delightful period setting.

🚩 Fort Calgary
Historic Park

750 9th Ave. SE. *Tel* (403) 290
1875. ⭕ daily. 🖼 ♿
Fort Calgary was built by the
North West Mounted Police in
1875 at the confluence of the
Bow and Elbow Rivers. The
Grand Trunk Pacific Railway
(later amalgamated with the
CPR), arrived in 1883, and the
tiny fort town grew to over
400 residents in a year. In
1887, a fire destroyed several
of the settlement's key
buildings and a new town
was built out of the more fire-
resistant sandstone. In 1914 the
land was bought by the Grand
Trunk Pacific Railway and the
fort was leveled. Pieces of the
fort were discovered during
an archeological dig in 1970,
and the well-restored site was
opened to the public in 1978.

Today, the reconstructed fort
offers an interpretive center,
which tells of Calgary's colorful
past through exhibits such as
a re-created quartermaster's
store and carpenter's
workshop. There are also
delightful walks along the river.

🍁 St. George's Island

St. George's Island sits on the
edge of the Bow River, near
downtown Calgary. The island
houses part of the magnificent
Calgary Zoo, Botanical Garden,
and Prehistoric Park.

The zoo prides itself on the
exciting presentation of its
animals, which can be seen in
their appropriate habitats. A
series of environments called
The Canadian Wilds has been
created, highlighting the diversity of the Canadian landscape
and its wildlife. There are
aspen woodlands where it is
possible to see the endangered
woodland caribou, and visitors
can wander the pathways of
the boreal forest environment,
maybe spotting the rare
whooping crane feeding in
the shallow wetlands area.

The zoo is surrounded by the
Botanical Gardens, which has
a vast greenhouse displaying
plants from different climate
zones from around the world.

The Prehistoric Park offers a
reconstructed Mesozoic landscape, where visitors can picnic
among 22 life-size dinosaurs.

The stately whooping crane at
Calgary Zoo, St. George's Island

🍁 Stampede Park

1410 Olympic Way SE. *Tel* (403) 261
0101. ⭕ daily. 🖼 some events. ♿
Famous as the site of the
Calgary Stampede, the park
offers year-round leisure and
conference facilities. There is
a permanent horse racetrack,
as well as two ice-hockey sta-
diums, one of which is housed
inside the striking Saddledome,
named for its saddle-shaped
roof. Trade shows, such as
antiques and home improvements, are also held here.

CALGARY STAMPEDE

An exuberant ten-day festival of all things western, the
Calgary Stampede is held every July in Stampede Park.
Originally established as an agricultural fair in 1886, the
Stampede of 1912 attracted 14,000
people. In the 1920s one of its
still-popular highlights, the risky
but exciting covered wagon races,
became part of the show.

Today's festival has an array of
spectacular entertainments that dra-
matize scenes from western history.
They can be seen both on site and
in Calgary itself. The fair starts with
a dazzling parade through the city,
and then features bull riding, calf
roping, and cow tackling. The
main events are the *Half-Million
Dollar Rodeo*, and chuck-wagon
racing which have combined prize
money of over Can$2 million.

Heritage Park Historical Village houses some 70 historic buildings

locals and visitors can enjoy the facilities all year round, including riding on the bobsleds and luge tracks. The views toward the Rockies and over Calgary from the 90-m (295-ft) high Olympic Ski Jump Tower are truly stunning.

Visitors can experience the thrills of the downhill ski run and the bobsleds on the simulators housed in the Olympic Hall of Fame and Museum.

🌿 Fish Creek Provincial Park

Bow Bottom Trail SE. **Tel** (403) 297 5293. ◯ daily. ♿ partial.
Established in 1975, Fish Creek Provincial Park is one of North America's largest urban parks, covering 13 sq km (5 sq miles) of forest along the Fish Creek valley. Park guides hold slide shows on both the ecology and history of the region, detailing the park's many archeological sites, such as buffalo jumps dated between 750 BC and 1800 AD.

The park's forest is a mix of white spruce, aspen, and balsam poplar. In winter, many of the hiking trails become cross-country ski trails, popular with locals and visitors alike. The Canada goose, the great blue heron, and the bald eagle are among a variety of birds that visit the park during both summer and winter.

🎡 Heritage Park Historical Village

1900 Heritage Drive SW. **Tel** (403) 268 8500. ◯ Village open May–Oct; museum and café open all year. ◯ Nov–Apr. ♿ ♿
www.heritagepark.ca
Heritage Park Historical Village sits on the shore of Glenmore Reservoir, and contains over 70 historic buildings, from outhouses to a 2-story hotel, which have been brought here from sites all over western Canada. The buildings have been organized into time periods, which range from an 1880s fur-trading post to the shops and homes of a small town between 1900 and 1914. Most of the 45,000 artifacts that furnish and decorate the village have been donated by residents of Calgary and the surrounding

towns, and vary from teacups to steam trains.

Among the most thrilling of the exhibits, a working 19th-century amusement park has several rides, and three original, operating steam locomotives. A replica of the SS Moyie, a charming sternwheeler paddle boat, takes visitors on 30-minute cruises around the Glenmore Reservoir. You can also ride one of two vintage electric streetcars to the park's front gates and walk down a 1930s–40s urban streetscape. The sense of stepping back in time is enhanced by the clip-clopping of horsedrawn carriages, and by the smells and sounds of shops such as the working bakery and the blacksmith's, which are all staffed by costumed guides.

Victorian drink container at Heritage Park

🌿 Canada Olympic Park

88 Canada Olympic Rd. SW. **Tel** (403) 247 5452. ◯ 10am–9pm Mon–Fri, 9am–5pm Sat & Sun. ♿ ♿
Canada Olympic Park was the site of the 1988 XV Olympic Winter Games. Today, both

🏛 Telus World of Science Calgary

Off Memorial Dr. NE., just north of Calgary Zoo. **Tel** (403) 268 8327. ◯ daily. ♿ ♿
www.calgaryscience.ca
Relocated and redesigned in 2011, the Telus World of Science is a popular interactive museum. It offers such exhibits as The Human Body, Earth and Space, and the Creative Kids Museum. The latest technology allows for a memorable experience of the center for both kids and adults alike. There is also an interactive outdoor playground.

🏛 The Military Museums

4520 Crowchild Trail SW. **Tel** (403) 974 2850. ◯ 9am–5pm Mon–Fri, 9.30am–4pm Sat & Sun. ♿ ♿
www.themilitarymuseums.ca
The Military Museums include naval, air force, and army museums under one roof. The focus is on the history of the Canadian Forces, from the Northwest Rebellion in 1885 to today.

Sherman tank on display outside the Military Museums

The mountain-ringed Waterton Lake in Waterton Lakes National Park

Fort Macleod ❷

🏃 3,100. 🚏 ℹ Fort Macleod
Museum, 25th St. (403) 553 4425.
www.fortmacleod.com

Alberta's oldest settlement,
Fort Macleod was established
in 1874 as the first North West
Mounted Police outpost in the
west. Sent to control lawless
whiskey traders at the Fort
Whoop-up trading post, the
Mounties set up Fort Macleod
nearby *(see p232)*.

Today's town retains over
30 of its historic buildings, and
the reconstructed fort palisades
(completed in 1957) house the
fort's museum, which tells the
story of the Mounties' journey.

The world's oldest and best-
preserved buffalo jump lies just
16 km (10 miles) northwest of
Fort Macleod. **Head-Smashed-
In-Buffalo Jump** was made a
UNESCO World Heritage site in
1981. This way of hunting
buffalo, in which aboriginal
people wearing buffalo skins
stampede herds of the animals
to their deaths over a cliff, was
perfected by the Blackfoot
tribe. The site takes its name
from the brave whose head
was smashed in when watching the kill from under the cliff.

🏛 **Head-Smashed-In-
Buffalo Jump**
Hwy 785, off Hwy 2. **Tel** (403) 553
2731. ⬤ daily. 🍴 🚻

Waterton Lakes National Park ❸

🚆 Calgary. ℹ Park Info Centre, open
mid-May–Oct (403) 859 2224. ⬤
daily. 🍴 🚻 partial. **www**.pc.gc.ca

Scenery as amazing as any
of that found in the Rockies'
other national parks characterizes the less-known Waterton
Lakes National Park. Located
in the southwest corner of
Alberta along the US border,
the park is an International
Peace Park and manages a
shared ecosystem with Glacier
National Park in the US.

The park owes its unique
beauty to the geological
phenomenon of the Lewis
Overthrust, which was forged
over a billion years ago (before
the formation of the Rockies)
when ancient rock was pushed
over newer deposits. Thus, the
peaks of the mountains rise up
sharply out of the flat prairies.

Waterton's mix of lowland
and alpine habitats means it
has the widest variety of wildlife of any of Canada's parks,
from bears to bighorn sheep,
and from waterfowl to nesting
species such as sapsuckers.

Crowsnest Pass ❹

ℹ Frank Slide Interpretive Centre
(403) 562 7388. ⬤ daily. ⬤ public
holidays. 🍴 **www**.frankslide.com

Crowsnest Pass is located
1.5 km (1 mile) off Highway 3,
in Alberta close to the border
with BC. Like most Rocky
Mountain passes, it is enclosed

Visitors on an underground tour of Bellevue Mine at Crowsnest Pass by snowcapped mountains. In the early 1900s this area was dominated by the coal-mining industry and was the site of Canada's worst mine disaster. In 1903, a huge mass of rock slid off Turtle Mountain into the valley below, hitting the town of Frank and killing 70 people. The Frank Slide Interpretive Centre offers two award-winning audio/visual presentations about this tragic event. A trail through the valley is marked with numbered stops and leads hikers to the debris left by the disaster. Visitors can learn more about the history of local mining communities at the Bellevue Mine, which offers tours through the same narrow tunnels that working miners took daily between 1903 and 1961. Tours are available of Leitch Collieries, a fascinating early mining complex. Sleepovers are also available.

The Rocky Mountains tower over houses in the town of Fernie

Fernie ⑤

🏚 4,200. ✈ ❙ 102 Commerce Rd, off Hwy 3. (250) 423 6868.
www.tourismfernie.com

Fernie is an attractive, tree-lined town set amid a circle of pointed peaks on the British Columbia side of Crowsnest Pass. The town owes its handsome appearance to a fire that burned it to the ground in 1904 and again in 1908, since when all buildings have been constructed from brick and stone. Among several historic buildings, the 1911 courthouse stands out as the only

château-style courthouse in BC. Fernie is known for its winter sports, and boasts the best powder snow in the Rockies. The skiing season runs from November to April. The nearby Fernie Alpine Resort is huge and capable of taking over 13,000 skiers and riders up the mountain every hour. During the summer, the Mount Fernie Provincial Park offers a broad range of hiking trails through its magnificent mountain scenery. Boat trips on the many nearby lakes and rivers are popular, as is the fishing.

Helicopter trips take visitors close to the mountains to see the formations and granite cliffs particular to this region of the Rockies.

Fort Steele Heritage Town ⑥

9851 Hwy 95. **Tel** (250) 417 6000.
◯ daily. 🎟 ♿ www.fortsteele.ca

A re-creation of a 19th-century pioneering supply town, this settlement was established in 1864, when gold was discovered at Wild Horse River. Thousands of prospectors and entrepreneurs arrived by the Dewdney Trail, which linked Hope to the gold fields. The town was named after the North West Mounted Police Superintendent, Samuel

19th-century barber's shop at Fort Steele Heritage Town

Steele, who arrived in 1887 to restore peace between warring groups of Ktunaxa native peoples and European settlers. The town underwent a brief boom with the discovery of lead and silver, but the mainline railroad was routed through Cranbrook instead, and by the early 1900s Fort Steele was a ghost town.

Today, there are over 60 reconstructed or restored buildings, staffed by guides in period costume, including the general store, livery stable, and Mountie officers' quarters, where personal items such as family photographs, swords, and uniforms create the illusion of recent occupation. Demonstrations of traditional crafts such as quilt- and ice cream-making are also held here. Tours at the nearby Wild Horse River Historic Site include the chance to pan for gold.

THE BUFFALO

The large, shaggy-headed type of cattle known as buffalo are really North American bison. These apparently cumbersome beasts (a mature bull can weigh as much as 900 kg/1,980 lbs) are agile, fast, and unpredictable.

Before European settlers began moving west to the plains, in the 18th and 19th centuries, the buffalo lived in immense herds of hundreds of thousands. It is estimated that as many as 60,000,000 roamed here. Initially hunted only by the Plains Indians, who respected the beasts as a source of food, shelter, and tools, the buffalo were subsequently hunted almost to extinction by Europeans. By 1900 less than 1,000 animals remained. In 1874 a rancher called Walking Coyote bred a small herd of just 716 plains bison whose descendants now roam several Canadian national parks.

A North American plains bison

The luxurious dining car on a restored train at Cranbrook's rail museum

Cranbrook **7**

🏔 19,000. ✕ 🚉 ℹ 2279 Cranbrook St. N. (250) 426 5914.

Cranbrook is the largest town in southeast BC and lies between the Purcell and the Rocky Mountain ranges. A major transportation hub for the Rocky Mountain region, Cranbrook is within easy reach of a variety of scenic delights, including alpine forest and the lush, green valleys of the mountain foothills. A range of wildlife such as elk, wolves, cougar, and the highest density of grizzlies in the Rockies, may be spotted on one of many hikes available here.

The town's main attraction is the **Canadian Museum of Rail Travel**, which includes a collection of deluxe "hotels on wheels" dating from between the 1880s and the 1950s that can be used for touring the facilities.

🏛 **The Canadian Museum of Rail Travel**
57 Van Horne St. S. **Tel** (250) 489 3918. ◯ Apr–mid-Oct: daily; late Oct–Apr: Tue–Sat. 🖼 🖺

The Purcell Mountains **8**

🚉 Kamloops. ℹ 500 10th Ave. N./ Hwy 95, Golden (250) 344 7125.

The rugged and beautiful Purcell Mountains face the Rockies across the broad Columbia River Valley. The region is one of the most remote in the Rockies and attracts hunters and skiers from across the globe. A high range of granite spires, called the Bugaboos, also draws mountain climbers. In the north of the Purcell range, and in one of its few accessible areas, the Purcell Wilderness Conservancy, covers a vast 21 sq km (8 sq miles). Carefully regulated hunting expeditions for bear, mountain goats, and elk are permitted here.

From the nearby pretty town of Invermere, it is possible to access one of the most difficult trails in Canada; the Earl Grey Pass Trail extends some 56 km (35 miles) over the Purcell Mountains. It is named after Earl Grey, Canada's Governor General from 1904 to 1911, who chose the Purcell range as the place to build a vacation cabin for his family in 1909. The trail he traveled followed an established native route used by the Kinbasket natives of the Shuswap First Nations. Today the trail is notoriously dangerous; bears, avalanches, and fallen trees are often hazards along the way. Hiking along it requires skill and experience and should not be attempted by a novice.

Glacier National Park **9**

🚉 Revelstoke/Golden. ℹ Revelstoke (250) 837 7500. ◯ daily. 🖼 🖺 **www**.pc.gc.ca

Glacier National Park covers 1,350 sq km (520 sq miles) of wilderness in the Selkirk Range of the Columbia Mountains. The park was established in 1886, and its growth was

The Purcell Mountains are noted for remote rivers, forests, and mountains

For hotels and restaurants in this region see pp362–3 and pp388–9

The Illecillewaet Glacier is one of 420 glaciers in Glacier National Park

linked to the growth of the railroad, which was routed through Roger's Pass in 1885. Today, many of the park's most accessible walking trails follow abandoned railroad lines. Other trails offer visitors stunning views of the park's 420 glaciers, including the Great Glacier, now known as the Illecillewaet Glacier.

The park is known for its very wet weather in summer and almost daily snowfalls in winter, when as much as 23 m (75 ft) of snow may fall in one season. The threat of avalanche is serious here, and visitors should stop at the Roger's Pass Center for up-to-date information.

The Roger's Pass line was abandoned by the CPR due to avalanches, and a tunnel was built underneath it instead. The Trans-Canada Highway (Hwy 1) follows the route of the pass as it bisects the park, en route to the lovely town of Revelstoke. From here visitors may access the forests and jagged peaks of Mount Revelstoke National Park.

Radium Hot Springs ⓾

🏘 1,000. ℹ Chamber of Commerce, 7556 Main St. E. (250) 347 9331, 888 347 9331. **www**.radiumhotsprings.com

This small town is famous for its mineral springs and is a good base for exploring the nearby Kootenay National Park. In the summer, flower-filled pots decorate the storefronts of the many coffee shops and pubs along the main street, and the town has more motel rooms than residents. Many of the 1.2 million annual visitors come to bathe in the healing waters of the springs. There are two pools, a hot soaking pool for relaxing in, and a cooler swimming pool. Locker rooms, swimsuits, showers, and towels can all be rented, and massages are readily available. Visitors can explore the nearby Columbia Valley Wetlands too. Fed by glacial waters from the Purcell and Rocky mountains, the Columbia River meanders through these extensive marsh lands, which provide an important habitat for over 250 migratory waterfowl such as Canada geese and tundra swans.

Taking the waters at Radium Hot Springs

Kootenay National Park ⓫

🚌 Banff. ℹ Park Info Centre, open May–Sep (250) 347 9615. ◯ daily. 📷 ♿ 🛒 **www**.pc.gc.ca

Kootenay National Park covers 1,406 sq km (543 sq miles) and is known for its ecology, climate, and diversity of landscape. The 94-km (58-mile) Kootenay Parkway (Hwy 93S) bisects the park from north to south. It winds through the narrow gorge of Sinclair Canyon, past the world famous Radium Hot Springs Pools, along the deep red cliffs of the Redwall Fault, and up over the Sinclair Pass. The road continues into the Kootenay River Valley, past Hector Gorge, and into the Vermilion Valley. Short nature trails introduce you to magical Paint Pots, iron-rich mineral springs with rust-colored clay banks. Visitors will see the Marble Canyon, whose 5 J-m (96-ft) deep dolomite walls are carved by the glacial waters of Tokumm Creek. The Fireweed Trail at Vermilion Pass features vibrant regenerating forests growing along the Continental Divide, in the wake of old forest fires.

The ochre-colored Paint Pot pools in Kootenay National Park

Kananaskis Country ⓬

🚌 Canmore. ℹ Suite 201, 800 Railway Ave., Canmore. (403) 678 5593. **www**.kananaskisalberta.ca

Kananaskis Country is a verdant region of the Rocky Mountain foothills, with mountain peaks, lakes, rivers, and alpine meadows. Located southwest of Calgary on the boundary of Banff National Park, this 4,000 sq km (1,544 sq miles) of wilderness is popular for hiking and viewing wildlife such as eagles, wolves, and bears. The town of Canmore serves as the center of this large recreational area, and has plenty of accommodations, as well as information on outdoor activities such as wildlife tours.

Banff National Park ⑬

The best known of the Rockies' national parks, Banff was also Canada's first. The park was established in 1885, after the discovery of natural hot springs by three Canadian Pacific Railroad workers in 1883. Centuries before the arrival of the railroad, Blackfoot, Stoney, and Kootenay native peoples lived in the valleys around Banff. Today, Banff National Park covers an area of 6,641 sq km (2,564 sq miles) of some of the most sublime scenery in the country. The park encompasses impressive mountain peaks, forests, glacial lakes, and mighty rivers. Some four million visitors a year enjoy a range of activities, from hiking and canoeing in summer, to skiing in winter.

Peyto Lake
One of the most rewarding walks in Banff is a short stroll from the Icefields Parkway, near Bow Summit, which leads to a vista over the ice-blue waters of Peyto Lake.

View from Icefields Parkway
Renowned for its stunning views of high peaks, forests, lakes, and glaciers, this 230-km (143-mile) road runs between Lake Louise and Jasper.

Saskatchewan River Crossing lies at the junction of three rivers, along the route used by explorer David Thompson, who first came here in the late 1700s and began mapmaking.

BEAR SAFETY

Both grizzly and black bears are found in the Rockies' national parks. Although sightings are rare, visitors should observe *The Mountain Guide*, a Parks Canada publication free to all park visitors that provides wildlife safety tips. The fundamental rules are: don't approach the animals, never feed them, don't run, and stay calm. Bears have an excellent sense of smell, so if you are camping be sure to lock food or trash inside a car or in the bear-proof boxes provided.

Grizzly bear in Banff

Valley of the Ten Peaks
A scenic road from Lake Louise winds to Moraine Lake, which is ringed by ten peaks each over 3,000 m (10,000 ft) high.

For hotels and restaurants in this region see pp362–3 and pp388–9

Johnston Canyon

This spectacular gorge boasts two impressive waterfalls, and is one of the most popular trails in the park. The walk can be reached from the Bow Valley Parkway (see p302), and has walkways close to the falls. Displays along the way explain the canyon's geology.

VISITORS' CHECKLIST

Hwys 1 & 93. ℹ *Banff Visitor Centre, 224 Banff Ave., Banff (403) 762 8421.* 🚌 *Brewster Bus Depot, 100 Gopher St.* 📅 *Daily.* 🅿 ♿ 🍴 📷 🚻
www.banfflakelouise.com

KEY

▬	Highway
▬	Major road
▬	Rivers
🅰	Camping
ℹ	Visitor information
☆	Viewpoint

Lake Minnewanka
is Banff's largest lake and is a popular place for picnics and boat trips.

Bankhead
An interpretive hiking trail displaying historic photographs leads visitors around this coal mine and ghost town.

Lake Louise
The turquoise waters of Lake Louise are an abiding symbol of the beauty of the Rockies. It was here that one of the first resorts was established in Banff, with visitors beginning to arrive in 1885.

Exploring Banff National Park

Wild goat by the Icefields Parkway

It is impossible to travel through Banff National Park and not be filled with awe. There are some 25 peaks that rise over 3,000 m (10,000 ft) in Banff, which are magically reflected in the turquoise waters of the park's many lakes. Banff townsite offers visitors a full range of facilities, including the therapeutic hot springs that inspired the founding of the park, and is an excellent base for exploring the surrounding country. Even the highway is counted an attraction here. The Icefields Parkway (Hwy 93) winds through stunning mountain vistas and connects Banff to Jasper National Park, beginning from the renowned Lake Louise.

Icefields Parkway (Highway 93)

The Icefields Parkway is a 230-km (143-mile) scenic mountain highway that twists and turns through the jagged spines of the Rocky Mountains. The road is a wonder in itself, where every turn offers yet another incredible view as it climbs through high passes from Lake Louise to Jasper.

The road was built during the Depression of the 1930s, as a work creation project. Designed for sightseeing, the highway was extended to its present length in 1960, with plenty of pull-offs to allow visitors to take in the views.

Bow Summit is the highest point on the highway, at 2,068 m (6,785 ft), and has a side road that leads to the **Peyto Lake** viewpoint, which looks over snow-topped peaks mirrored in the brilliant blue of the lake. In summer, Bow Summit's mountain meadows are covered with alpine flowers. From here, it is also possible to see the Crowfoot Glacier, a striking chunk of ice in the shape of a crow's foot, hanging over a cliff-face. Farther north a trail leads down from a parking lot to **Mistaya Canyon** with its vertical walls, potholes, and an impressive natural arch. The highway passes close by the Icefields (which cross the park boundaries into Jasper National Park), and the Athabasca Glacier is clearly visible from the road. Mountain goats and bighorn sheep are drawn to the mineral deposits by the roadside.

The Bow Valley Parkway passing scenic country along the river

The Bow Valley Parkway

The Bow Valley Parkway is a 55-km (35-mile) long scenic alternative to the Trans-Canada Highway, running between Banff and Lake Louise. The road follows the Bow River Valley and offers visitors the chance to explore the gentle country of the valley with

many interpretive signs and viewpoints along the way. From the road it is possible to see the abundant wildlife such as bears, elk, and coyotes.

About 19 km (12 miles) west of Banff, one of the best short walks leads from the roadside to the **Johnston Canyon** trail. A paved path leads to the canyon and two impressive waterfalls. The path to the lower falls is wheelchair accessible, and the upper falls are a slightly longer 2.7-km (1.5-mile) hike. A boardwalk along the rock wall leads to the floor of the canyon, offering valley views close to the railroad crossing through the mountains. One of the most striking natural phenomena in the canyon is the Ink Pots, a series of pools where vivid blue-green water bubbles up from underground springs. Interpretive signs explain how this fascinating canyon took shape, and how the water created its unique rock formations.

Lake Minnewanka Drive

This narrow, winding 14-km (8.5-mile) loop road begins at the Lake Minnewanka interchange on the Trans-Canada Highway. From here it is a pleasant drive to picnic sites, hiking trails, and three lakes. Lake Minnewanka is Banff's biggest lake, almost 28 km (17 miles) long.

A popular short trail leads to **Bankhead**, the site of an abandoned coal mine that was the first settlement in Banff and whose heyday was in the first half of the 19th century. The footpath displays old photographs and notices which depict the life of the miners.

Lake Minnewanka, the largest lake in Banff National Park

Banff Springs Hotel, styled after the baronial castles of Scotland

Banff

The town of Banff grew up around the hot springs that were discovered here in the 1880s. The Canadian Pacific Railroad's manager, William Cornelius Van Horne, realized the springs would attract visitors, so he built the grand Banff Springs Hotel in 1888. The resort was very popular, and the town expanded to accommodate the influx. Located at the foot of Sulphur Mountain, the **Cave and Basin National Historic Site** is the site of the original spring found by the railroad workers in 1883 and is now a museum telling the story of Banff's development. The **Upper Hot Springs Pool**, also at the base of Sulphur Mountain, is a popular resort where visitors can relieve their aches in the mineral-rich, healing waters.

At 2,281 m (7,484 ft) above sea level, Sulphur Mountain provides a spectacular view of the surrounding area. Although there is a 5-km (3-mile) trail to the top, a glass-enclosed gondola (cable car) carries visitors to the summit in eight minutes. Here the viewing platforms offer beautiful vistas of the Rockies.

Banff is busy all year round. In winter, snow sports from skiing to dog-sledding are available, while summer visitors include hikers, cyclists, and mountaineers. The **Banff Park Museum** was built in 1903 and houses specimens of animals, plants, and mineral samples.

🏛 Banff Park Museum
91 Banff Ave. **Tel** *(403) 762 1558.*
⭘ *daily.* ⬤ *Jan 1, Dec 25.* 🎟 ♿

Gondolas or cable cars taking visitors up Sulphur Mountain

Lake Louise
ℹ *by Samson Mall (403) 522 3833.*
One of Banff National Park's major draws, the beauty of Lake Louise is an enduring image of the Rockies. Famed for the blueness of its water and the snow-capped peaks that surround it, Lake Louise also boasts the Victoria Glacier, which stretches almost to the water's edge. Trails around the lake offer exhibits that explain the lake's formation some 10,000 years ago, at the end of the last Ice Age. The amazing color of the water of this and other lakes in the park comes from deposits of glacial silt, known as rock flour, suspended just beneath the surface. Dominating the landscape at one end of the lake is the imposing hotel Château Lake Louise, built in 1894.

During the summer, a gondola carries visitors up to Mount Whitehorn for stunning views of the glacier and the lake. In winter, the area attracts large numbers of skiers, ice-climbers, and snowboarders.

In Lake Louise village visitors can stock up on supplies, such as food, clothes, and gas.

Moraine Lake
Less well known than Lake Louise, Moraine Lake is every bit as beautiful, with its shimmering turquoise color. The lake has a pretty waterside lodge that offers accommodations, meals, and canoe rentals. There are several trails that all start at the lake: one lakeside path follows the north shore for 1.5 km (1 mile), while the climb, which leads up Larch Valley-Sentinel Pass trail, offers more stunning vistas, ending at one of the park's highest passes.

Yoho National Park ⑭

Inspired by the beauty of the park's mountains, lakes, waterfalls, and distinctive rock formations, this area was named Yoho, for the Cree word meaning "awe and wonder." Yoho National Park lies on the western side of the Rockies range in BC, next to Banff and Kootenay National Parks. The Park offers a wide range of activities, from climbing and hiking to boating or skiing. The

Shooting star flower

park also houses the Burgess Shale fossil beds, an extraordinary find of perfectly preserved marine creatures from the prehistoric Cambrian period, over 500 million years ago. Access to the fossil beds is by guided hike and is limited to 15 people each trip.

WAPTA ICEFIELD

Emerald Lake
The rustic Emerald Lake Lodge (see p363) provides facilities at this quiet, secluded place in the middle of the park. The lake, which is named for the intense color of its waters, is a popular spot for canoeing, walking, and riding horses.

Natural Bridge
Found in the center of the park, over the waters of the Kicking Horse River, Natural Bridge is a rock bridge formed by centuries of erosion, which have worn a channel through solid rock.

VANCOUVER, GLACIER NATIONAL PARK

KEY

═══	Highway
━━━	Major road
───	Rivers
⛺	Campsite
🏞	Picnic
ℹ	Visitor information
☙	Viewpoint

Hoodoo Creek
These fabulous, mushroom-like towers of rock have been created by erosion and can be accessed from a short, but very steep, trail.

VISITORS' CHECKLIST

Hwy 1. ￼ Park Info. Centre, Field
(250) 343 6783. ◯ daily.
￼ ￼ ￼ ￼
www.parkscanada.gc.ca/yoho

The Yoho Valley is noted for its stunning scenery, including the Takakkaw Falls.

Takakkaw Falls
Takakkaw means "it is wonderful" in the language of the local natives, and these are among the most impressive falls in Canada, having a drop of 254 m (833 ft). The falls can be accessed along the Yoho Valley Road, which is open seasonally.

Burgess Shale is a UNESCO World Heritage Site set up to protect two fossil beds. Day-long guided hikes here are by reservation only.

CALGARY, BANFF NATIONAL PARK

Kicking Horse River
This wild river rushes through Yoho alongside the original 1880s railroad. Today the tracks carry freight and the "Rocky Mountaineer" tourist train (see p423).

ANBURY GLACIER

Lake O'Hara
Shadowed by the majestic peaks of Mounts Victoria and Lefroy, Lake O'Hara is astonishingly beautiful. However, guests wishing to use the area's excellent hiking trails must book in advance as access is limited to protect this fragile environment.

0 km   3
0 miles   3

The Valley of the Ten Peaks reflected in the stunning turquoise waters of Moraine Lake ▷

Jasper National Park ⓰

The most northerly of the four Rocky Mountain national parks, Jasper is also the most rugged and the largest, covering an area of 10,878 sq km (4,199 sq miles) of high peaks and valleys dotted with glacial lakes. The Columbia Icefield *(see p310)*, a vast area of 400-year-old ice that is 365 m (1,197 ft) thick in places, is part of the national park. From the icefield, fingers of ice reach down through many of Jasper's valleys.

Some of the most accessible hiking trails in the park start from the Maligne Lake and Canyon, and the town of Jasper. The town is located roughly in the park's center and is the starting point for many of the most popular walks and sights here.

Pyramid Lake
Ringed by jagged peaks, both Pyramid and nearby Patricia Lake lie close to Jasper town.

The Jasper Tramway
Only a few kilometers out of Jasper town is the popular Jasper Tramway, which takes visitors to a viewing platform near the summit of The Whistlers at 2,277 m (7,472 ft). Panoramic vistas take in the park's mountains, forests, and lakes.

Snake Indian River

Jasper Lake

VICTORIA CROSS RANGE

PRINCE GEORGE

16

93a

0 km	20
0 miles	20

KEY

▬	Major road
═	Minor road
▬	Rivers
Ⓐ	Camping
🅟	Picnic
🅘	Visitor information
☀	Viewpoint

Mount Edith Cavell
It is possible to drive up this mountain as far as Cavell Lake from where the trail leads to Angel Glacier and to the flower-strewn Cavell Meadows.

309

Maligne Canyon
One of the most beautiful canyons in the Rockies, its sheer limestone walls and several impressive waterfalls can be seen from the many footbridges that are built both along and across its walls.

VISITORS' CHECKLIST

Hwys 93 & 16. ⓘ 409 Patricia St., Jasper (780) 852 3858. VIA Rail, Connaught St. Greyhound Bus Station. daily. www.jaspercanadianrockies.com

Miette Hot Springs
Visitors here enjoy relaxing in the warmest spring waters in the Rockies. The springs are said to have healing effects because of their high mineral content.

Medicine Lake
Renowned for its varying water levels, Medicine Lake is drained by a series of underground tunnels and caves. It is also one of Jasper's prettiest lakes.

EDMONTON

Rocky River

Maligne Lake

Athabasca River

BANFF NATIONAL PARK
YOHO NATIONAL PARK
CALGARY

COLUMBIA ICEFIELD

Sunwapta River offers white-water rafters a choice of conditions, from calm to turbulent.

Athabasca Falls
The dramatic, rushing waters of these falls are the result of the Athabasca River being forced through a narrow gorge.

Exploring Jasper

Established in 1907, Jasper National Park is as staggeringly beautiful as anywhere in the Rockies, but it is distinguished by having more remote wilderness than the other national parks. These areas can be reached only on foot, horseback, or by canoe, and backpackers need passes from the Park Trail Office for hikes that last more than one day. Jasper also has a reputation for more sightings of wildlife such as bear, moose, and elk than any of the other Rockies' parks.

Although most of the park services are closed between October and Easter, visitors who brave the winter season have an opportunity to cross-country ski on breathtaking trails that skirt frozen lakes. In addition, they can go ice fishing, downhill skiing, or on guided walking tours on frozen rivers. In the summertime there are a range of daytrips which are easily accessible from the park's main town of Jasper.

Downhill skiing is just one of the outdoor activities around Jasper

Columbia Icefield and Icefield Centre

Icefields Parkway. *Tel* (780) 852 6288. ☐ May–Oct: daily. ♿
www.pc.gc.ca
The Columbia Icefield straddles both Banff and Jasper national parks and forms the largest area of ice south of Alaska. The Icefield, which covers 325 sq km (125 sq miles) and can be as thick as 365 m (1,197 ft), was created during the last Ice Age.

Around 10,000 years ago, ice filled the region, sculpting out wide valleys, sheer mountain faces, and sharp ridges. Although the glaciers have retreated over the last few hundred years, during the early years of the 20th century ice covered the area where the Icefields Parkway now passes.

An interpretive center explains the Ice Age and the impact of the glaciers on the landscape of the Rockies. Tours of the Athabasca Glacier, in 4-wheel drive Sno-coaches, are available from the center, which also has information on local trails.

Athabasca Falls

Located at the junction of highways 93 and 93A, where the Athabasca River plunges 23 m (75 ft) to the river bed below, these are among the most dramatic waterfalls in the park. Despite being a short drop compared with other falls in the Rockies, the force of the waters of the Athabasca River being pushed through a narrow, quartz-rich gorge transforms these waters into a powerful, foaming torrent.

Jasper

The town of Jasper was established in 1911 as a settlement for Grand Trunk Pacific Railroad workers, who were laying track along the Athabasca River Valley. As with Banff, the coming of the railroad and the growth of the parks as resorts went hand-in-hand, and the town expanded to include hotels, restaurants, and a visitor center. Today, many of the park's main attractions are close to the town, which is located at the center of the park, on both Highway 16 and Icefields Parkway (Hwy 93).

Just 7 km (4.5 miles) out of town is the Jasper Tramway station, from where visitors may take a brisk, 7-minute ride up **The Whistlers**. The trip whisks visitors up to the upper terminal at 2,277 m (7,472 ft), where there is a clearly marked trail leading to the summit at

The wild waters of Athabasca River make it a popular venue for white-water rafting

For hotels and restaurants in this region see pp362–3 and pp388–9

2,470 m (8,100 ft). On a clear day the view is incomparable. For those who would rather walk than ride the tram, there is a 2.8-km (1.7-mile) trail to the top of the mountain. The trail winds upward, offering panoramic views of both the Miette and Athabasca valleys, and, in July, the lush meadows are blanketed with colorful wild flowers.

Patricia and Pyramid Lakes
North of Jasper townsite, the attractive Patricia and Pyramid lakes nestle beneath the 2,763-m (9,065-ft) high Pyramid Mountain. A popular daytrip from the town, the lakes are noted for windsurfing and sailing. Equipment rental is available from two lakeside lodges.

The deep blue waters of Pyramid Lake beneath Pyramid Mountain

Maligne Lake Drive
Maligne Lake Drive begins 5 km (3 miles) east of Jasper townsite and leads off Hwy 16, following the valley floor between the Maligne and the Queen Elizabeth ranges. This scenic road travels past many magnificent sights, with viewpoints along the way offering panoramas of Maligne Valley. Among the route's most spectacular sights is the Maligne Canyon, reached by a 4-km (2.5-mile) interpretive hiking trail that explains the special geological features behind the gorge's formation. One of the most beautiful in the Rockies, Maligne Canyon has sheer limestone walls as high as 50 m (150 ft) and many waterfalls, which can be seen from several foot bridges. The road

A boat cruise on Maligne Lake, the largest natural lake in the Rockies

ends at Maligne Lake. The largest natural lake in the Rockies, Maligne is 22 km (14 miles) long and surrounded by snowcapped mountains. There are several scenic trails around it, one of which leads to the Opal Hills and amazing views of the area. Guided walks around here can be organized from Jasper, and it is possible to rent fishing tackle and canoes and kayaks to go out on the lake.

Medicine Lake
Medicine Lake is also reached from a side road off Maligne Lake Drive. The lake is noted for its widely varying water levels. In autumn the lake is reduced to a trickle, but in springtime the waters rise, fed by the fast-flowing Maligne River. A vast network of underground caves and channels are responsible for this event.

Miette Hotsprings
Tel (780) 866 3939, 1 800 767 1611. ⬜ *May–Oct: daily.* 🅿 ♿
Located 61 km (38 miles) north of Jasper along the attractive Miette Springs Road, these springs are the hottest in the

Rockies, reaching temperatures as high as 53.9°C (129°F). However, the thermal baths are cooled to a more reasonable 39°C (102°F) for bathers. The waters are held to be both relaxing and healthy – they are rich in minerals, such as calcium, sulfates, and small amounts of hydrogen sulfide (which smells like rotten eggs). The resort of Miette Springs houses two pools, including one suitable for children. The springs are part of a leisure complex that offers both restaurants and hotels.

Mount Edith Cavell
Named after a World War I heroine nurse, this mountain is located 30 km (18.5 miles) south of Jasper townsite. The scenic road that climbs it is paved but has some rough sections and narrow switchbacks. The road ends at Cavell Lake by the north face of the mountain. From here, a guided trail leads to a small lake beneath the Angel Glacier. A three-hour walk across the flower strewn Cavell meadows has views of the glacier's icy tongue.

A peninsula of ice from Angel Glacier seen from Mount Edith Cavell

Typical kitchen of the late 1900s at Grande Prairie Museum

Prince George ⓰

🏛 70,000. ✕ 🚊 🚉
ℹ 101-1300 First Ave.
(250) 562 3700.
www.tourismpg.com

The largest town in Northern British Columbia, Prince George is a bustling supply-and-transportation center for the region. Two major highways pass through here, the Yellowhead (Hwy 16) and Highway 97, which becomes the Alaska Highway at Dawson Creek. Established in 1807 as Fort George, a fur-trading post at the confluence of the Nechako and Fraser rivers, the town is well placed for exploring the province.

Today, Prince George has all the facilities of a larger city, including a university specializing in First Nations history and culture, as well as its own symphony orchestra and several art galleries.

The **Fraser-Fort George Regional Museum** lies on the site of the original Fort, within the 26-ha (65-acre) Fort George Park, and has a collection of artifacts from native cultures, European pioneers, and early settlers.

Over 1,600 lakes and rivers are within an hour's drive of the community, making Prince George an ideal location for angling enthusiasts.

🏛 Fraser-Fort George Regional Museum
333 Becott Place, at the Exploration Place. **Tel** *(250) 562 1612.* ◯ *daily.*
● *Jan 1, Dec 25.* 🏷 ♿
www.theexplorationplace.com

Grande Prairie ⓱

🏛 50,000. ✕ 🚊 ℹ 11330 106th St. *(780) 539 7688.*
www.gptourism.ca

Grande Prairie is a large, modern city in the northwest corner of Alberta. Surrounded by fertile farming country, the city is a popular stop for travelers heading north toward Dawson Creek and the Alaska Highway *(see pp262–3).* The city is the hub of the Peace River region; it offers extensive opportunities for shopping in its giant malls and many downtown specialty stores, with the added draw of having no provincial sales tax *(see p392).*

Running through the city center is the attractive wilderness of Muskoseepi Park. Covering 405 ha (1,000 acres), the park offers a variety of outdoor activities including walking and biking trails, and cross-country skiing.

The **Grande Prairie Museum** is also housed in the park and has 10 buildings containing over 16,000 historical artifacts. There are several reconstructions, including a 1911 schoolhouse, a rural post office, and a church. A renowned display of dinosaur bones recovered from the Peace River Valley are also on display at the museum.

Bear Creek, which runs through Muskoseepi Park, has become a magnet for bird watchers as sightings of eagles are common. The Grand River wetlands, particularly those at Crystal Lake, located in the northeast corner of the city, contain one of the few breeding grounds for the rare trumpeter swan.

🏛 Grande Prairie Museum
Cnr 102nd St. & 102nd Ave.
Tel *(780) 532 5482.* ◯ *daily.*
● *Jan 1, Dec 25.* 🏷 ♿

Fort St. John ⓲

🏛 21,000. ✕ 🚊 ℹ 9523 100th St. *(250) 785 3033.* **www**.fortstjohn.ca

Fort St. John is located at Mile 47 of the Alaska Highway among the rolling hills of the Peace River Valley. During the construction of the Highway in 1942, the tiny town dramatically expanded from a population of about 800 to 6,000. When completed, the highway turned Fort St. John into a busy supply center that caters to visitors exploring the area, as well as

Lush farmland along the Peace River in northern British Columbia

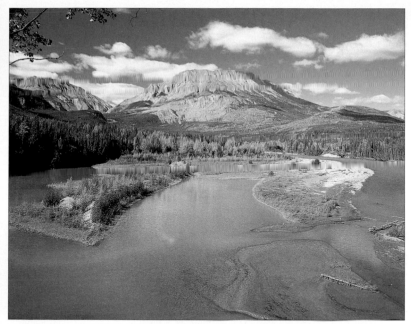

The green waters of Muncho Lake framed by mountains in Muncho Lake Provincial Park

supporting the growth of agriculture in the surrounding countryside. However, the town boomed when oil was found here in the 1950s, in what proved to be the largest oil field in the province. Today, Fort St. John's pride in its industrial and pioneering heritage is reflected in the local museum, which has a 41-m (136-ft) high oil derrick at its entrance and a range of exhibits that tell the story of the local oil industry.

Fort Nelson ⑲

🏛 6,000. ✈ 🚌 ℹ 5319 50th Ave. S. (250) 774 2541. www. tourismnorthernrockies.ca

Despite the growth of the oil, gas, and lumber industries in the 1960s and 70s, Fort Nelson retains the atmosphere of a northern frontier town. Before the building of the Alaska Highway in the 1940s, Fort Nelson was an important stop on route for the Yukon and Alaska, and until the 1950s was without running water or electricity. Fur trading was the main activity until the energy boom; even today both native

and white trappers hunt wolf, beaver, and lynx, for both their fur and their meat.

Today, the town has an air and bus service, a hospital, and good visitor facilities such as motels, restaurants, and gas stations. Local people are famous for their friendliness, and during the busy summer months run a program of free talks describing life in the north to visitors. A small museum displays

Lynx near Fort Nelson

photographs and artifacts that tell the story of the building of the 2,451-km (1,523-mile) Alaska Highway.

Muncho Lake Provincial Park ⑳

Off Hwy 97. **Tel** (250) 776 7000. ◯ daily.

One of three provincial parks (including Stone Mountain and Liard River Hot Springs) that were established after the building of the Alaska Highway in 1942, Muncho Lake occupies the most scenic

section of the road. The park encompasses the bare peaks of the northern Rockies, whose stark limestone slopes incorporate the faults, alluvial fans, and hoodoos that are a testament to thousands of years of glacial erosion. The Highway skirts the eastern shoreline of the 12 km (7.5-mile) long Muncho Lake before crossing the Liard River where the Mackenzie Mountain range begins. In early summer, passing motorists are likely to see moose grazing among meadows filled with colorful wildflowers. The park's bogs are popular with botanists eager to see the rare yellow Lady's Slipper orchid. The roadside also attracts goats, sheep, and caribou, drawn by delicious deposits of sodium, known as mineral licks.

Visitors may stay in the park at one of the campgrounds or lodges in order to explore its 861 sq km (332 sq miles) of wilderness. The deep waters of Muncho Lake house a good supply of trout for anglers.

SOUTHERN AND NORTHERN BRITISH COLUMBIA

Southern British Columbia covers the region south of Prince George, down to the US border. There is a vast variety of natural beauty here, including the forests and waterfalls of Wells Gray Provincial Park, and the lush valleys, wineries, and lake resorts of the Okanagan Valley. One of the most stunning wildernesses in North America, northern British Columbia spreads north of Prince Rupert, between the Coast Mountains in the west, the Rockies in the east, and the Yukon. Its dramatic landscape ranges from the volcanic terrain around Mount Edziza, with its lava flows and cinder cones, to the frozen forests of Atlin Provincial Park. Haida Gwaii can be accessed by ferry, and much of the trip is across open ocean. For 10,000 years the archipelago has been home to the Haida people, famous for their totem-carving.

SIGHTS AT A GLANCE

Historic Towns and Cities
Castlegar **5**
Hope **3**
Kamloops **9**
'Ksan Village **13**
Nakusp **7**

Nelson **6**
Prince Rupert **14**
Quesnel **12**
Sicamous **8**
Whistler **1**

National and Provincial Parks
Bowron Lake Provincial Park **11**
Northern Parks **16**
Wells Gray Provincial Park **10**

Historic Sites and Areas of Natural Beauty
Fraser River **2**
Haida Gwaii **15**
Okanagan Valley **4**

KEY

✈ International airport

━━ Highway

━━ Major road

── Major rail routes

▪-▪ International border

0 km   200
0 miles   200

◁ The Fraser River flowing through Fraser River Canyon in the midst of wooded winter scenery

The Trans-Canada Highway overlooking the Fraser Canyon along the Fraser River

Whistler ❶

🏔 10,000. 🚉 ℹ️ 4230 Gateway
Drive (604) 935 3357.
www.whistler.com

Whistler is the largest ski
resort in Canada. Set among
the Coast Mountains, 125 km
(78 miles) north of Vancouver,
the resort is divided into four
distinct areas: Whistler Village,
Village North, Upper Village,
and Creekside. Whistler and
Blackcomb mountains have
the greatest vertical rises of
any ski runs in North America.
The skiing and snowboarding
here can be among the best
in the world, with mild Pacific
weather and reliable winter
snow. In summer, there is
snowboarding and skiing on
Blackcomb's Horstman Glacier,
and mountain biking.
  Whistler Village offers visitors
a full range of facilities, from
comfortable bed-and-breakfasts
to luxurious five-star hotels.
Café-lined cobbled squares and
cozy bars and restaurants cater
to all tastes, while a
range of stores
sells everything

from ski-wear to native arts
and crafts. Whistler was the
2010 Winter Olympics venue
for most snow sports, from
downhill skiing to luge.

Fraser River ❷

ℹ️ Vancouver 1 800 667 3306.

The majestic Fraser River
travels 1,375 km (854 miles)
through some of BC's most
stunning scenery. The river
flows from its source in the
Yellowhead Lake, near Jasper,
to the Strait of Georgia, near
Vancouver. Along the way, it
heads north through the Rocky
Mountain trench before turning south near the town of
Prince George. It continues by
the Coast Mountains, then west
to Hope through the steep
walls of the Fraser Canyon,
and on toward Yale.
  It was Fraser Canyon that legendary explorer Simon Fraser
found the most daunting when
he followed the river's
course in 1808. How-
ever, when gold

was discovered near the town
of Yale 50 years later, thousands of prospectors swarmed
up the valley. Today, Yale is a
small town with a population
of 200 and the delightful **Yale
Museum**, where exhibits focus
on the history of the gold rush,
as well as telling the epic story
of the building of the Canadian
Pacific Railroad through the
canyon. This section of river
is also a popular whitewater
rafting area, and trips can be
arranged from the small town
of Boston Bar. At Hell's Gate
the river thunders through the
Canyon's narrow walls, which
are only 34 m (112 ft) apart.

🏛 **Yale Museum**
31187 Douglas St. **Tel** (604) 863 2324.
◯ May–Oct: Thu–Mon. 🎟 ♿
www.historicyale.ca

Hope ❸

🏔 6,100. 🚉 ℹ️ 919 Water Ave.
(604) 869 2021.

Located at the southern end
of the Fraser Canyon, Hope
is crossed by several highways,
including Hwy 1 (the Trans-
Canada) and Hwy 3. Hope is
an excellent base for exploring
the Fraser Canyon and southern BC, as well as being within
easy reach of several provincial
parks. The beautiful country
of Manning Provincial Park,
with its lakes, mountains, and
rivers, is noted for its outdoor
activities – swimming, hiking,
fishing, and sailing in summer,
and downhill and cross-
country skiing in winter.

The ski resort at alpine Whistler Village in British Columbia

For hotels and restaurants in this region see pp363–4 and p390

Okanagan Valley Tour ●

Okanagan

The Okanagan Valley is actually a series of valleys, linked by a string of lakes, that stretches for 235 km (146 miles) from Osoyoos in the south, to Salmon Arm in the north. The main towns here are connected by Highway 97, which passes through the desert landscape near Osoyoos, and on to the lush green orchards and vineyards for which the valley is most noted. Mild winters and hot summers have made the Okanagan one of Canada's favorite vacation destinations.

TIPS FOR DRIVERS

Starting point: On Highway 97 from Vernon in the north: Osoyoos in the south.
Length: 175 km (109 miles).
Highlights: Blossom and fruit festivals are held in spring and summer, when roadside stalls offer a cornucopia of fruit, and wine tours are available year-round.

Kelowna ④
The biggest city in the Okanagan, Kelowna lies on the shores of Lake Okanagan between Penticton and Vernon, and is the center of the wine- and fruit-growing industries.

Summerland ③
This small but charming lakeside resort boasts several 19th-century buildings and stunning views from the top of Giant's Head Mountain.

Penticton ②
This sunny lakeside town is known for the long Okanagan Beach, windsurfing, and local winery tours, as well as for its Peach Festival, held every August.

SALMON ARM

Armstrong

Vernon ⑤
Surrounded by farms and orchards, Vernon owes its lush look to the growth of irrigation in 1908. Several small resorts are set around the nearby lakes.

Lake Country

Peachland

Okanagan Lake

Naramata

Lake Skaha

Okanagan Falls

HOPE, VANCOUVER

CASTLEGAR NELSON

Historic O'Keefe Ranch ⑥
Founded by the O'Keefe family in 1867, this historic ranch displays original artifacts belonging to the family who lived here until 1977. The original log cabin remains, as does the church and store.

```
0 km          25
0 miles       25
```

US BORDER

Osoyoos ①
Visitors are drawn here by hot summers, the warm waters and sandy beaches of Lake Osoyoos, and the nearby pocket desert.

KEY

■ Tour route
= Other roads

Impressive and historic stone buildings in the attractive town of Nelson

Castlegar ❺

🏠 7,000. ✈ 🚌 ℹ️ 1995 6th Ave. (250) 365 6313.

Located in southeastern BC, Castlegar is a busy transportation hub. The town is crossed by two major highways, Hwy 3 and Hwy 22, and lies at the junction of the important Kootenay and Columbia rivers.

In the early 1900s, a steady influx of Doukhobors (Russian religious dissenters fleeing persecution) began arriving here. The **Doukhobor Discovery Centre** reflects the group's heritage and houses a variety of traditional clothes and tools, and antique farm machinery.

Traditional Doukhobor tunic

🏛️ **Doukhobor Discovery Centre**
112 Heritage Way. **Tel** (250) 365 5327. ◯ May–Sep: daily. 📷 ♿

Nelson ❻

🏠 9,300. 🚌 ℹ️ 225 Hall St. (250) 352 3433. **www**.discovernelson.com

One of the most attractive towns in southern British Columbia, Nelson overlooks Kootenay Lake. Established in the 1880s as a mining town, with the coming of the

railroad in the 1890s, Nelson flourished as a center for transporting ore and timber. The town owes its good looks to its location on the shores of the lake and to the large number of public buildings and houses that were constructed between 1895 and 1920. British Columbia's best-known architect, Francis Rattenbury (see p280), played a part in the design of some of the town's most prestigious and beautiful structures, such as the elegant Burns building which was built in 1899 for millionaire cattle rancher and meat packer, Patrick Burns. Rattenbury also designed the Nelson Court House in 1908, a stately stone building with towers and gables.

Today, the town has a thriving cultural scene, with an art walk during the summer, as well as numerous cafés, book, and craft shops. Visitors also enjoy the short ride on Car 23, a 1906 streetcar that operated in the town between 1924 and 1949 (it was restored in 1992), and which today travels along Nelson's delightful waterfront. The infocenter provides visitors with a map and guide for the heritage walking tour of the town's historic buildings.

Nakusp ❼

🏠 1,800. ℹ️ 92 6th Ave. NW. (250) 265 4234.

With the snow-topped Selkirk Mountains as a backdrop, and overlooking the waters of Upper Arrow Lake, Nakusp is a charming town. Originally developed as a mining settlement, the town is now known for its mineral hot springs. There are two resorts close to town; the Nakusp and Halcyon Hot Springs, both of which provide therapeutic bathing in hot waters, rich in sulfates, calcium, and hydrogen sulfide, said to be good for everyday aches, as well as arthritis and rheumatism.

The town of Nakusp overlooking picturesque Upper Arrow Lake

Roughly 40 km (25 miles) to the south of Nakusp, in the Slocan Valley, are two fascinating abandoned silver mining towns, New Denver and Sandon. Sandon had 5,000 inhabitants at the height of the mining boom in 1892. It also had 29 hotels, 28 saloons, and several brothels and gambling halls. A fire in 1900, poor metal prices, and dwindling ore reserves crippled the mines, and Sandon became a ghost town. Today, the town has been declared an historic site, and its homes and businesses are being carefully restored. The nearby town of New Denver suffered a fate similar to Sandon's, but is also noted as the site of an internment camp for the Japanese during World War II. The Nikkei Internment Centre on Josephine Street is the only center in Canada devoted to telling the story of the internment of over 20,000 Japanese Canadians. The center is surrounded by a formal Japanese garden.

Houseboats moored along the waterfront at Sicamous

Sicamous ❽

🏠 3,200. 🖼 ℹ️ 110 Finlayson St. (250) 836 3313.

Sicamous is an appealing waterfront village known for its 3,000 houseboats, as well as its charming cobblestone streets hung with flower-filled planters. Located between Mara and Shuswap lakes, at the junction of the Trans-Canada Highway and Highway 97A, the town is ideally placed for touring the lakes, and the town of Salmon Arm, at the northern end of the Okanagan Valley (see p317). Over 250 houseboats are available for renting in the summer, and there are 12 marinas and a houseboat store. From the boats it is possible to view the inlets and forested landscape of Lake Shuswap where wildlife such as black bear, deer, moose, coyote, and bobcat have been spotted along the shore. In summer, visitors and locals enjoy both the good public beach on the lake, as well as the pleasant walk along a marked waterfront trail.

Kamloops ❾

🏠 90,000. ✈️ 🖼 🖼 ℹ️ 1290 West Trans-Canada Hwy (250) 372 8000, 1 800 662 1994. **www**.tourismkamloops.com

Kamloops means "where the rivers meet" in the language of the Secwepemc First Nations. The largest town by area in BC's southern interior, it lies at the crossroads of the north and south Thompson Rivers. Three major highways also meet here; the Trans-Canada, Hwy 5, and Hwy 97 to the Okanagan Valley, as do the Canadian Pacific and Canadian National railroad.

European settlement began in 1812, when fur traders started doing business with local natives. The **Secwepemc Museum and Heritage Park** focuses on the cultural history of the Secwepemc First Nations and has a variety of artifacts, including a birch-bark canoe, hunting equipment, and cooking utensils. Outside, short trails lead visitors through the archeological remains of a 2,000-year-old Shuswap winter village site, which includes four authentically reconstructed winter pit houses and a summer camp. The village has a

A horse's snow shoe on display at Kamloops

hunting shack, a fish-drying rack, and a smoke house. The museum store sells pine-needle and birch-bark baskets, moccasins, and a wide variety of beaded and silver jewelry.

In the town center, the Art Gallery has a small but striking collection that features landscape sketches by A.Y. Jackson, one of the renowned Group of Seven painters (see pp164–5).

🏛 **Secwepemc Museum and Heritage Park**
355 Yellowhead Hwy. **Tel** (250) 828 9801. ◻ Jun–Sep: daily; Sep–May: 8:30am–4.30pm Mon–Fri. 🖼 ♿

Wells Gray Provincial Park ❿

Tel (250) 674 3334. 🖼 Clearwater. 🖼 Clearwater. ◻ daily. **www**.wellsgray.ca

Wells Gray Provincial Park is one of the most beautiful wildernesses in British Columbia, and offers wonders comparable to the Rockies in the east. The park was opened in 1939 and is distinguished by alpine meadows, thundering waterfalls, and glacier-topped peaks that rise as high as 2,575 m (8,450 ft). The Canadian National Railroad and Hwy 5 follow the Thompson River along the park's western edge, offering stunning views.

From the Clearwater Valley Road, off Hwy 5, there are several trails, from easy walks to arduous overnight hikes in remote country. A selection of small trails, just a few minutes from the road, lead to the spectacular sight of Dawson Falls.

Bowron Lake Provincial Park ⓫

Tel *(778) 373 6107.* 🚌 *Quesnel.*
🚍 *Quesnel.* ⬜ *May–Sep.* 🛶 *(canoe trip)* ♿ *partial.*

Bowron Lake Provincial Park is located about 120 km (75 miles) east of Quesnel on Highway 26 in the Cariboo Mountains. The park is renowned for having a 112-km (70-mile) rectangular waterway composed of nine lakes, three rivers, streams, small lakes, and many portages (trails linking the waterways). There is a week-long canoe trip here, but it is limited to 50 canoeists at a time, and passes must be obtained from the visitor center. It is a special trip that allows visitors to come quietly upon wildlife such as moose or beaver. In late summer, bears come to feed on the spawning sockeye salmon in the Bowron River.

A grizzly bear standing up

Quesnel ⓬

🏚 *9,500.* ✈ 🚌 🚍 ℹ *703 Carson Ave. (250) 992 8716.*

Quesnel is a busy logging town that started life as a gold rush settlement between 1858 and 1861. The town was the last along the Gold Rush Trail, or Cariboo Road (now Hwy 97),

A 19th-century horse and carriage in the streets of Barkerville

which was lined with mining towns between here and Kamloops. Quesnel occupies an attractive position in a triangle formed by the Fraser and Quesnel rivers. The town's sights include the Riverfront Park Trail System, a tree-lined 5-km (3-mile) path that runs along the banks of both rivers. Just outside the town's limits, Pinnacles Provincial Park features the geological wonder of hoodoos, rocky columns formed 12 million years ago when the volcanic surface was eroded by Ice Age meltwaters. From Quesnel, 87 km (54 miles) east on Hwy 26, lies the historic mining town of **Barkerville**. The town was born when Englishman Billy Barker dug up a handful of gold nuggets in 1862. Today, it is a good example of a perfectly preserved 19th-century mining town, with over 120 restored or reconstructed buildings and costumed guides. Visitors can see a blacksmith at work in his forge, watch showgirls put on the kind of display the miners would have seen at the theater, or take a ride on a stagecoach.

🏛 **Barkerville Historic Town**
87 km E. of Quesnel, Hwy 26.
Tel (250) 994 3332. ⬜ *daily.* 🎦 ♿

'Ksan Village ⓭

Tel (250) 842 5544, 1 877 842 5518.
⬜ *grounds: year round; houses: Apr–Sep: daily.* 🎦 ♿ **www**.ksan.org

Some 290 km (180 miles) east of Prince Rupert, 'Ksan Village is a re-creation of an 1870 native settlement, established in the 1950s to preserve the culture of the Gitxsan First Nations. Gitxsan natives have lived in the area for thousands of years, particularly along the beautiful Skeena River valley. Their way of life was under threat by an influx of white settlers who arrived in the 1850s at Prince Rupert to work their way up river to mine or farm. Noted for their skill in carving and painting masks, totems, and canoes, Gitxsan elders are

Gitxsan carved cedarwood totem pole in 'Ksan Village

now schooling new generations in these skills at 'Ksan Village. Within the complex are seven traditional long houses containing a carving school, museum, and gift shop.

Prince Rupert ⓮

🏚 *13,000.* ✈ 🚌 🚍 ⛴ ℹ *100 1st Ave. W. (250) 624 5637, 1 800 667 1994.* **www**.tourismprince rupert.com

Prince Rupert is a vibrant port city, and the second-largest on BC's coast. Located on Kaien Island, at the mouth of the Skeena River, the city is circled by forests and mountains, and overlooks the beautiful fjord-studded coastline. The busy harbor is the main access point for the Queen Charlotte Islands and Alaska.

Like many of BC's major towns, Prince Rupert's development is linked to the growth of the railroad. Housed in the 1914 Grand Trunk Railroad Station, the Kwinitsa Railway Museum tells the story of businessman Charles Hay's big plans for the town, which were largely unfulfilled: he went down with the *Titanic* in 1912.

Tsimshian First Nations were the first occupants of the area, and as recently as 150 years ago the harbor was lined with their large cedar houses and carved totems. The **Museum of Northern British Columbia** focuses on northwest coast First Nations culture and history. Tsimshian dance, song, and drama are performed in a traditional long house and there are Archaeological tours.

🏛 **Museum of Northern British Columbia**
100 1st Ave. W. **Tel** (250) 624 3207. ⭘ Jun–Aug: daily; Sep–May: Mon–Sat. ⬤ Dec 25, 26. ▣ ♿ ▯

Haida Gwaii ⓯

▣ & ▣ Prince Rupert. ▯ 3220 Wharf St, Queen Charlotte, (250) 559 0316 (open all year). **www**.gohaidagwaii.ca

Shaped like a bent ice-cream cone, the Haida Gwaii (previously called Queen Charlotte Islands) are an archipelago of about 150 islands across from the city of Prince Rupert.

The islands were left untouched by the last Ice Age, and have an eco-system unique to Canada. The forests house distinctive species of mammal such as the dusky shrew and short-tailed weasel. There is also a large population of bald eagles, and the spring brings hundreds of migrating gray whales past the shores.

The islands have been the home of the Haida people for thousands of years. Today, the Haida are recognized for their artistic talents, particularly their carvings and sculptures from cedar wood and argillite (a black slatelike stone found only on these islands).

It was the Haida who led environmental campaigns against logging companies in the 1980s, leading to the founding

Atlin Lake in remote Atlin Provincial Park

of the **Gwaii Haanas National Park Reserve and Haida Heritage Site** in 1988. The park has centuries-old rainforest, with 1,000-year-old Sitka spruce, red cedar, and western hemlock.

🌿 **Gwaii Haanas National Park Reserve and Haida Heritage Site**
Tel (250) 559 8818. ⭘ daily. ▣ (no fee in winter).

Northern Parks ⓰

Mount Edziza, Spatsizi; Hwy 37. Atlin; Hwy 7. ▯ (250) 771 4591.

The provincial parks of northern British Columbia comprise Mount Edziza Provincial Park, Spatsizi Plateau Wilderness Provincial Park, and, farther north, Atlin Provincial Park. These offer remote landscapes, with high peaks, icefields, and tundra.

Established in 1972, Mount Edziza Provincial Park is distinguished by its volcanic landscape which includes lava

rivers, basalt plateaus, and cinder cones. The park can be reached by boat or float plane. There is no vehicle access within the park, and only long, rugged overland trails or chartered float planes take visitors through open meadows, arctic birch woods, and over creeks.

Across the highway lies the even more rugged country of Spatsizi Plateau Wilderness Provincial Park, which includes the snow-capped peaks of the Skeena Mountains. Gladys Lake, a small lake in the center of the park, is an ecological reserve for the study of sheep and mountain goats. Access to the park is again limited to a small road leading from the village of Tatogga along Hwy 37. The village also offers guides and float plane hire.

The spectacular Atlin Provincial Park is only accessible from the Yukon on Hwy 7, off the Alaska Hwy. About one-third of the park is covered by large icefields and glaciers.

Masset, one of three major towns on Graham Island, Haida Gwaii

NORTHERN
CANADA

Introducing Northern Canada

Northern Canada covers the Yukon, Northwest Territories, and Nunavut, and stretches up to within 800 km (500 miles) of the North Pole, and from the Atlantic Ocean west to the Pacific, 37 percent of Canada's total area. The landscape is incredibly harsh: barren, treeless, frozen tundra dominates most of the year, with subarctic forest, mountains, glaciers, and icy lakes and rivers. Nonetheless, an abundance of wildlife flourishes, with musk ox, caribou, polar bears, and seals. At the height of the brief summer the "midnight sun" provides 24-hour days, while the Aurora Borealis *(see p337)* illuminates dark winters with ribbons of colored light. Development in the far north has occurred only where conditions are hospitable, often where the land is most scenic and varied. Populated by First Nations people some 25,000 years ago and the Inuit about 3000 BC, this uniquely dramatic land is enjoyed by 500,000 visitors a year.

BANKS ISLAND

VICTORIA ISLAND

INUVIK

DAWSON CITY

YUKON

MAYO

NORTHWEST TERRITORIES

Great Bear Lake

KUGLUKTUK

HAINES JUNCTION

WHITEHORSE

FORT SIMPSON

FORT PROVIDENCE

YELLOWKNIFE

Great Slave Lake

HAY RIVER

Glorious flaming fall colors rise above the evergreens in the north of the Yukon

GETTING AROUND

The watchword when traveling in this region is cost; trips, accommodations, and even food are all far more expensive than in the rest of the country. In the Yukon all major towns are connected by bus, but the most flexible way to travel around is by car. Air is the best means of traveling in Nunavut and the Northwest Territories. There are 600 landing strips and small airports here. Visitors should be aware that accommodations are equally restricted. In many settlements only one hotel is available, but the Yukon towns are well equipped with places to stay.

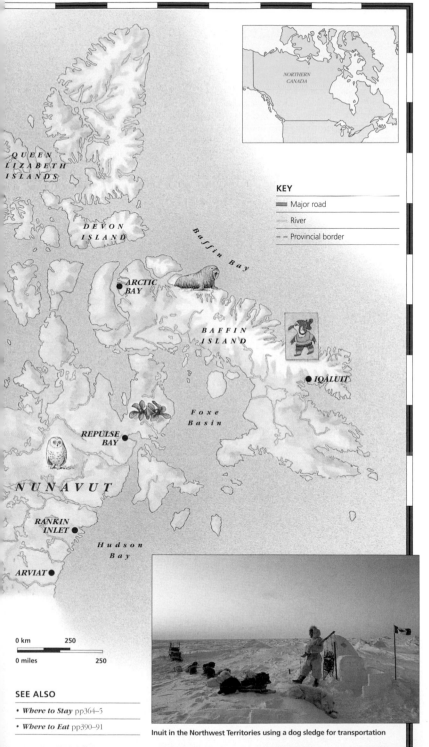

NORTHERN CANADA

QUEEN
LIZABETH
ISLANDS

DEVON
ISLAND

Baffin Bay

KEY

Major road

River

Provincial border

ARCTIC
BAY

BAFFIN
ISLAND

IQALUIT

Foxe
Basin

REPULSE
BAY

NUNAVUT

RANKIN
INLET

Hudson
Bay

ARVIAT

0 km   250

0 miles   250

SEE ALSO

Inuit in the Northwest Territories using a dog sledge for transportation

Inuit Art and Culture

For centuries, the hunting and trapping lifestyle has created a distinct culture for the Inuit. Their customs have remained largely the same throughout the communities of eastern and central Northern Canada, although regional differences can be seen in the varied artforms. The Inuit have a limited written tradition, and much of 21st-century culture is still oral. It might seem surprising, given the outstandingly harsh environment and limited natural resources, that their communities offer a flourishing artistic output, but it is the hardship of northern life that has promoted artistic achievement. For example, the Inuit use their tool-making skills for sculpture. Inuit culture is closely tied to their landsdcape and environment, which has inspired many artists and mythmakers.

This woodblock print *of a girl meeting a polar bear represents an artform developed in the 1950s. Stone cuts and stencils are also used to interpret drawings by older artists.*

Warm clothing is both functional and decorative. Often painstakingly handwoven from scraps from the remains of a kill, women dress their families mostly in fur and wool.

Inuit beadwork and jewelry *was made in earlier times from bone and ivory; colored stones and beads are now used. Each piece shows birds, animals, or people, and is unique. Western influences include new designs in silver and gold.*

This soapstone carving *of an Inuk (Inuit person) with a seal reflects the vital role seals have always played in Inuit culture.*

INUIT WOMAN PREPARING CHAR

The outdated, if not offensive, name for the Inuit people is "eskimo," a native Cree word meaning "eaters of raw meat." The Inuit traditionally eat their meat uncooked, as the Arctic has no trees for firewood. Much of the caribou, polar bear, and fish was sundried or mixed with sauces made from summer fruits and berries. The arrival of the stone and modern fuels has changed the menu somewhat, although tradition remains at the heart of the community's eating habits.

These dancing costume ornaments *are carved from ivory or whalebone and worn by Inuit dancers to celebrate ceremonial events. As with clothing, Arctic bird feathers are used for decoration.*

Inuit father and son in parkas, *which are traditionally made by the women of the family. They use caribou, wolf, and polar bear fur. Today, imported Western fabrics are added for decoration.*

Inuit Homes are no longer the traditional igloo. Most people have moved to camps or community housing.

Inuit fishermen *have made the best possible use of their often limited natural resources and still rely largely on small-scale fishing for food.*

INUIT MYTH

Carving of Inuk fighting his spirit

Set on the very fringes of the habitable world, the Inuit guarded against the threat of starvation with a supernatural belief system based on the respect of the animals they hunted, being careful to guard against divine retribution. Their myths promote the belief that every living creature has a soul, and that the village shaman could travel between the upper and lower worlds to commune with, and appease, the spirits in control of the hunt and the weather. Since earliest times hunting tools and weapons have been carved with the representations of the appropriate guardian spirit, and singers and musicians are well versed in legends of sea spirits and human heroes.

Traditional hunting and fishing remains at the core of Inuit culture, although in the 1960s the Ottawa government unsuccessfully tried to stop these ancient practices.

Drum dancing *is one of the varied forms of traditional music, and plays an important part in most of life's great events: births, weddings, a successful hunt, and honoring a person who has died. Another form of music, throat singing, is usually performed by two women facing one another to recount a legend, life event, or myth.*

NORTHERN CANADA

S till one of the most remote destinations on Earth, Northern Canada's Arctic beauty is now accessible to adventurous travelers in search of untouched terrain for superlative, challenging hiking and exploring. Many of the settlements at this brink of the world were established only in the 20th century. Some of the first towns grew up around RCMP outposts, established to monitor trappers, explorers, and whalers in Canadian territory; more recently defense outposts have developed new settlements. Local Inuit communities have gradually given up their nomadic life, and many are now settled around these outposts. These small towns are bases for exploring the stunning surroundings. In the winter the north is cold, descending to -50°C (-58°F), yet in summer warm air sweeps over the cold land, and the tundra bursts into bloom. The thaw acts in defiance of eight long months of winter when everything is draped in a blanket of white. This is a startlingly beautiful land with deserted plains, icy trails, rare wildlife, and gentle people, and is ripe for discovery.

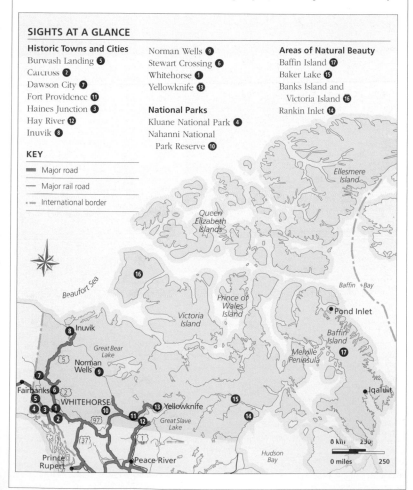

SIGHTS AT A GLANCE

Historic Towns and Cities
Burwash Landing ❺
Carcross ❷
Dawson City ❼
Fort Providence ⓫
Haines Junction ❸
Hay River ⓬
Inuvik ❽

Norman Wells ❾
Stewart Crossing ❻
Whitehorse ❶
Yellowknife ⓭

National Parks
Kluane National Park ❹
Nahanni National
  Park Reserve ❿

Areas of Natural Beauty
Baffin Island ⓱
Baker Lake ⓯
Banks Island and
  Victoria Island ⓰
Rankin Inlet ⓮

KEY
▬ Major road
— Major rail road
∙— International border

Ellesmere Island
Queen Elizabeth Islands
Beaufort Sea
Baffin Bay
Prince of Wales Island
Pond Inlet
Victoria Island
Inuvik ❽
Great Bear Lake
Baffin Island ⓱
Melville Peninsula
Norman Wells ❾
Fairbanks ❼
WHITEHORSE
Iqaluit
Yellowknife ⓭
Great Slave Lake
Prince Rupert
Peace River
Hudson Bay

0 km   250
0 miles   250

◁ The frozen seas surrounding the coast of Baffin Island

Whitehorse **❶**

Whitehorse takes its name from the local rapids on the Yukon River that reminded miners in the gold rush of "the flowing manes of albino Appaloosas." The town evolved when 2,500 stampeders on the hunt for gold braved the arduous Chilkoot and White Pass trails on foot in the winter of 1897–98 and set up camp here by the banks of Lindeman and Bennett Lakes. Boatmen made over 7,000 trips through the rapids during the spring thaw of 1898 before a tramway was built around them. On the spot where gold miners could catch a boat downstream to the mines of the Klondike and the glittering nightlife of Dawson City in the Yukon, a tent town sprang up and Whitehorse was born. This regional capital is the fastest-growing town in the northern territories, but despite all modern amenities, the wilderness is always only a few moments away.

🏛 MacBride Museum of Yukon History

1124 First Ave. **Tel** *(867) 667 2709.*
◯ *mid-May–Sep: daily; Sep–mid-May: Tue–Sat.* 🖼 🚻
www.macbridemuseum.com
The MacBride Museum is housed in a log cabin along the river. From Gold Rush fever to the birth of Whitehorse, this is the place to learn about the history of the Yukon. Gold to Government – Yukon's Modern History is one of several fascinating galleries. Other galleries cover wildlife, archaeology, and beadwork from the area's First Nations. Among the special features are Engine 51 from the White Pass and Yukon Route railway, and a log cabin depicting fictional character Sam McGee. In the summer there are daily talks and skits.

🏯 Log Skyscrapers

Lambert St. & Third Ave.
🅸 *(867) 667 3084.*
Two blocks away from the Old Log Church Museum on Elliott Street are the unique log skyscrapers. Now several decades old, these log cabins have two or three floors. Currently used for giftshops and exhibits, one was home to a Yukon member of parliament. Worth a detour, the cabins offer a pleasing diversion from the rather functional architecture that characterizes much of the rest of town.

🏛 Old Log Church Museum

303 Elliott St. **Tel** *(867) 668 2555.*
◯ *May–Aug.* 🖼 🚻
In August 1900, Anglican missionary Rev. R. J. Bowen was sent to Whitehorse to build a church. He held services in one

tent and lived in a second, as the log building took shape. The church opened on October 17 and the log rectory was built that winter. These buildings are among the few remaining here from the gold rush period. In 1953, the log church became the Diocese of Yukon cathedral and is said to be the only log cathedral in the world. Now, exhibits and interactive programs feature Inuit and First Nations cultures, missionaries, and the development of the Anglican church in the north.

The Old Log Church, constructed entirely from local timber

🏛 S.S. Klondike National Historic Site

End Second Ave. **Tel** *(867) 667 3910.*
◯ *mid-May–mid-Sep: 9:30am–5pm daily.* 🖼 🚻 www.pc.gc.ca
Originally built in 1929, the S.S. *Klondike* paddle-steamer sank in 1936. Rebuilt from its wreckage, the *Klondike* made 10 supply trips each season to Dawson City. In the early 1950s, bridges along the road to Dawson were built too low, blocking the passage of the sternwheelers, so all journeys

The city center of Whitehorse, sheltered in the Yukon River valley

For hotels and restaurants in this region see pp364–5 and pp390–91

S.S. *Klondike* in its permanent home in Whitehorse

stopped. The *Klondike* ceased operating in 1955 and was beached forever in Whitehorse. It is now restored to its heyday in every detail, right down to the 1937 *Life* magazines on the tables and authentic staff uniforms. Although no longer operational, the boat is a National Historic Site, with regular guided tours of the interior on offer.

Lake Laberge
Klondike Hwy. ***Tel*** *(867) 667 3084.*
☐ *daily, weather permitting.*
Largest of the lakes in the area, Lake Laberge is 62 km (39 miles) from Whitehorse along the Klondike Hwy. Frozen for

half of the year, with temperatures dropping below -30°C (-22°F), this popular summer swimming, fishing, and boating destination comes to life during the annual thaw. The lake is famous among locals as the site of the funeral pyre of Yukon poet Robert Service's *Cremation of Sam McGee*, which relates the demise of a fictional local hero. Trout fishing is excellent; fish were barged here by the ton during the Klondike gold rush to feed the hordes of hopeful miners.

Local mountain goat

VISITORS' CHECKLIST

🏘 *25,000.* ✈ 🚌 *Greyhound bus depot, 2191 2nd Ave.*
🛈 *Whitehorse Visitor Reception Centre, 100 Hanson St. (867) 667 3084, 1 800 661 0494.* 🎭
Yukon Quest, Yukon Sourdough Rendezvous, Frostbite Music Festival (Feb). **www**.travelyukon.com

Yukon Wildlife Preserve
Takhini Hot Springs Rd. ***Tel*** *(867) 458 7300.* ☐ *daily.* 🛒
This sanctuary was set up in 1965 for research and breeding purposes and lies about 25 km (16 miles) from the town off the Klondike Hwy on the Takhini Hot Springs Road. A beautiful reserve of forest, grassland, meadows, and water areas, it has ten species of northern mammals in large enclosures. Moose, bison, elk, caribou, mountain goats, deer, Dall sheep, as well as musk ox and lynx, can all be seen here protected in the 300-ha (750-acre) parkland of their natural roaming habitat.

WHITEHORSE CITY CENTER

Log Skyscrapers ②
MacBride Museum of Yukon History ①
Old Log Church Museum ③
S.S. *Klondike* ④

Lake Laberge, Yukon Wildlife Preserve

Airport 5 km (3 miles)

① MacBride Museum

WOOD STREET
STEELE STREET
MAIN STREET
ELLIOTT STREET
FIRST AVENUE

Old Log Church Museum ③
② Log Skyscrapers

SIXTH AVENUE
LAMBERT STREET
FOURTH STREET
HANSON STREET
HAWKINS STREET
FIFTH AVENUE
SECOND AVENUE
THIRD AVENUE

Yukon River

LEVES BLVD

HOGE STREET
④ S.S. Klondike

JECKELL STREET

ROBERT SERVICE WAY

0 meters 250
0 yards 250

Key to Symbols *see back flap*

Male caribou resting near Carcross, as herds migrate across the Yukon

Carcross ❷

🏛 *450.* 🚂 🛈 *(867) 821 4431.* ◯ *mid-May–Sep daily.*

Carcross is a small village that lies at the picturesque confluence of Bennett and Tagish lakes, an hour's drive south of Yukon's regional capital, Whitehorse. Early miners crossing the arduous Chilkoot Pass on their journey to the bounty of the gold mines in the north named the site "Caribou Crossing" after herds of caribou stormed their way through the pass between Bennett and Nares lakes on their biannual migration. The town was established in 1899 in the height of the gold rush with the arrival of the White Pass and Yukon railroad. "Caribou Crossing" was abbre-

viated officially to Carcross to avoid duplication of names in Alaska, British Colombia, and a town in the Klondike.

Carcross has a strong native tradition, and was once an important caribou hunting ground for the Tagish tribe. Tagish guides worked for US Army surveyors during the building of the Alaska Highway in 1942 *(see pp262–3)*.

Just 2 km (1 mile) north is the "smallest desert in the world", Carcross Desert. Blasted by strong winds, the sandy plain is barren, and the only remnant of a glacial lake that dried up after the last Ice Age. The strength of the winds allows little vegetation to grow, but the spot is memorable.

Haines Junction ❸

🏛 *589.* 🚂 🛈 *Kluane National Park and Reserve (867) 634 7207.*

Haines Junction is a handy fuel and food stop for visitors on the way to the impressive Kluane National Park and Reserve. The town has a post office, restaurant, and hotels. Trips into the park for rafting canoeing, and various hiking excursions can be organized from the town, as the park's administrative headquarters are here. Those wishing to raft should book well ahead. Haines Junction was once a base

camp for the US Army engineers who in 1942 built much of the Alcan Highway (now known as the Alaska Highway) that links Fairbanks in Alaska to the south of Canada. The St. Elias Mountains tower above the town, and air trips can be taken from here to admire the views of the frozen scenery, glaciers, and icy peaks of this wilderness.

Kaskawulsh Glacier rising over Kluane National Park and Reserve

Kluane National Park and Reserve ❹

Tel (867) 634 7207. 🚂 *Haines Junction.* ◯ *year round.* 🏛 ⓓ 🅿 **www.pc.gc.ca**

This superb wilderness area is a United Nations World Heritage Site. Covering 21,980 sq km (8,487 sq miles) of the southwest corner of the Yukon, the park shares the St. Elias mountain range, the highest in Canada, with Alaska. The whole park comprises one of the largest nonpolar icefields in the world.

Two-thirds of the park is glacial, filled with valleys and lakes that are frozen year-round, broken up by alpine forests, meadows, and tundra. The landscape is one of the last surviving examples of an Ice Age environment, which disappeared in the rest of the world around 5,000–10,000 BC. Mount Logan, at 5,959 m (19,545 ft), is Canada's tallest peak. Numerous well-marked and established trails make

The St. Elias range dominates the small town of Haines Junction

Kluane National Park and Reserve displays radiant foliage in fall, as seen here in the Alsek River area

for excellent hiking here, and several conveniently start from the main road. There are some less defined routes, which follow the old mining trails. There are trails to suit both the novice and experienced hiker, ranging from a 2-hour stroll to a ten-day guided trek.

Kluane's combination of striking scenery and an abundance of wildlife, including moose, Dall sheep, and grizzly bears, make it the Yukon's most attractive wilderness destination. Trips into the park are organized from nearby Haines Junction. Due to the hazardous weather, untamed wildlife, and isolated conditions, safety measures are mandatory here.

Burwash Landing ❺

🏠 88. ⓘ Whitehorse (867) 667 3084.

Northwest of Haines Junction by 124 km (77 miles), this little village at the western end of Kluane Lake lies just outside Kluane National Park on the Alaska Hwy. A community was established here in 1905, after a gold strike in a local creek, and Burwash Landing is now a service center. Visitors can also enjoy stunning panoramas of Kluane Lake to the south.

The village is noted for the **Kluane Museum of Natural History**, with many animal-related exhibits, including a mammoth's tooth and numerous displays on local natural

history. Focus is also given to the traditional lifestyle of the region's tribe of Southern Tutchone people.

🏛 Kluane Museum of Natural History
Burwash Landing. *Tel (867) 841 5561.* ◯ mid-May–mid Sep: daily. 🈺 &

Stewart Crossing ❻

🏠 35. 🚉 ⓘ Whitehorse (867) 667 3084.

Approximately 180 km (113 miles) east of Dawson City *(see p336),* Stewart Crossing is a small community at the junction of the Klondike Hwy and the Silver Trail, which leads to the small mining settlements of Mayo, Elsa, and Keno, once famous for their silver trade. During the gold rush in the late 19th century, the area was referred to as the "grubstake," because enough gold could be panned from the river sandbars here during the summer to buy

the following year's stake. Stewart Crossing is a modest service center that also operates as the starting-point for canoe trails on the Stewart River. Unusual for this wild terrain, these boat trips are suitable for children and beginners. Trips should be organized in Whitehorse or Dawson City.

About an hour north, at Km 655.1, is the **Tintina Trench Rest Area**. Providing in a glance visible proof of the geological theory of plate tectonics, the trench itself stretches for several hundred kilometers across the Yukon, with layers of millennia-old rock gaping open to the skies. "Tintina" means "chief" in the local native language, and this is one of the largest geological faults in the Yukon system. This area is an ideal place to view the trench, which runs up to here along the route of the Klondike Hwy, from a course parallel with the Yukon River that begins at Fortymile village.

Broad Valley by Stewart Crossing near the Yukon River, Yukon

The stunning beauty of a Yukon river valley in summer ▷

The Gaslight Follies Theatre in Dawson City

Dawson City ❼

🏠 1,350. ✕ 🚌 ℹ️ *cnr Front & King Sts. (867) 993 5575.* www.dawsoncity.ca

The town of Dawson City came into prominence during the Klondike gold rush of 1898 (see pp50–51), when the population boomed and the city grew from a moose pasture into a bustling metropolis of some 30–40,000 people, all seeking their fortune in the new "Paris of the North." The town continues to mine gold, but tourism is now one of Dawson City's key sources of income.

Dawson City Museum has exhibits on the Klondike, with features on the gold rush and artifacts from that period. A popular attraction is **Diamond Tooth Gertie's**, the gambling hall complete with a honky-tonk piano and can-can girls.

🏛 **Dawson City Museum**
595 5th Ave. *Tel (867) 993 5291.* ⭘ *mid-May–Sep: 10am–6pm daily; late Sep–May: by appointment.* 🎫 ♿

🎰 **Diamond Tooth Gertie's**
Cnr 4th Ave. & Queen St. *Tel (867) 993 5525.* ⭘ *mid-May–mid-Sep: 7pm–2am daily.* 🎫 ♿

Inuvik ❽

🏠 3,500. ✕ ℹ️ *2 Firth St. (867) 777 8600.* www.inuvik.ca

About 770 km (480 miles) north of Dawson City, Inuvik lies at the tip of the Dempster Hwy, the most northerly road in Canada. Inuvik has only a very recent history. Founded in the 1950s as a supply center for military projects in the NWT, the town prospered in the oil boom of the 1970s. Full of functional contemporary architecture, Inuvik's charm lies more in its location as a good visitors' center for the region – there are a few hotels and several shops, no mean feat for a town that boasts just a single traffic light. It is, nonetheless, the most visited town in the northern Arctic, popular as a craft center for the Inuit and as a starting point for a tour of the far north.

Inuvik welcomes its visitors

Environs

The settlement of Paulatuk lies 400 km (250 miles) east of Inuvik and is one of the smallest communities in the territory. It is well placed for hunting, fishing, and trapping game; these activities remain its staple support after many centuries. Its location is also useful as a stepping-stone to the wilderness. Tourism is becoming popular, and trips into Tuktut Nogait National Park with Inuit guides are available. The unusual Smoking Hills, which are composed of sulfide-rich slate and coal can be seen when flying to and from Paulatuk.

Norman Wells ❾

🏠 800. ✕ ℹ️ *Visitor Information Center and Museum, 23 MacKenzie Drive (867) 587 2415.* ⭘ *daily.* www.normanwells.com

In 1920 crude oil discoveries were made here near a small Dene settlement. Oil production surged in World War II when the US established a pipeline to supply oil to the Alaska Highway while it was being built, and the town grew.

Today Norman Wells is the starting point for the Canol Heritage Trail, a long-distance path of wilderness trail through to the Canol Road above the Ross River in the Yukon Territory, which links up with the Yukon Highway system. There are few facilities along the trail, making it one of the toughest trekking paths in the world. Despite the difficulties, this is a popular destination with experienced hikers.

Nahanni National Park Reserve ❿

Tel (867) 695 3151. ✕ *Fort Simpson.* ⭘ *year round.* 🎫 ℹ️ *Nahanni National Park Reserve, 10002-100 Street, Fort Simpson, NWT.* www.pc.gc.ca

Nahanni National Park Reserve sits astride the South Nahanni River between the border with the Yukon and the small settlement of Fort Simpson.

Inuvik's town church and hall, shaped like an igloo against the climate

The vast expanses of Nahanni National Park in summer

In 1978, it was one of the first places in the world to be designated a UNESCO World Heritage Site to protect its geological history. The park is a great wilderness with four vast river canyons, hot springs, and a spectacular undeveloped waterfall, Virginia Falls. The falls, at 90 m (295 ft), are twice the height of Niagara but have less volume, and boast excellent flora and fauna. At least 16 species of fish enjoy the cascades, and more than 180 varieties of bird live overhead. Wolves, grizzly bears, and woodland caribou move freely in the park.

The park's main activities are whitewater rafting and canoeing. In summer, watersports take precedence over walking tours, as the rivers thaw, and the landscape bursts into bloom with wild flowers. The park is usually reached by float plane.

Fort Providence ⓫

🏠 750. 🚌 ⓘ NWT Tourism Office, 52nd St., Yellowknife 1 800 661 0788, (867) 873 7200.

The Dene people call this village "zhahti koe," which means mission house in their native tongue. Fort Providence began life as a Catholic mission and was later enlarged by the Hudson's Bay Company (see pp162–3), which set up an outpost here in the late 19th century. Attracted by this and the prospect of employment, the local Dene First Nations people settled here permanently. Today the town is a Dene handicrafts center.

Just north of the village lies the Mackenzie Bison Sanctuary. The sanctuary is home to the world's largest herd of 2,000 rare pure wood bison. The park stretches for 100 km (60 miles) north along the banks of Great Slave Lake, and bison can be seen along the road.

Hay River ⓬

🏠 3,700. ✈ 🚌 ⓘ MacKenzie Hwy (867) 874 3180. ◯ Jun–Sep.

Set on the banks of Great Slave Lake, the small community of Hay River is the major port in the Northwest Territories. A lifeline, the town supplies the High Arctic settlements and the northernmost towns in the country, particularly Inuvik, with essentials. When the river thaws in spring, it supplies freight. The town looks designed for the purpose it serves – the wharves are lined with barges and tugs, as well as the local fishing fleet.

Unusually for this area, Hay River's history stretches back over a millennium. The Dene moved here centuries ago, lured by the town's strategic position at the southern shore of the Great Slave Lake, for its hunting and fishing. Attractions here are based on local industry; as a shipping center, the harbor is a bustling place to spot barges. The original Dene settlement, now a village of 300 people, sits across the river north from the Old Town and welcomes visitors.

THE NORTHERN LIGHTS

The Northern Lights, or *aurora borealis*, are believed to be the result of solar winds entering the Earth's ionosphere some 160 km (100 miles) above the surface of the planet. Emanating from the sun, these winds collide with the gases present in the Earth's upper atmosphere, releasing energy that becomes visible in the night sky. The stunning consequences are visible in the Yukon and the NWT, most often from August to October. Some aboriginal groups attach religious significance to the Lights, believing them to be the spirits of dead hunters, while 19th-century gold prospectors mistook them for vapors given off by ore deposits. Whatever one's beliefs, the sparkling ribbons of light are an awesome sight.

Yellowknife ⑬

Originally a native Dene settlement, Yellowknife is named after the yellow-bladed copper hunting knives used by its first residents. The Hudson's Bay Company closed its outpost here in 1823 due to failing profits, but the Old Town thrived again with gold mining in the 1930s and again after 1945. With improved road communications, the city became the regional capital of the Northwest Territories in 1967. Growing bureaucratic needs and four diamond mines 300 km (186 miles) north of Yellowknife have helped it flourish.

Makeshift houseboats on the Great Slave Lake

The Old Town

Just 1 km (0.5 mile) north of downtown, the Old Town is situated on an island and a rocky peninsula on Great Slave Lake. By 1947 Yellowknife had outgrown itself, and the New Town rose from the sandy plain southward. An unusual community thrives here on Yellowknife Bay, many living on makeshift houseboats. Also interesting is the variety of older architecture that can be seen from a stroll around this now residential area. Shops and accomodations are found farther south in the New Town. A good vantage point from which to survey the area is the Bush Pilots Monument (a blue Bristol airplane) at the north end of Franklin Avenue.

The Wildcat Café

3904 Wiley Road. **Tel** (867) 873 4004. ◐ Jun–Sep: 11am–9pm daily. ♿
The oldest restaurant in Yellowknife, this institution is open only during the summer. A true frontier stop, the sagging log cabin is set under

YELLOWKNIFE CITY CENTER

Legislative Assembly ④
Prince of Wales Northern
   Heritage Centre ③
The Old Town ①
Wildcat Café ②

Wildcat Café ②
Bush Pilots Monument ①
Back Bay
OLD TOWN
Niven Lake
Airport 4 km (2.5 miles)
INGRAHAM DRIVE
McAVOY RD.
NIVEN DRIVE
49TH AVE.
FRANKLIN AVENUE (50TH AVENUE)
48TH ST.
45TH ST.
46TH AVE.
Yellowknife Bay
SCHOOL DRAW AVENUE
④ Legislative Assembly
INGRAHAM TRAIL
DOWNTOWN
③ Prince of Wales Northern Heritage Centre
49TH AVENUE
49TH ST.
52ND ST.
50TH AVENUE
50TH ST.
47TH ST.
51ST AVE.
52ND AVENUE
48TH ST.
44TH STREET

| 0 meters | 400 |
| 0 yards | 400 |

Key to Symbols *see back flap*

the hill of the Old Town and has been refurbished in 1930s style. Its atmospheric interior is reminiscent of the pioneer days. Perhaps understandably, this establishment is the most photographed building in Yellowknife. It underwent renovations in 2011 but retains its authenticity.

Sampling the fare at the Wildcat Café is a truly northern experience

🏛 The Prince of Wales Northern Heritage Centre
4750 48th Street. *Tel* (867) 873 7551. ◯ *daily.* ⬤ *public holidays.*
♿ www.pwnhc.ca
This local museum's displays feature typically northern artifacts such as a mooseskin boat, as well as items illustrating the history of flying in the north. Changing exhibits explain life in the subarctic and Beaufort Delta regions.

🏛 The Legislative Assembly
Frame Lake. *Tel* (867) 669 2230, 1 800 661 0784. ◯ *Mon–Fri.*
♿ 🕐 *Jul & Aug.*
www.assembly.gov.nt.ca
Built in 1993, this headquarters of local government has a tall domed roof. Signifying equal rights for all ethnic groups, the government chamber is the only round one of its kind in the country, with a large oval table to give all delegates equal responsibility, in the manner practiced by aboriginals. Decorated with paintings and Inuit art, the chamber is graced with a large polar bear rug. The official public government rooms can be toured when the council is not in session.

Rankin Inlet ⑭

🏠 2,300. **ℹ** *Kivalliq Regional Visitor Centre (867) 645 3838.* ✈

Founded in 1955 when North Rankin Nickel Mine opened, Rankin Inlet is the largest community in the stony plateau of Kivalliq, which stretches east of the Canadian Shield to Hudson Bay. This small town is the government center for the Kivalliq region, whose population, now 85 percent aboriginal, has settled mainly on the coast.

This region is characterized by its rural way of life and stunning scenery. **Iqalugaarjuup Nunanga Territorial Park**, 10 km (6 miles) from the town center, contains a traditional Thule (ancestor of the Inuit) restored native site with stone tent rings, meat stores, and semi-subterranean winter houses.

🌿 Iqalugaarjuup Nunanga Territorial Park
10 km (6 miles) NW of Rankin Inlet, on the Meliadine River. *Tel* (867) 975 7700. ◯ *daily, weather permitting.*

Baker Lake ⑮

🏠 1,700. ✈ **ℹ** (867) 793 2456.

Baker Lake is geographically at the center of Canada and is the country's only inland Inuit community. Located at the source of the Thelon River, the area has always been a traditional summer gathering place for the Inuit. Today it is an important center for Inuit art, especially textiles. Heading westward, the **Thelon Wildlife**

Sanctuary can also be visited. Visitors can see herds of musk ox in their natural habitat and glimpse other indigenous animals and birds.

✈ Thelon Wildlife Sanctuary
300 km (200 miles) w. of Baker Lake. *Tel* (867) 975 7700. ◯ *daily*

Banks Island and Victoria Island ⑯

ℹ (867) 979 4636.

Located in the Arctic Ocean, Banks Island is home to the largest herds of musk ox in the world. They dwell in **Aulavik National Park**, on the remote northern tip of the island. This numbers among the world's most remote wildlife destinations, and is accessible only by plane. Note that the park is best accessed from the Northwest Territories.

Split between the Northwest Territories and Nunavut, Victoria Island has a town in each – Ulukhaktok in NWT and the Inuit Cambridge Bay in Nunavut, where local native people traveled each summer for char fishing and caribou and seal hunting. The town today is a service center for locals and visitors along the Arctic coast. Polar bears, musk ox, wolves, and Arctic birds live nearby.

🌿 Aulavik National Park
Sachs Harbour. *Tel* (867) 690 3904. ◯ *daily, weather permitting.* 🖼
www.pc.gc.ca

An Inuit igloo builder near Baker Lake, practicing this traditional skill

Baffin Island ⑰

Purple Saxifrage in summer

Part of Nunavut, Baffin Island is one of the most remote places in North America. At 500,000 sq km (193,000 sq miles), the island is the fifth largest on the planet, with more than 60 percent of its landmass lying above the Arctic Circle. Sparsely populated, the island is inhabited by just 11,000 people, 9,000 of whom are Inuit. Most people live in one of eight settlements scattered throughout the island, the chief of which is Iqaluit, capital of the territory of Nunavut.

With its spectacular fjords and knife-edged mountains sparkling with glaciers, Baffin Island offers a chance to experience all the outdoor activities of the Arctic. Canoeing, kayaking, trekking, and thrilling walks are all unbeatable here. Many of the activities often take place in the company of abundant wildlife, including polar bears and whales.

0 km   100

0 miles   100

BYLOT ISLAND

BRODEUR PENINSULA

ARCTIC BAY

SIRMILIK NATIONAL PARK

BORDEN PENINSULA

PRINCE CHARLES ISLAND

Pond Inlet

Pond Inlet is a jewel in Nunavut's twinkling crown. Blessed with stunning scenery of mountains, glaciers, and icebergs, it is surrounded by abundant Arctic marine life. Snowmobiling and dogsledding to the floe edge are popular.

AUYUITTUQ NATIONAL PARK

Auyuittuq is the third-largest national park in Canada at 21,470 sq km (8,300 sq miles). It is one of the few national parks with land above the Arctic Circle. A spectacular destination, the park displays a pristine wilderness of mountains, valleys, and fjords. In spring the meadows thaw out from under their snowy coverlets, and wildflowers burst into bloom. Within the park, wildlife abounds, with animals ranging from snow geese and arctic foxes to polar bears sharing the territory. Even in the brief summer, the weather can be tricky, with the risk of snow. Be prepared for cool weather, though temperatures can rise. The nearby town of Pangnirtung is a craft center.

Wildflowers flourish beneath Auyuittuq's frozen peaks

Cape Dorset is of interest archeologically because predecessors of the modern Inuit, the Thule and Dorset peoples, lived in this area. Cape Dorset is also known for its print-making tradition.

KEY

— River

— National Park boundary

☼ Viewpoint

☒ Domestic airport

Pangnirtung
*This little town of 1,300 residents sits at the
southern end of the Pangnirtung Fjord, the
100-km (62-mile) biking trail which is the most
popular on Baffin. Some of the cliff faces here
are more than 1,500 m (4,921 ft) high.*

VISITORS' CHECKLIST

11,400. Nunavut Tourism,
Iqaluit (1 866 686 2888).
Toonik Tyme (Apr), Iqaluit;
Alianait Arts Festival (Jun), Iqaluit.
www.nunavuttourism.com

ACCESSING CANADA'S NORTH

*While tourism to Nunavut
increases every year, the
only access to these remote
settlements is by air, which
is very expensive compared
to mainline routes. Despite
the cost, however, every
community has its own airport.*

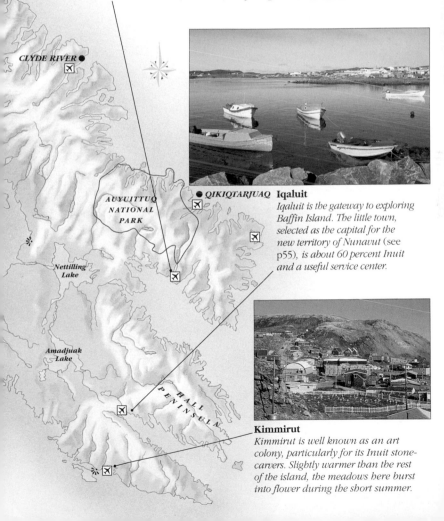

CLYDE RIVER

AUYUITTUQ
NATIONAL
PARK

QIKIQTARJUAQ

Nettilling
Lake

Amadjuak
Lake

HALL PENINSULA

Iqaluit
*Iqaluit is the gateway to exploring
Baffin Island. The little town,
selected as the capital for the
new territory of Nunavut (see
p55), is about 60 percent Inuit
and a useful service center.*

Kimmirut
*Kimmirut is well known as an art
colony, particularly for its Inuit stone-
carvers. Slightly warmer than the rest
of the island, the meadows here burst
into flower during the short summer.*

TRAVELERS' NEEDS

WHERE TO STAY

As one might expect in a country of its size, Canada has a wide range of places in which to stay: from stately, world-famous hotels such as the Château Frontenac in Quebec City, to family-run bed-and-breakfasts in the countryside, the variety is immense. Canada offers excellent middle-range accommodations, and you will find rural inns, cottages to rent in scenic spots, elegant town apartments, hostels, houseboats, and the most popular choice of all, the convenient motel. Whether you need a mid-journey bed for the night or a seasonal rental, you can always find the right place and may not even need to book in advance. The listings on *pp346–65* describe in full a selection of destinations for every taste and budget.

Hotel doorman

A rental lodge in Banff National Park

GRADING AND FACILITIES

There is no government-sponsored hotel grading system in Canada, but the voluntary program "Canada Select" is usually very accurate. Each establishment is rated by numbers of stars. It is worth bearing in mind, however, that a 4-star hotel in a large city such as Toronto, for example, might not have the same level of facilities as one with the same rating in a small upscale resort with a château hotel.

The Canadian Automobile Association also operates an assessment system, mostly for hotels and motels along main highways, and these, while also non-official, are largely recognized as consistent and accurate. Air-conditioning comes as standard in most of the country during summer, except in national park lodges and cooler coastal and northern regions. Central heating country-wide is efficient. Cable TV, radio, irons and ironing boards, and coffee-making facilities are standard. Private bathrooms are usual, but you will need to specify a bathtub or shower – also remember to ask for double or twin beds when booking a double room.

PRICES

With such a wide range of accommodations, prices vary hugely. In a major town, the top hotel's presidential suite may command a daily rate in excess of Can$1,000, while a hiker's hostel will provide a dormitory bed for under Can$25. Budget hotels and B-and-Bs charge Can$50–75 a night per person. Some prices rise in high season, but rates are discounted in low season.

RESERVATIONS

Advance reservations are always recommended in the main cities, where festivals, conventions, meetings, and major sports and musical events are held year-round (see pp38–41). Provincial tourist offices or airlines (see p409) will assist in suggesting and arranging bookings.

CHILDREN

Traveling with children is relatively easy. Nearly every property will supply a cot or junior-sized bed in a parents' room. Major hotels offer baby-sitting services. A lone parent traveling with children may need written consent from the other parent under anti-abduction regulation. For more information, visit www.servicecanada.gc.ca under "Citizenship and Immigration."

DISABLED TRAVELERS

All new public buildings provide wheelchair facilities with ramps and wide doors. However, many rural hotels date from the 19th century, so always check in advance.

Imposing façade of The Fairmont Royal York in Toronto (see p355)

LUXURY HOTELS

The major cities in Canada boast some truly world-class establishments. The railroad age of the late 19th century ushered in château-style

◁ Life jackets stored at the Madawaska Canoe Centre, Eastern Ontario

Bedroom at Elmwood Heritage Inn on Prince Edward Island *(see p348)*

hotels, which are unique Canadian architectural features. Nowadays, most of the castle-hotels, including the Château Frontenac, are owned and operated by Fairmont Hotels. Luxury chains are well represented: the Four Seasons, the Hilton, the Radisson, the Sheraton, and Westin chains operate in Toronto, Montreal, Calgary, and Vancouver.

CHAIN HOTELS

Canada offers numerous franchise and chain hotels and motels. Reliable and comfortable, if occasionally a little bland, chains vary in style and price from grand resort areas to the less expensive but equally well-known Best Western, Comfort, and Super 8. Popular with families and business travelers, many of the properties have offices for use, including fax, e-mail, and telegraph equipment. Children's facilities are usually good.

EFFICIENCY APARTMENTS

There is a tremendous variety of these options available in Canada in addition to the traditional cottage rental industry. Motorhomes or RVs (Recreational Vehicles) are gaining in popularity and can be leased in all the major cities. Most nowadays have air-conditioning, refrigerators, ovens, and bathrooms. Campgrounds are found all over the country, from lush fields in the fertile southern national parks to well-insulated zones partly inhabited by the Inuit in the north. The proliferation

of this choice guarantees high quality and a well-priced stay: electrical connections, as well as laundry facilities, general store, and sports programs are often available for all ages.

For many, the cottage or cabin option is traditionally Canadian. Ontario is famous for its selection of rural vacation homes, again very well equipped, which are available weekly, monthly, or seasonally, and are always well located for nearby attractions. National parks also rent lodges and offer campgrounds.

BED-AND-BREAKFASTS

The growing number of bed-and-breakfasts across Canada is testimony to their popularity. From historic inns to rustic quarters on vacation farms, each provides personalized service, a friendly local face, and insight into the region's way of life. Atlantic Canada is renowned for its

B-and-Bs, with many located in the elegant Victorian homes of historic towns. Call the provincial tourist office for a detailed list with tariffs. Most establishments have up to four rooms for rent.

ACCOMMODATIONS TAXES

Bear in mind that accommodations of almost every kind are subject to two taxes on top of the basic tariff. The first, Provincial Sales Tax (PST), varies from province to province and ranges from between 5 and 12 percent. It must be paid on accommodations as well as on goods and other services. Rules vary slightly between provinces: Alberta levies only the PST on hotel and motel stays, and campsites, B-and-Bs, and guesthouses are tax-free.

The Goods and Services Tax (GST) is a standard national charge of 5 percent throughout the country; this affects most accommodation classes. In some provinces the GST and PST are combined as Harmonized Sales Tax (HST) of approximately 13 percent. In Nova Scotia, New Brunswick, and Newfoundland and Labrador, the HST of 13 percent replaces the GST. Smaller hotels may not charge the GST, so inquire on arrival.

Since April 2007 the GST rebate program for non-residents of Canada has been eliminated.

A bed-and-breakfast in the Rocky Mountains

Choosing a Hotel

The hotels in this guide have been selected for their good value, excellent facilities, or location. This chart lists hotels under the region chapter headings in the same order as the rest of the guide, and grouped alphabetically by province and then by town. Entries are alphabetical within the price category. For restaurant listings, see pages 370–91.

PRICE CATEGORIES IN CANADIAN DOLLARS (CAN $)
For a standard double room per night, including breakfast (where served), taxes, and any extra service charges.
⑤ Under $100
⑤⑤ $100–$150
⑤⑤⑤ $150–$250
⑤⑤⑤⑤ $250–$350
⑤⑤⑤⑤⑤ Over $350

NEWFOUNDLAND AND LABRADOR

BAULINE EAST Celtic Rendezvous Cottages ⑤⑤⑤
P.O. Box 20, Tors Cove, Bauline East, Newfoundland, A0A 4A0 **Tel** *(709) 334 3341* **Fax** *(709) 334 2571* **Rooms** *23*

These are pine cottages with large picture windows and spectacular ocean views, within a bird sanctuary. Watch icebergs float by and whales play. There are private decks with barbecues. Horseback riding, fishing, boat tours, sea kayaking, and spa services are on site. **www.celticrendezvouscottages.com**

CORNER BROOK Bell's Inn ⑤
2 Ford's Road, Corner Brook, Newfoundland, A2H 1S6 **Tel** *(709) 634 1150* **Fax** *(709) 634 1114* **Rooms** *8*

This is Corner Brook's oldest bed & breakfast in a large, rambling, and modernized home. The host is happy to let guests use laundry facilities and is very knowledgeable about Newfoundland. There is a pleasant backyard garden. There are no set times for breakfast. A "make yourself at home" kind of place.

GRAND FALLS Mount Peyton Hotel ⑤⑤
214 Lincoln Road, Grand Falls - Windsor, Newfoundland, A2A 1P8 **Tel** *(709) 489 2251* **Fax** *(709) 489 6365* **Rooms** *150*

Medium-sized hotel with additional motel and holiday units. Staff are friendly and helpful. Close to shopping, arts, and culture center; great walking trails; and museum. For an intimate and quiet meal, check out Peyton Corral Steak House – one of two restaurants on site. **www.mountpeyton.com**

GROS MORNE Gros Morne Resort ⑤⑤
P.O. Box 200, Saint Paul's, Newfoundland, A0K 4Y0 **Tel** *(709) 243 2606* **Fax** *(709) 243 2615* **Rooms** *20*

Great views here at world famous Gros Morne. The resort has luxurious, extra large rooms. Amenities include hair salon, tanning salon, Internet café, and a bakery. The family restaurant has good food. There is an excellent golf course. Thursday nights feature Newfoundland kitchen parties and lively music. **www.grosmorneresort.com**

HAPPY VALLEY GOOSE BAY The Labrador Inn ⑤⑤
380 Hamilton River Road, Happy Valley Goose Bay, A0P 1C0 **Tel** *(709) 896 3351* **Fax** *(709) 896 3927* **Rooms** *66*

The largest and most modern hotel in Labrador on a landmark spot. This is pioneer country. The Labrador Inn proudly displays its heritage in the conference room with over 200 photos depicting life in the olden days. There is a NATO low-level flight training base close by. **www.labradorinn.nf.ca**

PORT REXTON Fishers' Loft Inn ⑤⑤⑤
Box 36, Mill Road, Port Rexton, Newfoundland, A0C 2H0 **Tel** *(709) 464 3240* **Fax** *(709) 464 3240* **Rooms** *21*

Located on a hillside between forest and ocean, this hotel offers wonderful views from every room. Staff are generous, and always helpful. There is a large selection of Newfoundland art and award-winning furniture, it has a garden, and the food is superb. There are amazing hiking trails close by. **www.fishersloft.com**

QUIRPON Quirpon Lighthouse Inn ⑤⑤⑤⑤⑤
Box 652 Corner Brook, Newfoundland, A2H 6G1 **Tel** *(877) 254 6586* **Fax** *(709) 639 1592* **Rooms** *11*

Built in 1922, this well-appointed, fully restored lightkeeper's home overlooking "Iceberg Alley" is a fascinating 45-minute jaunt from the mainland. Enjoy the whale-watching station and see Humpback, Orca, and Minke whales. Better yet, get in a kayak and paddle through the icebergs and whales. Rare spot, exquisite experience. **www.linkumtours.com**

ST. JOHN'S Compton House Heritage Inn and Apartments ⑤⑤
26 Waterford Bridge Rd., St. John's, Newfoundland, A1E 1C6 **Tel** *(709) 739 5789* **Fax** *(709) 738 1770* **Rooms** *12*

A grand old Victorian mansion with ornate woodwork, period furniture, interesting antiques, and working fireplaces. A great place to leave the world behind. Breakfast includes everything from fruit plates to wild berry pancakes. The library has over 1,000 books and a large selection of movies. **www3.nf.sympatico.ca/comptonhouse/**

ST. JOHN'S Sheraton Hotel Newfoundland ⑤⑤⑤⑤
P.O. Box 5637, 115 Cavendish Sq., St.John's, Newfoundland, A1C 3K2 **Tel** *(709) 726 4980* **Fax** *(709) 726 2025* **Rooms** *301*

The view alone from this hotel is worth the price. Think "relaxed elegance." Queens, movie stars, and prime ministers stay here. The hotel's Cabot Club offers fine dining (the only 5-Diamond rating in Newfoundland). There is a unique court garden on the lower level. City core and historic tours are within walking distance.

Key to Symbols *see back cover flap*

NEW BRUNSWICK, NOVA SCOTIA, AND PRINCE EDWARD ISLAND

ANNAPOLIS ROYAL Hillsdale House Inn

519 Upper St. George Street, Annapolis Royal, Nova Scotia, B0S 1A0 **Tel** *(902) 532 2345* **Rooms** *13*

The Hillsdale House Inn is a Registered Heritage Property dating back to 1859. Both public and guest rooms are furnished with Victorian antiques, and wireless Internet is available throughout the building. The grounds feature manicured lawns and stately trees. Breakfast included. Pets are welcome with prior notice. **www.hillsdalehouseinn.ca**

BAY FORTUNE Inn at Bay Fortune

RR 4, Souris, Prince Edward Island, C0A 2B0 **Tel** *(902) 687 3745* **Fax** *(902) 687 3540* **Rooms** *17*

This inn is in an idyllic rural setting overlooking the mouth of the Fortune River and harbor and has beautiful grounds and a large organic garden. Its kitchen is renowned for fine dining and for being the set of the famed TV show, "The Inn Chef." It has interesting architecture with a unique history and fascinating courtyards and towers. **www.innatbayfortune.com**

BOUCTOUCHE Auberge Le Vieux Presbytère

157 Chemin du Couvent, Bouctouche, New Brunswick, E4S 3B8 **Tel** *(506) 743 5568* **Fax** *(506) 743 5566* **Rooms** *19*

Originally built for a priest in 1880, then converted into a monastery-like operation replete with a chapel, in 1993 it opened as an inn. Popular place with travelers from all over the world. Exceptional views, expansive grounds, and peaceful surroundings. Easy driving distance to major attractions. **www.vieuxpresbytere.nb.ca**

CAPE D'OR Cape D'Or Lighthouse

Box 122, Advocate Harbour, Nova Scotia, B0M 1A0 **Tel** *(902) 670 0534* **Rooms** *4*

If you are looking for seclusion, this is the place. Be prepared to share a common room full of games and books. Guest rooms are not fancy but the spectacular location makes up for it. The owner is a fun-loving cook who serves gourmet cooking in the restaurant. **www.capedor.ca**

CARAQUET Hotel Paulin

143 Boulevard St-Pierre West, Caraquet, New Brunswick, E1W 1B6 **Tel** *(506) 727 9981* **Fax** *(506) 727 4808* **Rooms** *12*

A classic Victorian Hotel, built in 1891. This is a one-of-a-kind historical boutique-style hotel, still owned and operated by the Paulin family. Situated on the scenic Bay of Chaleur, it offers intimate surroundings with old-world French village charm. Long-standing reputation as a travel destination. Remarkable hosts. Incredible cuisine. **www.hotelpaulin.com**

CHARLOTTETOWN Elmwood Heritage Inn

121 North River Rd., Charlottetown, Prince Edward Island, C1A 3K7 **Tel** *(902) 368 3310* **Fax** *(902) 628 8457* **Rooms** *7*

Elmwood is an oasis in the heart of the city – an exquisite mansion on a secluded park-like acre, yet within easy walking distance to the downtown core. Breakfast is served by candlelight and features exotic entrées such as sundried tomato pecan pesto omelets. There are not enough superlatives to describe Elmwood. **www.elmwoodinn.pe.ca**

CORNWALL Howard Johnson Dutch Inn

Trans Canada Highway, Cornwall, Prince Edward Island, C0A 1H0 **Tel** *(902) 566 2211* **Fax** *(902) 566 2214* **Rooms** *58*

Known as "Ho-Jos," this family hotel has great seasonal packages including golf, geocaching, snowmobile, and romance getaways. Relaxed atmosphere. Check out the Windmill Lounge on Friday nights for a game of darts and Trivia. Henry's Restaurant is pretty laid back, has decent food, and will not break the bank. **www.hojopei.com**

EDMUNDSTON Clarion Hotel and Conference Centre

100 Rice Street, Edmundston, New Brunswick, E3V 1T4 **Tel** *(506) 739 7321* **Fax** *(506) 735 9101* **Rooms** *102*

The Clarion Hotel, "where every client is King", works hard to uphold this motto. It is also the only hotel downtown. Check out its special promotions, including great winter ski packages. Linked to the Carrefour Assomption shopping center, there is no need to go outside. There is free access to a gym close by.

FREDERICTON Carriage House Inn

230 University Ave., Fredericton, New Brunswick, E3B 4H7 **Tel** *(506) 452 9924* **Fax** *(506) 452 2770* **Rooms** *10*

The Carriage House Inn is a Victorian Queen Anne style mansion built in 1875. Hearty and delicious breakfasts are served in the elegant ballroom filled with interesting antiques. The owners have a very impressive collection of art that graces the walls. Close by are city attractions and the beautiful St. John River. **www.carriagehouse-inn.net**

GARDNER CREEK Moore's Specialties Tourist Home and Gallery

1254 Route 825, Gardner Creek, New Brunswick, E2S 2B2 **Tel** *(506) 696 4722* **Rooms** *3*

In a country setting with spectacular sunrises and sunsets overlooking the Bay of Fundy, this homestead with antiques, large verandas, and gardens is run by an artist who has painted murals throughout the home. Guests are allowed to use the kitchen and laundry facilities. The beach is within walking distance. **www.sjnow.com/moores**

GRAND TRACADIE Dalvay-By-the-Sea

Dalvay, Prince Edward Island, C0A 1P0 **Tel** *(902) 672 2048* **Rooms** *26*

Located at the east end of Prince Edward Island National Park, Dalvay-By-the-Sea offers a unique Maritime experience. Enjoy miles of beach and acres of manicured grounds. You can indulge in biking, picnics, canoeing, kayaking, and more. Staff go out of their way to help. **www.dalvaybythesea.com**

HALIFAX Halifax Waverley Inn

1266 Barrington Street, Halifax, Nova Scotia, B3J 1Y5 **Tel** *(902) 423 9346* **Fax** *(902) 425 0167* **Rooms** *34*

This bed & breakfast-style inn offers European-style canopies, feather beds, large Jacuzzi baths, and fluffy robes. Other pleasant surprises include antiques, free parking, Internet access, a delicious hot breakfast buffet, evening tea, coffee, and snacks. A historic building in an ideal downtown location. **www.waverleyinn.com**

HALIFAX Westin Nova Scotian

1181 Hollis Street, Halifax, Nova Scotia, B3H 2P6 **Tel** *(902) 421 1000* **Fax** *(902) 422 9465* **Rooms** *297*

This grand dame, built in 1930, is one of the first great CN railroad hotels. Guests' expectations are usually exceeded and it has won many awards. A live theater, museums, water tours, and nightlife are all within a short walk. Pets are welcome and also spoiled. Completely non-smoking. **www.westin.ns.ca**

INGONISH BEACH Keltic Lodge

383 Keltic Inn Road, Ingonish Beach, Nova Scotia, B0C 1L0 **Tel** *(902) 285 2880* **Fax** *(902) 285 2859* **Rooms** *105*

Set high on a cliff overlooking the Atlantic Ocean, the view here is breathtaking. This resort offers a spacious main lodge, a unique inn, and cozy upscale cottages. On site or nearby are tennis courts, a world class golf course, and wilderness trails. The Purple Thistle Dining room specializes in seafood delicacies. Breakfast and dinner included. **www.kelticlodge.ca**

LOUISBOURG Cranberry Cove Inn

12 Wolfe Street, Louisbourg, Nova Scotia, B1C 2J2 **Tel** *(902) 733 2171* **Rooms** *7*

Ideally located overlooking the harbor and only a ten-minute walk to world famous Fortress Louisbourg. Rooms at the inn are themed. If you stay in the Captain's Den, you will feel as if you are aboard an old time vessel. The food is superb and the staff friendly. **www.cranberrycoveinn.com**

LUNENBURG Lunenburg Inn

26 Dufferin Street, Lunenburg, Nova Scotia, B0J 2C0 **Tel** *(902) 634 3963* **Fax** *(902) 634 9419* **Rooms** *7*

This registered heritage property (Victorian building circa 1893) features a prominent tower. It is renowned for its attentive (but not intrusive) hospitality and exceptional breakfasts. Lunenburg is a UNESCO world heritage site and the inn is in a prime location. **www.lunenburginn.com**

MARGAREE VALLEY Normaway Inn and Cabins

P.O. Box 100, Margaree Valley, Nova Scotia, B0E 2C0 **Tel** *(902) 248 2987* **Fax** *(902) 248 2600* **Rooms** *29*

In an idyllic setting, this handsome lodge has tasteful cabins. A sunny dining room offers superb regional fare. The innkeeper is happy to help guests discover the magic of Cape Breton. There are tennis courts and bike rentals on site and a Weekly Three Fiddler Concert, Ceilidh, and Dance in the Blue Barn. **www.normaway.com**

MILL RIVER Rodd Mill River Resort

Woodstock, O'Leary, Prince Edward Island, C0B 1V0 **Tel** *(902) 859 3555* **Fax** *(902) 859 2486* **Rooms** *90*

Rodd Mill River is one of Canada's best golf resorts, ranking among the top 50 in Canada. Located within Mill River Provincial Park, it's an easy drive to Summerside and the Confederation Bridge. Canoe, kayak, bike, swim, windsurf, or play squash and tennis. Professional spa services. This place is tops. **www.roddvacations.com/**

MONCTON Crowne Plaza Hotels and Resorts

1005 Main Street, Moncton, New Brunswick, E1C 1G9 **Tel** *(506) 854 6340* **Fax** *(506) 382 8923* **Rooms** *191*

This is a landmark hotel in the heart of Moncton. Newly renovated guest rooms showcase the Sleep Advantage™ program with luxurious seven-layer bedding. There is free Internet and local phone calls are free. There is a cutting-edge fitness room and an exclusive saltwater pool. **www.cpmoncton.com**

NEW GLASGOW New Glasgow Inn

5673 Highway 13, New Glasgow, Prince Edward Island, C0A 1N0 **Tel** *(902) 964 2315 or (877) 862 0270* **Rooms** *4*

New Glasgow Inn is located in a small village with huge attractions, including the famous New Glasgow Lobster Suppers, PEI Island Preserve Company, and superb golfing. The inn is a heritage home dating back to 1861. Breakfasts are so hearty you won't be eating lunch. Its central island location is another plus. **www.newglasgowinn.com**

ST. ANDREWS Rossmount Inn

4599 Route 127, St. Andrews by the Sea, New Brunswick, E5B 3S7 **Tel** *(506) 529 3351* **Rooms** *18*

Rossmount Inn is part of an 87 acre estate, which includes a beautiful interpretive nature walk to Chamcook Mountain with breathtaking vistas. An ideal place to rekindle your spirits. Meander through the large organic garden, enjoy superb dining, or just relax on the large covered veranda overlooking the bay. **www.rossmountinn.com**

ST. ANDREWS The Fairmont Algonquin Hotel

184 Adolphus Street, St. Andrews, New Brunswick, E5B 1T7 **Tel** *(506) 529 8823* **Fax** *(506) 529 7162* **Rooms** *234*

This Maritime gem provides a superb culinary experience, hospitality, and lush gardens. Situated in the Bay of Fundy, it is close to Kingsbrae Gardens. It combines true old world charm with modern luxury and has an award-winning seaside golf course. Off the beaten track but worth the drive. **www.fairmont.com/algonquin**

SAINT JOHN Inn On The Cove & Spa

1371 Sand Cove Road, Saint John, New Brunswick, E2M 4Z9 **Tel** *(506) 672 7799* **Rooms** *9*

In an oceanside setting next to the Irving Nature Park yet very near the city center, this inn's guest rooms overlook the world's highest tides. There is a full service spa and hair salon and fine dining in the Ocean Room (reservations required). The hosts are well known TV personalities and provide memorable dining experiences. **www.innonthecove.com**

Key to Price Guide *see p346* **Key to Symbols** *see back cover flap*

SUMMERSIDE Willowgreen Farm Bed and Breakfast Ⓟ Ⓢ

117 Bishop Drive, Summerside, Prince Edward Island, C1N 5Z8 **Tel** *(902) 436 4420* **Rooms** *8*

This spacious country homestead in a unique pastoral farm setting is only a short walk from the city center and waterfront activities. It has a friendly, relaxed atmosphere and interesting themed rooms. Breakfasts are good. **www.willowgreenfarm.com**

TATAMAGOUCHE Train Station Inn Ⓢ Ⓢ

21 Station Rd., Tatamagouche, Nova Scotia, B0K 1V0 **Tel** *(902) 657 3222* **Rooms** *10*

Step back in time and experience Nova Scotia's railroad heritage brought to life in this award-winning country inn. Sleep in your own private railroad car that features a king-sized bed and fireplace. Evening meals served in 1928 dining car. Unusual experience! Train station itself houses guest rooms and unique museum café. **www.trainstation.ca**

WOLFVILLE Tattingstone Inn Ⓢ Ⓢ Ⓢ

620 Main St., Wolfville, Nova Scotia, B4P 1E8 **Tel** *(902) 542 7696* **Fax** *(902) 542 4427* **Rooms** *10*

This Designated Historical Property started life as the mansion of an apple baron; later it belonged to an architect. Guest rooms are tastefully decorated with period furniture, and there is wireless Internet throughout. Activities such as bird-watching, hiking and bicycling can be arranged by the front desk. Breakfast included. **www.tattingstone.ns.ca**

YARMOUTH MacKinnon-Cann Historic Inn Ⓢ Ⓢ Ⓢ

27 Willow Street, Yarmouth, Nova Scotia, B5A 1V2 **Tel** *(902) 742 9900* **Fax** *(902) 742 0326* **Rooms** *7*

Beautifully restored Italianate Victorian home (around 1887) located in the heart of the town's historic district, close to downtown. Guest rooms have decade themes, starting with the 1900s through to the 1960s. The interior is exquisite. Fun, entertaining, and thoughtful hosts. Delicious breakfasts, superb dinners. **www.mackinnoncanninn.com**

MONTREAL

CHINATOWN Holiday Inn Select Montréal Centre-Ville Ⓢ Ⓢ Ⓢ

99 Ave. Viger Ouest, H2Z 1E9 **Tel** *(514) 878 9888 or (888) 878 9888* **Fax** *(514) 878 6341* **Rooms** *235*

Two rooftop pagodas mean this modern hotel blends seamlessly into the cityscape. This member of the well-known chain offers an on-site fitness center, indoor pool, sauna, and whirlpool so you can relax after exploring the city. The lobby's miniature pond, pretty Chinese gardens, and the Chez Chine restaurant welcome you. **www.holidayinn.com**

DOWNTOWN Auberge de Paris Ⓢ

901 Rue Sherbrooke Est, H2L 1L3 **Tel** *(514) 522 6124 or (866) 266 5514* **Fax** *(514) 522 1387* **Rooms** *39*

This copper-roofed old graystone building with fanciful turret is a short walk from the nightlife of Rue St. Denis. The rooms are comfortable and the women's-only dorm has private bathrooms. There is an on-site free wireless Internet and computer workstation and a fully licensed bistro. **www.aubergemontreal.com**

DOWNTOWN Hôtel Viger Ⓢ

1001 Rue Saint-Hubert, H2L 3Y3 **Tel** *(514) 845 6058 or (800) 845 6058* **Fax** *(514) 844 6068* **Rooms** *21*

Tried and true, simple formula of clean, possibly unimaginative rooms all with private bath and television mean inexpensive rates at this Victorian hotel. Well known because of its good value, it is adjacent to Old (Vieux-) Montréal and Chinatown, close to Mont-Royal, and the Metro (subway) system. Rates include continental breakfast. **www.hotel-viger.com**

DOWNTOWN Residence Inn Ⓢ Ⓢ

2170 Lincoln Ave., H3H 2N5 **Tel** *(514) 935 9224* **Fax** *(514) 935 5049* **Rooms** *218*

Located just a few minutes' walk west of Montreal's entertainment district, the Residence Inn aims to be a "home away from home". All rooms, from studios to one- or two-bed apartments, have fully fitted kitchenettes and a dining/working area. There's high-speed Internet access and a breakfast buffet. **www.residencemontreal.com**

DOWNTOWN Delta Montreal Ⓢ Ⓢ Ⓢ

475 Ave. President Kennedy, H3A 1J7 **Tel** *(514) 286 1986 or (877) 286 1986* **Fax** *(514) 284 4306* **Rooms** *456*

Within walking distance of McGill University, Place des Arts, and trendy downtown shops, this grand, high-rise modern hotel also features an on-site spa, fitness center, and large indoor pool. Rooms are spacious, some with great views of the sprawling city and Mont Royal. The lobby is decorated with works by local artists. **www.deltamontreal.com**

DOWNTOWN Hôtel Château & Meridien Versailles Ⓢ Ⓢ Ⓢ

1659 Rue Sherbrooke Ouest, H3H 1E3 **Tel** *(514) 933 8111 or (888) 933 8111* **Fax** *(514) 933 6967* **Rooms** *181*

Located on what was Canada's "Fifth Avenue," this hotel is near chic galleries and stores. It consists of four distinguished residences owned by the likes of James Seath-Smith, architect, art collector, and owner of Montréal's first automobile. Today's luxury boutique hotel offers romantic packages. Award-winning French restaurant. **www.versailleshotels.com**

DOWNTOWN Hôtel du Fort Ⓢ Ⓢ Ⓢ

1390 Rue du Fort, H3H 2R7 **Tel** *(514) 938 8333 or (800) 565 6333* **Rooms** *124*

There is no on-site restaurant at the Hôtel du Fort, but Café Suprême in the lobby offers coffee and tea, and an elegant continental breakfast (not included in the room rate) is served daily in Louis XV Club Lounge (free for children under 5). Kitchenettes, available in well-lit spacious rooms, means this is a good choice for families. **www.hoteldufort.com**

DOWNTOWN L'Hôtel de la Montagne

1430 Rue de la Montagne, H3G 1Z5 **Tel** *(514) 288 5656 or (800) 361 6262* **Rooms** *135*

Richly decorated "belle époque" luxury hotel. You can select from several bars and restaurants, including Terrasse Magnétic rooftop terrace on the 20th floor, featuring panoramic views of the city. Les Beaux Jeudis restaurant offers jazz every Saturday while on Tuesdays you can enjoy the traditional all-you-can-eat leg of lamb. **www.hoteldelamontagne.com**

DOWNTOWN Le Nouvel Hôtel

1740 René Lévesque W., H3H 1R3 **Tel** *(514) 931 8841 or (800) 363 6063* **Fax** *(514) 931 5581* **Rooms** *171*

This hotel has elegant, bright rooms, tastefully appointed to maximize relaxation, some featuring old brick walls. It has an on-site Spa Tais and fitness room. Forty studios have kitchenettes so you can buy farm-fresh goodies at Atwater Market and create your own meals. **www.lenouvelhotel.com**

DOWNTOWN Marriott Residence Inn

2045 Rue Peel, H3A 1T6 **Tel** *(514) 982 6064 or (888) 999 9494* **Fax** *(514) 844 8361* **Rooms** *190*

Suites at this hotel are large and all have kitchenettes. There is a library with a fireplace. The "Hearth Room" offers a comfortable seating area where you can meet friends while enjoying a complimentary evening snack (Mondays through Thursdays only) such as nachos or a bowl of soup. **www.residenceinn-mtl.com**

DOWNTOWN Ritz-Carlton Montréal

1228 Rue Sherbrooke Ouest, H3G 1H6 **Tel** *(514) 842 4212 or (800) 363 0366* **Fax** *(514) 842 3383* **Rooms** *231*

Classic and classy, this oh-so-chic Edwardian "Grande Dame" was Richard Burton and Elizabeth Taylor's choice for one of their two weddings. Nestled beside Mont-Royal, in summer it makes a perfect choice for al fresco meals at Le Jardin du Ritz, a renowned urban garden. If nothing else, indulge in tea in the garden or at Café de Paris. **www.ritzmontreal.com**

DOWNTOWN Fairmont La Reine Elizabeth

900 René Lévesque W., H3B 4A5 **Tel** *(514) 861 3511* **Fax** *(514) 954 2296* **Rooms** *1039*

Situated downtown near the VIA rail station and the heart of the business area, the Fairmont has a distinguished charm and elegance from rooms through to lobby. Famous politicians and celebrities dine at chic The Beaver Club. You can reserve seasonal activities including skiing, river rafting, golf, and tennis through the concierge. **www.fairmont.com**

DOWNTOWN Loews Hotel Vogue

1425 Rue de la Montagne, H3G 1Z3 **Tel** *(514) 285 5555 or (800) 465 6654* **Fax** *(514) 849 8903* **Rooms** *142*

Priding itself on being child and pet friendly, the Vogue caters to your family's needs. Games, kid's menus, and VIT (Very Important Teen) treatment. This includes a library of DVDs, Gameboys, and more. Pet services include a pamphlet containing local dog walks or a kitty litter (extra charge applies). **www.loewshotels.com**

DOWNTOWN Marriott Château Champlain

1 Place du Canada, H3B 4C9 **Tel** *(514) 878 9000 or (800) 200 5909* **Fax** *(514) 878 6761* **Rooms** *611*

Close to shopping districts, a few steps from Old (Vieux-) Montréal, this tall white tower with arch-shaped windows has excellent views of Mont-Royal and the harbor on the St. Lawrence River. When you reserve specify whether you are bringing children, because some activities require reservations. **www.montrealchateauchamplain.com**

DOWNTOWN Montreal Bonaventure Hilton

900 de La Gauchetiere W., H5A 1E4 **Tel** *(514) 878 2332 or (800) 267 2575* **Fax** *(514) 878 3881* **Rooms** *395*

Built around a garden complete with ducks playing in a pool and an outside swimming pool open year-round, this Hilton is located over the Place Bonaventure exhibition halls. Each room has windows that open to let in fresh air. Connects to Montréal's Underground City shopping concourse. **www.hiltonmontreal.com**

DOWNTOWN Omni Mont-Royal

1050 Rue Sherbrooke Ouest, H3A 2R6 **Tel** *(514) 284 1110 or (800) 444 6664* **Fax** *(514) 845 3025* **Rooms** *299*

This first-class luxury hotel including heated pool, Amerispa, and large fitness centre (featuring dry sauna, steam room, and whirlpool) means you can enjoy resort living right downtown. Children become part of the Omni Sensational Kids program which includes a suitcase filled with games and books. Pets (under 25 lb) permitted. **www.omnihotels.com**

PLATEAU MONT-ROYAL Auberge de la Fontaine

1301 Rue Rachel Est, H2J 2K1 **Tel** *(514) 597 0166 or (800) 597 0597* **Fax** *(514) 597 0496* **Rooms** *21*

An open kitchen downstairs allows guests to help themselves to snacks, cookies, cheeses, and patés daily until midnight. This boutique hotel comprises two Second-Empire homes converted into a stylish, eccentrically decorated hotel. Some rooms overlook Parc La Fontaine. **www.aubergedelafontaine.com**

PLATEAU MONT-ROYAL Le Jardin d'Antoine

2024 Rue St-Denis, H2X 3K7 **Tel** *(514) 843 4506 or (800) 361 4506* **Fax** *(514) 281 1491* **Rooms** *25*

Find extra tranquility in deluxe rooms overlooking the small interior courtyard garden at the rear of this charming old home converted into a comfortable inn. All rooms are bright and airy, some have jacuzzis. A complimentary deluxe continental breakfast includes freshly made croissants. **www.hotel-jardin-antoine.qc.ca**

VIEUX-MONTREAL Auberge du Vieux-Port

97 Rue de la Commune Est, H2Y 1J1 **Tel** *(514) 876 0081 or (888) 660 7678* **Fax** *(514) 876 8923* **Rooms** *27*

Enjoy beverages on the roof terrace which overlooks the park lands, bike paths, as well as the boats and activities that make the Vieux Port an active, fun place to visit. Elegant, old-fashioned rooms feature hardwood floors and cut-stone walls. There is a prize-winning dining room – Narcisse Bistro-Wine Bar. **www.aubergeduvieuxport.com**

Key to Price Guide *see p346* **Key to Symbols** *see back cover flap*

VIEUX-MONTREAL Auberge les Passants du Sans Soucy

171 Rue Saint-Paul Ouest, H2Y 1Z5 **Tel** *(514) 842 2634* **Fax** *(514) 842 2912* **Rooms** *6*

This 1723 B&B in Vieux-Montreal contrasts lace curtains against cut stone and polished hardwood floors. The lobby serves as a gallery promoting local artists. Owners transformed this old warehouse by purchasing and installing European and Quebec antiques. Superb breakfast. Owners spin wonderful tales of the city. **www.lesanssoucy.com**

VIEUX-MONTREAL Hôtel Gault

449 Rue Saint-Hélène, H2Y 2K9 **Tel** *(514) 904 1616 or (866) 904 1616* **Fax** *(514) 904 1717* **Rooms** *30*

Enter this light-flooded boutique hotel where exemplary service matches contemporary design. Every room is uniquely interpreted but each has a flat-screen TV and bathroom with heated concrete floor. The Gault restaurant offers excellent meals. The lobby features an inviting recessed library where you can curl up with a book. **www.hotelgault.com**

VIEUX-MONTREAL Hostellerie Pierre du Calvet AD 1725

405 Rue Bonsecours, H2Y 3C3 **Tel** *(514) 282 1725 or (866) 544 1725* **Fax** *(514) 282 0456* **Rooms** *9*

There is opulent luxury in this 1725 merchant's house, now a boutique hotel. Fireplaces, oak paneling, and deep window seats let you slip back in time as horses trot past on the cobblestone streets of Vieux-Montréal. Breakfast is served in the atrium where parrots entertain with their antics. There are two superb restaurants. **www.pierreducalvet.ca**

VIEUX-MONTREAL Hôtel Inter-Continental Montréal

360 Rue Saint-Antoine Ouest, H2Y 3X4 **Tel** *(514) 987 9900 or (888) 424 6835* **Fax** *(514) 847 8550* **Rooms** *357*

This elegant, modern, high-rise hotel has fitness facilities that feature a lap pool, sauna, and massage services, making this a good choice for a "resort" hotel in the heart of Montreal's financial, shopping, and entertainment district. Babysitting services are also available. **www.intercontinental.com**

VIEUX-MONTREAL Hôtel Saint Paul

355 Rue McGill, H2Y 2E8 **Tel** *(514) 380 2222 or (866) 380 2202* **Fax** *(514) 380 2200* **Rooms** *120*

Described architecturally as "muscular Beaux Arts," this former bank enjoys new life as an award-winning boutique hotel where Canada's four elements of ice, fire, earth, and sky have been whimsically interpreted. Every chic room is eclectically furnished using such finishings as stone and silk, with heated tile floors in bathrooms. **www.hotelstpaul.com**

VIEUX-MONTREAL Hôtel le Saint James

355 St. Jaques, H2Y 1N9 **Tel** *(514) 841 3111 or (866) 841 3111* **Fax** *(514) 841 1232* **Rooms** *60*

The romanesque arched doorway sets a grand tone for this 1870 former bank where every sumptuously decorated room has a unique personality. A sweeping wrought-iron staircase leads from a balconied mezzanine to the Grand Salon restaurant which serves Quebec regional cuisine. There is an on-site spa. **www.hotellestjames.com**

QUEBEC CITY AND THE ST. LAWRENCE RIVER

BAIE SAINT-PAUL Auberge La Muse

39 Rue Saint-Jean-Baptiste, G3Z 1M3 **Tel** *(418) 435 6839 or (800) 841 6839* **Fax** *(418) 435 6289* **Rooms** *15*

This 1881 Victorian inn and spa with a secluded garden at the back is an oasis from the vibrant art galleries and stores. Well known as a health retreat, you can enjoy a rejuvenating massage and the restaurant's deservedly renowned haute cuisine. There are many packages and six styles of rooms, from "economic" to luxurious. **www.lamuse.com**

BAIE SAINT-PAUL Auberge La Maison Otis

23 Rue Saint-Jean-Baptiste, G3Z 1M2 **Tel** *(418) 435 2255 or (800) 267 2254* **Fax** *(418) 435 2464* **Rooms** *30*

Located in Quebec's stunningly spectacular Charlevoix region, this country-style inn features a superb restaurant – every first Thursday of the month a new artist is celebrated in the Café des Artistes. Salmon fishing, fly fishing, golf, and downhill skiing are nearby. **www.maisonotis.com**

COTE NORD Hôtel Tadoussac

165 Bord-de-l'Eau, Tadoussac, G0T 2A0 **Tel** *(418) 235 4421 or (800) 561 0718* **Fax** *(418) 235 4607* **Rooms** *149*

With its white clapboard façade and Mansard style, cherry-red roof, this hotel built in 1942 by Canada Steamships is a historic landmark overlooking the St. Lawrence River at the Saguenay River. Take binoculars as the area is famous for whale spotting. Tennis on-site. Closed Oct–May. **www.hoteltadoussac.com**

GASPE La Gîte du Mont-Albert

2001 Route du Parc, Sainte-Anne-des-Monts, G4V 2E4 **Tel** *(418) 763 2288 or (866) 727 2427* **Rooms** *60*

Resembling a hunting lodge, this rustic-looking inn is in the stunning Chic-Choc Mountains. Stay at the resort, lodge, or rent a cabin. Look for wildlife such as white-tailed deer and ask about caribou that eat the alpine tundra vegetation here. Varied open times (some cabins are open year-round for skiing, so check availability). **www.sepaq.com**

ÎLES-DE-LA-MADELEINE Hôtel au Vieux Convent

292 route 199, Havre-aux-Maisons, G4T 5A4 **Tel** *(418) 969 2233* **Fax** *(418) 969 4693* **Rooms** *10*

The old convent is a dominant stone landmark with the former dormitories converted into ocean-view rooms. The adjacent presbytery offers six apartments, some accommodating up to six people – good for families visiting these sandy islands. Excellent on-site seafood restaurant. Closed Jan–Mar. **www.domaineduvieuxcouvent.com**

LA MALBAIE Auberge and Restaurant Sur la Côte   ⅢⅠ P   ⑤⑤⑤⑤

205 chemin des Falaises, G5A 1T7 **Tel** *(418) 665 3972 or (800) 853 3972* **Fax** *(418) 665 3231* **Rooms** *11*

Find seclusion in this country hillside manor overlooking the spectacular St. Lawrence River. On a summer's eve watch the sunset while sipping drinks on the patio. Some rooms have fireplaces and there are river views. An on-site restaurant offers gastronomie based on Charlevoix foods. Meals included. Chalets available. **www.charlevoix.qc.ca/surlacote**

LA MALBAIE Manoir Richelieu   📺 Ⅲ ≋ 🏄 🍽 🗐 P   ⑤⑤⑤⑤

181 Rue Richelieu, G5A 1X7 **Tel** *(418) 665 3703 or (866) 540 4464* **Fax** *(418) 665 8131* **Rooms** *405*

Resembling a stone castle complete with turrets, this famous hotel perches on a cliff surrounded by gardens overlooking the St. Lawrence River estuary. As in all Fairmont hotels, with advanced notice your pet dog or cat is welcome. Stroll the beach nearby, bike along pathways, or play golf at heritage courses. **www.fairmont.com**

LAC-SAINT-JEAN Hôtel du Jardin   📺 Ⅲ ≋ 🍽 🗐 P   ⑤⑤

1400 Blvd. du Jardin, Saint-Felicien, G8K 2N8 **Tel** *(418) 679 8422 or (800) 463 4927* **Fax** *(418) 679 4459* **Rooms** *85*

This comfortable modern hotel with spacious rooms (some with whirlpool baths) is mere yards from the "Véloroute des bleuets" (Blueberry bike path) so it makes an excellent base from which to explore Lac-Saint-Jean. You can get a massage at the on-site massage center, Le Jardin d'Ô. **www.hoteldujardin.com**

L'ÎLE VERT (NEAR RIVIERE-DU-LOUP) Les Maisons du Phare de l'Île Verte   ⑤

28, Chemin du Phare, G0L 1K0 **Tel** *(418) 898 2730* **Fax** *(418) 898 4002* **Rooms** *8*

The rooms are simple in these two lighthousekeeper's buildings adjacent to a lighthouse. Breakfast is included, but bring groceries to prepare your lunch/dinner (there is a kitchen in the main building). Bikes and cars are prohibited. Payment is by Visa or cash only (there is no ATM on the island). Closed Nov–mid-May. **www.ileverte.net/maisonsduphare**

NEW RICHMOND (GASPE) Auberge Maison Stanley House Inn   P   ⑤

371 Perron Ouest, G0C 2B0 **Tel** *(418) 392 5560* **Fax** *(418) 392 5592* **Rooms** *11*

Formerly the fishing and hunting lodge of Canadian Governor-General Lord Stanley (who gave his name to the coveted Stanley Cup hockey award), this gracious estate home has a private beach overlooking the Atlantic Ocean. It has large lawns. Rooms are comfortably appointed in country-style furnishings. Closed Oct–May. **www.stanleyhouse.ca**

PERCE Hotel-Motel La Normandie   ⅢⅠ P   ⑤⑤⑤

221 Route 132 West, Percé G0C 2L0 **Tel** *(418) 782 2112 or (800) 463 0820* **Fax** *(418) 782 2337* **Rooms** *45*

Absorb breathtaking views of the ocean at this white clapboard inn overlooking local landmark, the Rocher Percé. In summer, sit on deck chairs placed on lawns stretching down to the sea. There are beautiful perennial gardens. The on-site fine seafood restaurant is open for breakfast and dinner only. Closed Oct–May. **www.normandieperce.com**

QUEBEC CITY Hôtel Particulier Belley   ⑤⑤

249 Rue Saint-Paul, G1K 3W5 **Tel** *(418) 692 1694 or (888) 692 1694* **Fax** *(418) 692 1696* **Rooms** *8*

This former tavern shelters beneath the old fortifications of the city, located next to the Marché du Vieux-Port, many antique stores, galleries, and museums. Along with the individually decorated small rooms, families/friends should ask about the small "conciergerie," a suite where up to four can stay for a monthly rental. **http://membre.oricom.ca/belley**

QUEBEC CITY Hôtel Clarendon   📺 Ⅲ 🍽 🗐 P   ⑤⑤⑤

57 Rue Sainte-Anne, G1R 3X4 **Tel** *(418) 692 2480 or (800) 222 3304* **Fax** *(418) 692 4652* **Rooms** *143*

After strolling Quebec City's cobblestone streets, step into old-fashioned luxury in this 1870 heritage hotel. Eavesdrop on Quebec news: this is a popular hangout for politicians, perhaps because Quebec's Premier lives in the adjacent Price Building when parliament is in session. **www.hotelclarendon.com**

QUEBEC CITY Le Priori   📺 Ⅲ 🗐   ⑤⑤⑤

15 Rue Sault-au-Matelot, G1K 3Y7 **Tel** *(418) 692 3992 or (800) 351 3992* **Fax** *(418) 692 0883* **Rooms** *21*

Stay in the former heritage residence of architect Jean Baillairgé, who designed many of Quebec City's religious edifices. This boutique hotel features intriguing rooms where contemporary furniture and art juxtaposes with walls of rough-cut stone. Located at the foot of Cap Diamant, it is a short walk to lively stores and galleries. **www.hotellepriori.com**

QUEBEC CITY Château Frontenac   📺 Ⅲ ≋ 🏄 🍽 🗐 P   ⑤⑤⑤⑤⑤

1 Rue des Carrières, G1R 4P5 **Tel** *(866) 540 4460* **Fax** *(418) 692 1751* **Rooms** *618*

Known as the castle on the cliff in the heart of old Quebec City, the baronial style exterior of this impressive landmark (*see p134*) is reflected inside with broad hallways and detailed stone-work. Rooms overlooking the St. Lawrence River offer magnificent views. Stroll Dufferin Terrace overlooking the river then retreat to the cozy bar. **www.fairmont.com**

RIVIERE-DU-LOUP Hôtel Levesque   Ⅲ ≋ 🏄 🗐 P   ⑤⑤

171 Fraser, G5R 1E2 **Tel** *(418) 862 6927 or (800) 463 1236* **Fax** *(418) 862 5385* **Rooms** *83*

Located on the St. Lawrence River's south shore, this hotel is ideal if you seek pampering. A waterfall courses through the tranquil gardens, which gently descend to the river. Many suites have whirlpools for further relaxation after spa treatments. The four-course "discovery menu" where regional foods are highlighted. **www.hotellevesque.com**

SEPT-ÎLES Hôtel Sept-Îles   Ⅲ 🍽   ⑤

451 Ave. Arnaud, G4R 3B3 **Tel** *(418) 962 2581 or (800) 463 1753* **Fax** *(418) 962 6918* **Rooms** *91*

Now a glorified three-storey motel, the bayside hotel has balconies overlooking the islands. Modernized rooms offer basic accommodations and there is an on-site fitness center for work-outs. The restaurant is open for breakfast only. **www.hotelseptiles.com**

Key to Price Guide *see p346* **Key to Symbols** *see back cover flap*

TROIS-RIVIÈRES Delta Trois-Rivières

1620 Rue Notre-Dame, G9A 6E5 **Tel** *(819) 376 1991 or (888) 890 3222* **Fax** *(819) 372 5975* **Rooms** *159*

This modern high-rise hotel overlooking the St. Lawrence River has an on-site health spa, steam room, sauna, and fitness center. Families welcome: kids can enjoy the pool as well as a Sunday breakfast buffet. Small pets are permitted – advise you are bringing an animal when reserving. **www.deltahotels.com**

SOUTHERN AND NORTHERN QUEBEC

GATINEAU Auberge de la Gare

205 Blvd. Saint-Joseph, J8Y 3X3 **Tel** *(819) 778 8085 or (800) 778 8085* **Rooms** *42*

Located in old Hull (Gatineau) this postmodern boutique hotel packs no pretensions yet offers courteous service and rooms that are extra quiet because of special construction considerations. Family packages available. Conveniently located near bridge to Ottawa, bike paths to Gatineau Park, museums, and restaurants. **www.aubergedelagare.ca**

LAURENTIAN MOUNTAINS Hotel La Sapinière

1244 Chemin La Sapinière, Val-David J0T 2N0 **Tel** *(819) 322 2020* **Fax** *(819) 322 6510* **Rooms** *68*

The beautiful lakeside setting of this award-winning hotel coupled with its excellent facilities make it a popular getaway. Past guests have included Norwegian royalty and G7 and NATO conference attendees. The fine dining here is complemented by an extensive wine cellar, boasting some 370 different wines. **www.sapiniere.com**

LAURENTIAN MOUNTAINS Auberge de la Montagne-Coupée

1000 Chemin Montagne-Coupée, Saint-Jean-de-Matha, J0K 2S0 **Tel** *(450) 886 3891* **Fax** *(450) 886 5401* **Rooms** *47*

With rates that include breakfast and dinner, this comfortable auberge is good value. Its name means "cut mountain" because of a piece of rock that slipped from the face of the mountain that the inn overlooks. There is a health spa, fine regional dining, and near trails for cross-country skiing, and hiking. **www.montagnecoupee.com**

LAURENTIAN MOUNTAINS Château Mont-Tremblant

3045 de la Chapelle, J8E 1E1 **Tel** *(819) 681 7000 or (866) 540 4415* **Fax** *(819) 681 7099* **Rooms** *314*

Luxury in the Laurentian mountains. Comfort and elegance await you after your ski or mountain bike experience on Mont Tremblant's trail network. Luxuriate in the spa. Enjoy artwork depicting Quebec legends as well as Canadian wildlife such as moose and bear. Superb restaurants serve delicious Fairmont brunches and regional fare. **www.fairmont.com**

MAGOG Auberge l'Étoile sur le Lac

1200 Principale Ouest, J1X 2B8 **Tel** *(819) 843 6521 or (800) 567 2727* **Fax** *(819) 843 5007* **Rooms** *52*

The only inn on the lake, this postmodern style hotel has many rooms with balconies overlooking pretty Lac Memphremagog. During summer, meals are served on the lakeside terrace. It is situated close to the village of Magog for stores, pubs, and restaurants. There are on-site spa facilities. **www.etoile-sur-le-lac.com**

NORTH HATLEY Hovey Manor

575 chemin Hovey, J0B 2C0 **Tel** *(819) 842 2421 or (800) 661 2421* **Fax** *(819) 842 2248* **Rooms** *41*

This charming, romantic, historic inn is modeled on George Washington's Virginia home. Beautiful grounds overlook a lake with beaches. Rates include kayaks, canoes, paddleboats, and windsurfers. In winter sleigh rides, a skating rink, and ice fishing are available. There is an Aveda spa. Many rooms feature fireplaces and four-poster beds. **www.hoveymanor.com**

NUNAVIK Auberge Kuujjuaq

Kuujjuaq, J0M 1C0 **Tel** *(819) 964 2903* **Fax** *(819) 964 2031* **Rooms** *22*

The beautiful, elemental tundra wilderness of northern Quebec can be explored from this small lodge with restaurant featuring game and fresh-caught wild fish. Lodging in Quebec's far north is scarce, hence competitive and expensive so reserve well ahead for a comfortable, basic room with private bath and television – these are luxuries in the North.

OUTAOUAIS Château Montebello

392 Rue Notre-Dame, Montebello, J0V 1L0 **Tel** *(819) 423 6341 or (866) 540 4462* **Fax** *(819) 423 1133* **Rooms** *211*

The largest log hotel in the world stands on the shores of the Ottawa River. The six-sided fireplace is a perfect gathering spot for a scotch before a dinner of exquisite local cuisine. Sister property, Kenauk, has 4-star chalets on remote lakes. Horseback riding, skiing, and cross-country skiing trails conspire to make your stay memorable. **www.fairmont.com**

RICHELIEU VALLEY Hostellerie Les Trois Tilleuls

290 Rue Richelieu, St-Marc-sur-Richelieu, J0L 2E0 **Tel** *(514) 856 7787 or (800) 263 2230* **Fax** *(450) 584 3146* **Rooms** *41*

Luxurious Château & Relais auberge borders the historic Richelieu River. Every room has a balcony overlooking the water. There is an on-site Spa Givenchy, an art gallery, and beautiful gardens and walkways. Its restaurant is renowned for using the freshest regional produce. **www.lestroistilleuls.com**

ROUYN-NORANDA Hôtel Albert

84 Principale, J9X 4P2 **Tel** *(819) 762 3545 or (888) 725 2378* **Fax** *(819) 762 7157* **Rooms** *51*

With a completely unadorned façade, this old-fashioned downtown hotel built in the 1930s was renovated in 1997 and features large comfortable rooms with courteous service from friendly staff. Pets are allowed (please give advance notice). Located in the heart of the city, it is close to restaurants, stores, and pubs. **www.bestwestern.com**

TORONTO

AIRPORT Days Hotel & Conference Centre Toronto Airport East

$⑤⑤

1677 Wilson Avenue, M3L 1A5 **Tel** *(800) 267 0997 or (416) 249 8171* **Fax** *(416) 243 7342* **Rooms** *200*

This modern hotel for business leisure travel is near Pearson International Airport and the corners of major highways 400 & 401. It has friendly service, an airport shuttle service, and modern conference and banquet facilities. Rooms have data ports, high speed Internet access, and on-demand movies. Informal licensed restaurant. **www.daysto.com**

AIRPORT Hotel Indigo

⑤⑤

135 Carlingview Drive, M9W 5E7 **Tel** *(416) 637 7000* **Fax** *(416) 637 7001* **Rooms** *120*

A modern hotel across from the airport, close to major highways, with easy access to downtown Toronto. There is an airport shuttle service, indoor pool, whirlpool, meeting/event space, full catering services, restaurant, and lounge. Business services include wi-fi Internet access, business center, and a free local fax number. **www.hotelindigo.com**

AIRPORT Delta Toronto Airport West

$⑤⑤⑤

5444 Dixie Road, Mississauga, L4W 2L2 **Tel** *(905) 624 1144* **Fax** *(416) 675 4022* **Rooms** *297*

A large, modern, multi-story hotel, south of major highway 401, and close to major routes for easy access to downtown Toronto. Near the airport, the hotel caters primarily to corporate travelers, groups, and associations. Nearby attractions include corporate headquarters, shopping centers, theaters, and the Mississauga City Centre. **www.deltahotels.com**

AIRPORT Westin Bristol Place Toronto Airport

$⑤⑤⑤

950 Dixon Road, M9W 5N4 **Tel** *(416) 675 9444* **Fax** *(416) 675 4426* **Rooms** *288*

A business hotel with airport shuttle service. Rooms have fax/modem hook-ups and Internet access. There is an indoor pool and a restaurant, Zachary's Lounge. Close to major highways 401 and 427, downtown Toronto, the Woodbine Shopping Centre, and Paramount Canada's Wonderland amusement park. **www.westinbristolplace.com**

DOWNTOWN The Primrose Best Western Hotel

$⑤⑤

111 Carlton St., M5B 2G3 **Tel** *(416) 977 8000* **Fax** *(416) 977 6323* **Rooms** *335*

This hotel is situated in central downtown Toronto, with comfortable rooms and complimentary wireless Internet access. The Primrose Restaurant and Bar offers continental or breakfast buffets, and a full dinner menu. There is a seasonal swimming pool. **www.torontoprimrosehotel.com**

DOWNTOWN Delta Chelsea

$⑤⑤⑤

33 Gerrard Street, M5G 1Z4 **Tel** *(416) 595 1975* **Fax** *(416) 585 4375* **Rooms** *1590*

This entrally located hotel is within walking distance of the city's best shopping districts, world-class theaters, vibrant nightlife, and exciting attractions. It has three restaurants/lounges, an in-room spa service, and separate adult/family recreation facilities and pools, including "Corkscrew" – downtown Toronto's only indoor waterslide. **www.deltachelsea.com**

DOWNTOWN Hilton Toronto Hotel

$⑤⑤⑤

145 Richmond Street West, M5H 2L2 **Tel** *(416) 869 3456* **Fax** *(416) 869 3187* **Rooms** *600*

This modern 32-story hotel is situated near Queen's Park, trendy shopping on Queen Street West, the CN Tower, SkyDome, theaters, nightclubs, and the financial district. Rooms have cable TV, pay-per-view, a minibar, and high-speed Internet access. There are three restaurants, two bars, a pool, a fitness center, and multiple meeting rooms. **www.hilton.com**

DOWNTOWN Radisson Hotel Admiral

$⑤⑤⑤

249 Queen's Quay West, M5J 2N5 **Tel** *(800) 967 9182 or (416) 203 3333* **Fax** *(416) 203 3100* **Rooms** *157*

This waterfront hotel close to the CN Tower and Ontario Place has stunning views of the harbor and islands. As well as fitness and business centers and an outdoor pool, it has the award-winning Commodore's Restaurant and Bosun's Bar. **www.radisson.com/torontoca_admiral**

DOWNTOWN Strathcona Hotel

$⑤⑤⑤

60 York Street, M5J 1S8 **Tel** *(416) 363 3321* **Fax** *(416) 363 4679* **Rooms** *194*

This boutique hotel in downtown Toronto dating from 1945 has electronic locks and a 24-hour safety deposit. Corporate rooms include a desk, data ports, and high-speed wireless Internet access. Suites have a mini-fridge. There is access to the Wellington Club with full-service racquet and fitness clubs. There is no parking lot. **www.thestrathconahotel.com**

DOWNTOWN Le Royal Meridien King Edward

$⑤⑤⑤⑤

37 King Street East, M5C 1E9 **Tel** *(416) 863 9700* **Fax** *(416) 863 4102* **Rooms** *298*

The luxurious century-old 'King Eddy' has a Royal Club floor and offers Afternoon Tea. Visitors have included Rudyard Kipling, Mark Twain, and The Beatles. The architecture is French Renaissance style with marble columns, a lobby skylight, and sculptures. There is a spa and Internet access. **www.starwoodhotels.com/lemeridien**

DOWNTOWN Metropolitan Hotel

$⑤⑤⑤⑤

108 Chestnut Street, M5G 1R3 **Tel** *(416) 977 5000* **Fax** *(416) 977 9513* **Rooms** *422*

This spendidly located mid-range hotel in the financial and shopping district has elegant decor in muted shades, European linens, and windows that open. Eat at the modern Hemispheres restaurant or the luxurious Lai Wah Heen Asian restaurant. The dim sum here are said to be among the best in the city. **www.metropolitan.com**

Key to Price Guide *see p346* **Key to Symbols** *see back cover flap*

DOWNTOWN Sheraton Centre Toronto

123 Queen Street West, M5H 2M9 **Tel** *(416) 361 1000* **Fax** *(416) 947 4854* **Rooms** *1337*

In the center of the entertainment and business district, this hotel is close to shopping, theater, and restaurants, and connected to PATH – the 26-km (16-mile) underground complex of stores and services. Childcare available. There are a 43rd-floor Club Lounge and 24-hour room service. Pet friendly; provides dog beds. **www.starwoodhotels.com/sheraton**

DOWNTOWN Sutton Place Hotel

955 Bay Street, M5S 2A2 **Tel** *(416) 924 9221* **Fax** *(416) 924 1778* **Rooms** *294*

An elegant European-style downtown hotel that has original works of art and antiques. Amenities include the Relaxed Accents Restaurant & Bar, with continental cuisine; 10 function rooms; three ballrooms; residential apartments – La Grande Résidence; business center; indoor pool; sauna; beauty salon; and exercise room. **www.suttonplace.com**

DOWNTOWN The Fairmont Royal York

100 Front Street West, M5J 1E3 **Tel** *(416) 368 2511* **Fax** *(416) 368 9040* **Rooms** *1365*

A landmark luxury hotel across from Union Station, close to the harbor. It has 5 restaurants, 4 lounges, 24-hour room service, a Xerox Business Centre on the Lobby Level, and the Elizabeth Milan Spa. There is a 'Fairmont Gold' service with private check-in/check-out, concierge services, and exclusive lounge. Pet friendly. **www.fairmont.com/royalyork**

DOWNTOWN The Westin Harbour Castle

1 Harbour Square, M5J 1A6 **Tel** *(416) 869 1600* **Fax** *(416) 869 0573* **Rooms** *977*

A luxury waterfront hotel with twin towers, scenic views, two restaurants, and a glass-enclosed walkway to the conference center. Close to the financial and theater districts, it has a free local area shuttle service. There is a surcharge for multiline phones/Internet access. Outdoor tennis courts. **www.starwoodhotels.com/westin**

DOWNTOWN Four Seasons Hotel

21 Avenue Road, M5R 2G1 **Tel** *(416) 964 0411* **Fax** *(416) 964 2301* **Rooms** *380*

In the heart of Yorkville, Toronto's fashionable shopping, dining, and entertainment quarter, the Four Seasons has majestic chandeliers, high ceilings, wood paneling, a Regency Ballroom, panoramic views of the city from the 32nd floor, and full business servcies. Great for star-spotting during the Toronto Film Festival. **www.fourseasons.com**

DOWNTOWN Hyatt Regency

370 King Street West, M5V 1J9 **Tel** *(416) 343 1234* **Fax** *(416) 599 7394* **Rooms** *394*

An urban-chic hotel in the Entertainment District, next to the headquarters of the Toronto International Film Festival. The stylish design and cool ambience contribute to the hotel's sense of being a "social place," particularly in the trendy restaurant King Street Social Kitchen & Bar. The place to see and be seen. **www.hyattregencytoronto.com**

DOWNTOWN Windsor Arms Hotel

18 St. Thomas St., M5S 3E7 **Tel** *(416) 971 9666* **Fax** *(416) 921 9121* **Rooms** *28*

This neo-Gothic boutique hotel has a stone carved doorway and vestibule, mahogany furnishings, fireplaces, bathrooms with limestone floors/walls, and luxury suites with butler service. There is a Courtyard Cafe for fine dining, Tea Room for afternoon tea, Club 22 for casual dining, a spa, beauty salon, pool, and exercise facilities. **www.windsorarmshotel.com**

EAST END Delta Toronto East

2035 Kennedy Road, M1T 3G2 **Tel** *(416) 299 1500* **Fax** *(416) 299 8959* **Rooms** *371*

Near highway 401, with easy access to downtown, this hotel has a fitness center (24 hours), squash courts, indoor pool, Atrium with waterslide, and full business facilities. Restaurants include the Whitesides Terrace Grill, Sagano Japanese cuisine, and TW's Bar and Grill. Pets allowed. **www.deltahotels.com**

NORTH Delta Markham

50 East Valhalla Drive, L3R 0A3 **Tel** *(905) 477 2010* **Fax** *(905) 477 2026* **Rooms** *204*

The Delta Markham is a modern hotel in North York's hi-tech sector, in the north part of the Greater Toronto Area, and a 30-minute drive from the airport. It also provides convenient access to downtown Toronto. There is Internet access. Enjoy Sunday brunch at the Tivoli Garden Restaurant. **www.deltahotels.com**

NORTH Hilton Suites Toronto/Markham Conference Centre & Spa

8500 Warden Avenue, L6G 1A5 **Tel** *(905) 470 8500* **Fax** *(905) 477 8611* **Rooms** *500*

Located in the hi-tech area of Greater Toronto, the hotel caters to leisure, business, and convention travel. There are two-room suites with coffee/tea service, mini-bar/refrigerator, ironing boards/irons, hair dryers, and complimentary Internet access. Wheelchair accessible rooms are available. Three on-site restaurants. **www.hilton.com**

WEST END Drake Hotel

1150 Queen Street West, M6J 1J3 **Tel** *(416) 531 5042* **Fax** *(416) 531 9493* **Rooms** *19*

A historic (1890) establishment in Queen West Art and Design District, the Drake Hotel has a grand lobby staircase, mural that is over 60 years old, terrazzo floors dating back to the late 19th century, and exposed brick. Known as a Bohemian-inspired hotel designed for the local neighborhood. **www.thedrakehotel.ca**

WEST END Gladstone Hotel

1214 Queen Street West, M6J 1J6 **Tel** *(416) 531 4635* **Rooms** *37*

This unique 1889 landmark hotel has hardwood floors, high ceilings, exposed brick, and themed rooms – Teen Queen room, Skygazer Room – designed by a number of artists. Rooms include a large flat-screen TV with CD/DVD player, Internet access, and safety deposit box. Busy center for local art events. **www.gladstonehotel.com**

OTTAWA AND EASTERN ONTARIO

BROCKVILLE Quality Hotel & Conference Centre Royal Brock

100 Stewart Boulevard, Brockville, Ontario, K6V 4W3 **Tel** *(613) 345 1400* **Fax** *(613) 345 5402* **Rooms** *72*

In historic Brockville, 'City of the 1000 Islands', this hotel is close to highway 401, within walking distance of shopping, and an hour's drive to Ottawa. Among the many facilities are a sports club, indoor pool, hot tub, three squash courts, a business center and wireless Internet. **www.qualityhotelbrockville.com**

COBURG King George Inn & Spa

77 Albert Street, Cobourg, Ontario, K9A 2L9 **Tel** *(905) 373 9971* **Fax** *(905) 373 4514* **Rooms** *24*

A character inn built in 1906, the restaurant is in the former Jail's Administrative Office and the west buildings were former Jail Cells. The rooms reflect local history – names include the Warden's Keep, the Privileged Prisoner, and Albert's Library. Modern touches include high-speed Internet access. **www.thekinggeorgeinn.com**

COLLINGWOOD The Westin Trillium House, Blue Mountain

22 Mountain Dr., RR3, Collingwood, Ontario, L9Y 3Z2 **Tel** *(705) 443 8080* **Fax** *(705) 443 8081* **Rooms** *228*

A Georgian Bay lodge-style hotel at Blue Mountain ski resort. Facilities include the Oliver & Bonacini Café Grill, a 24-hour Gym, Kids Club®, a games room, outdoor heated swimming pool, and two hot tubs. Kitchenettes are available. There's also the'Plunge!' aquatic center and nearby championship golf courses. **www.westinbluemountain.com**

FENELON FALLS Eganridge Inn & Spa

26 Country Club Drive, RR3, Fenelon Falls, Ontario, K0M 1N0 **Tel** *(705) 738 5111* **Fax** *(705) 738 5111* **Rooms** *23*

Two hours' drive from Toronto, this upscale Kawartha resort has 12 guest rooms with private patio or balcony, private cottages, and a six-bedroom 1837 house built of square-cut logs. Local cottagers arrive by boat to sample the Swiss-influenced cuisine. There is a spa, tennis courts, and an interesting nine-hole golf course. **www.eganridge.com**

HALIBURTON Pinestone Resort & Conference Centre

4252 County Road 21, Haliburton, Ontario, K0M 1S0 **Tel** *(705) 457 1800* **Fax** *(705) 457 1783* **Rooms** *103*

A mecca for golfers and outdoor enthusiasts, this resort has over 100 ha (250 acres) in scenic Haliburton Highlands, an 18-hole championship golf course, tennis courts, an indoor and outdoor pool, and fitness facilities. Accommodations are in villas, chalets, and resort rooms, with fine dining and a casual restaurant and lounge. **www.pinestone-resort.com**

HALIBURTON Sir Sam's Inn & Waterspa

1491 Sir Sam's Road, Eagle Lake, Ontario, K0M 1N0 **Tel** *(705) 754 2188* **Fax** *(705) 754 4262* **Rooms** *25*

Historic, elegant inn on Eagle Lake, in Haliburton Highlands, with beachfront activities: water-ski, windsurf, sail, kayak, and canoe. Outdoor pool and indoor sauna. Dining room with wine cellar. Original stone and timber mansion, also 16 lakeside rooms, most with fireplace and whirlpool. Conference wing. Luxurious WaterSpa. **www.sirsamsinn.com**

HUNTSVILLE Delta Grandview Resort

939 Hwy 60, Grandview, Drive, Huntsville, Ontario, P1H 1Z4 **Tel** *(705) 789 4417* **Fax** *(705) 789 1674* **Rooms** *123*

A luxury Muskoka resort on Fairy Lake dating from 1911, with daily nature activities, including wildlife-watching. Accommodation is in contemporary condos and luxury suites with wood-burning fireplaces. The spa offers facials and massages. Many recreational activities are included in the rate. **www.deltahotels.com**

HUNTSVILLE Arowhon Pines Lodge

Algonquin Park, Box 10001, Huntsville, Ontario, P1H 2G5 **Tel** *(705) 633 5661* **Fax** *(705) 633 5795* **Rooms** *60*

This historic family-owned summer resort in Algonquin Park is 3 hours' scenic drive from Toronto. In a natural setting on a private lake, it has rustic log cabins and luxury suites along the shore. Food is well prepared from a renowned kitchen, and there are canoes, sailboats, kayaks, trails, tennis courts, and a sauna for use. Meals included. **www.arowhonpines.ca**

KINGSTON Days Inn Kingston Hotel & Convention Centre

33 Benson Street, Kingston, Ontario, K7K 5W2 **Tel** *(613) 546 3661* **Fax** *(613) 544 4126* **Rooms** *161*

A large hotel in downtown Kingston, near major highway 401. Some rooms have balcony and refrigerator. There is a seasonal outdoor pool, lobby business center, fitness facility, and 24-hour Denny's Restaurant. There are Custom Business and Group packages for groups from 5 to 500 people. **www.daysinnkingston.com**

KINGSTON Confederation Place Hotel

237 Ontario Street, Kingston, Ontario, K7L 2Z4 **Tel** *(613) 549 6300* **Fax** *(613) 549 1508* **Rooms** *95*

A modern five-story hotel in downtown Kingston, on the waterfront, within walking distance of Confederation Place park, stores, and theaters. There are conference facilities and Internet access. Popular stopover for student groups, hockey tournaments, and business travelers. **www.confederationplace.com**

KINGSTON Four Points by Sheraton Kingston

285 King Street East, Kingston, Ontario, K7L 3B1 **Tel** *(613) 544 4434* **Fax** *(613) 548 1782* **Rooms** *171*

This nine-story central hotel is located in downtown Kingston, near the waterfront, Norman Rogers Kingston Airport, and highway 401. Deluxe rooms and suites have high-speed Internet and Four Comfort Beds. The King Street Sizzle Restaurant & Bar has an open kitchen and outside patio. There are a pool, sauna, and whirlpool. **www.fourpointskingston.com**

KINGSTON Holiday Inn Kingston Waterfront Hotel

2 Princess Street, Kingston, Ontario, K7L 1A2 **Tel** *(613) 549 8400* **Fax** *(613) 549 3508* **Rooms** *197*

A waterfront hotel with conference facilities and a restaurant in Ontario's Thousand Island area, close to Lake Ontario and the St. Lawrence River. Annual events include the Kingston Buskers Rendezvous, Kingston Blues Festival, and the Kingston Film Festival. **www.hikingstonwaterfront.com**

MARKHAM Howard Johnson Hotel

555 Cochrane Dr. (Hwy 404 & Hwy 7), Markham, Ontario, L3R 8E3 **Tel** *(905) 479 5000* **Fax** *(905) 479 1186* **Rooms** *172*

Near highways 404, 7, and 401, and close to Toronto, this hotel has free Internet access, morning newspapers, parking, and a 24-hour business center. It also has an indoor pool, sauna, whirlpool, and exercise room. Rooms have a refrigerator. Deluxe Junior Suites have a microwave. **www.hojomarkham.com**

NORTH BAY Best Western North Bay Hotel & Conference Centre

700 Lakeshore Drive, North Bay, Ontario, P1A 2G4 **Tel** *(705) 474 5800* **Fax** *(705) 474 8699* **Rooms** *130*

This conference hotel across from Lake Nipissing is 19 km (12 miles) from Jack Garland Airport. Facilities include an indoor pool, exercise facility, hot tub, sauna, and restaurant. Farina, for dinner. Near museums, Chief Commanda Cruises, Celtfest, and Capitol Centre for the Arts. **www.bestwesternnorthbay.com**

OTTAWA Gasthaus Switzerland Inn

89 Daly Avenue, Ottawa, Ontario, K1N 6E6 **Tel** *(613) 237 0335* **Fax** *(613) 594 3327* **Rooms** *22*

This family-run boutique hotel in downtown Ottawa is situated amid restaurants, boutiques, world-renowned museums, the Rideau Canal, and the Parliament buildings. There are fireplaces in some rooms, Jacuzzi tubs in honeymoon suites, a large garden, and free high-speed wireless Internet access. Environmentally friendly. **www.swisshotel.ca**

OTTAWA Days Inn – Ottawa Airport

366 Hunt Club Road, Ottawa, Ontario, K1V 1C1 **Tel** *(613) 739 7555* **Fax** *(613) 739 7005* **Rooms** *81*

This modern hotel is very near Macdonald Cartier International Airport and capital city attractions such as Parliament Hill, Ottawa Carleton Race Tracks, Ottawa Flying Club, and downtown shopping, theater, and nightclubs. Honeymoon suites have Jacuzzis. There is a swimming pool, hot tub and fitness room. **www.daysinnottawa.com**

OTTAWA Lord Elgin Hotel

100 Elgin Street, Ottawa, Ontario, K1P 5K8 **Tel** *(613) 235 3333* **Fax** *(613) 235 3223* **Rooms** *355*

This downtown hotel across from Confederation Park, the National Arts Centre, the Rideau Canal, Parliament Buildings, and Ottawa Rideau Centre has picture windows and Biedermeier-style luxury furnishings. Facilities include a lap pool, whirlpool, sauna, and fitness equipment. **www.lordelginhotel.ca**

OTTAWA Sheraton Ottawa

150 Albert Street, Ottawa, Ontario, K1P 5G2 **Tel** *(613) 238 1500* **Fax** *(613) 235 2723* **Rooms** *236*

A modern downtown hotel close to Ottawa International Airport and near Parliament Hill, the National Arts Centre, and the National Gallery of Canada. There is a Starbuck's Coffee Bar, light meals at Sasha's Bar, and formal dining at the Carleton Grill, as well as an indoor heated pool and fitness center. **www.starwoodhotels.com**

OTTAWA Delta Ottawa

361 Queen Street, Ottawa, Ontario, K1R 7S9 **Tel** *(613) 238 6000* **Fax** *(613) 238 2290* **Rooms** *328*

This large hotel in downtown Ottawa has studio kitchenettes and bedroom suites with balconies. There is a health club with an indoor pool, whirlpool, children's activity and creative center, and two-story waterslide. The Trendy Sparks Lounge and Mystique Café serve dinners, and the 5-star Capital Dining Room has international cuisine. **www.deltahotels.com**

OTTAWA Fairmont Château Laurier

1 Rideau Street, Ottawa, Ontario, K1N 8S7 **Tel** *(613) 241 1414* **Fax** *(613) 562 7030* **Rooms** *429*

This landmark hotel (built in 1912 to resemble a French chateau) is steps away from Parliament Hill and the Rideau Canal. It has hosted royalty, heads of state, and celebrities. Facilities include an indoor swimming pool, landscaped outdoor gardens, wood-burning fireplaces, and massage. **www.fairmont.com/laurier**

SAULTE STE MARIE Days Inn Sault Ste. Marie

320 Bay Street, Sault Ste Marie, Ontario, P6A 1X1 **Tel** *(705) 759 8200* **Fax** *(705) 942 9500* **Rooms** *115*

A downtown hotel opposite Station Mall, adjacent to Steelback Centre and near the Agawa Canyon Tour Train. The Daybreak Café serves a continental buffet. There is an indoor pool, sauna, and fitness center and a business center with computer and Internet access. 24-hour front desk. **www.daysinnsault.com**

THUNDER BAY Best Western Nor' Wester Resort

2080 Highway 61, Thunder Bay, Ontario, P7J 1B8 **Tel** *(807) 473 9123* **Fax** *(807) 473 9600* **Rooms** *89*

This modern hotel close to Thunder Bay International Airport, Fort William Historical Park, and the Loch Lomond Ski Area, has a huge amethyst fireplace and is near golfing, fishing, dog sledding, and downhill and cross-country skiing. Amenities include Internet access, a fitness center, a heated indoor pool, and a sauna. **www.bestwestern.com**

TOBERMORY Blue Bay Motel

32 Bay Street Little Tub Harbour Tobermory, Ontario, N0H 2R0 **Tel** *(519) 596 2392* **Fax** *(519) 596 2335* **Rooms** *16*

This spacious motel has balconies overlooking Little Tub Harbour in Tobermory and is centrally located in the heart of a beautiful historic fishing village, within walking distance of stores, restaurants, tour boat docks, the Ferry dock, and the head of the Bruce Trail. **www.bluebay-motel.com**

THE GREAT LAKES

BAYFIELD The Little Inn of Bayfield $$$

26 Main Street, Bayfield, Ontario, N0M 1G0 **Tel** *(519) 565 2611* **Fax** *(519) 565 5474* **Rooms** *28*

A pretty boutique hotel with a veranda and traditional rooms in a historic Main House or contemporary Guest Cottage. With unique beds, custom-made duvets, and antique furnishings, many rooms also have large whirlpool tubs and gas fireplaces. Babysitting/dog walking services available. The menu features local Huron County products. **www.littleinn.com**

GUELPH Best Western Royal Brock $$

716 Gordon Street, Guelph, Ontario, N1G 1Y6 **Tel** *(519) 836 1240* **Fax** *(519) 763 5225* **Rooms** *104*

Across from the University of Guelph in park-like grounds, the Ramada offers high-speed Internet, free parking, the Gordon restaurant, and The Stone Lounge. Rooms have windows that open or a balcony with sliding door. There is an outdoor swimming pool and sundeck, open from May to September. **www.bestwesternontario.com**

HAMILTON Sheraton Hotel, Hamilton $$$

116 King Street West, Hamilton, Ontario, L8P 4V3 **Tel** *(905) 529 5515* **Fax** *(905) 529 8266* **Rooms** *301*

Located downtown in the business district, this Sheraton is close to Copps Coliseum and shopping malls. Rooms have views of Lake Ontario or the Niagara Escarpment. Chagall's On Two restaurant offers relaxed dining and Sunday Jazz brunch, and the Tonic Lounge has dancing. There is a pool, sun deck, and fitness center. **www.sheratonhamilton.com**

LONDON Four Points by Sheraton London $$$

1150 Wellington Road South, London, Ontario, N6E 1M3 **Tel** *(519) 681 0600* **Fax** *(519) 681 8222* **Rooms** *181*

This modern hotel is located less than a mile north of major highway 401, and within walking distance of downtown White Oaks shopping mall, restaurants, and movie theaters. Rooms include suites with separate living rooms and king bed or two double beds. There is a heated indoor pool and sauna. **www.starwoodhotels.com**

MIDLAND Howard Johnson Midland $$

751 Yonge Street, Midland, Ontario, L4R 2E1 **Tel** *(705) 526 2219* **Fax** *(705) 526 1346* **Rooms** *41*

This two-story building close to downtown overlooks Midland's Little Lake Park and has a sandy beach and lake activities. There are standard and deluxe rooms; executive suites; and a utility suite with two queen beds, sofa bed, full kitchen, dinning room, cable TV, VCR, and Jacuzzi. **www.hojomidland.com**

NIAGARA FALLS Comfort Inn Clifton Hill $$$

4960 Clifton Hill, Niagara Falls, Ontario, L2E 6S8 **Tel** *(905) 358 3293 or (800) 263 2557* **Fax** *(905) 358 3818* **Rooms** *185*

This modern hotel in the vibrant, colorful Clifton Hill Tourist District, 'The Hill', is close to museums, restaurants, nightlife, and the Niagara Falls. There is a tropical indoor pool, complimentary wireless Internet, and deluxe continental breakfast. **www.comfortniagara.com**

NIAGARA FALLS Sheraton on the Falls $$$

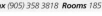

5875 Falls Avenue, Niagara Falls, Ontario, L2G 3K7 **Tel** *(905) 374 4444* **Fax** *(905) 371 0157* **Rooms** *670*

Directly across from Niagara Falls, this hotel is connected to the 8-ha (20-acre) Falls Avenue complex – Casino Niagara, Rainforest Café, Hard Rock Café and Club, MGM Studio Plaza, Hershey Store, and 4-D movie theaters. There is a work-out room, a spa, and Fallsview Restaurant. Rooms have floor to ceiling windows. **www.sheraton.com/onthefallshotel**

NIAGARA ON THE LAKE Harbour House $$$$

85 Melville Street, Niagara on the Lake, Ontario, L0S 1J0 **Tel** *(905) 468 4683* **Fax** *(905) 468 0366* **Rooms** *31*

A luxurious hotel in historic Niagara-on-the-Lake offering king-sized feather-top beds, quality linens, down duvet, a fireplace, whirlpool bath, flat screen TV, and DVD/CD players. Breakfast is served in the conservatory with baked goods and Niagara produce. There is wine and cheese sampling in the afternoons. **www.harbourhousehotel.ca**

NIAGARA ON THE LAKE Shaw Club Hotel $$$$

92 Picton Street, Niagara on the Lake, Ontario, L0S 1J0 **Tel** *(905) 468 5711* **Fax** *(905) 468 4988* **Rooms** *30*

Located next to the Shaw Festival Theatre, the Shaw Club Hotel has a cozy, private-club feel. Guest rooms are decorated with photographs taken by local artists, and they all boast the latest technological advances. Spa services are also available, as is a popular restaurant, Zees. **www.shawclub.com**

ST. CATHARINES Four Points by Sheraton St. Catharines $$$

3530 Schmon Parkway, St. Catharines, Ontario, L2V 4Y6 **Tel** *(905) 984 8484* **Rooms** *124*

This is an all-suites hotel in the center of the Niagara region, across from Brock University, near the Falls. There are suites for families and the physically challenged. Golf packages are available at Peninsula Lakes GC, Royal Niagara GC, Hunters Pointe GC, Rockway Glen GC, Whirlpool GC and Legends on the Niagara. **www.sheratonfourpointsniagara.com**

SAULT STE. MARIE Quality Suites Bay Front $$

180 Bay Street, Sault Ste. Marie, Ontario, P6A 6S2 **Tel** *(705) 945 9264* **Fax** *(705) 945 9766* **Rooms** *110*

This modern hotel is located directly across from Station Mall and Agawa Canyon train depot and near Casino Sault Ste. Marie. Facilities include an Indoor pool, whirlpool, sauna, exercise room, in-room coffee, wireless Internet access, and the Grand Festa Restaurant and lounge. **www.choicehotels.ca**

Key to Price Guide *see p346* **Key to Symbols** *see back cover flap*

STRATFORD Rundles Morris House   🔟 $$$$$
9 Cobourg Street, Stratford, Ontario, N5A 3E4 **Tel** *(519) 271 6442* **Fax** *(519) 271 3279* **Rooms** *1*

This ultra-modern house operates as a deluxe suite, with a bedroom, two bathrooms, and a living room. A two-course breakfast is included. Dinner may be arranged, upon request, during restaurant hours. There are splendid views of the lake and a fireplace in the lounge. **www.rundlesrestaurant.com/morrishouse.htm**

WINDSOR Hilton Windsor   🔲🔟🛏🍽📶🅿 $$$
277 Riverside Drive, Windsor, Ontario, N9A 5K4 **Tel** *(519) 973 5555* **Fax** *(519) 973 1600* **Rooms** *305*

A modern hotel in downtown Windsor across from Detroit, USA. All rooms have river views. There are suites on the top three floors with exclusive access to a private lounge with breakfast and evening reception. This hotel is connected to Cleary International Centre and is close to Casino Windsor. **www.hilton.com**

CENTRAL CANADA

CHURCHILL Lazy Bear Lodge   🔟🅿 $$$$$
313 Kelsey Blvd., Churchill, Manitoba, R0B 0E0 **Tel** *(204) 675 2969* **Fax** *(204) 663 8169* **Rooms** *33*

This is the place for the ultimate polar bear adventure in the fall. The lodge also offers whale tours, wilderness adventures, and kayaking and snorkelling packages. Accommodation is in rustic log cabins built by the owner, all en suite and with double beds. Rates include meals and airport/train pickups. **www.lazybearlodge.com**

DRUMHELLER Newcastle Country Inn   📶🅿 $$
1130 Newcastle Trail, Drumheller, Alberta, T0J 0Y2 **Tel** *(403) 823 8356* **Fax** *(403) 823 2373* **Rooms** *11*

This quiet country inn is just 1.7 km (1 mile) west of downtown Drumheller, in dinosaur country. The three-star inn has wireless Internet, and rooms include a small fridge. There are two decks with chairs. Price includes a self-serve continental breakfast. Check-in is generally 4–6pm. **www.bbalberta.com/newcastle**

EDMONTON Glenora Inn Bed & Breakfast   🔟📶🅿 $$
12327-102 Ave. NW, Edmonton, Alberta, T5N 0L8 **Tel** *(780) 488 6766* **Fax** *(780) 488 5168* **Rooms** *25*

Originally an apartment building in the heart of Edmonton's historic West End, the former Buena Vista Building has hosted colorful characters such as World War I pilot Wop May. Price includes a full breakfast served in the Glenora Bistro. Each room has its own Victorian decor. The inn also has a guest parlor and patio. **www.glenorabnb.com**

EDMONTON Union Bank Inn   🔲🔟🛏🍽📶🅿 $$$
10053 Jasper Ave., Edmonton, Alberta, T5J 1S5 **Tel** *(780) 423 3600* **Fax** *(780) 423 4623* **Rooms** *34*

This boutique hotel near Edmonton's arts and business district was built in 1911. Rooms are spread through two wings, one featuring contemporary styling, the other a distinctive heritage feel. The price includes breakfast, and wine and a cheese and fruit plate delivered to the rooms nightly. Room service 4–10pm. **www.unionbankinn.com**

EDMONTON Fantasyland Hotel   🔲🔟🛏🍽📶🅿 $$$$
17700-87 Ave. (West Edmonton Mall), Edmonton, Alberta, T5T 4V4 **Tel** *(780) 444 3000* **Fax** *(780) 444 3294* **Rooms** *355*

You can stay here and enjoy West Edmonton Mall's amenities – including an amusement park, water park, minigolf, and a skating rink – without setting foot outside. There are 120 themed rooms in 9 different styles including Hollywood, Polynesian, Roman, and Western. Room service available 6:30am–2am. **www.fantasylandhotel.com**

LETHBRIDGE Best Western Heidelberg Inn   🔲🔟📶🍽🅿 $$
1303 Mayor Magrath Drive S., Lethbridge, Alberta, T1K 2R1 **Tel** *(403) 329 0555* **Fax** *(403) 328 8846* **Rooms** *66*

Conveniently located near highways 3, 4, and 5. The rooms facing west on high floors have a mountain view on a clear day. Rooms have high-speed Internet and a complimentary newspaper delivered Monday–Saturday. The Fitness center has a steam room, sauna, and exercise equipment. Carmichael's Pub is located downstairs. **www.bestwestern.com**

MAPLE CREEK Historic Reesor Ranch   🅿 $$
Box 1001, Maple Creek, Saskatchewan, S0N 1N0 **Tel** *(306) 662 3498* **Rooms** *4*

This ranch house B&B is tucked away in the Cypress Hills. Two rooms have a private balcony. The large shared bathroom has an antique tub and the kitchen features an old stove. This cattle ranch has been in the Reesor family for five generations. There is a cowboy poet in residence. Breakfast is included in the price. **www.reesorranch.com**

MOOSE JAW Temple Gardens Mineral Spa Resort   🔲🔟🛏🍽📶🅿 $$$
24 Fairford St. East, Moose Jaw, Saskatchewan, S6H 0C7 **Tel** *(306) 694 5055* **Fax** *(306) 694 8310* **Rooms** *179*

This downtown hotel offers different packages. Swim inside or out in the natural geothermal mineral pool. Some rooms have views of Crescent Park. Parking is $5 per car per day. There is an outside terrace on the fourth floor by the Morningsides Café. Room service 7am–11pm. **www.templegardens.sk.ca**

REGINA Regina Inn Hotel & Conference Centre   🔲🍽📶🅿 $$$

1975 Broad St., Regina, Saskatchewan, S4S 7K3 **Tel** *(306) 525 6767* **Fax** *(306) 352 1858* **Rooms** *235*

Located in Downtown Regina, near the area's biggest shopping center (the Cornwall Centre), Casino Regina, and the tranquil Wascana Park. Choose from suites, double rooms, or business-class rooms offering city views. Make use of the hotel's gym and free Internet access. **www.reginainn.com**

REGINA Hotel Saskatchewan   🖥 🍴 🍷 ☰ 🅿   ⑤⑤⑤

2125 Victoria Avenue, Regina, Saskatchewan, S4P 0S3 **Tel** *(306) 522 7691* **Fax** *(306) 757 5521* **Rooms** *224*

This deluxe hotel was renovated in 1992. The rate includes a continental breakfast but there are different room packages. Built in 1927, the hotel is downtown and overlooks Victoria Park. It has a day spa, whirlpool, and sauna in the fitness center. There is Internet access and valet parking. Room service is 6am–midnight. **www.hotelsask.com**

REGINA Delta Bessborough Hotel   🖥 🍴 ≋ 🏃 🍷 ☰ 🅿   ⑤⑤⑤⑤

601 Spadina Crescent East, Regina, Saskatchewan, S7K 3G8 **Tel** *(306) 244 5521* **Fax** *(306) 665 7262* **Rooms** *225*

Wander around the hotel's 2-ha (5-acre) Elizabethan-style gardens overlooking the South Saskatchewan River. This stately historic hotel first opened in 1935. It offers complimentary high-speed Internet and a pool. There is a Japanese restaurant, a café, and a lounge. **www.deltahotels.com**

RIDING MOUNTAIN NATIONAL PARK Clear Lake Lodge   ≋ 🅿   ⑤

Wasagaming, Manitoba, R0J 2H0 **Tel** *(204) 848 2345* **Fax** *(204) 848 2209* **Rooms** *16*

In Riding Mountain National Park the lodge is a short walk from the beach, boat rentals, stores, restaurants, and the park interpretive center. The main lobby has a piano, and fireplace. A hot tub, barbecues, and picnic tables are in the back. Guests are welcome to use the guest kitchen and the dining area. **www.clearlakelodge.com**

WINNIPEG Fort Garry Hotel   🖥 🍴 ≋ 🏃 🍷 ☰ 🅿   ⑤⑤

222 Broadway Ave., Winnipeg, Manitoba, R3C 0R3 **Tel** *(204) 942 8251* **Fax** *(204) 956 2351* **Rooms** *246*

Situated near the Forks, this hotel was built in 1913 and is a national historic site. The Palm Lounge has live jazz nightly. The hotel has a spa. The Assiniboine Athletic Club is across the skywalk. There is a pool, hot tub, steam room, and workout facilities. Room service 6am–midnight. **www.fortgarryhotel.com**

WINNIPEG Inn at the Forks   ☰ 🅿   ⑤⑤⑤

75 Forks Market Rd., Winnipeg, Manitoba, R3C 0A2 **Tel** *(204) 942 6555* **Fax** *(204) 942 6979* **Rooms** *115*

A luxurious hotel surrounded by parkland in the heart of downtown Winnipeg, close to all the major attractions. Enjoy fine dining in the Current restaurant, or relax in the Riverstone Spa with a massage. The suites are especially spacious, and some offer sweeping city views. Wireless Internet available. **www.innforks.com**

VANCOUVER AND VANCOUVER ISLAND

BARKLEY SOUND Eagle Nook Resort & Spa   🍴   ⑤⑤⑤⑤⑤

Box 1068, Tofino, Barkley Sound, British Columbia, V0R 2Z0 **Tel** *(604) 357 3361* **Rooms** *23*

Stunning cedar lodge. Floor-to-ceiling windows bring the outside – where bald eagles soar above forest-clad shorelines offset by stunning mountain backdrops – inside. Spy ocean views of Vernon and Jane bays from luxurious rooms. Rates include all meals. Minimum stay of two nights. **www.eaglenook.com**

NORTH VANCOUVER Thistle Down House   ☰ 🅿   ⑤⑤⑤⑤

3910 Capilano Rd., British Columbia, V7R 4J2 **Tel** *(604) 986 7173 or (888) 633 7173* **Fax** *(604) 980 2939* **Rooms** *6*

Pretty 1920 craftsman-style heritage home with airy, bright rooms, some with fireplaces, some opening onto a balcony or private patio, where comfortable deck chairs await. European and Canadian antiques decorate the entire B&B. The garden awaits gentle exploration or enjoyment with a book or beverage. **www.thistle-down.com**

PARKSVILLE Sunrise Ridge Waterfront Resort   🖥 🍴 ≋ 🏃 🍷 ☰ 🅿   ⑤⑤⑤⑤⑤

1175 Resort Drive, Parksville, British Columbia, V9P 2E3 **Tel** *(250) 248 4674* **Rooms** *65*

This resort is located above the sandy beaches of Craig Bay, overlooking the Strait of Georgia. Fully furnished luxury suites include a stocked kitchen, BBQ on a private patio, fireplace, and complimentary Wi-Fi. The resort also offers kayaking. You can walk from here to the popular Rathbone Beach Provincial Park. **www.sunriseridge.ca**

SOOKE Sooke Harbour House   🖥 🍴 🏃 🍷   ⑤⑤⑤⑤⑤

1528 Whiffen Spit Rd., British Columbia, V9Z 0T4 **Tel** *(250) 642 3421 or (800) 889 9688* **Fax** *(250) 642 6988* **Rooms** *28*

The oldest B&B on the island, most of the spacious, individually designed rooms at this award-winning clapboard inn overlook the ocean. Activities include kayaking, biking, and hiking, or enjoying the art gallery. The menu changes daily in the outstanding restaurant. Pets welcome (extra charge). **www.sookeharbourhouse.com**

TOFINO Middle Beach Lodge   🍴 🏃 🍷 🅿   ⑤⑤⑤

400 Mackenzie Beach Rd., British Columbia, V0R 2Z0 **Tel** *(250) 725 2900* **Fax** *(250) 725 2901* **Rooms** *64*

In a fabulous setting on a stretch of private beach amid mountains, forests and ocean, this consists of two rustic lodges and 20 housekeeping cabins on 16 ha (40 acres). One resort is for families, one strictly for adults. Hike rainforest paths where ancient trees still exist; explore rocky shoreline where kids find sea life in tidal pools. **www.middlebeach.com**

TOFINO Clayoquot Wilderness Resort   🍴 🏃 🍷 🅿   ⑤⑤⑤⑤⑤

Box 130, Tofino, British Columbia, V0R 2Z0 **Tel** *(250) 726 8235 or (888) 333 5405* **Fax** *(250) 266 0412* **Rooms** *20*

A "21st-century eco-safari." An enclave of deluxe suite, dining, spa, and lounge tents offers a unique interpretation on discovering the wilderness. Families welcome. Center of "camp" is a cedar-log, ranch-style cookhouse with an open kitchen and stone fireplace. Horses on site. Rates include meals. **www.wildretreat.com**

TOFINO Wickaninnish Inn 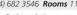 $$$$$

500 Osprey Lane, Chesterman Beach, Box 250, British Columbia, V0R 2Z0 **Tel** *(250) 725 3100* **Rooms** *75*

This elegant Relais and Châteaux property features the octagonal Pointe Restaurant jutting over rocks on the ocean. Famous for winter storm watching, "the Wick" offers supreme rest and relaxation in a spectacular setting. Cedar construction throughout emphasizes Zen-like rooms where balconies overlook the ocean. **www.wickinn.com**

VANCOUVER Best Western Sands by the Sea $$$

1755 Davie St., British Columbia, V6G 1W5 **Tel** *(604) 682 1831 or (800) 663 9400* **Fax** *(604) 682 3546* **Rooms** *119*

In a perfect location adjacent to a bike and pedestrian haven leading to English Bay, Stanley Park, and city stores and restaurants on Davie Street, the rooms here boast ocean or mountain view; some are pet friendly. Bayside Lounge for drinks and pub food offers view of Vancouver's inner harbor. **www.bestwesternsandshotelvancouver.com**

VANCOUVER Days Inn Downtown $$$

921 W Pender St., British Columbia, V6C 1M2 **Tel** *(604) 681 4335* **Fax** *(604) 681 7808* **Rooms** *85*

This boutique-style hotel has cozy, small, and clean rooms and is conveniently close to the YMCA (passes available), Stanley Park, Gastown, and all stores, museums, and galleries. There is a complimentary shuttle service into the downtown area and a restaurant and pub. **www.daysinnvancouver.com**

VANCOUVER Georgian Court Hotel $$$

773 Beatty St., British Columbia, V6B 2M4 **Tel** *(604) 682 5555* **Fax** *(604) 682 8830* **Rooms** *180*

An intimate European-style boutique hotel, where high-ceilinged rooms with opening windows emphasize the feeling of luxury. There are two on-site restaurants, and the hotel features in-room spa service; close to jogging/walking/cycling paths. **www.georgiancourthotelvancouver.com**

VANCOUVER Quality Hotel Inn at False Creek $$$

1335 Howe St., British Columbia, V6Z 1R7 **Tel** *(604) 682 0229 or (800) 663 8474* **Fax** *(604) 662 7566* **Rooms** *157*

Located downtown, this trendy boutique hotel's decor features Mexican and Santa Fe art. There are 15 rooms suitable for families. The restaurant is open from 7am until 9pm. Long stays are possible. There is a complimentary pass to the nearby fitness center. **www.innatfalsecreek.com**

VANCOUVER Metropolitan Hotel Vancouver $$$$

645 Howe St., British Columbia, V6C 2Y9 **Tel** *(604) 687 1122 or (800) 667 2300* **Fax** *(604) 602 7846* **Rooms** *197*

A member of the "Boutique Preferred Hotel" group, this is primarily a business traveler's hotel with quiet, intimate rooms. It provides traditional luxury. Squash courts are included in the health facilities. Diva at the Met, serving Pacific Coast cuisine, is one of Vancouver's finest restaurants. Pets allowed. **www.metropolitan.com**

VANCOUVER Fairmont Waterfront $$$$$

900 Canada Pl. Way, British Columbia, V6C 3L5 **Tel** *(604) 691 1991 or (866) 840 8402* **Fax** *(604) 691 1999* **Rooms** *489*

A spectacular glass-and-steel hotel across from the Vancouver Convention Center. Ocean, mountain, and city views can be stunning, depending on your floor: ask when you reserve. The hotel is located beside pretty walkways. An outdoor pool allows you to swim and watch the mountain views. **www.fairmont.com**

VANCOUVER Four Seasons $$$$$

791 West Georgia St., British Columbia, V6C 2T4 **Tel** *(604) 689 9333* **Fax** *(604) 684 4555* **Rooms** *373*

A white tower rising above the Pacific Centre with its stores and conference facilities, this modern, luxurious hotel is close to Stanley Park with its bike paths and walking trails. Also features the Yew Restaurant & Bar. Children are well looked after here. There is an indoor-outdoor pool. **www.fourseasons.com**

VANCOUVER Hotel Vancouver $$$$$

900 W. Georgia St., British Columbia, V6C 2W6 **Tel** *(604) 684 3131 or (800) 257 7544* **Fax** *(604) 662 1929* **Rooms** *556*

The Fairmont chain evokes an old-time traditional ambience in its stately properties, as does this downtown, elegant site in a great location for shopping. There are marble floors in the bathrooms. The state-of-the-art spa is fabulous after a hike up the Lions or ski trip to Whistler. There are rooms for the hearing- or mobility impaired. **www.fairmont.com**

VANCOUVER Hyatt Regency Vancouver $$$$$

655 Burrard St., British Columbia, V6C 2R7 **Tel** *(604) 683 1234 or (888) 591 1234* **Fax** *(604) 689 3707* **Rooms** *644*

The usual Hyatt amenities belong to this upscale hotel within walking distance of major downtown shopping and sightseeing attractions. The outdoor pool and whirlpool are usually open year-round. There is an excellent fitness center. The higher the floor, the better the views of downtown, the mountains, or the harbor. **www.hyatt.com**

VANCOUVER Pan Pacific Vancouver 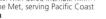 $$$$$

Suite 300, 999 Canada Place, British Columbia, V6C 3B5 **Tel** *(604) 662 8111* **Fax** *(604) 685 8690* **Rooms** *503*

This 23-story luxury hotel towers above the "white sails" of Canada Place, across the harbor from Stanley Park. There are bike, walking, and jogging paths nearby. Best views of Vancouver here include snow-capped peaks through to float planes taking off and landing in Burrard Inlet. **www.panpacific.com**

VANCOUVER Sutton Place Hotel $$$$$

845 Burrard St., British Columbia, V6Z 2K6 **Tel** *(604) 682 5511 or (866) 378 8866* **Fax** *(604) 682 5513* **Rooms** *396*

A five-diamond, four-star luxury modern high-rise hotel with all the amenities including a VIDA wellness spa with indoor heated pool and outside terrace. Please note that Robson Street can be noisy at night so avoid rooms overlooking it. Gerard Lounge attracts cinema celebrities so people watchers may be lucky. **www.suttonplace.com**

VICTORIA Ramada Victoria   🏨🍴🏊♨🛏🅿   ⑤⑤

123 Gorge Rd. East, British Columbia, V9A 1L1 **Tel** *(250) 386 1422 or (888) 468 3514* **Fax** *(250) 386 1254* **Rooms** *91*

Modern brick hotel offers comfortable, spacious, and peaceful rooms, suites, and apartments only a 5-minute drive from downtown Victoria. Each suite has a balcony, bedroom, and hide-a-bed in the living room: convenient for families. Welcoming family-style restaurant and a pub on-site. Heated outdoor pool good for children. **www.victoriaramada.com**

VICTORIA Humboldt House Bed & Breakfast   🅿   ⑤⑤⑤

867 Humboldt St., British Columbia, V8V 2Z6 **Tel** *(250) 383 0152 or (888) 383 0327* **Fax** *(250) 383 6402* **Rooms** *6*

This romantic hideaway in an 1893 Victorian clapboard B&B is a short walk from downtown Victoria. A gourmet champagne breakfast is delivered to your room. Themed rooms (Japanese, Victorian, Gazebo, etc.) feature Jacuzzi and wood-burning fireplace; views from rooms of apple orchard. Wireless Internet access. **www.humboldthouse.com**

VICTORIA Inn at Laurel Point   🏨🍴🏊♿🛏🅿   ⑤⑤⑤

680 Montreal Street, British Columbia, V8V 1Z8 **Tel** *(250) 386 8721 or (800) 663 7667* **Fax** *(250) 386 9547* **Rooms** *200*

Stunning contemporary waterfront hotel overlooks Victoria's protected Inner Harbor. From your bed look through glassed balcony walls to see nautical views of sailboats, busy tugboats, and float planes landing and taking off. Stroll around the Japanese gardens and enjoy the Inner Harbor view from the patio. **www.laurelpoint.com**

VICTORIA Delta Victoria Ocean Pointe Resort & Spa   🏨🍴🏊♿🛏🅿   ⑤⑤⑤⑤

45 Songhees Rd., British Columbia, V9A 6T3 **Tel** *(250) 360 2999 or (800) 667 4677* **Fax** *(250) 360 1041* **Rooms** *239*

Modern hotel with spectacular lobby boasting floor-to-ceiling windows overlooking Victoria's famous Inner Harbour with only the boardwalk between the hotel and the water's edge. World-class full-service European spa, excellent pool, outdoor tennis courts, some rooms accommodate persons of limited mobility; child-friendly. **www.deltahotels.com**

VICTORIA Fairmont Empress   🏨🍴🏊♿🛏🅿   ⑤⑤⑤⑤⑤

721 Government St., British Columbia, V8W 1W5 **Tel** *(250) 384 8111 or (800) 257 7544* **Fax** *(250) 381 4334* **Rooms** *477*

Built in 1908, this elegant, ivy-clad grande dame regally commands what is undoubtedly the best location overlooking the Inner Harbour. Pricey, excellent High Tea served daily in the grand lobby. Rose-beds and lawns slip down to the boardwalk surrounding harbour. Spectacular ambience. Caution: rooms are small and views limited. **www.fairmont.com**

WHITE ROCK/SURREY Pacific Inn Resort & Conference Centre   🏨🍴🏊♿🛏🅿   ⑤⑤⑤

1160 King George Hwy, British Columbia, V4A 4Z2 **Tel** *(604) 535 1432 or (800) 667 2248* **Fax** *(604) 531 6979* **Rooms** *150*

Tropical-style hotel features variety of simply designed rooms: some have private balconies overlooking a glass-roofed atrium with a swimming pool in the center. Families can choose over-sized rooms suitable for four. Outside, stroll White Rock's beaches and breathe in the ocean fresh air. Free parking also available for RVs. **www.pacificinn.com**

THE ROCKY MOUNTAINS

BANFF Rundlestone Lodge   🏨🍴🏊🛏🅿   ⑤⑤⑤

537 Banff Ave., Alberta, T1L 1A6 **Tel** *(403) 762 2201 or (800) 661 8630* **Fax** *(403) 762 4501* **Rooms** *96*

Modern interpretation of Rocky Mountain architecture complete with rugged stone fireplaces and an interior of rich natural shades, inspiring tranquility. Tooloulou's Bistro & Bar serves Canadian and Creole cuisine in a warm and welcoming atmosphere. **www.rundlestone.com**

BANFF Fairmont Banff Springs   ⑤⑤⑤⑤⑤

405 Spray Ave., Alberta, T1L 1J4 **Tel** *(403) 762 2211 or (800) 257 7544* **Fax** *(403) 762 5755* **Rooms** *768*

The "Castle of the Rockies" offers unmatched views of the Bow River Valley and Mount Rundle from many rooms and from the Rundle Lounge and outdoor pool. Rocky Mountain ambience is emphasized by rugged stone walls and fireplaces. Top-notch amenities include a golf course and Willow Stream Spa. Ask about naturalist-led hikes. **www.fairmont.com**

CALGARY Hotel Arts   🏨🍴🏊♿🛏🅿   ⑤⑤⑤

119 12th Ave. SW., Alberta, T2R 0G8 **Tel** *(403) 266 4611 or (800) 661 9378* **Rooms** *175*

A very hip "South Beach North" pool adds an extra perk to this chic boutique hotel located in downtown Calgary. Some rooms have marble bathrooms and two-person Jacuzzi tubs. There is a trendy Raw Bar and another restaurant serving award-winning Saint Germain French regional cuisine. **www.hotelarts.ca**

CANMORE Quality Resort Chateau Canmore   ⑤⑤⑤

1720 Bow Valley Trail, Alberta, T1W 2X3 **Tel** *(403) 678 6699 or (800) 261 8551* **Fax** *(403) 678 6954* **Rooms** *93*

There are great views of Three Sisters and other Rocky Mountains from this all-suite resort hotel. Suites have kitchenettes, and all feature stone, gas fireplaces. The spa offers esthetic and massage treatments as well as personal training. Children welcome: kids 17 and under stay free when with an adult. **www.chateaucanmore.com**

CRANBROOK Elizabeth Lake Lodge   🛏🅿   ⑤⑤

590 Van Horne Street South, Cranbrook, BC, V1C 4W7 **Tel** *(250) 426 6114* **Fax** *(250) 426 6221* **Rooms** *17*

All rooms at this reasonably priced inn have views of the adjacent Elizabeth Lake and Bird Sanctuary. Some suites have kitchenettes. Try a round of mini golf, or go for a pleasant stroll in the sanctuary. RV sites are also available. There is free Wi-Fi, and the hotel is pet-friendly. **www.elizabethlakelodge.com**

Key to Price Guide *see p346* **Key to Symbols** *see back cover flap*

FIELD Emerald Lake Lodge $$$$$

P.O. Box 10, British Columbia, V0A 1G0 **Tel** *(250) 343 6321 or (800) 663 6336* **Fax** *(250) 343 6724* **Rooms** *85*

Originally a Canadian Pacific Railway hotel, this log cabin resort is in spectacular Yoho National Park. The oak bar came from an 1890s Yukon saloon. Rustic luxury with exposed wood beams, stone fireplaces, chess sets, billiard table and cozy chairs establishes the mood for total relaxation. Rooms are in the lodge or in cabins. **www.crmr.com**

FORT NELSON The Blue Bell Inn 　 $$

4203 50th Ave. S., British Columbia, V0C 1R0 **Tel** *(250) 774 6961 or (800) 663 5267* **Fax** *(250) 774 6983* **Rooms** *57*

A bright, modern, two-story motel on Mile 300 on the Alaska Highway. The complete complex includes a 24-hour convenience store with stamp sales and mailbox, laundromat, fuel station, and RV park with 47 sites. Rooms are basic, comfortable, and clean, half with kitchenettes. Pets permitted in smoking rooms. Airport shuttle. **www.bluebellinn.ca**

GOLDEN Vagabond Lodge 　 $$$

1581 Cache Close, Golden, British Columbia, V0A 1H0 **Tel** *(250) 344 2622 or (866) 944 2622* **Fax** *(250) 344 2668* **Rooms** *10*

Spectacular log lodge tucked into the mountainside at the base of Kicking Horse Mountain Resort. Some rooms have private balconies or lofts. There are no telephones or TVs. There is a split-log bar for serving the alcohol you bring (no liquor licence). No children under 8; no pets. Price includes breakfast. There is a restaurant next door. **www.vagabondlodge.ca**

LAKE LOUISE Fairmont Chateau Lake Louise $$$$$

111 Lake Louise Drive, Alberta, T0L 1E0 **Tel** *(403) 522 3511 or (866) 540 4413* **Fax** *(403) 522 3834* **Rooms** *555*

Since 1890, Chateau Lake Louise has attracted adventurers to view the world-famous lake and explore breathtaking mountain scenery. Visitors can enjoy canoe rentals, a spa, and trail rides. Ask about the Heritage Mountain Guide program where naturalists lead hour/half-day trips (extra fee). Children, pets welcome. **www.fairmont.com**

LAKE LOUISE Simpson's Num-Ti-Jah Lodge 　 $$$$$

Mile 22, Bow Lake Icefield Parkway, Alberta, T0L 1E0 **Tel** *(403) 522 2167* **Fax** *(403) 522 2425* **Rooms** *16*

An authentic log cabin off Icefields Parkway on the shore of spectacular Bow Lake originally built in 1937 by legendary guide Jimmy Simpson. There is no telephone or TV. Special events such as artists-in-residence programs take place here. Closed in winter. **www.sntj.ca**

PRINCE GEORGE Economy Inn 　 $

1915 Third Ave., British Columbia, V2M 1G6 **Tel** *(250) 563 7106 or (888) 566 6333* **Fax** *(250) 561 7216* **Rooms** *30*

This is a two-story motel with comfortable and clean rooms and very basic amenities, but it is located minutes from downtown Prince George, with its museums, heritage river trail, parks, bookstores, and cafés. There is a choice of smoking and non-smoking rooms. Free wireless Internet access is available. **www.economyinn.ca**

RADIUM HOT SPRINGS The Radium Resort $$

8100 Golf Course Rd., Hwy 93/95, British Columbia, V0A 1M0 **Tel** *(250) 347 9311* **Fax** *(250) 347 6299* **Rooms** *100*

This is a golf resort. A three-story boutique hotel features mountain views. All rooms face one of two golf courses. Tennis and squash courts are on site. Good for bird watching. The Golf academy offers lessons (for a fee). There is a two-day minimum booking on weekends. **www.radiumresort.com**

WATERTON LAKES Prince of Wales Hotel $$$$

Waterton Lakes National Park, Alberta, T0K 2M0 **Tel** *(403) 236 3400* **Fax** *(406) 892 7375* **Rooms** *86*

This 1927 historic hotel enjoys a resplendent setting amid the grandeur of the Rocky Mountains in Waterton Lakes National Park. The gable roofline and ornate balconies create a stately alpine-lodge look on a bluff overlooking the lake. Rooms are small but well maintained with oak wainscoting. Closed Oct–Apr. **www.glacierparkinc.com**

SOUTHERN AND NORTHERN BRITISH COLUMBIA

108 MILE RANCH The Hills Health Ranch $$$$$

4871 Hwy 97, British Columbia, V0K 2Z0 **Tel** *(250) 791 5225* **Fax** *(250) 791 6384* **Rooms** *45*

This is a Western ranchhouse on sprawling acreage where gentle horses wander. "Dude ranch" trail riding, cowboy cookouts, and a health spa are all on site. The rate is for two nights, including six gourmet meals, full use of spa pools, fitness center, and one massage. **www.thehillshealthranch.com**

BARKERVILLE King and Kelly House B&B 　 $$

2nd St., British Columbia, V0K 1B0 **Tel** *(866) 994 0004* **Rooms** *6*

Lodging is in two heritage buildings in this authentically restored gold rush town. Highlights include delicious breakfasts and the sound of music from the nearby theater or from stagecoach rides going past. The whole bed & breakfast (sleeps eight) can be rented for $280. Some rooms share bathrooms. **www.kellyhouse.ca**

CHASE Quaaout Lodge 　 $$$$

1663 Little Shuswap Rd. West, British Columbia, V0E 1M0 **Tel** *(250) 679 3090* **Fax** *(250) 679 3039* **Rooms** *72*

This Shuswap First Nations' People resort overlooks Little Shuswap Lake and its sandy beach; many rooms offer views of the lake. The restaurant menu features native foods, while the Shuswap interpretation center provides an insight into native culture. Activities include horseback riding, canoeing, fishing, hiking, and golfing. **www.quaaoutlodge.com**

HARRISON HOT SPRINGS Harrison Hot Springs Resort and Spa ⬚ 🅼 ♨ 🏕 🗐 🅿 ⓈⓈⓈ
100 Esplanade Avenue, British Columbia, V0M 1K0 **Tel** *(604) 796 2244* **Fax** *(604) 796 3682* **Rooms** *337*

This relaxing retreat is great for single travelers and families alike. Sitting in one of the five mineral hot spring pools while gazing at the stars and mountains makes for a truly unique experience. Harrison Hot Springs is a 90-minute drive from Vancouver. **www.harrisonresort.com**

HOPE Manning Park Resort 🅼 ♨ 🏕 🗐 🅿 ⓈⓈⓈ
7500 Hwy 3, Manning Provincial Park, British Columbia, V0X 1L0 **Tel** *(250) 840 8822* **Fax** *(250) 840 8848* **Rooms** *73*

In this year-round family resort, choose from cabins, chalets, or lodge rooms. Activities include tennis, volleyball, ping pong, bocce, croquet, and horseshoes, plus video games, billiards, and movies. Loon Lagoon features a heated indoor pool. In winter there is a skating rink, cross-country and downhill skiing, and snowboarding. **www.manningpark.com**

KAMLOOPS Comfort Inn & Suites ⬚ 🅼 ♨ 🏕 🗐 🅿 ⓈⓈⓈ
1810 Rogers Place, British Columbia, V1S 1T7 **Tel** *(250) 372 0987 or (888) 556 3111* **Fax** *(250) 372 0967* **Rooms** *89*

Comfortable rooms are spacious in this three-story stucco-faced property. Kitchen units and Jacuzzis are available in some suites. Rates include continental breakfast. A waterslide in the pool and a family restaurant make this inn ideal for families. **www.comfortinnkamloops.com**

KELOWNA Lake Okanagan Resort ⬚ 🅼 ♨ 🏕 🗐 🅿 ⓈⓈⓈⓈ
2751 Westside Rd., British Columbia, V1Z 3T1 **Tel** *(250) 769 3511 or (800) 663 3273* **Fax** *(250) 769 6665* **Rooms** *146*

This family-oriented destination borders the beach on Lake Okanagan. Activities include horseback riding, golf, tennis, interpretive trails, mountain bike trails, and a children's playground. There is a full service spa. Spacious rooms have kitchen, balconies, and lake views. Rate is for a minimum two nights during May–Sep. **www.lakeokanagan.com**

PENTICTON Penticton Lakeside Resort ⬚ 🅼 ♨ 🏕 🗐 🅿 ⓈⓈⓈ
21 Lakeshore Drive West, British Columbia, V2A 7M5 **Tel** *(250) 493 8221 or (800) 663 9400* **Fax** *(250) 493 0607* **Rooms** *204*

A family resort in the center of Penticton with a private beach, pier, jet-skiing, and parasailing on Lake Okanagan. Suites have Jacuzzis. All rooms feature balconies. Equipment rental is available for all watersports. There is a children's play center and a casino. Pet friendly. **www.pentictonlakesideresort.com**

PRINCE RUPERT Prince Rupert Crest Hotel ⬚ 🅼 🗐 🅿 ⓈⓈⓈ
222 W. First Ave., British Columbia, V8J 1A8 **Tel** *(250) 624 6771 or (800) 663 8150* **Fax** *(250) 627 7666* **Rooms** *108*

Situated on a bluff close to historic Cow Bay area, this is the only four-star hotel in the north with wonderful harbor views, especially of Kaien Island. Choose your view: harbor, city, or mountain. Most rooms have window seats. The hotel is pet-friendly too. **www.cresthotel.bc.ca**

WHISTLER Holiday Inn Whistler Village ⬚ 🅼 🏕 🗐 🅿 ⓈⓈⓈ
4295 Blackcomb Way, British Columbia, V0N 1B4 **Tel** *(604) 938 0878 or (800) 229 3188* **Fax** *(604) 938 9943* **Rooms** *115*

A modern hotel located right in the heart of Whistler Village and a 5-minute walk from Blackcomb Village lifts. All rooms are equipped with kitchenettes, jetted soaker tubs, and gas or electric fireplaces. Deluxe suites have washers and dryers. Some have lofts, dens, and balconies. Children are welcome and eat for free. **www.whistlerhi.com**

WHISTLER Fairmont Chateau Whistler ⬚ 🅼 ♨ 🏕 🗐 🅿 ⓈⓈⓈⓈⓈ
4599 Chateau Blvd., British Columbia, V0N 1B4 **Tel** *(604) 938 8000 or (800) 606 8244* **Fax** *(604) 938 2291* **Rooms** *550*

Copper-roofed, gabled, castle-like luxury resort situated adjacent to Whistler and Blackcomb ski hills and gondolas, as well as hiking trails and a golf course. Nanny Network Ltd. (an external company) provides childcare including storytime and crafts. **www.fairmont.com**

WHISTLER Pan Pacific Whistler Mountainside ⬚ 🅼 ♨ 🏕 🗐 🅿 ⓈⓈⓈⓈⓈ
4320 Sundial Crescent, British Columbia, V0N 1B4 **Tel** *(604) 905 2999* **Fax** *(604) 905 2995* **Rooms** *121*

Pedestrian-only Whistler Village is home to this luxurious boutique-hotel property featuring floor-to-ceiling windows. Suites all come with fireplaces and a full kitchen, as well as stunning valley and mountain views. Float in the outdoor heated saltwater pool and watch dawn or a canopy of stars. **www.panpacific.com**

NORTHERN CANADA

CAMBRIDGE BAY Arctic Islands Lodge 🅼 ⓈⓈⓈⓈ
26 Omingmak, P.O. Box 38, Cambridge Bay, Nunavut, X0B 0C0 **Tel** *(867) 983 2345* **Fax** *(867) 983 2480* **Rooms** *26*

This lodge sits on the banks of the river that forms the historic and coveted Northwest Passage. The Northwest Passage meeting room has rare artifacts from the famed Franklin expedition. An airport shuttle service is available. This hotel is known for its range of sporting activities. Wireless Internet. **www.cambridgebayhotel.com**

DAWSON CITY Downtown Hotel 🅼 🏕 🅿 ⓈⓈ
1026 Second Ave., Dawson City, Yukon, Y0B 1G0 **Tel** *(867) 993 5346* **Fax** *(867) 993 5076* **Rooms** *59*

Locally owned and operated, this hotel has a Klondike-era look. Rooms are in the main building or annex. There is a jacuzzi and glass-roofed atrium with plants. Room service is available 7am–9pm. Sourdough Saloon has swinging doors and is home to the famed "Sourtoe Cocktail." **www.downtownhotel.ca**

Key to Price Guide *see p346* **Key to Symbols** *see back cover flap*

DAWSON CITY Midnight Sun Hotel

1054 Third Ave., Dawson City, Yukon, Y0B 1G0 **Tel** *(867) 993 5495* **Fax** *(867) 993 6425* **Rooms** *44*

Open since 1972, this three-story building was rebuilt in 1984. The hotel has a historic gold rush-era look. Located downtown, it has a variety store and business services. The Midnight Sun lounge offers nightly entertainment and a signature drink menu. Room service is available 6am–1am. **www.midnightsunhotel.com**

FORT PROVIDENCE Snowshoe Inn

1 Mackenzie Drive, Fort Providence, Northwest Territories, X0E 0L0 **Tel** *(867) 699 3511* **Fax** *(867) 699 4300* **Rooms** *35*

Located on the banks of the Mackenzie River, this family owned inn has a store featuring traditional local crafts such as moose hair tuftings and porcupine quill work and prints by area artists. Rooms have satellite TV and high-speed Internet; some have kitchen facilities. The restaurant is just across the street. **www.ssimicro.com/snowshoe**

FORT SIMPSON Janor Guest House

10003 99B Ave., Fort Simpson, Northwest Territories, X0E 0N0 **Tel** *(867) 695 2077* **Fax** *(867) 695 3030* **Rooms** *6*

The price at this centrally located guest house includes a continental breakfast and a large vegetable garden for the use of guests. The owners live next door in this side-by-side duplex. The house is wired up with satellite television, movie channels, and wireless Internet. There is a free on-site laundromat. Airport pickup is available for a fee. **www.janor.ca**

HAINES JUNCTION Raven Hotel

181 Alaska Hwy, Haines Junction, Yukon, Y0B 1L0 **Tel** *(867) 634 2500* **Fax** *(867) 634 2517* **Rooms** *12*

A gourmet breakfast is included in the price of your room at this family-run hotel. It has been awarded a four-star rating from Canada Select and is located at the base of the spectacular St. Elias Mountains. The restaurant is excellent, although expensive. Open May–Sep. **www.ravenhotelyukon.com**

HAY RIVER Ptarmigan Inn

10 J Gagnier Street, Hay River, Northwest Territories, X0E 1G1 **Tel** *(867) 874 6781* **Fax** *(867) 874 3392* **Rooms** *42*

Located in the center of town. Some rooms have kitchenettes; alternatively, the Keys Dining Room and Doghouse Sports Bar provide two dining and entertainment options. The full-service fitness center has a sauna. There is no pool but guests receive a complimentary pass to the town's aquatic center. High-speed Internet. **www.ptarmiganinn.com**

INUVIK Nova Inn Inuvik

300 Mackenzie Road, Inuvik, Northwest Territories, X0E 0T0 **Tel** *(867) 777 6682* **Fax** *(867) 777 4522* **Rooms** *42*

This is a clean, inexpensive option at the end of town (opposite the hospital). Rooms all have fireplaces for winter and air-conditioning for summer, and some have full kitchen facilities. A small canteen sells drinks and snacks on site. There is complimentary parking too. **www.novainninuvik.ca**

IQALUIT Frobisher Inn

The Astro Hill Terrace, Iqaluit, Nunavut, X0A 0H0 **Tel** *(867) 979 2222* **Fax** *(867) 979 0427* **Rooms** *95*

This inn has deluxe rooms that feature original Inuit artwork and views of Baffin Island and Iqaluit. Rooms have wireless Internet and coffeemakers. Some have kitchenettes. The complex in which the hotel is located has a pool, movie theater, drugstore, stores, restaurants, and a café. There is also a business centre. **www.frobisherinn.com**

WHITEHORSE Best Western Gold Rush Inn

411 Main Street, Whitehorse, Yukon, Y1A 2B6 **Tel** *(867) 668 4500* **Fax** *(867) 668 7432* **Rooms** *101*

Within walking distance of numerous attractions. Some rooms in this hotel have Jacuzzis and some have kitchens. The decor is 1898 gold-rush style, including a lobby filled with relics from the goldfields. The hotel has the Gold Pan Saloon and The Office lounge. Wireless Internet and airport shuttle. **www.goldrushinn.ca**

WHITEHORSE Edgewater Hotel

101 Main Street, Whitehorse, Yukon, Y1A 2A7 **Tel** *(867) 667 2572* **Fax** *(867) 668 3014* **Rooms** *31*

This locally owned downtown vintage hotel overlooks the Yukon River and is across from the historic White Pass Railway depot. Rooms are comfortable, with high-speed Internet. There is a nice steakhouse and a wine bar downstairs. **www.edgewaterhotelwhitehorse.com**

WHITEHORSE High Country Inn

4051 Fourth Ave., Whitehorse, Yukon, Y1A 1H1 **Tel** *(867) 667 4471* **Fax** *(867) 667 6457* **Rooms** *100*

A 12-m (40-ft) wooden Mountie guards the hotel's entrance. Located near walking trails, three blocks from the waterfront and six blocks from downtown, this stylish and comfortable hotel in a quiet part of town has antique furniture and a brick fireplace in the elegant lobby. Complimentary wireless Internet and hotel shuttle. **www.highcountryinn.yk.ca**

YELLOWKNIFE Bayside Bed & Breakfast

3505 MacDonald Drive, Yellowknife, Northwest Territories, X1A 2H2 **Tel** *(867) 669 8844* **Fax** *(867) 669 8843* **Rooms** *5*

The price includes a nice hot breakfast served in the lovely sunny tearoom overlooking Yellowknife Bay. The house has a wraparound deck and dockside views. A guest lounge is upstairs. Located in the heart of scenic and historic Old Town with buildings full of character, it is a 20 minute walk to downtown. **www.bbcanada.com/4822.html**

YELLOWKNIFE Explorer Hotel

4825 49th Ave., Box 7000, Yellowknife, Northwest Territories, X1A 2R3 **Tel** *(867) 873 3531* **Fax** *(867) 873 2789* **Rooms** *187*

Situated downtown, near Frame Lake and the Legislative Assembly. Good food is served at the Traders Grill and Trapline Lounge restaurants. Prominent guests have included Queen Elizabeth, Prince Phillip, Prince Charles, and actor Leonard Nimoy from *Star Trek*. **www.explorerhotel.com**

WHERE TO EAT

What makes Canadian cuisine unique is its regional specialties: Alberta beef, goldeye fish in Manitoba, salmon from BC, Nova Scotia lobster, and Quebec French pies and pastries. Game, including rabbit, caribou, and bison, which have been served in aboriginal homes for centuries, are now considered gourmet dishes at cosmopolitan restaurants. A tradition of French haute cuisine is evident in most of the country's major cities, particularly in top hotels. However, as Canada is a nation of immigrants, ethnic restaurants

Seafood on offer in Atlantic Canada

are common everywhere. German, Greek, Chinese, Thai, Indian, Ukrainian, African, and Italian cuisines, along with other international favorites, provide a wide range of choice at a price to suit every budget. Regional specialties can be sampled in their place of origin, but most of the larger towns will also offer a choice of the country's best local produce, and in some areas this includes Canadian wines and beers (see p369). The listings on pp370–91 describe a selection of restaurants chosen for their variety, service, and good value.

The Five Fishermen restaurant in Halifax, Nova Scotia *(see p372)*

TYPES OF RESTAURANTS

Eating out in Canada is surprisingly easy on the pocket, particularly compared to European and American prices. This makes a trip to a top restaurant to sample international cuisine (often made with local produce) very worthwhile. Eating places are extremely varied, with the tearoom, bistro, brasserie, and theater café competing with the more usual café, restaurant, and fast food outlet. Many pubs also serve excellent bar food, at reasonable prices. More unusual, but no less worthwhile, is the uniquely Canadian dining experience of the delicious lobster supper. Held throughout the summer on Prince Edward Island, these lively gatherings usually take place in church grounds

on wooden tables surrounded by local fishermen. Equally unique, though by no means public, are Inuit dinners. Traveling through the Arctic north may result in an invitation to join an Inuit family for the evening meal. Traditional dishes might include sun-dried caribou sweetened with berry sauces or smoked and dried local fish. These family dinners are usually alcohol-free and very lively.

VEGETARIAN

Vegetarian options are on the increase throughout the country. Expect to see at least one vegetarian dish on each menu. For those who eat fish, seafood has something of a national reputation. "Health Canada," the government plan for healthy eating, took

effect in the 1990s. Restaurants that subscribe to the plan sign menus with a heart symbol denoting low-fat dishes. Anyone on a special or weight-loss diet can feel free to ask the chef to leave out certain high-calorie ingredients. Fresh fruits are easily obtained throughout the south of the country, and are abundant and often day-old in the main growing areas of Ontario and BC's Okanagan Valley. Some of the best berries and peaches in the world can be enjoyed here in the summer. It is worth remembering that most food in the Northwest Territories and Nunavut is imported, and largely canned or frozen; apart from Inuit game kills, fresh food is hard to obtain, and very expensive, in these distant Arctic regions.

Open-air dining in downtown Montreal *(see pp373–5)*

Arowhon Pines Lodge in Algonquin Provincial Park, Ontario *(see p356)*

ALCOHOL

The minimum age of public purchase and consumption of alcohol is 19 throughout the country, except in Quebec where it is 18. Canada produces some fine wines *(see p369)*, which are becoming more widely available.

Throughout much of Canada, the distribution of alcohol is controlled by the provincial government. It is not sold in corner stores or supermarkets, but liquor stores sell a good range of wine and spirits. A separate government run store sells only beer. Beer and liquor stores are not usually open on Sundays, so expect long line-ups before long weekends and holidays.

EATING HOURS AND RESERVATIONS

Lunch tables are usually available from noon to 2pm, and dinner reservations from 6pm to 9pm, although later bookings should be accepted in larger cities. Reserving a table in advance is generally a good idea. It is considered polite to call ahead and cancel if you are unable to make your reservation.

PAYING AND TIPPING

It is possible to eat well in Canada for a bargain price. A snack in a café seldom costs more than Can$7. In a good restaurant, a three-course meal with wine often costs between Can$30–$60. Even gourmet dinners can start at Can$50. Luncheon items are generally less expensive, and are often similar to the evening menu. Restaurant tax is the 5 percent GST (Goods and Services Tax), plus a varying provincial sales tax, applicable everywhere except Alberta. Some provinces also add a separate liquor tax. Taxes are included on the final check. Tipping is generally expected, and should be about 15 percent of the net check. Service charges are rarely included, but might be included in the bill for a large group. In common with most countries, a tip should increase if you are bringing a larger party to a restaurant and for any exceptional service. Europeans should note that tipping is expected in bars and nightclubs. Penalizing staff for bad service is not common.

CHILDREN

Canada is a child-friendly society. Most restaurants offer high chairs or booster seats. The more upscale the venue, the more parents are required to keep children seated at table and to take noisy or upset youngsters outside until they calm down. A children's menu or half-portions may well be available for those under eight years old.

DISABLED FACILITIES

All new restaurants, as well as existing establishments undergoing renovation, have made their sites accessible to wheelchair users. A wide bathroom door and no interior steps from entrance to dining table are now compulsory across the country in new buildings. However, older, rural establishments should be checked out in advance.

DRESS CODE

Vacationers need not worry unduly about bringing formal clothes with them on a trip. Most restaurants operate "smart-casual" policy, especially at lunchtime, but exceptions to this can include sneakers (trainers), cut-off jeans, and dirty or ripped clothes. The rule generally runs as follows: the more expensive and exclusive the restaurant, the more formal the attire required. Evening dress is very rarely required in any venue.

SMOKING

More than 70 percent of Canadians do not smoke, and local by-laws restrict where the dwindling minority of smokers can smoke. Smoking is not allowed in any public places, including bars, cafés, and restaurants. A note of caution: when picnicking in a park, be sure to extinguish your cigarette for fear of starting a forest fire.

Café-bars in cities are mostly inexpensive and popular options

The Flavors of Canada

With a rich history of multiculturalism, Canada's culinary heritage is as diverse as it is intriguing. Although there is no national cuisine as such, regional specialties have their own strong identities. Seafood dominates Atlantic Canada and BC menus, while steaks and burgers are best in the ranching areas of Alberta and Saskatchewan. Acadian cuisine, reminiscent of French country food, is found in New Brunswick and Nova Scotia. In Northern Canada, age-old Inuit techniques produce a variety of sundried caribou and fish dishes. But the Canadian specialty that is famous the world over is maple syrup.

Vegetable squash

Pacific salmon, caught in the Khutzeymateen River, BC

FISH AND SEAFOOD

Bordered by oceans on three sides, Canada offers great seafood, particularly on its east and west coasts. Produce from here can easily make it from the ocean to the dinner plate within 24 hours. Oysters, clams, and scallops are a main feature of East Coast menus. Prince Edward Island is famous for its lobster; those who don't like crustacea can try Atlantic salmon. Pacific salmon, crab, shellfish, and shrimp (prawns) dominate British Columbian fare, along with a typically northern fish, Arctic char. More unusual dishes, often incorporating historic preserving methods, include Solomon Grundy (Nova Scotia's fine marinated herring), and cod tongues, as well as tasty seal flipper pie from Newfoundland.

Freshwater fish, both the farmed and wild versions, is caught in the two million lakes dotted across Canada, and offers a delicate contrast to seafood. In the west of the country, the tender Winnipeg goldeye, trout, and pickerel, which is often cooked over open fires at informal summer outdoor shore lunches throughout the central region, are a uniquely Canadian treat.

Scallop   Crab   Sardines   Lobster   Mussels   Oysters   Salmon   Clams

Selection of superb seafood from the clear waters of Canada

FRENCH-CANADIAN DISHES AND SPECIALTIES

The center of French-style gourmet cuisine in Canada is Quebec. Dishes here are reminiscent of the best European food. For some more traditional French-Canadian dishes, cities and towns in the province usually serve specialties. These include *creton, tourtière,* and many varieties of pâtisserie. Smoked beef is another popular local delicacy. The Maritime Provinces offer excellent, originally French, Acadian dishes from recipes which are hundreds of years old. As well as meat pies, patés, and stews, rich desserts and cakes feature in their filling menus. Vieux-Montréal's bistros offer many classic delights, such as *escargots à la bourguignonne.* French-Canadians are known for their rich desserts, such as *trempettes* (fried bread soaked in maple syrup) and *pudding au chomeur.*

Maple sypup

Creton *is a coarse, spicy, pork pâté. It is delicious served on hunks of fresh baguette with cornichons (gherkins).*

Baskets of rosy apples outside a Nova Scotia farm shop

MEAT AND GAME

Alberta's cattle ranches are the source of Canada's finest beef. Most beef in rural areas is served simply, with salad and fries, but one much-loved local dish is Calgary beef hash – corned beef with baked beans and fried potatoes. Lamb and buffalo are also farmed, in smaller numbers. The Yukon, North-west Territories, and Nunavut supply much of the country's game; caribou, musk ox, and moose are all sent south to be cooked in the European style. Local people, especially the Inuit, smoke meat for the winter months. Their smoked caribou is delicious and very popular. Famous for making the most of a kill, native people use every part of the animal for either clothing or food – even moose fleas are

something of a delicacy. Goose, duck, and fish are all smoked or sundried too, providing staples for the very long, harsh winter. Caribou and birds are preserved by being hung out on lines to dry in the Arctic sun.

Fiddlehead fern shoots for sale in a New Brunswick market

FRUIT AND VEGETABLES

Ontario is the fruitbowl of Canada. In addition to its burgeoning wine industry, the area is famous for its strawberries and cranberries. Peaches and apples are also cultivated here in large quantities, as are blueberries, which also flourish in Nova Scotia and Quebec. Corn, black beans, and vegetable squash (collectively known as the "three sisters") are produced in Ontario along-side zucchini (courgettes), huge tomatoes, and fresh herbs. In New Brunswick, fiddleheads (fern shoots) and dulse (seaweed) are sautéed as a vegetable side dish.

WHAT TO DRINK

Two popular Canadian beers, always served chilled, are the lagers Molson "Canadian" and Labatt "Blue." Canada also produces some excellent wines from hybrid grapes, thanks largely to European winemakers who have emigrated here. Most wine comes from three areas: a pocket in the southern Okanagan Valley of British Columbia *(see p317)*, the Annapolis Valley of Nova Scotia, and a narrow strip along the Niagara Penin-sula of southern Ontario. Grape varieties include such familiar names as Chardonnay, Riesling, and Pinot Noir. Rye whisky is distilled in BC; Canadian Club is the most popular brand, but local dis-tilleries produce specialties.

Escargots à la bourguignonne *are snails cooked in garlic and parsley butter and served in their shells.*

Tourtière, *a pastry-topped pie filled with meat and vegetables flavored with spices, is country fare.*

Pudding au chômeur *(literally "unemployed pudding") is an upside-down cake with a rich caramel base.*

Choosing a Restaurant

The restaurants in this guide have been selected across a range of prices for their exceptional food, good value, or interesting location. This chart lists restaurants under the region chapter headings in the same order as the rest of the guide, grouped alphabetically by province and then by town. Entries are alphabetical within the price category.

PRICE CATEGORIES IN CANADIAN DOLLARS (CAN $)
For a three-course meal for one, including half a bottle of house wine (where served) and service.
$ Under $30
$$ $30–$40
$$$ $40–$60
$$$$ $60–$80
$$$$$ Over $80

NEWFOUNDLAND AND LABRADOR

L'ANSE AU CLAIR Northern Light Inn $$
82–86 Main Street, L'Anse Au Clair, Labrador, A0K 3K0 **Tel** *(709) 931 2332*

At this popular family restaurant you'll find everything from pizza and fried chicken to a large assortment of scrumptious seafood. Ask for traditional Newfoundland fare like salmon, halibut, or cod, and their famous bread pudding with plum sauce. In the summer try the popular house specialty, roasted caribou. There is a historic lighthouse nearby.

CORNER BROOK Sorrento $$$
18 Park Street, Corner Brook, Newfoundland, A2H 2W9 **Tel** *(709) 639 3466*

A feast for the eyes and ears as well as a feast for the body, with an upscale decor, lovely outdoor (screened) patio, and live musicians on the weekends, the menu at the Sorrento features unique pizzas, hand kneaded pastas, a great grill, and European specialties. Tiramisu, the original Italian "pick-me-up," is a must.

COW HEAD Bayview Restaurant at Shallow Bay Motel $$
193 Main Street, Cow Head, Newfoundland, A0K 2A0 **Tel** *(709) 243 2471*

Its location in Gros Morne National Park, overlooking the Atlantic Ocean a few feet away, is just one of the perks here. Newfoundland fare, cheesecakes and parfaits laced with Newfoundland bakeapple and partridge are a huge hit here. There are frequent stage shows on site, and dinner theater performances accompany codfish dinners.

FERRYLAND Lighthouse Picnics $
Lighthouse Road, Ferryland, Newfoundland, A0A 2H0 **Tel** *(709) 363 7456*

This award-winning eating experience consists of a historic lighthouse, magical scenery, and gourmet picnics. After ordering, guests are given a picnic blanket and books of local interest and are asked to find the perfect spot. The distinctive menu ranges from crab cakes to curried chicken salad. There are complimentary interpretive tours of the lighthouse.

LA SCIE The Outport Tea Room $
101 Water Street, La Scie, Newfoundland, A0K 3M0 **Tel** *(709) 675 2720*

Located inside a small museum, this cozy restaurant is surrounded by local history and relics and provides a great view of the harbor. Meals are served in period costume. The amazing food is traditional Newfoundland cooking at its best: fish cakes, chowder, fisherman's brewis, pea soup, and more. Incredible value. No alcohol served.

PORT AU CHOIX Point Riche Restaurant $$$
41 Fisher Street, Port Au Choix, Newfoundland, A0K 4C0 **Tel** *(709) 861 3777*

This family restaurant with a wide menu selection, famous for Fish Chowder, home-style cooking, and homemade desserts, is proud to offer "a taste of Newfoundland." The decor throughout has a lighthouse theme. The service is fast and efficient. There is a lounge attached to the restaurant. Both lounge and restaurant have great views of the harbor.

PORT BLANDFORD The Clode Sound Restaurant 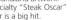 $$$
Port Blandford, Newfoundland, A0C 2G0 **Tel** *(709) 543 2525*

There is a breathtaking view of Clode Sound from this restaurant with cathedral ceiling, and Newfoundland artwork. Wait staff are knowledgeable about the area. The varied menu focuses on regional fare. House specialty "Steak Oscar" is grilled to perfection, topped with shrimp and scallop in hollandaise sauce. Mouthwatering lobster is a big hit.

ST. JOHN'S The Gypsy Tea Room $$$
315 Water Street, St. John's, Newfoundland, A1C 6J9 **Tel** *(709) 739 4766*

Smack in the middle of town this popular restaurant with old brick walls, hardwood floors, and casual decor really hums. European style dishes are prepared with a Mediterranean flair. Duck Confit (marinated for 24 hours and slowly cooked for 6 hours) is hugely popular, along with fresh seafood straight from the boats.

ST. JOHN'S Velma's $$$
264 Water Street, St. John's, Newfoundland, A1C 1B7 **Tel** *(709) 576 2264*

Velma's captures the spirit of Newfoundland. Located in the downtown core, it is a busy family restaurant frequented by locals and visitors. It has a homey atmosphere and an odd collection of bric-a-brac for decor. You will be called "me love" and treated as if you were family. Cod tongues and scrunchions are all-time favorites.

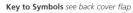
Key to Symbols *see back cover flap*

NEW BRUNSWICK, NOVA SCOTIA, AND PRINCE EDWARD ISLAND

ANTIGONISH Gabrieau's Bistro $$$$$

350 Main Street, Antigonish, Nova Scotia, B2G 2C5 **Tel** *(902) 863 1925*

Picture this: creamy custard walls, inset burgundy ceiling, lots of fine art. Cuisine is international in flavors with a creative edge. Lunch features hearty sandwiches, fresh salads, thin crust pizzas, and flavorful pastas. At night, the Bistro transforms to fine dining replete with creative appetizers, delicious entrees, and decadent desserts.

BADDECK Telegraph House $$$

479 Chebucto Street, Baddeck, Nova Scotia, B0E 1B0 **Tel** *(902) 295 1100*

Huge, beautifully decorated dining room in an old Victorian styled inn (circa 1860) serves superb seafood including fresh seafood every evening. An old-fashioned turkey dinner replete with dressing and cranberry sauce is another daily feature. Telegraph House is famous for its oatcakes. Celtic artists (fiddle and keyboard) perform from July.

BLACKVILLE Darlene's Family Restaurant and Tea House $$

186 Barnettville Road, Barnettville, New Brunswick, E9B 1X6 **Tel** *(506) 843 7979*

This charming restored 1896 grocery store is perky, bright, and colorful. The tried-and-true family recipes are truly amazing, including fiddlehead chowder and freshly baked blueberry pie. Rustic antiques, lace and hand-embroidered tablecloths, and bone china tea cups add to the ambience. Tasty food and exceptional value.

CARAQUET Le Caraquette $$$

89 Boulevard St.-Pierre Est., Caraquet, New Brunswick, E1W 1B6 **Tel** *(506) 727 6009*

This restaurant always amazes visitors with the quality of food and the friendly service. Its big bonus is eating on the large terrace overlooking the Bay of Challeur and watching the activity at the wharves. Renowned for the seafood omelet, lobster club sandwich, and seafood platter. Bring a big appetite.

CHARLOTTETOWN Piece A Cake Restaurant $$$

119 Grafton Street, Charlottetown, Prince Edward Island, C1A 1K9 **Tel** *(902) 894 4585*

Eclectic, fun menu featuring steak, seafood, and pasta. Hugely popular is ginger tiger prawn penne with cashews and dates. Dietary concern? No problem. The chefs can adapt any recipe, and they specialize in gluten-free pastas. The restaurant has an airy bistro feel, lots of windows, and funky unusual decor.

CHARLOTTETOWN Sirenella Ristorante 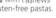 $$$$

83 Water Street, Charlottetown, Prince Edward Island, C1A 1A5 **Tel** *(902) 628 2271*

Northern Italian cuisine at its best, featuring homemade ravioli and gnocchi as well as grilled fish dishes. Warm and cozy decor, with large paintings on the walls. Located in the historic part of town, Sirenella chefs use fresh, local ingredients whenever possible. Try the tasty Vitello Pizzaiola and Mussels "In Love."

DALHOUSIE Le Menuet Dining Room and Restaurant $$$

Best Western Manoir Adelaide, 385 Adelaide Street, Dalhousie, New Brunswick, E8C 1B4 **Tel** *(506) 684 5681*

Elegant, cozy, fine dining. Large solarium windows, spectacular views of Bay des Chaleurs, Gaspé Coast, Appalachian Moutains. Wide variety of homemade Canadian dishes, from seafood and steaks to mouthwatering desserts. Hungry patrons go for the Fisherman Platter or the Surf and Turf. Excellent service. Bilingual. Scenic and cultural experience.

EARLTOWN Sugar Moon Farm $

221 Alex MacDonald Road, Earltown, Nova Scotia, B0K 1V0 **Tel** *(902) 657 3348*

Organic buttermilk pancakes, artisanal sausages, maple baked beans, maple butter, organic coffee, and more make up a wholesome traditional all-day breakfast with a gourmet twist at this eatorie housed in a hand-crafted log cabin with a stone fireplace and trestle tables, also attached to a working maple sugar camp and interpretive center (seasonal hours).

FREDERICTON Asia Beef Noodle $$

624 Queen Street, Fredericton, New Brunswick, E3B 1C2 **Tel** *(506) 472 6240*

Situated in the downtown core, Asia Beef Noodle is a popular addition on the restaurant scene. It serves an excellent selection of Viet-Thai food at modest prices, the staff are friendly, and the portions are large and very tasty. Any soup with noodles is a meal in itself. For fun, sit by the large fish tank.

FREDERICTON Luna Pizza $$

91 York Street, Fredericton, New Brunswick, E3B 3N4 **Tel** *(506) 455 4020*

Soft peach walls, tasteful decor, and white leather chairs say it all. A classy place with great Italian food in the downtown core, yet a surprisingly modest price tag. Food is prepared from scratch. Local favorites are the Caesar salad, seafood lasagna, and Marquerita pizza. Accommodating and friendly service.

FREEPORT Lavena's Catch Café $$

15 Highway 217, Freeport, Nova Scotia, B0V 1B0 **Tel** *(902) 839 2517*

A step from the ferry to Briar Island, this small restaurant has a big heart and a great reputation. Menu has interesting comments from visitors. Simple tasty food prepared by good cooks. Seafood fresh from the boats. Generous portions. Try the Solomon Gundy for appetizer. It's unique. Great kids' menu.

GLEN HAVEN White Sails Bakery and Tea Room   ⑤

12930 Peggy's Cove Road, Tantallon, Nova Scotia, B3Z 2S2 **Tel** *(902) 826 1966*

They are experts at serving simple and hearty food. People from all over the world have found this small restaurant tucked away on the ocean. You can't go wrong with their homestyle chili, baked beans, soups, and chowders. The bakery has a full line of goodies including diabetic and gluten-free specialties.

GUYSBOROUGH Days Gone By Bakery   ⑤⑤

143 Main Street, Guysborough, Nova Scotia, B0H 1N0 **Tel** *(902) 533 2762*

You won't find a deep-fat fryer here but you'll find lots of great "down-home" cooking like moist panfried haddock and roast turkey dinners. The view of the river is lovely from this 1790 home filled with antiques. All the baking is done from scratch. No preservatives are used. The breads, cakes, and pies are worth writing home about.

HALIFAX Chives Canadian Bistro   ⑤⑤⑤⑤

1537 Barrington Street, Halifax, Nova Scotia, B3J 1Z4 **Tel** *(902) 420 9626*

Located near the waterfront, this bistro has a strict policy of seasonality. In addition, they try to use locally sourced ingredients for dishes such as maple smoked chicken breast with potato rosti, caramelized onion, and maple balsamic jam, or Steak Diane with wild Nova Scotia mushroom risotto and spiced buttermilk onion rings. Open 5–9:30pm.

HALIFAX The Five Fishermen   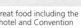 ⑤⑤⑤⑤⑤

1740 Argyle Street, Halifax, Nova Scotia, B3J 2W1 **Tel** *(902) 422 4421*

The Five Fishermen has provided popular fine dining since 1974. The building originally housed the first National Art School in North America and is full of character. Good spirits match the superb food. Seafood is delivered daily from dayboats. This multiple award-winning restaurant includes a world-famous mussel bar and features Nova Scotia wines.

KINGS LANDING Kings Head Inn, Kings Landing   ⑤⑤⑤

Exit 253 Route 2, Kings Landing, New Brunswick, E6K 3W3 **Tel** *(506) 363 4999*

In an 1855 setting, with candlelight ambience, and costumed staff, there is always a mouthwatering aroma from the scrumptious meals served here that feature traditional and tempting Loyalist feasts such as beggar's purse, Acadian tourtière, ploughman's lunch, fish cakes, and maple brandy squash pie. A cultural experience with exceptional food.

MONCTON McGinnis Landing   ⑤⑤⑤

499 Paul Street, Dieppe, Moncton, New Brunswick, B1A 6S5 **Tel** *(506) 856 6995*

McGinnis Landing Restaurant, one of Moncton's most popular restaurants, is known for its great food including the award-winning Seafood chowder. Located in Crystal Palace together with the Ramada Plaza hotel and Convention Center, it offers a menu for all appetites.

MONTAGUE Windows On The Water Restaurant   ⑤⑤

106 Sackville Street, Montague, Prince Edward Island, C0A 1R0 **Tel** *(902) 838 2080*

You will want to return again and again: first for excellent, fresh seafood, lobster, and fine steaks; second for the pleasure of eating out on the deck next to two large maple trees; and third for the view of Montegue Harbour. Be sure to have some seafood chowder, one of their signature dishes.

NEW GLASGOW New Glasgow Lobster Suppers   ⑤⑤⑤

604 Route 258, New Glasgow, Prince Edward Island, C0A 1N0 **Tel** *(902) 964 2870*

Opened in 1958, this restaurant is famous for preparing community-hall style lobster suppers. Two-level dining areas overlook the River Clyde. Checkered tablecloths and a large painted mural add to the decor. Fresh rolls are baked daily, and hot or cold lobster is served in the shell. Your meal includes PEI mussels and mile-high lemon meringue pie.

PUBNICO Red Cap Restaurant and Motel   ⑤⑤

1034 Route 335 South, Middle West Pubnico, Nova Scotia, B0W 2M0 **Tel** *(902) 762 2112*

Spacious and inviting, the Red Cap Restaurant has been serving great food since the 1940s. Located in a fishing community, fresh fish is popular. The menu also features Acadian cuisine, like its famous "rappie pie." Large windows overlook Pubnico Harbour. The restaurant showcases local art and photographs of the region.

QUISPAMSIS Hammond River Country Café   ⑤⑤⑤⑤

954 Hampton Road, Quispamsis, New Brunswick, E2G 1Z5 **Tel** *(506) 849 4726*

This is Polish cuisine at its best. Indulge in aromatic soups and meats prepared in unique ways. Specialties include borscht, pierogi, goulash, beef rolady, stuffed cabbage, schnitzel, and crepes. You will need a hearty appetite for the Polish sausage platter. In a comfortable setting, with Polish folk art, the river is close by with lots of migratory birds.

RUSTICO Dayboat   ⑤⑤⑤⑤

5033 Rustico Rd., Hunter River, Prince Edward Island, C0A 1N0 **Tel** *(902) 963 3833*

This upscale, simple, modern, casual restaurant with rave reviews and sparkling, intelligent service has a million-dollar view of Rustico Bay. A creative menu features PEI produce, meats, and lobster prepared three different ways. Meats are cooked to perfection, including their famous ribs. Great deck dining. Enjoy nature and the antics of the osprey.

ST. ANDREWS Kingsbrae Arms   ⑤⑤⑤⑤⑤

219 King Street, St. Andrews, New Brunswick, E5B 1Y1 **Tel** *(506) 529 1897*

This is fine dining featuring local and regional fare at its best in a tasteful heritage estate home. The chef raises organic and heirloom vegetables like purple peacock beans and Aztec red spinach. The menu reflects his simple "slow food" philosophy and features wild game and farmed sturgeon with osetra-style caviar. Attentive staff. Memorable food.

Key to Price Guide *see p370* **Key to Symbols** *see back cover flap*

SAINT JOHN Billy's Seafood Co.

Saint John City Market 49–51 Charlotte Street, Saint John, New Brunswick, E2L 2H8 **Tel** *(506) 672 3474*

Seafood lover's heaven. A fish market is part of the restaurant and fresh fish is delivered daily. They also pack live or cooked lobsters to go. Billy's is where the Maritime custom of cooking "cedar planked salmon" originated. This is a gastronomical delight in a relaxed, casual atmosphere in the historical Farmer's Market with lovely outdoor dining.

SHELBURNE Charlotte Lane Café

13 Charlotte Lane, Shelburne, Nova Scotia, B0T 1W0 **Tel** *(902) 875 3314*

An innovative menu features seafood, creative meat dishes, flavorful pastas, Swiss specialties, and luscious desserts. There is an outstanding wine selection. Housed in a 160 year-old heritage building, the Charlotte Lane Café has a welcoming interior and a peaceful garden patio. An in-house gift store has a great selection of hand-crafted Nova Scotian items.

SOURIS Sheltered Harbour Café

2065, Highway 2, Souris, Prince Edward Island, C0A 2B0 **Tel** *(902) 687 1997*

Known far and wide, this open concept kitchen uses locally grown ingredients. The Island Bar Clam Chowder is superb. You'll need a bowl since a cup is just a tease. The daily "alternative" menu, offered from 4 until 8pm, allows the owner/cook to step things up a notch, providing upscale selections at downscale prices. Large portions.

SUMMERSIDE Brothers Two Restaurant

618 Water Street East, Summerside, Prince Edward Island, C1N 4K2 **Tel** *(902) 436 9654*

With informal dining, cozy booths, Tiffany lamps, and a log room with a fireplace, the Brothers Two offers over 75 items and a menu just for kids. There is a great selection of beef, chicken, and seafood. Steamed lobster dinners are popular. The restaurant is home to Feast Dinner Theatres, where actors and actresses serve a four-course meal between hilarious scenes.

SUSSEX Broadway Café

73 Broad Street, Sussex, New Brunswick, E4E 2J7 **Tel** *(506) 433 5414*

Broadway Café exudes a rustic atmosphere with warm earth tones, lovely local art, wide planked floors with tile inserts, and large wooden booths. The menu changes frequently to reflect the seasons. Everything is made from scratch including blends of curry. The seafood is exceptional. Vegetarian friendly. Home to a definitive carrot cake.

WEST POINT West Point Lighthouse Inn, Restaurant and Museum

364 Cedar Dunes Park Road, West Point, Prince Edward Island, C0B 1V0 **Tel** *(902) 859 3605*

Twenty meters (65 ft) from the beach, this lighthouse restaurant has a historical significance that the staff love to talk about. Take a tour to the top! It is family oriented, with a fast service, but a casual and relaxed atmosphere. There is a big deck for sunny day eating. The chowder and fish burgers are a treat.

WOLFVILLE Acton's

406 Main Street, Wolfville, Nova Scotia, B4P 1C9 **Tel** *(902) 542 7525*

In the heart of downtown Wolfville, this friendly and intimate restaurant serves a range of dishes influenced by the cuisines of France and Italy. One of the menu highlights is the Nova Scotia Pan Roast: lobster, scallops, shrimp, and salmon in a lobster sauce, served with asparagus and rice.

MONTREAL

CHINATOWN Maison Kam Fung

1111 Rue Saint Urbain, H2Z 1Y6 **Tel** *(514) 878 2888*

The best dim sum in Montreal in a vast space adorned with pillars entwined with dragons, Chinese posters, and embroidery that fittingly sets the mood for the famous Peking Duck. Choose from a varied menu of Szechwan and Cantonese dishes that feature lots of dinner-for-two combinations and many tofu, chicken, pork, and other dishes.

DOWNTOWN Phayathai

1235 Rue Guy, H3H 2K5 **Tel** *(514) 933 9949*

Classic, delicious Thai dishes are served in a friendly ambience where staff are helpful and the seating is spaced for privacy. Try warming soups in which pungent fragrances of ginger, coriander, and lemon refresh the senses. The pad thai is excellent, and the curried chicken (gaeng gai sai nor mai) is also good.

DOWNTOWN Le Caveau

2063 Rue Victoria, H3A 2A3 **Tel** *(514) 844 1624*

An oasis in Montreal's downtown business core, this 1901 Victorian residence features intimate dining rooms spread over three floors where superb French meals are served. Specialties include fish, steak, rack of lamb, and the best liver in town. The pastry chef creates temptations such as Quebec maple pie.

DOWNTOWN L'Orchidée de Chine

2017 Rue Peel, H3A 1T6 **Tel** *(514) 287 1878*

Renowned for its Hunan Pekinese and Szechwan cuisine, this restaurant boldly offers non-standard, more upscale Chinese decor with floor-to-ceiling windows overlooking the street. Diners in romantic booths feast on Chinese delicacies such as Crispy duck in pastry or sautéed lamb with spicy sauce. The lemon chicken is delicious. Closed Sunday.

DOWNTOWN Restaurant & Taverne Magnan

2602 Rue Saint-Patrick, H3K 1B8 **Tel** *(514) 935 9647*

This legendary Montreal tavern used to serve gigantic platters to Lachine dockworkers. Nowadays, aficionados claim it has the best roast beef (Alberta beef) in North America. This is a sports bar where a wide-screen TV lets you catch up on the teams. There is a good selection of draft beers.

DOWNTOWN L'Actuel

1194 Rue Peel, H3B 2T6 **Tel** *(514) 866 1537*

This cheerful Belgian-style brasserie serves several dozen variations of mussels and French fries as well as other classic dishes such as smoked herring with potatoes. Daily luncheon and dinner table d'hôte offers three choices. Come for a drink (good choice of Belgian beers) at the lounge. Closed Sunday.

DOWNTOWN Chez la Mère Michel

1209 Rue Guy, H3H 2K5 **Tel** *(514) 934 0473*

Opened in 1965, this is one of the most traditional French restaurants in Montreal. Located in a Victorian residence, today's style is Provençale, where exposed wooden beams with copper detailing evoke countrified elegance. Try Dover sole à la meunière or classic coq au vin. Select from more than 7,000 mostly French wines.

DOWNTOWN Restaurant Julien

1191 Union, H3B 3C3 **Tel** *(514) 871 1581*

Parisian-influenced decor plus, in summer, a generous canopied terrace make this French restaurant a charming dining spot. The traditionally inspired menu features salmon fillet with sorrel cream sauce, or duck-breast tournedos. Desserts include the delicious chocolate marquise. There is an extensive wine list.

DOWNTOWN Café de Paris

Ritz-Carlton Hotel, 1228 Rue Sherbrooke Ouest, H3G 1H6 **Tel** *(514) 842 4212*

Whether you want afternoon tea or a romantic dinner, the formal Edwardian dining room in the luxurious Ritz serves exquisite elegance along with impeccable service. In summertime, doors are opened and you can dine overlooking the garden. The wine cellar is superlative. This is classic French interpretation of Quebecois regional foods.

DOWNTOWN Nuances

Casino de Montréal, 1 Ave. du Casino, H3C 4W7 **Tel** *(514) 392 2708*

This elegant, modern French restaurant with a magnificent panorama of the city marries taste, aroma and color in a new way. Nuances promises its guests a memorable culinary experience that will awaken the senses. The air of sophistication is well matched by an excellent by-the-glass wine selection.

DOWNTOWN Queue de cheval

1221 René-Lévesque Ouest, H3G 1T1 **Tel** *(514) 390 0090*

Very popular restaurant in heritage building, so reservations are recommended. Locals go for steaks, service, and ambience. Beef is from Colorado and comes in many forms: the specialty, the Kansas cut, is either a sirloin or filet mignon. In summertime 80 people can dine on the outdoor terrace.

DOWNTOWN The Beaver Club

Fairmont La Reine Elizabeth, 900 René-Lévesque Ouest, H3B 4A5 **Tel** *(514) 861 3511*

The Queen's popular landmark restaurant, The Beaver Club, exudes elegant sophistication, where jackets for men are suggested and reservations recommended. Exquisite dishes highlighting seasonal, regional fare are prepared with inspiration, served by knowledgeable staff. Choose from classic roast beef, grilled salmon, or lamb. Best martinis in town.

HOCHELAGA-MAISONNEUVE Chez Clo

3199 Rue Ontario Est, H1W 1P1 **Tel** *(514) 522 5348*

Locals pack this boisterous eatery where hurried staff serve traditional Quebecois favorites. Enjoy the rush, as well as hearty servings of shepherd's pie, pork and beans, and *pouding chômeur*, a hearty "poor man's pudding" featuring a thick caramelized maple syrup topping. Poutine is a specialty – really!

ILE SAINTE-HELENE Hélène de Champlain

200 Tour-de-l'Isle, H3C 4G8 **Tel** *(514) 395 2424*

Opened in 1983, this French restaurant situated in a historic mansion on Parc Jean-Drapeau boasts an incredible setting and fabulous food. The terrace, which is open for lunch and evening cocktails, offers a lovely view of the rose garden. During evenings a pianist underscores the mood of elegance.

OUTREMONT Faros

362 Ave. Fairmount Ouest, H2V 2G4 **Tel** *(514) 270 8437*

Fine, fresh seafood prepared Greek style is served in this cozy down-to-earth restaurant full of nooks and crannies for romantic meals where gracious but friendly staff help make this a city favorite. Choose from seafood such as crab, lobster, and grilled squid. Faros Feast allows pairings of appetizer and main course. Reservations recommended.

OUTREMONT Maïko Sushi

387 Rue Bernard Ouest, H2V 1T6 **Tel** *(514) 490 1225*

Diners enjoy more than just sushi here: steaks, tempura, and teriyaki are also available. Service may be slow, so watch the chefs prepare tastefully designed morsels at the sushi bar. Glass-encased lighting and sparse blue tones evoke a modern mood. Other "fusion" items have crept onto the menu, such as flambéed scallops. Reservations advisable.

Key to Price Guide *see p370* **Key to Symbols** *see back cover flap*

PLATEAU MONT-ROYAL Café Santropol 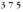 $

3990 Rue Saint-Urbain, H2W 1T7 **Tel** *(514) 842 3110*

A hippy atmosphere in a funky home with beautiful gardens. In summer tables spill out onto the lawn where you can dine beside the fish pond. Salads and sandwiches feature eclectic combinations, such as Hazel Brown, with bananas, cream cheese and other ingredients to tantalize the taste buds. No alcohol served. Exotic selections of tea.

PLATEAU MONT-ROYAL L'Anecdote $

801 Rue Rachel Est, H2J 2H7 **Tel** *(514) 526 7967*

Touted as serving the "best burgers in town," homemade mayonnaise gives L'Anecdote the edge over some stiff competition. Movie posters and chrome fittings lend this burger joint a 1950s feel but concessions to modern tastes include a vegetarian club sandwich. There is a strong wine list.

PLATEAU MONT ROYAL Schwartz's (Montréal Hebrew) Delicatessen $

3895 Blvd. Saint-Laurent, H2W 1X9 **Tel** *(514) 842 4813*

Jewish immigrants from Romania made smoked brisket a staple of the Montreal diet in 1928 when they opened this Montreal classic deli. Expect long lines. Choose from delicious lean, medium, or fatty smoked meat (lean can be dry). They have good rye bread though there is no seeded rye. No alcohol served.

PLATEAU MONT-ROYAL Au Pied de Cochon $$$$

536 Ave. Duluth Est, H2L 1A9 **Tel** *(514) 281 1114*

Soothing pleasures of tender meat, succulent sauces, and crisp salads await at this packed bistro serving traditional Quebecois cuisine, so make a reservation. Tuck into ample portions of venison, duck, bison, pork, or lamb roasted in a wood-fired oven. End your evening with sweet sugar pie. Closed Monday.

PLATEAU MONT-ROYAL L'Express $$$$

3927 Rue Saint-Denis, H2W 2M4 **Tel** *(514) 845 5333*

This almost perfect re-creation of a Paris bistro is extremely popular for its lively ambience with good and reasonably priced food, plus a great wine cellar containing many varieties available by the glass or half bottle. The long bar is the perfect setting for drinks before or after dinner. The specialty is fish soup with Gruyère croutons.

PLATEAU MONT-ROYAL Moishe's $$$$

3961 Blvd. Saint-Laurent, H2W 1Y4 **Tel** *(514) 845 3509*

The Jewish Quarter is home to this local tradition. Yes, it's noisy; yes, the staff are harried. But the Lighter family keep on serving their excellent thick steaks to an appreciative host of carnivores. Try the popular appetizer of chopped liver, but don't miss a side of twice-baked Monte Carlo potatoes.

PLATEAU MONT-ROYAL Café Méliès $$$$

3540 Boulevard Saint-Laurent, H2X 2V1 **Tel** *(514) 847 9218*

Located in the city's best indy film center, Ex-centris, at the Sherbrooke Metro. You can enjoy a coffee and sandwich for lunch or a glass of wine before or after seeing the show at this bistro-café. On weekends, it's popular for generous breakfasts. Alternatively, go for bistro-dinners such as duck confit or quiche.

SAINT URBAIN Wilensky's Light Lunch $

34 Rue Fairmount Ouest, H2T 2M1 **Tel** *(514) 271 0247*

Inexpensive Jewish corner-shop and tiny diner. Order the "special:" mustardy salami and Bologna served in a roll, along with a hand-pulled cherry cola. Or, try the chopped egg sandwich. Featured in Canadian author Mordecai Richler's classic *The Apprenticeship of Duddy Kravitz*, Wilensky's harks back to the 1930s. A true Montreal experience.

VIEUX-MONTREAL Stash's Cafe Bazaar $$$

200 Rue Saint-Paul Ouest, H2Y 1Z9 **Tel** *(514) 845 6611*

Casual Stash's Polish kitchen serves rib-sticking soul food, such as hot borscht, pierogis, nalesniki, and a deliciously unusual sausage salad. Don't know Polish food? No worries: that's why "le debutant" exists. This menu offers combinations so guests can sample different items. Diners sit at pews from a demolished convent.

VIEUX-MONTREAL Le Club Chasse et Pêche $$$$

423 Rue Saint-Claude, H2Y 3B6 **Tel** *(514) 861 1112*

The coat of arms over the doorway depicting moose antlers and flying fish introduces the cavernous interior where exceptional game and fish dishes are served. The leather-bound menu features iconic Canadian fare: deer, duck, salmon, oysters, and scallops. An affordable wine list complements the offerings: a don't-miss experience. Closed Sun–Mon.

VIEUX-MONTREAL Narcisse Bistro-Wine Bar $$$$

93 Rue de la Commune Est, H2Y 1J1 **Tel** *(514) 392 1649*

This elegant restaurant in Old Montreal offers splendid views of the St. Lawrence River and the Old Port. The chef prepares contemporary French seasonal delights, such as snails Provençal-style and beef bavette with a French shallot sauce and fries. The menu changes every week. Excellent wine list. Live jazz music Thu–Sat.

VIEUX-MONTREAL Toqué! $$$$$

900 Place Jean-Paul-Riopelle, H2Z 2B2 **Tel** *(514) 499 2084*

Normand Laprise and Christine Lamarche have reigned as Montreal's most innovative chefs for more than a decade so reservations are de rigeur here. Memorably flavorful, beautifully presented fusion meals fashioned from duck, venison, Arctic char, lamb, and salmon are served. There is an excellent wine list. Dress up and enjoy. Closed Mon & Sun.

QUEBEC CITY AND THE ST. LAWRENCE RIVER

BAIE SAINT-PAUL Le Mouton Noir 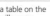 $$$
43 Rue Sainte-Anne, G3Z 1N9 **Tel** *(418) 240 3030*

The "Black Sheep", a small unpretentious restaurant, overlooks the Gouffre River: in summer request a table on the terrace overlooking the water. The European menu lists dishes such as seared tuna with tomato ratatouille as an entrée, and crème brulée for dessert. The staff are welcoming. Reservations (particularly in summer) are prudent.

BAS ST. LAURENT, NOTRE-DAME-DU-LAC Auberge Marie Blanc $
1112 Rue Commerciale S., G0L 1X0 **Tel** *(418) 899 6747*

William Bishop, a New York lawyer, built this romantic clapboard lodge on the shores of Lake Temiscouta for his Creole mistress, Marie Blanc Charlier. In summer, a beautiful terrace overlooks the lake. The restaurant with regional Quebecois cuisine focuses on locally grown produce *"pour votre santé"* (for your health). No wine. Closed mid-Oct–May.

CHARLEVOIX, SAINT-SIMEON Auberge sur Mer $$$
109 Rue du Quai, G0T 1X0 **Tel** *(418) 638 2674*

Unpretentious, family style Canadian restaurant with a children's menu that also serves beer and wine. Find basic meals such as salads, sandwiches, and soups along with pasta. Table d'hôte may include soups such as crab bisque, Matane shrimps, fresh lobster, or Doré (local fish), followed by Quebecois specialty, sugar pie.

HAVRE-SAINT-PIERRE Restaurant Chez Julie $
1023 Rue Dulcinée, G0G 1P0 **Tel** *(418) 538 3070*

This quaint, popular local seafood restaurant in what was once a tiny fishing village has absolutely no pretensions and you receive a genuine welcome and friendly service here. Look forward to generous portions of local seafood – try either the smoked salmon pizza or seafood pizza with béchamel sauce.

ILE D'ORLEANS, SAINT PIERRE Le Vieux-Presbytère $$$$
1247 Ave. Msgr-d'Esgly, G0A 4E0 **Tel** *(418) 828 9723*

This former priests' stone presbytery offers grand views of the St. Lawrence River. The dining room in the solarium provides a panorama of the Laurentian Mountains. View buffalo and elk wandering about the game farm next door – the source of the delicious steaks you'll be enjoying, probably as part of the daily table d'hôte specialties.

ILES-DE-LA-MADELEINE, CAP-AUX-MEULES Auberge Les Pas Perdus $
169 Chemin Principale, G4T 1C4 **Tel** *(418) 986 5151*

Cheerful owner Sebastien Cummings runs a funky hostel with deliciously creative bistro food. The staff are friendly and bilingual. Guests are invited to play the piano, wander with coffee and read the library of books, or view local art. A "don't miss" hangout with a spectacular view of the ocean as well as busy ferry docks.

LA MALBAIE Auberge des Peupliers $$$$
381 Rue Saint-Raphaël, G5A 2N8 **Tel** *(418) 665 4423*

This gabled farmhouse is one of Charlevoix's oldest auberges, with a gracious lawn overlooking the St. Lawrence River. Gastronome chef Dominique Truchon creates inventive dishes obtained fresh from regional producers. He is a founder of "La Route des saveurs" – the Charlevoix Flavor Trail, and this establishment is, of course, a member.

LAC-SAINT-JEAN, SAINT-GEDEON Restaurant le Parcours des Saveurs $$$$
255 Rue Dequen, G0W 2P0 **Tel** *(418) 345 2115*

An old-fashioned dining room where dark hardwood floor and wainscoting contrast pleasantly with sunflower-colored walls. This restaurant prides itself on being a certified "terroir cuisine," meaning "cuisine of the country," where health, seasonality, and freshness are paramount. Local game, meats, herbs, and vegetables are delectably prepared.

LES EBOULEMENTS Les Saveurs Oubliées $$$
350 rang Saint-Godefroy (route 362), G0A 2M0 **Tel** *(418) 635 9888*

Basque chef Régis Hervé offers a warm welcome to his airy restaurant overlooking *"la mer"* – the St. Lawrence River. This is a perfect setting for sampling traditional Charlevoix recipes that Hervé researched with assistance from older residents – hence the name, which means "Forgotten Flavors." Organic salt-grass-fed lamb and pine jelly are a specialty.

METIS-SUR-MER Au Coin de la Baie $
336 Route 132, G0J 1S0 **Tel** *(418) 936 3855*

This unpretentious motel dining room overlooks a lawn slipping down to Métis Bay, a view particularly lovely in summer. The scallops and cod filets are excellent. The motel also sells *"produits du terroir"* such as carrot marmalade and *rillettes de lapin* – so fill up your picnic hamper here. Closed mid-Sep–mid-May.

PERCE La Maison du Pêcheur $$$
155 Place du Quai, G0C 2L0 **Tel** *(418) 782 5331*

Located on a boardwalk overlooking the Atlantic, this cheerful establishment serves generous portions of fresh seafood. See and hear the ocean waves while dining on lobster, or specialties such as cod's tongue and seaweed soups. The extensive menu includes pasta, pizza, venison burgers, raclette, and grilled meats. Closed Nov–May.

Key to Price Guide *see p370* **Key to Symbols** *see back cover flap*

QUEBEC CITY Restaurant-Bistro Le Hobbit

$$⑤⑤

700 Rue Saint-Jean, G1R 1P9 **Tel** *(418) 647 2677*

Hobbit-inspired artworks decorate this casual city-center hangout frequented by locals wanting affordable, delicious bistro fare. The menu changes regularly, but includes both international and French dishes. Quaff a refreshing McAuslan microbrew with your meal.

QUEBEC CITY Le Cochon Dingue

⑤⑤⑤

46 Blvd. Champlain, G1K 4H5 **Tel** *(418) 692 2013*

Local institution that buzzes with activity. Children under 10 receive a special menu and games. In good weather, the Parisian style terrace lets everyone people watch while enjoying steak *frites*, mussel trios, spare ribs – or the Cochon's (Piggy's) famous hearty breakfast. A fun if eccentric choice.

QUEBEC CITY Aux Anciens Canadiens

⑤⑤⑤⑤

34 Rue Saint-Louis, G1R 4P3 **Tel** *(418) 692 1627*

The oldest house in Quebec (1675) lets you step through its threshold into a different century. Staff dressed in period costumes serve authentic, traditional Quebecois dishes such as venison in blueberry wine and ham in maple syrup, followed by sweets such as delicious maple syrup pie.

QUEBEC CITY Café de la Paix

⑤⑤⑤⑤

44 Rue des Jardins, G1R 4L7 **Tel** *(418) 692 1430*

Several intimate rooms and dependably excellent service offer a good balance of elegant yet casual dining inside the fortifications of Quebec. Reserve in advance: locals love the escargots, Caesar salad, caribou with juniper berries, beef Wellington, and other mouthwatering French dishes. Lingering is de rigueur over fine coffee and dessert.

SOUTHERN AND NORTHERN QUEBEC

CHAMBLY Fourquet-fourchette

⑤⑤⑤

1887 Ave. Bourgogne, J3L 1Y8 **Tel** *(450) 447 6370*

A summertime terrace overlooks historic Fort Chambly in this unique restaurant serving native foods along with recipes from early settlers and explorers. Wait staff are dressed in First Nation's and other early pioneers' or coureur-du-bois costumes. Unibroue microbrewery beer (the brewery is down the street and can be visited) is well matched to the foods.

GATINEAU Le Pied de cochon

⑤

248 Montcalm, J8Y 3C1 **Tel** *(819) 777 5808*

A Gatineau institution for over 30 years, this French bistro's white linens set the tone for romantic dining. Gracious wait staff serve you in the dining room, or on the terrace in summer. Fine dining at its best, with the "goût-du-jour" (taste of the day) being a special delight. Closed Sun–Mon.

GATINEAU Le Tartuffe

⑤⑤⑤

133 Notre-Dame-de-l'Île, J8X 3T2 **Tel** *(819) 776 6424*

An unpretentious French restaurant in a small historical house close to the Canadian Museum of Civilization, Palais du Congrès (Convention Centre), and downtown Ottawa. The menu is French origins with Outaouais influences, based on Quebec local/seasonal products, including Charlevoix veal, venison, lamb, and duck.

GATINEAU Le Twist Café Restaurant Bar

⑤⑤⑤

88 Montcalm, J8X 2L7 **Tel** *(819) 777 8886*

All-you-can-eat mussels on Sunday and Monday attract locals to this trendy café/bistro where contemporary music plays. Mussels, salmon pie, and homemade Belgian mayonnaise are specialties. The choice of the day often features fresh fish. There is also a range of microbrewery beers to try.

LAURENTIAN MOUNTAINS, SAINTE-ADELE L'Eau à la Bouche

⑤⑤⑤⑤⑤

3003 Blvd. Sainte-Adele, J8B 2N6 **Tel** *(450) 229 2991*

The discovery menu lets you explore new taste sensations coupled with fine wine. The fare is regional cuisine, with organic foods, game, and plants foraged from the wild are used whenever possible. Experience this restaurant's name, "mouth watering," while dining on such meals as roast veal in Xerxes sauce with wild mushroom risotto.

LAURENTIAN MOUNTAINS, VAL-DAVID A la Chocolaterie Marie-Claude

⑤

1090 Rue Valiquette, J8B 2M3 **Tel** *(450) 229 3991*

A charming house of small pleasures where over 30 varieties of quality chocolates are made the old-fashioned way. The menu includes waffles, croissants, salads, soups, and desserts like Italian gelato or chocolate fondue. Excellent espresso and café au lait. Closed Mon, Wed, and Thu.

LAVAL Derrière les fagots

⑤⑤⑤⑤⑤

166 Boulevard Sainte-Rose, Laval, H7L 1L4 **Tel** *(450) 622 2522*

White-clothed tables and warm earth tones in a Quebec-style house establish an atmosphere of relaxed elegance. In summer, dine outside on the small terrace. Seafood and fresh produce are the specialties. The mouthwatering French-inspired menu changes frequently. Superb sommelier, attentive service.

MONTEREGIE, SAINTE-MARTHE L'Auberge des Gallants   ⑤⑤⑤⑤⑤

1171 Chemin Saint-Henri, J0P 1W0 **Tel** *(450) 459 4241*

With a spa, hotel, restaurant, and sugar shack, this gracious inn situated in the heart of a wildlife sanctuary offers delicious food amid tranquility. Sugar shack (open late Feb to end Apr) serves traditional meals of maple sausages, beans, and pancakes while the gastronomical menu emphasizes regional, seasonal Quebec fare.

OUTAOUAIS, SHAWVILLE Café 349   ⑤

349 Rue Main, J0X 2Y0 **Tel** *(819) 647 6424*

Owner Ruth Smiley-Hahn bakes muffins, mouthwatering desserts, and serves tasty all-natural country-style meals seasoned with fresh herbs. Portions are generous. From quiches with salad to hearty soups, Ruth's menu changes every 6 weeks, celebrating the seasons. Local musicians entertain some Thursday nights, while local artists' creations are for sale.

OUTAOUAIS, WAKEFIELD Chez Eric Café   ⑤⑤⑤

28 Valley Drive, Wakefield, J0X 3G0 **Tel** *(819) 459 3747*

Named after a fish from a Monty Python skit, this quirky restaurant in an old house is a popular local hangout so reservations are advisable. Delicious homemade bistro food: try grilled salmon sandwich or wild boar ragout served by friendly staff. In summer, dine at tables in the flower garden.

OUTAOUAIS, CHELSEA Les Fougères   ⑤⑤⑤⑤

783 route 105, Chelsea, J9B 1P1 **Tel** *(819) 827 8942*

This is country elegance in the forested Gatineau Hills, popular with discerning locals who share a passion for fresh regional foods partnered with sommelier-selected fine wines. Staff are extremely knowledgeable. Les Fougeres is renowned for its 11-course tasting menu. The monthly table d'hôte features seasonal, organic local foods. There is a children's menu.

OUTAOUAIS, CHELSEA L'Orée du Bois   ⑤⑤⑤⑤

15 Chemin Kingsmere, J9B 1A1 **Tel** *(819) 827 0332*

A log building tucked into mature hardwood forest beside the entrance to Gatineau Park. The French menu features seasonal foods such as asparagus, mushrooms, raspberries, and regional meat wherever possible, as well as herbs from the kitchen garden and homemade chocolate desserts. The on-site smokehouse uses maple to season fish, poultry, and meat.

RIGAUD Sucrerie de la Montagne   ⑤⑤⑤

300 Rang Saint-Georges, J0P 1P0 **Tel** *(450) 451 0831*

One of Quebec's first "sugar shacks" to remain open year-round. In season (late Feb to end Apr), there is tour sap gathering and syrup production. This is an all-you-can-eat sugaring-off feast of maple-cured sausages and ham, beans, or pancakes with maple syrup (different grades: you choose). Finish with sugar pie.

ROUYN-NORANDA Restaurant Brochetterie Grecque   ⑤⑤⑤

152 Rue Principale, J9X 4P7 **Tel** *(819) 797 0086*

Welcoming atmosphere with Greek music playing in background where you can sample delicious homemade Greek fare such as locally smoked fish, grilled meats, and baklava dripping with honey. The specialty is brochettes – a variety of kebabs (usually meat roasted on skewers) – such as rosemary-rubbed lamb. Service is attentive, not fussy.

SHERBROOKE L'Arlequin   ⑤⑤

875 Belvédère Sud, J1H 4B9 **Tel** *(819) 573 2818*

Reasonably priced table d'hôtes attracts regulars who bring their own wine to this French restaurant known for its adventurous gastronomique menu. Seasonal creations include such foods as smoked venison or lamb with five pepper sauce. For dessert, try Quebec's famous regional cheeses such as Charlevoix region's Le Migneron.

SHERBROOKE La Mare au Diable Microbrewery   ⑤⑤

151 Rue King Ouest, J1H 1P4 **Tel** *(819) 562 1001*

There is a great view from this hillside French restaurant, which is also the first microbrewery in the city's downtown core. In summertime, the terrace affords panoramic views of the surrounding countryside. All beers are brewed on-site (tours available). Wait staff are well trained to assist you in matching your menu selection to the right beer.

TROIS-RIVIERES Il Circo Pâtes et passion   ⑤

1140 Saint Prosper, G9A 3V9 **Tel** *(819) 374 0008*

The cheerful bright yellow and royal blue exterior is matched by a bright interior, where the owner's passion for the circus is evident by his collection of clowns and other artifacts. Serves fabulous breakfasts (such as crepes with strawberries and bananas), delectable Italian food – pastas (salmon, shrimp, or carbonara) or tempting chicken dishes.

TORONTO

DOWNTOWN Café 668   ⑤

885 Dundas St. West, Toronto, Ontario, M5T 1H9 **Tel** *(416) 703 0668*

Vegetarian cuisine of Southeast Asia with Vietnamese, Thai, and Chinese influences is served in a small space. The extensive menu includes tempura platters, seaweed tofu soup, julienne salad of shredded deep-fried tofu with grilled cashews in vinaigrette, and the House Special – Lor-Hon Style (mixed vegetables, tofu). No alcohol served.

Key to Price Guide *see p370* **Key to Symbols** *see back cover flap*

DOWNTOWN Ethiopian House

4 Irwin Avenue, Toronto, Ontario, M4E 1E4 **Tel** *(416) 923 5438*

A quaint restaurant where food is eaten with fingers. Pickled achards and stewed meats are scooped up with injera bread. Service can be slow but prices are reasonable and portions generous. A great introduction to the cuisine. Vegetarian dishes include spicy split peas, chick peas in garlic, lentils, crunchy collard greens, and smooth-roasted potatoes.

DOWNTOWN Lil Baci

892 Queen Street E., Toronto, Ontario, M4M 1J3 **Tel** *(416) 465 4888*

This casual neighborhood spot is located in the heart of Leslieville dictrict and is known for its southern Italian pizzas, fresh pastas, salads, and diverse. There is a **C19** lunch menu (soup or salad with a panino, pizza, or pasta dish), served from Monday to Friday. Ontario craft beers are available on tap, as well as Canadian and Italian wines.

DOWNTOWN 309 Dhaba

309 King Street West, Toronto, Ontario, M5V 1J5 **Tel** *(416) 740 6622*

Traditional Indian food is served in a friendly, unpretentious location in the downtown theater/entertainment district. Pre-theater prix fixe; an extensive menu with butter chicken, sizzling tandoori dishes, lamb aubergine, and okra chicken; or all-you-can-eat lunch buffet (more than 50 items). There is a six-course tasting menu. Reservations recommended.

DOWNTOWN Big Daddy's Crab Shack & Oyster Bar

212 King Street West, Toronto, Ontario, M5H 1K5 **Tel** *(416) 599 5200*

In the downtown theater district, this spicy Cajun and Creole seafood restaurant decorated with images of jazz singers and New Orleans streetscapes is good for casual dinner before a show. Bar specialties include New Orleans Hurricane Cocktail. A courtyard dining area serves lunch and dinner.

DOWNTOWN Fressen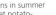

478 Queen Street West, Toronto, Ontario, M5V 2B2 **Tel** *(416) 504 5127*

Modern American vegan meals are prepared to order from fresh ingredients at Fressen. The front opens in summer onto Queen Street. The Tapas-style menu is good for sharing. Other items include exotic salads, sweet potato-coconut milk soup, freshly squeezed juices, and organic wines. Bring your own bottle – corkage $25.

DOWNTOWN La Palette

492 Queen Street West, Toronto, Ontario, M5V 2B2 **Tel** *(416) 603 4900*

This French bistro is popular with locals looking for a romantic dinner *à deux*, or an evening with friends. Fresh market fare is done in the French style, and dishes include 12-hour-braised venison side ribs with parsnip mash, red cabbage and molasses, and wild caught Ontario whitefish with potato and leek gratin and sweetcorn *beurre blanc*.

DOWNTOWN Marcel's Bistro

315 King Street West, Toronto, Ontario, M5V 1J5 **Tel** *(416) 591 8600*

Above Saint Tropez restaurant on trendy King Street West, downtown Toronto. Marcel's Bistro serves authentic southern French cooking, bouillabaisse-style fresh fish and seafood stew, mussels, pheasant, snails, venison, and frites. Classical music is played. Good for casual chic lunches or a romantic evening rendezvous.

DOWNTOWN N'Awlins Jazz Bar & Grill

299 King Street West, Toronto, Ontario, M5V 1J5 **Tel** *(416) 595 1958*

Popular downtown bar and grill in the entertainment district with live jazz, excellent Cajun-Creole food, and a romantic, eclectic atmosphere. House specials include spicy seafood, Surf'N'Turf, jambalaya, and pasta. There is also excellent gumbo, blackened catfish, rack of lamb, and cajun-seasoned alligator.

DOWNTOWN Niagara Street Café

169 Niagara Street, Toronto, Ontario, M5V 1C9 **Tel** *(416) 703 4222*

Niagara Street Café is an unpretentious but stylish café/bistro with French Mediterranean cuisine, great for vegetarian dishes. It has an organically based menu, and uses naturally raised meats and local products. The dining room is warm/romantic and service is excellent. The seasonal menu includes wild fish, squid, pork.

DOWNTOWN Segovia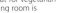

5 St. Nicholas Street, Toronto, Ontario, M4Y 1W5 **Tel** *(416) 960 1010*

The decor is cheerful and colorful in this casual Spanish restaurant in mid-town Toronto. Favorites include tapas, snails in wine and cream, mussels in saffron, and squid with traditional aioli. Entrees include paella, scallops, and lamb. Portions are generous. There is live music and dancing. Reservations recommended.

DOWNTOWN 5th Elementt

506 Queen Street West, Toronto, Ontario, M5S 3A5 **Tel** *(416) 504 3213*

This fusion Indo-American restaurant with a large space and two tier patio is good for business lunches and large parties. A new *à la carte* menu is created every 30 to 45 days, but original dishes could include Goan-style sirloin steak, coriander-crusted halibut, and rack of venison.

DOWNTOWN Ame

19 Mercer Street, Toronto, Ontario, M5V 3C6 **Tel** *(416) 599 7246*

Ame boasts one of the most beautiful interiors in the city. The food is almost as artful, featuring creative twists on Japanese fare. It is a contemporary take on a Japanese supper club offering wonderful cocktails, delicious dinners, and entertainment. A DJ plays from Thursday to Saturday evenings.

DOWNTOWN Benihana
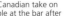
$$$$
100 Front Street West, Royal York Hotel, Toronto, Ontario, M5J 1E3 **Tel** *(416) 860 5002*

Part of the global Japanese restaurant chain, Benihana Toronto is located inside the Fairmont Royal York Hotel and is a traditional Japanese-style hibachi steakhouse ("teppanyaki.") Meals are prepared in front of you, from steak, to chicken, seafood, fresh vegetables, or sushi, in traditional Japanese style on a hibachi table. Reservations recommended.

DOWNTOWN Biff's
$$$$
4 Front Street East, Toronto, Ontario, M5E 1G4 **Tel** *(416) 860 0086*

This upscale bistro is located in the heart of the financial district. The cuisine is a contemporary Canadian take on bistro classics, such as steak frites, *boeuf bourgignon,* and haddock chowder. Oysters are available at the bar after 5pm, and the baked-to-order madeleines and profiteroles are exceptional. It's a popular pre-theater spot.

DOWNTOWN Biagio
$$$$
155 King Street East, Toronto, Ontario, M5C 1G9 **Tel** *(416) 366 4040*

Inside St. Lawrence Town Hall, the Biagio serves classic Italian food and has a formal dining room with a beautiful ceiling, and intimate garden patio with a fountain. Lunch choices include Risotto Tre Funghi, Rigatoni Amatriciana, and Cannelloni Pasticciati; dinner choices include Sella D'Agnello, Osso Bucco, and Dover Sole.

DOWNTOWN Rodney's Oyster House

$$$$
469 King Street West, Toronto, Ontario, M5V 1K4 **Tel** *(416) 363 8105*

Popular with downtown sophisticates, and busy at weekends, the specialty here is oysters – raw and in chowder – but there are also clams, mussels, lobsters, scallops, crab, and shrimp. Fresh salt and freshwater fish include halibut, salmon, walleye, and arctic char. There is a good wine list and cocktails. Open after midnight on weekends. Closed Sun.

DOWNTOWN Sultan's Tent and Café Moroc
$$$$
49 Front Street, Toronto, Ontario, M5E 1B3 **Tel** *(416) 961 0601*

On touristy Front Street, the Sultan's Tent has sophisticated, elegant Moroccan decor. Beautifully decorated tents serve as dining areas for groups, offering a traditional "diffa" (lavish banquet). Couples sit in the aisle outside the tents areas. The menu includes Keskesu Casablanca and rack of lamb. There are belly dancing performances.

DOWNTOWN Bistro 990

$$$$$
990 Bay Street, Toronto, Ontario, M5S 2A5 **Tel** *(416) 921 9990*

Hand-painted interior walls give this popular bistro a cozy feel. Offerings are meat-heavy, French and American bistro classics, such as French onion soup, snails with garlic, duck breast, steak tartare, and steak *frites.* Meat and poultry are additive-free, and all stocks and breads are made on the premises. It's popular with local and visiting celebrities.

DOWNTOWN Bymark
$$$$$
66 Wellington Street West, Toronto, Ontario, M5K 1J3 **Tel** *(416) 777 1144*

The Bymark is located in the Toronto Dominion Centre and was designed by Yabu Pushelberg. Main dining is on the concourse level with three separate dining rooms, a focal four-pillar sculpture fountain, and a glassed-in wine cellar. There is a courtyard bar with views of the Modernist Mies van der Rohe towers.

EAST END Beacher Café
$$
2162 Queen Street East, Toronto, Ontario, M4E 1 E4 **Tel** *(416) 699 3874*

A popular, busy landmark restaurant with a relaxing family atmosphere in Toronto's Beaches area with a seasonal patio and lines for Saturday and Sunday brunch. Original paintings and artwork (often for sale) are on display. The Beacher Café is famous for its homemade hollandaise sauce.

EAST END Kalyvia
$$$
420 Danforth Avenue, Toronto, Ontario, M4K 1P3 **Tel** *(416) 463 3333*

Home-style Mediterranean cuisine, taverna-style is served on a 'people-watching' patio in ethnic Greektown. Specialty dishes include seafood platter, Poikilia Kalyvia with spiced meats, onions, green peppers, mushrooms, tomatoes, hot peppers sautéed in white wine, and Melitzanosalata – a puree of eggplant dip, oil, garlic, onion, and Greek spices.

EAST END Rodeo Brazilian Steakhouse
$$$
95 Danforth Avenue, Toronto, Ontario, M4K 1N2 **Tel** *(416) 465 0969*

Toronto's first authentic Brazilian Rodizio, with an all-you-can-eat Brazilian menu and live music. The menu includes fried plantains, cheese breads, barbequed entrées, fish, roasted pineapple, and Brazilian Churrascaria. Within an authentic vintage building, this offers a unique dining experience. The Caipirinha cocktails are a speciality.

EAST END Embrujo Flamenco Tapas Bar

$$$$
97 Danforth Avenue, Toronto, Ontario, M4K 1N2 **Tel** *(416) 778 0007*

Originally established over 35 years ago, but located on Danforth since 2002, the regional Spanish dishes served include tapas and paella. The atmosphere is bohemian, with live flamenco Wed–Sun. There is an eclectic menu and a good selection of Spanish sherries and wines.

EAST END Lolita's Lust & The Chinchilla Lounge
$$$$
513 Danforth Avenue, Toronto, Ontario, M4K 1M8 **Tel** *(416) 465 1751*

Intimate, romantic, and trendy, with an upscale yet bohemian atmosphere and namesake martinis, this is the place to be seen – celebrities have been glimpsed dining here – in the heart of the Greek district. The Coach House (a retrofitted brick garage) extends the cozy space. The upstairs Chinchilla lounge is available for private parties.

NORTH Asian Legend
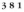 $

418 Dundas Street West, Toronto, Ontario, M5T 1G7 **Tel** *(416) 977 3909*

Located in trendy Chinatown west in a narrow space with modern decor, the menu serves traditional Northern dim sum and stir fry. Specialties include House Special Crispy Pancake with shredded shrimp, Chinese chives, and scallions; beef short ribs; Szechuan smoked duck; and bean curd with vegetables. There is a good range of tsingtao and jasmine teas.

NORTH Zaffron Ristorante
$$$

6200 Yonge Street, Toronto, Ontario, M2M 3X1 **Tel** *(416) 223 7070*

Authentic, upscale Persian restaurant, with California-style decor, stucco walls, and tiled floors and a wood oven. Specialties include Iranian flatbread, eggplant purée with goat yogurt cheese and deep-fried mint, Fusilli Saraceno, and skewers of lamb, tenderloin, sirloin and chicken, Persian tea, good wine list, and popular yogurt soda.

NORTH Wildfire Steakhouse & Wine Bar
$$$$

3438 Yonge Street, Toronto, Ontario, M4N 2N2 **Tel** *(416) 483 4800*

Upscale, uptown steakhouse with cozy, romantic candlelit atmosphere. Food is a combination of Portuguese and Californian cuisine. The house specialty is Sterling Silver steaks (aged for at least 4 weeks, enhanced with spices); churrasco meals include ribs, chicken, lamb dishes, and seafood.

NORTH Auberge du Pommier
$$$$$

4150 Yonge Street, Toronto, Ontario, M2P 2C6 **Tel** *(416) 222 2220*

Formal, elegant, upscale French dining in a building erected around rustic 1860s woodcutters' cottages. There are wood-burning fireplaces in winter and lush gardens in summer. Over 500 wine labels, mostly French and Californian, are on offer. The menu includes *tranche de foie gras sauté* and *grenouilles à la provençal*.

NORTH North 44
$$$$$

2537 Yonge Street, Toronto, Ontario, M4P 2H9 **Tel** *(416) 487 4897*

Named after Toronto city's latitude, North 44 serves excellent gourmet food in an elegant, contemporary setting with a neutral color scheme, wood, and accent lighting. A bar and lounge are on the upper level, as is a dining room that can seat 75. The restaurant also offers private rooms for 14–20 people.

WEST END Piri-Piri Churrasqueira Grillhouse
$$

1444 Dupont Street, Toronto, Ontario, M6P 4H3 **Tel** *(416) 536 5100*

Authentic Portuguese traditional dishes including fresh grilled fish, seafood, grilled sardines, sausages, and chicken are served at the Piri-Piri. Okra and mixed vegetables are particularly recommended. There is a wide selection of Portuguese wines and ports. Take-outs are available too.

WEST END Irie Food Joint
 $$$$

745 Queen Street West Toronto, Ontario, M6J 1G1 **Tel** *(416) 366 4743*

A relaxed Jamaican restaurant in trendy Queen west, with reggae music and a seasonal back patio, garden, and tiki lights. There is a small bar area. Traditional menu favorites include jerk wings, sweet corn, seafood gumbo, rice and peas, curried chicken, and homemade mango cheesecake. Corkage is $15.

FARTHER AFIELD Nice Bistro
 $$

117 Brock Street N., Whitby (near Hwy 401), Ontario, L1N 4H3 **Tel** *(647) 800 8837*

Bernard, a native of Nice, and his Canadian wife Manon have been serving classic French cuisine, mostly using seasonal and regional produce, at this popular location since 1993. Try the *bouillabaisse*, the traditional fish soup of Marseille, or *moules marinières et frites*, made with Prince Edward Island mussels. Closed Sun and Mon.

FARTHER AFIELD On the Curve Hot Stove & Wine Bar
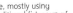 $$$

55 City Centre Drive, Mississauga, Ontario, L5B 1M3 **Tel** *(905) 804 9582*

In Mississauga, next to Square One Shopping Mall, is this upscale, hip restaurant/lounge with elegant candlelit dining, curved bar area, dance floor, plush sofas, and busy summer patio. Wednesday night is Latin Heat night with free dance lessons. Private party room available.

FARTHER AFIELD The Doctor's House
 $$$$$

21 Nashville Road, Kleinberg, Ontario, L0J 1C0 **Tel** *(416) 234 8080 or (905) 893 1615*

In picturesque Kleinburg is this elegant restaurant with superb food, favored for banquets, weddings, and film shoots. Restored to the original 1867 design, with a non-denominational wedding chapel on site, the dining room with patio and veranda overlook manicured lawns and flowers. Famous for Sunday brunch. Reservations recommended.

OTTAWA AND EASTERN ONTARIO

KINGSTON Candlelight Dining
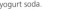 $$$

Fort Henry National Historic Site, Kingston, Ontario **Tel** *(613) 530 2550*

Travel back in time in the Officers' Dining Rooms at Fort Henry, a UNESCO World Heritage Site. Soldier-servants answer to a finger snap and guests dine on traditional British cuisine prepared from heritage recipes. Open for lunch and dinner during the months of July, August, and December, and on major holidays.

KINGSTON Chez Piggy

68-R Princess Street, Kingston, Ontario, K7L 1A5 **Tel** *(613) 549 7673*

Affectionately named by locals as "the pig," this restaurant in a secluded courtyard location in historic downtown Kingston was originally an abandoned limestone stable. It provides a great atmosphere for brunch, lunch, or dinner. There is also a related bakery, Pan Chancho, nearby at 44 Princess Street.

KINGSTON River Mill Restaurant

2 Cataraqui Street, The Woolen Mill, Kingston, Ontario, K7K 1Z7 **Tel** *(613) 549 5759*

In a historic woollen mill building, this elegant, relaxed restaurant serves contemporary cuisine with waterfront views. The wine selection is extensive, with vintage and private-order wines and an emphasis on French and Canadian wines. Sampling plate includes smoked breast of duck, bison carpaccio, smoked salmon, and roasted rack of lamb.

MUSKOKA Top of the Cove

375 South Bay Road, Honey Harbour, Ontario, M5H 2G4 **Tel** *(705) 756 3399*

Reached by water or road, this quaint, seasonal restaurant offers affordable waterside dining, overlooking South Bay Cove Marina on Georgian Bay. There are spectacular sunsets throughout the summer. Menus include pasta, burgers, prime steak, and international dishes in a casual dining atmosphere. Open Jun–Sep.

MUSKOKA Bartlett's Lodge

P.O. Box 10004, Algonquin Park, Ontario, P1H 2G8 **Tel** *(705) 633 5543*

Favored by gourmet diners, and located in Algonquin Provincial Park on the shoreline of Cache Lake, a short ferry ride by motorized freighter canoe, this restaurant serves contemporary cuisine. The table d'hote includes venison with port wine and cherry reduction, foie gras terrine, and chocolate and walnut tart. Open mid-May–mid-Oct.

MUSKOKA Bigwin Island Golf Club – Marine Dining Room

P.O. Box 5611, Huntsville, Ontario, P1H 2L5 **Tel** *(705) 635 2582*

In a building dating from the Roaring Twenties, visited by 1940s stars Clark Gable and Carole Lombard, the restaurant in the original dining room overlooks the Lake of Bays and serves 4-Diamond-rated classic French cuisine. Bigwin Island ferry departs Norway Point off Old Highway 117, 16 km (10 miles) east of Baysville. Reservations recommended.

OTTAWA D'Arcy Mc Gee's

44 Sparks Street, Ottawa, Ontario, K1P 5A8 **Tel** *(613) 230 4433*

This Irish-style pub near Parliament Hill and the War Memorial was shipped to Canada from Ireland and reassembled in Ottawa, with hand-crafted wood and mosaic tile floors in the bar and dining areas. There is live entertainment four nights a week – Celtic, Irish, and contemporary. The menu includes sandwiches, burgers, salads, and soups.

OTTAWA Domus Café

87 Murray Street, Ottawa, Ontario, K1N 5M5 **Tel** *(613) 241 6007*

This restaurant is located in the lively Byward Market. It is considered to be an excellent showcase for Canadian regional cuisine and has become a foodie destination. Menus are seasonal but could include pan-seared British halibut with mustard glazed beets or celeriac and apple-stuffed rabbit loin with homemade Worcestershire sauce.

OTTAWA Yang Sheng Cantonese

662 Somerset St. West, Ottawa, Ontario, K1R 5K4 **Tel** *(613) 235 5794*

Serving an authentic Cantonese/Szechuan menu, this fully licensed restaurant has a take-out service too. Traditional dim sum is served daily. It is popular with locals. The menu includes homemade rice noodle dishes, barbecued duck and pork, rice with chicken in curry sauce, and stir-fried Chinese vegetables. Open daily 11am–1pm.

OTTAWA Yangtze

700 Somerset Street West, Ottawa, Ontario, K1R 6P6 **Tel** *(613) 236 0555*

Slightly more expensive than normal, but good Chinese food is served at the Yangtze. Notable dishes include dim sum. The menu has everything from beef to shrimp, bean curd, pork, and squid. There is a late-night snack menu with smaller portions from 8:30pm. Take-out food is also available.

OTTAWA Haveli

39 Clarence Street Ottawa, Ontario, K1N 5P4 **Tel** *(613) 241 1700*

Family-owned and operated, with an extensive Indian menu, including tandoori and curries, the Haveli serves a daily lunch buffet and Sunday lunch/dinner buffets featuring Masala Dosa (potato-filled thin rice crepes served with tangy lentil soup). Spiciness ranges from mild to extra hot.

OTTAWA The Fish Market

54 York Street, Byward Market, Ottawa, Ontario, K1N 5T1 **Tel** *(613) 241 3474*

A renowned restaurant in historical ByWard Market, with a colorful, nautical theme, trout and lobster tanks and a fireplace in a heritage building. Generous portions of seafood, lobster, shrimp, crab, oysters, mussels, and scallop are served. The menu also includes salads, crusted fish, chowders, and cajun dishes. There is an extensive, eclectic wine list.

OTTAWA Wilfrid's

1 Rideau Street, Ottawa, Ontario, K1N 8S7 **Tel** *(613) 241 1414*

Located in the Fairmont Château Laurier hotel, here you will find upscale fine dining, including a popular buffet lunch which can be noisy. Large picture windows overlook Parliament Hill. There is a Canadian-themed menu which includes sautéed veal, Montreal smoked meat sandwiches, seafood chowder, and amazing desserts.

Key to Price Guide *see p370* **Key to Symbols** *see back cover flap*

THE GREAT LAKES

BAYFIELD The Little Inn of Bayfield
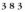
26 Main Street, Bayfield, Ontario, N0M 1G0 **Tel** (519) 565 2611

This restaurant at this pretty Colonial style inn is open to non-guests. It serves award-winning locally sourced cuisine, including air-dried bison proscuitto, seared duck foie gras brioche, and a fresh ginger crème caramel. There is a good wine cellar and a snug bar. Reservations recommended.

JORDAN On The Twenty
3836 Main Street, Jordan, Ontario, L0R 1S0 **Tel** (905) 562 7313

Nestled in charming Jordan Village, with a panoramic view over Twenty Mile Creek, On the Twenty is known for its excellent regional cuisine and exclusive Vintner's Quality Alliance wine list. There are tours of Cave Spring Cellars next door, with wine samples. A five-course Winemaker's Dinner is available. Booking is advised.

KITCHENER 20 King

41 King Street West, Kitchener, Ontario, N2G 1A1 **Tel** (519) 745 8939

A downtown restaurant in a historic 1800s building with upscale seasonal Canadian cuisine, leather booths, a rustic finish, and two private dining rooms. The eclectic menu includes bouillabaisse, vension, ossobuco, white chocolate and lavender cheesecake, and a cheese plate. There is an extensive wine list. A fee is charged for corkage.

LONDON The Waltzing Weasel

1324 Adelaide Street, North London, Ontario, N5X 1J9 **Tel** (519) 663 9194

Traditional pub food is served in this refurbished 1860s farmhouse. There is a bar area with high top tables and a private upstairs room with dartboards. A partially covered courtyard patio overlooking the North London Golf Center makes for pleasant al fresco eating. The menu includes finger foods, soups, salads, sandwiches, and steaks.

NIAGARA FALLS Milestone
6755 Fallsview Boulevard, Niagara Falls, Ontario, L2G 3W7 **Tel** (905) 358 4720

This restaurant on the second floor of the Sheraton Hotel has panoramic views of the Niagara Falls and offers a relaxed dining atmosphere with upscale decor and award-winning staff. Premium comfort food is on offer here; steakhouse specials include certified Angus beef, seafood, and pasta.

NIAGARA FALLS Table Rock Restaurant

6650 Niagara Parkway, Niagara Falls, Ontario **Tel** (905) 354 3631

On the upper level of Table Rock Center, close to the Niagara Falls, and with panoramic views, this casual restaurant serves fresh regional products. There is a children's menu, seasonal Sunday brunch, and early dinner specials. In the summer months you can eat outside on Horseshoe Landing patio.

NIAGARA FALLS Skylon Tower Summit Suite Dining Room
5200 Robinson Street, Niagara Falls, Ontario, L2G 2A3 **Tel** (905) 356 2651

A famous Niagara Falls landmark tower 236 m (775 ft) above the Niagara Falls this elegant restaurant provides a unique night atmosphere as the Falls are illuminated. A seasonal double-sided daily buffet consists of roast beef, fresh seafood, and French pastries. The revolving dining room is one floor down.

NIAGARA FALLS Watermark Restaurant

6361 Fallsview Boulevard, Niagara Falls, Ontario, L2G 3V9 **Tel** (905) 353 7138

A rooftop restaurant with a view of the Niagara Falls, the Watermark has a water theme including two aquariums, huge windows, and wave entrance. It is the best place to view the fireworks over the Falls. Continental cuisine, with breakfast buffet; lunch and dinner menus are served. The lounge offers cocktails and appetizers.

NIAGARA ON THE LAKE Shaw Café & Wine Bar
92 Queen Street, Niagara on the Lake, Ontario, L0S 1J0 **Tel** (905) 468 4772

Casual but elegant café-style cuisine is served here. There is an inviting patio with abundant plants and flowers. The Shaw Café & Wine Bar is open daily for lunch and dinner in summer and serves soup, sandwiches, salads, homemade entrées, decadent pastries, and cakes.

STRATFORD Bijou Restaurant
105 Erie Street, Stratford, Ontario, N5A 2M5 **Tel** (519) 273 5000

A popular restaurant serving modern French cuisine with Asian and Italian influences in a Parisian bistro setting. Local seasonal ingredients are used. The menu changes daily and may include chilled pea shoot soup, scallops with sliced shiitakes, spinach, zucchini, and a small wine list.

STRATFORD Church Restaurant

70 Brunswick Street, Stratford, Ontario, N5A 3M1 **Tel** (519) 273 3424

This is an upscale restaurant in a converted church with high ceilings and stained-glass windows that serves unusual food combinations. The varied à la carte menu changes frequently, with a focus on local flavors. There is a wine list of champagnes, burgundies, Ontario wines, and California reds. Closed Mon. Open Apr–Dec.

STRATFORD Rundles

9 Cobourg Street, Stratford, Ontario, N5A 3E4 **Tel** *(519) 271 6442*

Modern French cuisine is served here in a 100-seat pre-theater restaurant with stylish, elegant decor and service. There are also some influences on the menu from Italy, Japan, and Morocco. There are à la carte and three-course menus. Reservations recommended.

THUNDER BAY Hoito Restaurant

314 Bay Street, Thunder Bay, Ontario, P7B 1S1 **Tel** *(807) 345 6323*

This authentic Finnish restaurant in Big Finn Hall historic landmark building was established in 1918 to offer hearty meals at low prices to the Finnish bushworkers. It is now a café-style restaurant with individual tables and home-style food, including many Finnish dishes. Specialties include piles of Finnish pancakes for a hearty breakfast.

THUNDER BAY Bistro One

555 Dunlop Street, Thunder Bay, Ontario, P7B 6S1 **Tel** *(807) 622 2478*

A comfortable, upscale bistro with elegant decor and a private dining area. Menu highlights include sea scallops in a maple syrup champagne sauce and rosemary roasted rack of New Zealand lamb with gorgonzola butter. It is known for its decadent desserts, including warm chocolate gateau.

WINDSOR Motor Burger

888 Erie Street East, Windsor, Ontario, N9A 3Y6 **Tel** *(519) 252 8004*

This neighborhood spot serves deluxe variations on the burger theme: Angus beef burger, shrimp burger, lamb burger, sausage burger, and more. There are also salads for the health-conscious and a varied children's menu. A full bar offers specialty beers, wines, and cocktails, as well as milkshakes.

CENTRAL CANADA

EDMONTON Sherlock Holmes

West Edmonton Mall, Edmonton, Alberta, T5T 4V4 **Tel** *(780) 444 1752*

Part of a locally owned chain of restaurants, this British-style pub has traditional fare such as fish and chips and 17 types of beer on tap. There is live music nightly and karaoke on Sundays. The walls are adorned with British memorabilia, photos, and team jerseys. Open 11:30am–2am daily.

EDMONTON La Ronde

10111 Bellamy Hill, Edmonton, Alberta, T5J 1N7 **Tel** *(780) 420 8366*

La Ronde sits atop the Crowne-Plaza Château Lacombe Hotel downtown. It takes 90 minutes for this revolving rooftop restaurant to make a full rotation offering a panoramic view of the city. The menu features local Alberta cuisine including bison, venison, beef, and Arctic char. Open for dinner daily and for brunch Sun.

EDMONTON Unheardof Restaurant

9602 82 Avenue NW., Edmonton, Alberta, T6C 1A1 **Tel** *(780) 432 0480*

In business since 1980, the menu at the Unheardof Restaurant includes salmon, chicken, tuna, bison, and caribou. It uses symbols to help customers tailor their meal to their dietary restrictions such as gluten-free food. Open Tue–Sun dinner only. Reservations recommended.

MOOSE JAW Harwood's Dining Room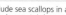

24 Fairford St., Moose Jaw, Saskatchewan, S6H 0C7 **Tel** *(306) 693 7778*

Set inside the Temple Gardens Mineral Spa Resort, the menu at Harwood's Dining Room includes fish, pasta, and beef. It also serves Sunday brunch. This restaurant has a relaxing atmosphere but dresses up in the evening with linens and fine china for a touch of elegance. Open 7am–11pm.

RED DEER La Casa Pergola

4909 48 St., Red Deer, Alberta, T4N 1S8 **Tel** *(403) 342 2404*

The Casa features Italian decor and tantalizing dishes made with care. The menu includes Al Tartufo ravioli with truffle brandy cream sauce and rack of lamb with rosemary and raspberry vinaigrette. There is a patio just off the lounge and live music on Saturday nights in summer. Open for lunch and dinner.

REGINA John's Place

379 Albert St., Regina, Saskatchewan, S4R 2N6 **Tel** *(306) 545 3777*

The menu at John's Place features prime rib steak, seafood, pasta, and pizza. The restaurant is decorated with live trees inside, lots of plants, a large fireplace, and skylights. There are also antiques on display, including an old butter churn. Open 11am–10pm Mon–Sat and 4pm–9pm Sun.

REGINA Willow on Wascana

3000 Wascana Drive, Regina, Saskatchewan, S4P 3B2 **Tel** *(306) 585 3663*

In a beautiful setting on Wascana Lake, the patio at Willow on Wascana offers a good spot from which to enjoy the view. The menu focuses on Prairie cuisine, using local ingredients as much as possible. A tasting menu is offered. Open daily for dinner and lunch from Tue–Sat.

REGINA Diplomat Steakhouse

*2032 Broad St., Regina, Saskatchewan, S4P 1Y3 **Tel** (306) 359 3366*

This elegant restaurant has a fireplace and lounge, polished oak and red velour booths. Pictures of Canadian prime ministers adorn the walls. The menu offers fine dining, and features steak and seafood. The Diplomat has received eight Wine Spectator awards. Open for lunch and dinner weekdays and only for dinner on weekends.

SASKATOON Wanuskewin Restaurant

*Wanuskewin Heritage Park RR 4, Saskatoon, Saskatchewan, S7K 3J7 **Tel** (306) 931 6767 or (877) 547 6546*

This eatery in Wanuskewin Heritage Park 5 km (3 miles) north of Saskatoon overlooks a scenic valley. Buffalo signs mark the way as you get closer to the park. The cafeteria-style service features First Nations cuisine such as bison stew, bannock, and wild rice salad. Open 9am–5pm (to 8pm in summer).

SASKATOON The Granary

*2806 8th St. East, Saskatoon, Saskatchewan, S7H 0V9 **Tel** (306) 373 6655*

This Saskatoon landmark is in a building shaped like a country grain elevator – the sentinels of the prairies. Highlights on the menu are prime rib, steak and seafood. The funky decor has a prairie theme – the walls showcase antique farm memorabilia such as old tools. Open for dinner only.

SASKATOON Saskatoon Station Place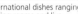

*221 Idylwyld Drive N., Saskatoon, Saskatchewan, S7L 6V6 **Tel** (306) 244 7777*

The decor here evokes the golden age of train travel with its vintage rail dining car. Step into the past with period artwork and antiques such as an English street clock and Victorian era chandeliers. The menu features Canadian specialties and offers a luxury dining experience. Open for lunch and dinner.

STEINBACH Livery Barn Restaurant

*Mennonite Heritage Village, Steinbach, Manitoba, R5G 1T8 **Tel** (204) 326 9661*

Learn about the Mennonite lifestyle from the 16th century to the present in the Heritage Village; then try the food at the red Livery Barn, reminiscent of the old rest stops for weary travelers. Eat locally prepared Foarma Worscht, vereniki, Komst Borscht, and stoneground bread. Open May–Sep for lunch daily.

WINNIPEG Wagon Wheel Restaurant

*305 Hargrave St., Winnipeg, Manitoba, R3B 2J7 **Tel** (204) 942 6695*

This lunch stop is best known for its clubhouse sandwiches. Open more than 50 years, it has an old-time feel with orange booths and one-legged yellow tabletops. There are wagon wheels on the ceiling and a spot for people to sit at the counter. Open weekdays from 8am–5pm.

WINNIPEG Restaurant Dubrovnik

*390 Assiniboine Ave., Winnipeg, Manitoba, R3C 0Y1 **Tel** (204) 944 0594*

Located in an elegant mansion on the Assiniboine River, this restaurant offers French and international dishes ranging from bison and lamb to New York steak, venison, and vegetarian options. There are three dining rooms and live piano music is played in the lobby on Fri and Sat evenings. Winner of Wine Spectator Award. Open for dinner only.

WINNIPEG Resto Gare

*630 Des Meurons, St. Boniface, Winnipeg, Manitoba, R2H 2P9 **Tel** (204) 237 7072*

Serving a menu of French cuisine that changes with the seasons, this hip restaurant is in the old St. Boniface train station in Winnipeg's French Quarter. Built in 1913, it became a restaurant in 1970. The lounge is in a former rail car, and there is a trained sommelier. Open for dinner daily. Lunch Mon–Fri.

VANCOUVER AND VANCOUVER ISLAND

CAMPBELL RIVER Legends Dining Room

*1625 McDonald Rd., British Columbia, V9W 4S5 **Tel** (250) 286 1102*

Overlooking Discovery Passage, at Legends patrons indulge in delectably fresh, exquisitely prepared and finished West Coast fare while watching ships cruise by. Waiters are on hand to suggest excellent local wines. Brandy is served in the fireside lounge. Sunday brunch is a local tradition. Reservations recommended.

DUNCAN Genoa Bay Café

*5000 Genoa Bay Road, Unit 9, Duncan, British Columbia, V9L 5Y8 **Tel** (250) 746 7621*

Perched on the water's edge overlooking Genoa Bay marina, this romantic café offers good food in a welcoming, casual atmosphere. The restaurant is known for its clam chowder and other Pacific Rim delights, and for its desserts. There is outside seating in summer. Reservations recommended.

NANAIMO Wesley Street Restaurant

*321 Wesley St., British Columbia, V9R 2T5 **Tel** (250) 753 6057*

An intimate café with pretty harbor views. The contemporary cuisine focuses on Vancouver Island produce, including a tasting menu featuring locally farmed products. With its excellent, prompt service, good food and wine list, this restaurant has been voted one of the top five restaurants on Vancouver Island.

NANAIMO Mahle House Restaurant

2104 Hemer Rd., British Columbia, V9X 1L8 **Tel** *(250) 722 3621*

This 1904 farmhouse set in an English garden includes "Adventure Wednesday" when the chef cooks a five-course surprise dinner. Even so, the main menu changes every week. Owner-chefs use their garden herbs with locally raised meats such as rabbit, venison, and chicken. Try porcupine prawns or calamari dijonnaise.

SALT SPRING ISLAND Hastings House

160 Upper Ganges Rd., British Columbia, V8K 2S2 **Tel** *(250) 537 2362 or (800) 661 9255*

Set in a historic English manor overlooking Ganges' harbor, the homegrown cuisine here includes herbs, fruits, and greens grown in the estate's orchards and gardens. Island produce features such as highly regarded Salt Spring Island lamb, served elegantly in a wood-beamed dining room. There is an award-winning wine cellar.

SOOKE Sooke Harbour House

1528 Whiffen Spit Rd., British Columbia, V92 0T4 **Tel** *(250) 642 3421 or (800) 889 9688*

An unusual, innovative culinary adventure awaits here, where the award-winning menu changes daily in order to present absolutely fresh ingredients. Choices will include marine edibles such as sea asparagus and sea urchins, partnered with vegetables and herbs from the seashore and gardens on the site.

TOFINO SoBo

311 Neil St., British Columbia, V0R 2Z0 **Tel** *(250) 725 2341*

SoBo, which stands for "sophisticated Bohemian," is housed in Tofino's stylish Conradi Building. Owner-chefs select organic vegetables, wild-caught BC salmon, and island-raised poultry, transforming them into tempting sensations such as "Gringo soft chicken tacos," and crispy shrimp cakes.

TOFINO Wickaninnish Inn & Pointe Restaurant

500 Osprey Lane at Chesterman's Beach, British Columbia, V0R 2Z0 **Tel** *(250) 725 3100*

This Relais & Châteaux property features a stunning dining room of West Coast cedar featuring a circular fireplace. Octagonal room juts out over the Pacific Ocean, providing an extraordinary setting in which to enjoy fresh seafood or exquisite lamb or beef dishes well-married with Pacific Northwest wines.

VANCOUVER Planet Veg

1941 Cornwall Ave., British Columbia, V6J 1C8 **Tel** *(604) 734 1001*

With an uncompromisingly plain ambience, this cafeteria-style little nook dishes up tasty vegetarian fare such as delicious roti rolls (including a basmati rice pot), or a yam and apple veggie burger – voted the city's best. Service is extremely friendly with staff who patiently wait while you try to decide what to order. No alcohol served.

VANCOUVER East is East

3243 W. Broadway, British Columbia, V6K 2H5 **Tel** *(604) 734 5881*

A unique experience awaits you at East is East on Broadway. With low tables, plenty of decorative cushions and live dancing, you may feel temporarily enchanted by this restaurant's exotic atmosphere. Try the chai tea, yoghurt lassis, and for the main meal, the all-you-care-to-enjoy Eastern plates.

VANCOUVER Foundation Lounge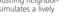

2301 Main Street, British Columbia, V5T 3C9 **Tel** *(604) 708 0881*

This is hipster hangout territory, with casual, retro decor; low lighting; and no heating, even in winter, in order to conserve energy. There's good, no-nonsense vegan and vegetarian food at inexpensive prices. It is a relaxed, casual place, although the music can get loud later on.

VANCOUVER Nyala

4148 Main St., British Columbia, V5V 3P7 **Tel** *(604) 876 9919*

A local favorite for more than 20 years, Nyala serves Ethiopian, Moroccan, and South African meals with wine or beer from South Africa and BC. Highlights include fresh ingredients, exotic spices, and a warm ambience featuring North African decor. There is a wide selection of vegetarian dishes.

VANCOUVER Havana

1212 Commercial Drive, British Columbia, V5L 3X4 **Tel** *(604) 253 9119*

This authentic Cuban restaurant shares space with an art gallery and theater, located in a diverse, bustling neighborhood. Breakfast is served (until 2pm), as well as sandwiches, tapas, and entrées. This popular spot simulates a lively slice of Havana, a feeling enhanced by old photographs haphazardly hung on graffiti-clad walls.

VANCOUVER Kirin Restaurant

555 W. 12th Ave., British Columbia, V5Z 3X7 **Tel** *(604) 879 8038*

At Kirin Restaurant, located across the road from Vancouver City Hall and near the Sky Train, you'll find Chinese fine dining, with excellent seafood dishes, dim sum, and a variety of set menus. The flavors are authentic and the service is consistently good. Try the baked tapioca for dessert.

VANCOUVER Maenam

1938 4th Ave. W., British Columbia, V6J 1M5 **Tel** *(604) 730 5579*

Located in the heart of the trendy Kitsilano neighborhood, Maenam serves Thai dishes, ranging from such classics as pad thai to more complex flavors, including a wonderful green papaya salad. Many of the menu items are meant to be shared, and a chef's set menu is also on offer. Try the chocolate *pot de crème* for dessert.

VANCOUVER Stepho's Souvlaki Greek Taverna

1124 Davie Street, British Columbia, V6E 1N1 **Tel** *(604) 683 2555*

Come very early to avoid the lines at this highly popular local favorite where portions are huge. Greek salad is "the city's best," while roasted potatoes jostle for room amid the lamb. Authentic dishes and crowds of happy customers means this is a fun if noisy place to eat.

VANCOUVER Chambar

562 Beatty Street, British Columbia, V6B 2L3 **Tel** *(604) 879 7119*

Hip Chambar offers Belgian dishes such as an exquisite interpretation of *coquilles St-Jacques* – maple-seared scallops served with lentils and sweet potato crisps. Specialties include mussels Congolaise, where smoked chillies, cilantro, lime, and coconut cream create a mouthwatering sensation. The cheesecake for dessert is a highlight.

VANCOUVER Cin Cin Restaurant & Bar

1154 Robson St., British Columbia, V6E 1B5 **Tel** *(604) 688 7338*

Pronounced chin-chin (a toast to good health), this popular restaurant featuring tasting menus is decorated in Italian style. A clattering open kitchen features a rotisserie, wood-fired oven, and a sizzling grill. There both local and imported Italian ingredients become mouthwatering sensations. Pasta (such as hand-rolled gnocchi) is homemade.

VANCOUVER Lupo

869 Hamilton St., British Columbia, V6B 2R7 **Tel** *(604) 569 2535*

Romance is in the air in this downtown Victorian-era building with large bay windows overlooking the city and an open fireplace. It is a favorite with local diners intent on mouthwatering Mediterranean food such as grilled quail or sablefish in vermouth and fennel broth.

VANCOUVER Refuel

1944 West 4th Avenue, British Columbia, V6J 1M5 **Tel** *(604) 288 7905*

Refuel is located in the trendy Kitsilano neighborhood, and here you'll find comfort food, such as fried chicken and baked beans on toast, albeit high-end interpretations. The menu also features interesting dishes such as roasted bone marrow and crispy pork cheek terrine. This is definitely a place for meat-lovers.

VANCOUVER The Fish House

8901 Stanley Park Drive, British Columbia, V6G 3E2 **Tel** *(604) 681 7275*

This fine fish restaurant is a Vancouver institution in Stanley Park, surrounded by greenery and panoramic views of English Bay. There is an excellent oyster bar. Superb flaming prawns (ouzo fuels the fire) are served. There is a choice of 20 wines served by the glass.

VANCOUVER Bishop's

2183 W. 4th Ave., British Columbia, V6K 1N7 **Tel** *(604) 738 2025*

The regional menu here changes weekly, so all the organic ingredients reflect the season. Highlights may include smoked fresh halibut, sockeye salmon, or venison, and desserts such as butterscotch rhubarb tart with mascarpone cream. Owner John Bishop displays a superb collection of First Nations art. Closed Jan 1–15 and Dec 24–26.

VANCOUVER C Restaurant

2-1600 Howe St., British Columbia, V6Z 2L9 **Tel** *(604) 681 1164*

With minimalist decor that emphasizes the old warehouse architecture, trendy, contemporary C also claims an attractive waterfront patio featuring white linens and tiles. Not limiting itself only to local ingredients, discover classic foods (especially seafood) with a contemporary flair: rabbit and prawn terrine, or slow-cooked sturgeon.

VANCOUVER Diva at the Met

Metropolitan Hotel, 645 Howe St, British Columbia, V6C 2Y9 **Tel** *(604) 602 7788*

The terraced floors and open-style Waldorf kitchen at this restaurant create a casual flair. Pre-theater menus feature eclectic takes on seafood and game such as black cod. Here you'll find Vancouver's largest selection of cheeses and decadent desserts – try warm upside-down chocolate soufflé.

VANCOUVER Gotham Steak House & Cocktail Bar

615 Seymour St., British Columbia, V6B 3K4 **Tel** *(604) 605 8282*

Canadian prime beef produces exceptionally tender steaks here, under the attentive hands of Chef Jean Claude Douget. There is an elegant ambience in this steakhouse with Art Deco-inspired touches. Linger over juicy steaks – many with bone in – or else select from a wide variety of seafood, pork, and lamb. Reservations recommended.

VANCOUVER Tojo's Japanese

1133 West Broadway, British Columbia, V6H 1G1 **Tel** *(604) 872 8050*

Since opening in 1988, chic Tojo's has served award-winning Japanese food that attracts diners from all over the world. Choose from 21 estate sakes while at the sushi or robata bar, or dine in semi private enclaves on such delights as charcoal-grilled tapas, individually prepared sushi, or entrées such as Shiitake Shinjo.

VANCOUVER West

2881 Granville St., British Columbia, V6H 3J4 **Tel** *(604) 738 8938*

West Coast takes on tradition in this award-winning restaurant with dramatic, modern decor. Organic and local ingredients are used, with dishes such as Haida Gwaii Ling cod, Yarrow Meadow duck, or Pemberton beef tenderloin with seared foie gras. Martinis are a specialty here, made with juices pressed to order.

VICTORIA Red Fish Blue Fish Ⓢ

1006 Wharf Street, British Columbia, V8W 1T4 **Tel** *(250) 298 6877*

This is a fantastic fish and chips shack located right by the water in Victoria's Inner Harbour. It's 100 percent Oceanwise, which means the menu only has sustainable, fresh choices, including wild salmon tacones, Fanny Bay oyster sandwiches, and Pacific Rim chowders. Outside seating only.

VICTORIA J & J Wonton Noodle House ⓈⓈ

1012 Fort St., British Columbia, V8V 3K4 **Tel** *(250) 383 0680*

This noodle house has a cozy atmosphere and serves fresh, home-made Chinese noodles to locals and those lucky tourists who go out of their way to find it. Handmade noodles are a specialty. The Szechuan braised beef hot pot is delicious. Closed Sun–Mon.

VICTORIA Spinnakers ⓈⓈⓈ

308 Catherine St., British Columbia, V9A 3S8 **Tel** *(250) 386 2739*

Spinnakers is the city's foremost brewpub where knowledgeable staff help you marry the brew to your pub fare meal. Enjoy handcrafted artesinal ales and specialty beers on tap. The on-site bakery creates amazing herb, olive, tomato, and other breads, while main dishes include brick oven pizzas and chicken fettuccini.

VICTORIA Il Terrazzo ⓈⓈⓈⓈ

555 Johnson St., British Columbia, V8W 1M2 **Tel** *(250) 361 0028*

In Old Town, in an original 1890 building, this restaurant has a fabulous courtyard patio with six fireplaces. Come for superb northern Italian fare where market- and seasonally-fresh foods are presented daily. The wood-burning oven turns out sensational Salmone al Forno – almond and black pepper encrusted salmon filet.

VICTORIA Fairmont Empress Room ⓈⓈⓈⓈⓈ

Empress Hotel, 721 Government St., British Columbia, V8W 1W5 **Tel** *(250) 381 4334*

The Empress Room is an elegant tradition, in architect Frances Rattenby's 1908 landmark hotel. You may pay handsomely for Afternoon Tea, but it is worth it simply for the sense of tradition and history, not to mention the scones, strawberry jam, and cream. In the evenings a harpist emphasizes the air of elegance.

THE ROCKY MOUNTAINS

BANFF Buffalo Mountain Lodge Dining Room ⓈⓈⓈ

700 Tunnel Mountain Rd., Alberta, T1L 1B3 **Tel** *(403) 760 4484*

Airy, delightful wood-beamed Sleeping Buffalo Restaurant and Lounge is ever-so-slightly off the beaten track. The specialty is delectably prepared, beautifully presented Canadian Rockies fare: venison, caribou, deer, lamb, salmon, and beef. Game is raised at the Canadian Rocky Mountain Resorts own ranch.

BANFF Coyote's Southwestern Grill ⓈⓈⓈ

206 Caribou St., Alberta, T1L 1A2 **Tel** *(403) 762 3963*

A small but highly regarded restaurant that focuses on Southwestern cuisine. Arizona-style prints adorn the walls to complete the regional effect. The ambience is casual and the varied menu includes pizza or calzones with spicy peppers, barbequed flank steak, spice-rubbed beef tenderloin, a good selection of salads, and some vegetarian choices.

BANFF Le Beaujolais 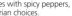 ⓈⓈⓈⓈ

212 Buffalo Street, Alberta, T1L 1B5 **Tel** *(403) 762 2712*

The menu at this award-winning restaurant in downtown Banff includes dishes such as braised elk with wild-boar bacon, champignons, and fried onions, and Atlantic lobster salad with avocado, mango, spring greens, and a citrus vinaigrette. For serious gastronomes, there is also a six-course tasting menu with wine pairings.

BANFF The Bison ⓈⓈⓈⓈ

The Bison Courtyard, 211 Bear Street, Alberta, T1L 1E4 **Tel** *(403) 762 5550*

Relax in summertime on an expansive patio, or during other seasons find cozy comfort in the lounge at this bistro where you can discover a choice of local beers or indulge in a signature cocktail before dinner. This is an elegant, airy, and trendy dining room where helpful wait staff serve organic and regional cuisine, with an emphasis on game.

CALGARY Ranchman's Cookhouse and Dancehall Ⓢ

9615 McLeod Trail South, Alberta, T2J 0P6 **Tel** *(403) 253 1100*

A Calgary tradition, this cowboy barbeque café and country music club displays trophy rodeo saddles and a chuck wagon above the stage. The menu features beef and chicken prepared in Texas-style smokers. Go here for the featured beer rather than for wine. This is a Calgary Stampede "place to be seen" for dining and dancing.

CALGARY River Café ⓈⓈⓈⓈ

25 Prince's Island Park, Alberta, T2P 4R5 **Tel** *(403) 261 7670*

This distinctly Canadian restaurant is located in Prince's Island Park, surrounded by a peaceful wooded garden with no car access. Wild game and the very best fresh, seasonal local produce are served. Try the fish and game platter with native candied trout, steelhead lox, salt-cured bison, duck rillettes, and more.

Key to Price Guide *see p370* **Key to Symbols** *see back cover flap*

CALGARY Saltlik Steakhouse

101 8th Ave. SW., Alberta, T2P 1B4 **Tel** *(403) 537 1160*

The portions are known for being generous at this upmarket, modern restaurant. As would be expected, the Alberta beef steaks are particularly noteworthy. This is an extremely popular restaurant, so reservations are recommended. Try the Almost Famous Dry Ribs with a tamarind honey glaze.

CALGARY Catch
100 8th Avenue SE., Alberta, T2G 0K6 **Tel** *(403) 206 0000*

Located on the second level of the historic Bank of Canada building, at Catch you will discover succulent seafood such as wild spring salmon gravlax with Digby scallops. Fish and shellfish are extremely fresh and are flown in daily. There is an excellent wine cellar with a special, private "red wine" dining room. Closed Sun.

CALGARY Rouge
1240 8th Avenue SE., Alberta, T2G 0M7 **Tel** *(403) 531 2767*

In the 1891 home of Calgary pioneer A.E. Cross on the Bow River embankment, this city landmark draws locals. The menu features home-grown herbs and vegetables, and fresh local ingredients. The specialties are black candied breast of duck or rack of lamb. Closed Sun.

FAUQUIER Mushroom Addition
129 Oak St., British Columbia, V0G 1K0 **Tel** *(250) 269 7467*

Delectable, delicate wild mushrooms are harvested locally at the Arrow Lakes and transformed into succulent creations at this restaurant. The menu is seasonal, depending upon what is growing. In winter it is only open Friday through Sunday – contact the restaurant to ensure it is open. There are a few dishes without mushrooms.

GOLDEN Eagle's Eye Restaurant

1500 Kicking Horse, British Columbia, V0A 1H0 **Tel** *(250) 439 5400*

Take a gondola up to this eyrie 2,410 m (7,906 ft) above sea level for panoramic views of Purcell, Rocky, and Selkirk ranges while dining at Canada's highest restaurant. Specialties include Alberta lamb, buffalo, and BC salmon. Dogtooth Patio serves drinks with spectacular views. Closed mid-Apr–mid-May and mid-Oct–mid-Dec.

JASPER The Emerald Lounge & Outdoor Patio

1 Old Lodge Road, Alberta, T0E 1E0 **Tel** *(780) 852 3301*

With stunning views of Lake Beauvert and Whistler's Mountain, don't miss The Emerald's expansive patio in summer, or the log interior at other times. There's a varied menu with delicious, beautifully presented grilled meats taking pride of place. Go with a hearty appetite, and hike around the lake afterward.

KIMBERLY The Old Bauernhaus
280 Norton Avenue, British Columbia, V1A 1X9 **Tel** *(250) 427 5133*

This 17th-century Bavarian barn was disassembled, shipped to Canada, and rebuilt in 1989, so the owners mean it when they say their food – and ambience – features old-world charm. Hearty fare is served. Specialties include the Bauernplatte (sliced meats and cheeses) and the Bavarian Feast. Closed Tue & Wed.

LAKE LOUISE Poppy Brasserie

Château Lake Louise, 111 Lake Louise Dr., Alberta, T0L 1E0 **Tel** *(403) 522 1818*

Cheerful as a poppy in a wheat field, this airy family restaurant commands views of Lake Louise. Children are particularly welcome: they'll find comfort foods like burgers, while adults select from salads, prime rib, or fish. This means Poppy's caters splendidly to everyone. An excellent buffet-style breakfast offers a surfeit of choices.

LAKE LOUISE Elkhorn Dining Room

Mile 22 Bow Lake Icefield Parkway, Alberta, T0L 1E0 **Tel** *(403) 522 2167*

Don't miss this authentic Canadian restaurant off the Icefields Parkway. The historic lodge was originally constructed by renowned guide, explorer, and tall-tale-spinner Jimmy Simpson. The Elkhorn's walls are festooned with trophy heads of moose, mountain goats, and other game: vegetarians beware! Unsurprisingly, the superb cuisine focuses on local game.

LAKE LOUISE The Post Hotel Dining Room

The Post Hotel, 200 Pipestone Road, Alberta, T0L 1E0 **Tel** *(403) 522 3989*

There is renowned fine dining at this Relais and Châteaux log-cabin luxury hotel, where wait staff are superbly informed about every nuance of your meal – and how to marry the perfect wine to your dinner. Swiss Executive Chef Hans Sauter produces memorable meals such as succulent rack of lamb.

NELSON The Outer Clove

536 Stanley St., British Columbia, V1L 1N2 **Tel** *(250) 354 1667*

If you love "the stinking rose," then rush here to sample garlicky treats, from appies to mains to desserts. Every day chefs here use 5 pounds of garlic in a variety of ways, including in the desserts, in this brightly painted old brick building. There is frequent live music. Closed Sun.

REVELSTOKE One Twelve Restaurant

112 First St. E., British Columbia, V0E 2S0 **Tel** *(250) 837 2107*

With white linen, heritage photos of the Canadian Pacific Railway, and a fireplace, the "112" offers friendly elegance. Dine on BC salmon, charbroiled steaks, or Caribbean lobster. Enjoy a locally brewed Mt. Begbie draft beer while admiring the world's largest grizzly bear carved in soapstone.

SOUTHERN AND NORTHERN BRITISH COLUMBIA

FORT LANGLEY Bedford House $$$$
9272 Glover Rd., V1M 2R7 **Tel** *(604) 888 2333*

Located in historic Fort Langley, this restaurant with several little dining rooms is on a spacious lot with lovely river views. It is very popular with locals, so reservations are a must, particularly for Sunday brunch. Enjoy good Canadian food in a relaxed atmosphere with attentive staff and fine wines.

HARRISON HOT SPRINGS Harrison Hot Springs Restaurants $$$
100 Esplanade Avenue, V0M 1K0 **Tel** *(604) 796 2244*

Three restaurants inside the Harrison Hot Springs Resort. A stellar Okanagan wine list, featuring many labels by the glass, complements a regional-based menu. Signature dishes include Fraser Valley duck with candied ginger glaze, sustainable, organic wild caribou, and pan-seared tenderloin medallions with blackberry jus.

KELOWNA The Yellowhouse Restaurant $$$
526 Lawrence Avenue, V1Y 6L7 **Tel** *(250) 763 5136*

Everything is homemade here – the stock, soup, sauces, and desserts. Dine on mouthwatering entrées such as warm seafood salad, rack of lamb, or wild BC salmon with strawberry beurre blanc. The casual ambience of this 1906 Victorian residence is enhanced before dinner while you sip a signature martini or award-winning BC wine.

OSOYOOS The Diamond Steak and Seafood House $$
8903 Main St., V0H 1V0 **Tel** *(250) 495 6223*

Popular with local residents, The Diamond's three dining rooms specialize in Greek and Italian cuisine with steaks, seafood, pasta, and many varieties of pizza. Prime rib is a house specialty but go for the Greek dishes such as calamari with Greek Salad.

PRINCE GEORGE Shogun Japanese Steakhouse $$$$
770 Brunswick St., V2L 2C2 **Tel** *(250) 563 0121*

Go for the Shogun Combo at this excellent Japanese steakhouse where quality meets quantity. Reserve ahead so you can sit around the Teppan grill where the chef creates your meal. If a romantic meal is in order, book a private Shojii room. Specialties include fresh sushi. Shogon, or Ozeki combo platters.

PRINCE RUPERT Cow Bay Cafe $$$
205 Cow Bay Rd., V8J 3Y1 **Tel** *(250) 627 1212*

Locals love this casual spot located right on the docks overlooking the harbor. There are many vegetarian options here, including salads and soups as well as freshly caught fish of the day. Those in the know order dessert along with their entrée – otherwise you'll find they may have sold out.

WHISTLER Black's Restaurant Pub and Patio $$$
4270 Mountain Square, V0N 1B4 **Tel** *(604) 932 6408*

An open-style Mediterranean restaurant located at the base of Blackcomb and Whistler mountains, this is an après-ski favorite, so check out the authentic local scene here. Turkey roast is served on Sundays, and the Canadian pub upstairs specializes in a large selection of beer on tap.

WHISTLER Bearfoot Bistro $$$$$
4121 Village Green, V0N 1B4 **Tel** *(604) 932 3433*

Brown leather chairs, live jazz pianist, and a large selection of Cuban cigars create a sophisticated air. This bistro serves innovative French cuisine specializing in seafood and game, particularly caribou. Tasting menus feature seasonal regional food paired with BC and other wines. There are après-ski specials.

NORTHERN CANADA

CAMBRIDGE BAY Arctic Islands Lodge Restaurant $$$
26 Omingmak P.O. Box 38, Nunavut, X0B 0C0 **Tel** *(867) 983 2345*

Located inside Arctic Island Lodge, this restaurant has specials almost every night. It serves traditional and Canadian cuisine including muskox steak, muskox stew, and Arctic char fillets. A gift case displays carvings from local artists. Open weekdays 7am–6pm and weekends 9am–6pm.

DAWSON CITY Bonanza Dining Room $$$
902 3rd Ave., Yukon, Y0B 1G0 **Tel** *(867) 993 5451*

This restaurant located in the Eldorado Hotel offers nothern fare such as Yukon salmon and Alaskan halibut alongside not-so-northern flambée desserts. The wait staff are dressed in gold rush era costumes. Evenings offer a fine dining experience. Open weekdays 6:30am–10pm and weekends 7am–9pm.

Key to Price Guide *see p370* **Key to Symbols** *see back cover flap*

DAWSON CITY Klondike Kate's

1102 3rd Ave., Yukon, Y0B 1G0 **Tel** *(867) 993 6527*

This popular family restaurant with a friendly atmosphere is located on 3rd and King Street. Serving Canadian, vegetarian, and ethnic food, it also offers espressos, lattes, and fruit smoothies. This gold rush era building dates back to 1904 and has an outdoor heated patio. Open Apr–Sep 7am–11pm.

FORT PROVIDENCE Snowshoe Inn Café

⑤

1 Mackenzie Drive, Northwest Territories, X0E 0L0 **Tel** *(867) 699 3511*

Located on the banks of the historic Mackenzie River, this café is across from the Snowshoe Inn. This local hangout serves Canadian fare including the Snowshoe burger, a bison meat patty. Open year round 7am–8pm (10am–8pm Sun & holidays). No alcohol served.

HAINES JUNCTION Raven Gourmet Dining

Box 5470, 181 Alaska Highway, Yukon, Y0B 1L0 **Tel** *(867) 634 2500*

Located in the Raven Hotel, this restaurant serves an international menu and even makes its own pasta. The food is cooked fresh to order, and the menu changes weekly. Highlights include dishes prepared with locally sourced wild game. It serves dinner only. Open May–Sep.

HAY RIVER Back Eddy Cocktail Lounge & Restaurant

⑤⑤⑤

6 Courtoreille St., Northwest Territories, X0E 1G2 **Tel** *(867) 874 6680*

This restaurant and lounge is open 11am–2am except on Sundays; the kitchen closes at 9pm. This local hangout is above Ring's Pharmacy in the center of town. The menu includes steak, seafood, burgers, and fish in a relaxed atmosphere that is a mix of sports bar and restaurant. There is also a good choice of finger foods and lighter fare.

INUVIK Tonimoes

⑤⑤⑤⑤

185 Mackenzie Road, Northwest Territories, X0E 0T0 **Tel** *(867) 777 4900*

This family steakhouse is in the Mackenzie Hotel across from the Igloo Church. There is a waterfall in the front and a fireplace in the back. The menu offers steaks, burgers, pasta, and fish and chips for Friday lunch. There is a delicious Sunday brunch offering too. Open daily.

IQALUIT Gallery Fine Dining Room

⑤⑤⑤⑤

The Astro Hill Terrace, Nunavut, X0A 0H0 **Tel** *(867) 979 2222*

This restaurant is housed in the Frobisher Inn. It offers northern cuisine in a fine dining atmosphere. Artists come in and sell their wares in what amounts to a bit of a dinner and art show. A place to spend the evening, especially when artists are around.

IQALUIT The Granite Room

⑤⑤⑤⑤⑤

P.O. Box 387, Iqaluit, Nunavut, X0A 0H0 **Tel** *(867) 979 4433*

Situated in the Discovery Lodge Hotel, the Granite Room serves up fine northern cuisine in elegant surroundings. The yellow walls give it a cheerful feel. The place offers table d'hôte specials and Sunday brunch. Signature dishes include Arctic char, caribou steak, Pangnirtung halibut, and tundra mushroom caps.

WHITEHORSE The Deck

⑤⑤⑤

4051 Fourth Ave., Yukon, Y1A 1H1 **Tel** *(867) 667 4471*

Located inside the High Country Inn, this restaurant offers northern cuisine such as caribou steak and fresh salmon in rustic surroundings. Among the beer on offer is Grizzly Beer, produced exclusively for the restaurant by the Yukon Brewing Company. There is a heated patio. Open 11:30am–1:30am.

WHITEHORSE Cellar Steakhouse and Wine Bar

⑤⑤⑤⑤

101 Main St., Yukon, Y1A 2A7 **Tel** *(867) 667 2572*

On the lower level of the Edgewater Hotel, this restaurant serves tapas, prime rib, crab, steak, lamb, and seafood in elegant surroundings and a relaxed atmosphere. There is also a wine bar. The hotel and steakhouse are located downtown near the historic White Pass Railway depot. Open Tue–Sat 6–10pm.

YELLOWKNIFE Bullocks' Bistro

⑤⑤⑤

3534 Weaver Drive, Northwest Territories, X1A 2J6 **Tel** *(867) 873 3474*

With its hand-scrawled appreciation and stickers on the wall, this place oozes character. Sit at the bar and banter with the cook as he whips up muskox, caribou, bison, and fresh fish from Great Slave Lake, served with healthy portions of salad, fries, and bread. Select your own drinks from the fridge. Top fish and chips too.

YELLOWKNIFE Le Frolic Bistro/Bar

⑤⑤⑤⑤

5019 49th Street, Northwest Territories, X1A 2N6 **Tel** *(867) 669 9852*

This lively downtown bistro/bar shares a wine cellar with the more upscale and formal L'Heritage Restaurant Français upstairs. Le Frolic's menu offers typical Northern specialties – such as Arctic char and bison – with a touch of French flair in an intimate setting. Open 3pm–1am Mon–Sat.

YELLOWKNIFE Wildcat Café

⑤⑤⑤⑤

3904 Wiley Road, Northwest Territories, X1A 2N6 **Tel** *(867) 873 4004*

A real slice of northern Canadian life, the Canadian Museum of Civilization in Ottawa has a replica of this café. This institution in historic Old Town is a log cabin that opened as a restaurant in 1937. It serves local fare in a convivial atmosphere. Share tables and meet people. Closed in winter.

SHOPPING IN CANADA

Shopping in Canada offers more than the usual tourist fare of Mountie dolls and maple leaf T-shirts. Visitors can choose from a wide range of products, and buy everything from electronic equipment to clothes and jewelry. There is also a variety of goods unique to the country – maple syrup from Quebec, smoked salmon from British Columbia, and cowboy boots from Alberta, to name a few. Native art inspired by centuries-old tradition, includes carvings by west-coast peoples and Inuit paintings and tapestries. In each major city there are covered malls, chainstores, specialty shops, and galleries, as well as street markets to explore. In country areas, beautifully-made crafts by local people can be found. Be aware that sales taxes are added to the price of many items.

Doll from Charlottetown

SHOPPING HOURS

Store hours vary, but in larger cities most stores are open by 9am and close between 5pm and 9pm. However, some grocery and variety stores are open 24 hours a day, and in major towns several pharmacies are also open for 24 hours. In most towns, stores have late closing until 9pm on Friday evening. However, in smaller towns and villages you should not expect any store, including the gas station, to be open after 6pm. Sunday openings are increasing: usually hours run from noon to 5pm but vary from province to province. Check first, as many may be closed in rural areas.

HOW TO PAY

Most Canadian stores accept all major credit cards, with VISA and MasterCard being the most popular. Some stores require a minimum purchase in order to use the card. They may limit the use of cards during summer and winter sales. Direct payment, or "Switch" transactions, are also widely used, with point-of-sale terminals for bank cards available in most supermarkets and department stores. Travelers' checks are readily accepted with proper identification; a valid passport or driver's license are the usually accepted forms.

US dollars are the only non-Canadian currency accepted in department stores. Bear in mind that the exchange rate is usually lower, sometimes as much as 15 percent, than a bank will give. Large stores may offer money-changing facilities within the store.

SALES TAXES

In Canada there are three types of sales taxes: Provincial Sales Taxes (PST), the federal Goods and Services Tax (GST), and the Harmonized Sales Tax (HST). Every province except Alberta implements a PST which varies between 5 and 12 percent, on store-bought items. The Yukon Territory, Northwest Territories and Nunavut are the exceptions and these do not have any type of regional sales tax. In Nova Scotia, New Brunswick, and Newfoundland and Labrador, an HST of 13 percent replaces both the GST and the PST and is applied on the same basis as the GST.

Canadians love to curse the GST, which currently runs at 5 percent. It is added to most retail transactions; the major exception is basic food items. Since the beginning of April 2007 the GST rebate program for non-residents of Canada has been eliminated.

CONSUMER RIGHTS AND SERVICES

Smart shoppers always check a store's refund policy before buying an item. Policies vary, some stores will refund money on unwanted items, others offer store vouchers, and many will not exchange or refund sale merchandise. Reputable stores will take back defective merchandise within 28 days as long as it is accompanied by the original bill. As credit card fraud increases, it is wise to be cautious about buying by telephone using cards.

Native Canadian Wayne Carlick, carving soapstone, British Columbia

COMPLETELY CANADIAN

Products made in Canada offer shoppers a wide variety of choice. Although most specialty items are on sale across the country, many goods are less expensive in their province of origin. Hand-knitted sweaters and pottery are particularly good value in Atlantic Canada, as is the much-praised Seagull pewter made in Nova Scotia. The Prairie provinces and Alberta specialize in cowboy attire; tooled belts, vests, cowboy hats, and boots. Farther west, British Columbian artisans produce elaborate carvings,

Shopkeeper at the Lonsdale Quay market in Vancouver *(see p278)*

including totem poles. Jade jewelry, from locally mined stone, is also reasonable here. Local specialties from Quebec and Ontario include maple syrup and sugar-related products. Quebec artisans make beautiful wood carvings too. In Ontario, native basketwork is good as a lasting souvenir. For those who need an extra suitcase to carry their finds home, the renowned Tilley travel cases and products are made and sold locally throughout Ontario.

Native carvings can be found across Canada, especially in the far north. Genuine Inuit carvings are inspected and stamped by the federal government. A sticker featuring an igloo marks a true piece; it will also be signed by the artist. Since the 1950s, the Inuit have been producing prints of traditional scenes, which are popular, as is native jewelry. Beautifully handmade parka jackets, embroidered panels, and soft deer hide moccasins make excellent gifts.

Contemporary Canadian art features highly in gift shops and galleries countrywide. Photographs and prints are recommended for the budget-conscious shopper. Recordings of Canadian music are freely available: Europeans will be pleased to find that tapes and CDs are at least 50 percent cheaper in Canada.

Modern sportswear and outerwear is both durable and beautifully designed. Camping, hiking, and boating equipment

Pottery jar, Nova Scotia

are fine buys, as is fishing tackle. With such a strong tradition of outdoor life, a wide range of products is usually available at well below European prices.

DEPARTMENT STORES

The Bay is the major middle-range department store chain across the country. Canadian department stores have suffered financially during the last years of the 20th century. They are changing to meet the competition of US chains, such as Wal-Mart and discount stores, and membership stores including Costco and Price Club. Chains such as Sears and Zeller's occupy the middle to lower end of the market place. Canadian Tire sells everything from auto parts to sporting goods and has become a national institution.

MALLS AND SHOPPING CENTERS

Suburbia may not offer the most culture in Canada, but some of the malls are fine destinations in themselves. The renowned modernist Eaton Centre in Toronto is enclosed by a glass and steel arched roof, with a wonderful sculpted flock of geese soaring over shoppers. Over 42 million visitors annually enjoy this showcase of modern architecture, though it has been derided as "brutalism" by conservative Torontonians. Canada has the world's largest mall, the West Edmonton Mall in Edmonton, Alberta. Over 800 stores, more than 100 restaurants, 34 movie theaters, a huge water park, an amusement park, a theme hotel, a mini-golf course, an ice rink, and a zoo with dolphins are just some of the sights that draw Canadians and visitors alike to this retail paradise.

Exclusive stores are largely found in the country's retail capital, Toronto. Bloor Street and Yorkville Avenue are lined with status brands known the world over, such as Tiffany, Holt Renfrew, Ralph Lauren, and Gucci. Both Vancouver and Montreal have their own selection of world-class luxury stores. Montreal is notable as the fur capital of the country; good department stores will stock a selection of winter and summer furs at very reasonable prices. For those unable to travel to the north, Inuit art features highly in craft shops here.

The Underground City, with hundreds of boutiques, in Montreal

Shopping in Montreal, Toronto, and Vancouver

Canada's three largest cities offer shopping experiences with one thing in common: international fare! Montreal's cosmopolitan edge complements its wide-ranging stores, from chic boutiques to antique shops to an underground network of stores and services. Toronto's shop-'til-you-drop attitude includes the Bay/Bloor neighborhood and Yorkville as well as dozens

Market vegetables

of ethnic communities selling wares from their home countries. Vancouver shows off with about ten great shopping areas, as befits a spreading coastal city, with *haute couture* alongside art, furniture, and much more.

Eaton Centre in Toronto, containing hundreds of stores

DEPARTMENT STORES AND MALLS

Canada's most well-known department store is **The Bay/ La Baie**, a modern moniker for the Hudson's Bay Company, which started here in the 17th century as a trading post between the early settlers and the aboriginal peoples. The Bay is found in all three cities, and its distinctive brand of rainbow-striped blankets, sweaters, and coats have always been a hit with visitors. In downtown Toronto, the mammoth **Eaton Centre** shopping complex, which stretches a full city block, contains two well known stores – Sears and the Swedish retailer H&M – as well as hundreds of smaller stores. Theater impresario Ed Mirvish started his empire with a small discount department store, **Honest Ed's**, which today covers a city block and remains exceptionally popular, especially with new immigrants to Toronto. Montreal's **Place Montréal Trust** is home to 70 boutiques, including several

major retailers. A good rendezvous point is the mall's soaring 30-ft fountain. In Vancouver, the **Pacific Centre** is arguably the city's premiere shopping mall downtown, but in nearby Richmond, the **Aberdeen Centre** plays host to a bevy of Asian stores, restaurants, and services.

MARKETS

Vancouver's milder climate allows for longer seasons of the outdoor markets, but Canada's two other large cities do not shy away from this popular shopping experience. Montreal's **Jean-Talon Market**, with over 100 vendors, is mainly outdoors from May until October, although it is open year round and contains 20 indoor stores over the underground parking lot. In Toronto, the **St. Lawrence Market**, with 60 vendors, is much loved by locals as much for its fresh produce and meats as for the quirky indoor shopping it offers. Vancouver's **Granville Island**

boasts an authentic farmer's market along with several galleries, boutiques, and artisans' stores.

ANTIQUES AND CRAFTS

Toronto's antique and craft stores are located throughout the city, but **Yorkville** has the higher end items. This is also the location for **The Guild Shop**, featuring beautiful items from the Ontario Crafts Council. The **Harbourfront Antique Market**, south by the lakeshore, is also a must-visit. In Montreal, **L'Art des Artisans du Québec** is a perfect store for original gifts made of wood, pewter, and glass, designed by talented Quebec artists. Local crafts are also on sale in the 15 boutiques of **Marché Bonsecours**. In Vancouver, **Antique Row** has both valuable and kitschy antiques. The city's **Antique Warehouse** is an attractive stop for aficionados.

DESIGNER FASHION AND JEWELRY

In Montreal, women's fashion by exclusively Quebec designers can be found at **Boutique Diffusion Griff'3000**, while there is a wide variety of designer menswear at **L'Uomo Montréal**. La Maison Ogilvy has been a respected fashion retailer in Montreal since 1866, and is also worth a visit for high-end items.

In Toronto, most designer stores, including **Tiffany & Co.**, **Royal de Versailles**, and **Gucci**, are centered in the Bloor-Yorkville area, including the flagship store for

The market on Granville Island in Vancouver

Holt Renfrew, a Canadian retailer known for its fine products, especially in cosmetics, fashion, and jewelry, Vancouver's Robson Street contains the high fashion stores, with Armani, Chanel, Louis Vuitton, and Canada's own **Roots** all catching the shopper's eye.

ART, BOOKS, MUSIC, AND GIFTWARE

The largest bookstore chain in the country is Chapters/Indigo/ Coles, and the large outlets in major centers have excellent music offerings as well (and

cafés). The **Canadian Guild of Crafts** in Montreal not only displays fine giftware in wood, ceramic, blown glass, metal, and handmade jewelry, but also has a permanent collection of Inuit art worth perusing. In Vancouver, rare books or early titles on western Canadiana can be found at **MacLeod's Books**.

SPECIALTY STORES

Canadian Maple Delights in Montreal is the quintessential homage to maple syrup: here there's everything from gelati, pastries, mustards, vinaigrettes,

and jams to 100 other maple treats. Elsewhere in the city, **La Casa del Habano** is the best place to enjoy a fine Havana cigar with a Cuban cocktail or coffee. And for those so inclined, **Héritage** is a furrier as well as an art gallery in the heart of Vieux-Montréal. In Toronto, the city's Yorkville neighborhood plays host to Canada's oldest sex toy store, **Lovecraft**, which is now considered to be decidedly upscale. Vancouver's **Mountain Equipment Coop** will ensure the buyer is outfitted with the very best in outdoor gear and supplies.

DIRECTORY

DEPARTMENT STORES AND MALLS

Aberdeen Centre
4151 Hazelbridge Way, Richmond, Vancouver. *Tel (604) 270 1234.* www.aberdeencentre.com

The Bay/La Baie
585 Rue Ste-Catherine Ouest, Montreal; 176 Yonge St., Toronto; 674 Granville St., Vancouver. www.hbc.com

Eaton Centre
Yonge and Dundas St., Toronto. *Tel (416) 598 8560.* www.toronto eatoncentre.com

Honest Ed's
581 Bloor St. W., Toronto. *Tel (416) 537 1574.* www.honesteds.sites. toronto.com

Pacific Centre
550–700 W. Georgia St., Vancouver. *Tel (604) 688 7235.* www.pacificcentre.com

Place Montréal Trust
1500 McGill College Ave., Montreal. *Tel (514) 843 8000.* www.place montrealtrust.com

MARKETS

Granville Island
South shore under the Granville Street Bridge, Vancouver. www.granvilleisland.com

Jean-Talon Market
7075 Ave. Casgrain, Montreal. *Tel (514) 277 1588.* www.montreal food.com/jtalon.html

St. Lawrence Market
92 Front St. E., Toronto. *Tel (416) 392 7120.* www.stlawrence market.com

ANTIQUES AND CRAFTS

Antique Row
Main St., Vancouver (betw. 16th and 25th Ave).

Antique Warehouse
226 S.W. Marine Dr., Vancouver. *Tel (604) 324 3661.* www.antique warehouse.net

L'Art des Artisans du Québec
Complexe Desjardins, 150 Rue Ste-Catherine Ouest, Montreal. *Tel (514) 288 5379.*

The Guild Shop
118 Cumberland St., Toronto. *Tel (416) 921 1721.* www.craft.on.ca

Harbourfront Antique Market
390 Queens Quay W., Toronto. *Tel (416) 260 2626.*

Marché Bonsecours
350 Rue St-Paul Est, Montreal. *Tel (514) 872 7730.* www.marche bonsecours.qc.ca

Yorkville
Betw. Avenue Rd. and Bay St., north of Bloor St. W., Toronto. www.bloor-yorkville.com

DESIGNER FASHION AND JEWELRY

Boutique Diffusion Griff'3000
Marché Bonsecours, 350 Rue St-Paul Est, Montreal. *Tel (514) 398 0761.* www.diffusiongriff 3000.com

Gucci
130 Bloor St. W., Toronto.

Holt Renfrew
1300 Rue Sherbrooke Ouest, Montreal; 50 Bloor St. W., Toronto; Pacific Centre, 633 Granville St., Vancouver.

La Maison Ogilvy
1307 Rue Ste-Catherine Ouest, Montreal. *Tel (514) 842 7711.* www.ogilvycanada.com

Roots
1001 Robson St., Vancouver. *Tel (604) 683 4305;* 1035 Rue Ste-Catherine Ouest, Montreal. *Tel (514) 845 7995;* 100 Bloor St. W., Toronto. *Tel (416) 323 3289.* www.roots.com

Royal de Versailles
101 Bloor St. W., Toronto. *Tel (416) 967 7201.*

Tiffany & Co.
85 Bloor St. W., Toronto. www.tiffany.ca

L'Uomo Montréal
1452 Rue Peel, Montreal. *Tel (514) 844 1008.*

ART, BOOKS, MUSIC, AND GIFTWARE

Canadian Guild of Crafts
1460 Rue Sherbrooke Ouest, Suite B, Montreal. *Tel (514) 849 6091.* www.canadianguild.com

MacLeod's Books
455 West Pender St., Vancouver. *Tel (604) 681 7654.*

SPECIALTY STORES

Canadian Maple Delights
84 Rue St-Paul Est, Montreal. *Tel (514) 765 3456.*

La Casa del Habano
1434 Rue Sherbrooke Ouest, Montreal. *Tel (514) 849 0037.*

Héritage
30 Rue St-Paul Est, Montreal. *Tel (514) 392 9272.*

Lovecraft
27 Yorkville Ave., Toronto. *Tel (416) 923 7331.*

Mountain Equipment Coop
130 W. Broadway, Vancouver. *Tel (604) 872 7858.* www.mec.ca

ENTERTAINMENT IN CANADA

Entertainment in Canada boasts all the sophistication tourists have come to expect from a major North American country, coupled with delightful rural entertainments in relaxing local venues. Covering mainstream world-class productions in Ottawa and the larger cities, Canada also offers the latest in alternative acts and traditional artforms, particularly in its exceptional folk music heritage. Music of the highest quality, both classical and modern, is offered throughout the country, and major cities provide first-rate theater, dance, and film, not to mention many musical shows and film festivals.

Royal Winnipeg Ballerina

INFORMATION

Provincial daily newspapers are the most reliable sources of information about forthcoming events; the *Vancouver Sun*, *Montreal Gazette*, *Ottawa Citizen*, and *Toronto Star* are the most popular. Listings are usually published at least once a week. The *Globe & Mail* and *National Post* are produced in Toronto but are sold countrywide and have excellent arts sections containing reviews of the latest attractions. Tourist offices *(see p409)* are helpful; some operators may assist in booking tickets. Visitor centers and hotel lobbies have weekly entertainment guides, such as *Where*, a magazine covering Vancouver. In Quebec, French-language entertainment is chronicled by two papers, *La Presse* and *Le Devoir*. *Macleans* is a national weekly magazine with arts coverage.

BOOKING

Ticketmaster outlets are found in many shopping malls and represent major halls across the country. Tickets to venues in Quebec are available from Admission Network. Different offices cater to different sports and artistic events in each city. Most venues, however, can be contacted directly for tickets.

DISABLED VISITORS

Major Canadian venues are well equipped to deal with wheelchair users. All interior halls contain ramps and restroom access. Parking lots will have designated disabled spaces nearby. A hearing loop system is available at Ottawa's National Arts Centre *(see p197)*,

and at most other major venues. Call ahead to check their availability. Outside ramps and elevators are provided to reach concerts halls and theaters at most large centers.

THEATER

Toronto, Ottawa, Vancouver, Montreal, Stratford, and Niagara-on-the-Lake are the top theater centers in Canada (most of their productions are in English). Homegrown talent mixes here with shows imported from Europe and the US. Musicals and classical theater are always popular, as is Shakespeare, but there is a wide spectrum of shows for example, Toronto's Princess of Wales and Royal Alexandra Theatres mount Broadway productions, as well as world premieres, such as *Lord of the Rings*. The main theaters have a principal season from November to May, but summer attractions are on the increase. Musicals and historical reconstructions provide family entertainment; the best-known is the musical *Anne of Green Gables*, performed year-round in Charlottetown.

FILM

Hollywood block-busters have no better chance of success than in Canada, where premieres are often parallel with the US, so visitors may well see films in advance of a showing in their own country. Huge IMAX™ and OMNIMAX™ movie theaters can be found in the center of major cities, particularly in Ottawa and Hull.

Canada has a fine history of filmmaking: the documentary genre was invented here, and more recently its art films have attracted a wider audience. The main centers to see the new trends are Montreal, Vancouver, and Toronto. Robert LePage, Canada's own theater and movie impresario, has an international following among the cognoscenti. The surrealist David Cronenberg, director of *Spider* (2002) and *A History of Violence* (2005), is also Canadian. Quebec's Denys Arcand is admired for his intensely human dramas, such as *Jesus of Montreal* (1989), *Love and Human Remains* (1993) and *The Barbarian Invasions* (2003). The National Film

Façade of The Royal George Theatre, Niagara-on-the-Lake, Ontario

The Ontario Place IMAX™ giant movie theater in Toronto

Board selects and releases a work by native talent each year, comprising feature films, animations, and documentaries. Ideal for spotting new talent, every year the Toronto International Film Festival provides a lively magnet to moviegoers, as do parallel festivals held in Montreal and Vancouver.

CLASSICAL MUSIC, BALLET, AND OPERA

Classical music and opera draw large audiences in Canada, and this is reflected by the high quality of performers and venues. The Canadian Opera Company is based at the Four Seasons Centre for the Performing Arts *(see p174)* in Toronto, with a repertoire ranging from Mozart to cutting-edge pieces sung in English. The National Ballet of Canada is also based here, rival to the Royal Winnipeg Ballet; both companies feature period pieces and experimental work in their seasonal run. Fringe theater takes off in Toronto each summer with 400 shows selected by lottery. Well over 100,000 people annually visit the state-of-the-art Jack Singer Concert Hall in the EPCOR Centre for the Performing Arts to hear the celebrated Calgary Philharmonic Orchestra. The Vancouver Symphony Orchestra plays at the Orpheum Theatre in Vancouver.

ROCK, FOLK, AND POP MUSIC

During the 1990s, Canadian pop music acquired a credibility even its kindest supporters would admit had previously been lacking. Quebec's Celine Dion is a superstar and Shania Twain, Bryan Adams, and k.d. lang are international stars. Alanis Morissette and Sarah McLachlan are worthy successors to their country's heritage of folk rock. Young pop icons Avril Lavigne, Nelly Furtado, and Leslie Feist have been wooing teenagers worldwide with their youthful anthems.

Canada is perhaps most famous for its folk music, with such stars as Leonard Cohen, Neil Young, and Joni Mitchell being the best-known

Celine Dion, one of Canada's best-selling international artists

faces from a centuries-old tradition. The product of an intensely musical rural people, the nature of Canadian song changes across the country, moving from the lonesome Celtic melodies on the east coast to the yodeling cowboys in the west. Atlantic Canada has numerous tiny, informal venues, where an excellent standard of music can be found. Quebec's French folksters include singer Gilles Vigneault *(see p28)* who is also admired in Europe. The Yukon's memories of the gold rush surface in 19th century vaudeville, reenacted by dancing girls and a honky-tonk piano in Whitehorse.

DIRECTORY

TICKET AGENCIES

Admission Network
Tel 1 800 361 4595.
Tel (613) 755 1111 Ottawa.
Tel (514) 790 1245 Montreal.
Tel (416) 861 1017 Toronto.

Ticketmaster
Tel (416) 870 8000 Toronto.

MAJOR VENUES

Bell Centre
Tel (514) 932 2582.

Calgary Philharmonic Orchestra
Tel (403) 571 0270.

EPCOR Centre for the Performing Arts
Tel (403) 294 7455.

Four Seasons Centre for the Performing Arts
Tel (416) 363 6671.

The National Ballet of Canada
Tel (416) 345 9686 Toronto.

The Newfoundland Symphony Orchestra
Tel (709) 722 4441.

Orpheum Theatre
Tel (604) 665 3050.

Roy Thomson Hall
www.roythompson.com

Royal Winnipeg Ballet
Tel (204) 956 0183.

Vancouver Symphony Orchestra
Tel (604) 876 3434.

Entertainment in Montreal, Toronto, and Vancouver

A visit to the three largest cities in the country will not disappoint when it comes to great entertainment. Each is rich in theatre, film, and music venues. Montreal has spawned both French and English musical artists, and annual festivals abound, such as the Festival International de Jazz de Montréal.

Avril Lavigne The renowned Toronto International Film Festival attracts the cream of Hollywood celebrities every September, and Vancouver is no slouch with its vibrant live music scene, dance clubs, and Irish pubs in numerous neighborhoods.

Giant banner in the parade at the annual Toronto Pride Festival

FESTIVALS

Festival fever hits Canada's three largest cities in the summer, but late spring and early fall can offer unique events too. Montreal's own **Cirque du Soleil** often premieres its new productions in its home city, and the **Festival International de Jazz de Montréal** is known for its 350 free concerts. The **Contact: Toronto Photography Festival** enables new artists to exhibit alongside internationally famous photographers. The **Toronto Pride Festival** has grown tremendously to include thousands of people of all orientations and gender identities. The city also hosts the **Caribana Festival** on the first weekend in August. The **Vancouver International Film Festival** is fast becoming as popular as the **Toronto International Film Festival**. In July, Vancouver's **Dancing on the Edge Festival** showcases contemporary dance.

THEATER

Montreal has an important theater for the Anglophone enthusiast. **The Centaur** is housed in the former Montreal Stock Exchange building and stages high-quality English-language productions by both emerging and established playwrights. Both Canadian and international plays are performed regularly. Toronto's live theater community, the **Mirvish Theatres**, is considered to be the third largest in North America, and the city often showcases the continental premiere of large-scale productions, such as

Lord of the Rings. Vancouver's nonprofit **Arts Club Theatre Company** has had over 40 seasons of producing professional live theater. The city also hosts the **Bard on the Beach** – western Canada's largest professional Shakespeare Festival, performed in Vancouver's Vanier Park.

ROCK, FOLK, AND POP MUSIC

The premier location for rock and pop concerts in Montreal is the **Bell Centre**, while folk music and up-and-coming artists can be found in the Quartier Latin (Latin Quarter) at any of the trendy bistros and bars along Saint-Denis and Ontario Streets. Toronto's largest pop/rock concerts can be enjoyed at the **Rogers Centre** or the **Air Canada Centre**; smaller groups and retro/folk musicians are normally featured at the **Molson Amphitheatre** at Ontario Place (on the lakefront) during the summer months. In Vancouver, **General Motors Place** usually hosts the biggest rock and pop concerts, while the more intimate **Orpheum Theatre** plays host to single or smaller groups of musicians.

CLASSICAL MUSIC, BALLET, AND OPERA

The **Opéra de Montréal**, founded in 1980, is the largest francophone opera company in North America. For dance lovers, **Les Grands Ballets Canadiens de Montréal** has a wide repertoire and invites prestigious international ballet companies each year to Place des Arts. Toronto is home to the **Toronto Symphony Orchestra**, and to the **Canadian Opera Company**

The setting for Bard on the Beach – Vancouver's Shakespeare Festival

Performance by the Opéra de Montréal at the city's Place des Arts

Elizabeth Theatre plays host to both the **Vancouver Opera** and **Ballet British Columbia**.

BARS AND CLUBS

Montreal has two main clubbing areas: Rue Crescent, a two-block area packed with patios and pubs between Rue de Maisonneuve and Rue Ste-Catherine, and Rue St-Laurent, a predominantly French-speaking neighborhood with more upscale locations and most of the dance clubs. Toronto's Queen

and the **National Ballet of Canada**, which are showcased at the **Four Seasons Centre for the Performing Arts**. In Vancouver, the **Queen**

Street and King Street West neighborhoods (from University to Spadina Avenues) are where the bulk of dance clubs, comedy clubs, and other pubs are located. The city's gay village and its nightclubs are in the Church-Wellesley Streets area. Vancouver's bars and clubs are spread all over: from Robson Street downtown, to the East Side/Main Street where the artsy community owns galleries that double as bars. Kitsilano is the city's homage to California life, with pretty people and beachside bars and clubs.

DIRECTORY

FESTIVALS

Caribana Festival
Toronto. August.
www.caribana.com

Cirque du Soleil
Frequent premieres in Montreal.
Tel (514) 790 1245.
www.cirquedusoleil.com

Contact: Toronto Photography Festival
June.
Tel (416) 539 9595.
www.contactphoto.com

Dancing on the Edge Festival
Vancouver. July.
www.dancingonthe edge.org

Festival International de Jazz de Montréal
Late June–early July.
Tel (514) 871 1881.
www.montrealjazz fest.com

Toronto International Film Festival
Early September.
www.bell.ca/filmfest

Toronto Pride Festival
June.
www.pridetoronto.com

Vancouver International Film Festival
Late September–early October. www.viff.org

THEATER

Arts Club Theatre Company
1585 Johnston St., Vancouver.
Tel (604) 687 1644.
www.artsclub.com

Bard on the Beach
Vanier Park, Kits Point at the Foot of Whyte Ave., Vancouver. *Tel (604) 739 0559.* www.bardonthe beach.org

The Centaur
453 Rue Saint-François-Xavier, Montreal.
Tel (514) 288 3161.
www.centaurtheatre.com

Mirvish Theatres
Princess of Wales Theatre, 300 King St. W.; Royal Alexandra Theatre, 260 King St. W.; Canon Theatre, 244 Victoria St., Toronto.
Tel (416) 872 1212.
www.mirvish.com

ROCK, FOLK, AND POP MUSIC

Air Canada Centre
40 Bay St., Toronto. *Tel (416) 815 5500.* www. theaircanada centre.com

Bell Centre
1260 Rue de La Gauchetière Ouest, Montreal.
Tel (514) 932 2582.
www.centrebell.ca

General Motors Place
800 Griffiths Way, Vancouver.
Tel (604) 899 7400.
www.canucks.com

Molson Amphitheatre
909 Lakeshaw Boulevard W., Toronto.
Tel (416) 260 5600.
www.ontarioplace.com

Orpheum Theatre
884 Granville St., Vancouver.
Tel (604) 665 3028.
www.city.vancouver.bc.ca /theatres/orpheum/

Rogers Centre
(formerly SkyDome) Next to the CN Tower, Toronto.
Tel (416) 341 1234.
www.rogerscentre.com

CLASSICAL MUSIC, BALLET, AND OPERA

Ballet British Columbia
Vancouver.
Tel (604) 732 5003.
www.balletbc.ca

Canadian Opera Company
Toronto.
Tel (416) 363 6671.
www.coc.ca

Four Seasons Centre for the Performing Arts
145 Queen Street W., Toronto.
Tel (416) 363 6671.
www.fourseasonscentre.ca

Les Grands Ballets Canadiens de Montréal
Tel (514) 849 0269.
www.grandsballets.com

National Ballet of Canada
Toronto.
Tel (613) 755 1111.
www.national.ballet.ca

Opéra de Montréal
Tel (514) 985 2258.
www.operademontreal. com

Queen Elizabeth Theatre
649 Cambie St., Vancouver.
Tel (604) 665 3050.
www.city.vancouver. bc.ca/theatres/

Toronto Symphony Orchestra
Tel (416) 593 4828.
www.tso.ca

Vancouver Opera
www.vancouveropera.ca

SPECIALTY VACATIONS
AND ACTIVITIES

Hiking sign in National Parks

The sheer variety of the massive, unspoiled landscape is, in many ways, what attracts visitors to Canada. Taking advantage of the 39 national parks, several of which are UN World Heritage sites, most specialty vacations tend to revolve around Canada's spacious natural playgrounds. The range of activities available in this single country is wide: sledding and snowmobiling with Inuit guides or cruising in the spring through the flower-filled Thousand Islands of Ontario are both possibilities. Other choices include scenic train rides through the Rockies, trout-fishing in pristine secluded lakes, and adventurous world-class hiking.

HIKING

Canada is one of the world's top hiking destinations, with excellent facilities and a wide variety of terrain for beginners and experts alike. Hiking trails range from a leisurely two-hour nature walk to several days' physically demanding trek through starkly beautiful wilderness.

The preferred starting places for hiking trails in each national park are well marked. Accommodations for longer trips are often available in lodges or hostels within a park; alternatively you can bring your own tent or rent one in a nearby town. Large-scale maps of any area, including national and provincial parks, can be obtained from **Canadian Topographical Series** in Ottawa.

Most of the more popular hikes require little preparation and only basic training. The best-known hiking areas are found in Alberta and British Columbia, in particular in and around the "big four parks" of Kootenay, Yoho, Jasper, and Banff, which encircle the Rocky Mountains. The variety of lands here, from the lush, gently rolling country near Calgary to craggy mountain peaks, reinforces the popularity of the area. More centrally, the prairie provinces offer a surprising variety of walking, from the arid badlands of Alberta's dinosaur country to the wilderness hiking in Prince Albert National Park. In the east the mountains resume; the steep scenery of the Quebec park of Gatineau and the untamed wilds of the eastern and central Gaspé Peninsula both have wonderful scenery.

In northern Canada hiking is more demanding but equally rewarding. Most walking and hiking takes place from April to August, when temperatures do rise slightly, although drops to -30°C (-22°F) are not unusual. At best, the weather remains

Turquoise Lake O'Hara in Yoho National Park

unpredictable. The Chilkoot Pass is a 53-km (33-mile) trail that follows the path of early gold prospectors in the late 19th century from Bennett in northern British Columbia to Dyea in Alaska. For the area, this is a relatively easy path to follow and gives a good taste of northern scenery. More arduous, not to say dangerous, is the memorable Pangnirtung Trail through the southeast of Baffin Island, which even in the summer has a permanently frozen ice cap. Inuit guides will take hikers through the frozen wastes by arrangement.

Occasionally wildlife-watching hikes are available, and teams of husky dogs carry visitors on sleds across ice paths in the wilderness to reach remote destinations. An unforgettable experience, these tours are expensive due to their remoteness and a lack of other modes of transportation.

Hikers near Weasel River, Auyuittuq National Park, Baffin Island

SAFETY MEASURES

Training and safety procedures must be followed for any hike. Always contact the local park or provincial tourist office for their advice and route maps before setting off. Remote, and however unlikely a meeting may seem, wildlife can be aggressive; following instructions on bear safety is a must *(see p300)*. While less alarming, insects are a constant irritant: take all possible measures to repel blackflies and mosquitos. However clear and sparkling it may seem, do not drink stream or river water without thoroughly boiling it first as it may contain an intestinal parasite, which can lead to "beaver fever" or giardiasis.

In the far north, freezing weather conditions place a premium on safety measures. Never go on a trip without telling someone your planned route and expected time of arrival. Consult local wardens about wildlife and routes, and take the proper equipment. Even in the summer, freezing weather changes can be sudden, so be prepared. Those venturing into little-known territory must be accompanied by a trained guide or seek local advice on dealing with the unexpected.

EQUIPMENT

Most hiking areas offer rental outlets for tents and cold-weather clothing. Nonetheless, sturdy walking boots, rain gear, and a change of spare clothing are essentials that hikers have to bring themselves, or buy in a nearby town. Appropriate medication and a first-aid kit should also be taken, in particular bug

Rental lodge by Emerald Lake in Yoho National Park

repellent, and antihistamine. Exposure, resulting in either sunstroke or hypothermia, can be guarded against by using appropriate clothes and medication. On a long trip, carry energy-giving foods such as chocolate or trail mix.

NATIONAL PARKS

Canada's 39 national parks cover the country's most beautiful mountains, lakes, rivers, forests, and coastline. Areas of unspoiled peace, they are the ideal destination for those seeking an outdoor vacation filled with sports, activities, or even a natural spa. The most celebrated upland areas are the "big four" parks in Alberta and BC, Kluane in the Yukon, and the arctic

Swimmers at Radium Hot Springs in the Rockies

flower-filled tundra of Auyuittuq National Park in southern Baffin Island.

Most of the parks are administered by the government heritage body, **Parks Canada**, and each has a visitors' center or park office to welcome visitors. Here walking, hiking, canoeing, and fishing information is available, often from guides who know every detail of the terrain. These offices also issue permits for fishing, which are necessary in each park. Hunting of any kind and use of firearms are all strictly forbidden in national parks, as is feeding the wildlife and damaging any trees and plants. Most parks have camping facilities, or rustic lodges and cottages. The parks generally charge for these facilities, and most have a daily, weekly, or yearly entrance fee, but some are free. Season tickets are available from either the individual park or the Parks Canada office in Hull.

Canoeists on Lake Wapizagonke,
Parc National de la Mauricie

CANOEING

Native Canadians perfected
the canoe to maneuver around
the country's vast system of
waterways for food and
survival; today canoeing is a
largely recreational pursuit. In
provincial or national parks
with many lakes and rivers,
canoeists can portage (or trek)
to the backwaters, getting away
from the most populated
areas at a gentle pace.

Over 250,000 lakes and
35,000 km (20,000 miles) of
waterways in Ontario make
this the most accessible
canoeing destination. Rivers
and lakes making up more
than 25,000 km (16,000 miles)
of canoe routes run through
the Algonquin, Killarney, and
Quetico parks. The Rideau
Canal, which travels 190 km
(120 miles) from Ottawa to
Kingston is a favorite route
through the province, taking
in the capital, the sprinkling of
tiny islands near the historic
town of Kingston, and acres
of fruit orchards by the fertile
waterway. While traveling
through the islands, be careful
of the other marine traffic. The
Canal connects with the St.
Lawrence Seaway, the world's
largest draft inland waterway,
and shipping regulations are
tight. Smaller craft may have
to make way for tankers.

Most towns near canoeing
routes will rent boats by the
day, week, or month, and
wetsuits, oars, and life jackets
are usually available. Because
of the popularity of watersports, Canada is an extremely
reasonable place to buy fishing
and canoeing equipment;
many outfitters offer good-
quality products at almost
half European and US prices.

WHITEWATER RAFTING

Whitewater rafting may be
attempted in the national
parks of British Columbia. The
Mackenzie River system, which
runs from BC backwaters
through the Northwest
Territories, provides occasionally hair-raising rafting and
canoeing. Most routes in
the far north are for the
experienced only. The
toughest trek of all is the
300-km (180-mile) run of the
South Nahanni River near Fort
Simpson in the Northwest
Territories. New roads here and
in the Yukon have boosted
the number of visitors to yet
another grueling set of waterways, the Yukon River system.

Inexperienced boaters and
rafters can take advantage
of two-week basic training
courses offered all over the
country. Lake canoeing in
Wells Gray Provincial Park
is popular throughout the
province for those seeking
a more relaxing alternative.

Windsurfing in Georgian Bay
Islands National Park, Lake Ontario

OTHER WATERSPORTS

Although the season may be
short, sailing has always been
a popular summer pastime.
Canada contains a large
proportion of the world's fresh

Whitewater rafting on the Athabasca River, Jasper National Park in the Rocky Mountains

Snowmobiling in Ontario across virgin powder snow

water, and there are allegedly more boats per head here than anywhere else in the world. The Great Lakes are the prime sailing and windsurfing areas, as are both east and west coastal regions from May to September. Swimming is also a favorite in warm weather; beaches on Prince Edward Island and Cape Breton off the east coast offer warm waters and sandy beaches, while lakes in Ontario, such as Lake Huron, provide inland swims. Torontonians sometimes swim in Lake Ontario in the summer.

FISHING

Over three million square miles of inland waters go partway to justifying Canada's reputation as a paradise for anglers. There are countless varieties of sports fish *(see p25)*, not to mention the charterboat ocean fishing for salmon off the Pacific coast. Almost all parks offer fishing, often in secluded, pristine lakes and rivers. Be sure to contact the park's main office to obtain a fishing license. While most visitors fish in summer, a tiny wooden structure that sits on the frozen lake makes winter fishing more comfortable. These huts sit over a hole in the ice and are often heated. It may be worth buying rods and reels at your destination; Canadian fishing equipment is very high quality, with a good choice, and is usually very reasonably priced.

Canadian snowboard

SKIING, SNOWBOARDING, AND SNOWMOBILING

Not for nothing is Canada known as the Great White North, and its snowy terrain provides some of the world's best skiing. In the east, the Laurentian resorts of Mont Tremblant and Mont-Ste-Anne offer excellent downhill skiing. Moving west, the resorts of Whistler, Lake Louise, and Banff provide unforgettably dramatic skiing. High in the Rockies, powder snow awaits the adventurous; heli-skiing (lifting skiers by helicopter to pristine slopes) takes place on the deserted northern peaks. Many of the runs are higher than those in the European Alps, particularly in Banff and Lake Louise. These sites have held major competitions, including the Winter Olympics in 1976. Another advantage to skiing in Canada is the proximity of the mountains to major cities; it is perfectly possible to spend the day zipping down slopes and then dine out in town.

Cross-country skiing is available across the country, but is particularly fine on southern and central Ontario's rolling terrain and Quebec's Laurentian mountain range and Eastern Townships. Most downhill ski resorts have a network of cross-country trails, but there are also dedicated cross-country ski areas and numerous parks with trails.

Snowboarding has become increasingly popular in

DIRECTORY

MAPS

Canadian Topographical Series
Tel 1 800 214 8524.

Canada Map Office
Tel 1 800 465 6277.

Ulysses Travel Bookshop
4176 Rue St. Denis, Montreal.
Tel (514) 843 9447.

Rand McNally (maps)
Tel 1 800 333 0136.

Open Air Books & Maps
25 Toronto St., Toronto.
Tel (416) 363 0719.

USEFUL ORGANIZATIONS

Parks Canada
Tel 1 888 773 8888.
www.pc.gc.ca

Canadian Cycling Association
Tel (613) 248 1353.

Canadian Paraplegic Association
Tel (416) 422 5644.

Grand American Adventures
Tel 1 800 221 0596.

TRAVEL OPERATORS

Air Canada Vacations
Tel (905) 615 8000 Toronto.
Tel (514) 876 4141 Montreal.

American Express
Tel 1 800 668 2639.

Cosmos/Globus
Tel 1 800 556 5454.

Trek America
Tel 1 800 873 5872.

snowsports centers across the country. All downhill resorts have a few slopes set aside for boarders.

Snowmobiles are a necessity for many living in rural areas, but snowmobiling is also a popular winter sport. Ontario has almost 50,000 km (35,000 miles) of snowmobile trails. Seasoned riders can cover up to 500 km (300 miles) in two days. Traveling in groups is advised; there are many popular pitstops en route. These "snow inns" often offer package deals.

SURVIVAL
GUIDE

PRACTICAL INFORMATION

Canada is a popular holiday destination, and offers visitors a mix of urban sophistication and outdoor pleasures. Visitors' facilities are generally excellent. Accommodations and restaurants are of international standard *(see pp344–91)*, public transportation is efficient *(see pp414–27)*, and tourist information centers are found nearly everywhere. The

Whale-watching sign

following pages contain useful information for all visitors. Personal Security and Health *(see pp410–11)* details a number of recommended precautions, while Banking and Currency *(see p412)* answers the important financial queries, together with taxation details. There is also a section on how to use the Canadian telephone and postal services.

WHEN TO GO

Weather and geography dominate any visit to Canada. The vastness of the country means that most trips will be centered on one of the major cities, Vancouver, Toronto, Ottawa, and Montreal, although it is possible to stay in remote areas such as the isolated Inuit settlements dotted around Hudson Bay. Depending on each visitor's individual interests, the best time to go will be dictated by local climate and the time of year.

In general, the climates on both the west and east coasts are temperate, while harsher weather occurs in the center of the country, in Saskatchewan, Manitoba, and Alberta, where the summers are fine but the winters long and hard.

Northern Canada is at its most welcoming during July and August when the land thaws, and the temperature is more likely to climb above zero.

In eastern Canada, Nova Scotia, New Brunswick, and Prince Edward Island, there are four distinct seasons, with snowy winters, mild springs, and crisp falls; summer is still the best time to visit the provinces' resorts. Quebec and Ontario have hot, humid summers and cold winters, with snow lingering until late March. Spring and fall are brief but can be the most rewarding times to make a visit.

The northeastern province of Newfoundland and coastal Labrador have the most extreme temperatures, ranging on a winter's day from 0°C (32°F) to –50°C (–41°F) in St. John's on Newfoundland's

east coast. Winter visitors to British Columbia and the Rockies can enjoy some of the best skiing in the world. This region is also noted for its temperate weather but can be very wet in spring and fall as Pacific depressions roll in over the mountains.

ENTRY REQUIREMENTS

All visitors to Canada should have a passport valid for longer than the intended period of stay. Stricter US security regulations mean this now includes American citizens, who must show passports when returning to the US. Travelers from the UK, US, EU, and all British Commonwealth countries do not require a special visa to visit. Tourists are issued with a visitor's visa on arrival if they satisfy immigration

Children play in the Kids' Village at the Waterpark, the Ontario Place leisure complex in Toronto

◁ Queen of Surrey Ferry in Horseshoe Bay near Vancouver

officials that they have a valid return ticket and sufficient funds for the duration of their stay. Visitors can stay up to six months, but to extend their stay they must apply to Citizenship and Immigration Canada in Ottawa before expiration of their authorized visit. As visa regulations are subject to change, check with the nearest Canadian Consulate, Embassy, or High Commission before travel.

Anyone under the age of 18 traveling unaccompanied by an adult needs a letter of consent from a parent or guardian.

TOURIST INFORMATION

Canadian tourist offices are famous for the amount and quality of their information, offering everything from local maps to hotel, B-and-B, or campground bookings. Special tours such as wilderness camping, archaeological digs, and wildlife watching can often be arranged through the tourism service. All the provincial and national parks have visitors' centers, which generally provide maps detailing hiking trails and canoe routes.

The national Canadian Tourism Commission is the central organization, and each province has its own tourism authority. Most smaller towns also have their own seasonal tourist offices, which offer good free maps and detailed information. Each of the large cities has a main office as well as extra booths and kiosks open during busy summer months. Accommodations can usually be booked at the booths found in airports and regional offices.

OPENING HOURS AND ADMISSION PRICES

Most museums, parks, and other attractions throughout Canada charge an admission fee. The amount can vary enormously and many sights

CANADIAN TIME ZONES

Canada has six time zones spanning a four-and-a-half hour time difference from coast to coast. Between Vancouver and Halifax there are five zones; Pacific, Mountain, Central, Eastern, and Atlantic Standard Time, with an unusual half-hour difference between Newfoundland and Atlantic time. Every province except Saskatchewan uses Daylight Saving Time to give longer summer days from mid-March to October or November. Clocks go back an hour in October/November, forward an hour in March.

Time Zone	Hours minus GMT	Time Zone	Hours minus GMT
Pacific	-8	Eastern	-5
Mountain	-7	Atlantic	-4
Central	-6	Newfoundland	-3.5

offer a range of discount packages for families, children, and seniors. Tourist office leaflets, brochures, and local newspapers often carry discount coupons. Some galleries and museums have free-of-charge days, evenings, or a free hour daily before closing time.

Opening times vary according to the time of the year. As a rule, most of the sights are open for longer through summer

"The Small Apple" tourist booth in Ontario

but may close completely during the winter months. Many museums and galleries close one day each week, usually on a Monday or Tuesday, but not on weekends. Although many attractions are closed on major holidays, such as Christmas and New Year's Day, a surprising number are open all-year-round. School summer holidays in Canada are from June to Labor Day Weekend, which ends on the first Monday in September. Labor Day generally signifies the end of

summer. This is the weekend after which opening hours change over to shorter winter hours of operation. Rural sights generally have shorter hours year-round than those in cities.

SENIOR TRAVELERS

In Canada people over 60 are refered to as "seniors," and are offered a wide range of discounts. Reduced rates frequently apply to the cost of movie tickets, public transportation, entrance fees, and some restaurant menus. VIA Rail reduce their fares by 10 percent for seniors. When applicable, reductions range from 10 percent to 50 percent for people aged from 55, 60, or 65, depending on the province or attraction. If discounts are not advertised it is always a good idea to inquire.

Educational trips for senior citizens are run by **Elderhostel Canada**, a non-profit organization that offers good, cheap accommodation in university dorms. A typical holiday comprises morning lectures, guided tours in the afternoon, and a communal dinner.

Tourists enjoying the scenery of Niagara Falls

TRAVELING WITH CHILDREN

Although Canada lacks the numbers of theme parks of the US, its beach resorts, parks, and city centers have much to offer children and families. Most types of accommodation state whether or not they welcome children. Those hotels that do often do not charge for a child sharing a parent's room. They will also normally provide cribs and high chairs, and sometimes have baby-sitting services.

Restaurants now generally welcome children, and many offer kids' menus and high chairs, or will warm up milk and baby food. Some fast food outlets have play areas. It is best to check in advance with more upscale establishments.

Both international and internal airfares are often cheaper for children, and babies under two years old who are not taking up a seat may travel free. On public transportation children under five travel free, and those under 12 have lower fares. If you are renting a car you can reserve one or two car seats for children from your rental firm (see p427).

ETIQUETTE

Canada is very much a multicultural nation (see pp26–7), which welcomes and respects people and customs from the rest of the world. Native Canadians are never referred to as "Indians"; in general they are known as Canada's "First Nations" or "natives," while "eskimos" are always known as Inuit (see p31). In Quebec, be prepared to hear French spoken first. It is also appreciated if visitors show that they have tried to learn a few French words.

Canada's relaxed, informal atmosphere is evident in its dress codes, which tend to be practical and dependent on the climate. Canadians favor jeans and sweatshirts, and dress in layers so they can add or subtract clothing, especially when moving between well-heated malls and winter streets. However, in the cities and larger towns more formal clothing is expected, particularly in more stylish restaurants, theaters, and other formal places. Even the more humble eateries insist on proper attire, and the sign "no shoes, no shirt, no service" is frequently seen in many tourist areas. Topless sunbathing is generally frowned upon in Canada.

Drinking in non-licenced public places is illegal, and it is also illegal to have opened bottles of alcohol in the car when traveling. It is against the law to smoke in public places such as on buses and trains, in taxis, in public buildings, and most restaurants throughout most of the country. However, smoking rules vary depending on which town you are in.

A service charge is seldom included in checks at Canadian restaurants. Unless it is included, the standard tip in Canada is 15 percent (more if the service is exceptional). Taxi drivers expect a similar tip, while barbers and hairdressers should receive about 10 percent of the total. It is customary to tip porters at airports and train stations, cloakroom attendants, bellhops, doormen, and hotel porters Can$1 per bag, and to leave something for the hotel maids. Tipping bar staff in bars and nightclubs is also expected. Anyone in charge of a large party of visitors should prepare to be generous.

STUDENT TRAVELERS

With an International Student Identity Card (ISIC), full-time students are entitled to substantial discounts on travel as well as admission prices to movies, galleries, museums, and many other tourist attractions. The ISIC card should be purchased in the student's home country at a Student Travel Association (STA) office in the nearest city. There are also a wide range of bus and rail discounts available to students, such as the "Go Canada" Accommodation and Coach Pass, which offers both reduced cost travel and stays in youth hostels across the country. The pass can be booked through local agents specializing in student travel. VIA Rail also offers students the "Canrail Pass," which allows a period of unlimited travel on all routes. Reasonably priced accommodations are available on university campuses in the larger cities during local student vacations. There are also comfortable hostels throughout the country, most of which are affiliated with the International Youth

International student I.D. card

Hostelling Federation (IYHF). Eating out is inexpensive, so it's easy to find great food on a budget.

ELECTRICITY

Canadian electrical appliances come with either a two-prong or three-prong plug, and most sockets will accept either. The system is a 110-volt, 60-cycle system. You need an adaptor if you are visiting from outside North America. Batteries are universal and are readily available for all appliances. Bear in mind that bargain electrical goods purchased here will probably need modification for use in Europe.

TRAVELERS WITH DISABILITIES

Travelers with physical disabilities can expect some of the best facilities in the world in Canada. Increasingly, large towns and cities offer wheelchair access in most public buildings, as well as on public transportation.

Vancouver's buses all have low platforms, and VIA Rail trains can accommodate wheelchairs. Each province has varying requirements for disabled drivers and information on this is available through the **Canadian Paraplegic Association (CPA)**. This Ottawa-based association also has details on companies that rent specially adapted cars and RV vehicles. Parking permits can be obtained in advance through the CPA but require a doctor's letter and a small processing fee.

There is a wide choice of hotels with disabled facilities in Canada. Most of the big chains such as Best Western and Holiday Inn are easily accessible, as are some luxury hotels and youth hostels. The CPA also has details on the most disabled-friendly attractions. Many of the national and provincial parks have interpretive centers, short nature trails, and boardwalks that are wheelchair accessible.

CONVERSION CHART

Imperial to Metric
1 inch = 2.54 centimeters
1 foot = 30 centimeters
1 mile = 1.6 kilometers
1 ounce = 28 grams
1 pound = 454 grams
1 pint = 0.6 liters
1 gallon = 4.6 liters

Metric to Imperial
1 centimeter = 0.4 inches
1 meter = 3 feet, 3 inches
1 kilometer = 0.6 miles
1 gram = 0.04 ounces
1 kilogram = 2.2 pounds
1 liter = 1.8 pints

DIRECTORY

IMMIGRATION

Canadian High Commission
Macdonald House,
1 Grosvenor Square,
London, W1X 4AB.
Tel (020) 7258 6600.

Citizenship and Immigration Canada
Jean Edmonds Towers,
365 Laurier Ave. W,
Ottawa, ON K1A 1L1.
Tel (613) 954 9019.
www.cic.gc.ca *or*
www.servicecanada.gc.ca

Consulate General
1251 Avenue of the
Americas, New York, NY,
10020-1175.
Tel (212) 596 1628.

TOURIST INFORMATION

Canadian Tourism Commission
Suite 1400, Four Bentall
Centre, 1055 Dunsmuir
St., Vancouver, BC
V7X 1L2.
Tel (604) 638 8300.
www.travelcanada.ca

Tourism Canada
501 Penn Ave.,
NW Washington DC, USA
Tel (202) 682 1740.

Visit Canada
Tel 0870 380 0070.
www.canada.travel

PROVINCIAL OFFICES

British Columbia
Tourism British Columbia,
865 Hornby St., 8th floor,
Vancouver, BC V6Z 2G3.
Tel 1 (800) 435 5622.

Newfoundland and Labrador
Department of Tourism,
P.O. Box 8700,
St. John's, NF A1B 4J6.
Tel 1 (800) 563 6353.

Northwest Territories
NWT Arctic Tourism,
P.O. Box 610, Yellowknife,
NWT X1A 2N5.
Tel 1 (800) 661 0788.

Nova Scotia Tourism
P.O. Box 456,
1800 Argyle St., Suite 605,
Halifax, NS B3J 2R5.
Tel 1 (800) 565 0000.

Nunavut Tourism
PO Box 1450,
Iqaluit, NT X0A 0H0.
Tel 1 (866) 491 7910.

Ontario
Ministry of Tourism,
900 Bay St., 9th floor,
Hearst Block, Toronto,
ON M7A 2E1.
Tel 1 (800) 668 2746.

Travel Alberta
400, 1601-9 Ave. SE.,
Calgary AB T2G 0H4.
Tel 1 (800) 252 3782.

Travel Manitoba
155 Carlton St., 7th Floor,
Winnipeg, MB R3C 3HB.
Tel 1 (800) 665 0040.

Tourism New Brunswick
19 Aberdeen
Campbellton, NB E3N 2J6.
Tel 1 (800) 561 0123.

Tourism Prince Edward Island
P.O. Box 2000,
Charlottetown,
PEI C1A 7N8.
Tel 1 (888) 368 4801.

Tourism Quebec
P.O. Box 979,
Montreal, PQ H3C 2W3.
Tel 1 (877) 266 5687.

Tourism Saskatchewan
189–1621 Albert St.,
Regina, SK S4P 3S5.
Tel 1 (877) 237 2273.

Tourism Yukon
P.O. Box 2703,
Whitehorse,
Yukon, Y1A 2C6.
Tel 1 (800) 661 0494.

SENIOR TRAVELERS

Routes to Learning
4 Cataraqui St., Kingston,
Ontario, K7K 1Z7.
Tel (613) 530 2222.

STUDENT TRAVELERS

STA Travel
Tel (020) 7361 6262 UK.
Tel 1 (888) 427 5639.

DISABLED TRAVELERS

Canadian Paraplegic Association
1101 Prince of Wales Dr.,
Suite 230, Ottawa,
Ontario, K2C 3W7.
Tel (613) 723 1913.

Personal Security and Health

With its comparatively low crime rate, Canada is a safe country to visit. In contrast to many US cities, there is little street crime in the city centers, perhaps because so many Canadians live downtown that the cities are never empty at night. However, it is wise to be careful and to find out which parts of town are more dangerous than others. Avoid city parks after dark, and make sure cars are left locked. In the country's more remote areas visitors must observe sensible safety measures. In the remote country, wildlife and climatic dangers can be avoided by heeding local advice. If a serious problem does arise, contact one of the national emergency numbers in the telephone directory.

PERSONAL SAFETY

There are few off-limit areas in Canadian cities. Even the seedier districts tend to have a visible police presence, making them safer than the average suburban area at night. Always ask your hotelier, the local tourist information center, or the police, which areas to avoid. Although theft is rare in hotel rooms, it is a good idea to store any valuables in the hotel safe, as hotels will not guarantee the security of property left in rooms. Make sure you leave your hotel room key at the front desk.

Pickpockets can be a hazard at large public gatherings and popular tourist attractions, so it is a good idea to wear cameras and bags over one shoulder with the strap across your body. Try not to be seen with large amounts of cash, and if necessary use a coin purse

and a wallet for larger bills. Keep your passport apart from your cash and traveler's checks. Never hang your purse over the back of your chair in restaurants; put it on the floor beside your feet with one foot over the strap, or pinned down by a chair leg. Male travelers should not carry their wallets in their back pocket, as this makes a very easy target. Safe options for both sexes are zippered purse belts.

LAW ENFORCEMENT

Canada is policed by a combination of forces. The Royal Canadian Mounted Police (RCMP) operate throughout most of the country, while Ontario and Quebec are looked after by provincial forces. There are also city police and native police on the reserves. For the most part, the officers are noted for their helpful attitude, but it is illegal to comment on (or joke about) safety, bombs, guns, and terrorism in places such as airports, where it is possible to be arrested for an off-the-cuff remark. Drinking and driving is also taken seriously here, and remember that open alcohol containers in a car are illegal. Narcotics users face criminal charges often followed by moves for deportation.

Toronto policemen on duty

LOST PROPERTY

As soon as something is lost, report it to the police. They will issue a report with a number that you will need in order to make a claim on your insurance policy. If a credit card is missing, call the company's toll-free number and report it immediately. Lost or stolen traveler's checks must also be reported to the issuer. If you have kept a record of the checks' numbers, replacing them should be a painless experience, and new ones may be issued within 24 hours.

If you lose your passport, contact the nearest embassy or consulate. They will be able to issue a temporary replacement as visitors do not generally need a new passport if they will be returning directly to their home country. However, if you are traveling on to another destination, you will need a full passport. It is also useful to hold photocopies of your driver's license and birth certificate, as well as notarized passport photographs if you are contemplating an extended visit or need additional ID.

TRAVEL INSURANCE

Travel insurance is essential in Canada and should be arranged to cover health, trip-cancellation, and interruption, as well as theft and loss of valuable possessions.

Canadian health services are excellent, but if you do not wish to pay you will need insurance. If you already have private health insurance you should check to see if the coverage includes all emergency hospital and medical expenses such as physician's care, prescription drugs, and private duty-nursing. In case of a serious illness, separate coverage is also required to send a relative to your bedside or return a rented vehicle. Emergency dental treatment, and out-of-pocket expenses or loss of vacation costs also need their own policies. Your insurance company or travel agent should recommend the right policy, but beware of exclusions for pre-existing medical conditions.

MEDICAL TREATMENT

A comprehensive range of treatment centers are available in Canada. For minor problems pharmacies are often a good source of advice, and walk in clinics in the cities will treat visitors relatively quickly. In smaller communities, or in more difficult cases, go straight to the emergency room of the closest hospital, but be prepared for a long wait. In a serious medical emergency dial 911 in most areas, or 0 for the operator, to summon an ambulance.

Anyone taking a prescription drug should ask their doctor for extra supplies when they travel, as well as a copy of the prescription in case more medication is needed on the trip. It is a good idea to take a simple first-aid kit, especially for longer trips in the more remote or Arctic areas of the country. Generally this should include aspirin (or paracetamol), antihistamine for bites or allergies, motion sickness pills, antiseptic and bandages or band aids, calamine lotion, and bug repellent. Antibiotic creams are useful for intrepid wilderness hikers.

All the provincial capitals have dental clinics that will provide emergency treatment. The Yellow Pages telephone book lists dentists in each area together with opticians and alternative health practitioners.

NATURAL HAZARDS

There are times when Canada's mosquitoes and black flies can be so troublesome that moose and deer leave the woods for relief. Insects are a major irritant for tourists in rural areas. They are at their worst during annual breeding periods from late spring to midsummer, and until the temperatures drop in Northern Canada. There are precautions one can take to alleviate the misery, the most effective one being the regular application of insect repellant. Stick to light-colored clothes as the bugs are drawn to dark ones, and cover as much skin as possible with long sleeves, and pants tucked into boots and socks. It might even be worth investing in a gauze mask for your head and neck if you are planning to venture into deserted areas at peak breeding times.

Canada is notorious for cold winter weather, but tourists are not likely to suffer many serious problems. The media gives daily extensive coverage to the weather, and on days when frostbite is possible they offer detailed reports. Dressing in layers and wearing a hat is necessary. Sunscreen is needed in summer, even on overcast days.

Warning sign for motorists

BEARS

Canada's national parks service, particularly in the Rockies, supplies advice on bear safety *(see p300)*, but unless you are camping or hiking in the woods it is unlikely that you will come across them. Encounters can be avoided by following a few basic rules: never leave food or garbage near your tent, car, or RV, do not wear scent, and make a noise (many hikers blow whistles) as you walk, as bears are more likely to attack if surprised. If you do come across a bear, do not scream or run since bears are very fast, and do not climb trees – they are even better at that. Instead, keep still, speak to them in a low voice, and put your luggage on the ground to try and distract them.

A polar bear approaching a tourist Tundra Buggy, northern Manitoba

Banking and Currency

Royal Bank of Canada logo

Canadian currency is based on the decimal system, and has 100 cents to the dollar. Two of the most useful coins are the 25-cent and $1 pieces which operate pay telephones, newspaper boxes, and vending machines. They are also handy for public transportation in the larger cities, where as a matter of policy bus drivers often do not carry any change. It is a good idea to arrive with some Canadian currency, around Can$50–100 including small change for tipping and taxis, but to carry most of your funds in Canadian dollar traveler's checks.

DIRECTORY

CURRENCY EXCHANGE AND WIRING MONEY

American Express
Check replacement, Canada
Tel 1 800 221 7282.

Thomas Cook, Mastercard
Lost or stolen
Tel 1 800 223 7373.

Travelex
Tel 1 877 643 7778.

Visa
Tel 1 800 732 1322.

Western Union
Wiring money, Canada
Tel 1 800 235 0000.

Janustuny Tauc ur uμ Turntu Stath Frhmmm

BANKS

Canada's main national banks are the Royal Bank of Canada, Bank of Montréal, TD Canada Trust, Canadian Imperial Bank of Commerce (CIBC), Scotiabank, and National Bank of Canada. These banks generally accept foreign ATM (automatic teller machine) cards, although it is wise to check with your bank first. ATMs can be found at bank branches, as well as grocery stores, shopping centers, gas stations, train and bus stations, and airports.

Banks are usually open Monday to Friday, from 9am to 5pm; some stay open later on Fridays, and a few open on Saturday mornings. All banks are closed on Sundays and on statutory holidays.

Scotiabank logo

TRAVELER'S CHECKS

Traveler's checks issued in Canadian dollars are probably the safest and most con-venient way to carry money for your vacation. They offer

security because they can be easily replaced if they are lost or stolen. They are also accepted as cash in a range of gas stations, shops, restaurants and hotels across the country. Buy checks in smaller denominations such as $20 as most retailers out large amounts of change. It is a good idea to find out which Canadian banks charge commission for changing traveler's checks, as many have arrangements with certain issuers of checks and make no charge. The Royal Bank of Canada and TD Canada Trust, for example, charge no commission on American Express checks in Canadian dollars. A passport or other form of ID is needed to cash trav-eler's checks at a bank or at Bureaux de Changes offices such as American Express or Travelex.

CREDIT CARDS

Credit cards are used extensively in Canada, and American Express, Diner's Club, MasterCard/Access, and VISA are widely accepted. Credit cards are often asked for as a form of ID, and for placing large deposits – most car rental companies in Canada insist on a credit card or require a substantial cash deposit. Some hotels also pre-fer prepayment by credit card.

Credit cards can also be used to secure cash advances, but you will be charged interest from the date of withdrawal.

WIRING MONEY

If you run out of money or have an emergency it is possible to have money wired from home in minutes using an electronic money service. Both American Express and Travelex provide this service, as does Western Union which has 22,000 outlets all over North America.

Western Union's familiar logo

COINS AND BANK NOTES

Canadian coins are issued in denominations of one cent (the penny), five cents (the nickel), ten cents (the dime), 25 cents (the quarter), $1 (dubbed the "loonie" because it has an illustration of the bird, the Canadian loon on one side), and the $2 coin or "toonie," which replaced the old bank note in 1996.

Bank notes are printed in denominations of $5, $10, $20, $50, $100, $500, and $1,000. However, the larger denomi-nations such as $50 or $100 dollar bills are sometimes viewed with suspicion as they are not used very often in small stores, or even in cafés and gas stations.

Media and Communications

Canada has some of the most sophisticated communication systems in the world. There are public payphones everywhere – in cafés, bars, public buildings, gas stations, and post offices. Most operate with coins or cards, and while local calls are a bargain, international calls can be expensive. It is also possible to send telegrams, faxes, and even documents via Intelpost, a satellite communications system.

Canada Post, the country's mail service is certainly reliable, but it is renowned for being slow. It can be quick however, if you are willing to pay an extra fee for priority handling and delivery.

PUBLIC TELEPHONES

Public telephones operate on 25 cent coins, although there is an increasing number of phones that accept both credit and phone cards. Rates are generally cheaper between 6pm and 8am, and on weekends. All local calls cost 25, 35, or 50 cents (private subscribers have free local calls). For any call outside the local area, including international calls, the operator will tell you how much to pay for the initial period and will then ask for more money as your call progresses. It is usually easier to make long distance calls using a phone card than to have the stacks of change required.

Public roadside telephones are found countrywide

POSTAL SERVICES

All mail from Canada to outside North America is by air and can take between three and seven days to arrive. If you are sending mail locally, it can also take days – not including the postal code will make the service even slower. To send mail, look for signs that say "Canada Post" since some post offices are located in malls.

MOBILE PHONES AND E-MAIL

It is possible to rent a mobile phone while on vacation, or to have your own mobile tuned to local networks.

Visitors can use e-mail in the larger hotels or at one of many city-based Internet cafés.

FAX AND TELEGRAM SERVICES

It is possible to send a fax from the commercial outlets found in most towns. Telegrams are dealt with by Canadian National Telecommunications (CNT) or Canadian Pacific (CP). There are two main services, Telepost, which provides first-class delivery, and Intelpost, which sends documents abroad via satellite.

MEDIA

The only papers that see themselves as national publications are *The National Post* and *The Globe and Mail*, both based in Toronto. There

DIRECTORY

PROVINCIAL CODES

Alberta - 403 & 780.
British Columbia - 604 & 250.
Manitoba - 204.
New Brunswick - 506.
Northwest Territories - 867.
Nova Scotia - 902.
Newfoundland & Labrador - 709.
Ontario - 416, 647 & 905
(Toronto).
  705 - *(central and northeast).*
  519 - *(southwest peninsula).*
  613 - *(Ottawa region).*
  807 - *(northwest).*
Prince Edward Island - 902.
Quebec - 514 & 540 *(Montreal).*
  819 - *(north).*
  418 - *(east).*
Saskatchewan - 306.
Yukon & Nunavut- 867.

is also a national news weekly called *Maclean's*. Most cities have their own daily newspapers and some, such as Toronto, have several. Many cities and regions have free weeklies that provide excellent coverage of local events.

Canada has a national 24-hour public broadcasting corporation (CBC), 80 percent of whose programs are produced locally. CBC also provides an excellent radio service, and can be a good source of information on local happenings and weather for visitors. They also have a national service in French.

USEFUL INFORMATION

Canadian Post Customer Services line.
Tel 1 800 267 1177.

REACHING THE RIGHT NUMBER

- For calls to another area code: dial 1 followed by the area code and the 7-digit local number. (In Toronto, dial the area code for all local calls.)
- For international calls: dial 011 then the code of the country (Australia 61, the UK 44) followed by the local area/city code (minus the first 0) and the number. To call the US from Canada dial **1**, the area code, then the local number.
- For international operator assistance dial **0**.
- For information on numbers within your local area dial **411**.
- For information on long distance numbers call **1** followed by the area code then **555 1212**.
- An **800**, **866**, **877**, or **888** prefix means the call is toll free.

TRAVEL INFORMATION

**Maple leaf
Air Canada logo**

The majority of visitors to Canada arrive by air, usually at one of the country's three largest international airports – Vancouver, Toronto, or Montreal. It is also possible to fly direct to cities such as Halifax, Winnipeg, Edmonton, Calgary, and St. John's, Newfoundland.

The size of the country makes flying between locations popular with visitors who wish to see more than one part of Canada. For example, on a short stay, it could prove difficult to see Toronto and Montreal in the east, as well as the Rocky Mountains in the west without spending some time in the air. There are other transportation choices that allow visitors to see much of Canada. The national rail network, VIA Rail, links most major cities, while long-distance bus routes provide a delightful, and often less expensive, way to see the country. There are short cruises and ferry rides that take in some spectacular scenery. Exploring Canada by car is also a popular choice, enabling visitors to get to locations that can be difficult to reach any other way.

Air Canada is the country's major air carrier

ARRIVING BY AIR

Canada is a destination for several international airlines, and the country's major carrier **Air Canada** is linked with national airlines around the world. All Europe's principal airlines fly into Toronto or Montreal, while Vancouver is a gateway for carriers such as Cathay Pacific, Qantas, and national airlines from the Far East.

Visitors who intend to see parts of the US as well as Canada can find plenty of connecting flights to such principal US destinations as New York, Los Angeles, Dallas, Chicago, and Atlanta.

INTERNATIONAL FLIGHTS

Flights between Canada and Europe take from five to ten hours; from Asia or Australia, across the Pacific, you may be in transit for as long as 25 hours. Older travelers or those with children may wish to consider a stopover for the sake of comfort (Hawaii is a popular choice). It is also a good idea to plan flights so that they account for international time differences.

Canada has 13 international airports, the busiest being at Toronto, Montreal, and Vancouver. It is also possible to fly direct into airports in cities such as Edmonton, Halifax, Ottawa, Winnipeg, and St. John's, Newfoundland. All the major cities are connected with airports in the US. Several leading airlines offer special deals that allow visitors to fly to one part of North America and leave from another.

AIR FARES

Flights to Canada from Europe, Australia, and the US can be expensive, especially during peak holiday periods such as Christmas, New Year, and between July and

AIRPORT	INFORMATION
St. John's	(709) 758 8500
Halifax	(902) 873 4422
Montreal (Trudeau)	(514) 394 7377
Montreal (Mirabel)	(514) 394 7377
Ottawa	(613) 248 2100
Toronto	(416) 247 7678
Winnipeg	(204) 987 9402
Calgary	(403) 735 1200
Edmonton	(780) 890 8382
Vancouver	(604) 207 7077

mid-September. It is always cheaper to book an Apex (Advanced Purchase Excursion) fare, which should be bought no less than seven days in advance, (most major airlines, including Air Canada, offer them). These tickets generally impose such restrictions as a minimum (usually seven days) and maximum (of 3–6 months) length of stay. It can also be difficult to alter dates of travel, and it is worth considering insuring yourself against last-minute, unforeseen delays or cancellations.

Charter flights sometimes offer a cheaper alternative, with savings of 20 percent on some tickets. Round-the-world fares are increasingly popular, as are package vacations which provide a variety of choices. The kinds of deals available range from fly/drive vacations with a much reduced car rental as part of the price of the ticket, to a guided tour, including all accommodations, transportation, and meals.

ON ARRIVAL

Just before landing in Canada you will be given customs and immigration documents to fill in. On arrival you will be asked to present them, along with your passport, to the appropriate customs and immigration officials.

The larger airports offer a better range of services, but most airports have shops, medical and postal services, foreign exchange bureaus, newsstands, and bookstores. The major car rental companies have outlets at the airport, and buses, limousines, and shuttle buses into town are available. Most terminals offer facilities for disabled travelers.

Visitors hoping to catch a connecting flight to another part of the country will have to claim and

Roads to and from airports are well sign-posted

clear their baggage through customs before checking in with the connecting airline. Arrangements for transferring to domestic flights are usually made when you book your trip. Ask airline staff if you need more information; in large airports such as Toronto's Pearson International there are three separate terminals.

DIRECTORY

AIRLINES IN THE UK, US, AND CANADA

Air Canada
Tel UK: (0990) 247 226.
CAN and US: 1 888 247 2262.
www.aircanada.ca

American Airlines
Tel UK: (0345) 789789
(0208) 572 5555 (London only).
CAN and US: (1 800) 433 7300.
www.aa.com

British Airways
Tel UK: (0845) 77 99977.
CAN and US: (1 800) 247 9297.
www.britishairways.com

Globespan
Tel UK: (0871) 271 9000.
CAN and US: (1 800) 663 8614.
www.flyglobespan.com

DISTANCE FROM CITY	AVERAGE TAXI FARE TO CITY	BUS TRANSFER TO CITY
8 km (5 miles)	CAN $25	NO SERVICE
42 km (26 miles)	CAN $60	30–45 mins
22 km (14 miles)	CAN $40	25 mins
55 km (34 miles)	CAN $70	40–55 mins
18 km (11 miles)	CAN $35	20–30 mins
24 km (15 miles)	CAN $45	45–55 mins
10 km (6 miles)	CAN $20	20 mins
16 km (10 miles)	CAN $35	30 mins
31 km (19 miles)	CAN $50	45 mins
15 km (9 miles)	CAN $35–50	25–45 mins

Domestic Air Travel

Because of the distances involved, flying around the country has become an accepted part of Canadian life. There is a complex network of domestic flights, with numerous local airlines, some of which are linked to Air Canada. The smaller operators fly within provinces, and to remote locations where they are often the only means of transportation. In all there are some 125 domestic destinations. It is possible to book domestic flights with a travel agent before departure or, once in Canada, through local agents or on the internet. Domestic flights along the busier routes are becoming cheaper and discounts are often advertised in the local press. A range of pass deals are available exclusively for visitors from abroad. Light aircraft can also be chartered for fascinating but costly trips over far-flung landmarks such as Baffin Island.

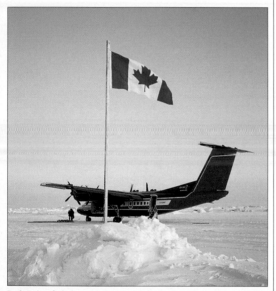

Dash-7 aircraft during a trip in Canada's far north

AIR ROUTES AND AIRLINES

The impressive array of domestic flights available here means that most of the nation's smaller urban areas are within reach of regular services. However, you will generally have to fly to the major city in the area, principally Vancouver, Toronto, or Montreal, and then take a connecting flight.

Some of the smaller airlines are connected with Canada's major carrier, **Air Canada**, and it is often possible to book your connection through the national airline. The majority of the country's long-haul domestic routes run east-to-west, connecting the cities from Halifax on the east coast, through to Montreal, Toronto, Ottawa, Winnipeg, Calgary, and Edmonton to Vancouver in the west. Longer north-to-south flights to places such as the Yukon and Northwest Territories usually originate from Edmonton and Winnipeg. In the remote north, light aircraft are the best way to reach a destination such as Baffin Island, (which can be reached by boat only in good weather) with the exception of Churchill, Manitoba, which is connected by train.

APEX FARES AND OTHER DISCOUNTS

There are several kinds of bargain tickets available within Canada, and low-cost airlines such as **WestJet** have increased competition and forced prices down. Charter airlines such as **Air Transat** fly between Canadian cities much like scheduled airlines. However, they are usually up to 20% cheaper than scheduled tickets and can be booked through tour operators. To take advantage of the reductions available through Apex (advanced purchase excursion) fares, you must book between 7 and 21 days in advance: the earlier the booking, the larger the discount. Each fare will have its own set of rules, which include restrictions on length of stay and time of travel (such as between certain hours or on certain days). Be aware that refunds are seldom given and it might be difficult to change your dates.

Seat sales are another bargain option whereby an airline will advertise exceptionally cheap tickets to boost travel on popular routes during quiet times of the year. There is, however, very little flexibility on these deals, and you have to fly within a specific period of time.

Air Canada offers pass deals for visitors who want to travel all over the country, as well as to the US. The passes are available only outside of North America. Most of the offers involve paying for a number of coupons, each of which represents a single flight within either the continent or a specific region. The passes also usually specify a period of time (7 to 60 days) for which they are valid.

FLY-DRIVE DEALS

A good way to make the most of a visit to Canada is to book a fly-drive vacation. The deal invariably involves a substantial cut in the cost of the car rental. Arrangements can also be made to pick up and drop off your vehicle in different places. It would be possible, for example, to pick up a car in Toronto, tour Ontario, dropping the car off in Ottawa before flying on to Vancouver on the west coast. Known as one-way car rental, these deals may involve large drop-off fees: from Toronto to Ottawa costs around Can$200. Travel agents offer a wide range of such packages.

BAGGAGE RESTRICTIONS

Passengers traveling economy on domestic flights should be aware that there are restrictions on the amount and weight of baggage that can be taken on board. The type of aircraft determines what can be carried, and light aircraft usually accept only hand-baggage.

WestJet logo

In general, passengers are entitled to have two suitcases, each with an average weight of 32 kg (70 lb) per item. Hand-baggage must fit safely under aircraft seats or in overhead lockers. Garment bags may be carried on board some aircraft but must be soft-sided and comply with size restrictions – length 112 cm (45 ins), depth 11 cm (4.5 ins) – so remember to check with your airline or travel agent when puchasing your ticket.

CHECKING IN

Security is a necessity nowadays and can make the boarding procedure take longer. Within Canada you must check in at least 30 minutes prior to departure; for flights to the US, allow 90 minutes; and for international flights, leave at least 2 hours. Visitors from other countries traveling within Canada should carry a passport to verify that he or she is the traveler named on the ticket.

It is also worth noting that the daily peak periods at the larger Canadian airports are usually from 7am to 9am and from 3pm to 8pm. Passenger volume also increases significantly during the winter holiday season, March break, and the summer, so it is wise to allow extra time for parking, check-in, and security screening during these periods.

DIRECTORY

DOMESTIC AIRLINES

Air Canada
Tel 1 888 247 2262.
www.aircanada.ca

Air North *(Yukon)*
Tel (867) 668 2228, 1 800 661 0407. www.flyairnorth.com

Air Transat *(charters only)*
Tel (514) 636 3630, 1 877 872 6728. **www**.airtransat.com

Bearskin Airlines
Tel (807) 577 1141, 1 800 465 2327. **www**.bearskinairlines.com

First Air
(Ottawa, for far north flights)
Tel 1 800 267 1247.
www.firstair.ca

Porter Airlines
Tel 1 888 619 8622.
www.flyporter.com

SkyService
Tel (416) 679 5700.
www.skyserviceairlines.com

Starlink Aviation
Tel 1 877 782 8247.
www.starlinkaviation.com

WestJet
Tel 1 800 538 5696.
www.westjet.com

PRINCIPAL DOMESTIC AIR ROUTES

Canada's major airline is Air Canada. It provides links to a number of regional carriers to form a comprehensive domestic air network, while WestJet specializes in western destinations.

GETTING AROUND CANADA'S CITIES

Although the car is a popular way to travel in Canada, the country is noted for the fast, frequent, and efficient public transit systems of its cities. In general, the best way for visitors to explore Canada's urban centers is primarily on foot, using public transportation as a back up. The streets are clean and safe, and strolling through different neighborhoods is a pleasant way to get to know them. Most municipal transit systems are reasonably priced, with discounted multi-ticket deals and

Tourbus in Toronto

day passes. Driving around downtown areas can be daunting, particularly during the rush hour, and parking tends to be both difficult and expensive.

Most transit systems offer free maps, available at stations or tourist information centers. The following pages detail how to get around Canada's three largest cities, Vancouver, Toronto, and Montreal *(see endpaper for detailed transit maps)*, as well as other provincial capitals and the most often visited towns and communities.

MONTREAL

Montreal's bus and subway network is integrated so that the stations connect with bus routes and tickets can be used on either. Be sure to get a transfer ticket, which should take you anywhere in the city for one fare. Known as the Metro, Montreal's subway is clean, safe, and air-conditioned in summer and heated in the winter. It is by far the fastest and cheapest way to get around town *(see endpaper)*. Free maps are available at any of the ticket booths. Visitors can buy a Tourist Pass for one or three days at major hotels and at the Visitor Information Office downtown.

Driving is not recommended here, as the roads are busy and parking is severely restricted, especially in the old town. It is best to use the city's park and-ride system. Cabs can be hailed in the street. They have a white or orange sign on the roof; the sign is lit up when the cab is available.

Many streets in Montreal now have bike lanes. The Great Montreal Bike Path-Guide is available free at the tourist office. Bikes can be taken on the Métro anytime except during rush hour, from about 7am to 10am and 5pm to 7pm on weekdays. There are some lovely bike paths, such as the waterfront trail on the historic Canal de Lachine, and those

that lead through Cité du Havre and across Pont de la Concorde to the islands. There are a number of bicycle shops offering daily or weekly rental; they generally require a deposit of Can$250 or more in addition to the daily rate.

TORONTO

The Toronto Transit Commission (TTC) operates a huge system of connecting subway, bus, and streetcar lines that serves the entire city. It is one of the safest and cleanest systems of its kind anywhere in the world. There are two major subway lines, with 60 stations along the way *(see endpaper)*. Be sure to get a free transfer pass if you

Scenic riverside cyling path in Quebec City

intend to continue your trip by bus or streetcar after you leave the subway.

To ride buses and streetcars, you must have exact change, a ticket, or a token. Tickets and tokens are on sale at subway entrances and stores. The "Pick up a Ride Guide" shows every major place of interest and how to reach it by public transit, and is available at most subway ticket offices. A Light Rapid Transit line connects downtown to the lakefront (called Harbourfront). The line starts at Union Station and terminates at Spadina/Bloor subway station.

It is easy to catch a cab in Toronto; they can be hailed in the street, called in advance, or found outside hotels. There are several outlets that rent bicycles, but as downtown Toronto is busy with traffic, it is best to confine your cycling to the parks. The Martin Goodman Trail is a well-marked scenic bicycle route along the long, scenic waterfront.

As in Vancouver, you will need the right coins for the bus. The regular adult fare is Can$2.75 across the whole system, and transfers are free for up to an hour. If you are going to be in Toronto for an extended period it is worth considering a monthly Metro-Pass, or you can buy 10 tickets or tokens for Can$21. There are day passes with unlimited access all day for Can$8.50.

Toronto taxicabs gather at a taxi stand

Ferries to the Toronto Islands run several times an hour at peak times in summer and continue well into the evening. There is also a road bridge.

VANCOUVER

Vancouver's well-organized network of light rail (called SkyTrain), bus, and ferry services is run by BC Transit. An inexpensive Transit Guide is available from newsstands and information centers. It includes a map of the city showing all routes. Driving is not the best way to see the city as congestion is heavy,

and you are unlikely to find a spot to park. There is a park-and-ride system, where commuters can leave their cars at certain points around the city center.

The SkyTrain is a light rail system of driverless trains that connects downtown Vancouver with the suburbs of Burnaby, New Westminster, and Surrey. It travels partially beneath ground and partially overground on a raised track. The main terminal is at Waterfront Station at the bottom of Seymour Street. An alternative to the SkyTrain is to use the city's downtown bus routes. These are worth riding as they offer delightful tours past the city's top attractions, although it is advisable to avoid rush hour traffic. Bus services end around midnight, but there is a scaled down "Night Owl" service.

One of the best ways to get around Vancouver is by water. The SeaBus is a 400-seat Catamaran that shuttles between Lonsdale Quay in North Vancouver and the downtown terminal at Waterfront Station. The trip takes around 15 minutes and includes wonderful

views of the mountains and Vancouver skyline. Aquabus Ferries connect stations on False Creek, Granville Island, Stamp's Landing, and the Hornby Street Dock.

If you want to take a cab it is best to call one of the main companies such as Black Top or Yellow Cab, as hailing a taxi in the streets is rarely successful. However, Vancouver is a great city for cyclists, with plenty of bike paths, including the 10 km (6 mile) road around Stanley Park. There is a park-and-ride service for bikes here, similar to the one elsewhere for cars.

Fares are the same for bus, SkyTrain, and SeaBus in the Vancouver area, but the price varies according to time of day and the distance you travel. Adult fares are cheaper after 6:30pm, and all day Saturday, Sunday, and holidays. There are three zones in the city, and the price of the fare depends on how many zones you cross. The off-peak adult fare in zone one is Can$2.25. There are a wide variety of discounts available: a FareSaver book of 10 tickets or a day pass are good value. Children under 4 ride free, and those between the ages of 5 and 13 pay less (as do students with a valid GoCard), and seniors over 65 also get concessions. A transfer ticket is free and lasts for 90 minutes of travel.

SkyTrain traveling over the city bridge in Vancouver on a summer evening

The scenic approach to Château Frontenac in Quebec City, best appreciated on foot

OTTAWA

Fortunately for visitors, many of the capital city's major tourist attractions are within walking distance of Parliament Hill. Ottawa's sidewalks are both wide and clean, and you can do most of your sightseeing on foot, using public transportation to cover the longer distances. The region of Ottawa-Carlton operates **OC Transpo**, a 130-route bus network. Fares are among the most expensive in Canada, with a two-tier system that charges more for traveling during rush hour, Can$2.60 per ticket. You need the exact fare unless you buy tickets in advance. These are available at newsstands and corner stores. If you need to change buses, ask for a transfer, which can be used for up to an hour. It is possible to get a transfer for use on the separate Hull bus system across the Ottawa River, although you may have to pay a little more. All routes meet downtown at the Rideau Centre, and the stops are color-coded according to the route.

If you are using a car there are several reasonably priced municipal car lots – look for a green 'P' sign. Taxis can be booked by phone or hailed at stands outside major hotels.

Bicycles are a good way to explore a city that has some 150 km (93 miles) of scenic paths. The Rideau Canal, that crosses the city from north to south, is bordered by delightful walking and bike paths.

CALGARY

Calgary transit operates buses and a light-rail transit system known as the C-Train. For a flat fare of Can$2.25 you can transfer to either using the same ticket, although day

Logo for the C-Train in Calgary

passes for around Can$6.75 are good value for visitors hoping to see several sights in one day. The C-Train travels north to the University and airport, and south to Macleod Trail. It is free in the downtown section between 10th Street and City Hall (buses are not). Maps are available from the **Calgary Transit** offices, where you can also buy tickets. C-Train tickets can be bought from machines located on the platforms.

If you wish to travel mostly within the city center, walking and public transportation are your best options. However, the city's blocks are long, (Calgary is Canada's second largest city by area) and any trip to the outskirts and beyond requires a car. There are several rental companies, including all the major outlets. Weekend car rental rates are cheaper than weekday car rental. Cabs are expensive here and cannot be hailed on the street, but they can be picked up at hotels or ordered by telephone.

WINNIPEG

Many of Winnipeg's attractions are within a 20-minute walk of one another in the downtown area, centered on the crossroads of Portage and Main Streets. **Winnipeg City Transit** operates an efficient bus system, which is also ideal for reaching farther-placed sights. There is a flat fare of Can$2.00, or you can purchase a book of 10 tickets for Can$18.00 from the Transit Service Centre based in the underground concourse at Portage and Main. (A transfer, valid for an hour, is available from the driver if you are changing buses.) The center is open weekdays between 8:30 am and 4:30 pm, and offers detailed information and a free route map of the city. There are also several pleasant bicycle paths that run through the city as well as to outlying districts.

QUEBEC CITY

The charming narrow streets of the old city are best seen on foot, especially since most of the historic sights are located within a small area of the walled city. If you need to travel farther to see one of the more distant sights such as the Musée du Québec, the bus system is frequent and reliable. Fares are cheaper if you buy a ticket before boarding and are on sale at several outlets in grocery stores costing Can$2.50 per person. There are also one-day passes for Can$5.95. The bus station is in the Lower Town on Boulevard Charest Est. Most of the main routes stop centrally on the Place d'Youville in the Old Town.

Taxi stands are located in front of the major hotels or outside city hall. Horse-drawn carriages or *calèches* may be hired for a gentle trot around the Old Town, but expect to pay Can$50 for 40 minutes.

HALIFAX

The compact city of Halifax is best explored on foot or bicycle, which can be hired for a half or full day. Driving around is difficult: parking is hard to come by. To reach outlying districts there is the **Halifax Metro Transit** bus system. Fares are cheap, with a flat fare of Can$2 charged downtown. It is also possible to purchase budget books of 20 tickets for Can$32. In the city from Monday to Saturday during the summer season, a free bus service called "Fred" circles the downtown area about every 20 minutes.

CHARLOTTETOWN

Since the completion of the Confederation Bridge in 1997, Prince Edward Island has become easily accessible by bus and car. Travelers still use the ferry service, which runs from New Glasgow, Nova Scotia between May and November. There is a shuttle bus service from Halifax that travels to the island by ferry. The island's public transportation system is limited to a bus service in Charlottetown run by **Trius Tours**; this operates all year round. However, touring by car is most popular, and it is a good idea to reserve a car during the busiest months of July and August. Several companies offer organized bus, walking, and cycling tours.

Driving over Confederation Bridge to Prince Edward Island

ST. JOHN'S, NEWFOUNDLAND

In comparison to most of Canada's cities, parking is easy in St. John's. It is possible to buy a parking permit from one of many well-placed machines. They take quarters (25 cents) or dollar coins. Car rental here is less expensive than in many other Canadian cities and there is a good choice of companies.

The local bus service is run by Metrobus, and tickets cost Can$2.00 every trip. If you are planning on spending some time here it is worth investing in a 10-ride card for Can$18.00. By riding on two routes, such as one downtown and one suburban bus, you get a bargain tour of the city.

Bus traveling over Harbour Bridge in Saint John, New Brunswick

Train Travel in Canada

The Canadian rail network is run by the government-owned VIA Rail. The service has been significantly reduced since the late 1980s when many cross-country services, along with other lines, were cut. VIA Rail still provides a service on the famed 1950s *Canadian*, a beautifully restored train that travels across the country between Toronto and Vancouver, passing through stunning Rockies' scenery between Jasper and Kamloops.

Increasingly, Canadians fly long distances or use their cars to cover most of the shorter hauls. For visitors, traveling by train remains a wonderful way to see large parts of Canada (especially in those trains that have glass-domed observation cars). Smaller commuter networks around the major cities are also useful for visitors who wish to explore an area in detail.

Specialty trips on the Rocky Mountaineer travel through the Rockies

SMALLER NETWORKS

Visitors should also be aware that VIA is not the only passenger rail service in Canada. The larger cities all have useful local commuter lines. Vancouver has **BC Rail** and the West Coast Express to Prince Rupert, while Toronto's Go Transit covers the city's outlying suburbs as far as Milton, Bradford, Richmond Hill, and Stouffville, and Montreal has AMT *(see p421)*.

SPECIALTY TRIPS

There are several lines that offer visitors the chance to enjoy Canada's best scenery in comfortable, often luxurious trains. Among the best trips is the **Algoma Central Railway** in Ontario *(see p225)*, which runs from Sault Ste. Marie to Hearst and has an excursion train from Sault Ste. Marie to the Agawa Canyon through spectacular landscapes from early June to October. There is a Snow Train excursion on weekends from late December to early March, also from Sault Ste. Marie.

Ontario Northland Railway operates both freight and passenger services on its main line from North Bay to Moosonee. *The Polar Bear Express* is a summer excursion to Moosonee, which provides a close-up look at the northern wilderness. The passenger service continues south of North Bay to Toronto.

The most spectacular train ride in Canada is probably in British Columbia, where, from mid-May until early October, **Rocky Mountaineer Railtours** runs two day excursions from Vancouver to Calgary via Banff or Jasper. The *Rocky Mountaineer* follows the original route of the Canadian Pacific Railroad. These trips operate entirely in daylight, and the package includes a night in Kamloops plus meals. There is also a dome car for viewing the stunning scenery that lies around every bend.

For a longer trip, visitors may want to take the six-day/five-night Golden/Crowsnest Tour, run by **Royal Canadian Pacific Luxury Rail Tours**.

THE CANADIAN RAIL NETWORK

Via Rail Canada Inc. operates Canada's national passenger rail service. Despite the closing of several lines there are still 400 trains every week, which cover some 13,000 km (8,000 miles) on major routes between Vancouver and Toronto, traveling on to Montreal, Quebec, and Halifax. It is possible to cross the country by train – a trip that takes five days – by connecting up with these lines. The longest continuous route remains the Vancouver–Toronto trip on board the stylish and luxurious 1950s *Canadian*, with its observation and dining cars. Places with no road link, such as the town of Churchill in northern Manitoba, rely on the railroad. The line between Winnipeg and Churchill is mostly used by visitors in October, heading north to see the polar bears *(see p253)*.

VIA Rail operates both long-haul trains in eastern and western Canada, as well as inter-city trains in the populous Ontario Corridor, from Quebec City to Windsor, passing through Kingston, Montreal, Niagara Falls, Ottawa, and Toronto. This is a fast service that offers snacks and drinks on board most trains.

It is easy to travel onward to the United States, as VIA connects with the American rail network, Amtrak, at both Montreal and Vancouver. VIA Rail and Amtrak jointly run the Toronto–New York line through Niagara Falls, and Toronto–Chicago trains through Sarnia/Port Huron. The VIA station in Windsor is only a few kilometers from the Amtrak station in Detroit.

The tour takes guests from Calgary, across the expansive prairie of Lethbridge, and on to Fort MacLeod, before entering the Rockies via the Crowsnest Pass. Guests can also learn about the history of the Canadian west from the area's most experienced naturalists and historians.

TRAVEL CLASSES

On long-distance routes there are two main classes of travel available, Economy and a variety of Sleeper classes, known as VIA 1. Economy Class offers comfortable, reclining seats in cars with wide aisles and large windows, as well as blankets and pillows for overnight trips. Passengers in Economy class also generally have access to one of the onboard snack bars or restaurants. Sleeper classes offer a range of options from double- and single-berth bunks to double bedrooms, which convert to luxurious sitting rooms by day. VIA services in Western Canada such as the *Canadian,* offer the choice of "Silver & Blue" first-class cars that have access to a private observation car, as well as plush dining cars.

TICKETS AND BOOKINGS

Reservations for rail travel can be made through travel agents or direct through VIA Rail. There are a variety of discounts available on both economy and sleeper classes if you book round-trip tickets or in advance. Reductions on Ontario corridor lines are available if you book five days in advance (on most other routes you need to reserve tickets seven days in advance.) There are also discounts for bookings made for travel during the off-peak period between October and December, and from January until the end of May.

The CANRAILPASS gives you 12 days of unlimited travel in economy class during a 30-day period. Just show your CANRAILPASS each time you obtain a ticket. The card is

Maple leaf on VIARail logo

valid on all VIA Rail routes, and you can make as many stops as you like during your trip. Up to three extra days' travel can be added, which can be bought in advance or at any time during the 30-day validity period. It is a good idea to reserve seats in advance during the summer as there are a limited number for pass holders. Throughout the VIA system, travelers over 60 are entitled to an additional ten percent reduction on fares.

DIRECTORY

VIA Rail
Tel (416) 366 8411 Toronto and most other Canadian provinces.
www.viarail.ca

Algoma Central Railway
Tel (705) 946 7300.
Toll-Free 1 800 242 9287.

Ontario Northland Railway
Tel 1 (800) 461 8558.

Rocky Mountaineer Railtours
Tel (604) 606 7245.
www.rockymountaineer.com

Royal Canadian Pacific
Tel (403) 508 1400.

PRINCIPAL RAIL ROUTES

VIA Rail is the main provider of passenger rail services throughout Canada. It is possible to reach all the major centers of the country, and regional operators link up with most town's outlying districts.

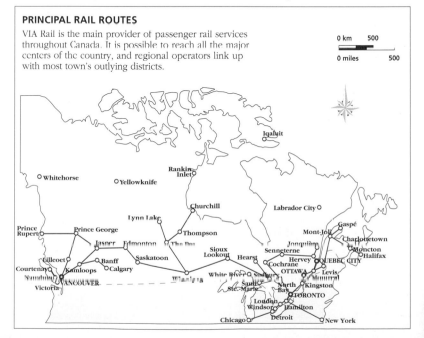

Traveling by Bus

Buses are the least expensive way to get around Canada. The majority of bus routes west of Toronto are run by Greyhound Canada, including the epic trip along the Trans-Canada Highway (Hwy 1) between Toronto and Vancouver. East of Toronto there are several smaller companies that cover most areas. Although a long bus trip can mean one or more nights spent sitting upright, the buses are generally clean and comfortable, and offer plenty of rest stops. The network is also reliable and efficient with buses usually arriving on time. In more remote regions, check timetables in advance as there may be no service or only one bus a week.

LONG-DISTANCE BUSES

Long-distance buses provide a cheaper and often faster option than the railroad. The main operator, Greyhound Canada, carries more than two million passengers each year to most of the towns and cities across the country. Although Greyhound lines operate in the west and center of the country, many routes are linked to bus lines in the east, and in the United States. West of Vancouver, Greyhound links up with Pacific and Maverick Coach Lines, east of Ottawa, with Voyageur Colonial, Orleans Express, and Acadian SMP. Greyhound's express services offer a faster, highway-based service on buses that have more leg room, movies, music, and snacks.

Although smoking is prohibited, most long-haul buses stop every three to four hours so that travelers can leave the bus for a rest break. Rest breaks or driver changes take place at both bus and service stations, where you will find a variety of facilities ranging from restaurants and cafés to snack vending machines. All the buses are air-conditioned and have washrooms. Buses also offer passengers the advantage of picking up and arriving in convenient downtown areas.

DISCOUNTS AND PASSES

There is a variety of discounted bus passes available to visitors. Children under five usually travel free, and travelers over 65 are entitled to discounts on both return tickets and pass deals. Fares are also cheaper if you book in advance or travel during the off-peak season, from January to June or from October to December.

The Greyhound Canada Pass offers unlimited travel on both Greyhound and many other lines, such as those running eastward between Ontario and Quebec or across Saskatchewan, for a range of time periods: 7, 10, 15, 21, 30, 45, and 60 days. Visit www.greyhound.ca for a list of fares. The Canada Coach

Greyhound bus logo

Pass Plus is similar, with the bonus of including travel across the country to Montreal, Quebec City, Halifax, St. John, and Charlottetown, as well as to New York City in the US.

Some pass deals booked overseas and through organizations such as Hostelling International include accommodation in more than 80 hostels from coast to coast; an example is the Go Canada Budget Travel Pass. This pass can also be used to travel on VIA Rail services between Toronto, Ottawa, and Montreal.

Rout-Passes offer access to some 35 intercity bus companies in Ontario and Quebec from mid-April to mid-November. Passengers do not need to decide on their itinerary in advance, and reservations are not necessary. There is a wide range of Rout-Passes to choose from, and some include accommodation vouchers. The 16-day Rout-Pass can be bought only by members of the International Hostelling Association.

BUS STATIONS AND RESERVATIONS

Buses from different carriers all operate from the same stations, making it easy to connect with other bus lines and municipal transit services. Reservations are not usually needed since buses are filled on a first-come, first-served basis. Passengers are advised to be there at least an hour ahead of departure time, leaving plenty of time to buy tickets and check their luggage. Do not panic if the bus fills up; it will generally be replaced with another one right away. Buying tickets in advance does not guarantee you a seat, and you will still have to line up to board the bus.

Most bus stations have a small restaurant or café where reasonably priced snacks and meals can be purchased. On long-distance journeys it is a

Boarding the bus on Ottawa's Parliament Hill

Tourists on a bus trip to the Athabasca Glacier, near Jasper

good idea to take some food with you, otherwise you will have to rely on the sometimes over-priced, unappealing food available in service stations. At the larger stations it is possible to rent luggage lockers, leaving you free to explore unencumbered by suitcases. In the major cities such as Toronto, you have the choice of boarding in the suburbs or in the city center. Choose the city center since the bus may be full by the time it reaches outlying

districts. Always ask if there is an express or direct service to your destination; as some trips involve countless stops en route and can seem very long. A small pillow or traveling cushion, a sweater (to counter the sometimes fierce air-conditioning), and a good book or magazine can often help to make a long trip more comfortable.

BUS TOURS

There are several tour companies that offer package deals on a variety of trips. An extensive range of tours is available, from city sightseeing and day trips to particular attractions, to expensive luxury, multi-day tours including guides, meals, and accommodations. There are specialized tours that focus on such activities as glacier hikes, white-water rafting, and horseback riding. A typical ten-day tour of the Rockies may take in everything from a cruise to Victoria, a hike in Banff, and a picnic on Lake Louise, to a trip to the Columbia Icefield, or a look at the history of gold rush country in the Cariboo

region. Most companies will send you detailed itineraries in advance, and it is a good idea to make sure that there are no hidden extras such as tips, sales taxes, and entry fees, as these are often included in the price of the package. Some of the most beautiful scenery can also be seen on regular Greyhound routes, such as those in the Rockies.

DIRECTORY

Greyhound Canada Inquiries
Tel 1 800 661 8747.
www.greyhound.ca

Timetable Information
(CAN & US) *Tel* 1 800 661 8747;
(UK) *Tel* 0870 888 0223.

Bookings (passes only)
(UK) *Tel* 0870 888 0223.

BUS TOUR COMPANIES

Brewster Transportation
for tours in the west *Tel* 1 877 791 5500. **www**.brewster.ca

Great Canadian Holidays
for tours in the east *Tel* (519) 896 8687, 1 800 461 8687.

BUS ROUTES

This map shows the main bus routes across Canada. It is possible to travel right across the country along the Trans-Canada Highway using Greyhound Canada and the bus companies that operate east of Toronto.

Driving in Canada

Driving Route tour sign

It is a good idea to rent a car when visiting Canada. Other modes of transportation will get you around the cities and from one rural town to another, but once you arrive in a remote country area, a car is the best way of exploring. Tours of regions such as Quebec's wild Gaspé Peninsula *(see pp144–5)*, or British Columbia's Okanagan Valley *(see p317)* are best made by car. Several aspects of Canadian life reflect the fact that this is a driver's country: there is an excellent, well-maintained highway network, and many places have huge out-of-town malls. However, city-center traffic congestion means that visitors to the major cities of Toronto, Vancouver, Montreal, and Ottawa may find that public transportation is quicker and cheaper than driving.

ARRIVING BY CAR

Many people drive to Canada from the US. The border here is the longest in the world. There are 13 major crossing points, the two busiest being from Detroit to Windsor and at Niagara Falls. Most of the highways entering Canada connect to the Trans Canada Highway, which is the longest highway through the country, running for some 5,000 km (8,045 miles) from Victoria, BC, to St. John's in Newfoundland. Customs control ask that visitors declare their citizenship, their place of residence, and proposed length of stay. You may be asked to show your passport and visa *(see pp406–7)*. It is a good idea to fill up with less expensive fuel on the US side. It is also possible to enter the country from the Alaska side by the famed Alaska Highway *(see pp262–3)*, which crosses the Yukon and ends in British Columbia at Dawson City.

DRIVER'S LICENSES

An up-to-date driver's license from your own country usually entitles you to drive in Canada for up to three months. There are some provincial variations: in British Columbia, Quebec, and New Brunswick your license will be valid for up to six months, in Prince Edward Island four months, and in the Yukon only one month. It is advisable to carry an International Driving Permit (IDP) with your license in case of problems with traffic officials or the police.

INSURANCE

Whether driving a rental or your own car you will need proof of insurance coverage, which is compulsory in Canada. If you are using your own car it is advisable to check whether your insurance is valid in Canada, as this may save money. The minimum liability cover is Can$200,000, except in Quebec, where it starts at Can$50,000. Most rental companies offer collision damage waiver and personal accident insurance for an additional charge; it is a good idea to have both. If you are driving a private car that is not registered in your own name, you will need to carry a letter from the owner that authorizes your use of the vehicle. For a rental vehicle you must carry the company's official documentation for the same reason. Arranging summer rentals and insurance in advance is recommended.

A Recreational Vehicle passes mountains and forests on a trip through Banff National Park, Alberta

CAR RENTAL

Rental cars are available just about everywhere in Canada. Most major rental car dealers such as Hertz, Avis, and Tilden, have offices at airports and in towns and cities across the country. Among the less expensive options are booking a fly-drive package from home, or there may be discounts if you rent your car in advance. The cost varies greatly depending on the season, type of vehicle, and length of rental. Ask about hidden costs such as drop-off charges, provincial sales tax, and the Goods and Services Tax (GST). When picking up your car you may be asked to show your passport and return airline ticket. The minimum age for renting a car is usually 25 or, in some cases, 21. You will need a credit card for the deposit as it is all but impossible to rent a car in Canada without one. Children under 18 kg (40 lbs) require a child seat fixed in place with a seat belt. Most companies will arrange for one with a little notice. The biggest rental companies offer a wide choice of vehicles, ranging from two-door economy cars to four-door luxury models. Most cars come with a radio and air-conditioning. Bear in mind that nearly all rental cars in Canada have automatic transmission. Manual models are unusual, although cars with specially adapted hand controls for disabled drivers are available from some of the larger companies. RVs (Recreational Vehicles) or camper vans can also be rented, but they are more expensive. They should be booked well in advance if you intend to travel in summer.

FUEL AND SERVICE STATIONS

Fuel prices are slightly higher than in the US and half the price you pay in the UK, especially in cities and large towns, although rural areas

often charge more. Unleaded gas and diesel only are available in Canada. Rental companies generally provide a full tank on departure, and give you the choice of paying for the fuel in advance or on return. Service stations are often self-service, which can be a problem if you need a mechanic. In major cities some stations are open for 24 hours, but in rural areas they often close at 6pm and are few and far between, especially in northerly regions. It is a good idea to fill up before setting off. Credit cards and traveler's checks are widely accepted.

RULES OF THE ROAD

Canada's highway system is well maintained and has mostly two-lane all-weather roads. They are all clearly numbered and signed. Most highway signs are in English, and some bilingual, except for those in Quebec where they are only in French. A good road map is essential and can be obtained from any auto club such as the **Canadian Automobile Association (CAA)**, which is affiliated with other similar clubs in the world. It is worth checking the rules of the road with them as there are numerous small provincial variations. In Canada you drive on the right. You can turn right on a red light everywhere, except in Quebec. The speed limits are posted in kilometers-per-hour (km/h) and range from 30–40 km/h (18–30 mph) in urban areas to 80–100 km/h (50–60 mph) on highways. On multi-lane highways you pass on the left for safety. Some provinces require cars to keep their headlights on for extended periods after dawn and before sunset, for safety reasons. Seat belts are compulsory for both drivers and passengers.

Driving in the north involves special procedures because most of the roads are extremely hazardous due to ice, and are passable only during the summer months.

Moose warning sign on highway

DIRECTORY

MAJOR RENTAL AGENCIES

Hertz
Tel 800 263 0600.
www.hertz.com

Avis
Tel 800 331 1212.
www.avis.com

National
Tel 800 387 4747.
www.nationalcar.ca

AUTO CLUBS

Canadian Automobile Association
Tel (613) 247 0117.

American Automobile Association
Tel (407) 444 7000.
24-hour emergency road service
Tel 1-800-222-help.

WINTER DRIVING AND SAFETY

Canadian winters are harsh, and you should always check road conditions and weather forecasts before setting out on trips. Drifting snow and black ice are frequent hazards in winter or in northern regions. When driving in remote areas, make sure you have a full gas tank, and carry blankets, some sand, a shovel, and emergency food, such as chocolate bars, in case you get stuck. Jumper cables are also useful because extreme cold can drain a car battery quickly. Studded tires are useful in winter conditions and are permitted in most provinces. Check with local tourist offices.

During the summer months animals such as bears and moose can be a hazard, especially in parts of British Columbia. They can suddenly appear on roads when they rush out of the woods to escape the blackflies during spring and summer. Watch for road signs, and take extra care when you see deer or moose road signs as these indicate an area where animals are most likely to appear suddenly.

General Index

Acknowledgments

Dorling Kindersley would like to thank the following people whose contributions and assistance have made the book possible:

Main Contributors

Paul Franklin has recently completed Nova Scotia's provincial travel guide, commissioned by the Government of Nova Scotia. A writer and photographer for both Canadian and world travel guides, he lives in Nova Scotia.

Sam Ion and **Cam Norton** live and work in Burlington, Ontario. A successful travel-writing team, they contribute to newspapers, magazines, and brochures as well as their most recent work, the Ontario Government's millennium website, celebrating the province.

Philip Lee has worked as a travel writer for over a decade, and is the author of numerous articles and travel books about countries throughout the world. He has lived and traveled extensively through the US and Canada and is now based in Nottingham, England.

Lorry Patton lives and works in British Columbia, having recently been travel editor of BC Woman magazine. She currently runs an online travel magazine which includes BC, and lives on the Gulf Islands just outside Vancouver.

Geoffrey Roy is an award-winning freelance travel writer and photographer, based in Surrey, England. He has published numerous articles on Northern Canada.

Donald Telfer is a Saskatchewan-based travel writer with over 20 years' writing experience of Central Canada. He contributes regularly to a variety of Canadian and international newspapers and magazines.

Paul Waters is a Montreal-based journalist who has lived and worked in several cities in Quebec and has written extensively on the province. He is currently the travel editor for *The Gazette*, a popular Montreal English-language daily.

Additional Contributors

Bruce Bishop, Alan Chan, Katharine and Eric Fletcher, Helena Katz, Ffion Llwyd-Jones, Sandra Phinney, Michael Snook.

Additional Photography

James Jackson, Gunter Marx, Ian O'Leary, Cylla Von Tiedman, Matthew Ward.

Additional Illustrations

Stephen Conlin, Eugene Fleury, Steve Gyapay, Chris Orr, Mel Pickering, Peter Ross.

Cartography

ERA-Maptec Ltd, Dublin, Ireland.

Proof Reader

Sam Merrell.

Indexer

Hilary Bird.

Design and Editorial Assistance

Gillian Allan, Emily Anderson, Claire Baranowski, Sonal Bhatt, Ilona Biro, Louise Bolton, Julie Bond, Vivien Crump, Flannery Dean, Hannah Dolan, Gadi Farfour, Emer FitzGerald, Joy Fitzsimmons, Camilla Gersh, Emily Green, Dr. Stephen Henderson, Jessica Hughes, Marie Ingledew, Steve Knowlden, Kathryn Lane, Patrick Lejtenyi, Hayley Maher, Mary Ormandy, Marianne Petrou, Rada Radojicic, Mani Ramaswamy, Lee Redmond, Sands Publishing Solutions, Susana Smith, Anna Streiffert, Geordie Telfer, Helen Townsend, Lisa Voormeij.

Additional Picture Research

Rachel Barber, Ellen Root, Marta Bescos

Special assistance

Canada Map Office, Ontario; Canadian Tourism Office, London, UK; Claude Guerin and Danielle Legentil, Musée d'art contemporain de Montreal; Jim Kemshead, Tourism Yukon; Wendy Kraushaar, RCMP Museum, Regina, Saskatchewan; 'Ksan Historical Indian Village &Museum, Hazleton, BC; Leila Jamieson, Art Gallery of Ontario, Toronto; Antonio Landry, Village Historique Acadien, New Brunswick; Marty Hickie, Royal Tyrrell Museum, Drumheller, Alberta; Mary Mandley, Information Office, Sainte-Marie among the Hurons; National Air Photo Library, Ottawa, Ontario; Liette Roberts, Manitoba Museum of Man and Nature, Winnipeg; Mark Sayers; Ernest D. Scullion, Aeriel Photography Services, Scarborough, Ontario; Visit Canada office, London, UK; Jennifer Webb, UBC Museum of Anthropology, Vancouver, BC.

Photography Permissions

Dorling Kindersley would like to thank everyone for their assistance and kind permission to photograph at their establishments.

Picture Credits

a = above; b = below/bottom; c = centre; f = far; l = left; r = right; t = top.

Works of art have been produced with the permission of the following copyright holders: © Bill Vazan *Shibagua Shard*, 1989 sandblasted sheild granite 189c.

The publishers would like to thank the following individuals, companies, and picture libraries for their kind permission to reproduce their photographs:

AIR CANADA: 53b, 414c/t; AKG, London: 51b; ALAMY IMAGES: Rubens Abboud 11cla; Bill Brooks 369tl; Jon Arnold Images 11br; Gunter Marx 368cl; mediacolor's 394cl; Megapress 394tl; Rolf Hicker Photography 317cla; Sean O'Neill 8tc; Pictures Colour Library 8br, 394br; Robert Harding Picture Library Ltd/Roy Rainford 10tr; Stephen Saks Photography 369c; John Sylvester 92c; Visual&Written SL/Dennis Fast/VWPics 10br; BRYAN AND CHERRY ALEXANDER: 20c, 24t, 25cr, 27c/cr/bl, 30t, 41t, 55c/b, 157t, 323c, 324, 326cb, 326-7, 327c, 334-5, 336t, 340t, 341t; ALLSPORT: Scott Halleran 36b; Jed Jacobson 37t; Jamie Squire 39b; Rick Stewart 36c; ANCHORAGE MUSEUM OF HISTORY AND ART, Anchorage, Alaska: B74.1.25 50t; courtesy of THE ANNE OF GREEN GABLES MUSEUM, Silver Bush, Park Corner, Prince Edward Island: 83b; ART CENTRAL: Jenny Tzanakos 292bl; ART GALLERY OF ONTARIO: 176tl, 178l Photo Resources/Sean Weaver 179cra; Edgar Degas *Grande Arabesque*, bronze 176b; Paul Gaugin French 1848–1903, HINA AND FATU c.1892, tamanu wood, 32.7 cm height, Gift of the Volunteer Committee Fund, 1980 178tl; Lawren H. Harris Canadian 1885–1970 *Above Lake Superior* c.1922 oil on canvas 121.9 x 152.4 cm Gift from Ruben and Kate Leonard Canadian Fund 1929 © Mrs. James H Knox 164b; Paul Kane *Scene in the Northwest* (1845–46) The Thomson Collection 179br; J.E.H. MacDondald Canadian (1873–1932) *Falls, Montreal River* 1920 oil on canvas 121.9 x 153cm Purchase 1933 Acc no 2109 Photo Larry Ostrom 165t; Henry Moore British (1898–1986) *Draped Reclining Figure* 1952 - 53 original plaster 100.4 x 160.4x 68.6 cm Gift of Henry Moore, 1974. The work illustrated on page 178cla is reproduced by permission of the Henry Moore Foundation; Robert Gray Murray (b1936) To 1963 painted aluminium, 2 units, tubular column H271.1cm planar column 275.0cm Gift from the Junior Women's Committee Fund 1966 65/60.1-2 33cb; Photographic Resources 32b; Peter Paul Rubens *Massacre of the Innocents* (1609-11) The Thomson Collection 178clb; Tom Thomson Canadian 1887-1917 *The West Wind* 1917 oil on canvas 120.7 x 137.2 cm Gift of the Canadian Club of Toronto, 1926 178cr; E.P Taylor Research Library and Archives 160tl; Axiom: Chris Coe 3c, 22c, 26tl, 27tr, 49bc, 88c, 205b, 234, 237t/c, 239c/br, 242c, 247t, 254-255, 277t, 278t, 310t, 317t, 332c/b, 367b.

Bard on the Beach Shakespeare Festival: David Blue 398bf; Bata Shoe Museum, Toronto: 103tl, Dibbuuuuu Arm Lubbum: London: Art Gallery of Ontario Paul Kane (1810–71) *Indian Encampment on Lake Huron* 6-7, Emily Carr (1871–1945) *Skidgate, Graham Island, British Columbia* 1928 (oil on canvas) Gift of the J.S. Mclean Collection by Canada Packers Inc. 1990 33t, Maurice Galbraith Cullen (1866–1934) *On the Saint Lawrence* 1897 (oil on canvas) Gift of the Reuben and Kate Leonard Canadian Fund, 1926 32c; British Library portolan by Pierre Descaliers Canada: *from the voyage of Jacques Cartier* (1491–1557) and his followers c.1534–41 44c, *Jacques Cartier* (1491–1557) *French navigator and discoverer of Canadian River St. Lawrence* (steel engraving after a portrait in St. Malo) 44b; Hudson Bay Company Lieutenant Smyth (19th Century) *Incidents on Trading Journey: HMS Terror Making Fast to an Iceberg in Hudson's Strait, August 18th, 1836* 163t; Private Collection "British Boys learn how to own your farm in Canada! Decide on Canada now" 30b; medal commemorating the British capture of Quebec, 1759 (bronze) 47b; engraving by Jean Antoine Theodore Gudin (1802–80) *Jacques Cartier* (1491–1557) on the St. Lawrence River, 1535 7; engraved by Charles Maurand by French School (19th century) *Delaware Indians Killing Bison* in the 1860's photo Ken Welsh 227c, litho by Howard Pyle (1853–1911) *The Capitualtion of Louisbourg, illustration from 'Colonies and Nation'* by Woodrow Wilson, pub. in Harper's Magazine, 1901 47t, Benjamin West (1738–1820) *Willaim Penn's Treaty with the Indians in November 1683* (oil on canvas) 26tr; Stapleton Collection engraved by Carl Vogel (1816–51) *Indian Hunting the Bison, plate 31 from volume 2 "Travels in the Interior of North America"*, 1844 (aquatint) by Karl Bodmer (1809–93) (after) 26br, engraved by Charles Geoffroy (1832–82) *Assiniboin Indians, plate 32 from volume 2 of "Travels in the interior of North America 1832–34"*, 1844 (aquatint) by Karl Bodmer (1809-93) (after) 247b; British Columbia Archives: Province of B.C. Photo 47cb.

Courtesy of Calgary Transit: 420c; Cephas: Fred R. Palmer 102tr; Pascal Quittemelle 102b; TOP/Hervé Amiard 28b; Bruce Coleman Ltd.: John Cancalosi 245c; Jean-Loup Charmet: 46t; Colorific!: Randa Bishop 411b; Terence LeGoubin 225t; John Moss 264; Black Star/Richard Olsenius 72b; Jeff Perkell 64; Michael Saunders 103b; Geray Sweeneyt 23b; Focus/Eric Spiegelhalter 321t; Corbis: 29t, 33b, 48b, 50c, 57c, 63br, 163br, 209, 211tl, 232bl, 250bl; Craig Aurness 232-233; David Bartruff 327b; Bettman 49bl, 51c, 52b; Bettman/UPI 203b; Daniel J. Cox 11tr; Peter Harholdt 326b; Hulton Deutsch collection 54cr/bl/br; Wolfgang Kaehler 332cl, Lake County Museum 431t; Library of Congress 15t/cb, 159t; Wally McNamee 125c; New York Public Library Picture Collection 44t; PEMCO-Webster & Stevens Collection Museum of History and Industry, Reuters 55bl; Seattle 51tl; Sygma/Touhig Sion 21b; UPI 35c.

Adrian Dorst: 256c, 288c, 289b. Empics Ltd:

Sportschrome 21c; Robert Estall Photo Library: 77b, 102–103, 104c, 156b; Mary Evans Picture Library: 47c, 51tr, 99c, 162tr, 255c, 343c, 405c.

Five Fishermen: 366cl; Four Seasons Centre For The Performing Arts: Sam Javanrouh 174tl; P.M. Franklin: 23t, 25tl, 60ca, 63tr/c, 74, 86-87, 95t; Winston Fraser Photos: 12–13, 68b, 73b, 102c, 103c, 105tr, 228b, 140b, 250t, 336b, 413, 415; Black Star 157c; Canada In Stock 219tr; Ivy Images/Don Mills 40c, 60br, 62t, 63tl, 72c, 73t, 151c, 229, 240–241; Ivy Images/Don Mills/© Gilles Daigle 78t,/© Sylvain Grandadam 403t; /© Tony Mihok 38b/ © Dan Roitner 81b; T.Klassen Photography 238c, 242t, 253t.

Getty Images: Dennis McColeman 194cl; First Light/ Alan Marsh 9tr; Photographer's Choice/Jeff Kobalenko 8cla; Stone/Alan Smith 10clb; Taxi/Walter Bibikow 9br; Courtesy of Greyhound Canada: 424t. Lyn Hancock: 338, 340b, 341b, 400b; Robert Harding Picture Library: 25cl, 27tl, 258cl; Charles Bowman 107; Philip Craven 38t; Robert Francis 404–405; Jeff Greenberg 262cb; Norma Joseph Frgs 233b; Maurice Joseph Frgs, Arps 38c, 425; Paolo Kotch 104c; R. McLeod 321b; Roy Rainford 180t; Walter Rawlings 305c; Geoff Renner 231tl; Ian Tomlinson 39t, 290, 294b; Dr A.C. Waltham 330b; Tony Waltham 216-217; Explorer 156t;/Patrick Lorne 144b; Publiphoto Diffusion 24cl;/Paul G. Adam 140t;/Yves Marcoux 120–121, 143t; Bild Agenteur Schuster GMBH 98–99; David Housef: 72t, 73c, 143t, 145bl; © Steve Cohen 99, 339t; Hudson Bay Company Archives, Toronto: 162tl; Provincial Archives of Manitoba 162b, 163c; Hulton Getty Collection: 54t, 95b, 104cb.

Inuit Art Foundation, Ontario: Sarah Joe Qinuajua, Puvirnituq *A Polar Bear Meets A Woman* QC1985 Black Stone Cut 326t.

Jasper Tourism and Commerce: 308t; Hugh Levy 309tr.

Wolfgang Kaehler: 144t, 145br; Robin Karpan: 19t, 31b, 226–227, 228t, 231c/b, 232tr, 236b, 238b, 243b, 244c/b, 245b, 246t/c/b, 249t/b, 250c, 251cl/cr/b, 331t, 339h; Joseph King: 267, 272–273, 275t, 320b; Kobal Collection: 21b, *Rose Marie*, MGM 233tr; *Anne of Green Gables*, RKO 34c.

Frank Lane Picture Agency: Dembinsky 24br; Michael Gore 61crb; John Hawkins 61br; FotoNatura/F.Hazelhoff 2-3; David Hosking 230cb, 260t, 297b; Maslowski 24bcr; C. Mullen 143c; Mark Newman 25crb, 260cb; C.Rhodes 25br; M.Rhode 77c; Leonard Lee Rue 25clb, 156c, 313b; Sunset/Brake 76t, 340c;/T.Leeson 260bl; John Watkins 60bca; L.West 304t; David Whittaker 260ca: Terry Whittaker 24bl; Leisurail/VIA Rail Canada: 423.

Courtesy of the Manitoba Museum of Man and Nature: 239bl; Arnold Matchtinger: 186b; McCord Museum of Canadian History, Montreal: Notman Photographic Archives 53t; McMichael Canadian Art Collection: Photo Arthur Goss/Arts & Letters Club 165b; A.V Jackson (1882–1974) *The Red Maple*, 1914 oil on panel, 21.6 x 26.9cm Gift of Mr. S. Walter Stewart 1968.8.18 164tr; courtesy of Molson Companies: 369b; Musee d'Art Contemporain de Montreal: Natalie Roy *Les Demoiselles de Montreal*, 11,1995 (sic!) Emploie gorro otjupon sous acrylique et bois 32 x 300 x 35cm Denis Farley et Natalie Roy Du Compagnonnage du 2 Juin au Septembre 1999 ©SODART/DACS, 2011 116t; Richard Long *Niagra Sandstone Circle*, 1981 32 pierres de gres © Richard Long 116c; Musee des Beaux-Arts de Montreal: Laurent Arriot *Teapot* Photo Christine Guest 1952 DS 41 118b; El Greco *Portrait of a young Man* 1945.885 119c; Harmensz van Rijn Rembrandt *Portrait of a Young Lady* 1949-1006 118cl; courtesy of the Museum of Anthropology, Univeristy of British Columbia, Vancouver, Canada: photo: Bill McLennan 276cb, 276b, Red Cedar Totem Poles in Great Hall, Haida and Tsimshian (Canada) 276t, Gift of Walter and Marianne Koerner 17c; Wooden Frontlet Bella Bella, (Canada) H.R. MacMillan Purchase 277c.

National Archives of Canada: C-011371 49t, C25739 263tr; National Ballet of Canada: C.Von Tiedmann 396t; National Gallery of Canada, Ottawa: 198c, Davidialuk Alasua Amittu (1910–76) *The Aurora Borealis Decapitating a Young Man* c.1965 purchased 1992 © La Fédération des Coopératives du Nouveau-Québec 198b; Louise Bourgeois *Maman* 1999 © Louise Bourgeois Trust 1999tl; Jackson Pollock (1912–56) No.29 c.1950 purchased 1968 © ARS, NY and DACS, London 2011 198t; Francesco Salviati *Virgin and Child with an Angel* c.1535–1539 199crb; Tom Thomson (1877–1917) *The Jack Pine* c.1916–1917 purchased 1918 199t; Natural History Photographic Agency: Brian and Cherry Alexander 61clb, 322–323; Dan Griggs 23, 163bc; Stephen Krasemann 24bcl, 60t, 261br, 332t, 333t, David E. Myers 18b; T.Kitchen and V.Hirst 25tr/bl, 60cb, 261tl/tr/cb, 262t, 289ca; Jean-Louis Le Moigne 261bl; Dr Eckart Pott 260bc; Kevin Schafer 60bl, 331b; John Shaw 61bl, 260br, 300b, 320c; Eric Soder 258t; NorbertWu 289cb; Naturpress: Roberto Olivas 337t; Peter Newark's American Pictures: 26cr/cl/bl, 42; 46–47, 46cl/b, 47tr, 48t, 49br, 50b, 52t/c, 53c, 62c/b; New Brunswick Tourism: 78b; Northern British Columbia Tourism Association: 312b.

Opera de Montreal: Yves Renaud 399tl; Oxford Scientific Films: Tui DeRoy 61cra; Breck P. Kent 61cla; Richard Herrmann 261bc. Parc Olympique, Montreal: 124tr; Parks Canada: Claude Picard *Acadians working the fields* commissioned by Canadian Heritage 62–63; PA Photos: AP/Aaron Harris 398cl; Photo Library: Imagestate Ltd/Steve Vidler 9cla; Robert Harding Travel/Alison Wright 341cr; Pictures Colour Library: 152–153, 416, 419b; Provincial Archives of Manitoba: neg no. CT16 49c; Publiphoto: 55t; Y. Beaulieu 29c; J.P. Danvoye 141br, 145t; Claude A. Girouard 141bl, 142b; Jean Lauzon 54cl, 144c; D.Oullette 142t; M.E.F. /Boulion 141c; S. Clement 28cr; G. Zimbal 28t, 29b.

Regié des Installations Olympique: 125t; Retna Pictures: Steve Granitz 397b; Phil Loftus 35b; Micheal Putland 34b; Richard Reyes 21tr; Reuters: Lucas Jackson 398tl; Rex Features: 35t; Courtesy of Royal Bank of Canada: 412t; Image courtesy of the Royal British Columbia Museum: 284t/cl, 285t/ca/cb; © Peter and Mabel Fox 284cr; courtesy of the Royal Canadian Mounted Police Museum, Regina: 232c/br; © Royal Ontario Museum: 184t, Man's painted caribou-skin coat, Innu, Quebec-Labradorc. 1805 184clb; David McKay 184cla; Royal Tyrell Museum,

Drumheller: Alberta Tourism Parks,Recreation and Culture 230ca/br, 230–231, 231tr, 248t/ca/cb/br. Courtesy of the Sainte-Anne-du-Beaupré Museum: 139bl/tl; photo courtesy of Saint Marie Among the Hurons: 220tl; Courtesy of Scotiabank: 412bl; Spectrum Colour Library: 333b, 336c; Spectrum Stock: 190, 206; Ottomar Bierwagen 40tl; Ron Erwin 224t/b; Henry Kalan 224c; Norman Piluke Photography 225b; STA Travel Group: 408crb; Tony Stone Images: Wayne R Bilenduke 325, 337b; Cosmos Condina 17b, 128, 300br; Richard Elliot 263b; John Edwards 173b; Suzanne and Nick Geary 232tl, 426b; Sylvian Grandadam 105tl; David Hiser 253b, 327tl; Susan Lapides 106; R.G.K Photography 328; Paul Souders 263tl; Jess Stock 37b; Chris Thomaidis 166.

Tate Gallery, London: The Honorable John Collier *Last Voyage of Henry Hudson* oil on canvas ©1988 45c; Donald L. Telfer: 24cr, 56–57, 238t, 242b, 243t/c, 244t, 245t, 252t/b; Travel Alberta: 301c, 312t.

University of Toronto: J.B Tyrrell Papers, Thomas Fisher Rare Book Library 26 230bl. Vancouver Public Library, Special Collections: 13220 50–51; Victoria University in the University of Toronto, Canada: Lawren S. Harris *Autumn Algoma*, 1920 © Mrs. James H. Knox 164–165; Village Historique Acadien: 79tl/tr/bl.

Courtesy of Western Union Money Transfer: 412c; Westjet: 417c; Wickaninnish Inn: Sairaa Astaria Thornton 288ca; Collection of the Winnipeg Art Gallery, Canada: Frank H Johnston *Edge of Forest*, 1919 watercolour, tempera on hardboard 52.2 x 62.8cm L26 Ernest Mayer 164c; World Pictures: 1c, 20t, 41b, 59b, 61t, 93br, 132t, 204b, 258b, 259t/c, 262b, 301t, 313t, 314, 320t, 327tr, 422, 424b. Yukon Government Communities: 330t.

Front endpaper: all special photography except Axiom: Chris Coe bcl; Colorific!: John Moss bl, Jeff Perkell tc; P.M. Franklin: trc; Robert Harding Picture Library: Ian Thomlinson cl; Spectrum Stock: bc, bcr; Tony Stone Images: Cosmo Condina c; Susan Lapides tr; R.G.K. Photography tlc; Chris Thomaidis br; World Pictures: tl.

Jacket
Front – Alamy Images: Jon Arnold; Back – Alamy Images: Rolf Hicker Photography tl; Piumatti Sergio bl, Paul Thompson cla; Dorling Kindersley: Francesca Yorke clb..

All other images © Dorling Kindersley.
For more information see:
www.DKimages.com

SPECIAL EDITIONS OF DK TRAVEL GUIDES

DK Travel Guides can be purchased in bulk quantities at discounted prices for use in promotions or as premiums. We are also able to offer special editions and personalized jackets, corporate imprints, and excerpts from all of our books, tailored specifically to meet your own needs.

To find out more, please contact:
(in the United States) **SpecialSales@dk.com**
(in the UK) **TravelSpecialSales@uk.dk.com**
(in Canada) DK Special Sales at **general@tourmaline.ca**
(in Australia) **business.development@pearson.com.au**